Jared Wicks demonstrates an admirable sensitivity for Luther's unique way of thinking, perspicaciously identifying his main topics and arguments, carefully analyzing them, and convincingly documenting his findings. With great respect, he describes how Luther cohesively reformulated the core of Christianity. Wicks sheds new light on aspects of Luther's thought that researchers formerly underestimated, for example on the church and sanctification, and uncovers the significance of lesser-known texts, such as the *Treatise on Indulgences*. He corrects Catholic misperceptions regarding Luther's alleged "subjectivism," emphasizing the objective, sacramental mediation of salvation in Luther's theology. The studies in the book count among the highlights of Catholic Luther research; they are also ecumenically important, as demonstrating how aspects of Luther's theology may also be appreciated by Catholics. Although written more than twenty years ago, these masterly studies have not lost any of their significance for understanding Luther properly. Reading them is still highly rewarding, eye-opening, and a pleasure.

THEODOR DIETER,
DIRECTOR
INSTITUTE FOR ECUMENICAL RESEARCH, STRASBOURG

For fifty years, Jared Wicks has been a clear, discerning, and indispensable voice in Luther-interpretation. In a field often dominated by religious and ideological agendas, praising or blaming Luther for "Protestantism" or "modernity," Wicks has demonstrated an unerring eye for the essential, presenting Luther as a man of his time whose own overriding concern was the gospel of salvation in Christ. The studies collected in *Luther's Reform* provide a lucid account of Luther's core theological and spiritual teaching, showing how it emerged it amidst controversy in the critical year 1518, and describing its relation to the larger program of church reform which it inspired. Wicks' rare combination of theological insight and historical concreteness makes visible both the ecumenical promise and the ecumenical problem of Luther and his Reform. This collection has been difficult to find in North America; its republication by Wipf & Stock is reason for celebration.

DAVID S. YEAGO
PROFESSOR OF SYSTEMATIC THEOLOGY AND ETHICS
THE NORTH AMERICAN LUTHERAN SEMINARY AND
TRINITY SCHOOL FOR MINISTRY

In the yeasty ferment of the years immediately before and after the second Vatican council, Father Jared Wicks played a leading role in the inauguration and shaping of serious Roman Catholic research into Luther's thought in a new ecumenical era. He has now served for more than a half century as a clear and careful expositor of Luther's way of thinking and as an ecumenical bridge and facilitator of conversation across the boundaries within the household of faith.

Wicks does not simply observe from the outside but has managed to enter into Luther's thought world and thought processes. His assessments of the way in which the reformer engaged the biblical text and the pastoral crisis of his time shed fresh light on the construction and maturing of the Wittenberg theology. This volume will continue to inform and guide those who are studying Luther's thought.

ROBERT KOLB
PROFESSOR OF SYSTEMATIC THEOLOGY EMERITUS
CONCORDIA SEMINARY, SAINT LOUIS

This fine collection by one of the leading Catholic Luther scholars stands at the intersection of historical Luther studies and ecumenical dialogue and shows creatively how the former can contribute fruitfully to the latter. The study of the past is used here to inform the Lutheran-Catholic dialogue of the present, and these dialogues in turn have obviously sharpened Wicks' eye for significant issues and details in the past. These studies offer insight without anachronism and challenge both their Lutheran and Catholic readers to take more seriously the abiding catholic in the teachings of Martin Luther.

MARK U. EDWARDS, JR.
AUTHOR, *LUTHER'S LAST BATTLES*

Jared Wicks has become an indispensable scholar in the field of Luther studies. He has taken up the torch of Catholic investigations of the reformer and shed so much light on his subject that Protestants are equally advised to pay heed. The essays in this book reveal a Luther who was not simply a sensational firebrand of ages past but a profoundly engaged theologian, probing matters personal and pastoral as well as ecclesiological, no less relevant today than he was five hundred years ago. The result is a Luther beyond confessional polemic, a Luther for the whole church.

SARAH HINLICKY WILSON
PASTOR, TOKYO LUTHERAN CHURCH
AUTHOR OF *A GUIDE TO PENTECOSTAL MOVEMENTS FOR LUTHERANS*

LUTHER'S REFORM

STUDIES ON CONVERSION
AND THE CHURCH

LUTHER'S REFORM

STUDIES ON CONVERSION
AND THE CHURCH

VON

JARED WICKS

WIPF & STOCK · Eugene, Oregon

Wipf and Stock Publishers
199 W 8th Ave, Suite 3
Eugene, OR 97401

Luther's Reform
Studies on Conversion and the Church
By Wicks, Jared, SJ
Copyright©1992 by Wicks, Jared, SJ
ISBN 13: 978-1-5326-7166-1
Publication date 1/28/2019
Previously published by Verlag Philip On Zabern, 1992

CONTENTS

Author's Foreword	VII
Abbreviations of Frequently Cited Sources	IX

1. Approaching Luther's Reform 1

Part I – Luther's Spirituality of Conversion

2. Justification and Faith in Luther's Theology 15
3. The Heart Clinging to the Word 43
4. Living and Praying as *simul iustus et peccator*:
   A Chapter in Luther's Spiritual Teaching 59

Part II – Critical Reformation Teachings and Responses to Luther

5. Luther's Treatise on Indulgences, 1517 87
6. *Fides sacramenti – fides specialis*:
   Luther's Development in 1518 117
7. Roman Reactions to Luther: the First Year, 1518 149
8. Luther and Lived Religiosity 189
9. Holy Spirit – Church – Sanctification: Insights
   from Luther's Instructions on the Faith 197

Part III – The Early Lutheran Church in Dialogue

10. Abuses Under Indictment at the
    Diet of Augsburg 1530 223
11. The Lutheran *forma ecclesiae*
    in the Colloquy at Augsburg, August 1530 279

Acknowledgment of Places of First Publication 318
Appendix – Books Reviewed on Luther and the
    Reformation by Jared Wicks, 1966-1991 319
Bibliography of Studies Cited 324
Index 341

AUTHOR'S FOREWORD

As this book goes out to those who remain fascinated with the drama of Martin Luther, with his doctrine, and with his reforming impact, the author is aware of a many-sided debt of gratitude. The studies collected here were written for different occasions and have been revised and updated in a variety of settings, and each of these found me receiving help and assistance from others.

I am, first, grateful to the journals and publishing houses that agreed to my reworking and republishing of materials that appeared under their copyright. This acknowledgment is made more specific on p. 318, below, giving the places of first publication of ten of the studies contained in this book.

I count myself fortunate to have spent a portion of each year in the past decade at the Newberry Library, Chicago, where the collection and services met the peculiar needs of a Luther scholar in exemplary fashion. Also, the Jesuit-Kraus-McCormick Library in Hyde Park, Chicago, and the Cudahy Memorial Library of Loyola University Chicago provided essential help. – During my work of revision and updating, I benefitted as well from the resources and assistance by staff at the Luther-Archiv of the Institut für Spätmittelalter und Reformation, Tübingen.

At the Seventh International Luther-Research Congress (Oslo, 1988), helpful comments on a draft-text of Study 4, on the *simul iustus et peccator*, were made by members of the Seminar on Spirituality and Meditation in Luther: T. Fabiny (Budapest), K. Hagen (Milwaukee), W.Y. Ji (Seoul), T. Mannermaa (Helsinki), P. Rajashekar (Geneva), M. Ruokanen (Helsinki), and H. Zschoch (Wald Michelsbach, Germany).

In the broader panorama of personal contacts, I recall profitable exchanges about Luther with Erwin Iserloh, James F. McCue, Kurt-Victor Selge, and Oswald Bayer. My work on the Diet of Augsburg in 1530, for Studies 10 and 11 in this volume, has benefitted by exchanges with Vinzenz Pfnür and Eugène Honée. The Bibliography of Studies near the end of this book is more than a scholarly convention. It is also an expression of esteem for those from whom I have learned much. In this regard, I mention the Lutheran historical theologians Martin Brecht, Wilfried Joest, Bernhard Lohse, and Bernd Moeller, with particular respect and gratitude.

I cherish the memory of the late Prof. Dr. Peter Manns, who was Director of the Institut für Europäische Geschichte Mainz, Abteilung Religionsgeschichte, when this book was proposed and then accepted for inclusion in the Institut's monograph series as a Beiheft. Prof. Dr. Rolf Decot has competently overseen the passage from first proposal to published book.

Finally, I gratefully acknowledge the contributors to a three-part financial subsidy of this publication: the McCarthy Family Foundation of East Boothbay, Maine, USA; the Detroit Province of the Society of Jesus; and my own university, the Gregorian of Rome.

January 1, 1991

ABBREVIATIONS

of Frequently Cited Sources

BS *Bekenntnisschriften der evangelisch-lutherischen Kirche* (Göttingen ^{5}1963). References give page and line numbers.

CR *Corpus reformatorum: Philippi Melanthonis opera* (Halle 1834ff, reprint New York and Frankfurt 1963). References give volume and column numbers.

WA *D. Martin Luthers Werke. Kritische Gesamtausgabe.* The Weimar Edition (1883-). References give volume, page, and line numbers.

WABr The Weimar Edition. *Briefwechsel* (Luther's Correspondence).

WADB The Weimar Edition. *Deutsche Bibel* (Luther's Biblical Translations and Prefaces).

LW *Luther's Works. The American Edition.* 55 vols. (St. Louis, Concordia Publishing House & Philadelphia, Fortress Press, 1955-86). References give volume and page numbers.

AWA *Archiv zur Weimarer Ausgabe.* Supplementary volumes to the Weimar Edition (Cologne 1981-). References give volume, page, and line numbers.

1

APPROACHING LUTHER'S REFORM

The studies offered in this book naturally rest on a set of specific assumptions and convictions. Taken together, these underlying beliefs add up to the author's approach to Martin Luther's teaching and reforming activity. Here, an introductory essay will break down this approach into some of its main component parts. I offer here an accounting of the foundations of my interpretation of Luther's texts.

A Developing Horizon of Understanding

In the normal course of a scholar's work, a cumulative process takes place, which should consist in development and growth. This means that one's approach to a subject is to a degree shaped by previous discoveries resulting from one's earlier investigations and insights. Later reading is then a work of interpretation partly under the influence of earlier understandings. To be sure, one has to be ready to absorb fresh evidence and revise previous insights and assessments in the light of new perceptions.[1] A warranted change of viewpoint can be a vital sign in an intellectual project. But past work is nonetheless an influential prelude to what follows.

Consequently, one component of my approach to Luther is what emerged early on from my study of his lectures from 1509 through 1517. There my first extended meeting with Luther's texts revealed an impressive account of conversion, penance, and personal growth.[2] In this collection, Study 5 brings

---

[1] Such a change of understanding and evaluation lies behind Study 6, on Luther's doctrine of faith in 1518. Note 5 of that study gives a more detailed reference.

[2] *Man Yearning for Grace. Martin Luther's Early Spiritual Teaching*, originally published in 1968 by Corpus Books (Washington) and then brought out by the Institut für europäische Geschichte, Mainz, in 1969 (Steiner Verlag, then in Wiesbaden). This was a dissertation done under the direction of Erwin Iserloh in Münster in 1964-67 and was accepted for re-publication in Mainz by Joseph Lortz. Naturally, the work bears a certain family resemblance to the interpretation of Luther proposed by these two major figures in Catholic Luther-studies.

together some of the results of what was the author's earliest work on Luther.³ Because of its foundational importance, Study 5 is a close reading of an illuminating but largely neglected text that Luther composed in the fateful year 1517. I argue, however, that that text, Luther's *Treatise on Indulgences*, nicely summarizes the major themes of his earliest theology and instruction on Christian life and prayer.

Other portions of this collection are shaped in part by the conviction, grounded in Study 5 as a key illustration, that Luther began his theological work as a teacher of conversion and lifelong penance. Study 4 takes up Luther's famous thesis that the believer is both »righteous and a sinner at the same time« (*simul iustus et peccator*). Here, his early spirituality of penance appears as an integral part of his mature teaching on the Christian life.⁴

A second foundational theme in this collection is featured in Study 6, on Luther's teaching on faith in 1518. Here I take up Luther's account of justification by faith from a special angle or perspective, namely, that of *fides sacramenti*, faith in the sacramental word of forgiveness spoken in virtue of promises made by Christ himself.⁵ Luther, we all know, taught people to relate to God, not by their own achievements, but by faith. However, it needs to be underscored that for Luther faith entails an essential orientation to words of grace and forgiveness spoken in the church. At the heart of Luther's theology, as he gained new clarity in 1518, the person relates to an objective mediation of salvation. Luther teaches believers to lay hold of specific words addressed to them, behind which stands another objective reality, the word of Christ's historic promise to effect in the believer what the sacramental words express. Study 6 argues that such a doctrine lays to rest a large complex of Catholic misgivings over Luther's teaching, namely the objections often clustering under the pejorative label »subjectivism«. Luther's view of the objective, sacramental mediation of salvation then recurs in Studies 8 and 9 as basic to his work of supplying pastoral resources for the churches of Electoral Saxony and other territories that espoused reform according to a Lutheran model.⁶

---

³ Also pp. 45-49 in Study 3 and pp. 118-122 in Study 6 set forth, in shorter resumés, the style of Christian self-understanding and prayer that Luther was teaching in lectures and publications from 1509 through 1517.

⁴ The author was given the opportunity to propose his insights into Luther as a master of spirituality in two entries in the encyclopedia, *Dictionnaire de Spiritualité*: »Luther (Martin),« in vol. 9 (1976), cols. 1206-1243, and »Simul iustus et peccator,« in vol. 14 (1989), cols. 921-931.

⁵ My understanding of this aspect of Luther's teaching emerged in the 1970s, when I was studying his argument with Cardinal Cajetan in October 1518 and re-reading his texts of that time. This revision was helped by the work of colleagues in Luther-research such as Oswald Bayer, Matthias Kroeger, and Kurt-Victor Selge. Study 6, on *fides sacramenti*, first appeared in *Gregorianum* in 1984.

⁶ Study 6, on Luther in 1518, is also the author's contribution to the debate over the date and content of Luther's »reformation breakthrough« to clarity over justification. See pp. 129 and 142-147, below. However, for understanding the origin of the church-dividing reformation, I argue, especially in the last part of Study 7, that greater importance must be ascribed to Luther's shifting conception of the norms of doctrinal truth. The two critical documents here are his *Responsio* to

1. Approaching Luther's Reform

An approach to a major figure in history is, however, more than one's beginnings and seminal discoveries. All the results of one's study fuse together to form the horizon of understanding within which one continues to read a transmitted work. Such a horizon shapes one's approach. This horizon, we all hope, will be coherent in itself, warranted by accurate reading, and such as to promote an alert sensitivity to perennial values of a theological and religious proposal. Consequently, one way to meet the approach underlying the studies presented here is simply to review the sets of conclusions given near the end of each study.

These conclusions form the author's present approach to Luther and have influenced the reworking of the following essays for their present publication. Let me now mention some of the important results that shape my fundamental view of Luther.

As stated in the conclusion of Study 5, Luther's religious and theological views are essential in understanding his work. This needs to be emphasized at a time in which the social history of the Reformation is engaging many scholars. Clearly it is significant for Luther's reform that the German peasants revolted against their feudal lords in 1525 and that in his day the newly empowered leaders of urban communes were taking responsibility for numerous dimensions of life in the cities of Germany and Switzerland. But without a specification of the doctrinal component, one's understanding of the Reformation and of Martin Luther remains truncated. Luther's impact on individuals and social groups was that of a religious teacher with a fresh and appealing message.

I note in the conclusion of Study 2, and again in Study 8, that Luther's message was a tightly coherent doctrine of salvation by Jesus Christ. Luther decisively overcame late-medieval diffusiveness in theology and Christian instruction to re-center teaching on the cross of Christ and on the word of grace derived from Christ. Luther could never dwell at length on the margins of the faith, but was driven to treat the whole by relating any part to the center, Christ and his saving grace. This characteristic of his message more than explains his transforming impact as an initiator of reform.

Luther taught an impressive personalizing of the individual believer's relation to God, but he went on to contribute as well to the doctrine of the church, or ecclesiology. Study 9 brings out an aspect of Luther's teaching on the church that even many Lutherans seem to neglect, namely, his close correlation between the mission of the Holy Spirit and the being and life of the church.

In this collection, Studies 10 and 11 deal more with the first Lutheran churches than with Luther himself. Here however we see the true radicality of Luther's work, from the perspective of those who swept away myriad abuses in everyday ecclesiastical life in order to carry out and institutionalize reforms of worship, clerical life, and church laws. Even though Studies 10 and 11 deal with events at Augsburg in 1530, where Luther was not present, he still was the causal force

---

Silvester Prierias (mid-1518) and a letter of January 1519 to Prince-Elector Frederick the Wise. I treat these on pp. 156-159 and 185-187, below.

behind the changes under discussion at Augsburg, because he taught people to take action under the force of imperatives stemming from God through his Scriptures. Thus, at the end, this collection presents Luther's reform as noteworthy and challenging because of the way he taught a fresh approach to the norms of true teaching and criteria of correct practice in the church.

These then are some leading characteristics of Luther's reform that I draw out of in his teaching on conversion and the church.[7]

A Critical Dialogue with Others

Another influence on a scholar's approach to documents is his or her ongoing discussion with others in the same field. An approach is shaped to a degree by what one sees as the positive contributions of other researchers. Also, there is the reverse influence of what one is against, for we are also shaped by our critical reactions to interpretations that we find unwarranted, wrong-headed, or skewed by unhelpful prejudice. The studies collected in the volume borrow from the works of others in a spirit of affirmative scholarly colleagueship, for example, from Erwin Iserloh in Study 4, from Oswald Bayer in Study 6, and Kurt-Victor Selge in Study 7.

Behind these investigations and essays lies one person's study of Luther's texts over a quarter-century, along with a dialogue over the same period with numerous others who have proposed interpretations of the Reformer and his work.[8]

One can become dependent on the work of others by taking over explicit themes, and then going on to develop the same themes further by presenting more evidence that warrants, and sometime nuances, the theme in question. Influence like this can go in the opposite direction, as is evident where I cite the studies of others who offer confirmation of what I claim to find in Luther.

More subtle, however, is the influence of others at the level of assessment and evaluation. Here my main connection is with the modern tradition of Catholic interpretations of Luther, and so the readers of this collection need to take some account of the larger enterprise of Catholic study of Luther. This collection itself extends the work of some Catholic scholars, while giving at the same time a critical alternative to other proposals. In other contexts, the author has sketched

---

[7] A broader horizon for reading Luther should make explicit one's views on the further implementation of the Protestant Reformation in the sixteenth century. Also it should sketch an account of early-modern Catholic reform and of the more general mentality-change that took place between 1500 and 1648. My view of these developments is given in an interpretive review of recent scholarship, »Reformation Studies,« *New Catholic Encyclopedia*, vol. 18, Supplement 1978-88 (Palatine, Ill. 1989), 415-424.

[8] As a partial accounting of this aspect of the background of this collection, an Appendix lists my published book reviews between 1965 and 1991. See pp. 319-323, below.

the historical development of Catholic views of Martin Luther's person and teaching.⁹ This is not the place to go over this material once more, but some brief observations are in order, to locate the present studies in the larger topography of present-day Catholic work on Luther.

Historians are aware of the importance of mentalities maintained over the long duration of time. Hence it is of relevance even today to recall that around 1850 Catholics began to work with a schematic account of modern European history. Luther, in this widespread view, stood at the head of a genealogy of modern errors. His subjectivism broke away from the salutary objectivity of medieval thought and life. His rejection of ecclesiastical authority opened the way to the proliferation of Protestant sects. The Enlightenment made a further application of critical principles enunciated by Luther when it mounted its corrosive attack on the supernatural, specifically on miracles and on the divinity of Christ. In the nineteenth century this led further to atheistic materialism and socialism, in which official Catholic teaching saw a dire threat to social order. Luther, thus, set in motion a destructive process and sowed disorder in the modern world.¹⁰

But this portrayal of Luther's calamitous role in history has been called in question, based on a more attentive study of Luther's teaching and impact. In this volume, Study 6 is such a more attentive study, and it shows that »subjectivism« is quite inappropriate for characterizing Luther's work, especially in the crucial year 1518. Then the final four studies treat from different angles the church life of early Lutheranism, with its own structure and coherence, as it issued from Luther's work as a reformer. As a whole, the present volume stands in contrast with the view of Luther that Catholics have long held.

Commonly we mark a decisive turning-point in Catholic attitudes to Protestantism with the appearance in 1939-40 of Joseph Lortz's study of the German Reformation.¹¹ This monumental work, translated in the 1960s and 1970s into French, Italian, English, and Spanish, centers on a 300-page interpretive essay on Martin Luther's life and thought. Lortz singled out Luther's central religious intention and all-consuming concentration on God's grace revealed in the cross of Christ. Luther did innovate doctrinally, but Lortz insists that one take careful account of the problems forced on Luther by elements of decadence in late-medieval Catholicism, and that we acknowledge as well Luther's teaching on life-long conversion, his account of faith as personal

---

9 »Luther through Catholic Eyes,« *Chicago Studies* 8 (1969), 275-285; and »Images of Luther,« Chapter 1, in *Luther and His Spiritual Legacy* (Wilmington, Del. 1983).

10 The mid-nineteenth-century dissemination of this interpretation, in which Pope Pius IX had an important role, has been described by G. Miccoli in the introduction to L. Perrone, ed., *Lutero in Italia* (Casale Monferrato 1983), xi-xix. Hilaire Belloc spread such an interpretation of modern history in numerous publications early in our own century, while Thomas P. Neill's *Makers of the Modern Mind* (Milwaukee 1949) formulated it for undergraduates.

11 *Die Reformation in Deutschland*, 2 vols. (Freiburg: Herder, 1939-40).

abandonment to God, and the many Catholic elements (doctrinal, sacramental, and structural) remaining as components of Luther's reformed Christianity. The work of Lortz is the milestone, and is deeply formative on the great majority of later Catholic studies of Luther, including the essays collected in this volume.[12]

In his history of the German reformation, Lortz was severely critical of Luther's emotional excesses and his passionate mode of interpreting Scripture and doctrines in terms of their relevance to himself personally. Lortz branded Luther as radically subjectivistic, However, Lortz did not stand still in the critical positions expressed in 1939-40. In the 1960s he produced a series of essays based on a fresh immersion in Luther's texts that notably nuanced the criticisms of his original statement.[13] The studies collected here in this volume intend to advance yet further the major reassessment of Luther that Joseph Lortz began and carried through.

The author is not deterred in this project by the work of two other Catholic authors, Paul Hacker and Theobald Beer, both of whom forcefully dissented from Joseph Lortz's revision of the Catholic assessment of Luther. Study 6, below, sets forth the grounds for not following Hacker's charge that Luther left a baneful legacy of »anthropocentric religion.«[14] Beer's lengthy critique of Luther came adorned with dust-jacket recommendations by Cardinal Joseph Ratzinger and Hans Urs von Balthasar. However, Beer's work turns out upon close examination to be filled with inaccurate readings and unsound interpretations of Luther's views of the incarnation, redemption, faith, and justification.[15]

Other scholars, both Catholic and Protestant, have had their moments of constructive influence on these studies. To them, the notes and bibliography give the conventional form of scholarly acknowledgment.

---

[12] A recent symposium in Mainz was dedicated to Lortz's work. See the papers: Rolf Decot and Rainer Vinke, eds., *Zum Gedenken an Joseph Lortz (1887-1975). Beiträge zur Reformationsgeschichte und Ökumene*. (Stuttgart 1989). I reviewed this volume in *Gregorianum* 72 (1991), 381-383.

[13] In the symposium volume, *Zum Gedenken an Joseph Lortz*, Boris Ullianich gives the text of a 1971 letter (pp. 193-195) in which Lortz summed up the points that he then saw differently than thirty years before, and which he would like to have seen presented in an introduction to the Italian translation of his Reformation book. Five of Lortz's later, revisionist studies are listed in our Bibliography, as entries for the years 1962-1969. These works are reprinted in the collection, *Erneuerung und Einheit. Aufsätze zur Theologie- und Kirchengeschichte*, ed. P. Manns (Stuttgart 1987), 540-717.

[14] The author knew Paul Hacker personally in Münster and, in *Theological Studies* 28 (1967), 374-376, wrote a positive review of his *Das Ich im Glauben* (Graz 1966), which came out in English as *The Ego in Faith* (Chicago 1970). But Study 6, below, amounts to a basic revision of this view.

[15] *Der fröhliche Wechsel und Streit. Grundzüge der Theologie Martin Luthers* (Einsiedeln 1980). I reviewed Beer in *Theologische Revue* 78 (1982), 1-12, and in *Gregorianum* 63 (1982), 162-164. See also Erwin Iserloh's portrayal of Beer's misinterpretations in »Der fröhliche Wechsel und Streit,« *Catholica* 36 (1982), 101-114.

Luther's Historical Context

A third factor in approaching a body of texts is the view one has of their immediate cultural surroundings. In the case of Luther, the important contexts for understanding and assessing his work are, first, the intellectual world of late-medieval theology, and, second, the church's preaching and pastoral care around 1500.

The author does not subscribe to the thesis that Luther came on the scene when Western Europe and the church were at a low ebb, after two centuries of decline from their thirteenth-century eminence. There were problems in theology and pastoral care in Germany around 1500 – and Luther pointed them out with all desirable incisiveness. But it is wrong to brand everything as corrupt and abusive. Many adherents of the Reformation did so brand the church of their ancestors and of their parents' pastors and bishops. But these were not objective assessments by persons attempting a comprehensive historical analysis. We can learn today from those who have done such analyses.[16] More importantly, we can review the evidence with the help of more recent editions of significant eve-of-reformation texts.

Let us now sketch some aspects of the situation in theology and the church at the time Luther entered upon the scene and began working out his impressive alternative to what was being taught. Our judgment on Luther's work will depend in part on the kind of contrast that emerges between his work and that of the teachers and preachers who immediately preceded him.

In the sphere of university theology, it is inevitable that one look to Gabriel Biel, the influential Tübingen professor who died in 1495 and whose systematic theology was published in 1501, the same year in which Martin Luther entered the University of Erfurt. Biel espoused the *via moderna* in theology, that is, the method and main theses of William of Ockham, as did two influential Erfurt professors whom Luther knew, Jodocus Trutvetter and Bartholomew Arnoldi of Usingen. As a young member of the Augustinian order, Luther prepared for his ordination to the priesthood by studying Biel's *Exposition of the Canon of the Mass*. Biel was thus a central figure in the theological thought-world in which Luther began his work.

As a follower of Ockham, Biel sought simple explanations and a rigorous treatment of evidence. A theme repeatedly emphasized in the *via moderna* is the total freedom and sovereign power of God. God is not bound by anything except his own decisions and commitments. Our universe is deeply marked by contingency, resulting from positive divine determinations – not by intrinsically necessary connections and sequences. Ockham and Biel, however, also showed considerable optimism about the scope of human freedom and the range of the human will's capabilities, both in the moral order and in relation to God. In fact

---

16 I list such works on the pre-reformation church at the end of Study 2, p. 41, n. 109, and briefly state my point of view in Study 8, p. 193, n. 22.

the Ockhamist wing of late-medieval theology had an exposed flank in its doctrine of our *liberum arbitrium* (free choice). On numerous occasions, Martin Luther successfully attacked this flank of the Ockhamist system.

In his *Collectorium* Biel argues that a fallen human person can, solely by his or her natural endowments and without the aid of divine grace, avoid mortal sin, keep the commandments, and even elicit an act of love of God above all things.[17] Biel further cites Alexander of Hales to the effect that a sinner can without grace use his remaining freedom to turn to God in obedience and love, begging with all his heart to be further enlightened unto salvation.[18] This account of human power reaches a climax in Biel's claim that a sinner can on his own change his consent to and delight over evil into hatred for sin and the aspiration for a good life.[19] We see that one current of late-medieval theology, one with which Luther was familiar, gave little heed to the consequences of sin in disorienting the human affective and moral life. Biel did not see that the person must be healed interiorly and receive from God that delight in the law that was so central to St. Augustine's view of conversion.

Biel of course states quite clearly that in themselves human moral achievements are not our way to salvation. Whatever the human will may do in preparing itself for salvation, it is God himself who forgives guilt, infuses saving grace, and ordains that our good actions in grace shall be rewarded in heaven.[20] But human actions in freedom nonetheless can have a positive relation to this complex of saving effects brought about by God in justification. For Biel holds that God does intend, by a contingent ordination of his own generosity, to respond to the good efforts elicited by free choice before justification. This accords with the medieval axiom, *Facienti quod in se est Deus non denegat gratiam* (To one who does his best, God does not deny his grace). The prior good effort required by this salutary divine disposition amounts to a momentous inner change in the person, namely, to cease delighting in evil and to move toward God in desire, obedience, and love.[21] By such actions, the human person can fulfil the conditions God has set for receiving his grace of salvation.[22]

---

[17] *Collectorium circa quattuor libros Sententiarum*, Lib. II, Dist. 28, art. 2 (conclusiones 1-3) and art. 3 (dubium 1); ed. W. Werbeck and U. Hofmann, 2 (Tübingen 1984), 538-540.

[18] Ibid., Dist. 27, art. 3 (conclusio 4); ed. cit., 518.

[19] »Potest [peccator] cessare a consensu et actu peccandi, immo odire peccatum et velle non peccare.« Ibid., art. 3 (dubium 4); ed. cit., 524.

[20] This is clear in Biel's definition of grace in the most proper sense (»donum supernaturale a solo Deo rationali creaturae infusum, quo ipsa redditur grata Deo et accepta ad vitam aeternam beatifice possidendam«) at the beginning of Lib. II, Dist. 26 (ed. cit., 498) and in his account of the merit of eternal life by actions done in virtue of *gratia cooperans* and God's free acceptance (Dist. 27, art. 2 [conclusio 1]; ed. cit., 512-514).

[21] Ibid., art. 2 (conclusio 5); ed. cit., 517f. Also Dist. 28, art. 3 (dubium 1); ed. cit., 539f.

[22] It should be noted that Biel softens considerably the optimism of his theological anthropology near the end of his treatise on grace and free choice. He admits that the human will is frequently seduced by error and evil. Wounded by original sin, the person is beset by endemic instability. These more realistic considerations lead to the conclusion that the true way to conversion is not that of moral self-actualization, but that of begging God for protection against

1. Approaching Luther's Reform

The optimistic theological anthropology of Gabriel Biel is one historical context in which to assess Luther's teaching on Christian conversion. Our essays on justification, faith, penance, and the word (Studies 2-6) present the doctrine of conversion from sin that Luther set forth in a host of treatises, commentaries, sermons, disputations, and popular instructions. Luther's notion of human abilities and our relationship to God's saving purposes resulted both from his fresh encounter with the Bible and St. Augustine and from his critical reaction against the optimistic moralism of Biel and the Erfurt exponents of the *via moderna*.[23] Our esteem for Luther as a Christian theologian can only grow when we contrast his work with Gabriel Biel's unrealistic and unbiblical theses about a notable complex of human abilities to seek and find the way to salvation.

A second figure of some importance when Martin Luther came on the scene as a teacher was his older confrere in the Augustinian order, Johann von Paltz, who lived from ca. 1445 to 1511. In 1490, when Paltz was preaching an indulgence to gain support for a papally-sponsored crusade against the Turk, Prince-Elector Frederick the Wise of Saxony, Luther's later patron, asked Paltz for a German text of some of his sermons. The little work that resulted from this request went through twenty printings between 1490 and 1520.[24] The booklet provides detailed instruction on devout meditation on Christ's passion; a brief treatise on how to prepare for death in imitation of the good thief crucified with Jesus; and short sketches of treatises on withstanding temptations to blasphemy and on the eight benefits of the sacrament of Anointing of the Sick.

Paltz's work belongs to the genre of »theology for piety,« and intends to help people as they experience the daily drama of sin and repentance and as they struggle with doubts in the quest of assurance.[25] Much of Luther's work was in this same genre of practical religious instruction, as I recall in Study 8 of this collection, and this makes quite pertinent the comparison and contrast of his

---

the tempter and for inner light and strength to find the right way to live. Ibid., art. 3 (dubium 2); ed. cit., 541f.

[23] More specific cases of Luther's critical reaction will be noted on pp. 19-21, 63-65, and 213 n. 79 (in Study 9). A recent current of interpretation sees Biel in a more positive light than is the case here. His theology is termed, e.g., in the writings of Alister McGrath (cf. Study 4, below, p. 65, n. 26, and Study 8, p. 195, n. 28), a systematization of »covenantal« relations between God and human beings. I doubt whether this is justified, in part because the meaning of »covenant« given us by biblical theology differs notably from what we find in Biel. Biel's theology, to characterize it in a global manner, rests on a perception of the radical contingency of the orders of creation and redemption. Regarding God's relations with human beings, it could be termed a »voluntarist« system or a »legal positivism.«

[24] *Die himmlische Fundgrube* (*The Mine, of Heaven*), originally published in Leipzig in 1490; available now in Johannes von Paltz, *Werke*, 3, *Opuscula*. ed. Christoph Berger et al. (Berlin-New York 1989), middle-high German text, pp. 201-253, low German text, pp. 254-284.

[25] Paltz has been studied most recently by B. Hamm, in *Frömmigkeitstheologie am Anfang des 16. Jahrhunderts* (Tübingen 1982). I reviewed this work, together with the recent editions of Paltz's main works, in *Gregorianum* 65 (1984), 200-204.

teaching with that of Paltz.[26]

At the turn of the sixteenth century Johann von Paltz was in Erfurt writing the first of his two major works. His book, the *Coelifodina*, came out in 1502 and was soon printed three more times (Leipzig, 1504, 1511, 1515). Long sections of this work set forth the considerations with which a pastor or friend should encourage persons being tempted to despair because of their sins. One should take hope, first, because the Blessed Virgin Mary and the saints are benevolent and powerful helpers. Further, one can go to confession, making use of a powerful sacrament to supply for what is imperfect in personal repentance. Ample opportunities are also at hand for gaining indulgences, by which one comes to share even more in the liberating benefits of Christ's redemption.

In 1502-03 Paltz was on the road preaching indulgences again, but this time he found himself frequently having to defend this institutionalized church practice against attacks on its validity. Paltz came back to Erfurt and set to work on a broad-based defense of indulgences, the *Supplementum Coelifodinae*, that came out in 1504 and was shortly after published twice more (Leipzig, 1510, 1516). This second major work by Paltz grew to the same size as the *Coelifodina*, as it returned to its author's favorite theme, help for sinners, and set forth the »seven gates of refuge« to which ordinary people should go in their quest for salvation.[27]

As a teacher and preacher, and especially as author of two lengthy works of pastoral theology, Johann von Paltz abhorred innovation. His works contain thousands of citations taken from the medieval authors he revered. He had been trained in the university and served as professor in Erfurt for a decade after 1483. So he could meet doubts and questions with clear answers backed up by theological authority, reasoning, and the example of holy people. More often, though, he tries to explain and urge on others the devotional and sacramental practices and the religious attitudes that lead one to peace of heart and to salvation.

In his treatment of the good thief crucified with Jesus, Paltz had recourse to the axiom about doing one's best, by natural effort, and so most assuredly being given God's saving grace. The bad thief was not mindful of his misery and felt no compassion for Jesus, and so he remained hardened in heart. But the good thief was impressed with Jesus' patient suffering, yearned to know the truth, and so disposed himself by his own effort for God's saving help, which he then received by congruous merit.[28]

However, such an application of a thesis akin to Biel's teaching in systematic theology was not typical of Paltz. More characteristic is his approach to the

---

[26] Study 6, below, will make more specific references to Paltz, as a way of situating Luther and understanding his view of sacramental absolution. See pp. 121f and 145f, in Study 6.

[27] Paltz's major works were recently published as volumes 1 & 2 of his *Werke*: the *Coelifodina*, ed. C. Burger et al., and the *Supplementum Coelifodinae*, ed. B. Hamm et al. (Berlin 1983).

[28] *Coelifodina*, ed. Burger, 213-217.

Immaculate Conception of Mary.[29] He takes this grace accorded her as the foundation and root of her other feasts and offers formulated prayers as ways of profitably observing each feast. Paltz teaches the devout to meditate on God's grace to Mary, to express one's lowliness and sin, to beg help, and so to gain Mary's benign protection from manifold dangers – from the elements and beasts, from plague and threat of miscarriage, from sin and *infamia*, from strife and lust, from diabolical vexation and final despair, and climactically from the pains of hell itself. Paltz knew the fears of late-medieval Christians beset by a phalanx of hostile forces, and he taught a fervent recourse to the devotional means to gain supernatural protection.

Just six years after Paltz's death, Martin Luther's first publication, a book of meditative comments on the Seven Penitential Psalms (1517), began spreading a renewed form of Christian spirituality. Luther was first read in the very Saxon-Thuringian milieu in which Paltz had worked and published his books shortly before. Many who responded avidly to Luther's first booklets and treatises may well have heard or read Paltz. Paltz's works show us the »normal science« that preceded Luther's new paradigm.

From the diffused way Paltz had been leading people to know Jesus Christ and pray to him and his Mother, we know why people responded so positively to Luther's sharply focused catechisms, sermons, biblical translations and prefaces, and devotional pamphlets. Luther reformulated the core of Christianity in a cohesive, unified way, as we set forth especially in Studies 3, 4, and 8 in this collection. We can see this in sharp relief by contrasting it with the diffuse devotionalism of Paltz's rambling, omnium-gatherum treatises. Again, our esteem for Luther grows and finds further warrant by consideration of his historical context.

Certainly, more could be said about Luther's historical context, but the foregoing notes on Gabriel Biel and Johann von Paltz should suffice to indicate some salient features of late-medieval theology and popular instruction. This is what Luther, as a young man, heard from his professors' podiums and from numerous pulpits. My book is about the noteworthy alternative that he came to offer to such teaching and preaching.

What follows in this book invites the reader on a journey through the thick forest of Luther's commentaries and treatises. I am aware that some aspects of Luther's teaching are not treated here in detail, for example, his articulation of the Pauline theme of Christian freedom. While my book is not comprehensive, still it does lead the reader to the heart of what Luther offers to theology and the church. Certain critical moments of the early Reformation, such as the indulgence controversy, Luther's hearing before Cardinal Cajetan, and the

---

29 *De septem foribus seu festis beatae Virginis / Die siben Porten oder Feste der Muter Gottes*. There were 5 Latin and 4 German printings, 1491-1501. This too was requested by Frederick the Wise, and represents an adaptation for pious usage of an earlier intervention by Paltz in the debate over the Immaculate Conception. The work is given in Paltz's *Werke*, v. 3, *Opuscula*, 285-358.

Augsburg Diet of 1530, are treated here in a new light. These studies intend to help the reader consider afresh a figure of transforming power in his impact on history. They offer as well an exploration of what is a major edifice of Christian thought. May Luther instruct us fruitfully on conversion and the church.

PART I

LUTHER'S SPIRITUALITY OF CONVERSION

2

JUSTIFICATION AND FAITH IN LUTHER'S THEOLOGY

An interpretation of Martin Luther must include an exposition of the heart of his theology, the doctrine of justification. Both for historical understanding and for theological reflection, Luther challenges his readers above all because of his probing questions about human sin, faith, God's grace, and the new life and activity given to believers by Christ the Redeemer. Luther's answers on this complex of issues provided the main grounds for his reforming impact on sixteenth-century Christianity. Today those same answers can well be fruitfully pondered by systematic theologians of every Christian confession. Luther, as a teacher of lived faith and faithful living and as a thinker who worked from a coherent doctrinal basis, repeatedly opens perspectives of enrichment for personal spirituality.

In his day Luther stood at the center of acrimonious controversy on numerous aspects of the doctrine of justification, but in this essay the emphasis will fall on historical retrieval and on what I hope will be a coherent exposition of Luther's central themes. The approach will be in part genetic and in part systematic. I distinguish (1) Luther's early theology of conversion (1513-17), (2) the transitional year 1518, and (3) Luther's maturing and mature teaching from 1519 onward. Many consistent lines of thought do, of course, appear throughout Luther's productive years, but other elements of considerable importance predominate only in certain periods or have an ascertainable time of emergence in his theology. I hope to convey something of the movement of his development, by first noting some of Luther's early insights into St. Paul and then sketching the developed formulation he offered to the church of his day.

The themes of a theology of justification include humankind's fall and the legacy of sin, God's merciful approach to sinners, the commitment of faith, reconciliation with God, and a graced life of righteousness. Luther at times showed impressive synthetic powers in drawing up comprehensive statements on these matters. One thinks of the Heidelberg Disputation (1518), *The Freedom of a Christian* (1520), the *Antilatomus* (1522), Luther's biblical prefaces (1522 and later), sections of *De servo arbitrio* (1525), and his exposition of the *Miserere* (1532). With Luther, a passage on justification often included important material on the doctrine of revelation, on God's rule of creation, and on the redemptive work of Christ. Justification frequently was the place where much of Luther's thought fused into cohesive unity.

Luther presents special problems for the historical theologian, both because of the abundance of his utterances and because of the profound influence of situations on his teaching. The give-and-take of disputation and controversy situated many of Luther's accounts of God's grace and of believing existence. But the work itself of articulating his perception of Christian conversion was for Luther a labor of searching the Scriptures and amassing texts and references. The Vulgate Bible must rank first among the situations affecting Luther's teaching. Consequently what he said is a classic part of the Christian heritage, and one approaching Luther today can reasonably expect to learn from him about conversion and the new life opened up for believers upon entry into the sphere of Christ's redemptive influence.

1. Luther's Early Theology of Conversion (1513-17)

Research on Luther in our own century has turned attentively to his early lectures and disputations, a considerable part of which were not published in the sixteenth century. In these works of the young professor of Scripture one finds the elements of a coherent doctrine of conversion to Christ and of God's justifying action in the human heart.[1] Extensive passages from this early phase contain positive, biblically-based instruction on the way God and human creatures interact in the drama of personal salvation. Other illuminating texts show us Luther beginning his polemic against theses of the scholastic theology then holding sway in university theology. Further passages manifest special theological convictions and characteristic formal and rhetorical patterns that constantly recur in Luther's long theological career.

Justification in the Form of »confessio peccati«

St. Paul's citation of Ps 51:4 (»That thou may be justified in thy words...«) in Rom 3:4 occasioned a lengthy reflection by Luther on faith and justification.[2] Faith is the act of »justifying God in His words,« that is, appropriating God's words and affirming that He speaks the truth. The special insistence here, though, is that the words to be assimilated contain the revelation of human sinfulness. As he expounded Rom 3:4, Luther knew he was dealing with the Pauline manifesto on God's charge against the humanity standing before Himself

---

[1] The author set forth this teaching of the young Luther in *Man Yearning for Grace* (Washington, D.C. 1968 and Wiesbaden 1969) under the rubric of the »spirituality« inculcated in Luther's works down to the end of 1517.

[2] WA 56, 214-234; LW 25, 199-218. This section of the Lectures on Romans (1515-1516) has been treated well by M. Kroeger in *Rechtfertigung und Gesetz* (Göttingen 1968), 41-72, highlighting the paradoxical identity of God's grace with his judgment and the consequence (1) that for Luther at this time *fides* was identical with *humilitas* and (2) that one was never certain of being in grace. Similarly, O. Bayer, *Promissio* (Göttingen 1971), 45-57, 118-123.

as guilty and liable to condemnation. Therefore a fundamental aspect of conversion is submission to this precise revealed truth, which should become a lived truth about oneself. The submission of faith comes to expression in the humble self-accusation, *Tibi peccavi*.³

Paradoxically, this confession of sin is a form of justification itself, and not simply a disposing precondition. Personal appropriation of God's verdict on human sinfulness transforms the self-understanding and self-assessment of the believer from the falsehood of secure self-approbation to the truth and righteousness of self-accusation. By so »justifying God in His words« the person is justified, that is, made just and truthful, in conformity with God's just and truthful words about the given human condition.⁴

In Luther's early lectures, crucial foundation stones were laid for his lifelong teaching. Among the themes of long-term importance, none is more characteristic than the certainty that before God the person must be stripped of a sense of personal power and achievement. This is not to be self-lacerating morbidity, but submission to God's word of judgment. Conversion occurs in the self-understanding, where the word makes one »become a sinner,« by a radical *metanoia* of self-assessment, in the midst of which God is making one righteous through a hidden but transformative action.⁵

Radical Sinfulness and Its Healing

A decisive event in Western ecclesiastical history was Luther's protest in October 1517 over the way papal indulgences were being offered in Germany and being avidly received by the people. In this intervention, however, Luther was only drawing a practical consequence from another central aspect of his early theology of sin, grace, and justification.

Luther had dwelt at some length on the words denoting »sins« in Rom 4:7, where St. Paul cited Ps 32:1f.⁶ By glancing ahead to Rom 7, especially to verses 5, 7, and 12, Luther realized that for St. Paul sin was not properly the discrete

---

³ WA 56, 229,28-33. Similarly at 218,7-13, leading to the conclusion »Ergo humiliate et fide opus est.« Also 221,24-34, 226,14-21, and 231,6-13.

⁴ WA 56, 226,23-227,6. The confession is, of course, made in virtue of God's gift: »Quia quod nos eius sermones iustificamus, donum ipsius est [WA: eius], ac propter idem donum ipse nos iustos habet, i.e., iustificat« (227,19f., corrected according to the reading of E. Vogelsang in *Luthers Werke in Auswahl*, 5 [Berlin, 3rd ed. 1963], 235).

⁵ WA 56, 233,5-9. But by such an operation of God the humble are justified, by both infused grace and imputation, when they come to »justify God,« that is, »quando [Deus] impios iustificat et gratiam infundit sive quando iustus esse in suis verbis creditur. Per tale enim credi iustificat, i.e. iustos reputat. Unde haec dicitur iustitia fidei et Dei« (220,9-11).

⁶ WA 56,268-291 (LW 25,257-278). I treated this section in *Man Yearning for Grace*, 99-101, 111-114.

thoughts, words, and deeds a person might mention in the self-accusation of confession, but instead the pervasive desires and orientations from which sinful human actions arise. Acts are the fruits or consequences of sin, while sin itself consists in the concupiscent inclination toward evil making one reluctant toward the good recognized as one's duty.[7]

Consequently sin is a pervasive infection of the heart with which even the righteous person must contend and struggle. God's forgiveness is nonetheless quite real, for in the case of those who confess their sin He does not impute this evil infection unto damnation. For the believer, however, having a disoriented and reluctant heart is a grave concern, and authentic faith includes the desire for its purification. So the righteous yearn and long for God's healing grace. Unfortunately, contemporary theology in Luther's day had lost sight of these truths and, according to his barbed charge, this theology was actually undermining the Christian struggle for personal liberation and integration.[8] In Luther's famous phrase the believer is *simul peccator et iustus*,[9] sinful because of the deep infection preventing one from delighting in God's law, but righteous because of God's mercy and the self-accusation affirming a true estimate of one's standing before God.[10] A related factor in present righteousness at this time is the trust that God will in time complete the cure He has begun.[11] But more emphasis falls on delighting in God's law than on trust in promises. Grace, for the early Luther, is *caritas* gradually instilling willingness, that is, *hilaritas* and *voluntas liberrima*.[12] Because such delight is always partial and flawed, the *simul* remains

---

[7] Luther uses these phrases in describing the nature of sin: »desideria, affectiones et inclinationes ad peccata« (WA 56, 271,3); »passio, fomes et concupiscentia sive pronitas ad malum et difficultas ad bonum« (271.7f); »voluntas, si liceret, nunquam faceret quae lex precipit. Invita enim est ad bonum, prona ad malum« (279,17f). Luther concluded that to reduce the notion of sin simply to an absence of righteousness, as the scholastics appeared to do, is to undermine the effort of penance and open the way to complacency (313,18-22). Still, in believers this many-sided evil is different than it is in the unrighteous, for in believers it is subject to the Spirit, who is preparing its destruction (314,5f).

[8] »Et error est, quod hoc malum possit per opera sanari... Sed misericordia Dei est, quod hoc manet et non pro peccato reputatur iis, qui invocant eum et gemunt pro liberatione sua« (WA 56,271, 24-28). Over against contemporary scholasticism Luther maintained: »Ista vita est vita curationis a peccato, non autem sine peccato finita curatione et adepta sanitate« (275,25f). But because people are not taught to yearn for healing grace, they become proud of a righteousness they think is perfect: »nihil solliciti sunt et concupiscentiis bellum indicere per iuge suspirium ad Dominum. Unde et tanta nunc in Ecclesia est recidivatio post confessiones« (276,8-12).

[9] WA 56,272,17. Study 4 in this collection treats Luther's doctrine of the *simul* across the full range of his teaching on Christian life and prayer.

[10] WA 56, 271,20-22.

[11] WA 56, 272,17-22, 274,2-11.

[12] E.g. WA 56, 257,18-29 and 358,1-8. Consequently caution is in order regarding the presence of a doctrine of justification by faith, in the classic reformation sense, in Luther's early work. Where a recent author, treating the Romans lectures, says, »Spirit is the whole person in its openness to God and in its trust in God's promises,« the texts referred to make no mention of trust or promises (D.C. Steinmetz, *Luther and Staupitz* [Durham, N.C. 1980], 117). Instead, Luther characterized »spirit« by a love for the law of God instilled by healing grace. The remedy for *caro* and its egotism is a gift of *caritas* (WA 56, 350,27, 352,6, 356,7). Luther can describe the

ever central to believing self-understanding.

In 1517 Luther grew seriously concerned over the way preachers were extolling the great »graces« of the papal indulgence offered to those who would contribute to the fund for the building of St. Peter's Basilica.[13] Sound instruction, he contended, would remind people of the pervasive infection of sin in their hearts and so would inculcate lifelong, penitential self-denial and especially the earnest petition for God's healing grace.

> We must be quite earnest in preventing indulgences ... from becoming a cause of security, laziness, and neglect of internal grace. Instead, we must be diligent to fully cure the infection of our nature and thirst to come to God out of love for Him, hatred of this life, and disgust with ourselves. That is, we must incessantly seek God's healing grace.[14]

Sad to say, Luther's plea for reform of indulgence preaching and for popular instruction on lifelong penance went unheard in 1517. Instead, he was cited to Rome, under accusation of heresy, because he was threatening the income needed by the Archbishop of Mainz and seemed to be derogating from papal authority.

Luther's Early Debate with Scholastic Theology

As Luther lectured on Romans in 1515-16, he articulated a series of judgments on elements of decadence present in society, the Church, and religious life in his day.[15] In theology certain errors verging on heresy were fostering attitudes of pride and were undermining morality.[16] Luther felt he reached the root of the

gospel as setting forth and offering *caritas et Jhesum Christum* (338,13-20).

[13] I offered an exposition of Luther's 1517 critique of indulgence preaching in *Man Yearning for Grace*, 216-264, with special attention to the otherwise neglected *Tractatus de indulgentiis* (1517), in which Luther formulated a constructive doctrine of penance and indulgences. This is treated in Study 5 of this volume. Examples of neglect of Luther's constructive *Tractatus* are not rare. S. Hendrix makes no mention of it in his account of Luther's 1517 intervention in *Luther and the Papacy* (Philadelphia 1981), 23-32. The *Tractatus* of 1517, with its engaging and theologically profound account of lifelong penance, was all the more reason why the papacy should have attended to Luther's intervention.

[14] *Tractatus de indulgentiis*, WABr 12, 9,152-156. Similar statements of this attitude normative in Luther's critique of indulgences had come in the Lectures on Romans, e.g. WA 56, 235,25-38 and 264,16-21. As Luther said, »Populus itaque fidei totam vitam suam agit in quaerendo iustificationem« (264,35).

[15] Luther's scholia on Rom 2:1-3 castigated the cruelty and avarice infecting government and the higher clergy (WA 56, 189f), which he interpreted as God's punishment meant to make people aware of the ruin that has come upon His holy Church (190,27-30). Numerous abuses in society and the Church were listed and lamented in Luther's comments on Rom 12-14. This material was studied by Gerhard Müller, »Ekklesiologie und Kirchenkritik beim jungen Luther,« *Neue Zeitschrift für systematische Theologie* 7 (1965), 100-128, reprinted in *Causa Reformationis*, ed. G. Maron & G. Seebass (Gütersloh 1989), 472-500.

[16] WA 56, 273,3-274,18, 276,6-12, 394,28-395,2.

abuses and laxity when, while commenting on Rom 14:1, he began unmasking pelagianizing attitudes and positions. Some forget that interior devotion is the ground of actions pleasing to God. Others feel that repentance is a matter of a relatively easy free decision. This superficial religiosity rests on a Pelagian belief about the power of the will to form a good intention which will work on God to certainly obtain His grace.[17] No one, of course, explicitly professes Pelagianism, but many in fact live according to its maxims, especially whose who are sure that they have on their own, independently of grace, the freedom and ability to act in a manner to which God is sure to respond by granting His saving grace. The whole Church, Luther maintained, is undermined by the false security instilled by this error.[18]

We cannot develop here the late-scholastic theological doctrine of the residual freedom of choice found in fallen humanity, of the responsible preparation or disposition required for the gift of grace, of merit for human actions, and of the final grace of God's acceptance of those whom He saves.[19] But it is essential to see Luther's early thought on justification in the context of his critical and increasingly polemical reaction to this current of thought, which he saw reviving the ethical optimism and salvation-by-achievement contested by St. Augustine and condemned by the church a millennium before.

According to Luther, a human being does not have a natural endowment for forming a good intention at will, as »the Scotists« teach. Instead of trying to arouse such an intention interiorly, one should fall prostrate before God and utter in prayer one's total dependence on God's gift of inward, transforming grace.[20] The scholastics in effect inculcate a sense of independence and autonomy, contrary to the New Testament's »fear and trembling« before God. The saints

---

[17] WA 56, 501,3-503,12 (LW 25, 494-497).

[18] WA 56, 503,1-6.

[19] Luther frequently recited the *monstra* taught in scholasticism: WA 2, 402,20-31; 8, 467,1-35 (LW 36, 214-216); 40I, 291,15-294,22 (LW 26, 173-175); 39I, 419,19-420,3; 50, 222ff. H.A. Oberman, *The Harvest of Medieval Theology* (Cambridge, Mass. 1963), 120-188, sets forth how Gabriel Biel, professor at Tübingen from 1484 to ca. 1490, treated these matters. We note that for Biel the human effort of »doing what lies in one« (*faciens quod in se est*) can be a purely natural actuation of the will (Oberman, 138), which is then the necessary disposition for the infusion of justifying grace (152). H. McSorley answered a qualified but definite »yes« to the question highlighted in his article, »Was Gabriel Biel a Semipelagian?« in L. Scheffczyk et al. eds., *Wahrheit und Verkündigung*, Festschrift Michael Schmaus (Munich 1967), 2, 1109-20. W. Ernst stressed Biel's seriousness about the effects of original sin, so that it would be nearly impossible for the fallen will to do good without grace. Still, Ernst ends by admitting that Biel's view of merit and freedom is doubtlessly close to Pelagianism. *Gott und Mensch am Vorabend der Reformation* (Leipzig 1972), 310-320, 332f.

[20] WA 56, 501,3-18 (LW 25, 494f).

were constantly begging for God's grace, ever fearful of doing evil on their own. Their way to God's favor was, therefore, their humble yearning for grace.[21]

Convictions and Thought Patterns

So far this essay has set forth the principal themes in Luther's early account of conversion and justification. I turn now to mention briefly some more pervasive convictions which gave rise to characteristic patterns of thought and language as Luther spoke of God and believers in interaction.[22]

1) Luther opened his exposition of Romans in 1515 by stating what he took to be the substance of Paul's message in the letter as a whole, namely, to pull down, to pluck out, and to destroy all human wisdom and carnal righteousness, so as to implant the reality of sin. Paul rates our own achievements as not worth anything at all, since it is by God's gift from beyond ourselves and not our achievements that we are saved.[23] This is a clear instance of Luther's penchant for thought and expression in terms of opposed totalities. Luther communicated the biblical call for conversion through rhetorical schemes of dialectical opposition, in which contents stand in sharp discontinuity with each other. Consequently the Reformation was being shaped by a trait of Luther's thought when it came to summarize its principles in the exclusive formulas of *sola fide*, *sola gratia*, and *sola scriptura*. As one schooled in St. Paul, especially in Gal 1-2 and 1 Cor 1, Luther found it second nature to highlight exclusive alternatives, oppositions brooking no compromise, and totalities set in complete discontinuity.

2) While lecturing on the Psalter in 1512-15, Luther came to characterize God's redemptive work as a hidden work, an *opus sub contrario absconditum*. The glory of the Church, accordingly, lies concealed beneath folly and weakness.[24] God regularly carries out His designs in a manner contrasting sharply with outward appearances. The sign does not represent the reality signified by being its

---

[21] WA 56, 503,18-22. In the Heidelberg Disputation of April 26, 1518, Luther concluded his exposition of human sinfulness with this instruction on begging God's grace as one takes refuge in Christ: »His auditis, procide, et ora gratiam, spemque tuam in Christum transfer, in quo est salus, vita et resurrectio nostra. Quia ideo haec docemur, ideo Lex notum facit peccatum, ut cognito peccato gratia queratur et impetretur« (WA 1, 360,35-38; LW 31, 50f).

[22] My presentation in this section has close affinities with three studies of Luther's thinking: Joseph Lortz, »Martin Luther, Grundzüge seiner geistigen Struktur,« in E. Iserloh et al., eds., *Reformata Reformanda*, Festschrift Hubert Jedin (Münster 1965), 1, 214-246 (in English in J. Wicks, ed., *Catholic Scholars Dialogue with Luther* [Chicago 1970], 3-33); Gerhard Ebeling, *Luther: Einführung in sein Denken* (Tübingen 1964) (English translation, *Luther: An Introduction to His Thought* [London and Philadelphia 1970]); and John O'Malley, »Erasmus and Luther: Continuity and Discontinuity as Key to Their Conflict,« *Sixteenth Century Journal* 5 (1974), 47-65.

[23] WA 56, 157,2-6; 158,10-14 (LW 25, 135-137). Later in the lectures this theme returned at 207,7-11, and implicitly at 305, 22-306,1.

[24] WA 4, 77,35-78,9 (LW 11, 226-228).

analogous and homogeneous expression, but instead stands in contrasting discrepancy with the reality. God is working out our renewal interiorly, but empirically one perceives weakness and diminishment – as occurred in the folly of the cross (1 Cor 1:21).[25] Consequently humility is required and a hesitant suspicion about what one senses and perceives outwardly, lest God's truth slip by unnoticed beneath its alien outward form. God's own proper work lies beneath his alien work.[26] In 1518, Luther's Heidelberg Disputation characterized God's revelation of sin, by which one comes to personal confession, as the alien work beneath which unfolds God's proper work of justification.[27]

3) The personal crisis initiated when God addresses His word to the person standing in complacent self-approval concerns a set of forensic relationships. The gospel calls in question the values that rate highly in the world and before our own eyes (*in conspectu hominum ... coram nobis*), to prepare us for God's own gift of righteousness and wisdom.[28] At issue is the adoption of the right perspective for judgment and assessment. What is valid *coram hominibus* must cede to what is valid *coram Deo*, that is, in the forum of God's judgment. Faith, consequently, represents a shift toward accepting and professing what one is *coram Deo*, or in God's estimate.[29] The worldly perspective is illusory and deceptive because of its false values. But faith initiates the person into God's perspective and assimilates one to evaluations valid *coram Deo*.

4) Thus the place in which the drama of personal justification unfolds is the conscience. Luther had an overriding concern with a person's self-estimate in relation to God's word. This judgment of conscience is not a matter of assessing particular acts in the light of the known norms of conduct, but a matter of the self in its global, yet simple, relation to God.[30] Conscience is at times troubled and distressed, fleeing from God's word of judgment on human self-seeking. But when the gospel announces Christ the Savior, then the same conscience is pacified and calmed by the gift of a reconciler and the promise of personal healing

---

[25] WA 4, 81,25-32; 82,17-27.

[26] WA 4, 83,3-7, and 87,22-25 (citing the Vulgate of Isa 28:21, »Opus eius alienum est ab eo, ut faciat opus suum«). The presence of the Spirit is concealed, as beneath many vexations (WA 56, 246, 12-20) or in words and teachings we might easily resist (256,10-23).

[27] WA 1, 360,37-361,5.

[28] WA 56, 157,2-6; 158,3-5.10-14 (LW 25, 135f).

[29] This is true, above all, in accepting God's judgment, that is, »quando nos credimus esse peccatores, mendaces, etc., et nostram virtutem atque iustitiam coram Deo penitus nihil esse. Ac sic tales efficimur in nobis intra nos, quales sumus extra nos (i.e., coram Deo)« (WA 56, 229,11-14).

[30] This has been acutely set forth by M.G. Baylor in *Action and Person: Conscience in Late Scholasticism and the Young Luther* (Leiden 1977), ch. 6, »Luther's New Object of Conscience,« pp. 209-272.

and renewal.³¹ The gospel dissipates the reproaches and accusations that often torment the conscience and so leads to *fides Christi*, in which the converted and transformed conscience finds itself sharing in the redemptive victory of God's own Son.

2. Christ and Faith in the Transitional Year 1518

In late 1517 Luther had invited his theological colleagues to join him in a disputation on the efficacy of papal indulgences. The disputation did not take place, but nonetheless Luther went on to think out his position on indulgences and a series of related topics. This occasioned theological reflection on the efficacy of the sacraments and especially on priestly absolution in the event of justification. Whereas his earliest thought had treated God's word primarily as a judgment to be appropriated in self-accusation, now Luther came to stress much more the effective offer of grace, expressed in the word of absolution, a word to be appropriated in joyous certainty of forgiveness. One expression of Luther's new articulation of justifying faith was a maxim he cited frequently in 1518: »It is not the sacrament, but instead faith in the sacrament that justifies« (*Non sacramentum sed fides sacramenti iustificat*). However, this shift of accent should not obscure the broader framework of Luther's conviction about the effective presence of Christ in the believer.

»Fides sacramenti«

A good example of the transitional phase in Luther's theology of justification is the set of disputation theses he composed in 1518 as »an inquiry into the truth and for the consoling of fearful consciences.«³² Luther distinguished between the remission of ecclesiastical penalties (by indulgences) and the more excellent remission of guilt before God (by sacramental absolution). The former reconciles

---

31 WA 56, 204,8-29 (LW 25, 188f). Also 411,4-21, 424,5-17, and 426,5-9. On the promise of healing, 272,3-21.

32 WA 1, 630-633. O. Bayer gave special attention to these theses, expounding them as the first consistent presentation of Luther's new Reformation theology of the word as gracious and forgiving promise (absolution) and of faith as certainty of forgiveness. *Promissio*, 166, 182-202. W. Schwab set forth perceptively Luther's transition in 1518 in *Entwicklung und Gestalt der Sakramententheologie bei Martin Luther* (Frankfurt-Bern 1977), ch. 2, »Die Entdeckung des Bußsakramentes,« pp. 77-144, in which the theses »Pro veritate« are studied on pp. 98-105. Martin Brecht's biography of Luther presents the theses as a milestone on the road to the Reformation. The theses result from a reflection of no little intensity in 1518 on the word and justification. They express the insight which has now become the heart of a new doctrine of penance, ecclesial mediation, faith, and certitude of God's grace. *Martin Luther, 1, Sein Weg zur Reformation* (Stuttgart 1981), 228-230; in English in *Martin Luther. His Road to Reformation* (Philadelphia 1985), 235-237.

with the church, while the latter brings peace of conscience by reconciling the penitent with God. But how is consoling remission of guilt attained? What is its basis? Luther's theses deny that the basis lies in the acts and attitude by which the penitent disposes himself in contrition. Also, Luther does not attribute fundamental importance here to the office and power of the priest. Instead, the basis of forgiveness is faith, by which one casts oneself upon the words of Christ to Peter. »Whatever you loose on earth will be loosed in heaven« (Mt 16:19).[33] Christ desires that our salvation rest on his creative word of power that cleanses hearts (Heb 1:3 and Acts 15:9). Consequently one being absolved must not doubt the effectiveness of the word of forgiveness spoken over him in virtue of the utterly certain promise of Christ the Savior.[34] The characteristic element in Christian sacraments is the word of Christ the author of the promise.[35] The disputation theses end with a concluding flourish from Paul: the righteous person does not live by works or the law, *sed ex fide vivit* (Rom 1:17).[36]

In the exegetical lectures on Hebrews in early 1518, Luther spoke in warm, positive tones about this faith in the word spoken in the Church, specifically in the proclamation of eucharistic consecration that Christ's blood is shed for the remission of sins. Faith in such a message is identical with a cleansed and quieted conscience filled with delight before God.[37] In another work of 1518 Luther called for a shift in Christian instruction on the sacrament of penance away from the reigning emphasis on the penitent's contrition and works of satisfaction, for this is producing bad consciences and making people self-reliant. Instruction should emphasize faith in the Christ who is active in the sacrament granting forgiveness mercifully and gratuitously. Luther was convinced that such teaching on faith would produce a new wave of Christian confidence and strengthen individuals for living the penitential life.[38]

Thus faith in Christ's promise is the essential pivot of Christian experience, by which one swings away from reliance on one's own religious achievement and

---

[33] WA 1, 630,5-631,6. There follows the dictum »Non sacramentum fidei, sed fides sacramenti... iustificat« (631,7-9). Luther had frequent« recourse to this probative sentence in the years 1518-20: WA 57III, 170,1; 1, 544,39, 595,33, 286,16, 324,15; 2, 15,32, 715,34; 6, 471,15, 532,29; 11, 301,16.

[34] WA 1, 631,9-22.

[35] WA 1, 632,38f. M. Kroeger brought out the great importance of Mt 16:19 in Luther's transition to his mature doctrine of justification, speaking of the discovery of this text as the hinge on which Luther swung towards a new integration of faith, word, and sacraments. *Rechtfertigung und Gesetz*, 173.

[36] WA 1, 633,12. Study 6, pp. 125-129, below, gives a fuller account of the 1518 theses *Pro veritate*.

[37] WA 57III, 208,22-209,3 (LW 29, 210). Also 169,10-171,7 (LW 29, 171-173).

[38] WA 1, 542,29-543,2 (LW 31, 103).

begins building a new existence in trust, peace, joy and certainty, out of which arise spontaneously the contrition and penance which another theology would make the precondition of justification. Whereas Luther had stressed a self-accusing faith in 1513-16, by 1518 a fiducial faith was coming to the fore, and conversion was now focusing on the appropriation of Christ's promise applied in the sacrament as valid *pro me*.[39]

»*Christus actuosissimus*«

Luther gave a concise account of conversion and justification in the Heidelberg Disputation (April 26, 1518). We cited this work above with reference to the hidden work of God. Other portions of the text show us essential Christological themes shaping Luther's view of justification.[40]

The initial movement of Luther's argument at Heidelberg concluded in theses 16-18, where the outcome of the insistent assertion of human sinfulness is the profound realization of the need of the grace of Christ, in whom alone is found salvation, life and resurrection.[41] Then, after a section on Christ's own self-emptying and crucifixion as the unique way to know God (theses 19-24), Luther sketched some dimensions of the new life of the righteous. In sharp contrast with an Aristotelian righteousness resulting from repeated righteous actions, revelation asserts that righteousness is infused into the hearts of those who believe in Christ. Righteous actions then result from the power of Christ, who makes the believer his operative instrument for doing good. Christ becomes present in transforming virtuality.[42] At its deepest level justification is union with the Christ who begins conforming the believer to his own action and behavior.[43]

---

[39] Personal assurance was stressed in the 1518 scholion on Heb 9:24 (WA 57III, 215,16-20). Study 6 of this collection gives a fuller account of Luther's transition in 1518 concerning faith and the word of sacramental absolution.

[40] Luther spoke pointedly of Christ as *sacramentum*, that is, the effective sign, of righteousness, as in the scheme *sacramentum/exemplum*, which he saw as positing the priority of grace over morality. See E. Iserloh, »Sacramentum et exemplum: ein augustinisches Thema lutherischer Theologie,« *Reformata Reformanda*, 1, 247-264. M. Lienhard focused on Luther's 1517-18 use of this formula in *Luther témoin de Jésus-Christ* (Paris 1973), 84-87. Most impressively, W. Joest brought out Christ's actuality for and in the new life of the believer: *Ontologie der Person bei Luther* (Göttingen 1967), 365-391.

[41] WA 1, 360,34-361,30 (LW 31, 50-52).

[42] WA 1, 364,4-16 (LW 31, 55f).

[43] WA 1, 364,23-28 (LW 31, 56f). In another 1518 text, the explanation of the 37th thesis on indulgences, Luther spoke with great conviction of the union of Christ and the believer, leading to the courage-filled delight of a conscience freed from the weight of sin and now sharing Christ's own righteousness (WA 1, 593,12-28 [LW 31, 190]).

Faith thus brings one into union with the Savior, who is active, not static or dormant. In a sermon in February 1517 Luther had anticipated this assertion of Christ's influence with a description of Christ's life in his members as one of superlative activity (*actuosissimus est, et ... cum omni suavitate et facilitate*).[44] Justification, consequently, has an assimilative and conforming effect in one who submits to God's word and work. Through Christ, now become through faith the inner principle of righteous living, God is creating in the believer a new behavior conformed to the conduct of His own Son, in whom He was well pleased.

Provisional Summary on »fides Christi«

The key elements, therefore, in Luther's early portrayal of justifying faith in Christ are the following. These motifs were sounded early and remain lasting elements of Luther's theological work and legacy.

1) Justifying faith can only occur in one who readily accepts God's just judgment against human sin. Faith must sense how forlorn and frustrating is the way of action and achievement for the fallen and diseased descendants of Adam. Faith appropriates God's judgment upon sin. God's primary instrument for impressing this sense of sin is His law.[45]

2) God's reconciling work entered the world in Jesus Christ and climaxed in his redemptive death. His cross is paradigmatic for conversion, but the actual communication of righteousness stems from his historical promises, especially the promise concerning the loosing of consciences by the word. Absolution and the other sacraments are essential, with the result that in the life of the Church justifying faith has the form of *fides sacramenti*. Thereby one accepts forgiveness and the conscience is renewed in joy before God.

3) More profound than the interaction of word and faith, however, is union with Christ through faith. Believing in Christ is to put on Christ and to have life in union with him who has been made our wisdom and righteousness. *Fides Christi* is thus transformative because of the action of Christ in the believer.

4) The experience of faith can be well expressed by a dramatic monologue of conscience under God's approach and address, as found in Luther's 1515 comment on Rom 2:15. The conscience, finding itself assailed by accusations of guilt, turns to Christ the redeemer. Here then is a refuge! He took on sin, and he alone has the righteousness needed! »And if he made his righteousness mine, then I am righteous in the same righteousness as he. But my sin cannot swallow him up, but is swallowed up in the infinite abyss of his righteousness, for he is God Himself, to whom be praise forever.«[46]

---

[44] WA 1, 140,20-23.

[45] An early formulation of the function of the law came in Luther's first lectures on Galatians (1516, extant in student notes): WA 57II, 59,18-60,13.

[46] WA 56, 204,8-29, citing lines 19-23 (LW 25,188f).

3. Justification In Luther's Mature Teaching

This section will offer a systematic account of the themes which coalesce in Luther's mature teaching on faith and justification. I want to show how his early discoveries found their place in his more comprehensive teaching. Some aspects of this doctrine are specific to Luther and represent historic contributions to forming the central Protestant tradition, such as the role of experience, the bondage of the will, and imputation. Some of these themes stirred controversy and even occasioned anathemas against Luther. Here I leave controversy aside, in order to concentrate on the contexts in which Luther developed his major theses and on the theological motivations that become evident when one reconstructs the arguments with which Luther supported the assertions of his mature doctrine.

Characteristics of Luther's Teaching on Justification

At times Luther attributed extraordinary importance to the correct doctrine of justification. Toward the end of his introduction to the *Lectures on Galatians* of 1531 (printed 1535) he states that one who loses the truth of this doctrine has thereby lost the whole of Christian doctrine. By this doctrine the church comes to be and perdures.[47] Justification was for Luther the real heart of his controversy with Rome: »Once this has been established, namely that God alone justifies us solely by His grace through Christ, then we will not only bear the pope aloft on our hands but also kiss his feet.«[48] The work of the authentic theologian is, therefore, concentrated on the cluster of themes that make up the doctrine of justification.

> The proper subject of theology is man guilty of sin and condemned (*homo... reus ac perditus*) and God the justifier and savior of man the sinner (*Deus iustificans ac salvator hominis peccatoris*). Whatever is asked or discussed in theology outside this subject is error and poison.[49]

Luther was convinced that all of Scripture sought to show God's merciful work of restoring to righteousness and life the humanity that had fallen into sin and condemnation. One who takes justification as the *scopus* (target, goal) in the

---

[47] WA 40I, 48,28f, 49,26f (LW 26, 9f). Also 441,29-31, on the doctrine of justification embracing all the other articles of faith. On justification as the *caput et summa* of Christian doctrine, WA 39I, 489,6. Further, WA 40III, 335,5-8 on justification as the one doctrine that preserves the church of Christ; for, »hoc amisso amittitur Christus et ecclesia.«
[48] WA 40I, 181,11-13 (LW 26, 99).
[49] WA 40II, 328,17-20 (LW 12, 311).

reading of Scripture will be nourished by the sacred text, because such a quest is thereby conformed to the biblical message itself.[50]

But the way to an adequate theology of justification was not simply the accurate reading of the text. One must have experience of sin and grace, and of life and death, to become a theologian worthy of the name.[51] Luther claimed that it was precisely his own experience of God and of sin that set him apart in the theological world, that is, from Thomas Aquinas, Erasmus, and the Antinomians.[52] Consequently, Luther's teaching on justification bears the marks of profound, often anguished, moments of personal involvement with deep feeling. Sin and guilt are terrifying in this world of thought, grace and forgiveness liberating and full of delight. Luther's theological discourse on justification is at times only the explanatory and protective superstructure built over the religious core and substructure of specific experiences of God.

Arising from experience, the theology of justification then serves further experience. The beginning concerns sin, which must not remain simply a concept in a thesis being asserted, but is to become a condition sensed with personal awareness of one's distance from God and of His fated condemnation. We know God's law well enough but we do not keep it. Realization of this occurs amid interior combat and struggle (*vera experientia et gravissimum certamen cordis*) and thus one comes to confess oneself a sinner.[53] Then the person is ready to appropriate another message, that of God's gracious design to raise the fallen in Christ. This dissipates all fears and lifts the spirit. Christ came for sinners. God is merciful precisely to the sinners who fear Him. Knowing self as sinful, one can move on to genuine theological knowledge of God, the God of the poor and afflicted upon whom He showers His mercy.[54] Then occurs the experience of faith, about which Luther's booklet *The Freedom of a Christian* (1520) has instructed so many readers. It is an experience of strength and courage now imperturbable, of trust and joy deep in the heart, and of a life transformed in Christ the Savior.[55]

---

[50] WA 40II, 328,20-29.

[51] »Vivendo, immo moriendo et damnando fit theologus, non intelligendo, legendo aut speculando« (WA 5, 163,29f). In a 1531 remark at table Luther went so far as to say, »Sola experientia facit theologum« (WA *Tischreden* 1, 16,13).

[52] WA 8, 127,24-26 (on Aquinas); WA *Tischreden* 1, 146,6-14 (on Erasmus); WA 39I, 490,16f (the Antinomians). Neither the *Rottengeister* nor the papists have experience of what they assert (WA 36, 505,1-506,2).

[53] WA 40II, 326,34-37, 327,21-26 (LW 12, 310f). On the distress of those truly struck by the demands of the law of God: WA 39I, 455,16-456,8.

[54] WA 40II, 327,26-35, 334,35-335,18, 361,15-18 (LW 12, 311, 316, 334).

[55] WA 7, 49,7-14, 59,1-20 (LW 31, 343, 357f).

Luther's orientation to personal experience had a number of consequences beyond the mark left on his works by tones of struggle, involvement, and deep feeling. He repeatedly tested doctrines and arguments with a view to their actual influence on one's lived relation to God. Luther, for instance, would not mitigate his insistence that »sin« remains after baptism, both because St. Paul said this in Rom 7 and because a change in terminology would likely make people cold and lethargic in praising God's mercy to people who are really sinners. They might glory in their incipient perfection and cease praying for forgiveness. They could come to rely on the purity and renewal given them, and not rely totally on Christ.[56]

The doctrine that salvation lies wholly outside the scope of our willing and striving is essential to the depth of humility God wants.[57] In fending off arguments from St. Augustine and St. Bernard for free choice having a role in justification, Luther asserted that one should not attend to their subtle disputations about the will and grace, but instead to their personal prayers to God. As they addressed God from the heart, they despaired of themselves and implored grace, only grace, without recourse to any power of choice.[58] An argument over the experiential outcome was one of Luther's last points in his refutation of Erasmus's case for free choice. Luther confessed that he had no desire to be free regarding his salvation. With freedom, how would he ever withstand the assaults of the enemy? How would he ever be certain of satisfying God's good pleasure by his free choices? But now because there is no free choice regarding salvation, the way opens to a special range of experience:

> Now, since God has taken my salvation out of my hands into His, making it depend on His choice and not mine, and has promised to save me, not by my own work or exertion but by His grace and mercy, I am assured and certain both that He is faithful and will not lie to me, and also that He is too great and powerful for any demons or any adversities to be able to break Him or to snatch me from Him... Moreover, we are also certain and sure that we please God, not by the merit of our own working, but by the favor of His mercy promised to us.[59]

---

[56] WA 8, 103,17-26, 108,2-9, 111,16f.27-36 (LW 32, 223, 230, 235). Study 4 in this collection treats this issue in greater detail.

[57] WA 18, 632,30-633,3 (LW 33, 62).

[58] WA 18, 644,5-16 (LW 33, 76f). This passage is used to good effect by Otto H. Pesch in his seminal essay »Existential and Sapiential Theology: The Theological Confrontation between Luther and Thomas Aquinas,« *Catholic Scholars Dialogue with Luther*, 61-81.

[59] WA 18, 783,17-39, citing lines 28-39 (LW 33, 289).

The Human Condition of Bondage

Any interpretation of Luther must take serious account of his massive broadside of 1525, *De servo arbitrio*, written as a rebuttal of Erasmus's *De libero arbitrio* (1524).[60] Justification is the central topic here, but Luther's argument entails treatises on biblical and doctrinal hermeneutics and ecclesiology, as well as numerous passages that amount to a tract on God's sovereign rule of His creation.

De servo arbitrio was a significant contribution to the process of clarification and demarcation by which Luther in 1525 defined with all desirable clarity the doctrinal character of the reform he had initiated. Early that year Luther completed *Against the Heavenly Prophets*, a defense of sacramental mediation that attacked the spiritualistic Christianity found in the pamphlets of his former colleague Andreas Karlstadt. Luther responded to the peasant uprisings of spring 1525 with a pamphlet calling upon the princes to use the power God had given them to suppress those who were rebelling against the established order. In autumn 1525 Luther turned to Erasmus's book on freedom, which was a subtle yet optimistic defense of human dignity, of the ethic of reward and punishment, and of the justice of God in His condemning or rewarding our responsible decisions and actions. Luther, in 1525, was making clear for all the differences between his reform and the projected reforms of revolutionary spiritualists and of those humanist theologians espousing an anthropological optimism.

De servo arbitrio represents a highpoint of dogmatic assertiveness in Luther's theology, as he ruthlessly condemned point by point Erasmus's gentle optimism about the human condition. God is to remain sovereign, Luther maintained, and not to be miniaturized in order to fit the contours of a sweetly reasonable religious-ethical piety. A topic of such importance as human freedom must be treated clearly and forcefully. One who is ignorant or unclear here will not know how to relate to God and what to expect from God's working. This is to undercut the worship and praise of God. »It therefore behooves us to be very certain about the distinction between God's power and our own, God's work and our own, if we want to live a godly life.«[61] What one must know is that God's power in fact does everything in our salvation, while our will does nothing. Before justification, there is no human activity in preparation for grace and renewal; once God has recreated the will, it does nothing toward preserving what has been given, »but the Spirit alone does both of these things in us,

---

[60] A basic ecumenical-theological study is H. McSorley, *Luther: Right or Wrong?* (New York and Minneapolis 1969). G. Chantraine has recently offered a useful historical account of the controversy between Luther and Erasmus, with special attention to their divergent theological approaches to Scripture: *Erasmus et Luther: Libre et serf arbitre* (Paris-Namur 1981), »Partie historique,« pp. 3-263.

[61] WA 18, 614,1-18, citing lines 15f (LW 33, 35).

recreating us without ourselves and preserving us without our help in our recreated state.«[62]

Luther's doctrine of human bondage, upon closer inspection, proves to be woven of three theological strands. Three distinct clusters of doctrinal convictions about the human condition fuse in *De servo arbitrio*.

1) Erasmus saw the will prior to justification as neutral and standing poised between God and Satan, poised, that is, between alternatives of choice. In response, Luther asserted that the fallen will is captive to evil and actually doing evil of its own accord and gladly (*sponte et libenti voluntate*).[63] The Creator supports the will's perverse actuation ontologically, but God does this in conformity with the given condition of the will, which is one of aversion to Himself and His law. The first type of bondage is thus the impossibility of altering this aversion: »It thus comes about that man perpetually and necessarily sins and errs until he is put right by the Spirit of God«.[64] Human bondage is first a captivity under the irresistible rule of evil in the fallen will, which is ever prompt and ready in its quest of the wrong.

2) Another strand in Luther's account of human bondage is his resolute exclusion of a free consent to grace which in any given case could in fact be dissent and refusal. The fallen will has no residual capacity out of which to freely comply with its own justification. Furthermore, when God turns the will to Himself, this is no weak and hesitant influence that awaits our ratification. »God's 'turning' ... is that most active working of God which a man cannot avoid or alter, but under which he necessarily has the sort of will that God both gives him and carries along, by His own momentum (*rapit suo motu*).«[65] God's gift is so dynamic and influential as to leave no place for a division of labor between the human will and the Spirit of God. Synergism is ruled out both by the ineptitude of the fallen will and by the efficacy, quite irresistible, of the Spirit.

The result, however, is not violent compulsion, for the will is swept along in a spontaneous movement of seeking the good.

> If God works in us, the will is changed, and being gently breathed upon by the Spirit of God, it again wills and acts from pure willingness and inclination and of its own accord, not from compulsion, so that it cannot be turned another way by any opposition ... but it goes on willing and delighting in and loving the good.... So not

---

[62] WA 18, 754,7-12, citing lines 11f (LW 33, 243).

[63] WA 18, 634,25. Also 670,7f, on the will being determined by either God or Satan: »Si Deus abest, Satan adest, nec nisi velle malum in nobis est.«

[64] WA 18, 709,21-710,10, citing 710,7f (LW 33, 176f). Further, 685,10-17, 768,17-26, 774,19-775,18, 786,7-14.

[65] WA 18, 747, 24-27 (LW 33, 233). Other references to God's work as *raptus*: 636,17, 699,13, 753,29-35, 782,10.33.

even here is there any free choice, or freedom to turn oneself in another direction or to will something different, so long as the Spirit and grace of God remain in a man.[66]

Therefore there is a bondage of subjection to God consisting in the passivity of the will under the active and enrapturing influence of God on the human spirit. Such is the way God works in His elect.

3) Finally, there is the total subjection of all creatures to the divine governance of the universe. God foreknows everything and He carries out His design in complete accord with His eternal, unchangeable, and infallible will. There is thus a cosmic subjection to God's rule that also shatters the pretensions of free choice.

> Everything we do, everything that happens, even if it seems to us to happen mutably and contingently, happens in fact nonetheless necessarily and immutably, if you have regard to the will of God. For the will of God is effectual and cannot be hindered, since it is the power of the divine nature itself; moreover it is wise, so that it cannot be deceived.[67]

Christian faith in divine providence means for Luther that God remains in such wise sovereign that creatures have no share in determining the governance of the world. Consequently one can believe with total assurance the word of God, because He carries out effectively all that He promises.[68]

An ultimate reason for the bondage of the will, in Luther's argument, is the subjection of all things to God's hidden preordination, according to which He carries out all He has determined. Why the design is such as it is and not different – that is God's own secret, far beyond the proper scope of our inquiry. Especially we are not to investigate why God gives His transforming grace to some and not to others. We have no right to ask about God's own counsels; instead, we are to attend to God as revealed and preached, that is, as merciful to all.[69] It may seem quite unjust for God to leave sinners in their rebellion and then to condemn them to hell for being children of wrath, but faith must bear with

---

[66] WA 18, 634,37-635,7 (LW 33, 65). Luther had in his *Operationes in psalmos* (1519-21) spoken of the way the will is passive in faith, hope and love, because in them »non est nisi passio, raptus, motus, quo movetur, formatur, purgatur, impregnatur anima verbo Dei« (WA 5, 176,12-14). Also 177,11-14. Similarly, in the 1519 *Resolutiones* of the Leipzig Disputation: WA 2, 421,7-15.

[67] WA 18, 615,25-616,12, citing 615,31-35 (LW 33, 37f). Also 714,38-722,29, where Luther argues at length from Rom 9:15-18 that what God foreknows then takes place of necessity. In addition, 752,12-15, 753,28-33.

[68] WA 18, 618,19-619,21. Also, 714,18f.

[69] WA 18, 684,32-686,13, 712,19-38. B. Gerrish brought out the distinctive character of Luther's position on the inscrutability of God in *De servo arbitrio*, noting the threat Luther thereby posed to his own central message by allowing such a forbidding presence to lurk at the edge of faith. »'To the Unknown God': Luther and Calvin on the Hiddenness of God,« *Journal of Religion* 53 (1973), 263-292.

this for the present, until in the light of glory God comes to be revealed as supremely just.[70]

Thus Luther has a variety of arguments against any human pretensions to autonomy before God. The ethical way of salvation by meritorious free choice of the good is walled off by three bulwarks that safeguard God's initiative and sovereign effectiveness in human salvation.

Structures of Justification Itself

The unique object of justifying faith is Christ and his redemptive work. This is the one way to encounter God and survive. As Luther laid down in the First Antinomian Disputation (1537), approaching »the naked God« in His majesty is perilous in the extreme. Instead, one must turn to the God who is given for us as Savior, the Word Incarnate whom the believer finds in the manger and hanging on the cross.[71] Specifically, justifying faith lays hold of the redemptive work of Christ – his delivery for sins, the shedding of his blood, his death, and his triumphant resurrection – all done out of merciful love for sinners. Luther would characteristically posit in one and the same article of faith both Christ's redemptive work and justification by faith alone. That Christ is Savior means that no works, merit, or performance according to precept can have a role beside him on whom faith focuses.[72] Faith, thus, is wholly soteriological in orientation and content, and it becomes authentic when it dawns on a person that the Redeemer did all this *for me*.

> True faith says, »I certainly believe that the Son of God suffered and rose, but that he did all this for me, for my sins, of that I am certain.«... Accordingly, that »for me« or »for us« if it is believed, creates that true faith and distinguishes it from all other faith, which merely hears the things done.[73]

By such faith Christ becomes active in one's existence against the malevolent forces of sin, guilt, and despair.

1) *The Savior's victory.* The fullest statement by Luther on redemption itself as an event came in his exposition of Gal 3:13 (»Christ redeemed us from the curse

---

[70] WA 18, 785,35-39. On Luther's own anguished struggle amid resentment over the mystery of predestination, 719,9f; also WA *Tischreden* 4, 641,14-642,2, where Luther observed that we have enough to do learning about God's revealed will, in the humanity of Christ, without probing mysteries meant to be hidden.

[71] WA 39I, 370,13-17, 389,10-15. Also WABr 1, 328,45-329,60 (a letter of Feb. 12,1519). As well, WA 40II, 329,19-35.

[72] Smalcald Articles (1537), Part 2, Article 1 (WA 50, 198,23-199,21; *The Book of Concord*, 292).

[73] WA 39I, 45,21-46,10, citing 45,33f and 46,7f. Some other representative passages on the *pro me* in genuine faith: WA 2, 458,22f, 490,35ff; 40I, 297,15-33.

of the law, becoming accursed for us...«).⁷⁴ Here Luther developed the conception of Christ taking upon himself all the sins of the human race, becoming thereby the willing *socius peccatorum*.⁷⁵ A theology that would segregate Christ from sin, say, to make him the supreme example of virtue, renders the Lord useless for sinners in need of deliverance.⁷⁶ Our consolation rests upon his being wrapped up in all the sins of the world. The event of redemption then transpired with the attack of sin, death, and the curse upon Christ laden with our sins. But in the drama of the Passion the malevolent forces did not see what was hidden in the person of Christ, namely, supreme and invincible righteousness.⁷⁷ Encountering divine power, the hostile forces were exhausted and suffered total defeat.⁷⁸ As the Easter Sequence celebrates, *Mors et vita duello conflixere mirando / Dux vitae mortuus regnat vivus*.⁷⁹ Justifying faith, thus, embraces Christ triumphant, for all of us, over sin, death, and the curse of condemnation.

2) *Communication by word and sacrament*. The link between Christ's redemptive work and believers is the proclamation of the gospel, the message of Christ's saving victory and legacy to humankind.⁸⁰ A narrative about Christ becomes »gospel« when you sense that Christ is offering himself to be your very own, so that all he has done becomes all yours (*totum tuum*).⁸¹ The privileged events of redemption-being-proclaimed are the sacraments, where words are spoken that make the individual utterly certain of God's grace in Christ.⁸² Justification can occur in one's accepting response to the baptismal formula, to the words of eucharistic institution, or to absolution, by hearing in delight

---

⁷⁴ WA 40I, 432-448 (LW 26,276-288).
⁷⁵ WA 40I, 434,17.
⁷⁶ WA 40I, 434,17.
⁷⁷ WA 40I, 439,13-24.
⁷⁸ WA 40I, 441,14-28.
⁷⁹ WA 40I, 439,32f. Perceptive on Luther's soteriology is Y. Congar, »Regards et réflexions sur la christologie de Luther,« in *Chrétiens en dialogue* (Paris 1964), 453-489, English translation as »Considerations and Reflections on the Christology of Luther,« in *Dialogue between Christians* (Westminster, Md. 1966), 372-406. Congar makes the point that Luther leaves the human subjectivity of the God-man passive in the divine work of redemption. Thus Luther is, in tendency, Alexandrine, not Antiochene, in his soteriology.
⁸⁰ WADB 5, 476,5-24 and 477,16-38 (LW 35, 358, 360). D. Olivier chose Luther's short instruction of 1522 on finding »the gospel in the Gospels« as an illuminating first example of Luther's discourse on faith. *La foi de Luther* (Paris 1978), 61-69, with commentary on pp. 69-72; in English in *Luther's Faith: the Cause of the Gospel in the Church* (St. Louis 1982).
⁸¹ WADB 5, 478,1-5.
⁸² WA 40I, 591,16-30 (LW 12, 388f).

(*auditus gaudii*). Works count for nothing here, where our hearing interacts with the *vox Dei*.[83] Luther can address Christ and say: »All our certitude rests upon your word, which reveals that the sins of the whole world have been expiated and destroyed by your sacrifice, death and resurrection.«[84]

3) *Grace frees from guilt; the gift purifies.* Luther elaborated a detailed account of what is conferred in justification by making use of the distinction in Rom 5:15 between *gratia* and *donum*.[85] This scheme served well in Luther's effort to articulate, on the one hand, the simple personal relationship between the merciful God and the believing person brought into the sphere of righteousness and, on the other hand, the complex historical process of lifelong struggle against sin in the power of God's Spirit shed abroad in the hearts of believers. God's *gratia* defines the relationship, while his *donum* animates the processes of new life.

»Grace« is God's mercy, benevolence, and favor, a reality ever outside a person but announced and come near in the gospel. God's grace stands opposed to His wrath, and each of them encounters the person in undivided totality, wrath upon the sinner and grace upon the righteous. God takes the person, that is, one who confesses his sin and believes the gospel-promise, wholly into the embrace of His mercy. Grace is consequently not a quality in the human heart but divine forgiveness of sin because of Christ. The believer's relation to grace proceeds from the conscience, where the power of sin to condemn has been broken. Before justification by God's grace, sin dominated (as *peccatum regnans*) and overwhelmed the conscience, but now it is dominated (as *peccatum regnatum*) and is no longer imputed, since guilt has been wiped away by God's merciful grace. The relationship is itself transformative, by bringing peace of heart, joy, assurance and courage – a totally new self-understanding before God. By grace the believer is wholly righteous because of Christ the Savior laid hold of in faith.[86]

The »gift« is directly opposed to our sinful and corrupt self-seeking. It is the Holy Spirit infused into the heart, where there unfolds the gradual process of

---

[83] WA 40II, 409,20-411,34 (LW 12, 368-370).

[84] WA 40II, 413,24-26.

[85] A fundamental treatment of this theme is E. Iserloh's study »Gratia und Donum: Rechtfertigung und Heiligung nach Luthers 'Wider den Löwener Theologen Latomus' (1521),« in L. Abramowski & J.F. Goeters, eds., *Studien zur Geschichte und Theologie der Reformation*, Festschrift Ernst Bizer (Neukirchen 1969), 141-156; reprinted in Iserloh, *Luther und die Reformation* (Aschaffenburg 1974), 88-105.

[86] In the *Antilatomus* (1522), WA 8, 88,25-29 (LW 32, 202), 94,8f, 106,10-15, 106,37-107,4, 107,13-23.32-36. In the prefaces to Romans (1522, 1529), WADB 7, 8,10-22; 5, 622,17-41, 623,26-32 (LW 35, 369f). In the exposition of Psalm 51 (1532, printed 1538), WA 40II, 350,33-37 (LW 12, 327), 351,23-25, 352,21-23, 352,36-353,21, 353,36-354,20, 357,35-358,19. In a disputation on justification (1536), WA 39I, 99,18-27 (LW 34, 168f).

eradicating and expelling the baneful complex of sinful drives and tendencies. One does not have the gift fully in this life, but there can be a gradual increment until complete purification is attained in death. The gift initiates a struggle of penitential transformation amid prayer for the healing of both soul and body, a struggle for which vitality and direction are supplied by the Holy Spirit (*ubi vita et gubernatio cordis sit Spiritus Sanctus*). The struggle, in Luther's late accounts, is against both egotistical flaws in one's love of God and perverse notions of God suggested by the flesh, which is ever ready to doubt God's favor by making it conditioned on our works. The Holy Spirit comes as the effective opponent of this pseudo-wisdom and as the animator of a holy life of unselfish service of others and growing dedication to God.[87]

4) *Imputation and union with Christ*. In the strict sense, the cause of justification is solely the meritorious work of Christ, the victor over sin in whom the believing heart lays hold of mercy.[88] The righteous are forgiven and acquitted before God, but not because of the beginning in them of purity and good deeds. At the stage of justification itself, righteousness is by imputation because of, and with regard to, Christ.[89] However, faith is a real relation to Christ, and his righteousness does become one's real possession by the promise of faith, although it is ever alien and external because we do not merit it.[90] The forgiveness, totally present by grace and imputation, begins at once to be cleansing and effective transformation by the gift.[91]

Luther's technical accounts of the diverse elements in justification should not obscure the more obvious character of the faith in Christ which justifies. By faith one clings to Christ and becomes one with him, sharing in all the righteousness and life that are his own.[92] Luther's stress on the unmerited *extra nos* of

---

[87] WA 8, 107,13-23.32-36; WADB 5, 622,18-24.34-37, 623,17 (cited); WA 40II, 351,26-352,17, 352,17, 352,33-36, 354,21-32, 355,16-24, 356,19-23, 357,20-31, 358,19-26. First Antinomiam Disputation (1537), WA 39I, 383,3-12. Third Antinomian Disputation (1538), WA 39I, 495, 11-26. Study 4, below, on pp. 70-74, develops in greater detail Luther's account of *gratia* and *donum*.

[88] WA 40II, 358,35-37 (LW 12, 332). In this context Luther would allow one to speak of the confession of one's sin as a *causa secunda* or *causa sine qua non*, which however has no independent causal influence: »quia sic est causa, ut tamen tota res pendeat ex misericordia Dei seu ex promissione.« There is no ground at all here for merit, since even one's confession is effected by God's promise (358,37-359,17 and 359,23-25).

[89] WA 39I, 83,18-27, 97,16-22, 492,2-23, 514,13-20.

[90] »Extra nos esse est ex nostris viribus non esse. Est quidem iustitia possessio nostra, quia nobis donata est ex misericordia, tamen aliena a nobis, quia non meruimus eam« (WA 39I, 109,1-3; LW 34,178).

[91] WA 39I, 98,5-11 (LW 34, 167). In the second Antinomian Disputation (1538) Luther repeatedly linked two modes of deliverance from sin: imputative and expurgative (WA 39I, 431,16-432,11, 434,3-12, 444,4-6).

[92] WA 2, 491,12-18, 504,6-8 (LW 27, 222, 241); WA 7, 54,31-55,35 (LW 31,351f.); WA 8, 599,2-7 (LW 44, 286).

righteousness and its imputation in no way prevented him from appropriating Gal 2:20 (»I live, now not I, but Christ lives in me«) as a testimony to Christ abiding »properly and inherently,« conferring his life, grace and salvation »by cementing and inherence in faith,« and becoming in a way one person with the believer.[93] It is not too much to say that justification entails a mystical union with Christ the Savior in the depths of the believing person.

Penance and Good Works in the New Life of Righteousness

The person once guilty but now saved by grace has been set right in relation to God, but God's design encompasses much more in his regard. Luther can compare one living this life to the heavens and earth in the beginning, since both are »matter,« even »pure matter,« for the future form of perfection God plans to bring forth, a form which in our case is in God's own image.[94]

The lifelong task remaining after justification is the purgation of the complex of sinful tendencies that remain. This is the daily cleansing, the renewal from day to day in groaning and struggle.[95] Sin's power in the conscience, where it once tyrannized and implanted guilt, has been broken, but the residue of sin is still present, as evidenced by reluctance in doing good and by recurrent temptations to satisfy God by achievements. But the state and condition of this sin is, after justification, changed decisively, for it is now subject, condemned, and bound over for eventual complete destruction.[96] The believer, therefore, does penance all his life, but with confidence as he confronts his lust, anger and pride. The internal *donum* of the Spirit and the external word work together to bring the whole person to health and well-being by expelling the poisoned complex of sinfulness.[97]

---

[93] WA 40I, 283,8f, 284,6f, 285,5 — all cited from the 1531 lecture script on Galatians, not from the text polished up by Luther's assistants for printing. The presence of Christ in the believer — as a central aspect of Luther's doctrine of justification — is a theme about which present-day Finnish Luther interpreters are doing much to remind us. See T. Mannermaa, »In ipsa fide Christus adest,« in *Der im Glauben gegenwärtige Christus. Rechtfertigung und Vergottung* (Hannover 1989), 11-93, and the papers by Mannermaa, U. Asendorf, and S. Peura in S. Peura and A. Raunio, eds., *Luther und Theosis. Vergöttlichung als Thema der abendländischen Theologie* (Helsinki & Erlangen 1990).

[94] WA 39I, 177,3-12 (LW 34, 139f). This text from Luther's Disputation on Man (1536) was used to good effect by K.-H. zur Mühlen to show the abyss separating Luther's biblical and eschatological view of the human situation from Aristotle's ontological and rational perspective. *Reformatorische Vernunftkritik und neuzeitliches Denken* (Tübingen 1980), 132ff.

[95] WA 2, 414,14-19, 536,3ff, 570,16ff (LW 26, 289, 340); WA 5, 299,30-34.

[96] WA 8, 88,25-29 (LW 32, 202), 91,15-25.35-40, 94,8f.

[97] WA 39I, 113,20-114,4 (LW 34, 182f), 394,13-19, 395,22-396,1, 398,11-20.

In the context of this lifelong penance, Luther comes to ascribe a role to good works. They clearly are not justifying and so one puts no stock in them as meritorious. The Spirit instills instead an uncalculating, free, and spontaneous desire of pleasing God and promoting His glory. No claim is made by one who does good only as God's instrument.[98] Works are not the cause of righteousness but its fruit.[99] The believer's delight in Christ frees him from the burden of meritorious achievement of status. Gratitude gives rise to joyful service in love unconstrained.[100] As Christ worked and suffered for us *gratis*, so those who believe in him, in whom he is now working, seek to benefit others without concern for gain.[101] Applying Phil 2:5-11, Luther presents Christ as the model who, being in the form of God and possessing all perfection, emptied himself in labors for others; just so, the righteous person, possessing righteousness in Christ and made free, is now to empty himself in service for the neighbor, dealing with others just as God dealt with him.[102] Thus faith and works are not to be separated. The distinction between them is radical, as between God and man in Christ or between the soul and body in a human being, but they are connected. Luther can speak of faith »growing fat« by works, as it makes its presence felt.[103]

Strange as it may seem, Luther's reform came to take pride in its instruction on good works.[104] The experience of conversion to Christ's salvation does lead,

---

[98] WA 5, 169,1-9; WA 6, 207,26-30 (LW 44,27).

[99] WA 6, 94,39f.

[100] WA 7, 60,6-9,27-29 (LW 31,359f.). Also WA 6, 207,15-30 (LW 44,27).

[101] WA 8, 608,24-32 (LW 44,301f).

[102] WA 7, 65,32-66,10 (LW 31, 366).

[103] *Rhapsodia de loco justificationis* (1530), WA 30II, 659,13-21. In a more technical mode, Luther could contrast *fides abstracta vel absoluta* (outside of good works) with *fides concreta, composita seu incarnata* (active in good works) and thereby he came to attribute qualified but definite significance to good works done in faith» (WA 40I, 414,24-416,27 [LW 26, 264-266]). On Luther's correlation of faith/works with Christ's divinity/humanity, and on the problems Luther's polemic brings in its train, see P. Manns, »Fides Absoluta — Fides Incarnata. Zur Rechtfertigungslehre Luthers in Großen Galaterkommentar,« in E. Iserloh & K. Repgen, eds., *Reformata Reformanda*, Festschrift Hubert Jedin (Münster 1965), 1, 265-312; reprinted in P. Manns, *Vater im Glauben. Studien zur Theologie Martin Luthers*, ed. R. Decot (Stuttgart 1988), 1-48; English translation, »Absolute and Incarnate Faith: Luther on Justification in the Galatians' Commentary of 1531-1535,« in J. Wicks, ed., *Catholic Scholars Dialogue with Luther* (Chicago 1970), 121-156.

[104] Article 20 of the Augsburg Confession of 1530 points to the existence of Lutheran instructions on the Ten Commandments in its refutation of charges that their reform undermines good works. Lutheran teaching »is rather to be praised for teaching that good works are to be done and for offering help as to how they may be done.« Cited from *The Book of Concord*, ed. T.G. Tappert (Philadelphia 1959), 46. Similarly, Luther said in his apologetic *Admonition to All the Clergy Assembled at Augsburg* (also 1530) that now even young children in the reformed territories are learning about the Ten Commandments in catechism. WA 30II, 301,5-16 (LW 34, 28). Luther had explained the Decalogue in his *Treatise on Good Works* of spring 1520 (WA 6, 202-76; LW 44, 21-114). His catechisms of 1529 begin with instructions on the Ten Commandments before taking up the Lord's Prayer and the sacraments. The Small Catechism finishes with a concise table of the duties incumbent on members of the various estates.

according to Luther, to a movement of descent into the world and society to meet human needs. »When I have this righteousness within me, I descend from heaven like the rain that makes the earth fertile. That is, I come forth into another kingdom, and I perform good works whenever the opportunity arises.«[105] The relation to God given by reconciling grace leads the believer to take up gladly a vocation in which God has stipulated needed tasks in the basic sectors of worldly life. These are the spheres of service in which to work for others in obedience to God's calling.

The »estates,« in which one works for others as an instrument of the Creator's bounty, are generically the Church, the family, the economy, and civil government.[106] This, then, is the context of Luther's stress on the dignity of the most ordinary occupations instituted by God the Creator – and the context of his attacks on doctrines of higher states in monastic and religious life. Marriage, government and the ministry are God's own »orders,« in which true good works can be done in abundance. But systematically these spheres of service belong to the first article of the Creed, on creation, and not to the second article, on redemption and its appropriation in justification.

Still the believer is freed by faith in Christ to attend to the needs of others. Service of the neighbor is clearly a consequence of, not a means to, a saving encounter with God's loving-kindness in Christ. The person returns again and again to be confirmed in God's freely given grace and forgiveness, by hearing the preached word and receiving the assuring sacraments in faith. Then the movement outward into service can commence again: feeding the hungry, giving drink to the thirsty, forgiving enemies, praying for all living on earth, and suffering trials and pain. But none of these good actions serve in gaining salvation, since that is found uniquely in clinging to Christ the Redeemer in faith.[107]

4. Concluding Evaluative Reflections

Some generalizing reflections can serve to highlight points of special significance in Luther's account of justification. I would indicate five contexts in which his work is of fundamental significance.

First, numerous points of Luther's theology occasioned dissenting and opposed reactions first by Catholic controversialist theologians, beginning in 1518, and then by the theologians and bishops gathered at the Council of Trent. Two of Luther's teachings presented in this essay caused a perceptible contrary

---

[105] WA 40I, 51,21-23 (LW 26, 11).
[106] WA 26, 504,30-505,10 (LW 37, 364f.). See P. Althaus, *Die Ethik Martin Luthers* (Gütersloh 1966), 43-48; in English as *The Ethics of Martin Luther* (Philadelphia 1972), 36-42.
[107] WA 26, 505,11-20.

movement in the formulation of doctrine basic to modern Catholicism.

Trent, and the theological instruction then shaped by the Council, singles out the role played by human freedom in the assent or dissent by which the movements of heart initiated by God's grace are appropriated by the person or sinfully resisted. Catholic theology, faced with the excesses of *De servo arbitrio*, came to be confirmed in its own kind of synergism as a mark of its account of faith and justification, quite convinced that God's efficacy in and upon the human spirit does not exclude but includes a movement of freely given compliance with the divine project of salvation. Thereby, this theology can ascribe human guilt for non-compliance with God's saving action.

Also early modern Catholicism, differing with Luther's »first-article« theology of good works, asserted that righteous persons act under the influence of Christ and his Spirit poured out into believing hearts. This is a »third-article« view of works, in which believers are members moved by the head or branches become fruitful because of Christ the living vine. This emphasis corresponds with a characteristic spirit in the men and women of early-modern Catholicism, an activist spirit of constant struggle, zeal for missions all over the world, and discipline and self-sacrifice in everyday life.[108] Typical representatives of this Counter Reformation spirituality were convinced of the supernatural and salvific value of their activity in a manner not open to Christians instructed by Luther.

On these two points at least, Luther's doctrine of justification had added historic significance, because of the contrary emphases that shaped a whole era in Catholicism. The contemporary dialogue between Lutherans and Roman Catholics is struggling hard to overcome the doctrinal impasse that is especially represented by these two doctrinal oppositions.

Second, looking to the positive side of Luther's message, one should first single out an element of basic and perennial Christian value. This I find in the way Luther confronts our secure, complacent, and proud humanity with a powerful evangelical witness to the primacy, yes even the sovereignty, of God's agency in what is most intimately human, namely, personal development. Luther demonstrated, on his Pauline basis, the inadequacy of our ethical striving toward the goals of humane living. Against various mentalities stressing achievement – whether in theology, popular piety, or humanistic »philosophies of life« – Luther set forth the cross of Christ as the paradox-filled paradigm for life. One finds life by losing it, that is, by delivering oneself over to God's own redemptive project. Then a new life can begin, but even this is predominantly a penitential existence, ever in needy dependence, ever on the way, ever being purified. Luther's theology of justification has a fundamental religious significance.

---

[108] H.O. Evennett, *The Spirit of the Counter-Reformation*, ed. J. Bossy (Cambridge 1968 & Notre Dame 1970). More recent perceptions of this phenomenon are surveyed in J.W. O'Malley, ed., *Catholicism in Early Modern History. A Guide to Research* (St. Louis 1988), especially in the Editor's Introduction and in the reports by M. Marcocchi on spirituality, by J.W. Witek on the missionary expansion, and by P.F. Grendler on schools and catechetics.

Third, Luther posited soteriology in the center of theological work. His thought was dominated by the effort to bind faith and theology in single-minded attentiveness to Christ as Savior. Turning from personal dispositions, intentions, and achievements as values regarding salvation, faith focuses exclusively on the redemptive mystery of Christ. Theology then strives to serve this orientation by constantly reaffirming redemption and continually connecting all other topics to the central event, Jesus Christ crucified for sin and risen. In this, Luther was offering a significant alternative to the schools or *viae* of late-medieval university theology, with their broad systematic attention to the levels of creation and all the stages and instruments of the human way to God. Thomists stressed the harmonious interrelation of all elements under divine wisdom, while Scotists and Ockhamists accented the freedom of God's unbounded will over against the contingent universe. But Luther posited a new foundation by expounding theology tightly unified in and around soteriology.

Fourth, there is Luther's drive to relate theological discourse to experience or lived religious existence. Here his work is of monumental importance, especially when seen in the perspective of the fateful divorce in the West of academic theology from monastic theology and spirituality beginning in the twelfth century, as with Abelard and St. Bernard of Clairvaux. In the new departure which is Luther's doctrine of justification, the systematic and experiential concerns came together again in creative renewal. Luther did argue from texts to conclusions; he defended theses and gave elaborate, often ingenious, explanatory accounts. Thus he stood in dialogue, to say nothing of stormy polemic, with the academic tradition of disciplined, warranted discourse. But all Luther's warrants and explanations serve religious living of a particular style. His theses relate directly to humility *coram Deo*, to the laying hold of redemption in audacious confidence, and to living then in penitential purification. Theology, rediscovering a center in the Pauline writings, is in Luther's work vitally connected with lived religion.

Fifth, Luther's theology of justification was undoubtedly a major achievement of Western thought at the beginning of the modern age. A crisis of basic institutions had afflicted western Europe in the fourteenth century, but this gave way to a many-sided recovery in the fifteenth century in which economic systems, governments, and schools began to provide a better context of order and more adequate nurture for humane living. The Church, it is clear, lagged behind this broad growth of competency. The Renaissance papacy (1450-1521) was victorious over conciliarism, but it did not effectively supervise the pastoral ministry of Europe's bishops. The late-medieval German episcopate was thoroughly politicized, being one of the main fields of aristocratic pursuit of power. Homiletics, with rare exceptions, remained beholden to old schemes of moralizing and to the support of devotional religion. Popular piety, in lush growth around 1500, was not checked and controlled by doctrine.[109] But reform

---

[109] These few lines can only suggest an understanding of the church-historical situation in

did come in the sixteenth century, with the formulation of new ways of faith, preaching, and worship which have proven viable over the long haul of subsequent centuries. Among these new ways, Luther's striking account of *homo reus ac perditus* and *Deus iustificans ac salvator* laid a foundation of truly historic significance.

which Luther emerged as a reformer. I stated a view more at length in *Luther and His Spiritual Legacy* (Wilmington, Del. 1983), ch. 2, »The Eve of the Reformation,« pp. 35-54. For basic insights I remain in debt to the following works. J. Lortz, »Zur Problematik der kirchlichen Mißstände im Spät-Mittelalter,« *Trierer Theologische Zeitschrift* 58 (1949), 1-26, 212-227, 257-279, 347-357; reprinted in *Erneuerung und Einheit. Aufsätze zur Theologie- und Kirchengeschichte*, ed. P. Manns (Stuttgart 1987), 295-370. B. Moeller, »Frömmigkeit in Deutschland um 1500,« *Archiv für Reformationgeschichte* 56 (1965), 5-31; in English as »Piety in Germany around 1500,« in S. Ozment, ed., *The Reformation in Medieval Perspective* (Chicago 1971), 50-75; also in G. Strauss, ed., *Pre - Reformation Germany* (London & New York 1972), 13-42. J.R. Strayer, »The Fourth and the Fourteenth Centuries,« *American Historical Review* 77 (1972), 1-14. F. Rapp, *Réform et Réformation à Strasbourg. Église et Societé dans le diocese de Strasbourg (1450-1525)* (Paris 1974). F. Oakley, *The Western Church in the Later Middle Ages* (Ithaca, N.Y. 1979). – A more incisive view will emerge in Study 10 of this collection, through investigation of the ways Lutheran leaders legitimated the reforms introduced by 1530.

3

THE HEART CLINGING TO THE WORD

Annually Reformation scholars and theological libraries around the world receive copies of the *Lutherjahrbuch*, with essays, book reviews, and an extensive bibliography of works on Martin Luther. The cover of each volume bears a sketch of the coat of arms Luther chose for himself in 1530. The Reformer stipulated that a golden ring should encircle a field of blue. The petals of a white rose open on the field, and in the center of the rose stands a human heart. On the heart, a black cross is embossed.

Luther explained that his chosen emblem gave compendious expression to his theology.

> There is first to be a black cross upon the heart, but with the heart having its natural color. Thus I would remind myself that faith in the Crucified saves us. For whoever believes from the heart becomes righteous. Being a black cross, it mortifies and means to bring pain, yet it leaves the heart still its own color, not ruining our nature. Thus the cross does not kill, but keeps alive. *Iustus enim ex fide vivet, sed fide Crucifixi.* Such a heart should stand in the center of a white rose, to show that faith gives joy, consolation, and peace.... The rose is in a field of heavenly blue, to show that our joy in the Spirit and in faith is a beginning of heavenly happiness to come, which we already have by laying hold of it in hope, although it is not yet manifest.[1]

Martin Luther understood himself as a teacher of the existential meaning of faith in Jesus Christ. On the one hand, he set forth the »theology of the cross,« for in Christ Crucified the wisdom of God has paradoxically made itself known. The message, however, conveys to the believer a consoling grace of certainty and conviction about God's mercy and loving-kindness. The fretful heart finds peace and assurance in the word God has spoken through his crucified Son.

Luther's concern over fixing the mystery of Christ upon the believing heart became explicit at times in his preaching. On December 27, 1533, he explained the responses of Mary and the shepherds of Bethlehem to the coming of Christ.[2] Although the shepherds came to see the new-born baby and later told others about the marvelous events, few in fact came to genuine faith. This reveals the

---

[1] Letter of July 8, 1530, from Castle Coburg, to Lazarus Spengler of Nürnberg. WABr 5, 445,5-18, but following variant readings given in WABr 13, 155.
[2] WA 37, 245-248.

inconstancy of the human heart, so liable to forget if God does not supply new signs and wonders. But Mary kept the words in her heart, meditating and pondering the significance of what had happened. Mary became deeply convinced that this child of hers was the Savior.

> Just so our Lord God wants us to cradle his word diligently in our hearts and so impress it that it becomes second nature. As in the Canticle, »Fix me on your heart like a seal« and indelible character. The word is not to sit lightly on the heart, like a swan on water.... She said, »I want God's word so impressed on my heart that it is a mark no one can remove, like a natural growth no one can uproot.« Such was the heart of Mary, where the words remained as she absorbed them. And whoever so retains the word has in fact the true »character« of Christ which they allow no one to take away.[3]

In an earlier exposition of the same Nativity gospel, Luther was more specific on the nature of faith and more positive on the shepherds. Divinely-given faith is one that ascribes little importance to the speaker serving as God's intermediary. Such faith is lasting:

> Godly faith clings to the word, which is God himself; it believes, trusts, and honors the word not on account of the one who has spoken it, but feels that here is such a certainty of truth that nobody can ever tear it away.[4]

The shepherds attended solely to what was said, not being overly fascinated with the extraordinary way in which it came to them. And Mary was not disturbed by the low estate of the shepherds as she fixed the words themselves in her heart.

> The word itself, as you disregard the person, must satisfy the heart, must embrace and capture the believer so that he, like one who is imprisoned in it, feels how true and right it is, even if all the world, all angels, all the princes of hell, had a different message.[5]

Luther had not always been so clear on just how, and with what attitude, the believing heart clings to God's word of grace and thereby finds the work of Christ operative in itself. The Reformer's accounts of both the content and the mediation of salvation show development. His autobiographical flashbacks, which recur with some frequency after 1531, stress that he had moved ahead in spurts, under providential guidance, in his understanding of God and of saving

---

[3] WA 37, 246,1-9, citing Cant 8:6. But Luther improvised the citation expressing Mary's heartfelt desire. The reference to »character« offers Luther's alternative to the traditional doctrine of the permanent, indelible effect of baptism, confirmation, and ordination.

[4] From Luther's *Church Postil* of 1522 on the liturgical readings of the Christmas season. WA 10I/1, 130,3-6, in translation from LW 52, 33.

[5] WA 10I/1, 130,14-17.

faith. There were breakthroughs and liberating discoveries.[6] These reminiscences are notoriously hard to correlate with the actual contents of Luther's extant early works and letters, but his works show clearly enough that his teaching underwent development.

In the present context, concerning the heart and the word, we will present three distinct emphases that successively came to the fore in Luther's theological work. There was early emphasis on the heart confronted by Christ's call to conversion and life-long purification. But beginning in 1518, Luther sounded a new accent as he laid great emphasis on how the heart is given a consoling gift mediated by Christ's sacramental word of forgiveness and life. However, in the later 1520s Luther was teaching with yet another emphasis, as he also called hearts to be obediently submissive to the words and signs we encounter in the dispensation willed by God and instituted by his Son's own decisions.

These stages of development are naturally of considerable importance in interpreting Luther's works, since the different contexts have to be taken into account. However, it is also true that in his work, earlier themes do not at a certain point simply disappear from his doctrinal and spiritual instruction. In Luther's later phases, many earlier themes remain, but they come to be repositioned around new central emphases that have emerged. In Luther's development, personal insight into Scripture interacted with defensive and clarifying responses to the views of adversaries, and the intensity of this interaction, especially in 1518 and again in 1525-26, changed the overriding emphasis of the instruction he gave to the believing heart.

»Poenitentiam agite« (Mt. 4:17)

No action taken by Martin Luther is better known than his protest, under date of October 31, 1517, over the way Johann Tetzel, O.P., was promoting the indulgences offered by the popes to those who would contribute to the building fund for the new St. Peter's basilica.[7] Less well known is the tight connection between Luther's 1517 protest and the coherent doctrine of sin and repentance he had been working out since the beginning of his career as Scripture professor in Wittenberg University in 1513. By late 1517, Luther had given lectures on the

---

[6] The following are some of the numerous texts in which Luther reminisces over his own development. WA *Tischreden* 3, 228; 4, 72f; 5, 210 (LW 54, 193f, 309, 442f). From the 1532 lectures on Ps 51, published in revised form in 1538: WA 40II, 331,26-332,18, 411,36-412,26 (LW 12, 313f, 370). From lectures on Genesis in 1542 and 1543: WA 43, 536,40-537,25 (LW 5, 157f) and WA 44, 485,25-486,38 (LW 7, 251f). The preface of 1545 to vol. 1 of Luther's collected Latin works: WA 54,179-187 (LW 34, 327-338).

[7] On Luther's intervention: Erwin Iserloh, *Luther zwischen Reform und Reformation*, 2nd ed. (Münster 1967), in English as *The Theses Were Not Posted* (Boston & London 1968). This work shows in a still convincing way that according to Luther's own accounts it is quite unlikely that any public or semi-public protest, such as an open posting of theses, occurred at any of Wittenberg's church doors in autumn 1517.

Psalter (1513-15), Romans (1515-16), Galatians (1516-17), and the early chapters of Hebrews (1517). He had also published an edition of the vernacular mystical treatise, *A German Theology* (December 1516), and had brought out his own first independent work, an exposition of the seven penitential psalms (Spring 1517).[8]

In October 1517 Luther then addressed himself, by mail, to the Archbishop of Mainz and Magdeburg, the prelate who had given Tetzel his commission to proclaim the abundant graces of the St. Peter's indulgence. Luther sent Archbishop Albrecht a letter of thoughtful admonition, a list of ninety-five propositions Luther wanted taken up in theological debate, and a short treatise on indulgences setting forth a better grounded view of sin and repentance than was implied in Tetzel's campaign.[9]

Both the spirit and the sense of Luther's alternative proposal are captured well in the opening statements of the list of theses:

> 1. When our Lord and teacher Jesus Christ said, »Repent (*Poenitentiam agite*),« he meant that the whole life of believers should be one of repentance.
> 2. This text cannot be taken as referring to sacramental penance.
> 3. Nor does it refer solely to interior repentance, for this is nothing unless it produce outward mortifications of the flesh.
> 4. Therefore such penance continues as long as hatred of self (which is genuine interior repentance) remains, namely until one enters the kingdom of heaven.[10]

Following this forceful assertion of the normative character of the penitential life, Luther's theses offer some ninety statements on sin and its punishment, on remission of punishment here and in purgatory, on ecclesial aids conferred by use of the keys, and on rightly regulated preaching on this complex of themes. The concluding theses indicate the basic motif of proper preaching.

> 94. Christians should be exhorted to concentrate on following Christ their Head in penances and enduring death and hell.
> 95. So they seek to enter heaven more through many tribulations than by trusting in any present security of peace.[11]

Thus, Jesus' evangelical call for *metanoia* and his own example of patient suffering should shape the message announced by any Christian preacher, even on an indulgence campaign.

---

[8] The doctrine and spirituality taught in these works is the subject of my *Man Yearning for Grace* (Washington, DC 1968 & Wiesbaden 1969).

[9] Letter: WABr 1, 110-112; LW 48, 45-49. Ninety-Five Theses: WA 1, 233-238; LW 31, 25-33. The treatise: WABr 12, 5-9, translated into English in *Man Yearning for Grace*, 241-261 (with commentary) and in Study 5 of this collection. A German translation appears in an Appendix of the Wiesbaden 1969 edition of *Man Yearning*, pp. 431-438.

[10] My translation from WA 1, 233,10-17.

[11] WA 1, 238,18-21.

3. The Heart Clinging to the Word

Luther's treatise gave the rationale underlying the demanding message of the theses. Central in the treatise is the doctrinal distinction between a commutation, by an indulgence, of the satisfactory works once imposed by the priest in confession and the interior cleansing of concupiscence, a malady of the human heart, by God's healing grace. Since indulgences do not directly contribute to the latter, the preacher must take care not to mislead people into thinking that after gaining a plenary indulgence they are exempted from the penitential life. Characteristically, Luther emphasizes less believers' exertions of life-long mortification and much more God's work by grace in the affective center of the person. Contrasting with the extrinsic »grace« of an indulgence, there is God's inner transformation of the heart's aspirations.

> Infused grace is an interior illumination of the mind and a kindling of the will. This is an eternal illumination into the soul like rays of the sun, and it does not become inactive after a plenary indulgence. This grace is necessary for the extirpation of concupiscence, until it is completely rooted out. This process is complete when a person is so filled with disgust for this life that he sighs longingly for God and finally breaks free from the body out of desire for God.[12]

Whatever might be worked out for understanding purgatorial cleansing after death, the consequence for Christians in this life is ongoing concern over the sinful roots lodged deep in the human spirit. There is a »root sin« to be dealt with, which is both the legacy from the time of our origins and the residue of sinful acts.

> You must still make efforts to advance and take care not to grow lethargic and snore away thinking you are purified and thus secure. Then you must diligently crucify your members and mortify the source of sin, that is, your concupiscence.[13]

This penitential dedication was for Luther the source of a typical form of prayer, a yearning for God's healing grace.

> Therefore, we must be quite earnest is preventing indulgences, that is, satisfactions, from becoming a cause of security, laziness, and neglect of interior grace. Instead, we must be diligent to fully cure the infection of our nature and thirst to come to God out of love for him, hatred of this life, and disgust with ourselves. That is, we must incessantly seek God's healing grace.[14]

Further elucidation and grounding for Luther's 1517 views of repentance can be found in abundance in his treatment of sin and purification of heart in the corpus of his early biblical lectures. A fundamental conviction had emerged from his work on Psalm 51. Luther's exegetical comments of 1514 on this basic

---

[12] WABr 12, 6,36-40. I comment on this passage more at length in Study 5 in this collection, pp. 100-103, below.
[13] WABr 12, 8,109-112. Comments are given in Study 5, on pp. 110f, below.
[14] WABr 12, 9,152-156. Comments are given in Study 5, on p. 114, below.

penitential text emphasized the paradoxical identity which obtains between being righteous before God and making a heartfelt confession of sin: *Iustus enim primo est accusator sui et ... iudex sui.*[15] This holds because those who judge themselves are thereby agreeing with the truth of God's own fundamental word about humankind. God's light appeared in his Son's coming to save sinners (1 Tim 1:15).[16] When God lays scourges and crosses upon us, he shows we have sinned and deserve punishment.[17] While commenting on Romans in 1515, especially on the citation of Ps 51:4 in Rom 3:4, Luther spoke at length on how the faith by which one is justified involves taking to heart God's revelation of one's sinfulness.[18] The key to faith's genuine expression, in Luther's earliest extant lectures, is a heartfelt *Tibi peccavi*.

Luther was convinced that the Christian enters upon the way of conversion through submitting to God's words of judgment and thereby accepting a wholly new self-assessment.[19] This rests, of course, not upon the prescriptions of the law, against which we offend, but on the endemic root-sin we have inherited and further solidified by our choices. Confession of sin signals the start of a process of purification of heart lasting to the end. Rom 3:10 says laconically, »None is righteous.« For Luther this means that we are always underway in a penitential project and bound to beg for God's healing.

> Those therefore who are truly righteous yearn for and implore the grace of God not only because they see that they have an evil will and so by this are sinful before God, but as well because they see that they can never fully grasp how deep is the evil of their will and how far it extends. They thus always believe that they are sinners, as if the depth of their evil will were infinite. Thus they humble themselves, thus they plead, thus they yearn, until at last they are perfectly healed - which takes place in death.[20]

Luther therefore was acting with strong theological motivation when he first addressed a wider public than his Wittenberg students. He had good reason to publish, as his first book, a translation and exposition of the penitential psalms and then to register a critical word about the easily misunderstood »graces« of the

---

[15] In free translation: »The righteous person is marked first of all by self-accusation and self-judgment.« From WA 3, 288,31 (LW 10, 236), that is, the *Dictata super Psalterium* of 1513-15. Michael Baylor sees here a key to Luther's originality in understanding conscience. *Action and Person. Conscience in Late Scholasticism and the Young Luther* (Leiden 1977), 212-224.

[16] WA 3, 290,20; LW 10, 239.

[17] WA 3, 292,29; LW 10, 242.

[18] WA 56, 214-234; LW 25, 199-219.

[19] WA 56, 233,5-9; LW 25, 217.

[20] WA 56, 235,31-37; translation adapted from LW 25. 220f.

indulgences offered in 1517. In his earliest theology, the whole of the Christian life is subsumed under the heart's yearning for God's interior work of renewal.

> The whole life of the new people, the faithful people, the spiritual people, is nothing else but prayer, seeking and begging by the yearning of the heart, the voice of the mouth, and the labor of the body, always seeking and striving to be made righteous, even to the hour of death. They never stand still, are never in possession, and never in any work put an end to the acquiring of righteousness, but they always await it as something still dwelling beyond them, and always live as people who still exist in sin.[21]

Close in time to his intervention of October 1517 on indulgences, Luther spoke on Zaccheus' change of heart (Lk 19:8) as exemplifying the proper response to Jesus' call for repentance.

> Interior repentance is true contrition, true confession, and true spiritual satisfaction. Then penitents really and utterly displease themselves in all they do. They turn efficaciously to God in genuine admission of their guilt and they confess to God from the heart. Then their self-hatred gnaws at them interiorly and leads to self-imposed punishment. Thus they make satisfaction to God. Truly repentant persons desire that, if it were possible, all creation would see and hate their sin, and they are ready to be trampled on by all. They do not seek indulgences for the remission of punishments, but instead the actual bearing of punishments.[22]

Luther's earliest teaching, we see, was centered on the change of heart occurring in repentance. Such a personal shift of outlook rests on confession of sin before God and issues in the dedicated quest of purification under God's healing grace. The young Luther thus deserves to be ranked among the great Christian exponents of penitential and purificatory spirituality.

»Fides sacramenti«

In the wake of the indulgence controversy of 1517-18, Luther became greatly concerned with explaining the sacraments. Soon he began showing less concern about inculcating the inner spirit and outward performance of penance and much more about the certain and consoling gifts of forgiveness and grace conferred by the sacrament of penance to those confessing their sins. Luther's instruction in

---

[21] WA 56, 264,16-21; translation adapted from LW 25, 251f. Although the sense of sinful need dominates self-understanding, Luther did hold that God's gift is effective in the human heart. See, for example, the 1517 *Disputation against Scholastic Theology* (WA 1, 224-228; LW 31, 9-16), in the counterpointed theses 55, 67, 75, 84, 89, on the influence of grace, which thesis 55 describes as always a »vivus, mobilis, et operosus spiritus« (WA 1, 227,1f). Luther's 1536 *Disputation Concerning Justification* contains a vivid account of the ongoing cure of endemic sinfulness (WA 39I, 112-114; LW 34, 181-183). Luther had a solid doctrine of the Spirit's transforming work in the heart.

[22] My translation of WA 1, 99,1-8, from Luther's sermon of May 30, 1517. On the dating: N. Flörken, »Ein Beitrag zur Datierung von Luthers 'Sermo de indulgentiis pridie Dedicationis,'« *Zeitschrift für Kirchengeschichte* 82 (1971) 344-350.

Christian living marked a transition from emphasis on self-accusing faith to insistence on faith being made assured by laying hold of God's gift. Central now is the well-known »fiducial« faith, an act and attitude of wholehearted trust, which though has its ground and warrant in the sacramental word.[23]

It could be that this shift of emphasis in Luther's teaching was the consequence of a dramatic insight into a Scriptural text. Luther did claim that his life changed when he suddenly realized that »the righteousness of God« (Rom 1:17) is a quality of divine mercy toward human beings and of effective conferral of righteousness. It is difficult to pinpoint when this breakthrough took place, but it may well have brought with it a new understanding of faith, because right in Rom 1:17 Luther would find in his Vulgate Paul's brief citation from the Old Testament, *Iustus enim ex fide vivit* (»For the righteous person lives by faith,« from Hab 2:4).[24]

But, however the new emphasis arose, Luther's accounts in 1518-19 of sacramental reception make frequent appeal to an axiom which Luther says is very well known and often cited in theology. While commenting on Heb 5:1, Luther stressed the need that belief be focused on the actual efficacy of a sacrament, and gave as his warrant the »widely used and powerfully probative axiom, 'It is not the sacrament, but instead faith in the sacrament, that justifies.'«[25] By this principle, formulated in a widely known saying, Luther shows that his new instruction on the sacraments and justification by fiducial faith is not a dangerous innovation. Rather, it is a matter of axiomatic truth, and the theological community should recognize here a consequence of a widely accepted principle. Luther holds that *fides sacramenti*, faith *in* the sacrament, should be central in Christian existence, for by it the believer lays hold of God's gift present with its power to renew human hearts. The sacrament expresses and makes present an efficacious promise of Jesus himself.[26]

---

[23] I treat Luther's transition below in Study 6 of this volume. The best book-length treatment of Luther's teaching on the sacraments is the rarely cited work of Wolfgang Schwab, *Entwicklung und Gestalt der Sakramententheologie bei Martin Luther* (Frankfurt/M. & Bern 1977).

[24] Luther often spoke of his breakthrough to a new understanding of *iustitia Dei* in the autobiographical passages listed in n. 6, above. Some interpreters do place this breakthrough in early 1518 and relate it to Luther's new approach to the sacraments, e.g., Ernst Bizer, *Fides ex auditu*, 3rd ed. (Neukirchen 1966); Oswald Bayer, *Promissio* (Göttingen 1971); Martin Brecht, *Martin Luther*, 1, *His Road to Reformation, 1483-1521* (Philadelphia 1985), 221-237. Citations of »*Iustus ex fide vivit*« did occur in 1518 at the end of disputation theses on absolution (WA 1, 633, 11) and at the beginning of Luther's defense against Cardinal Cajetan's objection to the new doctrine (WA 2, 13,13; LW 31, 270).

[25] From the Lectures on Hebrews in early 1518, WA 57III, 170,2 (»vulgatissimum et probatissimum dictum, 'Non sacramentum sed fides sacramenti iustificat'«). Luther defended himself against an early attack by Johann Eck with another appeal to the axiom as »dictum illud communissimum« (WA 1, 286,17f). Other citations of the axiom: WA 1, 324,16, 544,40, 631,7; WA 2, 15,31, 715,34.

[26] Grammatically, *fides sacramenti* is a case of an objective genitive, with the sacrament's principal word, e.g., absolution, being that which one believes with all trust.

3. The Heart Clinging to the Word

In 1520, Luther explained Jesus' words of eucharistic institution as his testamentary promise of grace, which we encounter in every celebration of the Lord's Supper. Worthy participation is by faith in the sacramental promise, and this transforms the heart. Faith grasps Jesus' gift of himself, in his body broken and his blood shed for the forgiveness of our sins. Here faith receives an immense benefit.

> Hard upon this faith there follows spontaneously a most sweet affection of the heart, by which the human spirit is enlarged and enriched (in charity granted by the Holy Spirit in the midst of faith in Christ). Thereby one is swept toward Christ, who left this testament in his graciousness and bounty, and one becomes a completely new and different person. . . . How can one help loving so great a benefactor, who offers, promises, and confers the riches of this eternal inheritance to one who is unworthy and actually merits much different treatment![27]

Thus Luther instructed Christians to cut through the complexities of traditional sacramental doctrine, for example, the ingenious subdivisions of benefits or »fruits« of the mass for body and soul. The one benefit attached to Christ's supper is the forgiveness of sins, the grace expressed in the word of institution over the cup of his blood. His purpose was to give our lives a new existential basis,

> so that the human heart, clinging to these words by faith, should gain strength in everything good against sin, death, and hell. His word and work were not intended to help us in a temporal way, but in a spiritual and eternal way. . . . A person should receive the sacrament . . . and not doubt that in him there takes place the intent and content of those same words of Christ, namely, that Christ's body is given for him and that his blood is shed for him, and that he is an heir of the New Testament, that is, of God's grace and favor for eternal life.[28]

Luther's new configuration of doctrinal and spiritual themes in 1518 had first focused attention on sacramental penance where the words of absolution are a paradigmatic mediation of salvation. He could even say that our trust rests on what comes from the mouth of the confessor.[29] Troubled hearts are helped by the church's ministry of consolation and encouragement, centered on the sacramental word as Christ's effective address.

---

[27] *De captivitate Babylonica* (1520), WA 6, 515,29-516,2. This passage follows Luther's assertion of the correlation of God's promise and a dependent, trusting faith: »Ubi enim est verbum promittentis Dei, ibi necessaria est fides acceptantis hominis, ut clarum sit initium salutis nostrae esse fidem, quae pendeat in verbo promittentis Dei« (514,13-16). The whole passage is translated in LW 36, 38-44.

[28] »Sermon on Worthy Reception of the Sacrament« (1521), WA 7, 695,22-696,3; LW 42, 175 (cited).

[29] »ut ... in ore sacerdotis collocetur fiducia nostra.« WA 4, 657,15, from a sermon at the first mass of a newly ordained priest in Spring 1518.

> Our salvation therefore lies in the word, but not really in the word, for Christ is joined to the word. There must be no tottering here. A sacrament is a rock grounded in Christ.[30]

Other texts from 1518 had begun working out how this new insight into faith and the word had consequences for the proper reception of Holy Communion. Christ purifies and pacifies the troubled heart by his blood shed for us, but this gift is mediated by a word of Christ which we are to lay hold of in convinced belief, »This is the blood shed for you and for many for the forgiveness of sins.«[31]

With such a basic insight into the present gift of salvation, Luther felt well equipped to turn to the broader public of literate Germans in numerous short works on fundamental aspects of the Christian's relationship to God. The year 1519 saw eight such pastoral instructions appear, explaining the Our Father, meditation on Christ's passion, married life, petitionary prayer, preparation for death, and the sacraments of Penance, Baptism, and Holy Communion. Each work was quickly and repeatedly reprinted both in Wittenberg and in other cities such as Leipzig, Augsburg, Nürnberg, and Basel.[32]

Typical of these works was Luther's high recommendation of the power of the sacraments in overcoming the assaults on the heart by our spiritual enemies in the struggle preceding death.

> We must earnestly, diligently, and highly esteem the holy sacraments, hold them in honor, freely and cheerfully rely on them, and so balance them against sin, death, and hell that they will outweigh these by far. We must occupy ourselves much more with the sacraments and their virtues than with our sins.[33]

In the sacraments God gives the heart a sure sign of his grace in Christ, in an expression that does not deceive. God's own word resounds in absolution; the holy body of Christ is a gift of »communion«, not only with Christ but as well

---

[30] WA 4, 658,26-28.
[31] From Luther's comment on Heb 9:14. WA 57III, 207,23-208,4; LW 29, 208f.
[32] Original texts in WA 2; translations in LW, vols. 35, 42, and 44. These works were recently studied by Ursula Stock in *Die Bedeutung der Sakramente in Luthers Sermonen von 1519* (Leiden 1982). They constitute the sizeable beginning of the first wave of Luther's influence on his literate urban contemporaries. As Bernd Moeller has been pointing out, Luther had his first impact not primarily by polemic and social criticism, but far more by a constructive, religious message. The appeal was that of a new popular spirituality and form of personal piety. Moeller argues for the internal coherence of the first wave of reformation popular writing and preaching, a coherence with clear roots in Luther's principal insights. »Korreferat zu Wolfgang Reinhard: Luther und die Städte,« in E. Iserloh & G. Müller, eds., *Luther und die politische Welt* (Stuttgart 1984), 113-121, esp. 118-120, and »Was wurde in der Frühzeit der Reformation in den deutschen Städten gepredigt?« *Archiv für Reformationsgeschichte* 75 (1984), 176-193. Below, in Study 8, I treat more in detail Luther's works of pastoral assistance and instruction for the wider population of believers.
[33] WA 2, 686,19-23; LW 42, 100 (cited).

3. The Heart Clinging to the Word

with his angels and saints as helpers in my suffering.[34] Faith lays hold of these gifts offered.

> In the sacraments we find God's Word - which reveals and promises Christ to us with all his blessings and which he himself is - against sin, death, and hell. . . . The right use of the sacraments involves nothing more than believing that all will be as the sacraments promise and pledge through God's Word.[35]

Luther's insistence on clinging to the sacramental word of grace did not fade away in the years after 1518-20. Later it was second nature for him to refer to sacramental reception as the privileged case of faith in God's saving word. In 1532, explaining Ps 51:10 (»To my hearing you will give joy and gladness«), Luther expressed a basic tenet of his reformation.

> We attribute everything to hearing or to the Word or to faith in the Word - these are all the same - and not to our works. Yes, in the use of the sacraments and in confession we teach people to look mainly at the Word . . . so that the chief part of the whole action might be the voice itself of God and the hearing itself.[36]

> So turn your eyes far away from your contrition, and with your whole heart pay attention to the voice of the brother absolving you. And do not doubt that this voice of the brother in the Sacrament or in absolution is divinely spoken by the Father, Son, and Holy Spirit Himself, so that you completely depend on what you hear, not on what you think.[37]

In his Galatians course of 1531 Luther made clear the interrelation found between the action of the minister, whether of word or sacrament, and the work of the Holy Spirit in transforming the heart.

> For the word issues from the mouth of the Apostle and reaches the heart of the hearer; the Holy Spirit is at hand and, as the word sounds, he impresses it upon the heart.[38]

Luther's last great lecture-course, on Genesis, from 1535 to 1545, was laced with brief references to the sacraments, especially as the Christian analogues to God's promises to the patriarchs and to their responses of faith.[39] But a new accent had appeared in the mid-1520s, when Luther went to the defense of

---

[34] WA 2, 692,26-35; LW 42, 110f.
[35] WA 2, 695,6-12; LW 42, 111 (cited).
[36] WA 40II, 411,20-34; LW 12, 369f (cited with adaptations).
[37] WA 40II, 412,33-37; LW 12, 370 (cited with adaptations).
[38] WA 40I, 649,27f; LW 26, 430.
[39] This even began in comments on Gen 1:2, with an admonition to hold to the God who envelopes himself in baptism and absolution (WA 42, 10,3-8; LW 1, 11) and continued down to Jacob's blessing of Judah in Gen 49:8f (WA 44, 777,37-778,17; LW 8, 270f).

Christ's bodily gift of himself in the Lord's Supper against the spiritualism of Zwingli and his Swiss colleagues.

The heart submissive to God's ordinances

A well-studied phase of Luther's theological career is his spirited defense of objective sacramental mediation and the presence of Christ's body and blood in the eucharistic elements.[40] These concerns loomed large from 1525 into 1530 as Luther debated with his former colleague Karlstadt and with the Swiss reformers, Zwingli and Oecolampadius. In our context we will note only one aspect of Luther's extensive argumentation in these years, an aspect which does bring out a theme previously latent in his doctrine of the believing heart and God's word of grace.

Luther had to confront the Swiss application of John 6:63 (»The spirit gives life; the flesh is of no avail«) to the gift offered in Holy Communion. Zwingli had concluded that this text leaves only a spiritual »eating,« a rememorative act of devotion that is little more than faith in Christ's redemptive death. Luther's response did grant that »spirit« and »flesh« are basic anthropological categories, applicable to the whole person as believer or unbeliever. However, in the Supper, Christ's body is not »flesh« in the sense of the controverted text, but a gift which in fact avails in a grand and glorious manner. Receiving communion rightly, according to Luther, is to eat Christ's body physically *while* believing in one's heart in the redemptive gift of Christ. The gift however is not one that leads to escape from the body.

> The heart knows well what the mouth eats, for it grasps the words and eats spiritually what the mouth eats physically. But since the mouth is the heart's member, it also must live in eternity because of the heart, which lives eternally through the Word, because here it also eats physically the same eternal food which its heart eats spiritually at the same time.[41]

Thus, in binding together mouth and heart, Luther connected the eucharistic presence of Christ's body with a quite holistic view of salvation.

But a yet more fundamental religious issue was at stake in the debate with these adversaries. The Swiss were asking what need or use there was for a bodily presence of Christ over and above his spiritual and effective presence in the Gospel and the message formulated in the words of institution. But this kind of questioning, in Luther's estimation, revealed a proud heart. To ask why, in this manner, is equivalently to lay down limits that one wants to say Christ should not transgress.

---

[40] Mark Edwards inserts this controversy into the broader context of Luther's polemics against other adherents of the Reformation. *Luther and the False Brethren* (Stanford, Cal. 1975), 82-111.

[41] WA 23, 181,10-18; LW 37, 87 (cited).

3. The Heart Clinging to the Word

> A faithful, God-fearing heart does this: it asks first whether it is God's Word. When it hears that it is, it smothers with hands and feet the question why it is useful or necessary. For it says with fear and humility, »My dear God, I am blind; truly I know not what is useful or necessary for me, nor do I wish to know, but I believe and trust that thou dost know best and dost intend the best in thy divine goodness and wisdom. I am satisfied and happy to hear thy simple Word and perceive thy will.«[42]

In the Marburg Colloquy of 1529, Luther drew a sharp line between himself and those Protestants who were questioning God's own sacramental ordinances.

> I am not inquiring whether or not it is necessary; that has not been entrusted to us. In that case I could neither be baptized nor believe in Christ. Christ gives himself to us in many ways: first, in preaching; second, in baptism; [third] in brotherly consolation; fourth, in the sacrament, as often as the body of Christ is eaten, because he himself commands us to do so. If he should command me to eat dung, I would do it. The servant should not inquire about the will of his lord. We ought to close our eyes.[43]

Still, the Lord's Supper is not simply a matter of blind obedience to divine decrees. The Swiss adversaries were claiming that their view safeguarded the transcendent glory of the divine Savior, by denying that anyone handles and carries about the body of Christ. But Luther countered with his own account of the true glory of Christ, who treats humankind with marvelous mercy.

> It is a glory and praise of his inexpressible grace and mercy that he concerns himself so profoundly with us poor sinners and shows us such gracious love and goodness, not content to be everywhere in and around, above and beside us, but even giving us his own body as nourishment, in order that with such a pledge he may assure and promise us that our body too shall live forever, because it partakes here on earth of an everlasting and living food.[44]

Thus, the great debate of the late 1520s was much more than a reactionary phase in Luther's career as a Christian teacher. Deep truths emerged about God's redemptive intention, which embraces even our bodily existence, and about how that intention has concretized itself in Christ and his economy of grace. There is need, though, of hearts submissive to God's chosen ways or ordinances, if the grandeur of his saving dispensation is to break forth before the eyes of faith.

Thus we can mark out three different prevailing emphases in Luther's spiritual teaching. He moved from forming repentant hearts to an insistence on how the heart should cling to the liberating and consoling word of Christ encountered in

---

[42] WA 23, 247,32-249,3; LW 37, 127 (cited).

[43] WA 30III, 116,7-12; LW 38, 19 (cited). In his treatise, *The Keys* (1530), Luther insists on the divinely instituted means of forgiveness as what Christ commanded us to do in the church. This is Luther's basic framework for understanding Mt 16:19 and 18:18. See WA 30II, 497-501 (LW 40, 364-369 and 372-376). The divine ordinances should free people from the plague of uncertainty, as Luther explained in 1542, commenting on Gen 26:9 (WA 43, 457-463; LW 5, 42-50, especially 45).

[44] WA 23, 155,32-157,2; LW 37, 71 (cited).

the sacraments. But then, when a more radical spiritualism emerged as part of the Protestant movement, Luther responded with his emphatic case for a more humble submission of heart before the full range of God's gifts, even when it is not clear how God's manner of giving fits with my idea of what is needful or appropriate.

Still, these three repeated emphases are not the whole story. In addition to these spiritual themes recurrently present in the different periods of Luther's life, we find as well some particular teachings that broke forth only momentarily in Luther's works. We will conclude this essay by relating just two of these. First, Luther did offer at least once an account of the meaning of the term »heart«. And then, in a gem of spiritual instruction, he led the believing heart toward an encounter with the heart of God himself.

The believing heart and God's own heart

Psalm 51 expresses an aspiration Luther felt was the immediate consequence of receiving God's justifying grace of forgiveness: »Create a clean heart in me, O God.« The commentary of 1538, based on lectures of 1532, tells how one favored with a right relationship to God begs in this verse to be maintained and strengthened in certainty about God's mercy and in dedication to doing his will. All this takes place by the Spirit's creative work in the heart – a consideration that leads Luther to clarify the term »heart«.

> Just as such a clean heart is not by our powers but by divine creation, so we cannot ourselves preserve this creation against the devil. We see how often we are polluted by sudden troubles and sadness. Hence this prayer and preservation of a clean heart ought never to stop. . . . The word »heart« in German is almost the same as what the Hebrew calls »spirit«. What in Latin we call »mind, intellect, will, affections« - almost all this the Germans render as »heart«.[45]

The heart, thus, is the cognitive and affective center of the person, where faith and righteousness come to be implanted through the word in which God both reveals and effects the person's new relationship to Himself. A heart submissive to God and clinging to his chosen words of grace then yearns for ongoing confirmation, healing, and renewal. Such are in fact the basic structures of the Christian spirituality taught by Martin Luther. But there is more. Luther was, among everything else, an insightful teacher of prayer, especially of meditative prayer on the fundamental truths and realities of revelation.[46] A Christian should

---

[45] WA 40II, 424,34-425,20; LW 12, 379 (cited). In an earlier commentary on the psalms, treating the meaning of God's scrutinizing of »the heart and the loins« (Ps 7:9), Luther explained that »the heart« is the organ of our fear and trust, for it stands for one's »consilia, studia, mentem, iudicium, opinionem, affectum, cogitationes, aestimationes, et his similia.« WA 5, 236,13f; AWA 2, 421,8f.

[46] This has been systematically set forth by Martin Nicol in *Meditation bei Luther* (Göttingen 1984).

3. The Heart Clinging to the Word

go in spirit regularly to Christ on his cross, there to be impressed ever again with the costly manner in which God realized his dispensation of mercy, forgiveness, and new life.

Luther's 1519 instruction on meditating on our Lord's passion leads up to the recommendation to cast off all reliance on self-achieved goodness and to cling instead to the Scripture verses on the redemptive value of Jesus' suffering, such as Isa 53:6, »He has laid on him the iniquity of us all,« and 1 Pet 2:24 and 2 Cor 5:21. One casts one's own sin, guilt, and anxiety upon the Redeemer. Prayer, however, does not simply dwell upon texts, but becomes a more active and alert perception of the personal basis of redemption. Our last citations of Luther will be long enough to afford vivid contact with this articulate and profound exponent of a spirituality of the heart, to show the reach and depth of that spirituality, by reason of its attention to Christ's own heart and the heart of the Father.

> You can spur yourself on. First, no longer envisaging Christ's suffering in itself (for this has done its work and frightened you), you should pass through to see his friendly heart and how this heart full of love for you impels him to bear with pain your bad conscience and sin. Your heart will be thereby sweetened and the confident assurance of your faith strengthened. Then go on to rise through the heart of Christ to the heart of God to see that Christ would not have shown his love for you, had not God in his eternal love wanted this. For Christ in his love for you is obedient. Thus you will come to the divine, fatherly heart and, as Christ says, be drawn to the Father through him. Then you will grasp the saying of Christ, »God so loved the world that he gave his own son« (John 3:16). To know God rightly is to lay hold, not of his power or wisdom (which are terrifying), but of his kindness and love. Then faith and assurance can stand steadfast and one is truly reborn in God.[47]

In 1529, in his catechetical exposition of the Apostles' Creed, Luther summed up the meaning of the basic economy of creation, redemption, and sanctification – set forth in the Creed – as the revelation of the profound love of the Father's heart for his creatures.

> Here in the Creed you have the entire essence of God, his will, and his work exquisitely depicted in very short but rich words. In them consists all our wisdom, which surpasses all the wisdom, understanding, and reason of men. . . . In these three articles God himself has revealed and opened to us the most profound depths of his fatherly heart, his sheer unutterable love. He created us for this very purpose, to redeem and sanctify us. Moreover, having bestowed upon us everything in heaven and earth, he has given us his Son and his Holy Spirit, through whom he brings us to

---

[47] WA 2, 140,30-141,7. See the larger context of this passage in LW 42, 12-14. In 1526, on Pentecost Sunday, Luther was expounding Jesus' words in John 14:23 (»Those who love me will keep my word, and my father will love them, and we will come to them and make our dwelling with them«). Jesus' purpose is to replace our fear of a divine judge with trust in the Father's loving heart, into which a window is here opened: »Per hoc verbum fenestra quasi aperitur patris cor. Si aliter inspicis, vides iudicem iratum. Sed si ita Christus est in officio, ut patrem reconciliet et ut inheream illo, ich will gern schand haben, ut ipse magnus.« WA 20, 400,4-6.

himself. As we explained before, we could never come to recognize the Father's favor and grace were it not for the Lord Christ, who is a mirror of the Father's heart.[48]

Martin Luther thus directed the believing Christian heart first to a consoling and saving word of God. Such a word should dominate the foreground of the heart's concerns as it clings submissively to the promise of forgiveness and life in Christ. But Luther also led the heart further into the background and wellspring of the word, where the heart encounters in all amazement the loving heart of our God.

---

[48] *Large Catechism*, The Creed, nos. 63-65, cited from *The Book of Concord*, ed. T. G. Tappert et al. (Philadelphia 1959), 419. Original: BS 660,18-42 and WA 30I, 191,27-192,5.

4

LIVING AND PRAYING AS *SIMUL IUSTUS ET PECCATOR*: A CHAPTER IN LUTHER'S SPIRITUAL TEACHING

By any standard of ecumenical significance, the 1983 United States Lutheran-Catholic dialogue declaration, »Justification by Faith,« is a landmark. Earlier phases of the dialogue had discussed the sacramental mediation of salvation and the church's transmission of doctrine.[1] But »Justification by Faith« deals with salvation itself as present in lives now enveloped by God's gracious promise and saving work in Christ. The dialogue ending in 1983 ascertained a fundamental Lutheran-Catholic agreement that the believer's basic trust for justification and salvation is in Christ and his gospel. No extended Lutheran or Catholic reflections were needed to highlight the limits of such a basic consensus, as had occurred in earlier dialogues. There are, to be sure, remaining differences between the teachings of the two confessions, but these do not shake the fundamental agreement.[2] The differences on justification itself concern »theological formulations« and the way each tradition works out the relation between the doctrine of justification and church proclamation.[3]

One of the formulations of remaining divergence noted in »Justification by Faith« concerns the righteous person being »at the same time righteous and a sinner« (*simul iustus et peccator*). Lutherans see sin as an ongoing presence and serious concern in the justified person, a presence certainly different from sin in the not-yet-justified, but nonetheless such as to ground constant need of God's

---

[1] The author offered an analytical chronicle of twenty years of Lutheran-Catholic dialogue, »Temi di ecclesiologia nel dialogo luterano-cattolico (1965-1985),« in R. Latourelle, ed., *Vaticano II Bilancio e prospettive* (Assisi 1987), 2, 883-919. The English original is in the parallel edition of this work, *Vatican II: Assessment and Perspectives* (New York/Mahwah, N.J. 1988-89), 2, 305-346. Translations have also appeared in the French edition (Montreal & Paris 1988), 2, 331-371, and the Spanish edition (Salamanca 1989), pp. 663-689.

[2] Subsequent to »Justification by Faith,« the U.S. Lutheran-Catholic dialogue group turned to the role of Mary and the saints in the economy of salvation. At the present time, the international Lutheran-Catholic Joint Commission is seeking to clarify how the two traditions view the place or role of the church in salvation.

[3] U.S. Lutheran-Roman Catholic Dialogue, »Justification by Faith,« no. 157, found in *Origins* 17 (1983), 277-304, at 298. The declaration is also in H.G. Anderson et al., eds., *Justification by Faith*, Lutherans and Catholics in Dialogue, 7 (Minneapolis 1985), 13-74, at 72.

merciful acquittal. But Catholics hold that God's justifying action and gift is transformative, with the result that what remains wrong in the justified person is not truly sinful. More is at stake here than just a linguistic ruling over whether one may predicate »sinner« of one who is righteous. For the dialogue states that two divergent religious or spiritual approaches stand in apparent conflict here, with Lutherans determined to counter complacency in the righteous and Catholics convinced that one should not obscure God's healing and renewing action in those who are justified.[4] The differences are real, but there is hope that the contrasts can become a fruitful example of unity in reconciled diversity

In the dialogues, the confessional and dogmatic documents of the churches are the principal sources, with major figures such as Luther and Aquinas having subordinate functions. But for an issue like the *iustus simul peccator*, Martin Luther himself remains essential in any contemporary understanding, since both the terminology of the *simul* and the broader thesis on sin in the life of the righteous come directly from him. The following pages will treat selected components of Luther's own teaching on the sin that remains in the righteous. The author hopes that Lutheran teaching can thereby be enriched from its own origins. Correspondingly, Catholic assessment of the *simul*, at least as it comes directly from Luther, can surely move beyond the reserve evident in »Justification by Faith.«[5]

Approaching Luther's »simul«

With the concise formula *simul iustus et peccator*, Martin Luther gives a succinct account of the situation of the believer in Christ. Thereby Luther states two theses quite emphatically. First, righteousness is given to sinners as an unmerited benefit because of Christ, »who became for us wisdom from God, as well as righteousness, sanctification, and redemption« (1 Cor 1:30). The *simul* means to convey first the fact that saving righteousness does not arise from one's nature or moral achievements, since these bring forth sin, but from the alien and extrinsic holiness of Jesus Christ.[6] The believer is, by God's mercy, a forgiven sinner.

---

[4] »Justification by Faith,« nos. 102-104. Note that in no. 159/9 one component of convergence is an agreement that sin no longer reigns in the justified, although sinful inclinations and assaults are felt, which one cannot withstand on one's own. Here, Luther's imagery of »sin reigning« and »sin under rule,« formulated in his 1521 work against the Louvain theologian Latomus, has contributed an important element toward resolving a controversy which Luther started himself.

[5] Still further encouragement comes from the recently completed work of the German ecumenical working-group (the Stälin-Jaeger Kreis), which has reviewed the mutual anathemas of the sixteenth century, and on the sinfulness of the justified concluded that Trent's condemnation is not applicable — especially when one takes account of Luther's distinction between *peccatum regnans* (before justification) and *peccatum regnatum* (in the righteous). K. Lehmann & W. Pannenberg, eds., *Lehrverurteilungen-kirchentrennend?* vol. 1 (Freiburg & Göttingen 1986), 50-53.

[6] »Si sum peccator in me, in Christo non sum peccator, qui nobis factus est iustitia.« »Christianus ... est quidem iustus et sanctus aliena seu extrinseca sanctitate ... hoc est, est iustus misericordia et gratia Dei.« *Enarratio Psalmi LI*, 1538; WA 40II, 327,31 & 352,36; LW 12, 311,

The second truth expressed by the *simul* is that the believer who now shares in Christ's righteousness cannot rest secure, as if his or her spiritual goal were already reached. Although one's sin is truly forgiven, a believer has to contend each day against sin's endemic power as this is still lodged in his or her own person. A lifelong struggle ensues. One who is *simul peccator* cannot rest from the battle.⁷ Concerning the Christian life, Luther's formula is not just descriptive but prescriptive for all, enjoining a life-long therapeutic concern: »That life is one of ongoing healing from sin, not a life without sin with completed healing and acquired health.«⁸

The thesis that the believer is simultaneously righteous and a sinner is thus a point at which much of Luther's teaching, especially his doctrine of justification, comes together. The importance of the doctrine itself is clear enough. But the understanding of it requires attention to the consequences Luther drew from the *simul* for daily life and prayer. In the lived religiosity of the believer, the *simul* indicates the necessary primacy of a penitential spirituality in daily practice and prayer: »The whole of life is penance, prayer, and contrition.«⁹ The ascertaining in Luther's teaching of a penitential spirituality could be the starting point of a fresh reflection on Luther's affinities with notable figures and movements in the Christian tradition before and after the Reformation. It is also important for a better understanding of the emergence of Luther's main theses on sin and justification within the context of the observant or reform movement among the religious orders, including Luther's own Hermits of St. Augustine, in the

---

328. In technical terms, the cause of justification is solely the work of Christ. Luther would allow the person's confession of sin to be called a *causa secunda* or *causa sine qua non*, but there is no independent causing here, »quia sic est causa, ut tamen tota res pendeat ex misericordia Dei seu ex promissione.« WA 40II, 358,35-359,25; LW 12, 332.

7 » ... apud Christianos duplex est peccatum: peccatum remissum et peccatum reliquum, quod extirpandum et abluendum est.... Ergo Christianus ... non debet sic securus esse, quasi plane ab omnibus peccatis purus sit, sed demum ei perpetua haec incumbit lucta cum reliquiis peccati.« WA 40II 352,25; LW 12, 328.

8 »Ista vita est vita curationis a peccato, non sine peccato finita curatione et adepta sanitate.« *Lectures on Romans*, 1515-16; WA 56, 275,26 (LW 25, 262f). Here Luther is understanding the Christian as the robbers' victim in the parable of the Good Samaritan. A good topic for further study would be Luther's use all through his career of this Augustinian understanding of this parable. Other echoes in the Romans' lectures are at WA 56, 258,21, 272,11, and 441,14-17 (LW 25, 245, 260, 433). Later, in 1537, Luther said believers are those being healed (»sanandi«), for, »Samaritanus coepit sanare eum, qui in latrones ceciderat.« First Antinomian Disputation; WA 39I, 376,6.

9 »Totam vitam esse poenitentiam et orationem et contritionem.« *Resolutiones*, Leipzig theses of 1519; WA 2, 410,14. In 1537, in the First Antinomian Disputation, Luther said, »Omnis credens, qui coepit fide vincere terrores legis, tota vita poenitet. Nam tota vita fidelium exercituum est et odium quoddam contra reliquias peccati in carne, quae murmurat contra spiritum et fidem.« WA 39I, 394,13-16. Also, »Ubi illa cognitio et fides Christi est, sequitur continua poenitentia.« Ibid. 398,14f.

fifteenth and early-sixteenth centuries.[10] Here, however, we will concentrate on the retrieval of Luther's own teaching on the *simul* with attention to its ramifications in penitential living and prayer.

An account of the simultaneity of sin and righteousness is not dealing with a marginal aspect of Luther's teaching. The insights codified in the concise formula *simul iustus et peccator* underlay Luther's protest of October 31, 1517, against misguided indulgence preaching. The Ninety-Five Theses begin with an argument, in theses 1-4, that evangelical repentance is not a momentary act, but a life-long struggle against evil and sin. The theses end by stating norms for good preaching:

> 94. Christians should be exhorted to concentrate on following Christ their Head in penances and enduring death and hell.
> 95. So they seek to enter heaven more through many tribulations than by trusting in any present security of peace.[11]

Even more informative on the rationale of Luther's 1517 approach to the indulgence question is the treatise he submitted to a number of bishops along with his theses. Luther's treatise argues that preachers must carefully avoid misleading people about the »grace« they gain in an indulgence. It is no exemption from the penitential life, because in itself it does not heal the malady of sin in the human heart. Even after gaining a plenary indulgence, a person must still seek the »infused grace« that counteracts sinful infections of mind and heart. The disciplined life also plays a role in countering concupiscent drives. Basic, as well, is the prayer of yearning for inner illumination and purified affections.

> Therefore we must be quite earnest in preventing indulgences, that is, satisfactions, from becoming a source of security, laziness, and neglect of interior grace. Instead, we must be diligent to fully cure the infection of our nature and thirst to come to God out of love for him, hatred of this life, and disgust with ourselves. That is, we must incessantly seek God's healing grace.[12]

It is not too much to say that Luther's historic intervention at the beginning of the indulgence controversy was motivated in large part by the conviction summarized in the formula *simul iustus et peccator*. But this topic, along with certain other issues which have come to the fore in previous treatments of the *simul*, will not be pursued further in this investigation.[13]

---

[10] Penitential spirituality was a major theme in the fifteenth-century treatise, *Liber de vita monastica*, by the Nürnberg Observant Augustinian, Conrad of Zenn (died 1460). See the new study of this work by Hellmut Zschoch, *Klosterreform und monastische Spiritualität im 15. Jahrhundert* (Tübingen 1988).

[11] WA 1, 238,18 (my translation).

[12] WABr 12, 9,152. I present and comment on Luther's treatise in Study 5 of this collection, treating this paragraph on p. 114, below.

[13] R. Hermann published what remains a basic study: *Luthers These »Gerecht und Sünder zugleich«* (Gütersloh 1930, reprint 1960). Hermann draws largely on two polemical works of Luther, the 1515-16 Romans lectures and the 1521 response to Latomus. As a systematic

Here, I will take note of Luther's biblical sources for the *simul*, because his work with Scripture repeatedly draws out its ramifications in daily living. A biblically based spirituality must reckon with the *simul*. Also, the distinction between God's *gratia* and *donum* (grace and gift), deserves attention, to prevent study of the *simul* from falling into an anthropocentrism alien to Luther. Because God has two ways of treating our sin, we have two principal concerns as we live and pray. My main concern is to set forth the spiritual consequences of the *simul* in Luther's sketches of daily living and personal prayer. Thereby, I am in effect taking this doctrine as a notable moment in the history of spirituality and prayer.[14] A final section of this essay will look to the ecumenical situation, by touching briefly on recent and contemporary Catholic assessments and appreciations of Luther's formula.

At the Heart of a Biblical Anthropology

The knowledge of human sinfulness is for Luther central and basic in Christian teaching. Philosophy may treat a human being as *animal rationale* and the law may look on him as a holder of property and rights, but theology learns from God's own word to envisage the human creature as a sinner and to inculcate in people this very sense of themselves. Knowledge of our sinfulness is the essential point of departure for grasping God's loving design to save us through Christ.[15]

---

theologian, Hermann was very interested in the problem of the believer's consent/dissent regarding sin's drives. Sections of this work remain helpful, but the final section on the *simul* and prayer does not draw on the more constructive sources which are Luther's later works. – The *simul* has been treated with insight by W. Joest in a chapter of his study of the *tertius usus legis*, *Gesetz und Freiheit* (Göttingen 1951, 4th ed. 1968), 55-82. – K.O. Nilsson's *Simul. Das Miteinander von Göttlichem und Menschlichem in Luthers Theologie* (Göttingen 1966) ranges widely through Luther's teaching to demonstrate the centrality of simultaneous opposites, treating the believer's condition and action with helpful reference to the means of grace and union with Christ (pp. 309-357). – A suggestive historical contrast is given by J.F. McCue, »Simul iustus et peccator in Augustine, Aquinas, and Luther: Toward Putting the Debate in Context,« *Journal of the American Academy of Religion* 48 (1981), 81-96. – A recent exposition underscores the ontological basis of the *simul* in the believer, in whom Christ is present and active against sinful flesh: T. Mannermaa, »Der im Glauben gegenwärtige Christus und die Heiligkeit des Christen,« in *Der im Glauben gegenwärtige Christus* (Hannover 1989), 56-93.

14 This point has been taken up by Gerhard Ebeling, with his customary penetration, in the concluding pages of »Der Mensch als Sünder: die Erbsünde in Luthers Menschenbild,« *Lutherstudien* (Tübingen 1971-), 3, 74-107, an essay based on a 1984 lecture.

15 »Iureconsultus loquitur de homine possessore et domino suarum rerum, ... theologus autem disputat de homine PECCATORE. Haec hominis substantia est in Theologia et hoc a Theologo agitur, ut hanc suam naturam peccatis corruptam homo sentiat.« *Enarratio Psalmi LI*, 1538; WA 40II, 327,19 (LW 12, 310f). See also 328,30 on properly theological knowledge of oneself. In 1515-16, Luther claimed that all of Scripture aims to bring a person to »become a sinner« in one's own self-estimate: »Haec enim mutare intendit omnis sermo Scripturae et omnis operatio Dei.« WA 56, 233,8; LW 25, 218.

Theology itself, for Luther, is centrally about fallen and guilty humankind, to whom God intends to grant righteousness and salvation.[16]

Luther's thesis on the lasting presence of sin even after one is forgiven and justified resulted from his labors in 1515-16 to expound Rom 4:7, with its citation of Psalm 32:1 (Vulgate: »Beati quorum remissae sunt iniquitates et quorum tecta sunt peccata«).[17] Luther's first consideration of the text drew out the paradoxical contrast holding between the self-estimate of the saints and their estimation by God. The saints are those who admit and confess their sinfulness, while at the same time God is judging or accounting them righteous.[18] Luther found a first realization of the *simul* here, for God in his mercy has us at the same time as sinners and non-sinners. Sin remains – in our self-estimate – and at the same time does not remain – in God's accounting of us.[19]

But what exactly is meant by »sin« in this text, that is, in the psalm-verse cited by Paul? It is to this question that Luther devoted his long scholion on Rom 4:7. His momentous conclusion is that the text cannot be taken narrowly, as referring only to discrete actual sins of thought, word, and deed, which God does forgive and for which he no longer holds us guilty. Beyond these sins, and more important than them, there is sinful passion and concupiscence, which produces our sins of thought, word, and deed in particular choices and actions.

Luther eventually cited Johann Reuchlin as an authority for this interpretation, making reference to Reuchlin's explanation of the seven penitential psalms from the Hebrew, a book published in 1512.[20] But Luther's initial conclusion came from a glance ahead to Paul's reference to »sin« in Rom 7:20, »It is no longer I that do it, but sin which dwells within me.« Luther promises that the whole matter will become clear to a person pondering chapters 7 and 8 of Romans.[21] The conclusion on »sin« is not, strictly speaking, philological, but exegetical within Scripture itself. In a phrase Luther uses later,

---

[16] »Nam theologiae proprium subiectum est homo peccati reus ac perditus ac Deus iustificans ac salvator hominis peccatoris.« *Enarratio Psalmi LI*; WA 40II, 328,17; LW 12, 311.

[17] WA 56, 268-291; LW 25, 257-278.

[18] »Quia dum sancti peccatum suum semper in conspectu habent et iustitiam a Deo secundum misericordiam ipsius implorant, eoipso semper quoque iusti a Deo reputantur.« WA 56, 269,25. Luther had already dealt at length with the primary role in a devout life of a person's *confessio peccati* in his scholion on Rom 3:4-7 (WA 56, 212-234; LW 25, 197-219). This complex of texts alerts us to the fact that prayerful encounter with God, centered in a personal *confessio peccati*, is fundamental to the *simul*. See R. Hermann, *Luthers These*, 295, and »Das Verhältnis von Rechtfertigung und Gebet nach Luthers Auslegung von Röm 3,« in Hermann's *Gesammelte Studien* (Göttingen 1960), 11-43, esp. 18-23.

[19] WA 56, 270,9; LW 25, 258.

[20] WA 56, 277,5-13; LW 25, 264.

[21] WA 56, 271,1-15; LW 25, 259.

4. Living and Praying the *simul*

Scripture is self-interpreting (*sui ipsius interpres*), and one gains understanding of a text by making comparisons with other parts of the Bible.[22]

His comparison with Rom 7 led Luther to grasp the primary term for »sin« in Rom 4:7 and Psalm 32:1. Quickly other texts came to mind which refer to this pervasive *peccatum* which lies at the source of sinful acts:

> Ps 32:5f: »I said I will confess my transgressions to the Lord. ...Therefore let everyone who is godly offer prayer to thee.«
> Ps 51:3f: »For I know my transgressions, and my sin is ever before me. ...Against thee only have I sinned.«
> 1 Jn 1:9: »If we say we have no sin, we are liars.«

There is thus a sin which continues to loom large in the self-awareness of the believer and which flaws and infects those who are saints and righteous.[23]

This *simul* therefore has another side, going beyond the first aspect that Luther noted, where the opposites were held together by the overarching fact of God's way of merciful reckoning or accounting. The simultaneity of righteousness and sin is verified *in* the very person who has turned to God. Such a believer, precisely as converted and believing, is »at the same time sick and healthy« (*aegrotus simul et sanus*). Not perfectly whole, the believer is at the same time righteous and sinner, one who looks forward to being freed from sin and completely healed of its enduring infection.[24]

This view of sin, Luther affirms, was prevalent in the early fathers of the church, such as Ambrose and Augustine, but has been lost in scholastic theology.[25] Among the scholastics, a faulty idea of sin goes hand in hand with defective thinking about grace, which they came to see as a supernatural qualification of the soul that God requires people to have for salvation. Scholastic theology has lost sight of our dire need of healing through grace from endemic sin.[26]

---

[22] WA 7, 97,23, 99,20, from the preface of *Assertio omnium articulorum*, written in late 1520. On this, we now have the essay by W. Mostert, »Scriptura sacra sui ipsius interpres. Bemerkungen zum Verständnis der Heiligen Schrift bei Luther,« *Lutherjahrbuch* 46 (1979), 60-96.

[23] WA 56, 271,2-27; LW 25, 259.

[24] WA 56, 272,7.27; LW 25, 260.

[25] WA 56, 273,3 – 274,18, citing Augustine to the effect that in baptism sinful concupiscence is remitted »non ut non sit, sed ut non imputetur.« *De nuptiis et concupiscentiis*, I, 25, 28 (CSEL 42, 240), cited at WA 56, 273,10 (LW 25, 261). See also WA 56, 281,1 (LW 25, 268), for another appeal to Augustine and other fathers.

[26] At this critical moment of his development, Luther is not operating with a voluntarist or »covenantal« view of reality. Instead he sees such a view obscuring a right understanding of God's grace. To ground the need of grace on the divine *intentio praecipientis* or the decree of God's *potentia ordinata* would run counter to Luther's main point in this scholion, namely, that we need grace because human nature is radically debilitated by the inherited and acquired malady of sin. A recent exposition of the »covenantal« view of the *via moderna* (cf. Study 1, above, p. 9, n. 23) underscores its relativizing of the ontology of justification but also misleadingly regards it as a prelude to Luther's biblical realism. A. McGrath, *The Intellectual Origins of the European Reformation* (Oxford 1987), 77-85, with reference to Luther on p. 82. Luther is a biblical realist, to be sure, but in 1515-16 this meant being realistic about the human, fallen condition. Later,

Luther's scholion on Rom 4:7 ranges widely on the true nature of sin and righteousness. His conclusion is that *iustitia* must be seen more in a relational manner than as an inherent quality. The relation is constituted on God's side by the merciful accounting of a person as righteous and not as guilty and bound for punishment. Inherent sin is not imputed unto guilt and condemnation. This is God's merciful decision, which though corresponds to an attitude in the person being justified. Luther even says that God's non-imputation of sin takes place because of (*propter*) the person's heartfelt confession and self-accusation, which entails prayer imploring God's saving righteousness and faith in God's word. However, sin, that is, the drive of concupiscence, remains, and because of its presence the person now accounted righteous is at the same time a sinner.[27]

Luther began the conclusion of his long scholion by cataloging biblical testimonies to the universality of enduring sinfulness. The list stretches from the beginning of the Bible to the end, starting from Moses' witness to the human heart's evil designs (Gen 8:21), and advancing through Exodus, the words of Solomon and Qoheleth 7:20 (»There is no righteous one on the face of the earth who does not sin while doing good«), Job (throughout the book) and Psalms, and Isaiah and Jeremiah. Paul and James both state this view of humankind, as does John in his first letter and the last chapter of Revelation.[28]

Texts of this sort are, therefore, Luther's warrant for a key aspect of his early teaching on Christian life and prayer. On such a basis he could insist on the penitential spirituality he had already depicted in his comment on Rom 3:10:

> Those therefore who are truly righteous not only yearn for and implore the grace of God because they see that they have an evil will and so by this are sinful before God, but as well because they see that they can never fully grasp how deep is the evil of their will and how far it extends. They thus always believe that they are sinners, as if the depth of their evil will were infinite. Thus they humble themselves, thus they plead, thus they yearn, until at last they are perfectly healed - which takes place in death.[29]

---

however, McGrath speaks of the incompatibility of Luther's new theology with the soteriology of the *via moderna* (p.120). Yes, and that incompatibility was due primarily to the conviction about the human condition that grounds the penitential spirituality Luther inculcates.

[27] »Sed 'iustitia' Scripturae magis pendet ab imputatione Dei quam ab esse rei. Ille enim habet iustitiam, non qui qualitatem solam habet, immo ille peccator est omnino et iniustus, sed quem Deus propter confessionem iniustitiae suae et implorationem iustitiae Dei misericorditer reputat et voluit iustum apud se haberi. Ideo omnes in iniquitate, i.e., iniustitia nascimur, morimur, sola autem reputatione miserentis Dei per fidem verbi eius iusti sumus.« WA 56, 287,18-24; LW 25, 274f. The »propter confessionem ... et implorationem« was amply foreshadowed in the scholion at WA 56, 269,26-29, 271,21f.27f, 276,32-35 (»propter humilem fidei gemitum«), 278,13-16, 281,9-16, 281,18f (»statuerit Deus nulli velle non imputare nisi gementi et timenti ac assidue misericordiam suam imploranti«), 282,6.11-15, and 284,12-14. Also, 289,20f.30-32.

[28] WA 56, 287,25-288,32; LW 25, 275f.

[29] WA 56, 235,31-37; translation adapted from LW 25, 220f.

For popular instruction, Luther explained Ps 32:1-2 in his vernacular commentary on the seven penitential psalms in early 1517. »Sin« is the fundamental reality among the psalm's four terms for human evil. »Sin« is the perduring evil of our nature, a complex of drives and feelings from which arise evil actions (»iniquities«/»*Missetaten*«), but in the righteous God does not account this »sin« unto damnation. In those who confess their evil and take refuge in him, as expressed in Ps 32:6f, God does not impute sin, but begins to heal this deep-seated malady.[30]

Luther spoke of this penitential lifestyle in his published explanation and defense of the theses which he debated at Leipzig in 1519 against Johann Eck. Also he broadened the biblical basis for his thesis on the simultaneity of righteousness and sin. 1 Jn 1:8 speaks in the present tense about our defective observance of God's commandments: »Hence we sin daily, and daily we rid ourselves of sin.« The lusts of the flesh (Gal 5:17) are sin, which one can only counteract and cleanse by penance. The mandate of Luke 24:47 calls us to a penitential life: »Therefore the evangelical life is nothing else but penance.« Luther concluded from a batch of New Testament texts: »And so the whole of life is penance, prayer, and contrition« (*deinde totam vitam esse poenitentiam et orationem et contritionem*), precisely because of the sinful tinder of concupiscence.[31]

These Leipzig *Resolutiones* argue for the pervasiveness of sin even in the actions of the righteous, citing several of the same texts offered in the scholion on Rom 4:7 (Isa 64:6, Qoh 7:20, Rom 7:19.22, Ps 143:2), but Luther adds pointed arguments from Gal 5:17, on the drives of concupiscent flesh against the Spirit, and from the parable of the Good Samaritan (Luke 10), which Luther takes with Augustine as an allegory on our fall and rescue.[32] Here Luther concludes to the primacy of the therapeutic cure of sin in the daily life of the church, as is represented by the inn or hostel in the parable.[33] The first part of Job also contributes to Luther's case, but now with explicit reference to the patristic interpretation of Gregory the Great's *Moralia in Job*.[34]

---

30 WA 1, 168,11-29; LW 14, 149. This passage was unchanged in Luther's 1525 revised edition of the work.

31 WA 2, 409,5.24.35, 410,14.23.

32 The whole biblical argument is on WA 2, 411-415, with Gal 5 treated at 413,1-29 and Luke 10 at 413,30-35.

33 »Itaque ecclesia stabulum est, in quo accepta gratia baptismi quottidie curamur a peccatis.« WA 2, 413,32. The reference here to baptism reminds us of the importance of penitential dedication in Luther's *Sermon* of the same year (1519) on the sacrament of baptism (WA 2, 727-737; LW 35, 29-43). See below, pp. 74-76.

34 WA 2, 418,1-419,4.

After Pope Leo X censured certain formulations of the *simul* in »Exsurge Domine«, nos. 2,3,31,32, Luther gave spirited replies in *Assertio omnium articulorum* in 1520, adding new arguments from New Testament paranesis, such as 1 Cor 5:7, »Clear out the old yeast, so you may become a new batch of dough.«[35]

But Luther's most systematic defense of the *simul iustus et peccator* came in his 1521 writing against an adversary he later grew to esteem, Jacobus Latomus of Louvain.[36] Luther's rebuttal to Latomus included a lengthy interpretation of Isa 64:6 (»We have all become unclean, and all our righteous deeds are like a filthy rag«). Luther contends that the prophet is speaking simply and directly about sin being present even in our good works and righteous deeds, so that a person is made worthy before God only through the forgiving mercy for which we should be grateful from our inmost heart.[37]

In 1538 Luther countered the Antinomian interpretation of his teaching by insisting on how the Law makes clear to the believer that experienced movements and drives of unruly flesh are indeed sins displeasing to God. All of Scripture is filled with this teaching, especially Rom 7. Also, Psalm 31:1.6, and 1 Jn 1:8 add their witness, showing that the believer is both holy and a sinner: »Two contraries are in one subject and this at the same point in time.« One senses sin still clinging to one's person. So we pray that God's name be hallowed and his kingdom come, while we engage in a never-ending battle.[38]

Luther's most engaging passages on the *simul*, however, occur in a text little marked by argument and polemic, his exposition of Psalm 51, which was published by Luther's disciple Veit Dietrich in 1538 based on Luther's lectures of 1532. This psalm is for Luther filled with instruction in basic Christianity and serves to give a schooling beyond which the believer never advances.[39]

---

[35] WA 7, 106,36.

[36] The life and work of this little-known figure has been set forth by J. Vercruysse in »Jacobus Latomus und Martin Luther: Einführendes zu einer Kontroverse,« *Gregorianum* 64 (1983), 515-538, reprinted in E. Iserloh, ed., *Katholische Theologen der Reformationszeit*, 2 (Münster 1985), 7-26.

[37] WA 8, 59-69; LW 31, 161-176.

[38] Third Antinomian Disputation, WA 39I, 507,5-508,9, citing 508,1 (»Duo contraria in uno subiecto et in eodem puncto temporis«). Also 512,7-15, on Paul showing us »ingentem illam pugnam seu luctam spiritus Dei et carnis in sanctis.«

[39] »Haec est doctrina huius Psalmi et perpetua nostra schola, in qua nunquam perfecti Magistri evademus, non nos, non apostoli, non propheti. Omnes enim hic manemus discipuli et omnes petimus, dum vivimus, amplius lavari.« WA 40II, 357,31; LW 12, 331. Luther's commentary has been called »ein Grundkurs des christlichen Glaubens« by its recent translator. H. Kleinknecht, in the sub-title of *Der 51. Psalm* (Munich 1983).

4. Living and Praying the *simul*

We conclude our review of Luther's biblical warrants for the simultaneity of sin with righteousness by citing two instructions on normative self-understanding that Luther drew out of Psalm 51.

> It is useful to consider David's prayer well. After he has asked for the forgiveness of sins as far as their guilt is concerned, and rejoices in God's mercy, he still asks for what remains: that he might be washed from his iniquities; that he might be granted the Holy Spirit, the power and gift that lives within the heart and cleanses the remnants of sin, which began to be buried through Baptism but have not been completely buried. This is the Christian life. ... In all Christians there remain such defilements of the spirit, that is, evil opinions about God, and defilements of the flesh, that is, vicious lusts, and it should be our labor and effort to clean these out with the help of the Holy Spirit.[40]

> Having the forgiveness of sins and existing in grace, being neither accused nor condemned by any sin, David is nevertheless unclean and has a sin so unclean that all it lacks to make it a real sin is that it cannot condemn him. David the righteous and the justified still has sin, and is still partly unrighteous. He prays for the supreme gift of the Holy Spirit to clean out these dirty spots, and this gift surely proves that the washing is no game or joke. We must avoid minimizing the remnants of sin.[41]

Our initial survey of a series of works by Luther on the condition of the justified person has brought out the main lines of his teaching on the *simul*, with attention to the growing cluster of biblical texts which Martin Luther found testifying to and supporting his position.

Before we isolate the central theological grounding that Luther gave for this teaching, two points should be stated in connection with the biblical argument that concupiscence makes the righteous person as well a sinner. This position is closely connected with issues relevant for theological method and for personal religiosity.

First, when scholastic theology chose to treat the baptized as if no sin at all remained in them, but only a *fomes* or weakness, a momentous change was actually transpiring. For Luther this innovation in the theological *usus loquendi* was symptomatic of a broader process of humanization, by which theology in effect lost its grip on the genuine meaning of biblical discourse as a whole. Luther claims that his own study of this scholastic theology left him ignorant of the great personal religious issues of sin, righteousness, baptism, and Christian life, and of God's own power, work, grace, and righteousness. He had also imbibed much which had to be unlearned: »There I lost Christ, whom I now have found in Paul.«[42] Against Latomus, Luther justified his position on perduring sin by claiming to speak the plain speech of the Apostle Paul. Post-biblical distinctions,

---

[40] WA 40II, 354,33-355,24; LW 12, 329f (cited).

[41] WA 40II, 356,35-357,23. LW 12, 331.

[42] *Resolutiones* of the Leipzig Disputation, WA 2, 414,4-11.22-28, citing from line 28 (»Ego Christum amisi illic, nunc in Paulo reperi«).

by which Paul's *peccatum* is made to mean only a weakness or the punishment for sin, needlessly complicate theological work, lead theology away from Scripture, and give the theologian a weak foundation in mere human inventions.[43]

Second, these non-biblical terms of the scholastics serve instrumentally in a treatment of the human condition and grace that has the effect of minimalizing the reality of sin and trivializing the Christian struggle. After his first formulation of the *simul*, Luther charged that »our theologians,« that is, those who take no account of the sin that remains, were leading people to neglect earnest prayer for healing grace. The faithful do not make war against their concupiscence, »and consequently there is now in the church much falling back into sin after confession.«[44] Against Latomus, Luther repeated his charge that recent theology was religiously subversive.

> Those who deny this sin make people rest apathetically and carelessly in the gift they have received. In this way they cheapen Christ's grace and minimalize God's mercy, from which necessarily follow coldness in love, slackness in praise, and lukewarmness in gratitude.[45]

Theology has been undercutting lived religion and devotion. It should instead support the prayer of confession and plea for mercy.[46] A good theology of sin promotes gratitude and praise for God's forgiveness and as well earnest prayer for his gift of ongoing purification.

God's grace and gift (»gratia et donum«)

Luther's *simul* surfaced in the midst of a terminological clarification of a Pauline text and grew into an anthropological explanation and spiritual vision. But it also relates a central truth about God by mirroring just how he wills to work in the world to implement our salvation.[47] By God's grace the believer is

---

[43] WA 8, 107,37-42, 109,2-10; LW 32, 229f, 231. Later in the same work Luther says, »Scripturae enim sinceritas custodienda est, nec praesumat homo suo ore eloqui, aut clarius aut securius, quam Deus elocutus est ore suo.« WA 8, 118,4; LW 32, 244. Also, in the same vein: WA 8, 103,17-23; LW 32, 223. Pierre Fraenkel recently set forth this trait of Luther's work in »Luther et le langage de la théologie,« *Revue de théologie et de philosophie* 119 (1987), 17-32.

[44] »Unde et tanta nunc in ecclesia est recidivatio post confessiones.« WA 56, 276,11; LW 25, 263.

[45] WA 8, 114,39-115,1; LW 32, 240 (cited). Also WA 8, 103,19-25; LW 32, 223.

[46] Luther brought this out indirectly against Latomus, by showing how an impossible prayer would follow from Latomus's denial of sin's presence in good works. One could present such a work to God in utter confidence of a reward, without need of forgiving mercy, glorying in what one has done with the help of grace. WA 8, 79,21-27; LW 32, 190. Luther's view coheres closely with the confession of sin and plea for forgiveness which recurs in liturgical prayer.

[47] This point is well made by R. Hermann, *Luthers These*, 90-108, 274-278.

righteous; but because the same person is simultaneously a sinner, God's gift begins to work in him, meeting a dire need.⁴⁸ Luther found the distinction between *gratia* and *donum* a helpful means for bringing order and system into his insights into the divine work of justifying sinful humans. We cite here from Luther in order to show the precision with which he stated the significant duality of God's grace and gift.

> A righteous and believing person doubtless has both grace and the gift. Grace makes such a one wholly pleasing, so that the person is completely accepted, and there is no place for wrath in him any more, but the gift heals from sin and from all corruption of body and soul. ... Everything is forgiven through grace, but as yet not everything is healed through the gift. (*Against Latomus*, 1521⁴⁹)

> These two terms, grace and gift, differ in this way. »Grace« is the favor, mercy, and freely given good will of God in our regard. The »gift« is the Holy Spirit in person, whom God pours out into the hearts of those on whom he has mercy and whom he regards with favor. ... But we are not given the fullness of the gift or Spirit now in this life, and so the remains of sin remain in us, doing battle against the spirit. (*Preface to Romans*, 1529⁵⁰)

> These are the two parts of justification. The first is the grace revealed through Christ, that we have a gracious God, so that sin can no longer accuse us, but our conscience has been given peace through trust in the mercy of God. The second part is the conferring of the Holy Spirit with his gifts, who enlightens us against the defilements of spirit and flesh. Thus we are defended against the opinions with which the devil seduces the whole world. Thus the true knowledge of God grows daily. (*Enarratio Psalmi LI*, 1538⁵¹)

---

48 The basic study of this component of the *simul* is E. Iserloh, »Gratia und Donum, Rechtfertigung und Heiligung nach Luthers Schrift 'Wider den Löwener Theologen Latomus' (1521),« in L. Abramowski & J.F.G. Goeters, eds., *Studien zur Geschichte und Theologie der Reformation*, Festschrift Ernst Bizer (Neukirchen 1969), 141-156; reprinted in E. Iserloh, *Luther und die Reformation* (Aschaffenburg 1974), 88-105. — W. Joest treats this duality by contrasting the simple totality of God's intervention by grace with the gradual and progressive character of his work by his gift. *Gesetz und Freiheit*, 57-70.

49 »Iustus et fidelis absque dubio habet gratiam et donum: gratiam, quae eum totum gratificet, ut persona prorsus accepta sit, et nullus irae locus in eo sit amplius, donum vero, quod eum sanet a peccato et tota corruptione sua animi et corporis. ... Remissa sunt omnia [peccata] per gratiam, sed nondum omnia sanata per donum. WA 8, 107,13-21; LW 32, 229 (cited).

50 »Haec duo vocabula, gratia et donum, sic differunt. Gratia est favor, misericordia, gratuita benevolentia Dei erga nos. Donum est ipse Spiritus Sanctus, quem in eorum corda effundit, quorum est misertus et quibus favet. ... Tametsi nunc non contingat nobis plenitudo doni aut spiritus in hac vita, semper manentibus in nobis reliquiis peccati, quae pugnant contra spiritum.« WADB 5, 622,17-22.

51 »Haec sunt duae partes iustificationis. Prior est gratia per Christum revelata, quod habeamus placatum Deum, ut peccatum amplius non possit nos accusare, sed conscientia fiducia misericordiae Dei sit reducta in securitatem. Posterior est donatio Spiritus Sancti cum donis suis, qui illuminat contra inquinamenta spiritus et carnis, ut defendiamur ab opinionibus diabolicis, quibus orbem terrarum seducit, ut vera cognitio Dei in diem crescat.« WA 40II, 357,35-358,22; LW 12, 331.

> Christ did not earn only *gratia*, »grace,« for us, but also *donum*, »the gift« of the Holy Spirit, so that we might have not only forgiveness of, but also cessation from, sins. (*On the Councils and the Church*, 1539[52])

There are thus two simultaneous actions in the dispensation that God is now implementing in human lives in accord with his will and purpose: (1) the complete remission of guilt by divine grace, by which one's sin is no longer imputed unto condemnation, one is fully accepted and accounted righteous because of Christ, with whom one is truly united, and one no longer suffers under sin's dominance in conscience; (2) the gradual and laborious purification from all sin, in mind and body, spirit and flesh, by the gift of the Spirit, who heals the person by a life-long process.

Luther found Paul alluding to this distinction in Rom 5:15 (»...how much more did the grace of God and the gracious gift of the one person Jesus Christ overflow for the many«), and Psalm 51 reflects it, as verse 3 begs the grace of pardon and acceptance, and then verse 4 begins to plead for the gift of gradual liberation from the vexation of sin still left in the flesh.[53] The texts on *gratia* and *donum* are recurrent in Luther's works and they give ample evidence that this systematic distinction underlies Luther's *simul* and leads as well to his characteristic emphases in teaching conversion and the penitential life.[54] From these texts, we can elaborate the following summary account.

Gratia is God's own mercy, benevolence, and favor toward humankind redeemed by Christ. It remains God's attribute, but it comes to impinge on a person's life through the word of the Gospel offering and effecting a genuine – ontological – union with Christ. The effect of grace proclaimed is peace of heart, consolation, and courage. God's gracious benevolence is effective in a new self-understanding. The opposite of this *gratia* is God's wrath, with which the law threatens those outside Christ. *Fides* is solely God's work in the sinner who thereby passes into the realm of grace, admitting his sins, laying hold of Christ's righteousness now imputed as his own, and accepting an unmerited gift of pardon with full assurance.

One relates personally to God's grace in conscience, where sin's power to condemn is decisively broken. Where sin was once dominant, *peccatum regnans*, it does remain present, but now is »ground down and subject: in us but captive

---

[52] »Denn Christus hat uns nicht allein *gratiam*, die gnade, sondern auch *donum*, die gabe des Heiligen Geistes, verdient, das wir nicht allein vergebung der sunden sondern auch auffhören von den sunden hetten.« WA 50, 599,32-35; LW 41, 114.

[53] This was not developed in the 1515-16 course on Romans, but Luther stated it in his preface to Romans in his translation of the New Testament. On Psalm 51:3-4, see WA 40II, 350-358; LW 12, 327-331.

[54] Luther offers treatments of *gratia/donum* in these texts: WA 8, 106f (Response to Latomus); WADB 5, 622f (Pref. to Rom); WA 40II, 420-432 (on Ps 51:12f, »Cor mundum crea in me...«); WA 39I, 95-114 (*Disputatio de iustificatione*, 1536); ib., 431-440 (2nd Antinomian Disputation, 1538); WA 50, 599 (*On Councils and the Church*, 1539).

4. Living and Praying the *simul*

and condemned, utterly debilitated ... bound over to complete destruction: not imputed: *peccatum regnatum*.«⁵⁵ Luther has two main concerns in these texts on the simultaneity of sin with righteousness. First, he is ascribing the totality of the grace of pardon to God, who declares over us his merciful forgiveness not because of any worthiness of our own but »because of Christ ... and because of the down-payment and first-fruits, the Spirit.«⁵⁶ Second, this teaching means to instill courage in the heart of one now made free to face the toil and trouble of lifelong battle with the remaining disorders of sin. Although the doctrine of *gratia/donum* entails a precise theological explanation (»All is forgiven by grace, but all is not yet healed by the gift«⁵⁷), the end it serves is the lived religiosity of the penitential life.

God's gift is directly opposed to our sinful thoughts and corrupt tendencies in all their variety. *Fides* is but the harbinger of the Holy Spirit's manifold helps against sin with a view to penitential cleansing.⁵⁸ One who believes in God's mercy and senses God's nearness is naturally vexed over not loving God wholeheartedly and not being as chaste, peaceable, and generous as God commands – and so he begs to be washed and thoroughly cleansed.⁵⁹

The life of penitential purgation, unfolding in virtue of the *donum*, fits into a doctrinal context which deserves mention. In 1539, Luther spoke of his wayward disciples the Antinomians as only partially appropriating the Creed. They preach well the second article on our redemption by Christ. But they say nothing about the third article, in which we profess our faith »concerning sanctification and the vivifying work of the Holy Spirit,« that is, concerning the transforming of our old Adam into a new person. Neglect of faith's acknowledgement, in the third

---

55 Sin is »contritum et subiectum; in nobis captum, iudicatum, prorsusque infirmatum ... mandatur penitus abolendum; non imputatum; peccatum regnatum.« *Against Latomus*, WA 8, 88,28, 91,24f, 93,14, 94,10 (LW 32, 202, 206, 209, 210). R. Hermann's book on the *simul* begins by treating the images through which Luther characterizes the sin remaining after justification, e.g., as the old rulers of the land who still remained after the Israelites took possession, or as an imprisoned criminal awaiting execution. *Luthers These*, 10-18.

56 »Propter Christum ... et arrabonem et primitias spiritus.« WADB 5, 622,28f; see LW 35, 369f.

57 »Remissa sunt omnia per gratiam, sed nondum omnia sanata per donum.« WA 8, 107,21; LW 32, 229.

58 Regin Prenter treated Luther's doctrine of progressive sanctification at the 1956 Luther-Research Congress: »Luthers Lehre von der Heiligung,« in V. Vajta, ed., *Lutherforschung heute* (Berlin 1958), 64-74. But Prenter collapses the power of progressive expulsion of sin into the dynamic of *fides Christi*. Luther, however, makes quite explicit that it is by the *donum/dona* of the Holy Spirit that one is carried along toward full purification and holiness. Prenter's foreshortened account seems to leave little room for daily prayer for the Spirit's manifold gifts.

59 WA 40II, 354,20-27; LW 12, 329. W. Joest shows how Luther ascribed a true role in the life of the righteous sinner to God's law and commandments, as warnings and directives which guide the believer's struggle against endemic evil. *Gesetz und Freiheit*, 71-81.

creedal article, of the principal works of the Holy Spirit, makes one blind to both the gift and task of the penitential life.⁶⁰

The Holy Spirit counteracts a variety of sinful disorders, not only human lusts and aggressivity, but especially sins of spirit and mind: the merit-mentality, doubts about God's grace, murmuring against God, impatience. Our part here is patient endurance of the Spirit's purging work and prayer that the Spirit's help be equal to our need. One is not simply passive in this, for sin is resisted »with great exertion.«⁶¹ Believers accept the Spirit's disciplining of their concupiscence and give readily of themselves in the *officia humanitatis* in which we exercise soul and body.⁶² The gift, alas, is not one of full victory in this life, because we human beings are always to some extent reluctant followers of the Spirit given. But there can be gradual progress in virtue of the *donum*, which brings an animating and guiding presence.

Living the »simul« in faith and embattled prayer

Both aspects of the righteous sinner's condition call for corresponding responses in intentional activity, especially in prayer. Daily the believer should appropriate afresh, with humility and gratitude, the grace of God's freely given pardon; daily one takes up the struggle of driving out the enemy still occupying terrain in one's own person.

A concise early exposition of this duality of laying hold of a once-for-all gift and doggedly performing a life-long task, is Luther's 1519 *Sermon on the Sacrament of Baptism*. Early in the sermon Luther enunciates the *simul*:

> When someone comes forth out of baptism, he is truly pure, without sin, and wholly guiltless. Still, there are many who do not properly understand this. They think that sin is no longer present, and so they become remiss and negligent in the killing of their sinful nature, even as some do when they have gone to confession. For this reason, as I have said above, it should be properly understood and known that our flesh, so long as it lives here, is by nature wicked and sinful.
>
> With respect to the sacrament, then, it is true that he is without sin and guilt. Yet because all is not yet completed and he still lives in sinful flesh, he is not without sin. But although not pure in all things, he has begun to grow into purity and innocence.⁶³

---

⁶⁰ *On Councils and the Church*, 1539; WA 50, 599,26-35; LW 41, 113f.

⁶¹ This phrase, »*magno conatu*,« occurs in Luther's account of the »washing« sought by Ps 51:4. WA 40II, 354,25; LW 12, 329.

⁶² WA 40II,355,23f, 356,16-23, 407,16-22; LW 12, 330, 366. A recent, quite thoughtful, treatment of believers' »offices« in the world is O. Bayer, »Natur und Institution. Eine Besinnung auf Luthers Dreiständelehre,« *Zeitschrift für Theologie und Kirche* 81 (1984), 352-382.

⁶³ LW 35, 32 & 33, translating WA 2, 729,19-25 & 730, 7-10. Also in 1519, Luther's published commentary on Galatians treated the *simul* as it explained Gal 5:17 (WA 2, 585-587; LW 27, 362-365). On Gal 5:21: »Omnes ergo sancti habent peccatum suntque peccatores, et nullus peccat: iusti sunt iuxta illud quod gratia in eis sanavit, peccatores iuxta quod adhuc sanandi sunt.« WA 2,

Baptism expresses God's commitment to envelop a person's life with his grace. »God allies himself with you and becomes one with you in a gracious covenant of comfort.« Baptism marks as well the start of God's transforming impact on sinful nature. »He begins to make you a new person. He pours into you his grace and Holy Spirit, who begins to slay nature and sin.«[64]

God's two works should be distinguished but not separated: »It is one thing to forgive sins, and another thing to put them away or drive them out.«[65] In baptism, God establishes with a person a gracious and consoling covenant of forgiveness, not imputing the person's sin unto condemnation – and so I should in faith recall my baptism with firm assurance of God's sheer mercy. Faith embraces God's loving intention to deal graciously with me both now and in the judgment to come. In such faith, one can withstand the murmuring of conscience and cast oneself on God's intention and promise expressed once-for-all in baptism.[66]

Baptism is also God's commitment to making one's sinful flesh wholly new – and I must dedicate myself to patient suffering and to persevering in good works contrary to my endemic sinful appetites. The negativities of this life, both those coming over a person and those willingly embraced in penitential dedication, are all seen as serving the realization of the baptismal project of driving out sin.

> Fasting and all such exercises should be aimed at holding down the old Adam, the sinful nature, and at accustoming it to do without what is pleasing in this life, and thus preparing it more and more each day, so that the work and purpose of baptism may be fulfilled.[67]

592,19; LW 27, 372.

[64] WA 2, 730,21.27; LW 35, 33. Luther's language in the second of these citations, »[Gott] geust dyr eyn seyn gnad und heyligen geist, der anfahet die natur und sund zu todten,« indicates that it is inadequate to explain Luther's difference from the previous tradition simply in terms of the difference between imputed righteousness and infused grace. Luther will oppose conceiving grace as an accidental quality modifying one's substantial being, but the image of »infusion« is still one he finds useful.

[65] »Ist es eyn ander ding, die sund vorgeben und die sund abzulegen odder auß zu treyben.« WA 2, 734,1; LW 35, 38 (cited).

[66] These lines summarize nos. 12-15 of the *Sermon*, WA 2, 732-734; LW 35, 35-39. In 1518 Luther had come to ascribe central importance to the confessor's word of absolution in the life of faith. Here in the *Sermon* of 1519, Luther is applying his new doctrine of the sacramental word and *fides sacramenti* to baptismal consecration. I treat this in »*Fides sacramenti – Fides specialis*: Luther's Development in 1518,« Study 6 in this collection. – Luther's contemporary commentary on Galatians highlights the christological ground of what baptism confers: »Omnis qui credit in Christum iustus est, nondum plene in re, sed in spe.... Interim autem, dum iustificatur et sanatur, non imputatur ei, quod reliquum est in carne peccatum, propter Christum, qui cum sine omni peccato sit, iam unum cum Christiano suo factus, interpellat pro eo ad Patrem.« WA 2, 495,1-5; LW 27, 227.

[67] LW 35, 39f, translating WA 2, 734,37-735,2. Luther's 1519 commentary on Galatians attributes the purgative side of Christian existence to faith's action, which leads to an »incarnation« of willing obedience to the Spirit: »Fides enim ipsa, ubi nata fuerit, hoc sibi negotii habet, ut reliquum peccati e carne expugnet variis afflictionibus, laboribus, mortificationibus carnis, ut sic lex Dei non modo in spiritu et corde placeat et impleatur, sed et in carne, quae

Each one should choose that station in life (*Stand*) which most readily promotes the penitential realization of baptism, whether this be in family life or the »spiritual estate«.[68]

Luther concludes that baptism is a principal basis for grateful praise of God. In baptismal faith the believer is joyful in God. »If we hear and firmly believe that in the covenant of baptism God receives us sinners, spares us, and makes us pure from day to day, then our heart must be joyful, and love and praise God.«[69] The *iustus simul peccator* is put on guard against the threat of despair from one side and against the danger of false security from the other side. The enemy within is to be countered with unperturbed dedication.

> No one should be terrified if he feels evil lust or love, nor should he despair if he falls. Rather he should remember his baptism, and comfort himself joyfully with the fact that God has there pledged himself to slay his sin for him and not to count it a cause for condemnation, if only he does not say Yes to sin or remain in it. Moreover these wild thoughts and appetites, and even a fall into sin, should not be regarded as an occasion for despair. Regard them rather as an admonition from God that we should remember our baptism and what was there spoken, that we should call upon God's mercy and exercise ourselves in striving against sin, that we should even welcome death in order that we may be rid of sin.[70]

The intentional activity by which the believer corresponds to the condition of simultaneous righteousness and sin is also present in Luther's widely-read booklet of 1520, *The Freedom of a Christian*. One can amplify the famous paradox Luther placed at the head of this treatise by saying that as *iustus* and forgiven in Christ one is »perfectly free lord of all, subject to none,« while as *simul peccator* and aiming toward full healing one must be the »perfectly dutiful servant of all, subject to all.«[71]

Luther concludes the first part of his treatise on Christian freedom by describing faith as interior transformation amid profound joy and consolation over the saving work of Christ with all the benefits it brings. The believing heart is made firm against all hostile threats and dangers.

> If the knowledge of sin or the fear of death should break in upon it, it is ready to hope in the Lord. It does not grow afraid when it hears tidings of evil. It is not disturbed when it sees its enemies. This is so because it believes that the righteousness of Christ is its own and that its sin is not its own, but Christ's, and that all sin is

---

adhuc resistit fidei et spiritui amanti et implenti legem.« WA 2, 497,18-21; LW 27, 231.
[68] WA 2, 735,18-736,32; LW 35, 40-42.
[69] LW 35, 42, translating WA 2, 737,6-9.
[70] LW 35, 35; translating WA 2, 731,29-37.
[71] Based on LW 31, 344; translating WA 7, 49,22-25.

4. Living and Praying the *simul*

swallowed up by the righteousness of Christ. This ... is a necessary consequence on account of faith in Christ.[72]

Such faith, based proximately on a word of God's acquittal, does not remain an isolated interior factor in one's life. Faith initiates gradual growth toward the full integration of the rest of the person into the heart's righteousness in Christ. Here, discipline is needed, for a hostile force still has a foothold in one's person.

> Here the works begin; here one cannot enjoy leisure; here one must indeed take care to discipline the body by fasting, watchings, labors, and other reasonable discipline and to subject it to the Spirit so that it will obey and conform to the inner man and faith and not revolt against faith and hinder the inner man. ... One meets a contrary will in one's own flesh which strives to serve the world and seeks its own advantage. This the spirit of faith cannot tolerate, but with joyful zeal it attempts to put the body under control and hold it in check.[73]

Luther's characteristic instruction on Christian living thus comprises numerous elements, which fall into place around two clearly identifiable poles. One cluster of elements concerns the fundamental relation of the person, in faith, to God's gracious presence among us and his saving work in Christ. A second cluster concerns all the elements of a person's intentional activity in prayer, self-discipline, and service, which the Holy Spirit is eliciting by manifold gifts, with the aim of eventually overcoming and expelling sin through a lifelong process of purification and renewal of all one is.[74]

The fundamental exercise of faith is ever anew to lay hold of the reality of God's mercy. One is not righteous by one's achievement or merit, and this is of lasting relevance.

> Forgiveness of sins is not a matter of a passing work or action, but of perpetual duration. For the forgiveness of sins begins in baptism and remains with us all the way to death, until we arise from the dead, and leads us into eternal life. So we live continually under the remission of sins.
>
> God's mercy is pardoning and his love is meanwhile forgiving, and God really takes sin in such a way that it does not remain sin, because he begins materially to purge and to forgive completely. On no condition is sin a passing condition, but we are justified daily by the unmerited forgiveness of sins and by the justification of God's mercy.[75]

---

[72] LW 31, 357; WA 7, 59,10-15. On the theme of the »happy exchange« between Christ and the believer, see R. Schwager, »Der fröhliche Wechsel und Streit,« *Zeitschrift für katholische Theologie* 115 (1983), 27-66.

[73] LW 31, 358f; WA 7, 60,2-6.

[74] W. Joest calls the first moment the ever-renewed *transitus* from complete loss to reconciliation with God in Christ (*Gesetz und Freiheit*, 60-65) and the second the gradual *progressus* as the Spirit gains greater scope in a person's daily life (Ibid., 68-70).

[75] *Disputation on Justification*, 1536. LW 34, 164, 167; WA 39I, 94,37-95,3, 98,5-9.

Faith readily considers how, if God were judging according to the rigor of his law, outside of Christ, then I am totally lost and all my works are condemned. But Christ has come and God's mercy is announced in Gospel and sacrament for me to lay hold of, casting myself on divine mercy. In Christ my sin is not a matter for judgment.

> If I am truly a sinner, I am nevertheless not a sinner. I am a sinner in and by myself apart from Christ. Apart from myself and in Christ I am not a sinner, for he has blotted out my sin with his holy blood; I do not doubt that. [As proof] of this I have baptism and the absolution and the sacrament as sure seals and letters.[76]

Luther teaches the believer to see life as threatened by dire destruction and possible alienation from God, but also as sustained by mercy.

Faith's characteristic movement is to flee, in prayer, to the divine mercy that accepts the person in forgiving grace, lest we perish. Faith lays hold of what one is in Christ, righteous, holy, and a beloved son or daughter destined to share eternal life.[77]

Then, the long-term project of purification from endemic sin is a work energized and guided by God's Spirit of holiness. We profess belief in this in the third creedal article, as Luther indicated in the *Large Catechism* of 1529, where he set forth an ample notion of sanctification – as all that which the Spirit does in the church, for the overcoming of sin, until the final resurrection unto eternal life.

> Meanwhile, since holiness has begun and grows daily, we await the time when our flesh will be put to death and buried with all its uncleanness, but will come forth gloriously and arise to complete and perfect holiness in a new, eternal life. Now we remain only halfway pure and holy. So the Holy Spirit must continue to work in us through the Word, daily granting forgiveness until we come to that life where there will be no more forgiveness. ... All this, then is the office and work of the Holy Spirit, to begin and daily increase holiness on earth through these two means, the Christian church and forgiveness of sins.[78]

Above, we noted how Luther, in countering antinomianism, underscored the life-phase of penitential purgation and renewal of the person.[79] At the same time,

---

[76] *Von der Winkelmesse und Pfaffenweihe*, 1533. WA 38, 205,28-31; LW 38, 158 (cited). Luther inculcates this totalizing consideration of faith also at WA 2, 46,28-38; 8, 95,25-96,17 (LW 32, 212f); 39I, 508,1-9.

[77] »Oportet vos confugere ad misericordiam, aut perebis in peccatis vestris. Iam itaque est divinae misericordiae, quod recipit nos miseros in gratiam ac ignoscit nobis. Est et divinae misericordiae, quod facit ex peccatoribus iustos, sanctos, imo filios Dei et haeredes.« *Disputatio de veste nuptuali*, 1537; WA 39I, 299,8.

[78] Large Catechism, The Creed, 3rd Article; *Book of Concord*, ed. T.G. Tappert et al. (Philadelphia 1959), 418; BS 659,1-20; WA 30I, 190,37-191,11. Study 9, below, treats more at length Luther's notion of sanctification and its ecclesial mediation.

[79] See pp. 73f, above, with note 60.

he dedicated the third part of a major work, *On Councils and the Church* (1539), to an extensive treatment of the Holy Spirit's work of imparting and developing holiness, a new life shaped according to the Decalogue, in those now made part of »the holy Christian people.«[80]

The Spirit is the sanctifier, but the believer has a subordinate but essential role, with much expected by way of intentional acts and attitudes. In an illuminating early passage on the *simul*, Luther had described people who live out what they believe about the Spirit's work: »who call upon him and sigh in longing for liberation, ... they seek in all their efforts to be made righteous.«[81] As he first entered upon the interpretation of Paul's weighty seventh chapter of Romans, Luther stated clearly the appropriate petitionary prayer of one who is *iustus simul peccator*:

> So the first thing to do is to beseech grace, so that the person be changed in spirit and with a glad and willing heart desire and do all things, not with servile fear or childish cupidity, but with a generous and strong soul. But this only the Spirit brings about.[82]

It is thus the work of the Holy Spirit, through life under the cross and in the church, to purge out the *peccatum regnatum*, so that it will not rise up again to destroy us. But this gift of the Spirit by no means entails that our activity ceases: »still one must die to sin, you still have to labor against your sins.«[83]

Faith issues in a characteristic desire for personal wholeness: »Thus we want sin not only forgiven, but as well totally destroyed.«[84] Only then will the Holy Spirit be unimpeded in eliciting the ardent and generous response that God's law requires: »Such a new, ardent, and generous affection of the heart you attain ... only by the operation and inspiration of the Spirit.«[85]

---

[80] WA 50, 624-653; LW 41, 143-178.

[81] »... qui invocant eum et gemunt pro liberatione sua ... quaerunt iustificari omni studio.« Lectures on Romans, on Rom 4:7; WA 56, 271,28; LW 25, 260. My own dissertation, *Man Yearning for Grace*, is filled with citations of and references to this prayer of the *gemitus pro gratia*, by which the believer longs for healing. Through the present study, we see that this theme did not disappear after Luther's recomposition of his teaching around a new center, that is, the word and faith, in 1518, but remained as a feature of the second essential concern of Christian living.

[82] »Primum itaque gratia est imploranda, ut homo mutatus in spiritu hilari corde et voluntario omnia velit et agat, non servili timore aut puerili cupiditate, sed liberali et virili animo. Hoc autem solus agit Spiritus.« WA 56, 336,14-17; LW 25, 324.

[83] »... adhuc moriendum est, adhuc in peccatis laborandum.« *Against Latomus*; WA 8, 92,6f; LW 32, 207.

[84] »Vellemus igitur non solum peccatum remitti sed totum aboleri.« *Enarratio Psalmi LI*. WA 40II, 351,28; LW 12, 327.

[85] »Talem vero novum et ardentem ac hilarem cordis affectum non ex tuis ullis viribus aut meritis, sed sola operatione et afflatu Spiritus consequere.« Preface to Romans; WADB 5, 620,35-40.

But experience shows we are far from such heartfelt obedience, and thus we have to remain under therapeutic treatment, *sub medico, sub Christo*, and allow him to apply his instruments of purgation. Thus we have need of daily prayer and reading, of attending to the proclaimed word, and of receiving the sacraments.[86]

Luther's direct instructions on prayer repeatedly inculcate the movements of mind and heart that arise naturally from one who is righteous and at the same time a sinner. For example, the often reprinted account of fruitful meditation on Christ's passion (1519) has the believer brought first to fear and terror over the sins that are the cause of Jesus' sufferings. Then follows the appropriation of God's redemptive grace in the light of such basic texts as Isa 53:6, 1 Pt 2:24, 2 Cor 5:21, and Rom 4:25. Following this encounter with salvation at Christ's cross, the passion becomes for the believer the master-example of docility and patience, as one is conformed to it amid struggles against every vice and failing.[87]

Luther left hundreds of remarks on prayer in his several explanations of the Lord's Prayer and in his numerous lecture-courses and commentaries on various psalms. Many characteristic emphases came together in his 1535 booklet, *A Simple Way to Pray*, where he binds the believer's daily prayer to the classic texts of the Lord's Prayer, the Ten Commandments, and the Apostles' Creed. Some self-administered catechizing takes place here, in prayerful considering of God's works and the creature's duties, but each commandment leads to personal confession of sin and to earnest petition for God's support in the daily struggle to live in accord with his will in the power of his gift and assistance.[88]

Luther described this ongoing struggle in his preface to the Third Antinomian Disputation in 1538, with insistence on our being »strong battlers against sin present and still inhering in our flesh.« For this we take up the armor and

---

[86] »Interim patimur vivi medici, id est, Christi medelam; audimus verbum, oramus, legimus quantum possimus, sanamus per verbum. Nam quotidie audire et meditari verbum et accedere ad sacramentum et purgare saniem et putredinem debemus: ergo debemus uti his instrumentis, ut purgemur, mundemur ex sanie peccati, donec vere et prorsus purgetur.« *Disputation on Justification*, 1536; WA 39I, 113,25-114,3; LW 34, 182. The sacrament, for Luther, renews faith's encounter with God's grace in especially concentrated form, as the gospel of unmerited forgiveness is applied to the individual. I set forth Luther's earliest articulations of his characteristic sacramental conception in Study 6, below.

[87] WA 2, 136-142; LW 42, 7-14. M. Nicol gives extensive treatment of this text, with reference to late-medieval works of the same genre (Jordan of Saxony, Johannes Mauburnus), in *Meditation bei Luther* (Göttingen 1984), 117-150.

[88] WA 38, 358-375; LW 43, 193-211. The »third strand« with which the meditating heart should encircle each commandment and each creedal article is the admission of failing to meet God's requirement and respond to his provision of care and protection. Then the »fourth strand« is prayer for God's interior strengthening for life in steadfast opposition to evil. Faith is here being introduced to the penitential lifestyle of the *simul*. M. Nicol treats this passage instructively in *Meditation bei Luther*, 160-166. J. Happee shows the contemporary relevance of Luther's 1535 booklet on prayer in his translation and commentary, *Mediteren met Luther. De weg van meditatie en gebed* (Deventer 1983).

weapons described in Ephesians 6, to do battle with enemies all about us. In virtue of the Spirit given, »I start to struggle and battle with sin and blasphemy.«[89]

Shortly after, in the preface to Volume I (1539) of his collected German works, Luther set forth a way of daily converse with God's written word amid these hostile assaults and the effort to overcome sin. Traditional monastic prayer rested on the ideal pattern of a passage through four stages, *lectio / meditatio / oratio / contemplatio*. Luther, for his part, inculcates a different but characteristic sequence, that of *oratio / meditatio / tentatio*. He explains this as being, first, the earnest prayer for light and instruction by the Holy Spirit on the text; second, reflective rumination, without wearying in using eye, speech, and heart, to take possession of the Holy Spirit's intended meaning in the text; and, third, the painful daily experience of the trials by which one is brought to real depth in grasping God's revelation. Instead of ascent to joyous immediacy with God, Luther highlights temptation or *Anfechtung*. This account can stand as Luther's description of the storm-tossed daily experience of one who is righteous but at the same time a sinner. Such a person is subject to God's way of instructing in humble confession and ever-renewed trust in mercy, along with the patient endurance of the therapy that, often despite contrary appearances, is bringing one to complete righteousness.[90]

But Luther could be yet more succinct on the consequences of the believer's condition as *simul iustus et peccator* and on dealing with the threat it poses. For instance in a lecture of 1533, where he was expounding the text, »Those who sow in tears will reap in exaltation« (Ps 126:5), he gave this alternative to a questionable spirituality that makes much of ecstatic union with Christ the spouse of the soul.

> The Christian life consists in this: above all, to lay hold of the word. This is union with God, namely, that daily exercise and increase. For the devil, the world, and the flesh will come to tempt you. So, hold to prayer and the word, so you have both ready at hand when temptation comes, lest you despair. They are sent so that one might become yet more holy.[91]

---

[89] WA 39I, 489-496, citing here 492,6 (»fortes milites adversus peccatum praesens et haerens adhuc in carne«) and 494,2 (»incipio luctare et pugnare cum peccato et blasphemia«).

[90] WA 50, 658,29-660,16; LW 34, 285-287. Again, M. Nicol's analysis is helpful: *Meditation bei Luther*, 91-101.

[91] »Christiana vita est haec: ante omnia apprehendere verbum; haec unio cum Deo, illud quotidianum exerceri et augeri, quia diabolus, mundus, caro veniet et tentabit. Ideo tene te ad orationem et verbum, ut preces et verbum habeas in promptu, ubi venit tentatio, ne desperes; quae mittuntur, ut sanctificetur amplius, quia non vult eum derelinquere, sed exerceri.« WA 40III, 199,8-13. This text was cited by M. Nicol, *Meditation bei Luther*, 96, n.99.

In Appreciation of Luther's »simul«

Luther-scholars standing in the Catholic tradition are in a position to explain Luther's view of the *iustus simul peccator* with considerable penetration and appreciation. Examples lie to hand in the works of Otto Hermann Pesch, Erwin Iserloh, and Peter Manns.[92] More significant, however, because of their much wider readership, are the works of systematic theologians like Karl Rahner, Michael Schmaus, and Luis Ladaria.[93] Rahner saw that the justified person's faith remains existentially threatened by sin and the danger of loss. Schmaus was appreciative of how a personalist mode of thought must accept sin as a factor in a person's believing self-understanding before God. God's effective work in the righteous is threatened from within by a perduring egotism. Ladaria points to the destructive mediations of sin which continue to damage our world and human beings. Sinful reluctance sets a limit on every human response to God's love, even the response elicited by grace, and this curtails the scope of the Holy Spirit's presence in the righteous. Sin is a real influence, at the same time as God's gracious working, in the converted.

There are, thus, signs of a growing need felt by Catholic systematic theologians to consider elements of Luther's *simul* appreciatively and to appropriate aspects of it. This is all the more valuable because these writers are having an impact on the everyday teaching of Catholic theology and not just on a small group of ecumenical specialists. Luther is thus influencing some constructive proposals of a more adequate theological anthropology.

One can foresee even further Catholic appropriation of Luther's thesis as future systematic proposals are more deeply shaped by biblical testimonies and by liturgical sources. Theologians of the human condition cannot neglect the Scripture texts that constrained Luther to take his stand on the *simul*. It cannot be without theological relevance that every eucharistic celebration begins with a confession of sin, encounters Christ as the one now present whose blood was shed, »for you and for all, so that sins may be forgiven,« and begs mercy and peace from the Lamb of God who takes away the sins of the world. The saints

---

[92] O.H. Pesch, *Theologie der Rechtfertigung bei Martin Luther und Thomas von Aquin* (Mainz 1967, reprint 1984), 77-122, 526-552; and in *Mysterium Salutis*, vol. IV/2 (Einsiedeln 1973), 885-891 (Italian translation: *Mysterium Salutis*, 9 [Brescia 1975], 364-370). E. Iserloh, »Gratia und Donum«. P. Manns, »Zum Gespräch zwischen M. Luther und der katholischen Theologie,« in T. Mannermaa, et al., eds., *Thesaurus Lutheri. Auf der Suche nach neuen Paradigmen der Luther-Forschung* (Helsinki 1987), 63-154, at 76-84 and 93-99.

[93] K. Rahner, »Gerecht und Sünder zugleich,« in *Schriften zur Theologie*, 6 (Einsiedeln 1965), 262-276; in English, »Justified and Sinner at the Same Time,« in *Theological Investigations*, 6 (Baltimore & London, 1969), 218-230. M. Schmaus, *Der Glaube der Kirche*, vol. 2 (Munich 1970), 577-585; in English, *Dogma*, 6, *Justification and the Last Things* (Kansas City & London 1977), 53-65. L. Ladaria, *Antropología teológica* (Rome & Madrid 1983), 260-262, 356-362; in Italian, *Antropologia teologica* (Casale Monferrato & Rome 1986), 210f, 268-277. – The distance traversed from the unsympathetic and misleading views of Luther in earlier (pre-1965) manuals of Catholic theology can be measured with the help of A. Hasler, *Luther in der katholischen Dogmatik* (Munich 1968).

too give witness to a striking sense of being somehow also in sin, as in Augustine's *Confessions*, Book X, and Thérèse of Lisieux's revealing conversation, shortly before her death, of August 12, 1897.[94] The *simul iustus et peccator* finds backing in a variety of theological sources.

For a broadly based historical appreciation of Luther's teaching, account must be taken of the Reformer's forceful witness to the overarching role of God's action by grace and gift in any movement toward human wholeness and growth. Luther reminds all, in his own vivid way, that Christianity is after all a religion of redemption, as he confronts proponents of achievement-based human perfectibility with the Pauline and evangelical doctrines of repentance, forgiveness, and ongoing healing. Luther's theological systematization of the duality of grace and gift, correlated with faith and healing, is one component in his timely compression of theology around soteriology and his momentous reuniting – after long separation – of theology with the concerns of lived religiosity.[95]

These general considerations of values inherent in Luther's teaching on justification take on more force when we consider attentively his enlightening account of God's reconciling grace in Christ, laid hold of in faith, and the gift of the healing Spirit, ground of lifelong growth. Luther explains the real difference between *peccatum regnans* (sin reigning) in the not-yet-justified and *peccatum regnatum* (sin dominated) in the righteous with sufficient clarity to allay, for those formed in the Catholic dogmatic tradition, most fears of the *simul*. Most of all, Luther's convincing accounts of Christian existence as a life of healing from sin are clearly an instruction on daily religiosity – spirituality – that can add depth and urgency to one's life of prayer, while making evident the need of patience in suffering and discipline in personal living. This is the stuff of which good and salutary theology is made.[96]

---

[94] *St. Thérèse of Lisieux. Her Last Conversations* (Washington DC 1977), 147, translating *J'entre dans la vie. Derniers entretiens* (Paris 1973).

[95] This states concisely what I wrote in a more developed manner at the end of »Justification and Faith in Luther's Theology,« Study 2, above. Luther's relation to 12th century monastic theology, which united spirituality with systematic elaborations, is the main topic of Peter Manns' contribution to *Thesaurus Lutheri*, noted in n. 92, above.

[96] What Studies 2, 3, and 4 of this collection set forth constitutes the spirituality transmitted in Luther's principal publications. After writing these articles, I came across a small work that confirms the main lines of what I had worked out. This is the impressively concise and dense formulation by the late Albrecht Peters, »Die Spiritualität der lutherischen Reformation,« in W. Lohff and L. Mohaupt, eds., *Volkskirche – Kirche der Zukunft?* (Hamburg 1977), 132-148.

PART II

CRITICAL REFORMATION TEACHINGS
AND RESPONSES TO LUTHER

5

LUTHER'S TREATISE ON INDULGENCES, 1517

Martin Luther's initial intervention in 1517 to reform indulgence preaching is now much better known through the research of Hans Volz,[1] Erwin Iserloh,[2] and Klemens Honselmann.[3] The present essay seeks to complement their work by presenting the forgotten document in Luther's action. This is a short treatise sketching a tentative theology of indulgences, which Luther sent to Albrecht (von Hohenzollern) of Brandenburg, Archbishop of Mainz and Magdeburg, on the fateful October 31, 1517.[4] The other two documents Luther sent to the

---

[1] *Martin Luthers Thesenanschlag und dessen Vorgeschichte* (Weimar 1959). This collection of information pertaining to Luther's theses was written in the course of a discussion between Volz and Kurt Aland, carried on in the *Deutsches Pfarrblatt* in 1957-58, on whether Luther posted his theses of 1517 on October 31 (Aland) or November 1 (Volz). Volz's collection of texts on pp. 19-23 of his book provides the principal materials of the subsequent controversy over whether Luther posted his theses at all.

[2] *Luther zwischen Reform und Reformation* (Münster 1966); translated as *The Theses Were Not Posted* (Boston & London 1968). This is the expanded statement of the position that Luther did not publicly post his theses, which Iserloh maintained in his review of Volz (n. 1, above) in *Trierer theologische Zeitschrift* 70 (1961), 303-312. Iserloh then stated his position in a lecture given at the Institute for European History in Mainz, published as *Luthers Thesenanschlag: Tatsache oder Legende?* (Wiesbaden 1962). The further debate has been chronicled by R. Bäumer, »Die Diskussion um Luthers Thesenanschlag,« in A. Franzen et al., *Um Reform und Reformation* (Münster 1968), 53-95, a report then expanded in the 2nd edition of this work (1983).

[3] *Urfassung und Drucke der Ablassthesen Martin Luthers und ihre Veröffentlichung* (Paderborn 1966). This work organizes new evidence against the historicity of the posting of the theses and attempts to reconstruct the obscure history of their circulation and first printings. A more recent study by Honselmann is »Wimpina's Druck der Ablaßthesen Martin Luthers 1528,« *Zeitschrift für Kirchengeschichte* 97 (1986), 189-204. Konrad Wimpina, O.P., is shown to have received a copy of the Ninety-Five Theses from Luther around December 1, 1517. Wimpina, Professor in Frankfurt an der Oder, informed Johann Tetzel of Luther's attack, and prepared a list of counter-theses which Tetzel defended in a disputation held January 20, 1518.

[4] On the posting or non-posting of the theses, let the following summary suffice. There is firm documentary evidence for Luther's letter to the Archbishop being written on Oct. 31 and for it being mailed with enclosures. For a theses-posting on the door of the Castle Church of Wittenberg, a bulletin board for Luther's university, there is no eye-witness testimony and no direct evidence from Luther's own narratives of the events. Further, Luther argued in writing in ways that would exclude a theses-posting, e.g., by asserting that Archbishop Albrecht is at fault for the unrest caused by the theses, because Luther had warned him about Tetzel's work and had given him time to intervene. But if Luther posted his theses for his university colleagues or for notice by the crowds visiting the church – on its titular-feast of All Saints – then he offered no real grace period for Albrecht to react to the warning given. Luther's narratives can be consulted

Archbishop are relatively well known.

First, Luther addressed to Albrecht a respectful, though urgent, letter that related the misunderstandings being spread by the preaching of Johann Tetzel and others commissioned by the Archbishop. Luther begged Albrecht to issue new instructions which would bring Tetzel under the control of sound theology.[5] Second, Luther sent the Archbishop a list of ninety-five Latin theses which he wanted to use as the basis of a theological disputation on the doctrine and practice of indulgences, treating at the same time a series of related problems in this area of penitential and sacramental doctrine.[6]

The third document sent to Albrecht, Luther's treatise, has not received the attention it deserves from historians and theologians studying the beginning of the Reformation. This is regrettable, since the treatise sets forth in orderly and succinct fashion Luther's understanding of indulgences in 1517 and reveals his conception of their definite but limited role in Christian living. The treatise thus expresses an essential element of the theology on which Luther based his momentous intervention, and it shows in miniature the impressive Augustinian theology of penance and spiritual progress that he had forged in his early works.

This study will first narrate how Luther's treatise on indulgences was rediscovered in our century and indicate its relation to his letter to Archbishop Albrecht and to his ninety-five theses on indulgences. Then I shall present the treatise itself in my own English translation, adding a commentary on each of its eight sections.

Discovery of the Treatise on Indulgences

Volume 1 of the Weimar Edition of Luther's works gives an inferior text of the 1517 treatise on indulgences under the title *Ex sermone habito Dom. X post Trin. A. 1516.*[7] This edition followed the eighteenth-century edition of Valentin E. Löscher, who had supplied this title.[8] Löscher, and later the Weimar Edition, mistakenly include the treatise in a series of sermons which Luther gave between July 1516 and February 1517 as introductions to catechetical explanations of the ten commandments.[9] According to the Löscher-Weimar title, the text was

---

in Volz (n. 1, above) and in Iserloh (n. 2, above), pp. 49-53 in the original, and pp. 56-61 in the English translation. See also n. 21, below, in this study.

[5] The letter is given in its original Latin in WABr 1, 110-112; and in English in LW 48, 45-49.

[6] WA 1, 233-238; LW 31, 25-33.

[7] WA 1 (1883), 65,7.

[8] *Vollständige Reformations-acta und Documenta*, 3 vols. (Leipzig 1720-29), 1, 729. Unfortunately, nothing is known about the manuscripts used by Löscher for his edition of Luther's early sermons. On the problems with Löscher's edition, see WA 1, 18-19.

[9] WA 1, 60-140.

preached in the parish church of Wittenberg on Sunday, July 27, 1516, in connection with Luther's ongoing explanation of the first commandment. One grows suspicious, however, upon noting that the previous sermon in the series was given on the same tenth Sunday after Trinity and that it treated the Gospel of the day, Lk 18:9-14 (on the Pharisee and Publican).[10] This previous sermon fits well into the series on the commandments, since Luther explained how it was a sin against the first commandment that marked off the proud Pharisee from the humble Publican.[11]

The following text on indulgences makes no reference to this Gospel passage, nor to the first commandment. It is not built around a Scripture text and it is far more analytical in style than Luther's early sermons.[12] Furthermore, July 27, 1516, was fully seven months before the preaching of Johann Tetzel made indulgences into a burning theological and pastoral issue in the environs of Wittenberg.[13] Therefore we have to conclude that the Löscher-Weimar dating and title are in themselves very questionable.

The first documentary help toward a better placing of the text on indulgences came with the discovery of a copy of it among the papers making up the correspondence between Archbishop Albrecht and the Mainz University faculty of theology in December 1517. On December 1 the Archbishop had sent the Mainz professors certain writings of Doctor Martin Luther, Augustinian professor in Wittenberg, and had asked their opinion as to the orthodoxy of these works. On December 10 Albrecht wrote again to the faculty to remind it of the urgency of the matter and ask them to submit their report as soon as possible. On December 17 the professors finally sent a brief report to the Archbishop.[14] In

---

[10] WA 1, 63-65.
[11] Near the end Luther says, »Patet nunc, quod iste Pharisaeus primum praeceptum non fecit, sed habuit Deum alienum..., idolum scilicet iustitiae suae in corde statutum.« WA 1, 64,35.
[12] Henri Strohl noticed the pronouncedly scientific character of the text: »Ce sermon est une véritable dissertation sur la question.« *Luther jusqu'en 1520* (2nd ed., Paris 1962), 250.
[13] Tetzel was sworn in as general subcommissioner of the St. Peter's indulgence for the ecclesiastical province of Magdeburg on January 22, 1517. On April 10, he preached the indulgence in Jüterbog, which was near enough to Wittenberg to cause a stir among people with whom Luther came in contact as preacher and confessor. Hans Volz gathered the evidence on Tetzel's activities in *Martin Luthers Thesenanschlag*, 11-13, 58-69. A recent treatment of Tetzel is P. Fabisch and E. Iserloh, eds., *Dokumente zur Causa Lutheri*, vol 1. (Corpus Catholicorum 41; Münster 1988), 252f. The same volume includes an annotated edition of the *Instructio summaria*, the official guidelines for Tetzel's preaching (246-293), and three texts of early 1518 in which Tetzel sought to counter Luther's arguments (310-375).
[14] F. Herrmann published this correspondence in *Zeitschrift für Kirchengeschichte* 23 (1902), 263-268; it ist now given in *Dokumente zur Causa Lutheri*, 1, 299-303. Of special interest is the reaction of the Mainz theologians and jurists to Luther's theses on indulgences. They assumed that he had publicly defended them in a university disputation and therefore judged that he had maintained a doctrine departing from the common theological opinion concerning papal power to grant indulgences. The Mainz professors, however, would not presume to condemn Luther's position or to enter into dispute with him, since they felt bound by the canon *Nemini*, of Pope Nicholas I, prohibiting judgments or disputes concerning papal authority. The Mainz faculty advised the Archbishop to send Luther's writings on to Rome – which the Archbishop had

the Mainz archive, in the midst of this correspondence, lay our text on indulgences. Here, however, it bore the title *Tractatus de indulgentiis per Doctorem Martinum ordinis s. Augustini Wittenbergae editus*.[15] The report which the university professors sent to Archbishop Albrecht spoke of »*conclusiones seu propositiones*« and of »*propositiones*,« that is, Luther's theses. This does not, however, diminish the probability that they also received a copy of the *Tractatus de indulgentiis*, since their report was extremely brief, so much so that they explicitly begged Archbishop Albrecht's pardon for having offered him so little professional theological assistance.

Archbishop Albrecht himself is the source of more evidence that links the treatise on indulgences quite firmly to the more renowned ninety-five theses. On December 13, 1517, Albrecht wrote from his residence in Aschaffenburg to his diocesan officials in Magdeburg to acknowledge receipt of some documents they had sent him earlier. He describes these documents as »the treatise and conclusion about the holy *negotium indulgentiarum* and about our subcommissioners written by an audacious monk in Wittenberg.« The Archbishop informed the Magdeburg officials that the documents they sent were read in his presence and then he sent »the treatise, conclusions, and other writings« to the university professors in Mainz for a theological judgment. Albrecht also related that he had sent the »articles, position, and treatise« on to the Pope.[16] Thus, on December 13 Albrecht spoke three times of a treatise that had originally come into his hands along with the theses sent to him by the diocesan officials in Magdeburg. This treatise is clearly the *Tractatus de indulgentiis* found later in the Mainz archives, and is identical with the text given in the Weimar edition as a sermon of July 27, 1516.[17]

---

already done before receiving their opinion. We know, however, that Luther's theses were not disputed publicly in Wittenberg. Luther wrote about his invitation to hold a disputation: »Igitur cum in hanc arenam vocarem omnes, veniret vero nullus, deinde viderem disputationes meas latius vagari quam volueram.« Letter of February 13, 1518, to Bishop Hieronymus Schultze of Brandenburg; WABr 1, 139,46.

15 F. Herrmann reported the discovery of the treatise amid the Mainz documents in *Zeitschrift für Kirchengeschichte* 28 (1907), 370-373, listing forty-six corrections of the WA 1 text on the basis of the Mainz copy.

16 Albrecht's letter is given in *Dokumente zur Causa Lutheri*, 1, 305-309. He acknowledged receiving »ewr schreyben mit zcugesandten tractat und Conclusion eins vermessen Monichs zcw Wittenberg, das heilig *negotium Indulgenciarum* und unsere Subcommissarien betreffend« (305).

17 In 1917 G. Krüger reviewed the evidence concerning Luther's *Tractatus* and published a critical text of it with apparatus in *Theologische Studien und Kritiken* 90 (1917), 507-520. W. Köhler took over this critical text for the second edition of his *Dokumente zum Ablassstreit von 1517* (Tübingen 1934), 94-99, leaving, however, the Löscher-WA title untouched. G. Krüger had already argued persuasively in his 1917 article against a 1516 dating of the *Tractatus* because of its close relation to the content of the ninety-five theses and the *Resolutiones* (written probably in December-January 1517-18). The improved text of the treatise is now given in WABr 12, 5-9.

We know, however, of no contact between Luther and the Archbishop, whether in his Magdeburg or Mainz jurisdiction, before the well-known letter of October 31, 1517.[18] Thus, it can be concluded that Luther sent the *Tractatus de indulgentiis* to Albrecht under the date of October 31, 1517, along with a letter and the famous list of theses.[19] Luther sent this packet to Albrecht's residence for Magdeburg, and it was opened on November 17 by his diocesan officials in Calbe on the Salle.[20] They then sent the documents on to Albrecht in Aschaffenburg. From that day to the present, Luther's theses have commanded vast interest as the fateful assertions that set the Reformation in motion. Luther's letter to Albrecht has been printed and studied, but on the whole it has been overshadowed by the most-likely legendary scene of Luther posting his theses on the door of the castle church of All Saints in Wittenberg.[21]

Luther's short treatise on indulgences, which presents the theological basis of his intervention, has for all practical purposes been completely forgotten. One can understand this, in view of the popular need for dramatic images, like the scene at the church door, and considering the sparks emitted by Luther's challenging theses amid the tinder of Western Christendom in 1517-18. But the

---

18 E. Iserloh pointed out the evidence that excludes any contact before this date. *The Theses Were Not Posted*, 62.

19 This was the position of both F. Herrmann and G. Krüger in their articles of 1907 and 1917. Hans Volz accepted this conclusion after his painstaking review of the pertinent materials. *Martin Luthers Thesenanschlag*, pp. 18 and 26f. H. Bornkamm also accepted this understanding of the treatise. »Thesen und Thesenanschlag Luthers,« in *Geist und Geschichte der Reformation*, Festschrift Hanns Rückert (Berlin 1966), 188, n. 30. Martin Brecht interprets the *Tractatus* as the fruit of Luther's mid-1517 study on indulgences which documents his thinking just prior to the composition of the ninety-five theses and letter of October 31 to Archbishop Albrecht. *Martin Luther*, vol. 1, *Sein Weg zur Reformation* (Stuttgart 1981), 185-187. Actually the treatise shows better than the theses just why Luther criticized of Albrecht's *Instructio summaria* as a directive liable to undermine a sound spirituality of penance.

20 The Magdeburg officials marked this date on the letter itself, as illustrated in Volz, *Luthers Thesenanschlag*, opposite p. 33.

21 The theses-posting was asserted by Philip Melanchthon, in the preface to the second volume of Luther's collected works. This was written in 1546, after Luther's death. Melanchthon was not yet in Wittenberg at the end of October 1517, and the historical value of his preface was contested by H. Boehmer as early as 1914 in *Luthers Romfahrt*, p. 8. Against the historicity of a theses-posting by Luther are the four texts in which he stresses that he wrote to the bishops, including Archbishop Albrecht, before the theses became known to a wider public. See n. 4, above. Also the chronicles of the beginning of the Reformation which were written during Luther's lifetime contain no report of a theses-posting. One of these chronicles was actually written by Melanchthon himself, although it was then published under the name of Johann Carion. E. Iserloh, *The Theses Were Not Posted*, 68f. Thurman L. Smith's recent survey of the numismatic evidence, that is, the numerous medals and coins minted to commemorate the beginning of the Reformation, corroborates E. Iserloh's position, showing that the first depictions on coins of a theses-posting occurred in connection with the bicentennial celebration of 1717. »Luther and the Iserloh Thesis from a Numismatic Perspective,« *Sixteenth Century Journal* 20 (1989), 183-201.

neglect of the treatise is regrettable, for it is moderate, in places quite brilliant, and in comparison with other writings of its age it offers a penetrating theological study of indulgences in a Christian life of penance. The Luther of the treatise is not an unflawed genius, but his ideas on sin, forgiveness, and the Church's intercession deserve a hearing by Christians even today.

Let us seek to situate the treatise more exactly. In his letter of October 31, 1517, to the Archbishop, Luther mentions, apparently as an afterthought, that Albrecht can examine an enclosure, *has meas disputationes*, in order to understand how doubtful a matter is the doctrine of indulgences, which the preachers are presenting as utterly certain.[22] The theses, thus, stand in contrast with the exaggerated and often deceptive claims of the preachers, as these were already described in the body of Luther's letter.

However, Luther's theses do not present the matter as doubtful. They are categorical and lucid in what they assert. They offer (for debate, we note) a set of clearly-stated alternatives to the ideas the preachers are propagating. The text of Luther's ninety-five theses also stands in contrast to the hesitations and doubts that Luther underscored in his later narratives of his entry upon the public scene.[23] However, we know from Luther himself that he did not think of the ninety-five theses as giving his own position. In fact, he did not plan to defend every one of the theses in the proposed disputation.[24] But Luther's doubts and lack of clarity are not clear from the text of the theses. Most readers, both in the sixteenth century and today, sense nothing of his hesitations.

---

[22] After dating his letter, »Ex Vittenberga 1517. Vigilia omnium sanctorum,« but before signing it, Luther added, »Si t[uae] reverendissimae p[aternitati] placet, poterit has meas disputationes videre, ut intelligat, quam dubia res sit Indulgentiarum opinio, quam illi ut certissimam seminant« WABr 1, 112,66.

[23] For example, in 1538, Luther spoke of the »infirmitas et ignorantia, quae me in principio coergerunt rem tentare, cum summo tremore et pavore. Unus eram et per imprudentiam in istam causam lapsus...« And then, »Denique de indulgentiis quid essent, prorsus nihil sciebam, sicut nec ipse totus Papatus quidquam de eis sciebat. Tantum usu colebantur et consuetudine. Ideo non disputam ut eas tollerem, sed cum pulchre scierem, quid non essent, cupiebam discere, quidnam essent« WA 39I, 6,6.24. This is from the preface Luther wrote for an edition of his various disputation theses, and is used by Iserloh, *The Theses Were Not Posted*, 99f.

[24] On February 13, 1518, Luther wrote to his local ordinary, Bishop Hieronymus Schultze of Brandenburg, and after complaining that his theses were being taken »non ut disputabilia, sed asserta,« he spoke further about them: »Inter quae sunt, quae dubito, nonnulla ignoro, aliqua et nego. Nulla vero pertinaciter assero. Tamen omnia Ecclesiae sanctae suoque iudicio submitto.« WABr 1, 139,48. The sincerity of the last sentence is patent, since this letter is a covering letter for Luther's *Resolutiones* (his positions and their grounds concerning each thesis), which Luther is submitting to Bishop Hieronymus with a request for permission to publish. On March 5, Luther wrote to C. Scheurl about the theses, »Sunt enim nonnulla mihi ipsi dubia, longeque aliter et certius quaedam asseruissem vel omisissem, si id [their diffusion] futurum sperassem.« Ibid. 152,13. On May 9, 1518, Luther wrote in a similar vein to his former teacher J. Trutfetter (ibid. 170,41); and the same view of the original theses recurs in Luther's prefatory letter to Pope Leo X, printed with the *Resolutiones*: »disputationes enim sunt, non doctrinae, non dogmata, obscurius pro more, et enygmaticos positae« (WA 1, 528, 39). See also p. 114, n. 77, below.

Luther's treatise on indulgences, however, is quite different in tone. On the question of a remission of the pains of purgatory, Luther wrote in the treatise, »I do not understand it sufficiently, it is without doubt still uncertain whether God will release...« On the distinction between perfect and imperfect contrition, he wrote, »I must confess my ignorance.« He began the last section of the treatise, »One point, though, is still doubtful.«[25] A close reading of the treatise suggests that its overall aim was to draw the line between what is certain and clear in Luther's mind concerning the theology of indulgences and what is doubtful and obscure. The treatise could thus serve even better than the theses in realizing Luther's stated purpose of showing the Archbishop that the preachers were overstepping the limits of sound and certain doctrine.

Luther's 1517 treatise on indulgences is the record of how a theologian of no ordinary talent wrestled with a difficult problem in the midst of the open and indefinite theological situation on the eve of the Reformation. Amazingly, near the end of the treatise, once Luther had to some extent isolated what was clear in the matter, his position was that abuses should not keep people from this church institution, for it is most useful to grant and gain these indulgences![26]

We have, therefore, a treatise from Luther's own hand, probably written in early autumn of 1517, in which he unfolds systematically his idea of indulgences and strives to point out their rightful place in Christian living.[27] The issues Luther posed are of no little significance. For instance, what exactly is the grace granted by an indulgence? How is that grace related to the infused grace by which God transforms the affections? How are these graces related to the *fomes* or root-sin that infects and binds a person in attachments to this world? What is progress in grace? What is purgatory for? What is the ground or source of the help offered to people by the church through indulgences? What precisely is the pope doing when he grants an indulgence? And echoing in every line of Luther's treatise is the incessant question about the degree of certitude with which one may speak of indulgences having an effect.

The tone of the treatise enhances its value as a record of Luther's thought in late 1517. There is polemic in the paragraphs of the treatise, but polemic under rein. Luther sought clarity on the nature of indulgences and their function in Christian living, and he went about his task with remarkable objectivity. This is a far cry from the apocalyptic threats against the mendicant orders with which

---

25 Translating WABr 12, 6,52, 7,66, 8,134.

26 In the original: »Quae cum ita' sint, utilissimum est istas indulgentias dari et redimi, quidquid sit de avaritia et quaestu quae in illis exerceri timentur.« WABr 12, 8,141; in translation, p. 113, of this essay.

27 There is no internal or external evidence for determining more precisely the date of composition of Luther's treatise. It does not fit logically into the time before the start of Tetzel's preaching in early 1517, and it does echo in some places the Ninety-Five Theses sent to Albrecht of Brandenburg on October 31, 1517. Thus the period March-October 1517 seems most probable.

Luther concluded his remarks on indulgences in his first lectures on the Psalter in 1514.[28] Much like Luther's lecture-course on Hebrews, begun in the summer of 1517, the indulgence treatise is calmly engrossed in its subject and moderate in its polemical remarks about opponents.

So far we have examined the available evidence for situating Luther's 1517 *Tractatus de indulgentiis* historically. But it is not enough to simply juxtapose this document with the other two pieces, Luther's letter and his ninety-five theses, sent to the Archbishop. Can any internal connections be shown between these documents? The letter explains itself as an appeal to Albrecht's pastoral responsibilities. Luther asks him to withdraw the *Instructio summaria*, which gave Tetzel his official guidelines, and to supply the indulgence preachers with a more moderate document, in order to restrain the exaggerated preaching which is confusing and misleading the people.[29] Luther explained the purpose of his ninety-five theses in a letter to Christoph Scheurl of Nürnberg on April 5, 1518. Scheurl had complained that Luther had not sent him a personal copy of the theses. Luther responded that his purpose in composing the theses ruled out their wide circulation:

> First, as to your astonishment that I did not send you the theses, I answer that it was not my plan or my wish to make them public. Instead, I first wanted to discuss them with a small group here and in the vicinity. Thereby, based on the judgment of many, they could have either been condemned and destroyed or approved and then published.[30]

Luther went on to lament the amazing circulation of his theses. It is not that the truth should be kept from the people, but rather than the theses were not a proper form for use in instructing them. »For I have doubts about some of the theses, others I would have expressed much differently and more certainly, or I

---

[28] Luther criticized the irresponsible prodigality of prelates and religious orders in their granting for money a participation in their merits through brotherhoods and indulgences. WA 3, 424,12-425,11. The Catholic historian of indulgences in the Middle Ages, Nikolas Paulus, agreed with Luther on the excessive multiplication of indulgences. *Geschichte des Ablasses im Mittelalter*, 3 (Paderborn 1923), 470. Bernd Moeller has recently described the notable augmentation of indulgence-offerings, beginning in 1476, along with the systematizing of the indulgence »campaign« by Cardinal Raymond Peraudi (d. 1508). »Die letzten Ablaßkampagnen. Der Widerspruch Luthers gegen den Ablaß in seinem geschichtlichen Zusammenhang,« in H. Boockmann et al., eds., *Lebenslehre und Weltentwürfe im Übergang vom Mittelalter zur Neuzeit* (Göttingen 1989), 539-567.

[29] After citing two sentences from the *Instructio*, Luther made the main point of his letter: »Sed quid faciam, optime praesul et illustriss. princeps, nisi quod per dominum Jhesum Christum t[uam] reverendissimam p[aternitatem] orem, ... eundum libellum penitus tollere et praedicatoribus veniarum imponere aliam praedicandi formam.« WABr 1, 112,53; LW 48, 48. The official *Instructio* contained 94 numbered paragraphs, which is probably one reason why Luther's theses, which contest the doctrine of the *Instructio*, were 95 in number.

[30] WABr 1, 152,6.

would have omitted them, had I had any hope of this happening.«[31] Here we are reminded again that the famous ninety-five theses were not an exact statement of Luther's position on indulgences in October 1517. They were instead a basis for debate and discussion and Luther originally saw them as needing improvement before being made public.

What, though, was the status of the treatise on indulgences? A first bit of evidence comes from a passage in Luther's *Resolutiones*, written probably in January 1518. In this work Luther stated his position on each of the ninety-five theses and gave arguments for the position he took. On thesis 26, he was treating the different ways in which the merits of the Church militant can be applied to people's benefit. The pope can make such an application, Luther states, in three manners: as satisfaction for the benefit of penitents, as suffrages for the departed, and as the Church's praise and giving of glory to God. Luther explains about this schematic division, »For thus I once taught and wrote that there are three ways in which the Pope has power over the merits of the Church militant.«[32] The place where we find Luther teaching and writing about this threefold manner of application is precisely the *Tractatus de indulgentiis* submitted to the Archbishop with the theses.[33] Luther used this threefold division as he ordered his ideas in the last part of the treatise. The phrase in the *Resolutiones*, »et docui et scripsi,« serves to confirm that the treatise was not originally a sermon, but had a more academic purpose, as indicated by both the internal and external evidence we reviewed above. Further, this wording suggests that the division in question was a matter of conviction when Luther used it. Luther does not say this about the whole treatise, but still the reference to teaching and writing on this point stands in marked contrast to the reservations Luther uttered about the assertions advanced for discussion in his ninety-five theses.

This, however, is as far as the known documentary evidence will carry us in the attempt to situate Luther's treatise exactly. I can nonetheless propose a hypothesis about the precise character of the treatise. This is based on work with the text and on reflection about how Luther appears to have prepared for the disputation held at Heidelberg on April 26, 1518. I suggest that the treatise is probably a preparatory essay which Luther wrote in order to frame the position he would take in the intended discussion and disputation on indulgences. In the treatise Luther put down his own thoughts with remarkable order and with careful respect for the line running between what is certain and what is still doubtful on the topic. The treatise is thus similar to the essay Luther composed in preparation for the Heidelberg Disputation of 1518.[34] If this be true, the

---

[31] WABr 1, 152,13, cited in the original, p. 92, n. 24, above.

[32] WA 1, 580,11; LW 31, 167.

[33] WABr 12, 7,96 (in English, p. 110, in this essay). G. Krüger was the first to point out this reference by Luther to his own treatise. *Theologische Studien und Kritiken* 90 (1917), 509.

[34] WA 1, 365-374; LW 31, 58-70. E. Vogelsang termed this text a »preparatory essay« in the introduction to his edition of it in *Luthers Werke in Auswahl*, 5 (3rd ed., Berlin 1963), 392.

theological purpose of the treatise is clear: it proposes to set forth what efficacy or power indulgences do in fact have.[35] In the treatise, Luther sought to elaborate within his own emerging systematic theology of penance how, why, and to what extent indulgences can be said to have a *virtus* or salutary influence.

We will indicate in the commentary that follows the lines connecting the treatise with the theology of sin, grace, and Christian living that Luther had worked out in his first five years of lecturing as professor of Sacred Scripture in Wittenberg University.

In a sense, Luther's letter, theses, and treatise did not arrive at their intended destination. Archbishop Albrecht of Brandenburg was far too interested in the income from his »*negotium indulgentiarum*« to take serious notice of Luther's pastoral and theological protest. Albrecht had to clear the debts he had amassed in his sudden rise to power in the German Church and Empire.[36] After some circulation, Luther's ninety-five theses received theological answers from such men as Silvester Prierias, the Roman *Magister sacri palatii*, and Konrad Wimpina, Tetzel's mentor in Frankfurt/Oder. But these responses were superficial and marred by irresponsible dogmatizing of theological opinions of questionable character.[37] As we noted above, Luther's forceful phrasing of his theses helped them spread like wildfire over the Empire, less as the basis for theological discussion, and more as a pointed challenge to papal authority. Luther's own gifts of expression raced ahead of his actual intention, as his March 1518 letter to Scheurl witnesses. Then, there is as well the dusty oblivion in which Luther's constructive *Tractatus de indulgentiis* has lain. Thus, one can say that the texts making up Luther's initial intervention did not properly arrive at their intended destination.

One can take this presentation of Martin Luther's *Tractatus* by a Catholic scholar as an expression of the will to hear Martin Luther and to allow his powerful word in this small way to reach its original destination. Luther, of course, did not maintain the positions expounded in the 1517 treatise during the controversies of the following years. Nonetheless, the work marks an important

---

[35] This echoes of course the title Luther gave to the intended disputation for which he wrote his theses. B. Moeller's recent account of Luther's critique of indulgences greatly oversimplifies the doctrinal background of Luther's intervention by reducing the issue to the incommensurability of *fides Christi* with the gaining of an indulgence. »Die letzten Ablaßkampagnen,« in H. Boockmann et al., eds., *Lebenslehren und Weltentwürfe*, 563f. It is rather Luther's theology of penitential purification of endemic sin that underlay his misgivings over the effects of indulgence preaching. But, once indulgences are understood as the church's supportive *suffragium* for penitents, then Luther gave them a definite though limited role in the Christian life of penance.

[36] E. Iserloh, *The Theses Were Not Posted*, 18-27, and *Dokumente zur Causa Lutheri*, 1, 202-207.

[37] See Iserloh, *The Theses Were Not Posted*, 109f. Prierias's *Dialogus* is now edited in *Dokumente zur Causa Lutheri*, 1, 53-107, and Wimpina's theses are in the same volume, pp. 321-337.

starting point and deserves attention as one studies how the Reformation began on October 31, 1517.

Luther's Treatise: Text and Commentary

There follows our English translation of Luther's *Tractatus de indulgentiis*.[38] We use the text established by G. Krüger,[39] except that we introduce further paragraph divisions in the interests of improved readability. We add analytical comments, drawing mainly on Luther's earlier works to throw light on each of the eight sections of the treatise. One may recall that the copy of Luther's treatise made for the Mainz professors bore the title *A Treatise on Indulgences Published by Doctor Martin of the Order of St. Augustine in Wittenberg*.[40]

> [1.] On indulgences: Although indulgences are the very merits of Christ and of his saints and so should be treated with all reverence, they have in fact nonetheless become a shocking exercise of greed. For who in fact seeks the salvation of souls through indulgences, and not instead money for his coffers? This is evident from the way indulgences are preached. For the commissioners and preachers do nothing but extol indulgences and incite the people to contribute. You hear no one instructing people about what indulgences are, about how much they grant, or what purpose they serve. Instead, all you hear is how much one must contribute. The people are always left in ignorance, so that they come to think that by indulgences they are at once saved.
>
> Indulgences, however, do not, at least per se, confer the grace which makes a person righteous or more righteous. They grant instead only the remission of penance and of imposed satisfaction, which however does not mean that one who then dies goes immediately to heaven. But most of the people are simple and have been deceived into thinking that a plenary indulgence drives out all sin, and one is thereby at once ready for heaven. So they sin with abandon, and thereby burden themselves with the bonds of concupiscence.

Luther's first paragraph sketches the problematic within which indulgences must be discussed. There is a clear tension between the exalted matter, the merits of Christ and salvation, and the avarice evident in the administration of indulgences. The critical point is that the preachers give the people no adequate instruction on indulgences, but instead leave them under the impression that gaining an indulgence means instant salvation. In the final two sentences of this section Luther depicts four consequences of this manner of offering indulgences.

---

38 The text was not selected for translation in the Concordia-Fortress »American Edition« of Luther's works. A German translation is found in J. Wicks, *Man Yearning for Grace* (Wiesbaden 1969), 431-438.

39 *Theologische Studien und Kritiken* 90 (1917), 513-520; WABr 12, 5-9.

40 *Tractatus de indulgentiis per Doctorem Martinum ordinis s. Augustini Wittenbergae editus.* WABr 12, 5,1. H. Volz pointed out that »editus« is incorrect, since the work was not printed or otherwise made public in Luther's time. *Martin Luthers Thesenanschlag*, 18.

First, most of the people believe that a plenary indulgence drives out all sin. Luther uses here a phrase, »*peccatum auferri*,« which has a specific meaning in his early theology of forgiveness and penance. It indicates the expulsion of concupiscence through lifelong application to Christian penance. This is distinct from »*peccatum remittere*,« which takes place when one is sacramentally absolved from actual sins. Absolution brings the non-imputation of one's concupiscence and it sets in motion the work of expulsion of sinful concupiscence.[41]

Second, people think that a plenary indulgence brings as a consequence the immediate entry into heaven upon death. It must be noted that the theological literature of Luther's day did in some cases lay the ground for such a conviction.[42]

Third, sinful deeds abound. Indulgences have so focused people's attention on satisfaction, and have been presented as being so effective as a substitute for satisfactory punishment, that people have lost their fear of sin itself. This echoes Luther's sermon of February 24, 1517, in which he spoke of the effect of the great outpouring of indulgences as being equivalently an instruction more on fleeing the due punishment for sin that avoiding sin itself. This leads to security and even to permissiveness regarding sin itself. Instead, people should be exhorted to do penance and to embrace the cross of Christ.[43]

Fourth, the people fall all the more under the sway of concupiscence. Luther understands this condition in close connection with actual sins. It is not just an disorder left after original sin is forgiven in baptism, nor only a structural absence

---

[41] Luther had elaborated this distinction in his *Lectures on Romans* in 1515-16, especially in his long scholion on Rom 4:7 (WA 56, 268-291; LW 25, 257-278). As he explained, the distinction enabled him finally to see how he could imitate the saints who humbly thought of themselves as sinners even after sacramental forgiveness: »ego stultus non potui intelligere quomodo me peccatorem similem ceteris deberem reputare et ita nemini me praeferri, cum essem contritus et confessus....Ita mecum pugnavi, nesciens quod remissio quidem vera sit, sed tamen non sit ablatio peccati, nisi in spe, i.e., auferenda et data gratia quae auferre incipit, ut non imputetur ammodo pro peccato« (WA 56, 274,2; LW 25, 261). Repeatedly in this scholion, Luther stresses that a healing or purificatory process is the main concern of life. I develop this recurrent theme in Luther's teaching in Study 4, above, in this collection.

[42] In a theological dictionary first published in Hagenau in 1508, Oswald de Lasco wrote without qualification that one dying after gaining a plenary indulgence goes immediately to heaven. De Lasco concluded that when a person can gain a plenary indulgence, the doing of sacramentally imposed satisfaction is of no practical use. *Rosarium theologiae*, s.v. »Indulgentia.«

[43] WA 1, 141,23. Life under the cross was an emphatic theme of Luther's Ninety-Five Theses, resounding in nos. 1-4 and 94-95. While lecturing on Romans Luther had also argued that a superficial notion of sin and forgiveness, neglectful of personal purification and healing, was causing widespread falling-back into sin: »Nostri theologi peccatum ad sola opera deflexerunt et ea solum inceperunt docere, quibus opera caveatur, non quomodo per gemitum humiliter gratiam sanantem quaerant et se peccatores agnoscant. Ideo necessario superbos faciunt et qui dimissis operibus ad extra iam se iustos perfecte putent, nihil solliciti sint et concupiscentiis bellum indicere per iuge suspirium ad Dominum. Unde et tanta nunc in Ecclesia est recidivatio post confessiones« WA 56, 276,6; LW 25, 263.

of proper subordination of the flesh to reason, but instead the inclination unavoidably engendered by actual sins. Later in the treatise Luther will speak of concupiscence as an excessive affection for creatures that diminishes one's love for God.[44] Concern over concupiscence as sexual lust plays no role in the spirituality Luther unfolds in the course of his reflections on indulgences.

An important datum of this first section, however, is an initial, delimiting statement of what an indulgence grants. It does not of itself confer the grace of justification, but only the remission of satisfactory penances imposed on the penitent in confession.[45] Thus Luther begins his attempt in the treatise to dispel the cloudy imprecision of Albrecht's *Instructio summaria* with its many-sided use of the word *gratia*.[46] Also, by asserting that indulgences do not grant justifying grace, Luther feels he has cut the ground from under the idea that an indulgence means immediate entry into heaven.

Luther's initial general definition of indulgences indicates that he thinks of two distinct processes in the life of a Christian. On the one hand, there is justification, both as an event of grace and forgiveness, and as a process of growth. On the other hand, there are the satisfactory penances which the Church imposes in the sacrament of penance and can remit through indulgences. However, the distinction between the two is not total. By a slight qualification, a *saltem per se*, Luther held back from a complete separation of the true processes. He leaves a slight opening for a possible indirect effect of indulgences on the process of

---

[44] The third section speaks of those whose contrition was at the time of death made imperfect by concupiscence: »imperfecte amaverunt Deum et nimio affectu adhaeserunt creaturis et sic praeter peccata quae fecerunt et deleverunt ... adhuc immundae sunt propter talem affectum terrenum, cum quo decesserunt« (WABr 12, 6,54). In the fourth section Luther will speak of contrition and repentance »super fomite et reliquiis amoris terreni« (7,83). His norm is perfect love of God and perfect detachment from this world, as Luther will bring out in the following, second, section.

[45] In the original: »Non enim ea gratia ibi confertur, saltem per se, qua quis iustus aut iustior fiat, sed tantum remissio poenitentiae et satisfactiones iniunctae, qua dimissa non sequitur quod statim evolet in coelum, qui sic moritur.« WABr 12, 5,12-14. In his letter of October 31, 1517, to Archbishop Albrecht, Luther expressed a similar understanding of the limited scope of indulgences: »Cum indulgentiae prorsus nihil boni conferant animabus ad salutem aut sanctitatem, sed tantummodo poenam externam, olim canonice imponi solitam, auferant.« WABr 1, 111,34; LW 48, 47.

[46] On the four »graces« offered by the St. Peter's indulgence, see the text of the *Instructio*, in *Dokumente zur Causa Lutheri*, 1, 264-269. The first is described as »plenaria remissio omnium peccatorum; qua quidem gratia nihil maius dici potest, eo quod homo peccator et divina gratia privatus per illam perfectam remissionem et Dei gratiam denuo consequitur.« Ibid., 264. Erwin Iserloh analyzes this aspect of the *Instructio* in *The Theses Were Not Posted*, 23-27. – B. Moeller traces the systematization of four »graces« to the work of Raymond Peraudi in connection with the indulgence offered in 1476, under Pope Sixtus IV, for contributions to the building-fund for the cathedral of Saintes. »Die letzten Ablaßkampagnen,« in H. Boockmann et al., eds., *Lebenslehren und Weltentwürfe*, 547-550.

justification. We will see below how he explained this effect in the context of his account of one way indulgences help the souls in purgatory *per modum suffragii*.

In the next section of the treatise, Luther begins by explaining more about the two processes taking place in Christian life.

> [2.] We must therefore recall that grace is of two kinds, namely, the grace of remission, and infused grace, with the former being extrinsic and the latter intrinsic.
>
> The grace of remission is a release from the temporal punishment imposed by a confessor, which one must undergo either on earth or in purgatory, if it still remains [at death]. At one time, for instance, they gave seven years for one sin. But this release in no way diminishes concupiscence and the infection of our nature. Neither does it increase charity or grant grace and interior virtue. All these, however, must take place before one enters the kingdom of God, for »flesh and blood will not inherit the kingdom of God« [1 Cor 15:50] and »nothing defiled will enter« [Ap 21:27]. But no one knows how long this takes in purgatory.
>
> Nor can the pope in any way release a person [from this interior healing] by the authority of the keys, but only by applying the intercession of the whole Church. In the latter case, however, a doubt will remain whether God accepts the intercession for some part or for all [of the healing]. The pope can, of course, release a soul from purgatory with regard to the penance he has himself imposed or could impose. The wording of the papal bull indicates this: »so far as the keys of holy mother Church extend« and »we mercifully release from imposed penances.« Hence it is irresponsible to proclaim that by these indulgences souls are released from purgatory. For this statement is not clear, nor do they explain how it should be understood. Or else the pope is cruel, in not granting to the suffering souls gratis what he can grant for money contributed to the Church.
>
> Infused grace is an interior illumination of the mind and a kindling of the will. This is an eternal emanation into the soul like rays of the sun, and it does not become inactive after a plenary indulgence. This grace is necessary for the extirpation of concupiscence, until it is completely rooted out. This process is complete when a person is so filled with disgust for this life that he sighs longingly for God and finally breaks free from the body out of desire for God. Clearly, only a few who gain a plenary indulgence are so disposed. Further, a plenary indulgence is only granted to those who have proper sorrow and have confessed.

The systematic idea underlying Luther's argument is the distinction between *gratia remissionis* and *gratia infusionis*. These graces relate to the two distinct tasks a person must complete before entering heaven. First one must submit to the temporal punishments imposed by the confessor, which are to be worked out in this life or in purgatory. The *gratia remissionis* is the removal of this punishment by the power of the keys in the grant of an indulgence. The second task concerns concupiscence, a sickness of human nature, which, as we saw in the first section, grows with actual sins.

Before one enters heaven, concupiscence must be totally expelled and replaced by charity and interior virtue. This latter is the work of *gratia infusionis*, a distinct grace from the extrinsic remission of imposed punishments.⁴⁷ The great error of the indulgence preachers consists in giving the impression that indulgences grant the infused grace people must have to make them ready to enter heaven. Luther's aim is to show that in themselves (»*per se*«) indulgences have nothing to do with the Christian's more urgent task of rooting out concupiscence, growing in charity, and becoming detached from this world. When this distinction between the two Christian tasks is made clear, then the false security and certainty of immediate salvation based on indulgences will disappear.⁴⁸

Luther explains that the Church works to advance these two tasks in distinct ways. With the power of the keys the Church remits the imposed temporal punishments. The extent of this power of remittance would be the same as the power to impose these penalties, as Luther claims to find expressed in the papal bull.⁴⁹ Even in purgatory the pope can remit the punishments remaining from those he has imposed himself and which have not been worked out in this life.

But in the extirpation of concupiscence, the pope intervenes »only by applying the intercession of the whole Church.« This is not simply to grant, but to beg and petition the needed infused grace from God. The success of this intercession is not certain, since we do not know whether God will accept the Church's prayer of petition. Here Luther uses one of the favorite terms of late-medieval

---

⁴⁷ Luther's sermons of 1516-17 on the Decalogue had addressed the issue of the purification required for entry into heaven: »Nam oportet nos ita puros fieri, antequam in regno caelorum veniamus, ut nec motus mali in nobis sint nec ullus fomes ad malum inclinans, sed perfecta sanitas corporis et animae ab omni prorsus vitio, quod sane in hac vita non fiet nec est in potestate nostra.« *Decem praecepta praedicata populo*, 1518; WA 1, 515,14-17.

⁴⁸ A false security based on indulgences was the first of the four bad effects of Tetzel's preaching that Luther reported in his letter of October 31, 1517, to Archbishop Albrecht: »doleo falsissimas intelligentias populi ex illis conceptas, quas vulgo undique iactant. Videlicet, quod credunt infelices animae, si literas indulgentiarum redimerint, quod securi sint de salute sua« (WABr 1, 11,17; LW 48, 46). The polemic against false security had played an important part in Luther's early lectures. In his exposition of Psalm 69 in 1514, he excoriated the security of people in his own age and connected this with indulgences: »nunc est invalescentia tepidorum et malorum (pax et securitas). Quia accidia iam regnat adeo, quod ubique sit multus cultus Dei, scilicet literaliter tantum, sine affectu et sine spiritu, et paucissimi ferventes. Et hoc fit totum, quia putamus nos aliquid esse et sufficienter agere: ac sic nihil conamur et nullam violentiam adhibemus et multum facilitamus viam ad coelum, per Indulgentias, per faciles doctrinas, quod unus gemitus satis est.« WA 3, 416,17; LW 10, 351. *Pax et securitas* is the threat the Church faces in its third age of history, after times of persecutions and of heresy, according to the schematization Luther took over from St. Bernard. In lecturing on Romans, Luther complained how false security underlay people's falling back into sin: »Iustificandos sese nesciunt, sed iustificatos se esse confidunt, ac ita per securitatem suam sine omni labore diaboli prosternuntur.« WA 56, 276,12; LW 25, 263.

⁴⁹ The first of the two phrases cited by Luther occurs in the formula of absolution prescribed by the *Instructio summaria*, no. 75, for use in granting the St. Peter's indulgence. *Dokumente zur Causa Lutheri*, 1, 280. Neither phrase, however, is found in Leo X's bull, *Sacrosanctis Salvatoris*, extending the indulgence to the areas of Albrecht's jurisdiction (ibid., 212-224).

nominalism, referring to the divine *acceptatio*.⁵⁰ This context, however, is notably different from that of the nominalists' probing of the relation between grace, merit, and God's sovereignly free decision to reward good works. For Luther's context is a vision of the Church prayerfully interceding before God in aid of one of her members who is being healed or purified in purgatory. The point is that this prayer does not have automatic efficacy. Luther's main purpose, however, is to sharply distinguish the two actions of the Church; for the keys grant no healing grace, and the intercession does not bring the remission of sacramentally imposed penances.

The ground for uncertainty even after gaining a plenary indulgence is clear. The indulgence stems from the power of the keys and remits only the imposed temporal punishments. The indulgence does not directly touch the other hindrances blocking one's entry into heaven, which may well be quite considerable: concupiscence, the wound of human nature, a lack of charity, attachment to this world. In the case of the souls in purgatory, we have no idea how long such a purification takes, nor do we know whether and to what extent God accedes to the Church's prayer by granting healing grace. Therefore, Luther can turn conclusively against the phrase »*redimere animas*« used to denote the gaining of an indulgence for the dead.⁵¹ This is a careless use of words which the preachers themselves cannot explain. And if this deliverance from purgatory were so easy, then the pope would appear in a very bad light for not simply emptying purgatory by a generous use of the power of the keys.⁵² Many uncertainties surround this whole matter, and in recognition of this the preachers should accordingly moderate their language.

---

⁵⁰ W. Dettloff treated the doctrine of the divine acceptation in the later Middle Ages in his two dissertations, *Die Lehre von der acceptatio divina bei Johannes Duns Scotus* (Werl 1954) and *Die Entwicklung der Akzeptations- und Verdienstlehre von Duns Scotus bis Luther* (Münster 1963). The role played by this concept in the theology of Gabriel Biel is indicated by the fact that H.A. Oberman's summary of Biel's teaching on justification comes toward the end of a section entitled, »*Habitus* and *Acceptatio*.« *The Harvest of Medieval Theology* (Cambridge, Mass. 1963), 175-178.

⁵¹ For instance, Albrecht's *Instructio summaria*, no. 16, spoke thus of the duties of the indulgence preachers: »Praedicatores etiam in singulis suis sermonibus populum monere debet, ... ut in redimendis animabus negligentes non inveniantur.« *Dokumente zur Causa Lutheri*, 1, 262.

⁵² Gabriel Biel had made this same point in his argument against the very possibility of indulgences being extended to the dead. *Canonis missae expositio*, lect. 57 H (a text of 1488; ed. H.A. Oberman and W.J. Courtenay, 2 [Wiesbaden 1965], 401). Shortly after, Biel saw a papal bull, most likely Sixtus IV's *Salvator noster* of 1476, which explicitly extended an indulgence to the souls in purgatory *per modum suffragii* and Biel accordingly reversed his stand. In explaining his new position, Biel pointed out that the pope must observe moderation. Biel argues further that it is unlikely that the faithful will ever do enough pious works to enable the pope to empty purgatory. However, if sufficient works were forthcoming to match the souls' needs, then the emptying of purgatory would be »nihil inconveniens.« Ibid, lect. 57 N; Oberman-Courtenay edition, 2, 406-407.

Luther's idea of the healing process by which a person is made ready to enter heaven can be explained in three steps. First, the malady of concupiscence is engendered by actual sins, resulting in weakness in charity and attachment to this life. Second, infused grace effects a cure by illumining the mind and stirring the will. Luther thinks of this grace as lasting and in itself permanent, but he speaks as well of its appropriation as a process extending over time and succeeding gradually until concupiscence is wholly rooted out.[53] Third, at the terminal stage, one longs so purely for God and is so filled with disgust for this life as to be carried quite naturally to God.

The description of this healing process gives Luther more material for attacking a false security based on indulgences, for only a very few who obtain indulgences are so detached from this life that they can be judged ready for heaven. Further, a condition of true contrition is attached to indulgences. Luther does not develop this point, but the implication is clear enough, namely, that here too is another reason for rejecting a security about salvation based on indulgences. Who can say with certainty that his contrition is up to the level required for gaining an indulgence in the first place? With this question Luther then begins the next section of his treatise and he proceeds to draw conclusions from the uncertainties already singled out.

> [3.] Corollary: Since no one can be certain about himself, and still less about others, that he is perfectly and worthily contrite and has confessed, it is irresponsible to assert that one gaining indulgences goes immediately to heaven or that a soul is freed from purgatory. I could see this, if one indicated a soul about whose release I was already certain, say, one who had been contrite on earth and had merited to be freed, as St. Augustine said. But only God knows which souls are and are not so disposed.
>
> For otherwise one must suffer purgatory, because one has not merited to be helped, namely, by making oneself worthy through sufficient contrition and detachment from love of creatures. However this might be, for I do not understand it sufficiently, it is without doubt still uncertain whether God will release the imperfectly contrite through indulgences. For they have loved God imperfectly and they had an excessive affection attaching themselves to creatures. Thus, over and above the sins they committed and had forgiven by contrition, confession, and plenary indulgences, they are still befouled by reason of this attachment with which they died. This attachment

---

[53] The theme of progressive expulsion of sin is recurrent in Luther's early lectures, especially on Romans (1515-16). Concisely put, »ista vita est vita curationis a peccato, non sine peccato finita curatione et adepta sanitate. Ecclesia stabulum est et infirmaria aegrotantium et sanandorum. Coelum vero est palatium sanorum et iustorum.« WA 56, 275,26; LW 25, 262f. For us who are *in via*, the Church is the inn to which Christ brings the wounded for healing: »Samaritanus noster Christus hominem semivivum aegrotum suum curandum suscepit in stabulum et incepit sanare, promissa perfectissima sanitate in vitam aeternam.« WA 56, 272,11; LW 25, 260. In this context, Luther first used the formula »simul peccator et iustus« (WA 56, 272,15), the understanding of which calls for attention to the progressive healing depicted in the context. See J. Lortz, »Luthers Römerbriefvorlesungen: Grundanliegen,« *Trierer theologische Zeitschrift* 71 (1962) 129-153, 216-247, at 237. Study 4, above, in this collection gathers further texts on the long-term overcoming of sin.

surely cannot be removed by a plenary indulgence, when it has not been driven out by contrition.

Instead the attachment remains and is *actu* present in the separated soul and cannot be removed even in purgatory unless one first turns against it in contrition in repentance. Who, though, is sorry over having feared death? Or who puts this fear away, by ceasing to rebel against God's will? Do not they say this themselves, when they state that indulgences help only those who are contrite and have confessed, and no one else?

The last thought of the previous section grounds Luther's rejection of two formulations used frequently in indulgence preaching, *statim evolare*, regarding those who gain an indulgence and upon death go straightway to heaven, and *animam eripi*, describing the effect of an indulgence gained for a departed soul. The phrases are only verified in cases in which the indulgence is applied to one who is worthily and perfectly contrite, that is, »worthily« as a condition for gaining the indulgence and »perfectly« as the result of concupiscence being fully rooted out.

Luther then sought to explain a case in which such terms might be applicable. An indulgence would have such an effect if a certain person were contrite, and if he had further merited to be helped by the Church's prayer. The key issue is detachment from this world, by advancement of the healing process. Then a remission of imposed penalties would bring this deserving soul to salvation. Luther refers here to St. Augustine's words on the intermediate situation of the souls in purgatory, who in this life were evil enough to have to suffer confinement there, but also good enough to merit being helped by the Church after death.[54] But Luther stresses that only God knows who is deserving of the help of the Church in the manner described by Augustine.

Hence Luther can conclude to our uncertainty about the effect of indulgences gained for those who are still sick with concupiscence. Their contrition was imperfect and their love of God weak. And so, over and above the actual sins remitted by absolution and indulgences, they are still bound by affective ties to this earth. This attachment is not reduced by a plenary indulgence, but is only driven out by conversion and contrition. Luther specifies this conversion as acceptance of the will of God decreeing one's own death.[55] Thus the normative

---

[54] *Enchiridion* 29, 110 (PL 40, 283; CCSL 46, 108). G. Biel explained the ecclesial character of this latter merit. This is, »quod manserunt in unitate ecclesiae per caritatem in qua finaliter decesserunt, propter quod manserunt membra eiusdem corporis Christi cuius et vivi, ideo in bonis spiritualibus cum vivis communicant.« *Canonis missae expositio*, lect. 56 M; Oberman & Courtenay edition, 2, 380.

[55] In commenting on Heb 2:14 in the summer of 1517, Luther spoke of contempt for death as the goal of Christian striving. »Qui timet mortem aut non vult mori, non satis est Christianus, quia adhuc in fide resurrectionis deficiunt, dum plus diligunt hanc vitam quam futuram.« WA 57III, 131,5; LW 29, 137. And then, »ille contemptus mortis et gratia eius ab apostolo et sanctis praedicata est meta illa et perfectio, ad quam niti debet omnis Christianorum vita, licet paucissimi sint tam perfecti.« WA 57III, 132,24; LW 29, 139.

ideal for the souls in purgatory is the same ideal toward which we strive on earth as we are cured from concupiscence and brought to a purified longing for God. In purgatory as well, life's goal is perfect detachment from this life and willing acceptance of one's own death.[56] The problem still to be solved is just how the sufferings of purgatory effect such a change of affective attitude. Of itself, this conversion is a work of the infused grace Luther described in the second section. How is this grace connected with the pains of purgatory?

Again the structure of Luther's argument rests on the duality of two parallel tasks of penance. The first compensates for actual sins, as one submits to sacramentally imposed penances in this life or in purgatory, with the possibility of a remission being granted by the intervention of the keys in granting an indulgence. Second, one must root out attachment to this world, in submission to the infused grace which leads to real conversion. The term of the second process is willing resignation to God in accepting death. But here an indulgence appears to play no part.

Luther begins the next section of his treatise by posing an objection calling in question the utility of indulgences regarding one's entry into heaven, but then moves on to a new way of thinking about the Church's intercession.

> [4.] But you will say, »Perfect contrition of itself takes away all punishment, and hence indulgences are not needed, since the perfectly contrite person goes immediately and directly to heaven.« In answer I must confess my ignorance. The perfectly contrite person goes to heaven without indulgences, but the imperfectly contrite person cannot go there even with indulgences. For God places no demands upon one who is perfectly contrite, neither for actual sins, nor for habitual, that is, for the tinder and »original« sin.
>
> What good then are indulgences? Do they only serve to satisfy for actual sins? But how are souls saved when their actual sins are forgiven, but original or habitual sin remains? For those whose original sin is remitted, actual sin as well is remitted, but not vice versa. By »original sin« I mean the tinder left from our origin which has not yet been healed by grace nor overcome and mortified by our good efforts, as St. Paul indicates in chapters 6 and 8 of Romans.
>
> Could it be that those who have merited to be contrite over this tinder in purgatory or in death attain this contrition through indulgences? They do not consider this difficulty, since no one is concerned with mortifying this tinder and with the root-sin. They only think of lopping off actual sins by contrition, confession, and satisfaction. Then they quickly fall back into sin and »return to their vomit« [2 Pt 2:22], since they do not attend to the infection and to the root of sin. Thus they are like people cutting off rivulets flowing from a stream or the leaves from a tree, but

---

[56] This underlies nos. 14-18 of Luther's Ninety-Five Theses, and is Luther's 1517 formulation of the norm of agapaic love that underlies much of his thought on the human condition and life under God's rule. Peter Manns has made much of this theme as fundamental to Luther's whole work. »Was macht Luther zum 'Vater im Glauben' für die eine Christenheit?« in P. Manns, ed., *Martin Luther Reformator und Vater im Glauben* (Stuttgart 1985), 1-24, at pp. 12-15. See also »Absolute and Incarnate Faith,« in J. Wicks, ed., *Catholic Scholars Dialogue with Luther* (Chicago 1970), 121-156.

who leave intact the stream and root. They have no concern to sigh earnestly for the grace that destroys this body of sin and puts to death our sinful members.

Could it perhaps be that the term *per modum suffragii* means that this suffrage not only grants them remission of actual sins, but also impetrates contrition and repentance over the tinder and remaining earthly attachments, and that it confers the grace of perfect love of God and longing for God? For example, if a person about to die is not resigned, nor so desires to be released that he most gladly obeys God's will, then it is clear that he is dying in sin. I speak here of resignation of mind and will, even though the senses may rebel, as was the case with Christ and all the martyrs. This sin is not a mortal sin, but still it is nearly so, and the person has not repented for it in this life.

Could it be that one receives from God the grace of repentance in purgatory, and this through the suffrages of the Church, with the result that the person becomes willingly resigned to death? One cannot so repent by natural power nor can the fire of purgatory free one from this sin without grace. But the person did die in sin, since he did not love with his whole heart what God willed, but was unwilling, nor was »his delight in the law of the Lord« [Ps 1:2]. Even though he outwardly obeyed the command, still his heart was not in it.

Luther widens the scope of his inquiry through an objection, which leads him once more to emphasize the forgotten factor of concupiscence, or *peccatum radicale*. He then suggests a remarkable answer to the difficult problem of how concupiscent affections are overcome in purgatory.

In his third section, Luther had described how the affections are purified by contrition. This then becomes the basis for an objection. When such a conversion has taken place, are not indulgences superfluous? The perfectly contrite person has overcome the obstacles posed by both actual and radical sin. But one imperfectly contrite is still attached to this life, and so has still to overcome radical or habitual sin. Indulgences, however, are of no help to the latter, for what is needed there is mortification of the affections and conversion under grace to love of God. Luther goes at his problem with driving seriousness and deftly opens up all its aspects.

To make his point about root-sin quite clear, Luther gives a definition and contrasts his view with current theology. The tinder not yet healed or not yet mortified is what St. Paul described as the »body of sin« still to be destroyed (Rom 6:6), the »sin« that must not reign in us (6:12.14), and the »flesh« according to which we must not live (8:12f) and from which one longs to be freed (8:20). Basic to Luther's conception is a vision of the Christian life as progressive healing under grace.[57] Grace, though, is not alone, for Luther stresses as well the person's

---

[57] See n. 53, above. The healing power of grace underlay the theses against scholastic theology, mainly that of Ockham and Biel, which Luther defended in Wittenberg September 4, 1517 (WA 1, 224-228; LW 31, 9-16). This is clear in the counterpointed theses of the second half of the disputation: »55. Gratia Dei nunquam sic coexistit ut otiosa, sed est vivus, mobilis et operosus spiritus... 67. Gratiae Dei est nec concupiscere nec irasci... 75. Gratia autem Dei facit abundare iusitiam per Ihesum Christum, quia facit placere legem... 89. Necessaria est mediatrix gratia, quae conciliciet legem voluntati. 90. Gratia Dei datur ad dirigendum voluntatem, ne erret etiam in

efforts to go against selfish, earth-bound affections in the work of breaking the reign of concupiscence.

The view of the Christian life as the gradual overcoming of concupiscence is fully consistent with the main themes of Luther's *Lectures on Romans* of 1515-16,[58] and especially with the theology of justification he sketched in a sermon given January 1, 1517.[59] This is not the whole of his early teaching, since it does not directly develop the radical *metanoia* of self-estimate, by which one enters a truly Christian life.[60] Nor are the intriguing Christological themes of Luther's early works found in the treatise of 1517.[61] Still, the basic complaint of this

---

amando Deum.« I analyze this disputation, in the context of Luther's wider polemic against the scholastics, in *Man Yearning for Grace*, 190-199. This view of grace appeared in Luther's decalogue sermons of 1516-17, in connection with a passage on true, spiritual observance of the law: »solo spiritu impletur et spiritum requirit, hoc est, nisi corde et hylari voluntate impleatur, non impletur. Sed talis spiritus non est in nobis, sed datur per gratiam Spiritus Sancti, quae facit voluntarios in lege domini.« WA 1, 461,28. Here, *gratia* is identical with what Luther will call *donum* in his mature systematization of God's work, where *gratia* becomes the unmerited and undivided forgiveness of sin imparted because of Christ. See Study 4 of this collection, pp. 70-74, above.

[58] Luther spoke of earnest prayer and the efforts of penance as the »agricultura sui ipsius« by which one collaborates with healing grace. WA 56, 257,31; LW 25, 244. Doing to death the »corpus peccati« is taxing: »Sed hoc odium et hoc resistentia corporis peccati non est levis, sed laboriosissima, ad quam necessaria sunt tot opera poenitentiae, quot fieri possunt.« WA 56, 321,9; LW 25, 309. Baptism and confession give no basis for security, »non enim ad otium vocati sumus, sed ad laborem contra passiones.« WA 56, 350,8; LW 25, 339. In summary: »semper orandum et operandum, ut crescat gratia et spiritus, decrescat autem ac destruatur corpus peccati et deficiat vetustas. Non enim iustificavit nos, i.e., perfecit et absolvit iustos ac iustitiam, sed incepit, ut perficiat.« WA 56, 258,17; LW 25, 245. Note also the texts cited in n. 53, above.

[59] The feast of the Circumcision, centered on a good work carried out by Jesus and his parents, occasioned Luther's reflection on the relation of grace to good works. Programmatically: »Doctrina autem fidei hoc docet, quod homo iugiter debet intus gemere pro gratia, sciens quod cor eius non ideo est mundum, si opera sunt munda, nec ideo voluntas sana, quia mores sunt boni. Ista ergo displicentia sui, odium et taedium vitae suae non debet usquam cessare... Hoc suum absconditum peccatum (quod per gratiam sanari inceptum est) sancti assidue habent in oculis, ideo non possunt superbire de externis suis operibus.« WA 1, 118,37. Justification, however, does bring a transformation in its train: »Iustitia fidei sine quidem operibus datur, sed tamen ad opera et propter opera datur, cum sit res quaedam viva nec possit esse otiosa.« Ibid., 119,34. I treat this sermon in *Man Yearning for Grace*, 157-161.

[60] See, for instance, his remark in the Romans lectures on »becoming a sinner«: »tota vis huius mutationis latet in sensu seu aestimatione ac reputatione nostra. Hunc enim mutare intendit omnis sermo scripturae et omnis operatio Dei.... Ergo fieri peccatorem est hunc sensum destrui, quo nos bene, sancte, iuste vivere, dicere, agere pertinaciter putamus et alium sensum (qui ex Deo est) induere.« WA 56, 233,7; LW 25, 217f.

[61] Luther's career as a biblical expositor began with the option to understand the Psalms as written literally for Christ and about Christ. This made his *Dictata super Psalterium* of 1513-15 an extended meditation on Christ in the flesh, in the Church (allegorical sense), and in the individual believer (tropological sense). Gordon Rupp spoke felicitously of the »Christological concentration« of this work. *The Righteousness of God* (London 1953), 146f. I treated this Christocentric hermeneutics in *Man Yearning for Grace*, 42-51. Closer to the indulgence treatise, Luther spoke emphatically of Christ's life in the believer in a sermon on February 24, 1517: »Non sint otiosi in quibus sapientia Christus revelata est, et qui non iam ipse sed Christus in eo vivit; non est metuendum, ne Christus sit otiosus, immo actuosissimus est, et id ipsum cum omni suavitate et facilitate.« WA 1, 140,19.

treatise, namely, that people »have no concern to sigh earnestly for the grace that destroys this body of sin and puts to death our sinful members,« is the reverse-image of a basic leitmotif of Luther's early theology.[62]

The young Luther can best be understood as a theologian of the Christian life. He taught a spirituality of justification-as-process, tending toward complete personal purification. The main concern of his early works was not directly God's attribute of righteousness and not justification as a discrete event, but the lifelong task of refining and purifying human intentions and affections under the influence of healing grace.[63]

The discussion of concupiscence as root-sin occasioned an important question on Luther's part. Could indulgences be the means by which deserving souls gain the grace of contrition and so overcome their sinful affections? This question brought Luther to take another look at how indulgences work, and in the midst of this reflection he appears to have gained an insight into the meaning of the traditional phrase *per modum suffragii*. He explains his idea hypothetically, as a possible way the matter could be understood. The *suffragium* could well be a prayer of ecclesial impetration which gains from God the grace of conversion, that is, an interior movement of heart toward the pure love of God and resignation to God's will. As far as we can see, this is Luther's own insight. St. Bonaventure did speak of an indulgence for the departed as a type of *deprecatio* in aid of the souls in purgatory,[64] while St. Thomas saw the Church's help as a

---

[62] In the Romans lectures: »Tota vita populi novi, populi fidelis, populi spiritualis est gemitu cordis, voce oris, opere corporis non nisi postulare, quaerere et petere iustificari semper usque ad mortem, nunquam stare, nunquam apprehendisse, nulla opera ponere finem adeptae iustitiae, sed tanquam adhuc semper extra se habitantem expectare, se vero in peccatis adhuc vivere et esse.« WA 56, 264,16; LW 25, 251f.

[63] Thus Luther's later account of his wrestling with the meaning of *iustitia Dei* in Rom 1:17 is not a good guide to the content of his early theology. His preface to the 1545 first volume of his Latin works (WA 54, 179-187; LW 34, 327-338) is not historical-minded autobiography, but instead a text serving the purpose of orienting readers of the next generation in their understanding of the old documents contained the volume being introduced. – Martin Brecht places Luther's »Reformation breakthrough,« around March 1, 1518, seeing it as a shift in the understanding of justification, by which Luther left behind his early theology of humility, where the primacy was given to self-accusation, and moved to center justification in the accepting faith that lays hold of all that is offered to sinners in Christ. *Martin Luther*, 1, 215-230. In *Man Yearning for Grace*, I argue that the first phase of Luther's work yielded more than just a theology of humility, for he was teaching a comprehensive view of life, rich in its potential for spiritual growth and guidance. It was much more than the thesis that justification before God depends on a person's being humbled. In this collection, Studies 2-4 show how Luther's mature configuration of his teaching on the Christian life still incorporated valuable themes from his early work.

[64] *In 4 Sent.*, d. 20, art. un., q. 5.

dispensatio.⁶⁵ Late medieval canonists thought of this help as a gift of vicarious satisfaction offered out of the treasury of the Church on behalf of the departed.⁶⁶

Luther's idea does allow the Church to have an influence upon the purification of radical sin, but not by the power of the keys, by which she simply remits the penances imposed for actual sins. Instead, the Church offers a *suffragium* of petition which moves God to grant the needed grace of contrition and conversion to love and longing for Him. Apparently, this idea come to Luther while he was writing the treatise, and so he holds back from asserting this as certain. It would be a point to be tested in discussion and disputation.⁶⁷ The matrix of Luther's reflection would well have been the theology of Christian living he had worked out in lecturing on Romans, with its emphasis on root-sin and its purification by healing grace. Grace gives the *hilaritas* and good will in embracing God's law.⁶⁸ The way, however, to attain this grace is that of earnest and assiduous petition.⁶⁹ This prayer of the individual is but one step from thinking of the Church's intervention *per modum suffragii* as its prayer of petition that God grant the grace that is transformative of one's affections. What the Church does for the departed, according to Luther's proposal, is just what one must do for oneself in this life, that is, »we must incessantly seek God's healing grace.«⁷⁰

The final lines of this fourth section return to treating the ideal state one must reach before liberation from purgatory. Luther speaks of one who deep in the core of his person was not resigned to death. The work of grace gained by the prayer of the Church is to transform this reluctant heart and bring the person to accept death from God's hand. In this acceptance of death, Luther sees the ideal culmination of life, expressive of loving God with all of one's heart.

---

65 *In 4 Sent.*, d.20, q.1, art.5, q.4 ad 3; *Sum. theol. Suppl.* q. 27, a.4.

66 For example, Cardinal Raymond Peraudi (d. 1508), as related by N. Paulus, *Geschichte des Ablasses im Mittelater*, 2, 383-390.

67 Luther's notion anticipates the account of indulgences worked out by B. Poschmann in our century, which Karl Rahner took up in »Remarks on the Theology of Indulgences,« *Theological Investigations*, 2 (Baltimore 1963), 173-201.

68 For example, »Nisi per gratiam Dei (quam credentibus in Christum promisit et largitur) sanetur ista voluntas, ut liberi simus et hilares ad opera legis, quaerentes nonnisi Deo placere et eius voluntatem facere...semper sub peccato sumus.« WA 56, 235,21; LW 25, 220. See also n. 57 above. Other texts are drawn together in my *Man Yearning for Grace*, 104-106.

69 »Assiduis oporteat gemitibus ad Deum intendere, ut hoc taedium tollat et ad hilaritatem perficiat voluntatem auferatque per gratiam pronitatem illius ad malum.« WA 56, 257,26; LW 25, 244.

70 »Assidue sanantem gratiam eius quaeramus.« These are the final words of the treatise of 1517, given in section 8, p. 114, below.

The last sections of the treatise are calm and well ordered. Luther has gained a key insight into the material and can now make a more systematic presentation.

> [5.] Let us now draw the matter together, as far as we can. All the works and merits of Christ and the Church are in the hands of the pope and he can apply whatever good works are done through Christ in the Church in three ways, as follows: first, as satisfaction; second, as a suffrage; and third, as a votive offering or sacrifice of praise. In this same way Christ by his deeds glorified God, took away our sins, and merited grace.
>
> The pope makes an application as satisfaction in the indulgences he grants the living. The sense and intention of this is that if you have sinned and then in sorrow for your sins want to make satisfaction, you then come to the pope saying, »Holy Father, I beg you to direct the works and prayers of the Church [to satisfy] for my sins.« Then he answers, »Let it be as you ask.« Then all who offer Mass, pray, fast, labor, or do any other work pleasing to God do this for you, so that you are freed from the labor of penance and satisfaction.
>
> This is a plenary indulgence. This is, however, not all that you need, for thereby you neither receive interior grace, nor do you advance, but you remain in the same grace as you were when you made this petition. Therefore you must still make efforts to advance and you must take care not to grow lethargic and snore away thinking you are purified and thus secure. Then you must diligently crucify your members and mortify the source of sin, that is, your concupiscence. For just as it was the cause of the sins for which the indulgence was granted, so it will cause further sins, if you stand still in security.

First, Luther uses the three-part scheme taken over from Christology in order to set his proposals in order. The first way of applying the merits of good works done under Christ's influence in the Church is as satisfaction, which is the second member in the scheme in its application to Christ's life and death.

The ordinary way, therefore, in which an indulgence works is that of satisfying the debt of punishment owed by the living. The imposed penance of sacramental satisfaction is carried out vicariously by prayers and sacrifices pleasing to God in the Church. It is the pope who can direct these good works to the fulfillment of this purpose. To gain an indulgence is to have his assurance, in virtue of the power of the keys, that this is being supplied and thus the previously imposed vindictive penances are remitted. The text indicates Luther is well beyond the quantitative thinking dominating the theological manuals of his time.[71] He saw an indulgence in the framework of people helping each other.

The limitations of this indulgence are quite clear. For the application as satisfaction does not bring about any interior growth in the person gaining the indulgence. It confers no infused grace to help overcome concupiscence, and therefore it is no basis for spiritual security. It only frees a person to attend to the

---

[71] For this contrast, one can review J. Dietterle's ten-part survey of the explanation of indulgences in twenty-two manuals for confessors, or *summulae*, published from the thirteenth to the early-sixteenth century. *Zeitschrift für Kirchengeschichte*, Volumes 24 (1903) through 28 (1907).

much more important task of overcoming the radical sin that led to actual sin in the first place.

We see that Luther understood the satisfactory penances imposed in the sacrament of penance as severely and radically distinct from the »life-penance« of one seeking under grace to root out concupiscence. Luther made no connection between the prayers and mortification imposed in the sacrament to compensate for the sins being forgiven and the prayer and mortification demanded in the central task of Christian living. The former was for actual sins, the latter for radical sin. The former was imposed by the confessor or by the canons, while the latter grew out of our inability to love God because of our chronic infection by sin.

One can well lament this dualism separating the ecclesial action from the personal task and concern.[72] Still there is much to admire in the forcefulness with which Luther urges believers to advance in doing to death the roots of sin. He warns against any certainty of salvation being engendered by the »grace« of a plenary indulgence. Persons lolling in false security are certain to fall back into the same sins for which the remittance of punishment had been given to them in the first place.

Luther's systematic presentation on indulgences now turns to the question of indulgences granted to departed souls in purgatory.

> [6.] The pope makes an application as a suffrage in the indulgences he grants to the departed. Strictly speaking, these are not indulgences, because the pope cannot absolve or forgive the departed, but only make intercession that God will forgive and absolve them, whether from the punishment due for their actual sins, or from the root-sin that they did not mortify or cure in life. This is no doubt done by an infusion of grace, which they can in no way merit for themselves. I do not see that the pope makes this intercession for the living, although the Church as a whole intercedes for all before God.
>
> It is, however, something more when this suffrage is applied to a particular person by the pope or by anyone else. For the pope himself says that the departed become sharers, and he states quite clearly that he understands this as being by way of suffrage. However, those who gain these indulgences should not lightly declare that the soul they named is freed, for one does not know if that soul is worthy before God, or if perhaps another soul was more worthy. Therefore, the pope appears to do

---

[72] Erwin Iserloh laments that Luther did not see the taking on of ecclesial penance as expressive of one's commitment to the medicinal prayer and self-discipline of the penitential life demanded by the disorders of concupiscence. *The Theses Were Not Posted*, 42-44, 105. Konrad Wimpina was critical of this dualism in Luther in the theses against Luther which he wrote for defense by Johann Tetzel at Frankfurt/Oder in January 1518. For Wimpina satisfactory prayer and work is not simply an ecclesial imposition but can also be a requirement of *iustitia divina* (Theses 4, 7, 41; *Dokumente zur Causa Lutheri*, 1, 322f, 329). Tetzel made the same point in the 5th and 7th sections of his *Vorlegung* against Luther in April 1518 (Ibid., 345f, 347f). Johann Eck's second *obeliscus* on Luther's Ninety-Five Theses said it was wrong to see ecclesial penances as added to and concurrent with the penance God requires, for they declare and interpret the latter (Ibid., 405).

more by indulgences for the departed than for the living, since he impetrates infused grace for the former, but grants only a remission [of punishment] to the living.

The souls of purgatory are related to subsequent grace, that is, to increase of grace and to its completion in glory, as a sinner is related to first grace or justification. For neither can merit grace, but both are able to receive it. This is true of one who has the first grace, even though he is no longer in this life, and of one who is still in this life, but without the prior grace.

The second mode of applying the good works of Christ and the Church is by way of intercessory petition that God effect the purification of the souls in purgatory by infused grace. The intercession appears to request release from both punishments, both that for actual sins and that for the concupiscence remaining. This is a slight change from Luther's statement in the second section of the treatise that the pope could simply remit the imposed punishments of the departed souls by use of the power of the keys.

The expulsion of concupiscence in the departed is a work of God's infused grace. The question arises whether the Church in any way acts to gain this for the living. Luther points to the Church's regular prayers before God for this grace for all, but this is something other than an indulgence.[73]

At any rate, the elements of uncertainty are clear. One should not say that an indulgence effects the release of a particular person from purgatory, since we do not know if this person is ready to be freed from purgatory. Still, Luther's theological elaboration of the problem has shown that the Church's help for the suffering souls through indulgences is greater than what she does for the living. The former receive the infused grace that advances their conversion and purifies charity, while the latter are only freed from the vindictive punishments imposed by human agency.

Luther states that the departed can in no way merit the infused grace they need. But their previous merits do have an effect in preparing them to be helped by God through the Church's impetration. Thus, some are better prepared than others to receive this help. But the grace itself they do not merit. In fact they stand in relation to this grace and its flowering in heaven just as the sinner stands in relation to the first gift of justifying grace. Both can receive the gift, but neither can merit it.

The emphasis placed on the Church's intercession leads Luther quite naturally to the question of our certitude about God's acceptance of this prayer.

> [7.] One point, however, is still doubtful. If the pope only offers a suffrage and intercedes for souls, approaching God as a mediator and not as one having

---

[73] Luther is touching here on the problem posed by the third principal »grace« of the St. Peter's indulgence, a grant of »participatio omnium bonorum ecclesiae universalis,« accorded to those contributing to the St. Peter's building fund. *Instructio summaria*, no. 35; *Dokumente zur Causa Lutheri*, 1, 268f. Luther's treatise poses no basic problem here, although in the Ninety-Five Theses no. 37 asserts that the true Christian already shares in this treasure, even without such a special »grace.«

jurisdiction, how can he be certain that a soul is freed? For God is free to decide to what extent, how, when, where, and for whom He hears the prayers of His Church. Who is certain that God accepts in the manner in which we make the petition? Unless perhaps it is that God does not turn back the prayer of his Church, where Christ is praying with her. For He said, »Ask and it will be given you« [Mt 7:7], and again, »Whatever you ask in prayer, believe that you receive it, and you will« [Mk 11:24].

Since this is the case, the granting of and gaining of indulgences is a most useful practice, in spite of the commerce and avarice which we fear is involved with them. Perhaps God wants to show greater mercy toward the departed in our day, since He sees them forgotten by the living. Also, more souls go to purgatory today than earlier, since Christians today are lazier than earlier. Thus many go there, but few work on their behalf, since both the departed and their survivors were and still are quite lazy. The pope comes to their aid at least in this manner.

Finally, the pope applies the good works of the Church as a votive offering or in thanksgiving and in praise of God for the blessings granted himself and the elect.

The question of certitude crops up again. How can the pope be certain that some soul is freed by an indulgence for the dead? For the pope acts as a mediator, and the answer to the prayer depends wholly on the divine good pleasure. But Luther sees an answer even here, for Christ prays in his Church and with his Church when this suffrage of petition is offered. Thus the Church can be confident of being heard, just as Christ Himself exhorted her to be confident in prayer.

Luther's final evaluation of indulgences is thus based on the Church's certainty of being heard by God. Even the avarice of those running the indulgence campaign cannot tarnish the good done there. Luther's evaluation of this as »a most useful practice« is nonetheless startling. It must, of course, be understood within the limits of the proposal he has drawn up. Still, it stands in contrast to the sharp criticism Luther directed against indulgences while commenting on the Psalms and Romans.[74] In 1517 the pendulum swung, at least for a time, to a decidedly positive assessment, in spite of the abuses.[75]

Finally, Luther can even see a reason for the multiplication of indulgences in his own time. The Christian people are lazier than before, and God is coming to the aid of the departed souls in a more generous way. Also, with so little concern for rooting out concupiscence, many more come to purgatory. Thus it is good

---

[74] See p. 101, note 48, above.

[75] The principal documentation of Luther's changing evaluation of indulgences, after the intervention of Oct. 31, 1517, is his *Resolutiones*, which present a position on each of the Ninety-Five Theses. Luther submitted these in manuscript to the Bishop of Brandenburg in February 1518, then did some further work on the text, and sent it to Staupitz on May 30. It came off the press in August. One finds an unambiguous expression of a new stand on indulgences in Luther's letter to Georg Spalatin on February 15, 1518. Indulgences, he has come to hold, are delusions, of no help to serious Christians, and should be rated far below acts of charity in aid of the poor. WABr 1, 146,52-68.

that the pope is doing what he can for them. This is basically the same justification offered by Gabriel Biel in his *Expositio canonis missae*, when this problem came up.[76]

Luther concludes the *Tractatus de indulgentiis* by returning to the theme of Christian life as a healing process, and to the ardent prayer for the grace by which one is healed of the malady of concupiscence.

> Conclusion
> [8.] Therefore, we must be quite earnest in preventing indulgences, that is, satisfactions, from becoming a cause of security, laziness, and neglect of interior grace. Instead, we must be diligent to fully cure the infection of our nature and thirst to come to God out of love for Him, hatred of this life, and disgust with ourselves. That is, we must incessantly seek God's healing grace. This is the end of this matter.

Here, in miniature, is the spirituality of Luther's early works, especially the *Lectures on Romans*. Compressing his view of the human condition and the resulting task into a few lines, Luther addresses the problematic of indulgences in the life of the Church. The true enemy is *pax et securitas*, and hence, even though indulgences can well have a role in Christian living, one's main concern is not with them, but with the process of inner healing from sin and growth in love and longing for God. The focus of attention must therefore be prayer for the grace that enlightens and inflames the heart, cleansing and directing the affections to God.

Concluding Reflections

This, then, is how Luther ordered his thoughts and arguments in 1517 in preparation for a disputation with other theologians on the nature and efficacy of indulgences. His Ninety-Five Theses of October 31 aimed to stimulate discussion and debate. They were not his doctrine, but instead were meant to draw others into stating how they understood the issues and how they would argue for their positions.[77] The treatise, in contrast, shows us the quite moderate position, together with some brilliant insights, that Luther intended to offer in this discussion. One can lament the crevasse he left between imposed ecclesial penances and the intrinsically grounded penitential tasks incumbent on the believer. But far more lamentable is the fact that in late 1517 his barbed theses

---

[76] Lectio 57 O; Oberman-Courtenay edition, 2, 407f.

[77] See the letters cited in n. 24, p. 92, above. In his early 1518 explanations of the indulgence theses, Luther made it clear that he did not hold what was asserted in some of the theses. See WA 1, 567,29 (LW 31, 145) and WA 1, 596,38 (LW 31, 196). This was most explicit regarding the sixth thesis: »Quamquam igitur sextam conclusionem ipse non posui ex animo ... sed quia alii sic sentiunt.« WA 1, 544,33; LW 31, 106 (inexact rendering). Luther made the same point about the 6th thesis not representing his own view in his *Responsio* of August 1518 to the *Dialogus* of the pope's theologian Silvester Prierias. WA 1, 658,41.

5. Treatise on Indulgences, 1517

spread over Germany in a matter of weeks, while this penetrating expository treatise fell into dusty oblivion.

With the recovery of this enlightening document, we are at least in a much better position to understand the origin of the divisions under which the Western churches suffer today. This presentation of Luther's views of October 1517, especially on endemic sin and the penitential life, is offered in the belief that his theological convictions were a powerful motive force in the transformation of Western Christianity in the sixteenth century. I am reminded here, with a strong sense of agreement, how Joseph Lortz highlighted the importance of Luther's ideas and teaching on the first page of *Die Reformation in Deutschland* some fifty years ago.[78] The doctrinal component is essential for understanding the Reformation. Other dimensions and components were present in abundance, but the whole cannot be understood if the doctrines are neglected.[79]

Obviously, a process of reception and implementation, along with parallel refusals and opposition, followed hard upon Luther's publication in the years 1518-20 of his freshly minted set of teachings, but it was Luther's teaching that set the complex process in motion.[80] Some individuals and communities accepted his doctrines, and sought to walk in the light of Luther's vision. Others responded positively, but then selected certain themes, which in turn came to be amalgamated with other convictions and values not rated highly by Luther. But it was Luther's configuration of Christian doctrine that the first Protestants were encountering and appropriating in their own way. Others heard Luther, and in the light of their understanding of his aims, whether their grasp was accurate and sensitive or not, they rejected his program. But it was Luther's proposals that caused the reaction and to an extent shaped the new Catholic content through reversal.

Certainly, one has to attend to the social-historical changes that took place in towns and rural areas where Luther made his impact, and contemporary historians are doing this with energy and growing refinement of method. But social change, in the European sixteenth century, unfolded under the influence of

---

[78] »Die Reformation ist inhaltlich wesentlich bestimmt einerseits durch die religiöse-theologische Anschauungen Luthers und durch die Kirchenspaltung.« *Vorwort, Die Reformation in Deutschland*, 2 vols. (Freiburg 1939-40), 1, vii.

[79] B. Lohse recently underscored the enduring significance of Lortz's work, precisely with reference to the primacy Lortz accorded to Luther's thought and teaching, especially as the Reformer worked out positions in his early lectures and writings. B. Lohse, »Die bleibende Bedeutung von Joseph Lortz' Darstellung 'Die Reformation in Deutschland',« in R. Decot & R. Vinke, eds., *Zum Gedenken an Joseph Lortz (1887-1975)* (Stuttgart 1989), 337-351.

[80] I attempt to sketch a global view of what happened, in the form of an updated report on the Reformation and Counter-Reformation scholarship of the past quarter-century, in an entry »Reformation Studies,« *New Catholic Encyclopedia*, 18, *Supplement 1978-1988* (Washington, D.C. & Palatine, Ill. 1989), 415-424.

doctrines, forms of lived religiosity or spirituality, and various theologically grounded views of the urban and rural world. The study of Luther's thought and teaching is thus essential, if we want to grasp the Reformation adequately.

Luther's *Treatise on Indulgences*, especially in its insistence on penance and earnest prayer, displays the engaging set of ideas and ideals for living that Luther proposed in 1517 and with which the Reformation did in fact begin. Our scholarly consideration of Luther's proposal has obviously been informed by an appreciative sense of its value. This is not a Catholic ecclesial recognition of Luther, which Wolfhart Pannenberg recently called for, but it does clearly suggest that something other can well follow upon a reading and hearing of Luther's initial reforming proposal than what came in *Exsurge Domine*.[81] Luther spoke well on sin, healing grace, and the penitential life in his treatise.[82] He presented as well an uncommonly rich vision of the help that repentant Christians can give each other by their intercession with God. This was a timely message in 1517.[83] This final aspect, here newly discovered, can well be a point of intersection at which late-twentieth century Lutherans and Catholics meet and then learn together, with no little spiritual enrichment, from Luther's theology. May this be the ultimate sense of our presentation of this text. May Luther himself help us come together.

---

[81] W. Pannenberg's statement of what is needed came in his lecture, »Über Lortz hinaus?« in *Zum Gedenken an Joseph Lortz*, 93-105, esp. 98f and 101f.

[82] Recently Carl J. Peter raised the question whether certain recent statements of the Catholic doctrine of indulgences, marked by a personalist, spiritual, and analogical view of the *thesaurus ecclesiae*, do not meet the concerns that underlie the Lutheran rejection of indulgences and their supporting doctrines. »The Church's Treasures (*thesauri ecclesiae*) Then and Now,« *Theological Studies* 47 (1986), 251-272, at 272. Peter's historical-ecumenical essay makes no reference to Luther's 1517 *Tractatus de indulgentiis*, because the treatise did not enter into the crucial controversy between Luther and Cardinal Cajetan in October 1518. But the *Tractatus* does raise a question similar to the one posed by Peter, but directed to Catholics: are they disposed to learn – theologically and personally – from Luther's theology of endemic sinfulness and healing grace?

[83] Bernd Moeller's recent study of the indulgence-campaigns, especially between 1476 and 1517, notes how Cardinal Peraudi's influential systematization of the comprehensive »graces« of an indulgence left little or no room for a concern over penance and purificatory healing of spirit. »Die letzten Ablaßkampagnen,« in H. Boockmann et al., eds., *Lebenslehren und Weltentwürfe*, 550.

6

FIDES SACRAMENTI – *FIDES SPECIALIS*: LUTHER'S DEVELOPMENT IN 1518

When Joseph Ratzinger was lecturing at Münster in the 1960s, he observed on occasion that while Catholic doctrine holds that infallibility is part of the Church's empowerment for teaching, the Reformation, while denying ecclesial infallibility, has the individual grasp as an infallible truth the reality of his or her own justification before God. This may well be an enlightening way to frame a key difference between the Catholic and Lutheran traditions. The issue of the believer's certitude of grace in his own regard has been for centuries one of the divisive doctrinal issues, especially since the Council of Trent spoke forthrightly against such certitude in Chapter 9 and Canons 13 and 14 of the *Decree on Justification* in 1547.

However, some recent investigations and proposals, based in large part on source-documents published in the past century, have brought to light a far more complex relationship between the Catholic and Lutheran doctrinal positions on grace, faith, and certitude than is apparent in Trent's clear and categorical texts. The Tridentine theologians and bishops, schooled in the sophisticated conceptual systems of the late-medieval *viae*, did not grasp Luther's concentration on God's redemptive deed of mercy in Christ. Trent's reaction to the Protestant use of forensic language (»declare righteous,« »impute,« »righteous *coram Deo*«) produced a healthy stress on justification being a real change in the person, but the same reaction also made it difficult for them to articulate this change as God's work of unconditioned grace, as bound irrevocably to the cross of Christ, and as being a merciful pardon which places the believer's life on a totally new existential basis. The Tridentine Fathers thought of *fides* as the submissive acceptance of revealed truth, a conception conveying only part of St. Paul's *pistis* and very little of Luther's *fides Christi*. Consequently, a recent review of this problem by Juan Alfaro concludes with a denial that Trent accurately condemned what Luther had taught on the certainty of the *fides* or *Glauben* by which the sinner lays hold of God's righteousness given in Christ.[1]

---

[1] »...la conclusion s'impose que la 'certitude de la grace' enseignée par Luther n'est pas celle que Trente condamna. La position de Trente et celle de Luther sont différentes mais non pas opposée; elles ne coincident point parfaitement mais ne s'excluent pas non plus mutuellement.« Juan Alfaro, »Certitude de l'espérance et 'certitude de la grace,' « *Nouvelle Revue théologique* 104

These conclusions have their warrants in the results of modern research on Luther,[2] in investigations of the *acta* of the Council of Trent,[3] and in ecumenically sensitive comparative studies.[4] However, in this particular area of developing rapprochement on the doctrine of justification, there has not yet been a work of retrieval of the specific historical circumstances in which Luther himself came to insist on fiducial faith, the *pro me*, and the certitude one should have about God's gracious and effective action to forgive and overcome my sin. The present study aims to fill this lacuna and thereby to enlarge the basis of contemporary reflection on the complex set of oppositions, divergences, and complementarities central to the Lutheran-Catholic dialogue in our day.[5]

Faith and Conversion according to Luther, 1509-17
Luther's exegetical and pastoral works from the beginning through 1517 proposed an intense spiritual teaching on a faith-life that is ever in process, ever called out of satisfied self-reliance, and ever yearning to be more completely

---

(1972), 29.

[2] Paul Althaus, *Die Theologie Martin Luthers* (Gütersloh 1962), 48-62, 186-203; in translation, *The Theology of Martin Luther* (Philadelphia 1970), 43-63, 211-233. Gerhard Ebeling, *Luther. Einführung in sein Denken* (Tübingen 1964), 157-199; in translation, *Luther, Introduction to his Thought* (Philadelphia 1970), 141-199. Wilfred Joest, *Ontologie der Person bei Luther* (Göttingen 1967), 219-232, 290-310. Otto Hof, »Luthers Unterscheidung zwischen dem Glauben und der Reflexion auf den Glauben,« *Kerygma und Dogma* 18 (1972), 249-324; Wolfgang Schwab, *Entwicklung und Gestalt der Sakramententheologie bei Martin Luther* (Frankfurt & Bern 1977), 77-144. Martin Brecht, »Der rechtfertigende Glaube an das Evangelium von Jesus Christus als Mitte von Luthers Theologie,« *Zeitschrift für Kirchengeschichte* 89 (1978), 45-77.

[3] Adolf Stakemeier, *Das Konzil von Trient über die Heilsgewissheit* (Heidelberg 1947), especially pp. 90-92, 167-176. Hubert Jedin, *Geschichte des Konzils von Trient*, 2 (Freiburg 1957), 208-213, 251f, with bibliography in n. 5 on pp. 486f; in translation, *A History of the Council of Trent*, 2 (St. Louis 1961), 247-253, 297f, with bibliography in n. 1 on pp. 249f. J. Alfaro, »Certitude de l'espérance,« 10-35.

[4] Stephanus Pfürtner, *Luther und Thomas im Gespräch* (Heidelberg 1961); in translation, *Luther and Aquinas on Salvation* (New York 1964). Otto Hermann Pesch, *Die Theologie der Rechtfertigung bei Martin Luther und Thomas von Aquin* (Mainz 1967), 195-288, 719-757, 935-948. August Hasler, *Luther in der katholischen Dogmatik* (Munich 1968), 76-89, 180-204. Joseph Lortz, »Sakramentales Denken beim jungen Luther,« *Lutherjahrbuch* 36 (1969), 9-40; reprinted in *Erneuerung und Einheit. Aufsätze zur Theologie- und Kirchengeschichte*, ed. P. Manns (Stuttgart 1987), 646-677. Harry McSorley, »Luther and Trent on the Faith Needed for the Sacrament of Penance,« in E. Schillebeeckx, ed., *Sacramental Reconciliation* (Concilium, no. 61; New York 1971), 89-98.

[5] The present study develops the brief section on *fides sacramenti* in my »Justification and Faith in Luther's Theology,« Study 2, above, pp. 23-25, in this volume. The present study also represents a retraction of pejorative assessments on Luther's 1518 theology expressed in my *Man Yearning for Grace* (Washington 1968 and Wiesbaden 1969), 7f, 11, 271-273. The aim in the present essay, however, is less to reassess and more to explain the specific configuration of themes and convictions that Luther worked out in 1518.

penetrated by the spirit of love for God and others. One characteristic of these early works, contrasting with much late-medieval piety and with Luther's own later teaching, is the absence of extended treatments of the sacraments as bases of Christian existence.

The early focal point in Luther is conversion and the life-long process of penance, based especially on believing acceptance of God's word of judgment. The conversion to which Christ and the Apostle Paul invite people is a movement from secure self-approval to a personal appropriation of judgment, by which the believer »becomes a sinner« in his or her own conscience, that is, in one's self-estimate and self-understanding before God.[6]

The cross of Christ is the revelatory model of God's work of exalting the humble. Repentance embraces the cross by confession of one's sin before God. Thus a person comes to speak the truth about his or her status before God and in a fundamental way becomes thereby truthful and righteous.[7]

In this humble self-accusation, according to Luther's early account, sin is forgiven, that is, it is not imputed. Thereby a penitential life begins its further development. The dominant concern becomes the rooting out of inherent sinfulness – a complex of self-regarding and self-seeking tendencies – under the influence of God's healing and transforming grace. The believer then constantly yearns and seeks for God's grace to purify otherwise unruly and concupiscent affections. These themes recur in Luther's earliest lectures and they were set forth engagingly in Spring 1517 in Luther's first published work, a vernacular exposition of the seven penitential Psalms.[8]

This early, a-sacramental teaching on humility and penitential prayer was then the principal basis for Luther's criticism of indulgence preaching in 1517.

---

[6] Early in his 1515-16 lecture-course on Romans, Luther generalized: »Hoc est totum negotium Apostoli et domini eius, ut superbos humiliet et ad huius rei agnitionem perducat et gratia eos indigere doceat, iustitiam propriam destruat, ut humiliati Christum requirant, peccatores se confiteantur ac sic gratiam percipiant et salvi fiant.« WA 56, 207,7; LW 25, 191f. Central to conversion is »spiritualiter fieri ... peccatorem,« about which Luther specifies, »tota vis huius mutationis latet in sensu seu estimatione ac reputatione nostra. Hunc enim mutare intendit omnis sermo Scripturae et omnis operatio Dei.« WA 56, 233,5; LW 25, 217 (misleading translation).

[7] A fuller exposition is in my *Man Yearning for Grace. Martin Luther's Early Spiritual Teaching* (Wiesbaden 1969). See pp. 60-73, on *accusatio sui* in Luther's *Dictata super Psalterium*, 1513-15; pp. 95-97, on »becoming a sinner« in the 1515-16 lectures on Romans; pp. 45-51, on conformity to Christ and his cross in the *Dictata*; pp. 107f and 115, on confession and righteousness.

[8] *Man Yearning*, 88-94 (progressive purification in the *Dictata*); 99-101, 104-106, 111-114, 125-128 (yearning for healing grace to overcome endemic sin). The exposition of the penitential Psalms is now at WA 1, 158-220 (LW 14, 139-205), and is treated in *Man Yearning*, 165-177. Oswald Bayer called this work the »authentic compendium« of the first phase of Luther's theological work. *Promissio. Geschichte der reformatorischen Wende in Luthers Theologie* (Göttingen 1971), 144.

On February 24, 1517, Luther concluded a sermon with a criticism of the multiplication of indulgences in his day. He indicted current practice for promoting a sense of spiritual security instead of fostering love for the cross. At best, indulgences should be offered as a solace to the weak in faith, but not to people aspiring to bear the cross in meekness and humility. The latter acknowledge their sinfulness and so embrace suffering and the cross; in them Christ can become supremely active for their purification and renewal.[9]

Another sermon by Luther, probably preached on May 30, 1517, contrasted the humility of Zaccheus with the self-righteousness of those who murmured over Jesus' visit to Zaccheus's home.[10] The Lord could not come to the others, but in Zaccheus's lowliness he could be welcomed. Indulgences, as they are being offered, promote thoughts of one's own worthiness and distract from interior repentance by drawing attention to the external acts of confessing sins and doing imposed satisfactions. Normative for the Christian is instead a ruthless self-abnegation under God's word of judgment.

> Interior repentance is true contrition, true confession, and true spiritual satisfaction. Then a penitent really and utterly displeases himself in all he does. They turn efficaciously to God in genuine admission of their guilt as they confess to God from the heart. Then their self-hatred gnaws at them interiorly and leads to self-imposed punishments. Thus they make satisfaction to God. The truly repentant person desires that, if it were possible, all creation would see and hate his sin, and he is ready to be trampled on by all. They do not seek indulgences for the remission of punishments, but instead the actual bearing of punishment.[11]

In Luther's intervention of October 31, 1517, his *Treatise on Indulgences* formulated an ingenious account of the limited role indulgences can play in Christian penance.[12] More important than indulgences is the penitential sigh of

---

[9] WA 1, 141,22. On *Christus actuosissimus*, 140,15.

[10] WA 1, 94-99, and WA 4, 670-674. See *Man Yearning for Grace*, 261-264. I then inclined toward a January 1518 dating (ibid., 394f, n. 151). N. Flörken has advanced a coherent argument for the date of May 30, 1517, which was after Johann Tetzel had preached the St. Peter's indulgence in nearby Jüterbog. »Ein Beitrag zur Datierung von Luthers Sermo de indulgentiis pridie Dedicationis,« *Zeitschrift für Kirchengeschichte* 82 (1971), 344-350.

[11] »Nam poenitentia interior est vera contritio, vera confessio, vera satisfactio in spiritu. Quando poenitens vere purissime sibi displicet in omnibus quae fecit, et efficaciter convertuntur ad Deum pureque agnoscunt culpam et Deo confitentur in corde. Deinde per sui detestationem intus sese mordet et punit: ideo ibidem Deo satisfacit. Immo vere poenitens vellet, si fieri posset, ut omnis creatura suum peccatum videret et odisset, et paratus est ab omnibus conculcari. Non quaerit indulgentias et remissiones poenarum, sed exactiones poenarum.« WA 1, 99,1. These motifs echo in Luther's Ninety-Five Theses, especially in nos. 1-4, 39-40, and 93-95. On February 15, 1518, Luther instructed his friend Georg Spalatin that the dominant trait of the righteous person is self-accusation in conformity with God's judgment.

[12] WABr 12, 5-9; in English, with commentary, in Study 5 of this collection, above, pp. 97-114. A German translation is in *Man Yearning for Grace* (Wiesbaden 1969), 431-438.

longing (*gemitus*) for interior grace which purifies from concupiscence by transforming the affections. Thus Luther concluded his treatise:

> Therefore we must be quite earnest in preventing indulgences, that is, satisfactions, from becoming a cause of security, laziness, and neglect of interior grace. Instead, we must be diligent to fully cure the infection of our nature and thirst to come to God out of love for him, hatred of this life, and disgust with ourselves. That is, we must incessantly seek God's healing grace.[13]

Luther's early inculcating of self-accusation and life-long purification from sin went hand-in-hand with the traditional exclusion of certainty about one's being in the grace of God. Luther could cite the usual proof-text against such certainty: »Nescit homo, an odio vel amore dignus sit« (Ecclesiastes 9:1, Vulgate).[14] Enduring uncertainty of grace renders a valued service by promoting humility, that is, by driving the believer ever again to appropriate the cross of self-emptying dependence on God's work and grace.[15] Later, Luther worked out a new configuration of his spiritual teaching, in which certainty of grace came to have a central place, although this was not a certitude identical with that certitude discussed in Thomist and Scotist theologies of justification.

The characteristic emphases of Luther's early theology of conversion, taught from 1509 through 1517, have an internal coherence and impact as a penitential spirituality. This teaching becomes still more intelligible when seen in the framework of what Berndt Hamm has called the »theology-for-piety« proposed by different authors at the beginning of the sixteenth century.[16] Works of this genre had been appearing in German lands since the time of Jean Gerson (d. 1429). They sought above all to serve reform of life by facilitating repentance, fostering devotion, and inculcating prayer and virtuous living. The prevalent attempt in much recent scholarship to classify such writings according to their

---

[13] »Conclusio. Id itaque diligenter attendendum, ne indulgentiae, id est satisfactiones fiant nobis causa securitatis et pigritiae et damnum interioris gratiae. Sed sedulo agamus, ut morbus naturae perfecte sanetur et ad Deum venire sitiamus prae amore eius et odio vitae huius et nostri ipsius taedio, id est assidue sanantem gratiam eius quaeramus.« WABr 12, 9,151.

[14] Literally, »A person does not know whether he deserves hatred or love.« Cited by Luther in the Romans course, WA 56, 79,18; in the 1516-17 course on Galatians, WA 57II, 101,18. The text was also cited by Luther's student B. Bernardi, in the disputation of September 25, 1516: WA 1, 150,1. In the indulgence treatise of October 1517, Luther assumed that no one can be certain of the adequacy of his own contrition and confession: WABr 12, 6,44; in translation, p. 103, in this volume.

[15] This has been noted by M. Kroeger, *Rechtfertigung und Gesetz* (Göttingen 1968), 140, and by W. Schwab, *Entwicklung und Gestalt der Sakramententheologie*, 44f.

[16] *Frömmigkeitstheologie am Anfang des 16. Jahrhunderts* (Tübingen 1982), 222-247. Also, »Frömmigkeit als Gegenstand theologiegeschichtlicher Forschung,« *Zeitschrift für Theologie und Kirche* 74 (1977), 464-497.

adherence to one or other of the scholastic *viae* does not bring out the specific characteristics of their teaching.

Works of this type evince a notable diversity in the early sixteenth century, with an identifiable group of these theologians looking inward, where God exercises an intense direct influence on the human spirit. Luther's early a-sacramental instruction on interior, spiritual conversion was a creative new departure in this sub-type of theology-for-piety, but was akin to other instructions being offered in the elite circle of thinkers influenced by Luther's one-time personal mentor, Johann von Staupitz. But a notably different type of theology-for-piety was exemplified by another of Luther's older Augustinian confreres, Johann von Paltz, whose works of pastoral theology, especially those of 1502 and 1504, were helping preachers guide large numbers of ordinary folk to encounter God's mercy by the practice of ecclesially approved devotions, by reception of the ecclesial sacraments, and by sharing in the special largess of recent indulgences. Paltz sought to direct souls toward God's grace by teaching them to use the special endowments of the church, such as the saints, the priesthood, sacraments, the treasury of merits, and the well-defined practicable methods of attaining grace and salvation by these means.[17]

In 1518, as we shall see, Luther took up the concerns of this populist wing of early sixteenth-century theology-for-piety and began a renewal program of pastoral instruction focused on the utter credibility and reliability of sacramental absolution.

Absolution and Faith in early 1518

While Luther's systematic exposition, the *Treatise on Indulgences*, did not treat sacramental forgiveness of sin, his Ninety-Five Theses did include several clusters of lapidary assertions about priestly absolution in the sacrament. With these statements, which were meant to be clarified in the give-and-take of disputation, Luther began a reflection, amid moments of distress, on the implications of Christ's conferral of the power to bind and loose from sin (Matthew 16:19).[18] The outcome of these reflections on sacramental forgiveness are found in a cluster of statements Luther made in the first half of 1518.

The *Resolutiones* of the indulgence theses, written in early 1518, show in the materials on theses 7 and 38 a stage in Luther's thought in which priestly

---

[17] I reviewed B. Hamm's book on Paltz, mentioned in the previous note, and the new critical editions of Paltz's *Coelifodina* (1502) and *Supplementum Coelifodinae* (1504) in *Gregorianum* 65 (1984), 200-204. I also reviewed the recent edition of Paltz's *Opuscula*, in *Gregorianum* 71 (1990), 592-595.

[18] Binding and loosing is at issue in the indulgences theses, in nos. 5-8, 12-13, 20-23, and 38. These mark the beginning of a personal struggle that Luther described some months later. »Torsit diu animum meum haec auctoritas, 'Quodcumque ligaveris super etc.' et meditabar semper: Ey sso mag der Bapst mit uns thuenn was ehr will.« WA 4, 658,4.

absolution is an open declaration of the justifying and forgiving work of God that has already taken place in a hidden manner and *sub contraria specie*. God's hidden work grinds down the spirit, according to the root-sense of *contritio*, and in fact does give grace, but without the person knowing about the gift conferred. Then, the declaration made in absolution confers peace, through the sense and awareness of being graced and reconciled with God.[19] However, the latter is also a grace, in the form of »faith in forgiveness and present grace.«[20] In a first stage, the penitent has undergone anguish under God's severe judgment, but in a second stage consolation and assurance are offered as one is called to believe in the absolution on the basis of the power conferred in Matthew 16:19.[21]

Other formulations of early 1518 on absolution, forgiveness, and faith occur in two sermons, one given by Luther on February 2 and the other sometime in the Spring at the first mass of a newly ordained priest.[22] The means of true purification is not indulgences, nor the external acts of confessing and expressing sorrow for sins, but uniquely a faith that lays hold of the words which the priest says in virtue of Christ's conferral of the power to bind and loose.[23] Those thus

---

[19] WA 1, 540,8-541,24 (LW 31, 99-101), 543,14-24 (LW 31, 104), 545,1-4 (LW 31, 107), all in the 7th *resolutio*. In the 38th Luther admits his dissatisfaction with the declaratory understanding of absolution (WA 1, 594,5; LW 31, 191f), and defends himself against charges that he diminishes the power of the keys (WA 1, 596,24f; LW 31, 194). His view of absolution is moving from seeing it as a declaration of what has already been given (WA 1, 593,32-37, 594,25-32; LW 31, 190f, 192) toward holding that it is an effective conferral of forgiveness (WA 1, 595,10-18.33f; LW 31, 193f). O. Bayer finds a declaratory view of absolution also in Luther's scholion on Hebrews 7:12. *Promissio*, 173ff.

[20] »Igitur remissio Dei gratiam operatur, sed remissio sacerdotis pacem, quae et ipsa est gratia et donum Dei, quia fides remissionis et gratiae praesentis.« WA 1, 542,7; LW 31,102.

[21] The frequency of Mt 16:19 in Luther's texts of early 1518 is notable: WA 4, 637,3.13, 658,4; WA 1, 539,39, 541,4.8.22, 542, 18.32, 594,10.35,40, 615,23.38, 323,25, 288,8; WA 57 III, 192,9. M. Kroeger treated the discovery of this text as the hinge on which Luther's thought swung in the direction of his mature theology of justification and faith. *Rechtfertigung und Gesetz*, 173-175. Such a clear datum indicates the need of caution in efforts to interpret Luther's development in 1517-18 in conformity with the content of his later autobiographical passages about his struggle to understand Rom 1:17 and the *iustitia Dei* revealed in the gospel. Rom 1:17 did play a role in Luther's new articulation of the shape of conversion, but in subordination to the New Testament text standing behind the power of loosing from sin as this is actualized in absolution. See n. 18, above for a contemporary testimony by Luther to the effect that Mt 16:19 was a text that upset him for a while, before he saw its connection with the mercy of God revealed in a concentrated way in absolution.

[22] WA 4, 636-639, 655-659.

[23] WA 4, 636,25-637,35, including this forthright instruction on the practical implication of Mt 16:19 on loosing from sin: »Quidquid Christus Petro cum suis dixit, et nobis dictum est, ad nos potissimum concernit, praecipue qui mundandî sumus. Tantum autem mundamur in confessione, quantum credimus verbis sacerdotis et Christi potius, qui dixit, 'Quodcumque solveris, etc.' Restat quod sola confessio recta stat in fide. Si non credimus verbis sacerdotum ... certum est nos non purgatos a peccatis nostris, non curando quantum habueris contritionem, an bene peccata nostra recollegimus: si credimus nos verbis absolutionis, tunc peccata remittuntur« (637,9).

purified by *fides Christi* do not then sink into quiescent passivity, but instead burst forth with the good works that constitute a sacrifice to the Lord in righteousness (Malachy 3:3, Vulgate – read on February 2).[24] The second sermon then explained that God provided priests empowered to bind and loose, »so that our trust builds on the mouth of the priest.«[25] The honor shown to priests rests on their ministry of consolation and encouragement. But the source of the spiritual stability they confer is ultimately Christ himself.

> Thus our salvation lies in the word, but not really in the word, for Christ is conjoined to the word. There must be no tottering here. The sacrament is a rock grounded in Christ.[26]

Luther's issued a popular instruction, the *Sermo de poenitentia*, around Easter 1518 as guidance for people's annual confession. The text set forth a doctrine of forgiveness in which the critical moment, not so much for the essence of the sacrament as for lived realization by the penitent, is the utterance of the word of absolution by the confessor. Luther makes no reference here to a prior hidden work of God, but makes it central that the penitent give full credence and trust to the word addressed to him. Contrition should not loom large in one's personal concerns.

> See that you in no way trust that you are absolved because of your contrition,... but instead because of the word of Christ, who said to Peter, »Whatever you loose on earth will be loosed in heaven.« This is where to place your trust, if the priest has given you absolution. Believe firmly that you are absolved, and you are truly absolved, because he does not deceive, however it might be with your contrition.[27]

---

[24] WA 4, 638,29-34.

[25] »ut ... in ore sacerdotis collocetur fiducia nostra.« WA 4, 657,14. In an undatable marginal note to the *Sentences* of Peter Lombard, Luther disqualified the work of previous theology because it did not attend to the high dignity of the sacramental word as the very word of God himself: »Haec disputant non attendentes verbum vocale in sacramentis esse verbum ipsius Dei.« WA 59, 49,12. This theology treated only the relation of cause and effect in the sacrament, to the neglect of faith in the sacramental promise (WA 59, 49,24 and 51,26).

[26] »Ita salus nostra in verbo est et non in verbo, sed quia Christus in verbo est annexus, es muss nicht pampeln. Sacramentum ist ein fels in Christum gegrundtt.« WA 4, 658,26.

[27] » ... vide, ne ullo modo te confidas absolvi propter tuam contritionem (sic enim super te et tua opera confides, id est pessime praesumes), sed propter verbum Christi, qui dixit Petro: 'Quodcumque solveris super terram, solutum erit et in caelis.' Hic, inquam, confide, si sacerdotis obtinueris solutionem, et crede fortiter te absolutum, et absolutus vere eris, quia ille non mentitur, quicquid sit de tua contritione.« WA 1, 323,22. In a recent study, Carl J. Peter has traced the chapter of doctrinal history that begins with Luther's pastoral advice in the *Sermo* of 1518 about confessing all one's sins and ends with the Council of Trent's declaration (*Sessio* XIV, November 25, 1551; Chapter 5 and Canons 6-7) that the integral confession of all one's remembered mortal sins is a constitutive part of sacramental penance. »From *Sermo* to *Anathema*: a Dispute about Confession of Mortal Sins,« in N.H. Minnich et al., eds., *Studies in Church History in Honor of John Tracy Ellis* (Wilmington, Del. 1985), 566-588.

6. *Fides sacramenti* in 1518

In other texts from the first half of 1518, Luther applied his new insight into faith, forgiveness, and Christ's consolation to issues concerning proper reception of Holy Communion. One must not look to one's own preparatory acts and prayers, but instead to the promise of Christ, who invites the heavily burdened to come and be refreshed in him.[28] Commenting on Hebrews 9:14, Luther briefly touched on a theme that in 1520 would become central in his instruction on the Eucharist: a faith that purifies the conscience and consoles should believe the words of Christ, the giver of the new covenant (the *testator*), who addressed his people, »This is the blood shed for you and for many for the forgiveness of sins.«[29]

Where scholasticism had explained the words of absolution and consecration as the »form« by which sacraments are constituted, Luther was leading people to a direct faith in the words as personally addressed to themselves in the name of Christ. For Luther in 1518 *fides Christi* has changed its predominant content. It no longer lays hold of judgment but, instead, of merciful pardon communicated openly and explicitly in words spoken in virtue of Christ's institution and commission.

The new emphasis on believing the word of sacramental grace led naturally to a warning by Luther against interpreting Ecclesiastes 9:1 as referring to a person's present state and as inculcating uncertainty. In commenting on Hebrews 9:24f, Luther underscored that Christ entered heaven to appear before God *pro nobis*, and that authentic faith consequently entails certainty that Christ does this on one's own behalf. It is thus wrong to use the word of Qoheleth to make one uncertain of God's mercy and to undermine trust in his saving work: »For this is to completely ruin Christ and faith in him.«[30] Here is but one sign of the new configuration of central elements in Luther's teaching in 1518.

The clearest expression of Luther's theology of faith and sacramental forgiveness in 1518 is found in a set of theses formulated in the Summer Semester and transmitted under the title, *Pro veritate inquirenda et timoratis conscientiis consolandis* (»Seeking the Truth and Consoling Fearful Consciences«).[31] Here the new concerns and the central insight about absolution fuse into a coherent theology of conversion under the word of God for the overcoming of guilt and sin. Luther has transcended the transitional two-phase account of justification found in the *Resolutiones* and is now in firm possession of views contrasting sharply with the emphases of his teaching down through 1517.[32]

---

[28] WA 1, 255,24, 264,9, 330,36-331,25; WA 57III, 170,13-171,8 (LW 29, 172f).

[29] WA 57III, 207,23-208,4, 208,22-209,3; LW 29, 209f.

[30] »Hoc est enim funditus evertere Christum et fidem eius.« WA 57III, 215,16-216,6, citing 216,5; LW 29, 217f.

[31] WA 1, 630-633.

[32] In recent scholarship, O. Bayer has underscored the importance of these theses. *Promissio*, 166f, 182-202. W. Schwab presented them as formulating the result of the theological reflection and argumentation Luther began with his references to absolution in the Ninety-Five Theses. *Entwicklung und Gestalt der Sakramententheologie*, 98-105. In the new standard biography of

In the theses *Pro veritate*, nos. 1-7 contrast the excellence of the forgiveness of guilt (*culpa*) with the far less valuable remission of the debt of punishment (*poena*). Indulgences, which effect the latter, are thereby relegated to the periphery, while forgiveness of guilt is prized for the way it brings peace of heart and removes the true burden of sin, estrangement from God, from the heart (nos. 2-3). The focus is on reconciliation with God (no. 4) and salvation (no. 6), which leads even now to delight in bearing adversity and punishment (no. 5).

But what is the basis or ground for the forgiveness of guilt? Luther's theses 8-12 set this forth, giving the position in nos. 8-9 and a quick sketch of some backing for the position in nos. 10-12. Forgiveness rests on faith, which lays hold of the word by which Christ conferred the power to loose from sin (Matthew 16:19). Christ expressed his will once and for all (*voluit*, no. 11), in a word of divine mandate (no. 24), and so the absolution from guilt can be taken as authoritative and effective. Luther's warrant for such an account of forgiveness comes from an axiom in use in theology, *Non sacramentum fidei sed fides sacramenti ... iustificat* (Not the sacrament of faith, but faith in the sacrament ... justifies), and from the well known word of St. Augustine on sacramental effectiveness: ... *non quia fit, sed quia creditur* (Not because [the sacrament] is carried out, but because it is believed; no. 10).[33] Further, Christ wanted our salvation to rest on his word of power and thus on a faith that purifies hearts (nos. 11-12, citing snatches of Hebrews 1:3 and Acts 15:9), not on the human decision-making involved in indulgences (no. 11).

As Luther began stating his position of mid-1518 on the word and faith in thesis 8, he ruled out two other possible foundations of forgiveness, the contrition of the penitent and/or the authoritative action of the priest. These two issues were then taken up, the former in theses 13-22, and the latter in theses 23-41.

Contrition cannot have a key role in forgiveness because it is an uncertain human work (nos. 13, 18) and thus cannot confer stable peace and reconciliation with God. A contritionist view of the basis of forgiveness is tantamount to

---

Luther, M. Brecht presents the theses as a milestone in Luther's development on justification. *Martin Luther*, 1, *Sein Weg zur Reformation* (Stuttgart 1981), 228-230; *Martin Luther, His Road to Reformation* (Philadelphia 1985), 235-237.

[33] K.-H. zur Mühlen noted that Augustine had actually written »non quia *dicitur*, sed quia creditur,« with reference to the baptismal formula. »Zur Rezeption der Augustinischen Sakramentsformel ... in der Theologie Luthers,« *Zeitschrift für Theologie und Kirche* 70 (1973), 51, 55-57. T. Camelot indicated that there were two levels in Augustine's *fides sacramenti*, that is, both the faith of the church professed at the *redditio symboli* as the culmination of the prebaptismal catechesis, and the faith by which the person being baptized opens his spirit to the consecratory power of the sacramental formula given by Christ. »Sacramentum fidei,« in *Augustinus Magister* (Paris 1954), 2, 891-896. See also the recent concise exposition by Y. Congar of the current of medieval thought inspired by St. Augustine which tended toward ranking faith's direct relation with God above the mediated encounters with God's saving purpose in the sacraments. »Intentionalité de la foi et sacrament,« in H.J. Auf der Maur et al., *Fides Sacramenti – Sacramentum Fidei*. Festschrift P. Smulders (Assen 1981), 177-191.

despising the sacrament (no. 19), questioning God's truthfulness in his word (nos. 17, 20-21), and wanting to establish or constitute the word by one's own action instead of being passively established or constituted by God's word in faith (no. 22).[34]

Christ the Savior uttered his promise in Matthew 16:19 and so forgiveness has a firm basis outside oneself, where subjective uncertainties cannot corrode it (nos. 15, 17). The term *promissio* in thesis 15 anticipates a generalizing statement in thesis 45 on the correlation found between *verbum promittentis* and *fides recipientis*, that is, the word of one promising and faith receptive of the promise. This for Luther is a specific note of the sacraments of the Christian dispensation.[35] In receptivity vis-à-vis God's promise, the person being absolved sacramentally is to put off all self-regarding concern about his contrition and to respond to the word with *fides sacramenti* (no. 10). Here justifying faith takes the form of a firm conviction about the validity and effectiveness of the absolution (nos. 14-16, 19). Believing the absolution (no. 19) is the one way to the firm, confident stability of a renewed conscience (no. 20), based on the veracity of the divine declaration and mandate.

Luther's exposition in theses 24-41 of the role of the confessor who utters the sacramental word of absolution is both doctrinal (nos. 23-24, 30-33) and pastoral (nos. 25-29, 34-41). Since forgiveness stems from God, the priest has only a ministerial role in uttering the word to be accepted in faith (no. 23). The power of the keys is, however, a necessary factor in forgiveness (no. 33), and its action is by God's mandate a *firmum et infallibile opus* (no. 24). Consequently, when the minister forgives sin by absolution, precisely then and there the Spirit of God elicits justifying faith in Christ and in his word (nos. 30-34).[36] Thus, Luther has

---

[34] W. Schwab gives a brief account of Gabriel Biel's contritionist view of forgiveness. *Entwicklung und Gestalt der Sakramententheologie*, 83. It is treated more at length in Heiko A. Oberman, *The Harvest of Medieval Theology* (Cambridge, Mass. 1963), 146-160. But Biel's contritionism was having little influence on the confessional manuals of Luther's day. Although most of these did explain the nature of true contrition, all the manuals but one indicated that less was required of those approaching sacramental absolution. Thomas N. Tentler, *Sin and Confession on the Eve of the Reformation* (Princeton 1977), 241-243. According to Tentler, it was »an exceedingly common teaching« that one did not have to bring to confession the perfect sorrow required by Biel (Ibid., 273). Johann von Paltz, in his *Coelifodina* (1504), repeatedly spoke of how sacramental absolution supplemented the defective disposition (attrition, servile fear, flawed repentance) which people usually bring to the sacrament. Paltz, *Werke*, 1, *Coelifodina*, eds. C. Burger and F. Stasch (Berlin 1983), 211, 257-262, 298, 421.

[35] Here Luther anticipates the programmatic utterance on faith in God's promise that will come in *De captivitate Babylonica* (1520): »Ubi enim est verbum promittentis Dei, ibi necessaria est fides acceptantis hominis, ut clarum sit initium salutis nostrae esse fidem, quae pendeat in verbo promittentis Dei, qui citra omne nostrum studium gratuita et immerita misericordia nos praevenit et offert promissionis suae verbum.« WA 6, 514,13; LW 36, 39.

[36] »Sicut sacerdos docet, baptisat, communicat vere, et tamen haec solius sunt spiritus intus operantis, ita vere peccata remittit et absolvit a culpa, et tamen hoc solius est spiritus intus operantis. In iis omnibus, dum ministrat verbum Christi, simul fidem exercet, qua intus iustificatur peccator.« Theses 30-32; WA 1, 632,9. In other utterances in early 1518, Luther identified *fides* as *gratia iustificans*: WA 57III, 191,24; WA 1, 286, 16f, 542,7-9 (cited above in n.

come to set justification firmly in the context of an ecclesial sacrament and has systematically defined faith as *fides sacramenti*. Theses 30-33 show that fine balance between the inner spiritual realm and the external ecclesial realm that will mark Luther's later responses to Karlstadt and other »false brethren,« who in the mid-1520s will start from Luther's message of grace but will end with a very un-Lutheran view of grace given directly by God and experienced independently of sacramental mediation.

In the 1518 disputation *Pro veritate*, Luther's doctrinal clarification led to some indications of significant consequences for pastoral practice. Because contrition is less important than faith in the absolution and its effect, the confessor should not explore whether a person is contrite, but he should instead do what he can to encourage faith in the sacrament of forgiveness (nos. 25-28). The limits set by church authority on the actual use of the power of the keys, by specific terms of jurisdiction or faculties, and by reserving certain sins for absolution by higher authority, should be observed by confessors (no. 35), but they do not affect the validity of the absolution (no. 36). If one responds in sincere faith even to an illicit absolution, such a penitent is truly absolved (no. 38). In fact, the role of faith is so critical for the fruitfulness of the absolution that Luther can assert that in the hypothetical case of one who was not contrite, if such a person believed in the absolution, it would still be effective in his own case (no. 40).[37]

In the concluding parts of his theses, Luther first sets forth, in theses 42-45, his position on the specific difference between the sacraments of the old law and those of the Christian dispensation.[38] The central point is not precisely the efficacious character of the New Testament sacraments, which the Scotist tradition had been accentuating to the point of depicting a minimal kind of receptivity under the rubric *non ponere obicem* (no. 42). For Luther, receptivity is

---

20). Also, Luther spoke in a quite traditional manner on this grace of faith as an *infused* gift: WA 1, 364,4.8 (Heidelberg Disputation, Thesis 25); WA 2, 145,9, 146,24 (*Sermo de duplici iustitia*). – In a variety of ways, Luther expressed his conviction that *fides sacramenti* is given by God *intus operans* and is not worked up by rumination or by simply deciding to so believe. In commenting on Heb 5:1, Luther cited St. Bernard's *Sermo in annuntiatione* to show that such faith is not from ourselves, for this would be Pelagian, but is instead received as the Holy Spirit's testimony to the conscience. WA 57III, 169,10-23; LW 29, 171f. See also Luther's comment on Heb 11:6 (WA 57III, 233,1-12; LW 29, 235), to which reference is also made in n. 75, p. 137, below.

[37] Luther assumed that anyone coming to be absolved is in fact contrite, and that simply approaching the sacrament gives *evidentia contritionis signa* (no. 25; WA 1, 631,38). The point of his criticism of the view making contrition the essential disposition is not to deny a place to contrition for sin but instead to anchor one's confidence in the right place in the whole context of sacramental forgiveness. In the 7th *resolutio* on indulgences, Luther had charged that recent theologians were in fact teaching people to trust in their own *contritiones et satisfactiones* as effective in blotting out sin. If they only believed first in Christ's gratuitous forgiveness, then they would truly hate their sin, be contrite, and make satisfaction – doing all this *hilariter*. WA 1, 542,34; LW 31, 103.

[38] This standard topic of sacramental doctrine had cropped up in other contexts in Luther's works of the first part of 1518, e.g., WA 57III, 191,19-192,15; WA 1, 286,10-19, 545,1-7.

essential in every sacrament, so much so that an absence of faith undercuts the sacramental reality and brings down God's judgment. The distinguishing marks of the Christian sacraments are, first, their sphere of influence, that is, interior and spiritual justification, not the external ritual purity of the old law (no. 44), and, second, the structural correlation in the Christian sacramental dispensation between the word of God's promise and faith on the part of the person receiving forgiveness (no. 45).

Luther's theses close with a summary of the views he first set forth in the *Sermo de poenitentia*[39] on the proper way to confess (theses 46-50). The traditional norm that all mortal sins be explicitly confessed does not bind (no. 46), because it is impossible of fulfillment, given our deep infection with vainglory (nos. 47-48). So confess what stands out, while consigning all the rest to the mercy of God as you cast yourself on that mercy with complete trust in God's fidelity to his promise (nos. 49-50).

At the end, Luther looked back over his theses and their systematic exposition of the truth of God's historic promise and commitment, the power of the keys and absolution, *fides sacramenti*, forgiveness and justification, and consolation for fearful consciences. He sensed that the synthesis expressed here was in fact conformed to the heart of St. Paul's teaching on the appropriation of the Gospel by the person being made righteous. Consequently, Luther could formulate the *summa summarum* of his disputation from the last part of Romans 1:17, »The righteous does not live by works nor by the law, but by faith.«[40]

This concluding flourish may result from a sudden insight by Luther, but the Pauline half-verse that he cites does not bring out the specific way in which he had come to anchor justifying faith in the objective word of sacramental absolution. The theological gain in 1518 was not the realization that justification is by faith, but in the new sharpness with which Luther came to define faith. The objective word of forgiveness is the real discovery, for it overcomes any subjective doubtfulness troubling the conscience. The believer lays hold of a quite determinate expression of the will of God, that is, God's purpose to loose from sin through the keys and his doing this by the word of absolution. The objectivity and contentual specificity of such a word strikes a person in just the right manner as to allow the Spirit working within to elicit *fides sacramenti*, a certainty of conviction in which the believer, the *iustus*, now lives.[41]

---

[39] WA 1, 322,33-323,9.

[40] »Iustus non ex operibus neque ex lege, sed ex fide vivit.« WA 1, 633,11. See, however, n. 21, above, in this Study.

[41] This formulation of the specific character of the word and faith in the theses *Pro veritate* follows O. Bayer, *Promissio*, 193f and 200, and W. Schwab, *Entwicklung und Gestalt der Sakramententheologie*, 365f.

Cajetan's criticism of »fides sacramenti«

At this point in Luther's development, one of his major theological critics entered upon the scene. Thomas de Vio, Cardinal Cajetan, was in Germany in late Summer 1518 as Legate of Pope Leo X to the Diet of the German Empire being held at Augsburg. Cajetan had just completed ten years as Dominican Master General and had already published three-quarters of his monumental commentary on the *Summa theologiae* of St. Thomas Aquinas. Cajetan's principal mission in Germany was to promote official German support, by new levies of taxation, for the defense of Europe against the Turks. Eventually, however, Cajetan was delegated by the Pope to examine Luther's doctrine, and this led to a fateful exchange in October over indulgences, sacramental absolution, and *fides sacramenti*.[42]

In mid-July 1518 Cajetan forwarded to Luther the canonical summons issued in Rome by Bishop Girolamo Ghinucci, in which Luther was notified that a preliminary investigation had ascertained that he was suspected of teaching heresy and so had to come to Rome to respond to charges. Luther then appealed to his Saxon overlord, Prince-Elector Frederick, asking him to intervene in Rome to have the case transferred to a German ecclesiastical tribunal. But before Frederick reacted to Luther's request, the case sharply escalated on the basis of a denunciation of Luther before Leo X by Emperor Maximilian. In mid-August Luther was declared a known and obstinate teacher of heresy and Cajetan was charged to bring about Luther's arrest and to deliver to him the Pope's condemnation of his heresy.

Frederick of Saxony and Cajetan conferred in Augsburg about September 1, with the Prince-Elector seeking a *commissio ad partes*, a transfer of the case to Germany, and the Papal Legate hoping to gain the help of Luther's overlord in bringing the accused to Augsburg. The outcome of this conference was an agreement that Luther would, at the order of Frederick, appear before Cajetan in Augsburg. But to gain this, Cajetan had to compromise, by conceding the important point that Luther was not to be detained after the hearing. To obtain the Saxon Elector's cooperation, and so have Luther come before him, Cajetan had to agree to forego carrying out one part of the charge given him by Leo X. When Cajetan reported this to Rome, an answer was swiftly given that reformulated his commission. He was now charged with examining the case himself, reviewing the evidence carefully, and, based on the exchange he would have with Luther, possibly terminating the case in Germany. In effect, Rome suspended the determination of Luther's guilt and made Cajetan the judge of his orthodoxy. Once Frederick learned in mid-September that Cajetan had been

---

[42] A narrative of Cajetan's career is in my *Cajetan Responds. A Reader in Reformation Controversy* (Washington 1978), 3-46. The story down to 1521, with special attention to the 1518 encounter with Luther, is told in my *Cajetan und die Anfänge der Reformation* (Münster 1983), with the main points also given in Study 7 of this collection.

delegated to hear Luther, he sent word to Wittenberg that Luther was to come to Augsburg.[43]

About September 20 Cajetan began preparing for his meeting with Luther by examining two of Luther's recently published works, the *Resolutiones* of the theses on indulgences and the *Sermo de poenitentia*. The outcome of the Cardinal's study was a set of fourteen treatises, completed between September 25 and October 17.[44] On the basis of this work, Cajetan charged Luther on October 12 with two departures from normative church teaching and insisted that Luther revoke or modify his published views. The two points concerned the underlying foundation of indulgences (the *thesaurus* of merits and the power of the keys) and the type of faith necessary for fruitful reception of sacramental absolution.[45] From the second and the sixth of Cajetan's Augsburg treatises, we can see how the Legate perceived Luther's teaching on faith in the sacrament and why he felt obliged to censure this doctrine.

In Cajetan's reading of Luther on absolution and faith, special attention fell on four points. Luther's *Resolutiones* diverged from the traditional understanding of a sacrament as an efficacious sign of grace, stressing instead the declaration in sacramental penance that grace has already been given.[46] The fruit or benefit given in virtue of the power of the keys, in Luther's account, is peace of conscience, consolation, and certitude that my sins are forgiven and that I am in grace.[47] Luther had cast doubt on the importance of contrition both in the *Resolutiones* and in the *Sermo*, urging instead faith in the absolution and in its declaration of grace.[48] Cajetan noted how Luther had repeatedly insisted that believing I am really forgiven before God is a necessary component of authentic

---

[43] This compressed account of the Luther-case rests on the documentation given below in »Roman Reactions to Luther: the First Year (1518),« Study 7 of this collection.

[44] The texts are now in Cajetan's *Opuscula omnia* (many editions; I use that of Lyon 1581, where the treatises are on pages 91a-118b). English translations of six treatises, with synopses of the other eight, are in my *Cajetan Responds*, 47-91. The most recent study of Cajetan's Augsburg treatises is B. Lohse's »Cajetan und Luther - Zur Begegnung von Thomismus und Reformation,« *Kerygma und Dogma* 32 (1986), 150-169. More detailed observations on this study will be made in notes 56 and 63, below, in this essay.

[45] Luther reported this in the *Acta Augustana*: WA 2, 7,28-38; LW 31, 261.

[46] *Opuscula*, 111a,43f and 111b,30-34, critically noting Luther's statements now at WA 1, 324,8-11, 542,9-11, 545,1-4, and 595,5-8.

[47] *Opuscula*, 111a,50-55 and 111b,33, from Luther's texts now at WA 1, 540,34-41, 541,20-24, 542,7-9.15f, and 595,13-15. The benefit, according to Cajetan, is forgiveness of sins and grace, not a consoling certitude.

[48] *Opuscula*, 109b,70-77, 110a,2-6.11-13, reacting critically to points stated in Luther's texts now at WA 1, 323,23f.32-37, 342,2-6.11-13, 594,37-595,5, and 595,21-23.

faith. If this conviction be lacking, one frustrates God's work of grace leading up to the sacrament and his communication of forgiveness in the sacrament.[49]

Cajetan's second and sixth treatises formulated a sharp attack on Luther's notion of *fides sacramenti* as an unwarranted innovation.[50] To show the impossibility of this kind of faith, Cajetan organized his exposition around the distinction between infused and acquired faith. The God-given supernatural virtue, poured out from on high, does not include a conviction about the effectiveness of a particular sacramental event, nor does a person have grounds from perceived fact and reasonable illation for the certainty Luther said was based on the word of Christ.[51] Cajetan marshalled counter-arguments to show that Luther's theory was contrary to the sense and doctrine of the Church. Luther was extending the scope of *fides* beyond its proper content, which is divine revelation, to include a particular and singular case of sacramental efficacy.[52] Luther was calling for people to have a certitude of the grace given them, which theologians agreed was not possible.[53] On the one hand, for Cajetan, one cannot be sure of having the traditionally required dispositions for fruitful sacramental reception; but then Luther was making sacramental efficacy contingent upon a new kind of disposition, namely, faith in the actual reception of grace.[54] Luther had spoken disparagingly about contrition, which in sound theology and in the practice of confessors was central in the forgiveness of sins and justification through sacramental penance.[55] Finally, Luther proposed a revived form of the

---

[49] *Opuscula*, 109b,74-77, 110a,2-4, 111a,54-57, 111b,41-47, noting Luther's words at WA 1, 323,35f, 324,11f, 543,20-27, and 595,15-18.

[50] Cajetan judged that Luther had invented a new kind of faith, in which an non-essential aspect of belief was made into the necessary disposition for receiving grace through sacramental forgiveness. Luther had to be censured for saying that for one who is in fact contrite the sacrament would occasion damnation, »nisi credat se absolvi« (see WA 1, 323,27, 542,16, 543,9.24). This minimalizes what the church teaches about the requirements for receiving the sacrament (confession, contrition, and satisfaction), while insisting that faith in the actual sacramental effect is necessary for salvation. »Hoc est novam construere ecclesiam.« *Opuscula* 111a,1-8; *Cajetan Responds*, 55.

[51] *Opuscula*, 110a,16-110b,9; *Cajetan Responds*, 50-52. The background for Cajetan's analysis in terms of *fides infusa/acquisita* is his commentary on *Summa theologiae*, I-II, 112,5 (published in 1514), where he made the same distinction and went on to deny an infused *certitudo scientiae* of one's own faith, while admitting a *certitudo fidei*, in line with Aquinas's response to the second objection in this article. Aquinas, *Opera omnia*, Leonine edition, 7, 327.

[52] *Opuscula*, 110a,23-29.48-54; *Cajetan Responds*, 50f.

[53] *Opuscula*, 110a,76f, 111b,38-41. *Cajetan Responds*, 52, 66.

[54] *Opuscula*, 110a,57-65, 111b,2-8.14f, 111a,1-8; *Cajetan Responds*, 51, 52, 55.

[55] *Opuscula*, 110b,52-54.72-79, 111b,41-54; *Cajetan Responds*, 53f, 54, 65f.

declaration theory of absolution, once held by Peter Lombard, but which the Council of Florence had excluded from Catholic doctrine.⁵⁶

Among the criteria Cajetan applied in his negative evaluation of Luther's *fides sacramenti*, there is first his lapidary judgment, in the *sed contra* of the second treatise, that Luther's view went against the *communis ecclesiae sensus*.⁵⁷ Then, in elaborating his rejection, Cajetan appealed to the »ordinary norm« that one cannot have complete certainty about being in the grace of God. Cajetan noted that such a residual doubt was woven deeply into the concrete life of the church, being implicitly expressed both in postcommunion prayers of the mass that the sacrament not lead to condemnation and in the »Lord, I am not worthy« recited before communion even by those who have confessed and been absolved.⁵⁸ Such prayers illustrate the lived conviction of good Christians who neither have nor aspire to Luther's faith in the actual presence of grace given them.

For Cajetan, the *sensus ecclesiae* also accentuates the importance of contrition, in contrast with Luther's refusal to make it central in conversion. Cajetan claimed that the sacramental rite of the universal church makes clear that contrition is *summe necessaria*, and this point of doctrine is reflected in the practice of confessors who look for contrition in a penitent, not for explicit belief in the grace-effect being actually given by the sacrament.⁵⁹

---

56 *Opuscula*, 111a,54f, 111b,30-33; *Cajetan Responds*, 63f, 65f. B. Lohse concluded that Cajetan did not really confront Luther's position on the certitude of faith (»Luther und Cajetan,« *Kerygma und Dogma* 32 [1986], 168). For this judgment to stand, one would have to take more account of Cajetan's contextualization of the issue in sacramental theology. Reading Luther's *Sermo de poenitentia* and 7th indulgence *resolutio*, Cajetan perceived Luther as specifying certitude as the main disposition in sacramental reception. It was not directly a discussion of the theological virtues of faith and hope. Given the content of the two writings before him, Cajetan was certainly justified in bringing to bear on the argument the existing principles used in the sacramental theology of penance.

57 *Opuscula* 109b,83. Cajetan had spoken of the *sensus ecclesiae* in his commentary on Aquinas's theology of faith in *ST* II-II, 1,1 and 2,3 (Aquinas, *Opera omnia*, Leonine ed., 8, 8-10, 30). Faith, specifically as assent, is principally based on God himself, who sheds light upon the mind to enable one to assent supernaturally to his revelation. But faith, specifically as the appropriation of definite truths, is grounded, outside cases of direct revelation by God to the prophets and apostles, on an infallible rule provided in this world by the Holy Spirit. This rule is »the sense and doctrine« of the Church. The Church transmits the objects of faith as realities to which it is vitally assimilated by its *sensus fidei*.

58 *Opuscula*, 110b,15-20; *Cajetan Responds*, 52.

59 *Opuscula*, 110b,53b.74-79; *Cajetan Responds*, 54. Cajetan would not be referring to contrition in the strict sense. Earlier in 1518, treating what is required for forgiveness, he said that the issue is not »de contritione in veritate, hoc est de dolore caritate informato,« since this is always uncertain. In confession, it suffices that the penitent have attrition with a »vellietas« of being without sin. *Quaestio* of March 4, 1518, »Quando quis obligetur ad contritionem peccatorum mortalium,« in Aquinas, *Opera omnia*, Leonine ed., 12, 376f.

However, Cajetan did not brand Luther's teaching heretical.[60] The Cardinal had found a newly invented notion; a view put forth without backing of Scripture, the canons, church tradition, or theologians; presumptuous teaching; and an error requiring correction. Luther's declaratory view of absolution giving peace diverged from the Council of Florence's teaching that the sacrament effects remission of sins.[61] Still, neither in the treatises nor in the oral exchanges of October 12-14 did the Legate accuse Luther of heresy.[62]

We all know that Luther did not accept Cajetan's censure, but maintained tenaciously that his positions both on the *thesaurus* of indulgences and on *fides sacramenti* were supported by Scripture texts more authoritative than the norms Cajetan had applied. Luther submitted a written defense in the third meeting between the two, but Cajetan found the text offering no reason to drop his demand for the two recantations. On October 14, the hearings ended in an ominous impasse. However, as few know, after the October 14 exchange, Cajetan reassessed his position and apparently noted a sense in which Luther's *fides sacramenti* could bear an orthodox construction.[63] Accordingly, the Legate sent word to Luther to assure him that he was not accusing him of heresy and was not about to declare him excommunicated. There will be a delay while a clarification on indulgences comes from Rome, but for the present Luther's teaching on *fides sacramenti* can remain an open question, since with a slight redefinition the notion can stand.[64] Whatever the reason for this remarkable reevaluation, Cajetan

---

[60] In contrast, Silvester Prierias's *Dialogus*, on the basis of which the canonical *processus* against Luther had developed in June-July 1518, contained several outright accusations that Luther's Ninety-Five Theses taught heresy. *Dokumente zur Causa Lutheri*, vol. 1, ed. P. Fabisch & E. Iserloh, Corpus Catholicorum 41 (Münster 1988), 61, 70, 75, 78, 104f (»non modo hereticus, verum heresiarcha es, quantum ego sentio«).

[61] On Luther innovating: *Opuscula*, 110a,17, 110b,80, 11a,1f.50. On lack of warrant: 110b,6-9. On presumption: 110b,52f, 111b, 55ff. On error needing correction: 110a,64, 111a,5, 111b,42. On Florence: 111b,30-34.

[62] This is not just a conclusion from silence on Cajetan's part. In 1519, in Koblenz, the Cardinal was shown a copy of the Froben edition of Luther's works (Basel, late 1518) which the Louvain theologians had gone over, noting in the margins the numerous heresies they had detected. Cajetan observed tartly that these texts may contain errors, but not heresies. Most of the points could with some conceptual refinement (*distinctiones*) have an orthodox sense. This is related in Martin Bucer's letter to Beatus Rhenanus, July 30, 1519. *Briefwechsel des Beatus Rhenanus*, ed. A. Horowitz & K. Hartfelder (Leipzig 1886), 166.

[63] In his preliminary treatise of September 26, Cajetan had used a distinction that would allow Luther's notion of *fides* to stand: »Et dicito, quod fides certissima est, & esse debet etiam de effectu sacramenti particulari in me, quantum ex parte sacramenti; sed ex parte mei suscipientis licitum est dubitare de illius effectu in me.« *Opuscula* 110b,12-15; *Cajetan Responds*, 52. Here Cajetan had come much closer to grasping and saving Luther's proposal that B. Lohse gave him credit for in his »Cajetan und Luther,« *Kerygma und Dogma* 32 (1986), 165-168.

[64] Cajetan's modification of his demand for recantation is narrated in a report prepared for the Prince-Elector, *Lenger und weitleuffiger Bericht der Handlung D. Mart. Luth. ergangen zu Augsburg*, published originally in *Der Neundte Teil der Bücher des Ehrwirdigen Herrn D. Martin Lutheri* (Wittenberg 1551), fol. 38r. K.-V. Selge called attention to this in a book-review in *Archiv für Reformationsgeschichte* 60 (1969), 273, and has more recently had the text printed in his article, »La chiesa in Lutero,« in M. Marcocchi, ed., *Martin Lutero* (Milan 1984), 31f, n. 30.

communicated to Luther a reduced charge, in an act of keen discretion and forthcoming theological diplomacy, which however has not been noted or acknowledged in most all biographies of Luther and histories of the outbreak of the Reformation.[65]

Luther defends »fides sacramenti«

Luther published his written defense against Cajetan's censures in the *Acta Augustana*, which he assembled in early November 1518 after his return from Augsburg to Wittenberg. The *Acta* incorporated the defensive brief submitted to Cajetan on October 14, with an incisive section on *fides sacramenti*.[66] Here Luther restated his thesis quite precisely, assembled a battery of biblical proofs, and in the course of his argument developed an emphasis which then entered the mainstream of his theology of justification.

Luther set out to defend himself against Cajetan's charge that his seventh *resolutio* had proposed a non-traditional and erroneous notion of the correct and necessary way to approach a sacrament and receive the grace it offers. Luther had asserted that one must believe that God is actually giving his grace and justifying or else one is rejecting and opposing God's work.[67]

Reversing the order of the theses *Pro veritate*, Luther stated at the beginning of his defense the *infallibilis veritas* of Romans 1:17, that righteousness and life before God takes the form of *fides*,[68] a faith that arises simultaneously with God's

---

[65] Luther responded to Cajetan's reduced demand in a letter of October 17, in which he came half-way on the issue of the *thesaurus*, which still remained a bone of contention after Cajetan withdrew his demand for a recantation on *fides sacramenti*. Luther agreed to forego public discussion of indulgences, providing his adversaries would maintain a similar moratorium on the question. WABr 1, 221,30-33.

[66] WA 2, 13,6-16,5; LW 13, 270-274.

[67] Luther gave two formulations of Cajetan's charge. (1) »Secundo obiecit, quod propositione vii. inter declarandum docueram, necessariam esse fidem accessuro ad sacramentum aut in iudicium accessurum. Hanc enim novam et erroneam doctrinam putari voluit [Cajetantus], sed potius incertum esse omnem accedentem, gratiam consequeretur nec ne ...« (WA 2, 7,35-38; LW 31, 261). (2) »Obiectio altera est, quod in conclusione mea vii. declaranda dixi, neminem iustificari posse nisi per fidem, sic scilicet, ut necesse sit, eum certa fide credere sese iustificari et nullo modo dubitare, quod gratiam consequatur. Si enim dubitat et incertus est, iam non iustificatur, sed evomit gratiam. Hanc theologiam novam videri putant et erroneam« (WA 2, 13,6-10; LW 31, 270).

[68] WA 2, 13,12-14; LW 31, 270. This use of Paul's declaration that the just person lives by faith was of capital importance in Ernst Bizer's argument for a 1518 dating of Luther's momentous insight into the meaning of Romans 1:17. *Fides ex auditu* (Neukirchen ³1966), 117-119. However, as Luther's argument progresses in the *Acta Augustana*, one sees that the faith by which one lives is somewhat different from what Bizer proposed. Luther attributes overriding importance to Christ's historical promise of the power to loose from sin. See n. 21, above, in this essay.

word of promise.[69] The precise point then is to establish that justifying faith is a *certissima fiducia* in God's promise and effective word in one's own case.[70]

Two biblical texts have a privileged role in Luther's defensive exposition, the classic definition in Hebrews 11:6 of that faith by which one draws near to God, and the solemn determination by Jesus in Matthew 16:19 that grounds sacramental absolution. The Hebrews text supported a simple illation giving actuality to its content:

> If we must believe in God who rewards, then by all means also in God who justifies and gives grace at the present moment (*gratiae largitorem in praesenti*). Without such belief, no reward will be given.[71]

If you take Christ's promise of the power of loosing with the ultimate seriousness his word calls for, then you must receive the sacramental absolution in utter assurance of the effect, namely, that you are »loosed in heaven«. Otherwise, you fall into a horrible sin and risk damnation.[72]

A central part of Luther's defense offered a series of nine New Testament texts and references in support of this *fides sacramenti*.[73] What Jesus sought in four cases of those for whom he worked miraculous cures was the firm conviction of his power to heal, and this anticipates how one is to attain ecclesial forgiveness. New Testament commendations of adamantly confident prayer show the attitude one must bring to a sacrament – quite the opposite of the weak faith Jesus lamented in his disciples. The heroes of faith from Abraham down to Mary and Elizabeth held fast to definite words of promise, and so it must be with everyone who receives a sacrament.

---

[69] »Fides autem est nihil aliud quam illud, quod Deus promittit aut dicit, credere, sicut Ro. 4. 'Credidit Abraham Deo et reputatum est ei ad iustitiam.' Ideo verbum et fides necessario simul sunt et sine verbo impossibile est esse fidem, ut Isa. 55. 'Verbum, quod egreditur de ore meo, non revertetur ad me vacuum' &c.« WA 2, 13,18-22; LW 31, 270f.

[70] »Nunc probandum est, quod accessuro ad sacramentum necessarium sit credere, sese gratiam consequi, et in hoc non dubitare, sed certissima fiducia confidere, alioquin in iudicium accedit.« WA 2, 13,23-25; LW 31, 271.

[71] WA 2, 13,29f.

[72] »Necessarium est sub periculo aeternae damnationis et peccati infidelitatis credere his verbis Christi: 'Quodcumque solveris super terram, solutum erit et in caelis.' Ideo si accedas ad sacramentum poenitentiae et non credideris firmiter tete absolvendum in caelo, in iudicium accedis et damnationem, quia non credis Christum vera dixisse..., quod est horrendum peccatum.« WA 2, 13,31-14,4; LW 31, 271. Outside such faith, one attains nothing from God (14,29), and the entire Church totters (14,34f). Luther further alluded to Paul's threat of judgment in 1 Cor 11:29 against doubt in the efficacy in absolution (15,27f). O. Bayer borrowed the term, »ein Satz heiliges Rechtes,« from biblical study of divinely given revelatory mandates, to underscore the absolutely binding character of what the word addresses to faith. *Promissio*, 188.

[73] WA 2, 14,13-15,27; LW 31, 272f.

Beyond Scripture, Augustine and Bernard of Clairvaux add their testimony, especially to fend off Cajetan's charge that Luther is innovating with an untraditional notion of faith.[74] Augustine's declaration that the sacrament is efficacious *non quia fit, sed quia creditur* fused smoothly into a probative cluster of warrants for believing in the absolution: Jesus' words when he absolved Mary Magdalen, »Your faith had saved you« (Luke 7:50); the *dictum commune* that not the sacrament but *fides sacramenti* justifies; and the immediate connection Paul makes in Rom 5:1 between justifying faith and peace of conscience. Bernard had stated that authentic faith arises with the *pro me* in laying hold of forgiveness, a work of the Holy Spirit's interior testimony actualizing the content of the outer word spoken in absolution.[75]

Thus, under the pressure of Cajetan's accusation, Luther marshalled his arguments in rebuttal and came to formulate with all desirable clarity his convictions on *fides sacramenti*. Unmistakably, Christian existence is to have its unifying and vital center here, as one holds to Christ's intent and promise as this finds actualization in particular sacramental words.

Central in Cajetan's critique had been the charge that Luther had gone wrong by including within the scope of faith the fruitfulness of a particular and singular sacramental event. Thereby, Cajetan occasioned a characteristic emphasis in Luther's response, as the Reformer repeatedly concluded that his biblical warrants exemplified not a general faith in God and his revelation, but instead a *fides specialis* that with full conviction lays hold of a particular gift, effect, or grace.[76] This is what Jesus sought all through the gospels and what was evinced by the biblical heroes of faith.

> If you page through the entire Gospel, you will find many other examples, all of which present not a general but a particular faith, and which speak with reference to some effect right at hand....
>
> Wherever we read in the old and new law about some important event, we read that it came about by faith - not by works nor by a general faith, but by a faith oriented to a here-and-now effect. Hence, Scripture recommends nothing else but faith.[77]

---

[74] WA 2, 15,28-16,3; LW 31, 274.

[75] Luther cited from Bernard's sermon on the Annunciation, as he had in his 1515-16 elucidation of Rom 8:16 (WA 56, 370; LW 25, 359f). See also n. 36, above, in this essay. This Spirit-inspired inner assurance of forgiveness illustrates Luther's assertion in the theses *Pro veritate*, »[sacerdos] vere peccata remittit et absolvit a culpa, et tamen hoc solius est spiritus intus operantis« (thesis 31; WA 1, 632,11). On Hebrews 11:6 Luther had contrasted naturally acquired faith, which lacks the personal reference, and faith elicited by grace, which lays hold of God's design for me personally (WA 57III, 233,1-12; LW 29, 171f).

[76] WA 2, 14,15f.25, 15,2f.7f.23f. The first occurrence states that the gospel is not speaking of a type of general faith (*de fide illa generali*), such as Cajetan had expounded orally on the basis of his treatise. O. Bayer, *Promissio*, 195, and W. Schwab, *Entwicklung und Gestalt*, 121, n. 32.

[77] »Si totum Evangelium percurras, invenies exempla alia multa, quae omnia non de fide generali, sed particulari, et quae ad effectum aliquem praesentem pertineat, dicuntur.« WA 2, 15,1-3; LW 31, 273. »Breviter quidquid illustre factum legimus in veteri et nova lege, fide factum

Thus, what has entered the history of doctrine as Luther's characteristic insistence on the *pro me* as decisive in authentic faith became an explicit and emphatic concern in the Reformer's defensive brief against Cajetan in Augsburg.[78] Such *fides specialis*, one must note, is formed by two influences impinging upon the believer: first, the objective content of the word of absolution, which derives its certainty from the solemn declaration of Matthew 16:19, and, second, the interior witness of the Holy Spirit in the heart to actualize just what the word had addressed to this individual.

Luther's exposition, as we know, did not impress Cajetan when the Cardinal received it on October 14. Luther reported that Cajetan reacted contemptuously to the written brief, but still agreed to send it on to Rome.[79] Cajetan himself wrote to Frederick the Wise on October 25 that Luther had defended his view of *fides sacramenti* with Scripture texts that were both irrelevant and wrongly understood.[80] A day or so after the written defense had been submitted, Luther's confrere Wenceslaus Link sought to convince Cajetan of the cogency of Luther's defensive treatise,[81] and this probably contributed to the modification of the Legate's demand for a public recantation by Luther. However, Cajetan did not really change his mind on the erroneous character of Luther's *fides sacramenti*, which he later contested in writings of 1521 and 1532.[82]

Luther, of course, was utterly convinced of the validity of his thesis on *fides sacramenti*. On October 12 he had been both pained and astounded to hear it called in question by the Pope's Legate.[83] A few hours after handing in his

---

esse legimus, non operibus nec fide generali, sed fide ad praesentem effectum destinata: inde nihil aliud in Scriptura quam fides commendatur.« WA 2, 15,21-24; LW 31, 273f.

[78] Luther had anticipated this emphasis in the thirty-eighth *resolutio* on indulgences (WA 1, 596,31-33; LW 31, 196) and in his scholia on Hebrews 9:24 and 11:6 (WA 57III, 215,16-216,6, 233,7-12; LW 29, 217f, 235). I present some representative later texts on the *pro me* in my introductory volume, *Luther and His Spiritual Legacy* (Wilmington, Del. 1983), 130-135.

[79] WA 2, 16,22f; LW 31, 275.

[80] WABr 1, 234,46-48.

[81] WABr 1, 234,58f.

[82] Translations of Cajetan's later arguments are in my *Cajetan Responds*, 147, 219-223. W. Schwab contends that both at Augsburg and later Cajetan mistakenly attacked a certitude resulting from human natural striving, a *fides acquisita*, which he alleged that Luther posited as the needed disposition for the sacrament, while Luther had certitude being the effect of the sacramental word itself. *Entwicklung und Gestalt*, 118-120, 124f. It is true that Cajetan's quick perusal of Luther's brief of October 14 did not lead him to see how Luther has *fides* resulting from the work of the Holy Spirit, as the citation of Bernard of Clairvaux indicates. This should make it clear that *fides acquisita* is not the issue. Still, Cajetan would contest the claim that the Spirit works just so in every fruitful reception of sacramental absolution. – My own differentiated assessment of Cajetan's response to Luther in 1518 is found in *Cajetan und die Anfänge der Reformation*, 109-112.

[83] WA 2, 8,18-20; LW 31, 262.

written defense, Luther wrote to his colleague Andreas Karlstadt that a revocation in contradiction of this point would make him (Luther) a heretic and separate him from the idea on which his own personal Christian faith rests.[84]

The certain and convinced laying hold of forgiveness and grace has become for Luther not only a matter of biblically based doctrine, but of personal existence before God. A few weeks later, in the published *Acta*, Luther minimalized the religious import of whole discussion and heated argument with Cajetan over the *thesaurus* of indulgences. But regarding faith in the sacrament, the *summa salutis* is at issue. Luther can only be distressed over the fact that the Pope's spokesman had both denied *fides verbi Christi* and tried as well to force another to deny it.[85]

Echoes of Luther's defense against Cajetan

The *fides specialis* on which Luther's *Acta Augustana* were so emphatic soon resonated in other works. As Luther expounded Psalm 4:4-10 in early 1519 in his *Operationes in Psalmos*, he lashed out against the detestable theologians who inculcate in people a residual uncertainty about their actually being in God's grace. Especially pernicious is the distinction they propose between the sacraments in themselves, with the effect being certain, and the sacraments in the case of a particular recipient, with the effect being uncertain. This, for Luther, is to open the floodgates to doubts about God and thereby to undermine the whole church.[86]

From this polemical retort to Cajetan's qualification of Christian certainty, Luther's comment on Psalm 4 passes on to a positive recommendation of a quite characteristic style of belief.

> Each one should take care to avoid any and all doubt that he has a God, that is, a Father, Creator, Savior, and bountiful giver of all good. Thus one may dwell uniquely in hope (Ps 4:10) and not be tossed about on the choppy waters of inconstancy.... For if you believe that the saints are secure and confident, why don't you also believe the same concerning yourself - you who desire to be like the saints, and who have received the same baptism, the same faith, the same Christ, and all else that they have. It would be utterly wicked to believe one thing of yourself and another thing of the saints or to teach that all must doubt just as you doubt.[87]

---

[84] WABr 1, 217,60-63. The personal assurance in this letter signals the definitive ending of the struggle begun a year before over the import of Matthew 16:19. See n. 18, above.

[85] WA 2, 18,14-17; LW 31, 278. The same view recurs in Luther's report to Frederick the Wise on the Augsburg meetings: WABr 1, 237,59f, 238,71-82. Six months later, Luther charged that Cajetan had at Augsburg attempted to undermine his Christian faith. WABr 1, 402,38f.

[86] AWA, 2, 213,30-214,10, 215,1-6 (WA 5, 124,20-30, 125,1-5). Cajetan had made this distinction in his preparatory critical treatise on *fides sacramenti*. See note 63, above, in this study. Luther repeated his attack on Cajetan's distinction in his explanation of the first thesis of the *Disputatio de fide infusa et acquisita*, of February 3, 1520 (WA 6, 88,23-29).

[87] »Unusquisque id curare debet, ut nullo modo dubitet se habere Deum, hoc est, patrem, creatorem, salvatorem et omnium bonorum largitorem, ut possit 'singulariter et in spe habitare' et non sicut mare inconstantissimum fervere.... Si enim de sanctis id credis, quod sint securi et

In another contemporary passage, near the beginning of his 1519 commentary on Galatians, Luther broadened the scope of *fides specialis* from the particular moment of receiving a sacrament to make it central in one's faith in Christ's redemptive work as such. Christ gave himself for our sins (Gal 1:4), and so no one should harbor any doubt about actually being included among those who are said, by the phrase »our sins,« to be the beneficiaries of Christ's sacrifice of himself.

> It will avail you nothing to believe that Christ was delivered for the sins of the other saints, while doubting it was for your sins.... You must hold with adamant trust that he was delivered for your sins as well and that you are included. This faith justifies you and will cause Christ to dwell, live, and reign in you. This faith is the testimony the Spirit gives to our own spirit that we are children of God [Rom 8:16].... What the scholastic theologians hold is ridiculous, namely, that one is uncertain whether he is among the saved or not. Beware of ever being uncertain. You can be certain that of yourself you are lost; strive also to be certain and firm in your faith in Christ delivered for your sins.[88]

In these last texts, two main components stand out. On the one hand, Luther makes questionable insinuations about the pastoral impact of the Scholastic doctrine that divine grace transcends our faculties of creaturely knowledge. But there is, on the other hand, a positive teaching, namely, that *fides* entails a living and personal realization that God's redemptive intention actually bears on one's life. Luther urged every Christian believer to lay hold of the truth expressed by Paul that God, who is bountiful in giving all good, sent his Son »who loved me and gave himself for me« (Gal 2:20).

In a broader historical perspective, this doctrine of *fides specialis* is one articulation of a religious experience which Luther shared to a degree with a number of his contemporaries. One thinks of the personal turning-points

---

fidentes, cur non etiam de teipso idem credis, qui sanctorum similis esse cupis, qui idem baptisma, eandem fidem, eundem Christum et omnia eadem accepisti? Immo impiissime credis aliud de te et aliud de sanctis, qui doces oportere omnes dubitare, sicut tu dubitas.« AWA 2, 214,11-19 (WA 5, 124,31-39). This passage plays a key role in Horst Beintker's study of Luther's teaching in the *Operationes* on how the believer deals with trials and temptation, *Die Überwindung der Anfechtung bei Luther* (Berlin 1954), 126-131.

[88] »Nihil enim tibi profuerit credere, Christum esse pro peccatis sanctorum aliorum traditum, pro tuis autem dubitare. Nam hoc et impii et demones credunt. Verum constanti fiducia praesumendum est tibi, quod et pro tuis et unus sis illorum, pro quorum peccatis ipse traditus est. Haec fides te iustificat, Christum in te habitare, vivere et regnare faciet. Haec est testimonium spiritus, quod reddit spiritui nostro, quod sumus filii Dei... Fabulae ergo sunt opinatorum Scholasticorum, hominem esse incertum, in statu salutis esse necne. Cave tu, ne aliquando sis incertus, sed certus, quod in teipso perditus: laborandum autem, ut certus et solidus sis in fide Christi pro peccatis tuis traditi.« WA 2, 458,20-32 (my own translation). Precisely when Luther composed this passage is uncertain. He had given his manuscript on Galatians to the printer on January 1, 1519, but some time later he took it back for revision, which was finished in mid-April of the same year. Later in 1519 Luther made clear how absolution is God's own word of forgiveness, a word which leaves no room for doubt regarding its effectiveness. Sermon of October 30, 1519; WA 9, 415,23-29.

marking the lives of men like Gasparo Contarini of Venice, Erasmus of Rotterdam, Ulrich Zwingli, and Ignatius Loyola. Jacques Pollet has pointed out the parallels and described this as a spiritual »Copernican revolution,« by which a number of early-sixteenth-century Christians changed from seeing God primarily as the object of human devotional action, that is, of action exerting influence on God to draw down his gifts, to seeing God instead as the active source of good who goes ahead of our human effort. God, in Christ and in the Spirit, grants prevenient gifts which then call for a range of responses.[89]

In late 1518 and early 1519 Luther gave special articulation to his particular discovery of the God of prevenient grace, by insisting on the personal reference, the *pro me*, in faith. This *fides specialis* is a receptive faith that lays hold of the work of Christ with full assurance, especially as that work is made actual through the words one hears in the ecclesial sacraments.

Conclusions

This presentation of Luther's teaching on faith and God's word has given special attention to two 1518 expositions of his position, the theses *Pro veritate inquirenda* and the *Acta Augustana*. Because both of these texts are methodical and concise, a caveat seems in order, lest a false impression be given. The well-structured presentations of our two main documents do not give us the whole Luther. As Joseph Lortz observed in his 1969 treatment of Luther's sacramental thinking, Luther's discourse is fluid, shifting, at times careless, and often prolix.[90] The study of Luther must deal with thought that is on-the-move. The converse of this is, of course, the explosive force of much of Luther's prose and the engaging charm of many of his presentations of Christian existence in and under the dispensation of God's mercy. This is especially evident in four popular treatises of late 1519 in which Luther gave instruction aiming to foster faith in people finding themselves in the contexts of preparing for death and/or receiving absolution, baptism, and Holy Communion.[91] Thus, while Luther can expound doctrine with rigorous order, as in the two works of 1518, in other works on the same topics he keeps escaping the net of our analyses as we seek to mark off clear definitions, key causal factors, exact linkages of premise and consequence, and the ordered steps of beginning and completing a personal religious exercise.

---

[89] Jacques Pollet, *Huldrych Zwingli et la Réforme en Suisse* (Paris 1963), 44f.

[90] »Sacramentales Denken,« *Lutherjahrbuch* 36 (1969), 9f; *Erneuerung und Einheit*, 646f. Lortz also made the pertinent observation that Luther did not always attribute the same content to the term *fides* (p. 13; p. 650).

[91] Texts: WA 2, 685-697, 714-785 (LW 35, 3-11 and 42, 99-115). Ursula Stock studied these works in exhaustive detail in *Die Bedeutung der Sakramente in Luthers Sermonen von 1519* (Leiden 1982). I reviewed Stock's work in *Theological Studies* 44 (1983), 717-719. In this collection, Study 8, below, treats the popular writings that Luther brought out in the service of pastoral renewal.

Amid Luther's eruptive abundance, we have nonetheless seen a clear line of development in 1518. His notion of *fides* moved from its earlier, predominantly penitential, form through the initial sacramental emphasis in which it lays hold of peace and assurance. Then it became the lived form of righteousness itself as it appropriates a definite sacramental word of grace and forgiveness. From this point, Luther came to stress against Cajetan the personal actualization of the sacramental gift to me in *fides specialis de effectu praesenti*. This existential religious attitude then became in Luther's instruction what permeates any authentic acceptance of God's mercy in Christ.

I will add five specific observations which formulate provisionally the meaning and value of the teaching studied here.

First, we can characterize the main theological genre in which Luther's *fides sacramenti* emerged as an insistent motif of his teaching. In the wake of the aborted academic controversy over indulgences, Luther turned to pastoral sacramental instruction. In this area he quickly achieved a creative formulation – aiming at pastoral enrichment – of how grace is mediated through the rites instituted by Christ.

One aspect of Luther's creativity lay in his repeated emphasis on the sacramental gifts of assurance, consolation, and peace of heart. This fruit comes from the common rites of the church, especially absolution, in their impact on the lived religiosity of believers. Luther sought especially to break through any emphasis on a recurrent cycle of acts to be performed, such as the steps of self-examination, sorrow for sin, integral confession, and assigned penances (the »parts« of sacramental confession), where each step could give rise to doubt about adequately fulfilling the requirement. Luther shifted attention from the penitent's actions to what absolution expresses and means to convey. Looming in the background is an insistence on the certainty of Christ the Savior's promise.[92] Christ's declaration, »Whatever you loose on earth shall be loosed in heaven,« is to be believed, and so the absolution spoken in virtue of this promise is to be believed. This is the core conviction around which Luther constructed his pastoral instruction.

Another side of Luther's creativity was his introduction into popular sacramental teaching of a cluster of Pauline themes. One lays hold of absolution with *fides*, not meriting forgiveness by works. Reconciliation with God is God's own gift, given *gratis*, resting on the promise, not on performance conformed to the law. Joseph Lortz once spoke of Luther's sacramental theology as being a brilliant exemplification of his fundamental doctrine of justification by faith alone as God brings to reality in human hearts what Christ won by his passion, death, and resurrection.[93] The main thrust of this instruction was not to inculcate strenuous rumination in search of consolation, not to deflect faith back on the

---

[92] »Certa est Christi salvatoris promissio.« Theses *Pro veritate*, no. 15; WA 1, 631,18.
[93] »Sacramentales Denken,« *Lutherjahrbuch* 36 (1969), 12; *Erneuerung und Einheit*, 649.

6. *Fides sacramenti* in 1518

subject, but to help people set their lives on a new basis, namely, the word of merciful forgiveness spoken in the church in virtue of Christ's mandate and commission.[94]

Second, the theme of »reflexive faith« merits more detailed consideration, since it is at times posited by Catholic critics as one of Luther's significant departures from sound tradition.[95] But others have called in question whether Luther actually taught such a reflexive faith, because of his emphasis on response to the word and going out of oneself to live from the actuality of Christ.[96] We find good grounds for such questioning.

Clearly, Luther did in 1518 link *credere* with reflexive pronouns, as in *credit se consequi gratiam*[97] and in *si credideris te accipere, habes*.[98] At one time he even said that the person who is baptized must believe that he had rightly believed and approached the sacrament.[99] However, these passages result from a thought that is developing under the impact of a promise of Christ like Matthew 16:19, which extends its influence to the believing Christian by sacramental absolution. The reflexive clauses do not denote the principal movement of faith, but a consequent stage in which Christ's gift has resulted in a special kind of personal actualization. Clearly, Luther's reflexive or reduplicative sentences are inelegant in themselves, and misleading when taken alone. They mislead most when faith in my actual attainment of grace, that is, that grace has attained residence in my heart, is made an isolated condition of justification. But Luther did not so isolate these personalizing accounts. The disputation *Pro veritate* made it clear that forgiveness

---

[94] This is to take issue with the basic thesis of Paul Hacker's *Das Ich im Glauben* (Graz 1966), translated as *The Ego in Faith. Martin Luther and the Origin of Anthropocentric Religion* (Chicago 1970).

[95] E. Iserloh, in *Handbuch der Kirchengeschichte*, ed. H. Jedin, 4, *Reformation, Katholische Reform und Gegenreformation* (Freiburg 1967), 58f; in translation in *History of the Church*, 5, 56f. Also in »Luther und die Kirchenspaltung,« in H.F. Geisser et al., *Weder Ketzer noch Heiliger. Luthers Bedeutung für das ökumenischen Dialog* (Regensburg 1982), 80f, and under the same title in *Katechetische Blätter* 108 (1983), 32f.

[96] W. Joest, *Ontologie der Person bei Luther* (Göttingen 1967), 233-320, 355-394. My review-article on Joest is »Luther on the Person before God,« *Theological Studies* 30 (1969), 289-311. More directly in contestation of Paul Hacker's view of reflexive faith in Luther is O. Hof, »Luthers Unterscheidung zwischen dem Glauben und der Reflexion auf den Glauben,« *Kerygma und Dogma* 18 (1972), 294-324.

[97] Scholion on Heb 5:1; WA 57III, 169,25. Note also the texts we cited above in notes 27, 70, and 72.

[98] *Resolutio* of the seventh thesis on indulgences; WA 1, 543,8. Also 540,40 (»ne dubitet sibi remissa peccata sua«) and 542,16 (»certus fit, se esse remissum«). Also, in the *Sermo de poenitentia*, WA 1, 323,27.

[99] »Baptisatum oportet etiam credere, se recte credidisse et accesisse.« Seventh *resolutio*, WA 1, 542,12f.

rests on (*innitur*) a faith that principally lays hold of Christ's mandate to loose from sin (thesis 9). *What* is believed is the absolution spoken in virtue of this dominical mandate, and so this faith is also *fides Christi* (thesis 33).

There are formulations from this time in which Luther makes *fides* a predisposition for receiving a sacrament, and thus separates it somewhat from the sacramental word spoken *in* the sacrament. But in some of these passages faith is not specified by a content, and so it cannot be said to be reflexive or not reflexive.[100] Other passages on this predisposing faith refer to preparation for Holy Communion and teach a certain belief that one will receive grace from Christ as bread of life. But these latter passages include explicit citation of a promise of Christ upon which to base such certain expectation, for example, the promise found in Matthew 11:28, »Come to me, all you who labor and are heavy burdened and I will give you rest.«[101] This faith may include a movement of reflexive self-awareness, but its primary object is the divine word of promise, which a person lays hold of as concerning himself as he approaches a particular application of Christ's mercy in the sacrament. W. Joest remarked accurately how for Luther the believer is one fastened on another in complete dependence. This other is Christ, who becomes operatively present through his word.[102]

Third, the value of Luther's instruction on *fides* in 1518 is enhanced by his recurrent assertion that this blessed conviction is elicited or given by God himself. It is not a decision of the autonomous subject nor the product of mental or psychic effort. Luther's 1518 instruction on faith stood in continuity with his anti-nominalist views and arguments of 1515-17. Just as he had argued incisively against the salvific efficacy of »doing what lies in yourself« (*facere quod in se est*) and against the notion of congruously meriting grace by doing moral good by one's natural abilities (*ex puris naturalibus*), so here he drew a clear line against faith being a testimony arising by simply wanting to have such an outlook (*quod nobis ex nobis est*).[103] Correlative with Christ's historic mandate to loose from sins and his promise to refresh the burdened is the Spirit's work of eliciting peace and loving trust. The faith at issue is a grace, an infused gift, the Spirit's testimony; it is the work of God in the heart.

Fourth, although it is obvious that Luther's development on *fides* was notably discontinuous with scholastic theologies of sacramental forgiveness, grace, and justification – and his encounter with Cajetan made this quite clear – still, serious attention should be given to Luther's claim that he had backing in the

---

[100] WA 1, 286,15-18, 544,37-41.

[101] On approaching Communion: Scholion on Heb 5:1 (WA 57III, 170,3-171,8), *Sermo de digna praeparatione* (WA 1, 331,5-25), and *Instructio pro confessione peccatorum* (WA 1, 264,9-19). Matthew 11:28 is cited at WA 57III, 171,6; WA 1, 331,14, and 264,16.

[102] *Ontologie der Person*, 250 and 386-391.

[103] WA 57III, 169,21f. See also the texts given in notes 36 and 75, above, in this Study.

tradition for his notion of *fides sacramenti*. Three issues call for investigation, both to test Luther's claim and to gain a fuller historical understanding of his theses on the effect of believing the absolution.

(1) One should clarify the history of the theological axiom on faith in the sacrament (*Non sacramentum, sed fides sacramenti iustificat*) that Luther repeatedly cited in his own support in 1518.[104] However the saying may have been used and understood, the adjectives Luther used when he cited it do suggest that *fides sacramenti*, in some form at least, was known and discussed in the late-medieval theological community.

(2) A similar project for research should seek to clarify the import of the *pro me* in St. Bernard of Clairvaux's accounts of the believer's relation to God. More than once, historians have commented that Luther and Bernard are kindred spirits as they teach Christians the ways of faith.[105] This similarity needs to be tested at the precise point on which Luther claimed Bernard's backing in the *Acta Augustana* as he was fighting off Cajetan's charge of theological innovation.

(3) Finally, there is the issue of »trusting in your contrition« on the eve of the Reformation. Such trust, according to Luther (*Sermo de poenitentia*, theses *Pro veritate*), must stop. Those who inculcate it as the way to approach absolution were demeaning the sacrament and casting people into a morass of doubt. But just what were the theologians and spiritual guides saying around 1500 concerning the proper attitude for one who is approaching confession?

The late-medieval confessors' handbooks recently studied by Thomas N. Tentler do not seem to have treated directly the issue of personal trust and one's basis for assurance. Tentler does speak of a general tendency in these works to exalt the power of the keys.[106] This suggests a practice quite different from what Luther attacked. A good example of this exaltation of the keys and absolution is found in the work of Johann von Paltz, the Augustinian pastoral theologian who was publishing in the first decade of the sixteenth century. Paltz taught that the sacraments are so powerful that only a minimal disposition is required for their fruitful reception. Sacramental absolution from sin supplements, by virtue of the passion of Christ, the flawed repentance with which people often come to confession. Thus one does not need to be contrite and loving, for the sacrament transforms one's imperfect sorrow or attrition into contrition. In fact, Paltz was critical of there being any reference to contrition in the formulaic expressions by

---

104 WA 57III, 170,1 (Luther qualifies the axiom as *vulgatissimum et probatissimum*); WA 1, 286,18 (*dictum illud communissimum*), 324,15, 544,33, 631,7; WA 2, 15,32, 715,34.

105 I did this in *Man Yearning for Grace*, p. 267f, in a passage that generalized on Luther's early spiritual teaching and with a sense of following numerous observations made by Joseph Lortz. Also, E. Kleinaidam gives a systematic exposition of the affinities between Bernard and Luther in »Ursprung und Gegenstand der Theologie bei Bernard von Clairvaux und Martin Luther,« in *Dienst der Vermittlung*, ed. Wilhelm Ernst et al. (Leipzig 1977), 221-247.

106 *Sin and Confession on the Eve of the Reformation* (Princeton 1977), 293.

which priests granted absolution.[107] Paltz was thus teaching the opposite of the theology of self-reliance Luther attacked. For Paltz, if one is to build on anything, it is not oneself or one's efforts but instead the efficacy of absolution itself.

Thus, a number of issues call for further study in order to deepen our understanding of the doctrinal and pastoral situation in which Luther undertook his project of explaining sacraments and faith in 1518. We are not yet fully informed about the factors preparing the audience that welcomed Luther's instructions on *fides sacramenti* and *fides specialis*.

Fifth and finally, what should we say about Cajetan's incisive analysis and critique of Luther's new theology of faith? Basically, we conclude that there was much more to Luther's idea than the Dominican cardinal perceived as he studied Luther's two works in Augsburg. And Cajetan himself appears to have sensed this fact shortly after his third meeting with Luther.

Luther insisted that *fides sacramenti* is the form of the Christian's encounter with God's grace in one of the principal ways the Savior decided and determined to convey it. Luther, schooled in the thought of Ockham, gave far greater weight to positive historical mandates than did the Thomist Cajetan. Luther asserts that God has bound himself, and in the rites of the church he is faithful to his promises. Absolution, above all else, has an objective ground in Christ's institution.[108] But it also has a dimension of obligation as part of its full reality for Luther – an aspect not easily conceivable for a Thomist. Luther's Pauline thinking enters the picture as he specifies that the required response to such a word is confident submission, *fides*, to just what the word means to effect or convey. One is bound to believe this, even though the word is not one of law. Rather, in just this way ordinary people encounter the Gospel, which is »the power of God for salvation to every one who believes« (Rom 1:16).

The core of one's response is the realization in *fides specialis* that God is gracious *to me*. But this is not alien to the Catholic tradition, at least according to the precise wording of the Council of Trent. In 1547 Trent spoke of one of the dispositions people should have for justification as confident trust »that because of Christ God will be merciful *to themselves*.«[109] Luther's *fides* is not predominantly deflected back on the subject and on a subjective condition, but is an amazed rush of certainty that God's mercy has broken into my life. It is the acceptance, firm and unhesitating, of God's word of acquittal, given *gratis* but spoken on God's authority. A different kind of theology is unfolding here than

---

[107] Paltz, *Coelifodina*, 258-262, 263, 361f. Jean Gerson had also warned against absolution formulae which make reference to contrition (Tentler, *Sin and Confession*, 288f).

[108] This has been recently set forth by Jos E. Vercruysse in »Word and Sacrament in Luther's Theology,« in *Luther et la Réforme allemande dans une perspective oecuménique* (Chambésy-Geneva 1983), 197-211.

[109] »Fidentes Deum *sibi* propter Christum propitium fore.« *Decree on Justification*, ch. 6; DS 1526 (emphasis added).

that to which a scholastic thinker would be accustomed, and Cajetan did find it alien and peculiar. It is undoubtedly a theology-for-piety, and aims above all at being pastorally fruitful and directly helpful in living one's faith. This theology is embedded in experiences of guilt, fear, doubt, and joyful release. Its language is predominantly biblical. It wants to be effective in shaping religion actually lived out.

For all these reasons, Luther's 1518 theology of faith deserves respectful recognition. Of course, the idea of *fides specialis* brings certain dangers in its train, as do most all theological and religious proposals. If one detaches such *fides* from the work of the Holy Spirit working within to elicit whole-hearted trust, then it becomes self-achieved and Pelagian. If one detaches such *fides* from the mandates of Christ and the gracious words of address that are its grounds, then it becomes subjectivistic. A later Protestantism, alienated from the sacraments, may have interpreted Luther's *sola fide* in a subjectivistic manner, but in 1518 it is clear enough that Luther did not detach and isolate *fides* in such a way that he fell into subjectivism in his theology and pastoral instruction.

7

ROMAN REACTIONS TO LUTHER:
THE FIRST YEAR, 1518

By early January 1518, Roman officials had heard about Martin Luther, Augustinian Hermit and professor of Scripture at the Electoral Saxon university in Wittenberg. Albrecht of Brandenburg, Archbishop of Mainz and Magdeburg and Prince-Elector of the Empire, had sent to Rome Luther's Ninety-Five Theses and *Tractatus de indulgentiis*.[1] The Archbishop had received these materials in December 1517, forwarded to him from his diocesan curia for Magdeburg. In acknowledging their receipt, Albrecht described them as »the treatise and conclusion about the holy *negotium* of indulgences and about our subcommissioners, written by an impudent monk in Wittenberg.«[2] Luther's submitted works amounted to an acutely argued appeal for the reform of current preaching on indulgences, such as that being promoted by Johann Tetzel, O.P., one of Albrecht's subcommissioners for the St. Peter's indulgence.[3]

Luther's ideas of Christian penance struck Archbishop Albrecht and his council as novel and as likely to obstruct effective indulgence-preaching. Luther also seemed to be challenging current views of papal authority regarding grants of indulgences. Principally, however, Luther argued that indulgences should have only a peripheral place in the Christian life of penance, purification from sin, and growth under the work of God's healing grace.

---

[1] On the events and non-events of Luther's intervention regarding indulgences on October 31, 1517, see the opening pages of Study 5, above, in this collection. Luther's little known *Tractatus* is now given in WABr 12, 5-9; an English translation with commentary is a substantial part of Study 5, above.

[2] The letter is now given in *Dokumente zur Causa Lutheri*, 1, *Das Gutachten des Prierias und weitere Schriften gegen Luthers Ablaßthesen (1517-1518)*, eds. P. Fabisch and E. Iserloh (Münster 1988), 305-309.

[3] At the time, Luther was not isolated in his protest. On January 9, 1518, the Sorbonne resolved to inform the king and bishops of France about abuses due to indulgence preachers: »plerique falsa, ridiculosa, scandalosa et periculosa in fide et moribus predicant ad extorquendas pecunias a pauperibus.« A. Clerval, *Registre des procès-verbaux de la Faculté de Théologie de Paris*, vol. 1 (Paris 1917), 232. On May 6, 1518, the Parisian theologians formally censured a proposition claiming automatic effectiveness for indulgence grants gained for the deceased. Ibid., 237f. This action is described in the context of the Faculty's oversight of doctrine in France and beyond by James K. Farge, *Orthodoxy and Reform in Early Reformation France* (Leiden 1985), 164f.

The archbishop had, on December 1, 1517, asked the theologians and canonists of the University of Mainz to deliver a report on the orthodoxy of Luther's theses and treatise. The Mainz professors noted Luther's statements about papal authority, and so had told Albrecht, in a letter of December 17, that Luther's ideas were contrary to common theological opinion. Still, the Mainz faculty had to refrain from formally judging and condemning Luther, since the canon *Nemini* prohibited disputes on papal authority.[4] The professors advised the Archbishop to send the papers submitted by Luther to Rome for evaluation.[5]

Actually, while waiting for the report from the Mainz professors, Albrecht had gone over the matter with his advisors at his residence at Aschaffenburg, and had concluded that Luther's ideas constituted a threat against the successful preaching of the St. Peter's indulgence in his domains. This would seriously undermine the archbishop's plan, approved by the Roman curia, to apply half the income from this indulgence toward paying off the sizable loan he had taken from the Fugger Bank in order to pay the pallium-fee for his Mainz archbishopric and the cost of the dispensation he had gained in 1514 permitting him to hold three episcopal sees simultaneously.[6] Albrecht decided that a Roman intervention was urgently needed. Hence, he had sent the Luther materials to Rome for examination, even before he received the evasive answer of the Mainz professors.[7] In Rome, consequently, news about Luther's intervention would be on hand by early January, 1518, through the request of the Archbishop of Mainz for papal action to halt Luther's protests about indulgence preaching.

Response by Way of Internal Augustinian Discipline

In Rome, the Luther materials were examined in January 1518, probably by Silvester Prierias, O.P., the *Magister sacri palatii*, whose responsibilities as theologian of the papal court included theological censorship and the answering of doctrinal questions raised in the immediate ambience of the Pope.[8] However,

---

[4] *Decretum Gratiani*, Secunda Pars, Causa XVII, Quaestio IV, c. 30; ed. E. Friedberg, vol. 1 (Leipzig 1879), 823.

[5] The response of the Mainz professors is now given in *Dokumente zur Causa Lutheri*, 1, 301-303. It has been studied also by W. Borth, *Die Luthersache* (Lübeck and Hamburg 1970), 31f.

[6] *Dokumente zur Causa Lutheri*, 1, 203-209. Albrecht was also episcopal administrator of Halberstadt.

[7] Reported in Albrecht's letter to his Magdeburg officials, given in *Dokumente zur Causa Lutheri*, 1, 305-307.

[8] Silvestro Mazzolini was commonly known as Prierias from his birthplace, Priero, near Cuneo in Liguria. He had published his encyclopedic moral and canonistic manual, the *Summa summarum* (=*Summa silvestrina*), in 1514. On his duties in Rome after the appointment of late 1515, see R. Naz, »Maître du sacré-palais,« *Dictionnaire de droit canonique*, vol. 6 (1957), 711f.

six months were to elapse before Prierias raised his voice by publishing a critique alleging that Luther's Ninety-Five Theses contained error and heresy.

The result of the first Roman examination of Luther's writings was a letter of February 3, 1518, in which Pope Leo X called upon the Vicar General of the Augustinian Hermits, Gabriele della Volta of Venice, to take measures to silence the German priest of his order, Martin Luther, who was disseminating *novas res ... nova dogmata* among the faithful.[9] Thus the first Roman reaction to Luther initiated a disciplinary effort within his order, with this constituting the response to the complaint of the archbishop to whom Luther had directed his intervention of October 31, 1517. And the Augustinians were given time, as long as four months, to resolve the issue internally by making Luther desist from attacks on the St. Peter's indulgence and withdraw or recant his positions diverging from commonly accepted views of papal authority.

In February and March 1518, Luther was working industriously toward a further clarification of his understanding of indulgences and penance, through a comprehensive exposition of each of the ninety-five theses that he had formulated the previous October. A factor very much on Luther's mind in these days was the campaign being waged against him by Johann Tetzel and Tetzel's Dominican confreres in Germany. Tetzel had defended a series of theses attacking Luther at a regional chapter of the Dominicans held at Frankfurt an der Oder on January 20, 1518. And in his *Resolutiones* on the ninety-five theses Luther responded to several of Tetzel's key points, taking up, for instance, the heavily fraught concept of *iustitia divina* and its relationship to penitential satisfaction and to the remission of penitential obligations.[10] When copies of the Wimpina-Tetzel theses arrived in Wittenberg in mid-March, a gang of students snatched them away from the book-peddler and consigned them to a bonfire. One copy at least survived the flames and Luther answered it with a vernacular treatise, *Eyn Sermon von dem Ablass und Gnade*, which was circulating in print in early April 1518 among an increasingly interested lay audience.

In addition to Tetzel's academic disputing, Luther became aware of a campaign against him by Dominican preachers who, from numerous pulpits, were calling him a heretic and charging him with departures from traditional doctrine. Some even assured their hearers that Luther's heterodoxy would bring him down in disgrace and even to death at the stake.[11] This Dominican activity aiming to

---

[9] Text published by Leo X's Latin Secretary, Pietro Bembo, *Epistolarum ... nomine Leonis X. P.M. scriptarum Libri XVI* (Strassburg 1611), 379f.

[10] Tetzel's theses, actually composed by Konrad Wimpina, O.P., of the Frankfurt theology faculty, are given in *Dokumente zur Causa Lutheri*, 1, 321-337. Luther's responses are in WA 1, 532,33-533,33, 536,17-537,27 (with five references to *iustitia divina*), and 544,11-545,8; LW 31, 87f, 93-95, 105-107. Two further works of Tetzel against Luther are given in *Dokumente zur Causa Lutheri*, 1, 337-375, and have been studied by Scott Hendrix, *Luther and the Papacy* (Philadelphia 1981), 35-37.

[11] Reported in Luther's letter to Johann Lang, March 21, 1518. WABr 1, 154,11. Also mentioned in letters of February 15 (146, 69) and May 9 (169,15).

refute and discredit Luther sowed an animosity in his mind that prejudiced his literary exchange with Prierias in mid-1518 and his face-to-face interaction with Cardinal Cajetan later in the year at Augsburg. Luther came to blame the Dominicans for denouncing him in Rome. However, Johann Tetzel, at least, stoutly denied that had any role in a denunciation of Luther before Roman authorities.[12]

As the first stages of disciplinary action were taking shape in the spring of 1518, Luther showed a clear readiness to acknowledge the right of ecclesiastical authorities to judge the doctrines which were the fruit of his study and writing. Luther held back the text of his *Resolutiones* from the printer until he received an *imprimi potest* from his ordinary, Bishop Hieronymus Schultze of Brandenburg.[13] In late May, Luther composed a covering letter to Pope Leo X for printing with the *Resolutiones* in which he expressed a reverent acknowledgment of church authority and submissively asked the Pope to judge the content of his teaching: »... approve or condemn as seems fitting; I will acknowledge your word as the word of Christ who presides and speaks in you.«[14] Given such an attitude on Luther's part, it is all the more imperative to watch both the Roman reactions to him and his subsequent responses under pressure, in order to determine what it was that occasioned his later swing from docility to defiance of Roman censures of his teaching.

In March 1518 Luther was informed by his regional Augustinian superior, Johann von Staupitz, that disciplinary action against him had been ordered by Vicar General della Volta.[15] Luther was apparently told that he was to withdraw his theses and to forgo further public statements on indulgences. Furthermore, Luther was to attend the chapter of the German Observant Augustinians scheduled for late April in Heidelberg, where he was either to correct his errors concerning church authority or give an account of the bases of his positions. If this was not done satisfactorily in Heidelberg, he was to go to Rome where he could expect to face charges in a formal *processus*.[16]

---

[12] Letter of December 31, 1518, to Karl von Miltitz; cited in N. Paulus, *Johann Tetzel der Ablassprediger* (Mainz 1899), 48.

[13] Luther had sent the bishop the *Resolutiones* in manuscript February 13, 1518 (WABr 1, 138-140). In March the bishop asked Luther to hold off publication (162,10-23), but about April 1 he gave permission for their printing (164, Letter no. 70).

[14] WA 1, 529,24.

[15] In a later letter, on August 25, 1518, della Volta related how he had earlier admonished Luther and ordered him to come to Rome either to justify or recant his views that detracted from papal and church authority. Text given by T. Kolde, »Luther und sein Ordensgeneral in Rom,« *Zeitschrift für Kirchengeschichte* 2 (1878), 477.

[16] Luther reported in a letter of March 21 to Lang that many were urging him not to go to Heidelberg, in order to avoid being taken captive by stealth. But Luther will be obedient and go. WABr, 1, 155,16.

At this point a new factor entered upon the scene, the support given Luther by Prince-Elector Frederick the Wise of Saxony, the founder and proud patron of the University of Wittenberg. Earlier, Frederick had refused permission for the preaching of the St. Peter's indulgence in his lands, mainly as a measure against the ascending fortunes of the Brandenburg house of the Hohenzollern, whose offspring, Archbishop Albrecht, stood to profit considerably from the indulgence. Also, Frederick's young university, founded in 1502, was in the process of introducing significant reforms in the curriculum under the lead of Luther and Andreas Karlstadt. Scholastic philosophy and theology was being relegated to the periphery, so that biblical and patristic studies could occupy the central place in the theological program.[17] Other universities, however, were not in sympathy with this return to the sources in Wittenberg. Hostility had been evinced, especially in places known for their strong Dominican presence in theology, such as Cologne, Leipzig, and Frankfurt an der Oder.[18] Prince-Elector Frederick knew well of this opposition to the new directions of his school, and so he did not hesitate to defend his talented professor of Scripture against a censure from Rome which would bring discredit on his university.

When Luther requested the Prince-Elector's permission to absent himself from the university for the Heidelberg chapter and asked for a letter of safe-conduct for the journey, Frederick responded with a good deal more than Luther had sought. The Elector wrote to the Bishop of Würzburg and to the Count Palatine, ruler of Heidelberg, asking them to give Luther their protection while he was in their domains.[19] He further wrote to Staupitz, indicating that Luther's permission to be absent from the university was being given reluctantly and that Staupitz should see to it that Luther return immediately to Saxony after the chapter.[20] Frederick thereby blocked any move by Luther's Augustinian order to apply a more rigorous discipline, for instance, by an order for him to go to Rome to answer charges before his highest religious superior.

Frederick's interference in the disciplinary procedure of the order became known. Johann Tetzel attacked it in a set of theses in early May, charging that such an act was tantamount to aiding and abetting heresy and would bring a ruler

---

[17] See Luther's often cited report of May 18, 1517, on the predominance of »our theology and St. Augustine« at Wittenberg. WABr 1, 99,8; LW 48,42. On March 11, 1518, Luther sent to Georg Spalatin, Prince Frederick's chaplain and secretary, a list of proposed new courses, which however will entail considerable expense for the elector. But if the resources are provided, and new faculty members hired, the new plan will surely lead other universities to follow the Wittenberg example in eliminating the reigning barbarism. WABr 1, 153,3; also, 155,41.

[18] Borth, *Die Luthersache*, 25-29.

[19] »Princeps noster ... me et Carlstadium in protectionem non rogatus suscipit, nullo modo passurus, ut me ad Urbem trahant.« Luther to Lang, March 21, 1518; WABr 1, 155,20.

[20] Text given by T. Kolde, *Die deutsche Augustiner-Congregation und Johann von Staupitz* (Gotha 1879), 314, n. 1.

under ecclesiastical penalties.[21] When Frederick's action became known in Rome, it was certainly a factor in the raising of the Luther case to the level of a canonical *processus* carried out under papal authority. Rome felt constrained to apply a more powerful instrumentality after the Saxon Elector had blocked the procedure internal to the Augustinian order.[22]

The Heidelberg chapter was a notable success for Luther, because on April 26 he presided at a public disputation that offered an engaging presentation of his Pauline-Augustinian »theology of the cross.« Luther's theological claims and proofs of his twenty-eight theological theses defended in the Heidelberg Disputation remain to this day a fine short formula of his early theology of Christian conversion.[23] Also Luther responded to the communication from his order's superior general, who sought to silence him. Later, Luther spoke of the severe letter read out against him in chapter.[24] In response, Luther agreed to present to the Pope the explanations and proofs of his views on penance and indulgences, by submitting the *Resolutiones* once they were printed. The Prince-Elector's intervention stayed any further implementation of disciplinary action.

Shortly after he returned to Wittenberg, Luther issued a short *protestatio* in which he communicated to a wider public what was presumably the nub of his response to censure at the Heidelberg chapter.[25] Clearly hoping to protect the good name of his university, Luther affirmed that he could not recant just because some overly rash opponents were screaming that there was heresy in his writings. No academic, civil, or ecclesiastical condemnation had been issued against him. He challenged his attackers either to point out a better understanding of the matters he was treating or to submit their charges to a church tribunal. He would await a reputable judgment on his views, meanwhile paying no attention to the charges conjured up by hostile and prejudiced critics. Nonetheless, Luther did begin to consider what it might mean in fact if he were condemned and had to face the threat of excommunication.

In early May, Luther gave a thematic sermon on the subject of excommunication and its effects on the life of a Christian. He excoriated the

---

[21] Fifty theses (published in late April or early May), nos. 47-48. *Dokumente zur Causa Lutheri*, 1, 375.

[22] Borth, *Die Luthersache*, 39-45.

[23] WA 1, 353-374; LW 31, 39-45. A careful exposition of Luther's argument is Jos Vercruysse, »Gesetz und Liebe. Die Struktur der Heidelberg Disputation Luthers (1518),« *Lutherjahrbuch* 48 (1981), 7-43.

[24] Letter to W. Link, July 10, 1518; WABr 1, 186,51.

[25] WA 2, 620. Paul Kalkoff indicated the reasons for dating this piece in May 1518. »Luther vor dem Generalkapitel zu Heidelberg,« *Zeitschrift für Kirchengeschichte* 27 (1906), 320-323; also ibid. 32 (1911), 572-577. It is far from certain, however, that Luther was responding to Dominican denunciations in Rome, as Kalkoff maintained.

excessive use of this censure by church officials in his day, and then went on to maintain that the effect of excommunication in itself was to sever only the external bonds of a person's relationship to the church as a visible society. It did not, in itself, affect the bond of faith, hope, and charity by which a person could still be in interior, living communion with Christ.[26] In May 1518, Luther's Wittenberg printer, Johann Grunenberg, was straining his resources to bring out the *Resolutiones* and so there was no immediate way to print the short treatise on excommunication that was the basis of Luther's sermon. Consequently, instead of the full text, a set of »theses« drawn up by someone in the audience began to circulate as a report on the view Luther held on the Church's supreme canonical censure. In late summer, these theses turned up in Augsburg during the Imperial Diet and had the effect of prejudicing powerful figures, including Emperor Maximilian, against Luther.[27] In October 1518 a printed text of Luther's sermon-treatise was circulating, and Cardinal Cajetan composed a critical analysis of it in a *quaestio* completed on October 29, 1518.

The Ordinary Canonical Procedure

In Rome, probably in May, when it became known that the attempt to silence Luther through an admonition from his Augustinian superior had been blocked, curia officials opened a *processus ordinarius* against Luther as suspect of heresy.[28] Later, Luther asserted that it was the repeated delations by the Dominicans that caused this step to be taken in Rome.[29] This, however, is not otherwise documented. But there could have been an intervention by the Saxon Dominican provincial, Hermann Rab, who attended the order's general chapter in Rome, May 28-31, 1518.

In the *processus* the accusation was brought by the Pope's *procurator fiscalis*, Mario de Perusco, and in response Leo X commissioned the *Auditor camerae apostolicae*, Bishop Girolamo Ghinucci, to investigate the accusation in order to

---

[26] Text now given in WA 1, 638-643.

[27] Reported by Spalatin from Augsburg, September 5, 1518. WABr 1, 201,33. The same letter gives the information that Luther's alleged theses were circulating in Augsburg with an appended epigram casting derision on the Roman Curia (possibly from Ulrich Hutten).

[28] At this point, Luther had not been formally indicted, but was the object of accusation and rumor. The procedure did not simply begin with a formal accusation, but with the decision of church officials to investigate, that is, to conduct an *inquisitio* into, the accused person's utterances and deeds. In the early sixteenth century, the status *suspectus de haeresi* was not sharply defined, principally because *haeresis* could cover a wide range of outlooks contrary to the church and its faith. H. Flatten, *Der Häresieverdacht im Codex iuris canonici* (Amsterdam 1963), 32-34, 52-66.

[29] WA 2, 30,14-27, 38,30-18. These are significant descriptions of the procedures directed against Luther, but, unfortunately, documentary confirmation has not been found in the pertinent Roman archives.

determine whether the alleged suspicion of heresy rested on grounds that would justify summoning Luther to a formal hearing. To assist Ghinucci in his investigation, Silvester Prierias was commissioned to examine the evidence, which at this stage was taken to be Luther's Ninety-Five Theses.[30]

When Prierias went to work on the matter, he took only three days to write a doctrinal assessment of Luther's theses. This report gave Ghinucci ample grounds for summoning Luther to Rome to render an account of his views, now judged suspect, on indulgences and papal authority. Ghinucci drafted the summons, probably in early July, and sent it to Cardinal Cajetan in Augsburg for forwarding from the Imperial Diet to Luther in Wittenberg. Beginning on the day on which the summons arrived in Wittenberg, August 7, Luther had a sixty-day period for betaking himself to Rome to appear before Ghinucci, and canonical penalties were threatened in case of non-appearance. Along with the summons, Luther received a copy of Prierias's report, which had been printed in Rome under the title, *In praesumptiosas Martini Lutheri Conclusiones, de Potestate Papae, Dialogus*.[31]

The *Dialogus* of Prierias represented the first theological response to Luther emanating from Rome. Unfortunately for the present study, Silvester Prierias has not been the subject of adequate monographic study of his thought prior to 1518. The bare text of the *Dialogus* itself, however, yields three clusters of assertions which were influential in the later course of Reformation controversy, as can be shown by a brief reflection on each cluster.

(1) Prierias laid down as the fundamental criterion for judging Luther the doctrine and practice of the Roman Church. Divergence from this norm, according to the *Dialogus*, implicates one in heresy.[32] Consequently, any questioning of the legitimacy of Roman indulgence practice is heretical: »Whoever says regarding indulgences that the Roman Church cannot do what it *de facto* does, is a heretic.«[33] In setting forth his notion of the »treasury« of

---

[30] Karl Müller, »Luther's römischer Prozess,« *Zeitschrift für Kirchengeschichte* 24 (1903), 46-61. One wonders what became of Luther's *Tractatus de indulgentiis*, which systematically explained how the merits of Christ and the Church are applied by the Pope. See pp. 110-113, above.

[31] Text in *Dokumente zur Causa Lutheri*, 1, 52-107.

[32] Ibid., 55f.

[33] Ibid, 56. Late-medieval scholastics commonly defined both *fides* and *haeresis* in a global manner with reference to life and thought in conformity with, or diverging from, revelation. Heresy, for Aquinas, could even include »inordinata locutio circa ea quae sunt fidei.« *Summa theologiae*, II-II, 11, 2 ad 2. Obedience to church discipline is definitely included in the ambit of these notions. See Albert Lang, »Die Gliederung und Reichweite des Glaubens nach Thomas von Aquin und den Thomisten,« *Divus Thomas* (Freiburg/Switzerland) 20 (1942), 231f and 236. As well, Piet Fransen, in »Réflexions sur l'anathème au Concile de Trente,« *Ephemerides theologicae Lovanienses* 29 (1953), 659f. Cardinal Cajetan, however, influenced later development through a narrower concept of heresy as »error in fide pertinax,« limiting *fides* to divinely revealed truth. Comm. on *Summa* II-II, 11, 2, in the Leonine edition of Aquinas, vol. 8, p. 99.

indulgences, in answer to Luther's thesis 56, Prierias baldly stated that the authority of the Roman Church and the popes is greater than the authority of Scripture.[34] From the moment Luther read Prierias's concise statements on fundamental doctrinal norms, the question of the criteria of true Christian teaching became a key theme of his reflection and controversy. Luther's eventual contestation of papal authority is to a certain extent a reactive effort to vindicate the rightful authority of Scripture in the face of the one-sided claims made by Prierias for the papal magisterium.[35]

(2) Among the specific censures Prierias levelled against Luther's theses, there are (i) three assertions that Luther »thought wrongly« about the practice of the Church,[36] (ii) six charges that Luther was derogating from papal authority,[37] and (iii) five outright accusations that Luther was teaching heresy.[38] But Luther, so he will repeatedly assert, had not offered his Ninety-Five Theses as a definitive statement of his views and convictions. The theses were assertive, and for the most part quite clear, but nonetheless they were meant to initiate debate, in the course of which terms would be precisely defined, evidence presented, and a *determinatio* reached.[39] In the absence of an actual disputation, Luther had carried out this process for himself in the *Resolutiones*, which were still in the press when Prierias was attacking the Ninety-Five Theses. Luther complained, rightly it would seem, that he was being unfairly accused in the early stages of the Roman *processus*.[40] The perception of this Roman impropriety underlay Luther's subsequent efforts to have his case transferred to Germany.

---

[34] *Dokumente zur Causa Lutheri*, 1, 92

[35] Prierias's extremism appears in sharp relief when his foundational principles are considered in the light of the concise survey of late-medieval ecclesiological positions given by Brian Gogan in his study of Thomas More, *The Common Corps of Christendom* (Leiden 1982), 60-63, 328-341. Prierias may have been the pope's official theologian, but he was at the far end of the ecclesiological spectrum of his day. We will see in this essay that his views contrast with the working principles underlying Cajetan's review of Luther's teaching just three months later.

[36] *Dokumente zur Causa Lutheri*, 1, 60, 61, 70.

[37] Ibid., 70, 74, 78, 81, 84, 100.

[38] Ibid., 61, 70, 75, 78, 104f (»non modo haereticus, verum haeresiarcha es«).

[39] On February 13, 1518, Luther had lamented that his theses were being taken »non ut disputabilia, sed asserta,« claiming that he had his own doubts about some of them. »Nulla vero pertinaciter assero. Tamen omnia Ecclesiae sanctae suoque iudicio submitto.« WABr 1, 139,48.52. Similarly, in letters of March 5 and May 8: WABr 1, 152,13, 170,43. Also in the letter to Pope Leo X on May 31: WA 1, 528,39f.

[40] WA 1, 661,32-37. In his response to Prierias's *Dialogus* Luther repeatedly referred to the clarifications forthcoming in the *Resolutiones*: WA 1, 655,27, 656,22, 658,12, 661,38, 666,17, 681,38f, 684,8f.

(3) Prierias's *Dialogus* cited hardly any Scripture and no Fathers of the Church, but on seven occasions he asserted views contrary to Luther's theses and gave as warrant the teaching of St. Thomas Aquinas.[41] This fact contributed, on the one hand, to Luther's wary reserve in approaching Cajetan in October, 1518, since Cajetan was the best-known exponent of Thomism in his day. More importantly, Prierias stimulated a development in Luther's self-understanding in mid-1518, by which he came to see himself as expounding a broadly based theology drawn from Scripture, the Fathers, and the canonical tradition. In his *Responsio* to Prierias, Luther countered the Thomist views of the papal court-theologian with the refrain, *Rogo, ubi hic Scriptura, patres, aut Canones sonant?*[42]

If anything, Luther's reading of the *Dialogus* of Prierias was an experience that contributed to his self-confidence as he prepared his response to the summons of Bishop Ghinucci. Over against Prierias, Luther sensed that he was in fact well equipped to argue cogently and dispute successfully, because he was steeped in Scripture, St. Augustine, and the canons on ecclesial penance. Stated more pointedly, Luther felt that he was working out views in continuity with the central Catholic tradition, while the other side was innovating by appealing only to Aquinas and to recent *facta* of the Roman Church.[43]

---

[41] *Dokumente zur Causa Lutheri*, 1, 61, 66, 68, 70, 71, 81, 83. The paramount role of Thomism in Rome had grown from the time of initial decisions of Pope Nicholas V (1447-55), especially under the orchestration of Olivero Caraffa (d. 1511), long-time Cardinal Protector of the Dominicans. See John W. O'Malley, »The Feast of Thomas Aquinas in Renaissance Rome,« *Rivista di Storia della Chiesa in Italia* 35 (1981), 1-27.

[42] WA 1, 648,19. Equivalent expressions are at 647,32, 650,21, 656,19, and 664,40. At 649,14 Luther exclaimed, »Omnes Doctores Ecclesiastici sentiunt mecum, nullus autem tecum.«

[43] This interpretation of Prierias as a catalyst in Luther's development in the direction of divisive positions coincides with the view of Erasmus. Upon first seeing the *Dialogus*, Erasmus termed it »insulsissimam« (very ill-judged). Letter to J. Lang, October 17, 1518; *Opus Epistolarum*, ed. P.S. Allen et al. (Oxford 1905-58), 3, 409. Seven months later Erasmus said Prierias's criteria were fabricated new laws, »per quas doceant haereticum esse quidquid non placet.« To Prince-Elector Frederick, April 14, 1519; Allen, 3, 531. Six months later Erasmus explained Luther's daring views, probably in reference to the Leipzig Disputation, as reactions to Dominican exaggerations of papal power and the authority of St. Thomas. To Albrecht of Brandenburg, October 19, 1519; Allen 4, 105. Just after the publication of *Exsurge Domine*, Erasmus came back to the unconvincing work of the Pope's official theologian: »Quae Silvester Prierias scripserat adversus Lutherum, a nemine hactenus audivi probari, vel ex eorum numero quibus Lutherus est invisissimus.« To Lorenzo Cardinal Campeggio, December 6, 1520; Allen 4, 409. These passages may be consulted in English translation in *Correspondence of Erasmus*, ed. R.A.B. Mynors et al. (Toronto 1974–) 6, 137f, 298f, and 7, 112f, 120. From the distance of nearly a decade, Erasmus saw the origins of the Reformation tumult as a schematic pattern of action and reaction, with Prierias having a key role: »Tota haec Lutherana tempestas ex levioribus initiis huc usque incrudit. Dominicani commendabant impudentius indulgentias pontificias, Lutherus opposuit articulos, Silvester inepte respondit, Lutherus acriter resistit.« To J. Vergard, September 2, 1527; Allen 7, 167 (see also 211, 257f).

After receiving the *Dialogus* of Prierias on August 7, Luther composed a *Responsio* that was printed in Leipzig and was in circulation by August 31.[44] Three aspects of this work cast light upon Luther's attitude mid-way through the fateful year 1518.

(1) Luther saw his theological work in both the Ninety-Five Theses and *Resolutiones* as situated in an area of free opinion not yet settled by authoritative doctrinal decisions. On occasion Luther made reference to a coming determination by the Church or by a council.[45] He undercut Prierias by pointing out that only after such a declaration could there be question of heresy on the part of an obstinate dissenter.[46]

(2) Luther evinced concern over the way Pope Leo X might come to regard him, and in the last part of his *Responsio* he complained that Prierias was out to ruin his good name with the Pope.[47] Luther perceived a real danger in actions of inept members of the papal entourage who might be currying favor by calumniously attacking alleged enemies of the Pope.

(3) Luther's *Responsio* made one forthright assertion of the normative character for all Christians of the faith professed by the Roman Church, because Christ miraculously maintains that church in the truth and in continuity with original expressions of Christian belief.[48] This indicates, for August 1518, Luther's positive attitude toward judgments on doctrine emanating from the Roman See. Clearly it was a fateful development that Pope Leo's spokesman in the Luther case was eventually a Dominican confrere of Tetzel and Prierias, Tommaso de Vio, Cardinal Cajetan, whose reputation as a Thomist loomed large in early sixteenth-century academic circles. Doctrinal judgments delivered by Cajetan, acting as the Pope's legate, were to put a severe strain on Luther's submissive readiness to accept a Roman determination.

---

[44] Luther's answer is studied with penetration by K.-V. Selge in his Heidelberg Habilitationsschrift *Normen der Christenheit* (1968), 56-70.
[45] WA 1, 658,18, 681,4.
[46] WA 1, 655,28.
[47] WA 1, 665,6, 669,40, 673,18, 681,9-18.
[48] »... ad eam fidem, quam Romana ecclesia profitetur, omnium fides debet conformari ... Nam et ego gratias ago Christo, quod hanc unam Ecclesiam in terris ita servat ingenti et quod solum possit probare fidem nostram esse veram miraculo, ut nunquam a vera fide ullo suo decreto recesserit ...« WA 1, 662,30-34. The Roman Church for Luther is not properly called the »regula fidei,« as Prierias said, for it is instead ruled by the faith, in the sense of Gal 6:16 (622,25). Remigius Bäumer noted the neglect of this passage in the literature on Luther. *Martin Luther und der Papst* (Münster 1970), 24. S. Hendrix cites this passage in *Luther and the Papacy*, 51, as referring to Roman fidelity in the past, notwithstanding the present tense of *servat* in the passage cited above. Christ's miraculous preservation of the Roman Church from decreeing in divergence from the true faith has for Luther an extrinsic character, which is compatible with inherent fallibility, for the Roman Church can err (WA 1, 685,20).

In spite of his confession regarding the Roman Church, Luther remained quite suspicious of officials like Ghinucci and Prierias. Consequently, upon receipt of the summons and the *Dialogus*, Luther set in motion efforts aimed at avoiding the demanded appearance in Rome within sixty days. Luther wrote on August 8 to Prince-Elector Frederick, who was at Augsburg taking part in the Imperial Diet. Luther asked his overlord to intervene with the Pope to the end that the matter be remitted to Germany for settlement before an impartial judge. Luther construed the structure of the Roman *processus* as such that Prierias, his declared adversary, was a judge of the tribunal that would rule on the charges of heresy.[49] This request for remission to a local judiciary would not be unique in the early sixteenth century, when rulers frequently voiced concern that so many matters of ecclesiastical dispute were taken to higher courts for settlement far from the scene of the dispute. Civil intervention in a doctrinal issue would be extraordinary, but Frederick could allege that he had to be involved, since a condemnation would do serious harm to the good name of his Wittenberg university.[50]

Three weeks passed after Luther sent off his request for Frederick's help. By August 28, he had no word on whether he was to have the aid of a powerful German intercessor. Luther knew that Cajetan was in Augsburg, and he put the worst construction on the Dominican cardinal's mission in Germany. Luther imagined that the Pope had sent Cajetan with an express mandate to convince the leaders of Germany that Luther posed a dire threat to religion and society. Luther could see only one outcome, his own condemnation and excommunication, if Frederick's aid were not forthcoming. Still, Luther asserted that he would never hold obstinately to error in the face of correction. »I will never be a heretic. I may err while arguing in a disputation, but I do not want to assert conclusions.«[51]

At this time, the printing of Luther's *Resolutiones* was finally completed, and he had a number of copies sent on to Spalatin, who was with the Prince-Elector in Augsburg. Spalatin welcomed the clarifications contained in Luther's newly printed book and distributed copies to some figures of influence in Augsburg. At the end of September, Cajetan was using one of these copies as he undertook his own diligent study of Luther's doctrine. About September 10 Luther finally heard that the Prince-Elector was in fact taking initiatives calculated to gain Luther a hearing in Germany. Luther must have been amazed to hear that the

---

[49] WABr 1, 188,5-17; LW 48,71f. On Prierias: »Est idem homo suavissimus mihi simul adversarius et iudex.« WABr 1, 188,21.

[50] Borth, *Die Luthersache*, 46f.

[51] WABr 1, 190,21; LW 48,74. However, to Spalatin on September 1, Luther vented a real hostility toward Prierias and the Romans: »Horum enim studium est, ut video, ne regnum veritatis, id est Christi, sit regnum veritatis...« In contrast stand the people longing for the sound of the voice of Christ their shepherd and the Wittenberg students now enthusiastically studying Scripture. WABr 1, 194,20.

elector's ally in proposing the transferral of his case was none other than the papal legate himself, Cardinal Cajetan.[52]

In late April 1518 Cajetan had been named legate to the Diet of the German Empire, being a last-minute substitute for Cardinal Alessandro Farnese. At the time Cajetan was in the last weeks of his ten-year tenure as Dominican Master General, and so was something of a novice in diplomacy. At the Imperial Diet, beginning in August, his main task was to rally the German estates to the support of armed forces to defend against Turkish advances.[53] In spite of Emperor Maximilian's support for the new crusade,[54] the task given Cajetan was not an inviting one, because of the tensions and hostilities present in the assembly of German leaders with whom he and the Emperor would have to negotiate. A new tax-levy was sure to meet opposition. Smoldering resentments would need no time at all to flame forth with pointed *gravamina* against the Church's judiciary, church taxes, indulgences taking money out of Germany, clerical morals, and further specific practices such as the pallium-fees extracted from archiepiscopal sees at each accession of a new bishop.[55] But when Cajetan left Rome on May 5, there was no indication that he would eventually be delegated to conduct a hearing on the doctrinal issues raised by Luther.

In the first stages of the Diet, Cajetan's dispatches reported on Emperor Maximilian's efforts to secure the election of his grandson, King Charles of Spain, as King of the Romans and future Emperor. This issue brought Cajetan, representing Leo X, and Elector Frederick the Wise into common opposition to the Hapsburg dynastic project. The Pope wanted to avoid encirclement, since Charles already held title to the Kingdom of Naples, while Frederick judged the plan unconstitutional and was dismayed over the venality of his fellow electors in the face of Maximilian's offers of payment in exchange for their votes.[56]

---

52 Letter of Spalatin to Luther, September 5; WABr 1, 200,5-201,23. On September 16 Luther wrote Lang that the Prince was having Cajetan seek the *commissio ad partes* from Rome, and so Luther hoped to avoid censure. WABr 1, 203,16ff.

53 On this aspect of papal interaction with the great powers of Europe, see K.M. Setton, »Pope Leo and the Turkish Peril,« *Proceedings of the American Philosophical Association* 113 (1969), 367-424, reprinted as essay no. IX in Setton, *Europe and the Levant in the Middle Ages and the Renaissance* (London 1974).

54 Georg Wagner, »Der letzte Türkenkreutzzugsplan Kaiser Maximilians I. aus dem Jahre 1517,« *Mitteilungen des Instituts für österreichische Geschichtsforschung* 77 (1969), 314-353. Also, H. Wiesflecker, *Kaiser Maximilian I.*, 4 (Munich 1981), 227-232.

55 Bruno Gebhardt, *Die Gravamina der Deutschen Nation gegen den römischen Hof* (2nd ed., Breslau 1895), 94-102.

56 Hans von Voltelini, »Die Bestrebungen Maximilians I. um die Kaiserkrone 1518,« *Mitteilungen des Instituts für österreichische Geschichtsforschung* 11 (1890), 50-54, 58. August Kluckhorn, in *Deutsche Reichstagsakten*, jüngere Reihe, 1 (Gotha 1893), 91-97. Cajetan's dispatches are not extant, but they are reflected in a report of September 11 of the papal vice-chancellor, Cardinal Giulio de' Medici, to the legate in France: *Archivio storico italiano*, 3rd series, 24 (1876), 11.

Cajetan addressed the Diet on August 5 on the dire need of a grand effort to save Christian Europe, especially German lands, from the infidel.[57] But the days following Cajetan's oration revealed strong opposition to the papal project. A pamphlet in the form of an *oratio dissuasoria* began to circulate, attacking the papal request as a Medici subterfuge for acquiring more German money. The real Turk preying on Christians is not based in Asia, but in Italy.[58] But in spite of the hostility, Cajetan and Maximilian pushed ahead in negotiations with the estates in late August and September. Finally, the estates agreed that the support should take the form of a two-shilling alms from every adult communicant in each of the next three years, but it was stipulated that definitive approval of this levy would only be given at the next Diet. Cajetan, deeply frustrated, was forced to forward to Rome a list of German complaints for remedial action by the Pope.[59] Thus, reform was being made the price Leo X would have to pay for obtaining backing for his crusade project. However, the whole matter was suspended in the wake of Maximilian's death on January 12, 1519.

Escalation to a Summary Procedure against Luther

Even before Luther asked Prince-Elector Frederick's help in changing the summons to Rome, Emperor Maximilian had intervened and thereby set in motion a series of events that led to the encounter between Luther and Cajetan in Augsburg in mid-October. On August 5, Maximilian sent a letter to the Pope denouncing Luther for writing and preaching in a manner calculated to undermine both indulgences and the Church's disciplinary measure of excommunication. The Emperor referred to the accusation by Silvester Prierias that Luther was teaching heresy and went on to assert that he was in fact holding to his ideas obstinately *(pertinacius)* and was gaining both numerous adherents as well as powerful patrons for his cause.[60] The Pope thus came to hear on good

---

[57] Text in *Ulrichi Hutteni Opera*, ed. Edward Böcking, 5 (Leipzig 1861; reprint Aalen 1963), 163-167.

[58] Text, Ibid., 168-174. By September 2, Luther had seen the pamphlet, and it reinforced his negative attitudes to Roman craftiness and avarice. WABr 1, 196,33.

[59] Cajetan's bitter frustration was mentioned by the Polish envoys to the Diet, as cited by Xavier Liske, »Zur Geschichte des Augsburger Reichstages 1518,« *Forschungen zur deutschen Geschichte* 17 (1878), 644, 647. The final status of the negotiations was reported by the Frankfurt emissaries. *Frankfurts Reichscorrespondenz*, vol. II/2, ed. Johannes Janssen (Freiburg/B. 1872), 994-998.

[60] »Quae res eo magis displicuit, quo pertinacius dictus Frater, ut edocti sumus, doctrinae suae inhaerere, atque complures errorum suorum defensores et patronos, etiam potentes, consequutus esse dicitur.« Cited from *D. Martini Lutheri opera Latina varii argumenti* (Frankfurt and Erlangen 1865–), 2, 349. It is often said that Cajetan was behind the Emperor's letter, even to the point of furnishing a first draft, e.g., by Paul Kalkoff, *Forschungen zu Luthers römischem Prozess* (Rome 1905), 135-150. However, there is no direct evidence for this, and it requires postulating for Cajetan both considerable knowledge about the Wittenberg curriculum reform and a hostility to Johann Reuchlin, neither of which is verifiable. More probably, the letter stems from the Emperor's vexation with Frederick the Wise because of the latter's opposition to the plan to hold

authority that the Luther movement was making advances in Germany, while the accusation of obstinacy was calculated to cause an intensification of the canonical *processus* introduced some two months earlier. The Emperor asked the Pope to make expeditious use of his authority in order to stop the spread of Luther's ideas before they incited tumult with princely support. Maximilian declared himself ready to take action to see to the enforcement in the Empire of punitive measures against Luther.[61]

In Rome Maximilian's letter was taken as new evidence, having canonical relevance, against Luther and action was begun to have Luther apprehended for trial. By August 23 letters were composed in Rome that show that the character of the canonical proceeding against Luther had been changed. A *processus summarius* opened, in which Luther was now treated as a known and obstinate *(notorius et pertinax)* teacher of heresy. The accused was to be confronted with the simple alternative of recantation or condemnation.[62]

Cajetan was officially commissioned to play a role in the Luther case, that is, to take action to bring about Luther's arrest and detention. Acting in concert with Emperor Maximilian, Cajetan was to have Luther brought before him to hear the papal judgment on his heretical views. In the optimal-case scenario that Luther would recant and beg forgiveness for spreading heresy, Cajetan was delegated to reconcile him. But if Luther remained obstinate, he was to be held in custody until further instructions were forthcoming from Rome.[63] Thus Tommaso de Vio became the spokesman for the Pope against Luther and his powerful patrons in Germany.

Another letter of August 23 went from Rome to Prince-Elector Frederick in an effort to win his cooperation against the professor whom he was rumored to be protecting. This letter subtly concealed the precise stage of the juridical procedure, and spoke of a possible acquittal of Luther without mentioning the other provisions set forth in Cajetan's instructions.[64]

---

an early election of Charles of Spain as King of the Romans. On this point, Cajetan stood with Frederick, not Maximilian.

61 *Luteri opera Latina var. arg.*, 2, 350.

62 K. Müller, »Luther römischer Prozess,« *Zeitschrift für Kirchengeschichte* 24 (1903), 63-66; P. Kalkoff, »Zu Luthers römischen Prozess,« ibid. 33 (1912), 40-46; Borth, *Die Luthersache*, 48f. Cardinal Giulio de' Medici's October 7 letter to Cajetan mirrored the summary procedure in referring to Cajetan's original instruction in the Luther case: »...di qua fu iudicato che ne le cose notorie et publice non accadessi altra solennità o citazione.« *Archivio storico italiano*, 3rd series, 24 (1876), 23.

63 The text of Cajetan's instruction was published by Luther late in 1518 at the end of his *Acta Augustana*, WA 2, 23-25; LW 31, 286-289. Luther, not aware of the August intervention of Emperor Maximilian, an intervention that had transformed the *processus*, accused the Roman curia of impropriety in issuing notice of his guilt just sixteen days into the sixty-day period given him to answer the charges made in the first procedure. WA 2, 25,30.

64 *Lutheri opera Latina*, 2, 352-354. In hopes that Frederick would cooperate and thus be freed from any suspicion of complicity with Luther, and as well that he would promote the crusade-levy, Leo X announced in consistory on September 3 that Frederick was to receive the Golden Rose, in testimony of his Christian princely virtues. See Kalkoff, *Forschungen*, 56, based on a report of the English ambassador to the papal court.

The Augustinians were also involved, and by command of Leo X, the order's Vicar General della Volta instructed the conventual provincial in Germany, Gerhard Hecker, to have Luther taken into custody and held – handcuffed and chained – so he could be brought before the papal judiciary.[65]

The arrival in Augsburg of the August 23 letters from Rome brought Frederick to Cajetan for a long discussion of Luther's case.[66] The Elector assumed that while Luther was under suspicion, still no verdict had been given, and he simply asked Cajetan to intercede in favor of a transferral of the case to a German ecclesiastical and/or academic tribunal. Cajetan accepted that Luther should be heard before impartial judges who would give him a fair opportunity to disprove the accusations against him. Uppermost in the legate's mind seems to have been his instruction to have Luther brought before him, and so he naturally refrained from confronting Frederick with the harsh facts of the *processus summarius*.

In responding to Frederick, Cajetan discounted the possibility of a transferral to a German tribunal, while stressing that he did have faculties from the Pope to reconcile a repentant Luther. Cajetan assured Frederick that if he were to meet Luther, he would treat him gently and patiently. In effect, he agreed that if the accused were to come to Augsburg, he would be treated in a manner satisfactory to the Elector.[67] Frederick gave his word that he would never protect a person duly condemned by the Church, while Cajetan agreed to conduct the hearing informally and to allow Luther to leave Augsburg after their conversations. Frederick was satisfied with Cajetan's flexible approach and gave assurances that Luther would be properly docile under instruction.

Cajetan Delegated to Judge Luther

Cajetan immediately reported to Rome, asking for modification of his instructions. Cajetan's proven competence as a theologian and administrator made it easy for the Pope to expand considerably his role in the case. In addition, showing a favorable attitude to Frederick could lead to some progress on the

---

[65] Text given by T. Kolde, »Luther und sein Ordensgeneral,« 476-478.

[66] The sources for reconstructing this conversation are Spalatin's letter of encouragement to Luther on September 5 (WABr 1, 200f) and Luther's brief statement, in a letter of September 16, of what the Elector communicated to him (WABr 1, 203). Also, there is a November letter of Frederick to his counsellor, D. Pfeffinger (Luther, *Werke*, 1 [Jena 1555], 134r-135r), and a December letter to Cajetan (WABr 1, 250f) which throw light upon the meeting.

[67] Spalatin assured Luther that Cajetan was not hostile. »Cardinal Caietanus, nisi et Principem et me fallit, adeo abs te alienus non est, ut tantum in te mali moliatur apud Caesarem et Sacri Romani Imperii proceres. Locutus enim nuper cum Illustrissimo Principe nostro, qui eum accessit, et familiariter et copiose, magnam mihi spem fecit, multo futurum leniorem et tolerabiliorem in causa tua quam timebam.« The Cardinal is not to be identified with the uncultured German Dominicans aligned with Tetzel who scream about Luther's heresies from every pulpit. WABr 1, 200,5-201,18.

issue of the crusade levy. Consequently, on September 11 a new letter of instruction went from Rome to Cajetan.⁶⁸ Although an earlier instruction had assumed that Luther was a notorious heretic, the Pope was ready to follow Cajetan's suggestion for a hearing and possible settlement by him.⁶⁹

The Cardinal Legate was commissioned to have Luther arraigned before himself and, after careful examination of the charges, the evidence, and Luther's own responses, to proceed to terminate the case in an appropriate manner.⁷⁰ In effect the judgment against Luther was suspended, and Cajetan was made the judge of his orthodoxy.⁷¹ No mention was made of how Cajetan is to act if Luther comes to be adversely judged and remains recalcitrant, a fact that tacitly approved the crucial concession to Frederick that Luther be allowed to leave Augsburg after appearing before Cajetan. No mention of penalties was made, which left the Pope a certain scope for further adaptation once he learned the outcome of Cajetan's examination of Luther's works and of his hearing of the accused.

Cajetan would have received his revised instructions about September 18. He communicated the gist of his new commission to Frederick, who then sent word to Wittenberg that Luther was to come to Augsburg for a hearing before Cajetan. On September 20, Cajetan sent to Rome the official response of the imperial estates to the Pope's crusade-plan, and so he became free to prepare himself for the coming interview with Luther. In compliance with the Pope's instruction to examine the issue *diligenter*, Cajetan began studying two recently published works by Luther, the *Resolutiones* of the Ninety-Five Theses, and a short *Sermo de poenitentia*, published the previous spring.

---

68 The text is in V.M. Fontana, *Sacrum Theatrum Dominicanum* (Rome 1666), 346, but should be read in the light of the corrections given by Kalkoff, *Forschungen*, 57ff.

69 »...tamen crederes non ab re forsan fore, si causa eius, licet ex eis sit, quae apud hanc Sanctam Sedem agitari et cognosci deberet, per te istic audiri et terminari posset.« Fontana, 346; Kalkoff, 58.

70 »...eidem circumspectioni tuae committendum duximus, prout etiam committimus, ut eundem Martinum coram te accersiri facias, eiusque causam diligenter examines, eaque per te diligenter audita et examinata, ad illius absolutionem vel condemnationem, prout iustum fuerit procedas.« Fontana, 346; Kalkoff, 59. A further expression of the nature of the commission given Cajetan came in the bull *Cum postquam* drafted by Cajetan in Augsburg in the second half of October 1518 and issued by Pope Leo on November 9 as a concise clarification of the doctrine of indulgences. It refers back to Cajetan's mandate as »ut auctoritate nostra approbatione digna approbes, ea vero, quae minus recte dicta essent, etiam per eos, qui Romanae ecclesiae doctrinam se sequi paratos asserent, reprobare et damnare curares.« Given in Walther Köhler, *Dokumente zum Ablassstreit von 1517* (2nd ed., Tübingen 1934), 158.

71 K.-V. Selge emphasized the notable shift in the papal handling of the case, by which Cajetan's assessment was made decisive. *Normen der Christenheit*, 86f. In effect, Prierias's judgment on Luther was no longer relevant to the *processus*.

The direct outcome of Cajetan's study was a set of fourteen treatises, cast in the form of scholastic *quaestiones*, completed between September 25 and October 17.[72] Cajetan's treatises constitute a major early work of Reformation controversial theology. They identify, assess, and censure selected teachings proposed by Luther in two of his published works of 1518. On each point he takes up, Cajetan relates a series of particular arguments given in the *Resolutiones* and *Sermo de poenitentia*, usually citing verbatim. Then followes a brief, even cryptic, statement of a judgment on Luther's position, e.g., *In oppositum autem est communis Ecclesiae sensus*.[73] The central part of each treatise, a scholastic *corpus articuli*, sets forth the reasons and arguments that back up the judgment Cajetan had made. The final section of each treatise returns to Luther's arguments to show them to be erroneous or irrelevant to the point at issue.

In the unfolding of the early history of the Reformation, Cajetan's treatises were of enormous importance. The Pope had confided to him the task of deciding on Luther's orthodoxy. In the treatises Cajetan left firsthand evidence of the emergence in his mind of a considered judgment that Luther was in fact diverging from teachings then normative in the Church. In the last days of September, the Legate communicated to Rome the news that the Luther-case was not susceptible of a simple solution, since he was convinced that Luther's teaching had to be censured. There were various ways of doing this, for instance, with or without mention of Luther's name.[74] But the ecclesiastical *processus* could not simply be terminated, because the Cardinal-Legate's diligent examination of two of Luther's works had located some points which could not stand. Cajetan would have to try to elicit from Luther a retraction of at least some points. It was

---

[72] The treatises are now found, arranged according to subject matter, along with treatises written on other occasions, in the various editions of Cajetan's *Opuscula omnia* (usually in »Tomus I«). In the edition of Lyons 1581, the texts composed in preparation for the hearing with Luther are on pp. 97-118. English translations of six, and synopses of the other eight, are in my *Cajetan Responds* (Washington DC 1978), 47-91, followed by the translation of a *quaestio* on excommunication finished October 29, after Cajetan saw Luther's *Sermo de excommunicatione*. *Cajetan Responds* gives in the notes, pp. 266-273, references to the passages in Luther's works from which Cajetan formulated the positions he was assessing. – The most recent study of Cajetan's treatises is B. Lohse's »Cajetan und Luther - Zur Begegnung von Thomismus und Reformation,« *Kerygma und Dogma* 32 (1986), 150-169. Observations on Lohse's conclusions will occur below, in nn. 117, 130, and 152.

[73] Cajetan, *Opuscula* (Lyons 1581), 102b,13; *Cajetan Responds*, 56. This is Cajetan's basic censure of Luther's restriction of the efficacy of indulgences to the sphere of obligations to the Church, to the exclusion of any direct efficacy regarding a person's debt of punishment before God.

[74] Cardinal Giulio de' Medici communicated news about developments in Germany to the papal legate in France, Bernardo Bibiena, mentioning the following: »Il Legato vuole, che Fr Martin Lutero si condanni in ogni modo, o l'opere sue.« *Lettere di Principi*, 1 (Venice 1570), fol. 58r. The letter is given the date of March 27, 1519, but this is surely incorrect, since the letter reports the departure of Emperor Maximilian from Augsburg (September 27, 1518). Probably the letter was sent from Rome between October 10 and 15, 1518.

thus not so clear how the case could be solved in a way acceptable to Frederick of Saxony.

It is well known that in the momentous interviews of October 12, 13, and 14, Cajetan pointed out to Luther two censurable points in his writings and demanded that he revoke these teachings. The points concerned the underlying foundation of indulgences and the kind of faith necessary as a disposition in fruitful reception of the sacrament of Penance.[75] Through Cajetan's preparatory treatises we can determine quite precisely how the Pope's delegate had perceived Luther's teachings and why he felt obligated to insist on modifications.

On the nature of indulgences, Luther's assertions were under examination by Cajetan in the third and eighth of his treatises, completed on September 29 and October 7, respectively.[76]

The first of these works responded to arguments Luther had proposed in the *resolutio* of his fifth indulgence thesis. The conclusion, advanced by Luther as a disputation position, was that the Pope's power to »loose« in indulgences was limited in its scope to the purely ecclesiastical sphere of imposed satisfactory penances.[77] This, for Cajetan, was a improper restriction of what a pope does in granting an indulgence. Luther, in Cajetan's perception, missed or neglected the interrelation between a penitent's obligations in the ecclesial sphere and his obligations to God. The two spheres may be different, but they are connected, since an ecclesial penance only imposes a determinate form on the penitential obligations one has before God. Doing the penance specified by the Church fulfills a dual obligation, although the ecclesiastical prescription may fall short of the full demands of God's justice. In a parallel manner, an indulgence both exempts one from a stipulated church-penance and reduces one's obligation under divine justice to satisfy for sins committed.[78] Cajetan found Luther incorrectly dichotomizing the one sphere of Christian existence, which is both before God and in the Church.

Luther's stand on this point, according to Cajetan, goes contrary to the sense of the Church. For all the faithful see indulgences as affecting their debt of temporal punishment to God as well as their obligations to the Church. Cajetan added the *sensus doctorum* as a further criterion in the course of his argument. He was concerned as well to ward off a response that might denigrate such a

---

75 Luther reported this in the publication, *Acta Augustana* (November 1518); WA 2, 7,28; LW 31, 261.

76 Cajetan was not unprepared to evaluate a theology of indulgences. Less than a year before, on December 8, 1517, he had completed his own *Tractatus de indulgentiis (Opuscula omnia*, 90-97). This treatise betrays no knowledge of Luther, but deals with disputed questions arising from canonical and scholastic viewpoints.

77 WA 1, 536,6-13, 537,28-30; LW 31, 92, 95. Luther's statements on the papacy throughout the *Resolutiones* are reviewed by S. Hendrix, *Luther and the Papacy*, 39-43.

78 *Cajetan Responds*, 56ff.

combined criterion as theologically irrelevant. He asserted that the *sensus* is of such authority that one holding the opposed view must be judged rash or irresponsible *(temere)*.[79]

To confirm this criticism of Luther, Cajetan referred to the promise of Jesus in Matthew 16:19, where Peter received the privilege of »loosing« on earth with effect in heaven. Further, Cajetan mentioned the bull, *Unigenitus*, issued by Pope Clement VI in 1343 and recently incorporated into the promulgation of Holy Years of jubilee.[80] The bull shows the Apostolic See teaching without restriction that indulgences remit the temporal punishments due for sin. Thus, Luther's disputation position went contrary to a teaching backed by papal authority. Cajetan, one can see, worked over Luther's *Resolutiones* with the diligence the Pope had asked of him, as he deftly applied a series of criteria of assessment. The judgment formulated in the treatise of September 29 was, however, quite restrained, censuring Luther for alleged temerity, while making no mention of »heresy« or »error in faith«.

The direct source of the first censure Cajetan communicated to Luther in their first meeting on October 12 was his eighth treatise.[81] In this lengthy examination of the arguments in Luther's fifty-eighth *resolutio*, Cajetan gave a carefully crafted rebuttal of Luther's denial that the indulgences granted to the faithful are an application of the superabundant merits of Christ and his saints. The bull *Unigenitus* was cited near the beginning of Cajetan's *corpus articuli* as a declaration about the *thesaurus* of merits Christ left to his Church and which the saints augmented.[82] Cajetan did not, however, use his paragraph of papal doctrine apodictically, but went on to develop a series of supporting arguments. First, he cited the provisions in canon law which secure the normative character of Roman or papal teaching.[83] Biblical and theological considerations on merit and satisfaction, mutual help in the body of the Church, and the papal role in distributing the benefits of the *thesaurus* all point toward the doctrine formulated by Clement VI.[84] The bull, therefore, was on firm ground when it stated the view that Luther had called in question.

In the responses to the twenty-two arguments that he cited from Luther's *resolutio*, Cajetan urged that his high view of the *thesaurus* had stronger backing that just the endorsements of Saints Thomas and Bonaventure. The doctrine rests on Scripture texts, intellectual arguments, Roman decrees, as well as a theological

---

[79] *Opuscula omnia*, 103a,8; *Cajetan Responds*, 58.
[80] *Cajetan Responds*, 58f.
[81] *Opuscula omnia*, 97a-101a; *Cajetan Responds*, 68-85.
[82] *Cajetan Responds*, 71f.
[83] Ibid., 72.
[84] Ibid., 72-75.

consensus. Consequently, one holding the contrary must be judged rash and presumptuous.[85] On such a point the agreement of high-ranking theologians is a bulwark against the plague of confusion that would come over the Church if each theologian were to follow his own head. Again, however, the teaching subjected to assessment is branded »rash«, not »heretical«.

Three special aspects of this first critique of Luther's *Resolutiones* by Cajetan deserve mention. (1) Luther's *Tractatus de indulgentiis* of 1517 had taught that the works and merits of Christ and his members are in the hands of the Pope for distribution in indulgences. The *Tractatus* had not referred to a *thesaurus*, but it had nonetheless portrayed an indulgence granted to the living and one for the departed as each in its own way an application of the benefits accrued from the good done in the Church under the influence of Christ.[86] Luther's treatise, to be sure, sharply distinguished conferral of indulgences from God's gift of interior, healing grace,[87] but then Cajetan himself had alluded to the same kind of distinction in his treatises.[88] In comparison with the earlier *Tractatus*, Luther's *resolutio* on the *thesaurus* was a substantial innovation. It appears to be one consequence of Luther's new accentuation of the power of the keys in early 1518.[89] Cajetan surely would have preferred the doctrine expressed in the *Tractatus*, which Luther had submitted in 1517, over the *Resolutiones* of 1518. The former gave a dense ontological basis for indulgences, while the latter built its teaching around acts of will and decision, first by Christ in conferring the keys and then by the pope in voiding assigned penances.

(2) Cajetan did not explain the *sensus ecclesiae* in the Augsburg preparatory treatises, but only asserted its normative character. However, the term had

---

[85] »Doctrina haec, super scripturas & rationes & auctoritates Rom. Ecclesiae sanctorumque doctorum fundatur. Et non solum temerariae presumptionis est contrarium docere, verum indisciplinatae mentis est non acquiescere tot allatis.« *Opuscula omnia*, 99b,34.

[86] WABr 12, 7,96-98.107, 8,115-124. In English, in Study 5 of this collection, pp. 110 and 111f, above.

[87] WABr 12, 5,18-6,25, 8,108-114. In English, pp. 100 and 110, above.

[88] »Poenae inquantum sunt medicinae passionum non supplentur per indulgentias: & propterea debemus etiam indulgentiis acquisitis poenitentiam agere ... .« Treatise of September 29; *Opuscula*, 103a,59. Also in the treatise of October 7: ibid., 100b,27ff.51f; *Cajetan Responds*, 60, 84.

[89] In Thesis 58 Luther had been moving toward Thesis 60, which concludes that the treasure given to the Church is in fact the keys, »scilicet potestas Clavium« (WA 1, 615,11-15; LW 31, 228f). The text of Matthew 16:19, on binding and loosing in virtue of the keys, is so frequent in Luther's works of early 1518 that one analysis of his development makes the »discovery« of this text the hinge on which Luther's thought swung in, the direction of his mature theology of justification and faith. Matthias Kroeger, *Rechtfertigung und Gesetz* (Göttingen 1968), 173-175. In this collection, I treat this in Study 6, pp. 122f, 127, and 136, above.

occurred in Cajetan's explanation of the theology of faith in his commentary on Aquinas's *Summa theologiae*, in the exposition of Part II-II, published in 1517.[90] Faith, specifically as assent, is principally based on God himself, as the First Truth, who sheds his light upon the mind to make possible a supernatural act of accepting his revelation. However, faith, specifically as appropriation of revealed truths, grounds itself, for all who do not receive direct communications as prophets and apostles, on an infallible rule provided in the world by the Holy Spirit. This rule is not simply the Church's dogma, but is found in the »sense and doctrine« of the Church. The »sense of the Church,« consequently, belongs to the full reality of faith. The Church transmits the object of faith as a reality to which it is vitally assimilated by its sense of faith. Faith is assent of the mind to divine truth, but this truth is articulated in accord with the Scriptures and the sense of the Church. The believer, therefore, takes the sense and doctrine of the Church as a rule that proposes and explains what is to be believed. Church teaching is thus linked with a perception of the truth by which the Church is conscious of God and of the way to salvation.

(3) By way of historical assessment of Cajetan's critical analysis of Luther's views on indulgences in the *Resolutiones* of 1518, we can relate two observations made by Nikolas Paulus in the course of his exhaustive study of indulgences in doctrine, teaching, and practice at the end of the Middle Ages. Against the background of a massive store of information, Paulus studied Cajetan's treatises and did confirm the accuracy of Cajetan's contention that according to the *sensus ecclesiae et doctorum* indulgences did affect a penitent's obligations before God.[91] Paulus went on, however, to observe that when Cajetan cited the bull *Unigenitus* and proceeded to take it as having the force of a doctrinal utterance, then he was breaking new ground. No one to this time, Paulus contended, had used *Unigenitus* as documenting a binding doctrinal decision by the Pope.[92]

Cajetan's second censure of Luther on October 12 concerned the certainty of faith regarding the actual reception of grace. Luther had said, in his explanation of his seventh thesis on indulgences, that such certainty is necessary as one approaches sacramental absolution from sin. Cajetan's accusation of error on this point rested on the second and sixth of his preparatory treatises, completed on September 26 and October 1, respectively. These treatises were a penetrating

---

[90] On S.T. II-II, 1,1, in paragraphs III and X of Cajetan's commentary; also on II-II, 2,3, in par. VII. Leonine edition, 8, 8-10 and 30.

[91] Nikolas Paulus, *Geschichte des Ablasses im Mittelalter*, 3 (Paderborn 1923), 419.

[92] Ibid., 88. A year before, Cajetan had used the wording of *Unigenitus* as probative in his *Tractatus de indulgentiis* of late 1517. *Opuscula*, 92b,81ff, 93a,18f, 95b,1. K.-V. Selge pointed out that Luther, earlier in 1518, had referred to *Unigenitus* in his first exchange with Johann Eck (WA 1, 308,23-28; *Documenta zur Causa Lutheri*, 1, 439), but had called in question whether it was meant as a doctinal determination and whether it had been received, e.g. by a Council, as binding doctrine. *Normen der Christenheit*, 42, 107.

critique of the *Resolutiones* and of the *Sermo de poenitentia* published by Luther in late March as guidance for confessors just before Easter.

These texts by Luther represented one of his first attempts to treat technical questions of sacramental theology. Starting with the problem of the correct way to interrelate God's forgiveness with the priest's absolution in sacramental penance, Luther proposed theses which he knew diverged from what was held by the majority of his theological colleagues.[93] He felt he had backing for his new views, since they made sense of the loosing power conferred by Jesus in Matthew 16:19, were supported by a common axiom *(Non sacramentum, sed fides sacramenti iustificat)*, and were pastorally fruitful.[94] The *Resolutiones* contested the normal understanding of a sacrament as a *signum efficax gratiae*, stressing instead the declaration by the priest that God's grace had already been given.[95] The sacrament's fruit or benefit, given in virtue of the keys, is peace of conscience, consolation, and certitude both of the forgiveness of sins and of being in grace.[96] The *Resolutiones* cast doubt on the importance of contrition for sins, urging instead faith in what absolution declares, namely, that God's grace is given.[97] Repeatedly, Luther had insisted that believing one is really forgiven before God is a necessary component of authentic faith, for if it be lacking one frustrates both God's work of grace before the sacrament and his communication of assurance in the sacrament.[98] Luther's *Sermo de poenitentia*, shorter and more pointed than the rambling exposition in the *Resolutiones*, also contained Luther's relativization of contrition and pointedly set forth how believing in the effectiveness of the word of absolution is necessary in justification.[99]

---

[93] Luther's *resolutio* contained a strong challenge to other theologians: WA 1, 544,35-545,8; LW 31, 106f. Also, on his Thesis 38, where *fides absolutionis* was treated again: WA 1, 596,1-5 (against a popular view based on Jean Gerson), 596,24-36; LW 31, 195, 196.

[94] Matthew 16:19 occurs all through these and other works by Luther in early 1518. See above, n. 89. The axiom is cited at WA 1, 544,39, and then with some frequency in other works, e.g., WA 57III, 170,1; WA 1, 286,18, 325,16, 631,7; WA 2, 15,32. The pastoral aid given to penitents was noted at WA 1, 542,29 (LW 31, 103). Consequent on Luther's view is a different way for confessors to deal with those coming to them for confession and absolution: WA 1, 596,17 (LW 31, 195f); WA 1, 324,2.

[95] WA 1, 542,9, 545,1, 595,5; LW 31, 102, 107, 193.

[96] WA 1, 540,35, 541,20, 542,7.15f.24-27, 543,20, 595,13; LW 31, 100, 101, 102f, 104, 193f.

[97] WA 1, 542,39, 594, 37, 595,4.21f; LW 31, 103, 193.

[98] WA 1, 540,41-541,5, 543,20-25 (»Non enim sufficit remissio peccati et gratiae donatio, sed oportet etiam credere remissum ...«), 595,13; LW 31, 100, 104, 193f.

[99] WA 1, 323,32-324,19. As noted in Study 6 (p. 124, n. 27, above), Carl J. Peter recently studied Luther's 1518 *Sermo de poenitentia* with regard to its pastoral advice on the kind of effort to make toward confessing all one's sins. Cajetan's critique of this point of the sermon was the first in a series of Catholic reactions leading up to the Council of Trent's declaration on integral confession.

Cajetan's treatises formulate a sharp rejection of Luther's notion of *fides sacramenti* as an unwarranted innovation.[100] To show the impossibility of this kind of faith, the cardinal had recourse to the familiar distinction between infused and acquired faith. Neither the infused supernatural virtue is such as to include a conviction about a particular sacramental effect, nor does a person have grounds by perceived evidence and human trust for the certainty Luther wanted based on the word of Christ.[101]

The counter-arguments that Cajetan marshaled against Luther seek to show that such a theology of faith is contrary to the sense and doctrine of the Church. Luther had extended the scope of *fides* from its proper content, divine revelation, to include in this content a particular and singular case of sacramental efficacy.[102] Luther's thesis was proposing a certitude of grace that theologians agreed was not possible.[103] On the one hand, for Cajetan, a person cannot be certain of having the traditionally required dispositions for fruitful sacramental reception; but then Luther was making sacramental efficacy contingent upon a new kind of disposition, faith in the actual reception of grace.[104] Luther had also spoken disparagingly about contrition, which in sound theology and in the practice of confessors plays a central role in the forgiveness of sins and in justification through sacramental penance.[105] Finally, Luther's works proposed a repristinated form of the declaration-theory of absolution, once held by Peter Lombard, but which the Council of Florence had excluded from Catholic doctrine.[106] When one considers the range and force of Cajetan's arguments, it becomes clear why

---

[100] Cajetan perceived Luther as arbitrarily requiring »novellum et impertinens accidens pro dispositione necessaria ad gratiam Dei per absolutionem sacramentalem.« Luther had to be censured for saying that even if one were contrite, sacraments would occasion a person's damnation »nisi credat se absolvi« (cf. WA 1, 324,11). This is, in Cajetan's view, to oppose the Church by minimizing what it requires (confession, contrition, satisfaction) while insisting on faith in the sacramental effect and making this necessary to salvation – »Hoc est novam construere ecclesiam.« *Opuscula*, 111a,1-8; *Cajetan Responds*, 55.

[101] Ibid., 50-52.

[102] *Opuscula*, 110a,23-26.48-54; *Cajetan Responds*, 50f.

[103] *Opuscula*, 110a,76f, 111,38-41; *Cajetan Responds*, 52, 66.

[104] *Opuscula*, 110a,57-65, 110b,2-8.14f, 111a,1-8; *Cajetan Responds* 51, 52, 55. For the last text, see note 100, above.

[105] *Opuscula* 110b,52-54.72-79: »...probare enim seipsum (quod est conteri) iussit Apostolus [1 Cor 11:28], iubet Ecclesia, exigunt omnes communiter confessores. Credere autem se poenitentem omnino effectum habiturum novatorum exigit dogma.« Also 111b,41-45; *Cajetan Responds*, 53f, 54, 65f.

[106] *Opuscula*, 111a,45-55, 11b,30-33; *Cajetan Responds* 63f, 65f. W. Schwab describes accurately Luther's espousal of a declaratory understanding of absolution in early 1518, which Luther had not overcome in the writings available to Cajetan. *Entwicklung und Gestalt der Sakramententheologie bei Martin Luther* (Frankfurt/M. and Bern 1977), 81-97, especially 88-93.

he spoke so firmly in demanding Luther's recantation. While he did not accuse Luther of heresy, he still had to voice a serious censure of what Luther had published on *fides sacramenti*.[107]

Three aspects of Cajetan's encounter with Luther's thought on faith in the sacrament can be mentioned. (1) The *sed contra* of Cajetan's treatise of September 26 had given a lapidary judgment that Luther's view was contrary to the *communis ecclesiae sensus*. We saw above something of the theological density this »sense of the Church« had in Cajetan's thought. In elaborating his rejection of Luther's *fides sacramenti*, Cajetan appealed to »the ordinary norm« that one cannot have complete certainty about being in the grace of God. Cajetan added that such a residual doubt was woven deeply into the fabric of the life of the Church, being implicitly but clearly expressed both in postcommunion prayers that the sacrament not lead to condemnation and punishment and in the »Lord, I am not worthy« said before communion even by those who have confessed and been absolved.[108] Such prayers illustrate the lived convictions of good Christians who neither have nor aspire to Luther's *fides gratiae praesentis*.

The sense of the Church also accentuates the importance of contrition, in contrast to Luther's refusal to make it central in conversion. Cajetan claims that the sacramental rite of the Church makes clear the role of contrition as *summe necessaria*, and this point of doctrine is also reflected in the common practice of confessors who look for contrition in a penitent, not for explicit belief in the effect of the sacrament.[109]

However, Cajetan's appealing use of the *lex orandi* should not obscure the point that his precise and cogently argued treatises contrast sharply with the pastoral and spiritual themes present in Luther's writings on sacramental reception. In his *Resolutiones* Luther was concerned to set forth the paradoxical hiddenness of God's grace and the seriousness with which people should take Christ's historical institution of the keys of binding and loosing. Luther's *Sermo de poenitentia* sought to stimulate the coming alive of faith, over against a straining to feel sorry or a merely conventional fulfillment of ritual requirements.

---

107 Note that Cajetan rejected Luther's version of a particular kind of faith. In his own theology, he was resolutely opposed to a minimalizing form of the *obex*-doctrine, which would so stress sacramental efficacy as to require only the absence of a sinful intention in the recipient. Cajetan postulated the need of actual devotion (»actum ... actualiter tendentis in Deum justificatorem«) in the person being justified, whether outside or in a sacrament. Such devotion was a disposition freely chosen under the enabling influence of grace. Cajetan, Commentary on S.T., I-II, 113,3, paragraphs II-III (Leonine edition, 7, 333), and on 113,8, paragraph II (»gratia causat duos motus: alterum per modum liberi arbitrii, quasi imperando ei accessum ad Deum et recessum a peccato; alterum per modum naturae, quasi exequendo inductionem iustitiae et remissionem peccati.« Leonine edition, 7, 340). This part of Cajetan's commentary was written in 1511.

108 *Opuscula*, 110b,15; *Cajetan Responds*, 52.

109 *Opuscula*, 110b,53f.79 (see n. 105, above); *Cajetan Responds*, 54.

Luther's words resonate with themes stemming from prayer, personal struggle, and pastoral guidance. This experiential and religious coloration does not mean that Luther's positions were necessarily correct, but it does entail consequences for an effective counter-argument. Cajetan did not sense this, and so his treatises do not concern themselves with developing an engaging presentation of the doctrines he was setting forth as normative alternatives to Luther's proposals. Consequently, the encounter of the two at Augsburg was marked by a tragic difference in the levels of discourse, which explains why Cajetan did not convince Luther and win him over to an alternative view of sacramental forgiveness.

(2) From the viewpoint of Luther's theological development, we note that the materials from early 1518 studied by Cajetan included early and rambling attempts by Luther to formulate a doctrine of word, sacrament, and faith. Cajetan was studying transitional documents, beyond which Luther had in certain respects progressed by the time he arrived in Augsburg.[110] Parts of the *Resolutiones* bear some disclaimers on Luther's part that can alert the reader to the still tentative character of what is being proposed, and the first exposition of *fides sacramenti* is one of these texts.[111] Luther apparently felt the need of a more systematic and complete work than the 1518 *Sermo de poenitentia* studied by Cajetan, for he issued a German sermon-treatise on sacramental penance in 1519 which is much more than a translation of the 1518 work.[112] What Cajetan judged with his well-grounded severity in Augsburg were not works showing Luther at the top of his form theologically.

Furthermore, numerous key themes of Luther's theology of Christian conversion had been explained in works not published in the early autumn of 1518. Cajetan had no evidence before him, for example, of the engaging interweaving of Christology and justification found in Luther's 1517-18 lecture-course on the Epistle to the Hebrews.[113] Cajetan had no exposure to the central current of Luther's thought down to early 1518, namely his strong opposition to Ockhamist views of grace and human efforts to prepare for justification.[114]

---

[110] The transitional nature of Luther's *Resolutiones*, regarding their sacramental theology, has been pointed out by O. Bayer, *Promissio* (Göttingen 1971), 166, 182, 346, and by W. Schwab, *Entwicklung und Gestalt*, 90. In the summer of 1518 Luther made a concise and ordered presentation of his new notion of *fides sacramenti* in theses entitled *Pro veritate inquirenda et timoratis conscientiis consolandis* (WA 1, 630-633). The importance of these theses is noted by Bayer, 182-202, Schwab, 98-105, and M. Brecht, *Martin Luther*, vol. 1, *Sein Weg zur Reformation* (Stuttgart 1981), 228-230. I analyze them in Study 6, pp. 125-129, above.

[111] At the beginning of the 7th *resolutio*: »In eius intelligentia adhuc laboro.« WA 1, 539,36; LW 31, 98.

[112] *Ein Sermon von dem Sakrament der Buße*, WA 2, 709-723; LW 35, 9-22.

[113] I set this forth in *Man Yearning for Grace*, 199-207.

[114] Ibid., 178-199; more concisely, in Study 2, pp. 19-21, above.

Cajetan too opposed the positions on human ability and merit of grace that Luther had contested with his profound theological theses during the Heidelberg Disputation of April 1518.[115] There was more common ground between Cajetan and Luther than appeared during their exchange at Augsburg.

(3) In contrast with Silvester Prierias, Cajetan did not brand Luther's teaching heretical. He had detected errors requiring correction, but not evidence that Luther was diverging from revealed and defined truth.[116] It is well known, however, that Luther did not accept Cajetan's judgment on his two errors. In the interviews of October 12-14, Luther maintained instead that his positions on the *thesaurus* of indulgences and on *fides sacramenti* were supported by Scriptural texts more authoritative than the norms Cajetan was using in his censures. Luther submitted a written defense in their third meeting, but Cajetan found in it no reason to drop his demand for recantation on two points. Thus the hearing ended in an ominous state of impasse.

What is less well known is that after the three interviews Cajetan reassessed the cogency of the charges he had pressed against Luther. Perhaps he had re-read his treatises and noted a sense in which Luther's *fides sacramenti* would bear an orthodox construction.[117] He concluded that on this point his stand was not based on the same kind of provable evidence as given by the papal bull *Unigenitus* in showing Luther's error on indulgences. Therefore, a day or so after the third interview, in a conversation with Luther's Augustinian confrere, Wenceslaus

---

[115] WA 1, 355-365; LW 31, 42-58. This disputation is a basic text of Luther's theology. It gives focus to such a standard work as W. von Loewenich, *Luther's Theology of the Cross* (original, 1929; translation, Minneapolis 1976). Catholic appreciations of its content are Harry McSorley, *Luther: Right or Wrong?* (New York and Minneapolis 1969), and J. Vercruysse, »Gesetz und Liebe.«

[116] This is not argued just from silence. In 1519, Cajetan was shown a volume of Luther's works which the Louvain theologians had gone over, making frequent marginal notations where they found heresy. Cajetan was recorded as uttering the tart comment that these may be errors, but they are not heresies. Most of the points, he added, could stand as orthodox with some conceptual refinement *(distinctiones)*. Related in Martin Bucer's letter to Beatus Rhenanus, July 30, 1519; *Briefwechsel des Beatus Rhenanus*, ed. A. Horowitz and K. Hartfelder (Leipzig 1886), 166.

[117] In his treatise of September 26, Cajetan had used a distinction that would allow Luther's notion of *fides* to stand, in a certain sense. »Et dicito, quod fides certissima est, & esse debet etiam de effectu sacramenti particulari in me, quantum est *ex parte sacramenti*; sed *ex parte mei suscipientis* licitum est dubitare de illius effectu in me.« *Opuscula*, 110b,12 (emphasis added); *Cajetan Responds*, 52. Cajetan spoke similarly about certitude of the application of the merits of Christ in an indulgence: *Opuscula*, 100a,71; *Cajetan Responds*, 83. More notably, Cajetan applied such a scheme of thought to the value of the works of the saints, saying that »secundum se et secundum proprias vires« the saints and their works are evil, while »secundum gratiam Spiritus Sancti in ipsis et operibus suis« they fulfil the commandments and merit eternal life. *Opuscula*, 99b,53-73; *Cajetan Responds*, 79f. This Thomist papal legate was thus capable of applying modes of theological thought which later turned up in Luther's discourse on how one is *simul iustus et peccator*, and totally both, but from two different viewpoints. The absence of a reference to these passages in B. Lohse's study of the treatises undermines somewhat the cogency of his repeated claim that Cajetan really did not engage Luther's main proposals on faith and salvation. Cf. »Cajetan und Luther,« *Kerygma und Dogma* 32 (1986), 161, 166, 168.

Link, Cajetan gave assurances that he was not judging Luther a heretic and that he was not about to issue an excommunication. There would be some delay, since he was asking for an answer from Rome. But in the meantime Luther is to be told that the second of the two points, on *fides sacramenti*, could remain open, since with a slight redefinition Luther's view might stand. All that the Legate wanted from Luther was an expression of obedient agreement with the bull of Clement VI.[118]

Cajetan's modification of his charge against Luther, in a last attempt to bring the *processus* to a satisfactory end, is especially remarkable in view of the severity with which the legate had judged Luther in his second and sixth preparatory treatises. But aspects of Cajetan's earlier assessment could well have influenced him in his decision to suspend judgment on Luther's doctrine of sacramental disposition. First, Cajetan's treatises referred to the »ordinary norm« that one cannot attain certitude of being in grace. But this doctrine had been especially articulated by St. Thomas Aquinas, while some Scotists held that one could go beyond a merely conjectural knowledge of being in, or having, grace.[119] Cajetan may have realized that the theological consensus was not perfect on this key element in his verdict against Luther. Secondly, there was his appeal to the *sensus ecclesiae* manifested in the prayers of the Church. Could such a point be urged against Luther in a canonical *processus*? A heresy investigation calls for norms more precisely documented in the doctrinal tradition. Whatever may have been his reasons, the delegated spokesman for Pope Leo X communicated to Luther a reduced set of charges, in an act of keen discretion and diplomatic forthcomingness not recognized in most biographies of Luther and histories of the outbreak of the Reformation.

Luther's face-to-face exchanges with Cajetan in Augsburg constitute one of the great scenes of the Reformation. A critical moment came in the second meeting with Cajetan's agreement to accept from Luther a written defense of his stand on the foundation of indulgences and faith in sacramental efficacy. Luther composed

---

[118] Cajetan's changed judgment is narrated in a report prepared for Prince-Elector Frederick, who had left Augsburg, and printed as »Lenger und weitleuffiger Bericht der Handlung D. Mart. Luth. ergangen zu Augsburg,« *Der Neundte Teil der Bücher des Erhwirdigen Herrn D. Martin Lutheri* (Wittenberg 1557), fol. 38r. K.-V. Selge called attention to this report in his critical review of G. Hennig, *Cajetan und Luther* (Stuttgart 1966), in *Archiv für Reformationsgeschichte* 60 (1969), 273, and sought to explain why Cajetan shifted his position in *Normen der Christenheit*, 147f. Selge gave this important text in »La Chiesa in Lutero,« in M. Marcocchi et al., *Martin Lutero* (Milan 1984), 13-33, at 31f, n. 30. Luther himself wrote in early 1521, during his polemic with Jerome Emser, that at Augsburg Cajetan demanded his recantation only on the doctrine of indulgences, while the Cardinal granted that »the other« (*das ander*) could be handled by introducing a distinction. *Auf des Bocks zu Leipzig Antwort*, WA 7, 282,10; LW 39,134.

[119] Scotus held that a person has no reason to doubt about the sufficiency of his disposition for justification through a sacrament, especially penance. *In IV Sent.*, D.17, Q.1 (*Opera omnia*, 18, 510f). The Scotist position was argued at the Council of Trent in August 1546, with regard to certitude of being justified, by Giovanni Antonio Delfini, O.F.M., *Pro certitudine gratiae praesentis*, given in *Concilium Tridentinum* 12, 651-658.

his defensive brief and had it ready at the third meeting, on October 14.[120] Luther argued in his paper, first, that the bull *Unigenitus* could not be taken as binding doctrine. The decretal was at most a pious exhortation that did not give convincing grounds for what it declared. Further, its use of Scripture was such as to twist the meaning of texts. The notion of the saints' superfluous merits cannot stand examination, and so the *thesaurus* of merits is a question open for ongoing theological disputation. Luther then made a concise proposal of his own view of the role of the keys and papal authority in granting indulgences. For a settlement of the matter, he looked forward to an authentic declaration by Pope Leo.

On *fides sacramenti* Luther's written brief presented a tightly argued statement, climaxing with eleven biblical texts to show that one must believe most certainly in the grace attained in the sacrament or else one is rejecting Christ's promise and offer. One is to respond to God's word and grace with *fides specialis, fides de effectu praesenti*.[121] Luther begged Cajetan to appreciate how the texts bound him in conscience to hold the doctrine they contain. Demanding a recantation in the face of such evidence would be cruelty indeed. Still, Luther asked that Pope Leo be informed that he is an honest seeker after truth who is ready to change once he is shown his errors.

Cajetan immediately read through Luther's paper, but found in it no grounds for changing the demands that rested on his preliminary treatises. Luther was amazed at Cajetan's seeming insensitivity to his biblical arguments, and so evaded the Legate's renewed demand for recantation by saying that Pope Leo would have to give a binding verdict. Exasperated at seeing the hoped-for informal solution slipping away, Cajetan agreed to forward Luther's written defense to the Pope, although it would be accompanied by a refutation based on Scripture and the canons. As for any further conversation, Luther was not to return until he had a change of heart and was ready to stop trying to introduce new dogmas into the Church.

Cajetan did make an attempt to break the impasse by asking Staupitz, Luther's Augustinian superior, to persuade Luther to retract his errors. But Staupitz pleaded his own inability to keep pace with Luther when discussing Scripture texts. Cajetan did ask that Luther be assured of his own good will toward him.[122] However, this assurance was undercut, since on the same day Staupitz learned of harsh measures against Luther ordered in late August by the order's Vicar General, G. della Volta, namely, that Luther was to be captured, imprisoned, and delivered in chains to Rome.[123]

---

[120] He published the tenor of the text in the *Acta Augustana* in November. WA 2, 9-16; LW 31, 264-275.

[121] WA 2, 14,25, 15,2.7.23.

[122] The meeting between Cajetan and Staupitz is described in various letters, e.g., WABr 1, 214,39ff, 234,54-58, 241,227-232.

[123] Staupitz reported this to Frederick the Wise immediately, in a letter of October 15. T. Kolde, *Die deutsche Augustiner-Congregation*, 443f. Luther mentioned the disturbing fact in his mid-November report to the Elector: WABr 1, 241,224. Kolde also published the letter of della

Two letters to his friends back in Saxony, both dated October 14, reveal the immediate impact on Luther of Papal Legate Cajetan and the demands he made for a recantation.[124] Because of Cajetan's tenacity on the two points, Luther sees no hope of any good coming from him, no matter how fatherly and benevolent he says he is. Luther is sure he has refuted Cajetan on the two points, but the Cardinal is obtuse in the face of biblical arguments. Luther will hold to his two positions, especially faith in the sacramental word, since thereby he has become a Christian.[125] In case Cajetan tries to have him taken into custody, a formal appeal will be readied which will take the matter over Cajetan's head directly to the Pope himself. Another means of neutralizing the Legate will be the publication of the written brief defending against his two accusations of error. Luther is sure he can show the world that he had an incompetent judge in the Augsburg hearings. Luther asks for prayers, since a dire threat hangs over him as he does battle for faith in Christ and the grace of God.

Two days after writing the letters, on October 16, Luther had the text of his appeal to Pope Leo notarized before witnesses.[126] Luther protested that the procedures undertaken against him so far have been improper and unjust. First, his theses treated a legitimate matter of disputation, since on important aspects of indulgences no definitive, binding doctrine had been laid down by the Church.

Volta. »Luther und sein Ordensgeneral,« 476-478.

[124] (1) Letter to Spalatin, with information meant for Frederick: WABr 1, 241f; LW 48, 83-87. (2) Letter to A. Karlstadt, for the Wittenberg university faculty: WABr 1, 215-217.

[125] Luther told Karlstadt that he could obviously please the Pope's legate immensely by uttering the simple word »Revoco«. »Aber ich will nicht zu einem Ketzer werden mit dem Widerspruch der Meinung durch welchen ich bin zu einem Christen worden; ehe will ich sterben, verbrannt, vertriben und vermaledeiet werden etc.« WABr 1, 217,60. Clearly something more than a doctrinal position and its warrants in the theological sources is at stake here. Luther's personal relation to God must now include a certitude of grace on the basis of the actualizing word of absolution. It is a matter, for Luther, of biblically based teaching, and so of theology to be taught, but also a matter on which pastoral practice and personal appropriation have given further verification. O.H. Pesch highlights the importance of this utterance by placing it at the head of Ch. 6 of his *Hinführung zu Luther* (Mainz 1982), 103. At this climactic point in Luther's development, the personal conviction shaped by the Word of God has come to stand in critical tension with the church and its official teachers (Pesch, p. 110).

[126] WA 2, 28-33. The historical and legal context of Luther's two canonical appeals of late 1518 is greatly illuminated by the work of H.-J. Becker, *Die Appellation vom Papst an ein allgemeines Konzil* (Cologne & Vienna 1988), which treats Luther's first appeal on p. 245f. Early in his work, Becker specifies that such an appeal *ad papam melius informatum* was essentially a formal call for the Pope to review the grounds for his earlier decision (p. 10). Luther's appeal was quickly printed by Froeben in Basel together with the *Acta Augustana*. R. Bäumer treats this appeal in *Martin Luther und der Papst* (5th ed., Münster 1987), 33-35 and 125, with emphasis on Luther's profession of readiness to hear the voice of Christ speaking through the Pope (see n. 129, below). This utterance, as Bäumer points out, is not consistent with what Luther will say at the end of the *Acta Augustana*: »Veritas divina est etiam domina Papae: non enim iudicium hominis expecto, ubi divinum iudicium cognovi.« WA 2, 18,2.

Added to this, indulgences are not central to the faith, and so there was no *iusta causa* for citing Luther before an ecclesiastical tribunal with reference to his orthodoxy.[127] Second, it was wrong for the Roman officials Ghinucci and Prierias to have official roles in the *processus*, because the former is expert only in civil and not in doctrinal matters, while the latter as a Dominican comes from the camp of Luther's adversaries. Further, Prierias's *Dialogus* demonstrated deep-seated hostility as well as ineptitude in working with the normative sources, Scripture and the Fathers.[128] Third, Cajetan did not conduct himself properly in the three interviews, since he sought to pressure Luther into recanting on a matter not yet doctrinally determined. Further, he refused to instruct Luther on his errors, simply setting aside the defense submitted to him. Also, the Legate made use of threats of excommunication and interdict in a final effort to force Luther to modify his teaching.[129] Consequently, as the victim of a series of injustices, Luther appeals from the ill-informed Pope Leo, who has allowed the *processus* to unfold in such a manner, to a better informed Pope Leo, from whom Luther awaits a just judgment, as from the spokesman for Christ in his Church.[130] With such a legal instrument in hand, Luther remained in Augsburg awaiting further developments and the right moment to make his appeal public.

A first development came with the message from Cajetan that the second point of his censure, on *fides sacramenti*, was suspended for the present, and that the Legate was now asking Luther only to conform to the doctrine of *Unigenitus*. On

---

[127] »...cum in materia indulgentiarum variae et incertae sint opiniones doctorum, tam Canonistarum quam theologorum, nec in his usque hodie aliquid certum et determinatum habeat ecclesia.« Luther mentions two canons whose minimal teaching set the perameters of discussion, but adds, »nec satis constat nec per ecclesiam determinatum est, quid sit et quantum valeat modus ille suffragii, per quam conferuntur indulgentiae defunctis.« WA 2, 28,32-29,7. In such an open situation, disputing is licit, especially when done with a readiness to submit to the church's judgment: »Deinde sic disputavi, ut totam hanc disputationem submitterem non solum Ecclesiae, sed etiam cuiusque melius sentientis iudicio.« 30,1f.

[128] Luther states that the indulgence preachers had delated him before the Pope and his procurator. He evinces here no knowledge of Archbishop Albrecht's submission of his theses and treatise. WA 2, 30,20. Luther claims that Prierias knows only the practice of scholastic theology, which leaves him poorly equipped to treat the matter presently at issue, for »haec materia iudices quaerat in sacris literis et ecclesiasticis Patribus instructissimos.« 31,3.

[129] WA 2, 32,5-25. Luther refers to his readiness to submit to judgment on his teachings by the Roman Church or by university faculties, such as Basel, Freiburg, and Louvain, or even by the faculty of overarching authority, that of Paris.

[130] »Ex quibus me gravatum laesumque et oppressum sentio, cum et hodie fatear, solummodo me disputasse et omnia sub pedibus sanctissimi domini nostri Leonis x. subiecisse, ut occidat, vivificet, reprobet, approbet, sicut placuerit, et vocem eius vocem Christi in ipso praesidentis agnoscam.« WA 2, 32,24. Consideration of this text, along with Luther's assertion about the normativity of the Roman church in the *Responsio* to Prierias (cited in n. 48, above in this Study), could well lead to a nuancing of B. Lohse's indications that the real issue between Luther and Cajetan was papal authority in doctrinal matters. Cf. »Luther und Cajetan,« *Kerygma und Dogma* 32 (1986), 165, 169.

October 17, Luther wrote to Cajetan, and, apparently in response to the reduction of charges, Luther promised to observe a moratorium on indulgences, provided only that his opponents do the same.[131] However, and here Luther refers to Cajetan's remaining demand, conscience would not permit submission to a doctrine backed only by the theology of Thomas Aquinas. Since indulgences represent an uncharted theological area, Pope Leo should make a determination of binding doctrine.[132] The next day, October 18, Luther composed a farewell letter to Cajetan, informing him of his appeal and renewing his profession of submissiveness to the coming papal determination.[133] When three days passed without any further word from the Legate, Luther's Saxon advisors became fearful that word from Rome could suddenly unleash stern measures against Luther and his friends. So in the night of October 21/22, Luther left Augsburg, and the next morning his appeal was found posted on the door of the cathedral.

Luther arrived back in Wittenberg on October 31, just one year after his initial intervention on indulgences. He first took up the task of writing his account of the hearing before Cajetan. These *Acta Augustana (Proceedings at Augsburg)* included the text of the defense in which Luther had responded to the Legate's two accusations of error, and went on to show that papal decretals at times twisted the original, natural meaning of the text of Scripture.[134] Luther also

---

[131] »Immo promptissimus sum atque facillime promitto me posthac materiam de indulgentiis non tractare atque his finitis quiescere, modo illis quoque modus imponatur ... qui me in hanc tragoediam suscitaverunt.« WABr 1, 221,30.

[132] The situation Luther depicts seems open to different possibilities: it could be resolved by the Pope or it could lead to a conflict between authority and conscience. »Libentissime omnia revocarem, tam tuo quam Vicarii mei [Staupitz's] iussu et consilio, si ullo modo conscientia mea permitteret.« But nothing should be said or done contrary to conscience, no matter what the command, advice, or advantage offered. Aquinas and the other authorities cited so far do not satisfy: »Visae enim sunt non satis firmo niti fundamento.« Pope Leo should therefore intervene, »ut per ecclesiam haec dubia determinata ad iustam vel revocationem vel credulitatem possit compelli. Nihil alius cupio quam ecclesiam sequi.« WABr 1, 221,35-49. S. Hendrix pointed out correctly that Luther is not here asserting individual conscience over against the religious institution. Still the same author muddles the issue by identifying Luther's appeal to conscience as being »also an appeal to the conscience of the church« *(Luther and the Papacy*, 63). The church, in the present letter, is an external instance of judgment on teaching offered for public consumption, an instance which can speak to this conscientious theologian with more authority than the scholastic masters. – However, in a short time, the biblical text will be speaking to Luther's conscience with greater authority than Leo X has in Luther's eyes.

[133] WABr 1, 222f; LW 31,87-89.

[134] WA 2, 19,20-22,5; LW 31, 279-282. S. Hendrix underscores the importance of this section of Luther's *Acta* as indicating a shift in Luther's complex set of doctrinal norms. *Luther and the Papacy*, 67f. Especially significant for future developments is the inclusion of Matthew 16:18-19 as one of the misused texts, that is, when the decretals take it as proof of the divine foundation of the Roman primacy. Cajetan composed a rejoinder to Luther's charges, admitting that church teaching is not rigorously bound to the literal sense of Scripture. But he then showed that three examples cited by Luther were not cases of papal deviance from the literal sense, including the Matthew 16 text. Cajetan's treatise is translated in *Cajetan Responds*, 99-104.

included in the *Acta* the text of the papal brief of August 23 that had ordered Cajetan to take Luther into custody. Luther expressed his doubts that such a harsh letter could have come from the Pope, in view of its blatant departure from due process in a *processus ordinarius*.[135] The return journey from Augsburg had given Luther time to further assess the two teachings on which Cajetan had charged him with error. Luther was coming to see that indulgences were rather unimportant in comparison with faith in the effect of the sacrament. On the latter point, salvation itself is at stake. One's Christianity is not affected by Clement VI's *Unigenitus*, but a person becomes completely heretical by denying faith in the word of Christ.[136] In December, such assertions were circulating in Luther's printed *Acta Augustana*. In spite of Cajetan's suspension of his second charge, the fact that he had made it in the first place continued to affect Luther deeply. Six months later, Luther wrote to another papal emissary that in Augsburg Cajetan had tried to undermine his faith in Christ.[137]

Pope Leo X's Doctrinal Determination on Indulgences

In addition to his personal appeals to Luther, Cajetan began steps toward gaining the authentic papal decision Luther had repeatedly requested. On October 15, Cajetan completed a treatise in which he set down concisely the basis of indulgences in the power of the keys, and affirmed the special manner *(per modum suffragii)* in which indulgences are applied to the souls in purgatory.[138] Shortly after, he wove together passages from this treatise and from his October 7 treatise on the *thesaurus* of merits into a draft declaration on indulgences, which he sent to the Pope with the request that a bull of doctrinal clarification be issued. Thus, the points would be set forth authentically on which Luther had spoken in his theses and *Resolutiones*.[139]

---

135 The »leaked« letter: WA 2, 23ff. Luther's critical apparatus on Roman juridical malpractice: 25,16-26,2. In translation: LW 31, 286-290. What Luther did not know was that Emperor Maximilian's supplementary denunciation, in his letter of August 5, had occasioned a change in the type of *processus*.

136 WA 2, 18,7-16; LW 31, 290f. Shortly after, in his commentary on Galatians 1:4 (published in 1519), Luther added the certitude of grace to the set of doctrines about which he was attacking the scholastics. WA 2, 458,29; LW 27, 172f. A contemporary passage in the *Operationes in Psalmos* condemns the detestable theologians who approve a pious doubt about one's own being in God's grace. WA 5, 124,30. See p. 139, above, in this collection.

137 May 17, 1519, to Karl von Miltitz. Luther was grounding his refusal to come before a mixed commission – Roman and German, theological and ecclesiastical – made up of Cajetan and the Archbishop of Trier. In a flight of fancy, Luther asserts that if he had time he would delate Cajetan to the Pope, listing the errors the Cardinal should be made to recant. WABr 1, 402,37.

138 *Cajetan Responds*, 88-90.

139 Paul Kalkoff, »Die von Kajetan verfasste Ablassdekret,« *Archiv für Reformationsgeschichte* 9 (1911), 142-144; G. Hennig, *Cajetan und Luther* (Stuttgart 1966), 90-92.

In Rome Pope Leo X acceded immediately to Cajetan's request, and the bull *Cum postquam* was issued on November 9, with the stated aim of removing doubts about the basis and efficacy of papally sanctioned indulgences.[140] Cajetan was commissioned to have the bull published in Germany, so that no one might henceforth allege ignorance on this matter or fabricate excuses, protests, or appeals on the pretext that the Church has not enunciated its teaching on indulgences. Using Cajetan's draft, Leo X taught that indulgences have their ground in the power of the keys, by use of which the Pope opens heaven for the faithful by removing impediments blocking their entry. Absolution in the sacrament of penance removes personal guilt, while indulgences remove the debt of punishment by conferring a share in the superabundance of Christ's and the saints' satisfactory merits. Thus indulgences are not efficacious as bare acts of authority by the power of the keys, but as acts of distribution – to the living by an absolution from punishment, to the departed by suffrage – out of the *thesaurus* of merits.

With *Cum postquam* Leo X reinforced the account Clement VI had given in 1343, following the compressed formulation of Cajetan's draft of a doctrine of indulgences. Thus, the *processus* was set on a solid juridical basis by the fashioning of a clear and updated standard against which Luther's teaching could be measured. For the moment, Cajetan's second charge, namely, that Luther taught an erroneous kind of disposition for fruitful reception of sacramental absolution, was in abeyance, in spite of the great importance which both Cajetan and Luther attributed to this question. If only Luther would revoke his utterances that went contrary to *Cum postquam*, then the matter could be settled.

Parallel with his request for doctrinal clarification from Rome, Cajetan acted as the diplomat by writing on October 25 to Frederick the Wise.[141] Reporting on the hearing in Augsburg, Cajetan underscored that he had treated Luther *paterne*, in conformity with the agreement made with Frederick in early September. Cajetan dismissed Luther's defensive brief of October 14, asserting that it was disrespectful in speaking of the bull of Pope Clement VI, a document patently contrary to Luther's position. Also, Luther cited Scripture quite ineptly in favor of his notion of *fides sacramenti*. Cajetan complained that after the inconclusive personal meetings with Luther there were promising signs of progress by the exchange of messages. But then Luther left Augsburg, thereby frustrating the Legate's hope of a negotiated settlement.

Cajetan pleaded with the Prince-Elector not to bring the Saxon house into disrepute by protecting one who is trying to foist new dogmas on the Church. The matter will not be dropped, and it would be much better if Luther were sent away from Wittenberg before his errors are condemned. The best course of

---

[140] Text in W. Köhler, ed., *Dokumente zum Ablassstreit von 1517* (2nd ed. Tübingen 1934), 158-160.

[141] WABr 1, 233-235.

action, however, would be for the prince to send Luther to Rome for the completion of the canonical *processus*. Luther's views, Cajetan assured Frederick, are not authentically Catholic, and Luther has been stating them in sermons in the form of direct assertions of teaching. Luther's academic freedom to dispute questions is no longer a viable defense against the charges made.[142]

Even while Cajetan had been meeting with Luther in Augsburg, the Curia in Rome was preparing to approach Frederick the Wise in hopes of gaining his backing for the crusade-levy and his cooperation in silencing Luther. Frederick was designated recipient of the Golden Rose, in testimony to his princely Christian virtues, and a special nuncio, Karl von Miltitz, was being commissioned to bring the Rose to him. By mid-November, when Miltitz left Rome, it was known that Luther had returned to Saxony from Augsburg. Consequently, Miltitz was ordered to deposit the Rose with the Fuggers in Augsburg and to delay conferring it until Cajetan judged that Frederick was conducting himself in a manner appropriate for one receiving this papal honor.[143]

In November, Luther began formulating a further canonical appeal, this time from an expected excommunication by the pope to a future general council. In the ecclesiastical controversies of the previous century, such appeals had proliferated, notwithstanding the prohibition issued by Pope Pius II in *Execrabilis* (1460).[144] Luther was aware of the precedent given by the appeal to a future council made by the Sorbonne in March 1518, as a protest against Leo X's new concordat with King Francis I. Luther had his appeal notarized on November 29, and then asked a printer to secretly prepare copies in placard format, which Luther would then hold in readiness pending Rome's reaction to Cajetan's communiques from Augsburg. But the Wittenberg printer sensed he had a sensational piece in his hands and he sold most of them before Luther even heard of his demarche.[145]

---

142 »Dicta Fratris Martini, licet in Conclusionibus sint disputative, in sermonibus tamen ab eo scriptis affirmative et assertative esse posita, et confirmata in vulgari Germanico, ut aiunt. Ea autem sunt partim contra doctrinam Apostolicae Sedis, partim vero damnabilia. Et credat mihi Illustrissima Dominatio Vestra, quia vera dico et loquor ex certa scientia, non ex opinionibus.« WABr, 1, 234,70. Cajetan is giving reasons why Luther's appeal to a better informed Pope cannot stand.

143 The texts concerning Miltitz's mission are in Johann Georg Walch, ed., *Dr. Martin Luthers Sämmtliche Schriften*, vol. 15 (St. Louis 1899), 668-679. One report was that Miltitz was armed with more than forty papal letters to powerful figures in Germany bidding them to help bring Luther under rein. WABr 1, 279,4. As for the Golden Rose, Frederick quickly perceived that the Curia was trying to bribe him into expelling Luther from Saxony. Heinrich A. Creutzberg, *Karl von Miltitz* (Freiburg/B. 1907), 47.

144 H.-J. Becker, *Die Appellation vom Papst*, 120-243, with Luther's appeal treated on pp. 246-249. Such an appeal was held permissible by a minority group of canonists, even in the first years of the 16th century. Becker, 356-365.

145 The text is given at WA 2, 36-40. Erwin Iserloh suggests that Luther foresaw the diffusion of his appeal, but let it occur in the way it did so that he could excuse himself in the face of the Prince-Elector's desire that he restrain himself. In H. Jedin ed. *Handbuch der Kirchengeschichte*, 4, *Reformation, Katholische Reform und Gegenreformation* (Freiburg 1967), 61; in English in H. Jedin

Luther's appeal claims that multiple abuses of power have vitiated the Roman *processus* against him, with the very appointment of Cajetan being a calculated act of unfairness, since he was a Dominican just like Luther's accusers. Though the cardinal had received Luther *humaniter* in Augsburg, in the end he applied pressure and uttered threats, without making clear to Luther why he judged him to be in error. Now that the Curia is apparently rushing to judgment, in a tyrannous act of power, Luther asks for redress at a future council.

The last two months of 1518 were for Luther a time of brooding uncertainty and foreboding. His firmly held views may well be condemned, for the signs of the times indicate that the Antichrist has enlisted the Roman Curia as an ally in war against God's truth.[146] Condemnation of Luther would ruin the educational renewal now underway in Wittenberg and would mean banishment from the Empire for himself. For a while, even the support of Frederick the Wise appeared doubtful. But the elector did allow Luther to read the letter he had received from Cajetan and to help draft the response in early December.[147] Frederick refused to expel Luther from Saxony or have him delivered to Rome, and assured Cajetan that many learned men in Germany found no departures from orthodoxy in Luther's works. The elector asked that the matter be referred to universities for disputation and eventual judgment on Luther's doctrine. If Luther would be shown in a credible manner to be teaching error, Frederick would readily fulfil his duty as a Christian prince.

Cajetan had followed Emperor Maximilian to Linz in Austria, where on December 13 he promulgated *Cum postquam*. Later he distributed copies of the bull as he moved westward across Germany in early 1519. Karl von Miltitz missed seeing Cajetan in Augsburg, but after depositing the Golden Rose there, he went on to Saxony to confer with Frederick and even to meet with Luther on January 5-6, 1519. Out of this meeting there arose an agreement on a new moratorium on controversy, while the attempt was made to have a German bishop named to deal with the case. It was stipulated that Luther have clearly explained what he was to recant and what the grounds were for any admission of error on his part.[148] The early months of 1519 brought a pause in Luther's case, as

---

and J. Dolan, eds., *History of the Church*, 5, *Reformation and Counter Reformation* (New York 1980), 59f.

[146] WABr 1, 270,9, 282,17. K.-V. Selge has pointed out how Luther's application of apocalyptic themes of judgment against his papal foes was quite decisive for the beginning of the Reformation upheaval. »Das Autoritätengefüge der westlichen Christenheit im Lutherkonflikt 1517 bis 1521,« *Historische Zeitschrift* 223 (1976), 591-617, especially 608-611.

[147] Luther's comments on Cajetan's letter: WABr 1, 236-246; Frederick's answer to Cajetan: WABr 1, 230.

[148] Luther's letters describe the meeting: WABr 1, 289ff (LW 48, 97-100), 294,5-14, 299,14-20, 313,5-19. Miltitz's reports on his own negotiating generated an ungrounded optimism in Rome about Frederick's cooperativeness and Luther's readiness to submit. For his part, Luther quickly came to doubt that anything would come of the exchange with Miltitz. He claimed in late February that the moratorium was already broken by John Eck's publication of theses directed against the Wittenberg theology.

the principal participants waited to see the outcome of the intervention by Miltitz. And with the death of Emperor Maximilian on January 12, the pause was extended into late 1519, as the issues concerning the Imperial succession overshadowed those concerning Luther's orthodoxy.

In mid-January 1519 Luther received a copy of *Cum postquam*, with its formulation on indulgences. In an important letter, actually a concise position paper, Luther gave Frederick the Wise the reasons for his refusing to acknowledge *Cum postquam* as an adequate and therefore binding church teaching.[149] The bull, according to Luther, simply repeats old doctrine, without any reference to the many points Luther has raised in the past year, and even declines to deal with some papal texts that ground divergent conclusions. There were no Scriptural arguments, no use of the Fathers, no citation of canon law, and no rational arguments, but only an assertion of teaching claiming authority. At a time when many source-documents of the faith are circulating in new editions, and when a new critical spirit is widespread, it is only right that one be shown the basis for accepting a church teaching. This, Luther noted, is not just a matter of personal integrity and conscience, but a requirement for the good name and credibility of the Roman Church itself. Luther will not repudiate *Cum postquam*, but neither will he submit to it.[150] Later in 1519, during the Leipzig Disputation, Luther made public his dissent from *Cum postquam*, while offering some principles about doctrine in the church.[151] But this matter belongs to the next stage of argument in early Reformation controversy.

Reflections

At the end of our narrative of the five distinct reactions to Luther that emanated from Roman authorities in 1518, a number of observations suggest themselves. Three remarks can be made about Luther, along with an evaluative reflection on the Roman reactions themselves.

First, it is clear that Luther offered quite substantial answers to the early Roman response to his work. Cajetan, at one point, accused Luther of rashness, but another impression is left by Luther's *Responsio* to Prierias, his defensive brief against Cajetan's two charges, his appeal from Cajetan to the Pope, and his

---

[149] K.-V. Selge called attention to this letter by citing a key passage from it as an epigraph following the title-page of *Normen der Christenheit*. S. Hendrix saw the letter as the turning point in the case initiated by the papacy against Luther. *Luther and the Papacy*, 77.

[150] WABr 1, 306,6-10, 307,61-64; LW 48,103-106. Luther's demand for ecclesial competence arises from a sense of belonging to a new age and working with a new set of norms of truth. But the challenge is also implied that the papacy refute him in a manner *he* judges competent and adequate. The parting of the ways is at hand.

[151] Johann Eck introduced *Cum postquam* into the Leipzig debate, but Luther responded that papal decrees are to be accepted »cum iudicio«, and that this document is defective, »Nec satis exprimit nec probat una syllaba quae dicit.« WA 59, 559,3973.3978f, 569,4295-4308; WA 2, 349,5.10f, 357,3-15. Luther gave a more systematic case against Leo X's decree in the *Resolutiones* of the theses debated against Eck at Leipzig: WA 2, 427-429.

justificatory statement on his dissent from *Cum postquam*. All of these were incisive, well argued, and formally quite cogent. In content, they gave, among other points, a coherent criteriology of theological discourse. Luther's responses to Rome articulated a clear set of norms for judging doctrinal statements. In fact, the analysis of Luther's Ninety-Five Theses by the papal court-theologian, Prierias, prompted numerous concise formulations of Luther's set of criteria, as in the refrain, *Rogo, ubi hic Scriptura, patres, aut Canones sonant?*[152]

Second, Luther's appeals for reform of preaching and doctrinal clarification became embroiled in 1518 in a complex interplay with non-homiletical and non-doctrinal forces. Early on, we saw something of the tawdry arrangement between Albrecht of Brandenburg, an episcopal pluralist, and the Roman Curia. In mid-1518, Emperor Maximilian was seeking to secure the Hapsburg dynasty, and his vexation over being opposed by Frederick of Saxony apparently occasioned the harsh attack on Luther in the Emperor's letter to the Pope on August 5. This produced the canonical escalation of late August, in which Luther perceived a grave offense against due process. Leo X was trying to promote the defense of Europe against the Turks, but the notion of such a coordinated effort by the Western powers belonged to the already collapsed paradigm of »Christendom«. Faced with Leo's appeal, the German estates responded resentfully, pleading their many *gravamina* against Rome. Anti-Roman indignation grew and came in turn to fuel developments toward the divisive Reformation. All in all, these political dynamics posed dangers for that clarification of doctrine and that enrichment of Christian proclamation for which Luther had called out. These latter concerns demanded careful examination of multiple sources, thoughtful weighing of argument, and a passion for deeper insight into the human condition and God's redemptive work. The swirl of the political struggles of 1518 was not a good atmosphere for Luther's original »cause«.

Third, at the end of the year, Luther indicated that his response to Rome was coming under the influence of apocalyptic themes and convictions. This brought an uncanny, ominous factor into the picture. Such a mode of thought created a volatile context as Luther continued to study, lecture, write, and dispute in 1519.

The Roman reactions to Luther in 1518 leave the impression of notable variety, a variety both of kind and of quality. The initial response, applying disciplinary pressure within the Augustinian order, was moderate and measured. But in the summer of 1518 Silvester Prierias made his hostile march through Luther's theses, in a response not showing Roman theology at the top of its form. The measured pace of response by Pope and Curia to Luther swerved over the energetic pursuit of the man on the basis of the Emperor's harsh letter. Both

---

[152] The pluriformity of Luther's doctrinal sources and norms in 1518 deserves more attention than given in B. Lohse's study, »Cajetan und Luther,« *Kerygma und Dogma* 32 (1986), 150-169. The presentation suggests that Luther argued only from Scripture against the doctrinal tradition, papal authority, and church practices (pp. 160, 162f, 169). But Luther's *Responsio* to Prierias, the *Acta Augustana*, and the January 1519 letter on *Cum postquam* all show him appealing to a broader range of sources.

actions in August, imperial and papal, were in all likelihood motivated politically.

Cajetan stands out on the Roman side for his competence and restraint. At the end of three weeks of energetic theological assessment, in his fourteen Augsburg treatises, he was sure of Luther's errors, but his »theological note« on the positions he censured was no more than that of theological impetuosity. Upon reflection, Cajetan suspended one charge and sought a papal declaration with which to sustain the other. A very skillful performance indeed. Cajetan's proficiency, however, did not make the positive impression then needed to enhance Rome's credibility in Luther's eyes.

At the end, the critical point is that Luther changed in very late 1518 from a readiness to submit to Roman correction to a position of dissent from *Cum postquam*. He had made unambiguous statements of submissiveness to judgments by the Pope in the preface to his *Resolutiones* in May and in the August *Responsio* to Prierias. In Augsburg, he stated his readiness to receive Leo X's *determinatio* in his formal appeal of October 16 and in letters of October 17 and 18. But three months later, when faced with Leo X's declaration, *Cum postquam*, Luther did not assent.

Luther's dissent entailed a mystery of human development, as a person passed over from one mode of judgment to another, but that is not all. The Roman reactions themselves had contributed. Prierias had forced Luther to sharpen his operative criteria of truth, and he then applied these criteria to *Cum postquam* in mid-January 1519. Cajetan's censure of Luther's early teaching on *fides sacramenti* had left Luther astounded and outraged. Finally, the intercepted papal letter of August 23, which Luther obtained in late October 1518, fueled bitter reflections on Roman judicial procedures. This motivated Luther's legal appeals and conclusions about malfeasance, or even worse, in the Roman Curia. In the end, his dissent from *Cum postquam* was not so mysterious.

8

LUTHER AND LIVED RELIGIOSITY

Stefano Cavallotto's anthology of nine writings by Luther presents the Reformer to the Italian reading public in the role of a pastor concerned with the care of souls.[1]

The title given to this book, with its reference to minor pastoral works, could suggest that its contents are of little importance. But this is not the case, because of the way in which the works in this volume – translated, accurately introduced, and amply commented upon by Cavallotto – cast considerable light upon both the figure of Martin Luther and on Christian doctrine itself.

Ordinarily, theologians and church historians treat Luther with reference to his incisive doctrines on justification, ecclesiology, and the Christian in society. Cavallotto's collection invites us to take note as well of the instruction by Luther which contributed in his day to the formation of pastors and people for the actual living-out of Christianity.[2] In these works Luther was writing for a population which he saw as religiously underdeveloped. In a text cited in the notes of Cavallotto's volume, Luther lamented the sad and deplorable religious impoverishment of the people that he had ascertained during parish-visitations in Saxony. »Good God, what wretchedness I beheld. The common people, especially those who live in the country, have no knowledge whatever of Christian teaching, and unfortunately many pastors are quite incompetent and unfitted for teaching.«[3]

---

[1] Martin Luther, *Scritti pastorali minori*, translated and edited by S. Cavallotto, with Preface by Boris Ulianich (Naples: Ed. Dehoniane, 1987), lxxii + 328pp.

[2] Martin Brecht shows how Luther turned, in 1518-20, to promoting a program of renewal of the daily life of piety for ordinary believers, almost immediately after his discovery of the saving righteousness of God. *Martin Luther*, 1, *Sein Weg zur Reformation, 1483-1521* (Stuttgart 1981), 333-348; in English, *Martin Luther. His Road to Reformation, 1483-1521* (Philadelphia 1985), 349-365. The first text in Cavallotto's anthology, »A Sermon on Preparing to Die« (1519; LW 42, 99-115; WA 2, 685-697), belongs to this first phase of Luther's pastoral program.

[3] From Luther's 1529 Preface to his Small Catechism (*The Book of Concord*, ed. T. Tappert et al. [Philadelphia 1959], 338; WA 30I, 264,17-265,2; cited, *Scritti pastorali minori*, 188). On the visitations of 1527-28, and the impact of their results on Luther, see M. Brecht, *Martin Luther*, 2, *Ordnung und Abgrenzung der Reformation, 1521-1532* (Stuttgart 1986), 253-273.

But Luther was not an ivory tower professor who would only lament the low state of formation among pastors and the poor level of religious instruction among the people. Luther is in fact best seen as part of the tradition of »theology-for-piety« that goes back to the Parisian university chancellor Jean Gerson (1363-1429). A notable number of fifteenth-century theologians, sadly little known, had dedicated their thought and writing to the service of religious renewal. This theological effort reached its pre-Reformation high-point in the works of the two older Augustinian confreres of Luther, Johann von Paltz (died 1511) and Johann von Staupitz (died 1524).[4] Like these men, but much more effectively, Luther did not just wring his hands over the state of lived religion in his day. Instead, Luther worked energetically over a number of years to supply remedies for the situation he had perceived.

Consequently, a full and balanced perception of Martin Luther must include an explicit reference to his long career as a theologian in the service of popular piety and his extensive production of pastoral and catechetical resources. Cavallotto's anthology is especially valuable for setting in relief this component of Luther's legacy. The work is a small pastoral *summa* of the early Lutheran reformation.

The works collected here cover the whole course of the Christian life. First, there is the ritual of baptism,[5] from which one moves on logically to Luther's catechisms[6] and to his personal profession of faith.[7] There follows an instruction on the confession of sins[8] and the marriage ritual,[9] as well as Luther's primer on

---

[4] Cavallotto remarks on the tradition of theology-for-piety on pp. xxix-xxxii of his introduction to *Scritti pastorali*. John Gerson has been studied recently by C. Burger, *Aedificatio, Fructus, Utilitas. Johannes Gerson als Professor der Theologie und Kanzler der Universität Paris* (Tübingen 1986), and D. C. Brown, *Pastor and Laity in the Theology of Jean Gerson* (Cambridge 1987). On Staupitz: David Steinmetz, *Misericordia Dei. The Theology of Johannes von Staupitz in its Late Medieval Setting* (Leiden 1968). On Paltz and »theology-for-piety«: B. Hamm, *Frömmigkeitstheologie am Anfang des 16. Jahrhunderts* (Tübingen 1982). I reviewed the work of Burger in *Gregorianum* 69 (1988), 796-798, and the work of Hamm, ibid. 65 (1984), 200-204. The latter review covers as well the recent edition of the works of Paltz, and was recently completed in a further review, ibid. 71 (1990), 592-595. See pp. 9-11, above in Study 1, for a further report on and assessment of the work of Paltz.

[5] »The Order of Baptism« (1523): LW 53, 95-103; WA 12, 51-52.

[6] Cavallotto gives Luther's prefaces of 1529 and 1530 to the Large Catechism: WA 30I, 125-132; in English in Theodore G. Tappert et al., eds., *The Book of Concord. The Confessions of the Evangelical Lutheran Church* (Philadelphia 1959), 358-365.

[7] Cavallotto gives Luther's 1528 confession, which is the final part of his last major defense of the Eucharistic real presence against Zwingli. LW 37, 360-372; WA 26, 499-509.

[8] »A Short Order of Confession Before the Priest for the Common Man« (1529): LW 53, 117-118; WA 30I, 343-345.

[9] »The Order of Marriage for Common Pastors« (1529): LW 53, 111-115; WA 30III, 74-80.

daily prayer.[10] One text exemplifies pastoral encouragement for a person undergoing severe temptations,[11] while another sets forth a way to help one discouraged over his or her life of prayer.[12] Finally, Luther teaches preparation for death.[13]

We can well recall that the nine short works in Cavallotto's anthology represent only a part of a much larger corpus of writings in which Luther offered guidance, instruction, and encouragement to unlearned pastors and ill-instructed people. He turned out hundreds of short instructional treatises in the service of lived religion. For example, Luther expounded on many occasions the meaning of the Our Father, and he wrote in response to practical questions, like the propriety of a Christian fleeing from a plague-stricken area and the reasons for keeping children in school. Luther usually taught about such issues of daily life and daily prayer in vernacular pamphlets of twenty-five to thirty numbered paragraphs, which continued to be reprinted during his lifetime and after his death.

In response to a request from the Prince-Elector to help upgrade preaching in Saxony, Luther began in 1520 to work on his »postils,« which offer model sermons on the gospel-passages read on Sundays and the major feasts of the church year.[14] Especially notable in the postils are Luther's texts on the Christmas gospels, where he recommends that one contemplate the mystery of the Word made flesh with a faith that refers Christ's coming to oneself, namely, »that you firmly believe that Christ was born for you, that his birth is yours, because it took place for your benefit«.[15]

Another genre of Luther's pastoral publications is his famous vernacular translation of the Bible. Here one should speak in the plural, since the extended

---

10 »A Simple Way to Pray« (1535): LW 43, 193-211; WA 38, 358-375.
11 »Comfort When Facing Grave Temptations« (1521): LW 42, 183-186; WA 7, 784-791.
12 »Ein kurzer Trostzettel für die Christen, daß sie im Gebet sich nicht irren lassen« (probably from 1540): WA 51, 455-457.
13 »A Sermon on Preparing to Die« (1519): LW 42, 99-115; WA 2, 685-697.
14 These works came out over the course of time extending from 1522 to 1544, with many of them being based on notes taken by students during Luther's own sermons. The Advent, Christmas, and first Summer Postils are in WA 10I; the Lenten Postil and a second Summer Postil (1526) in WA 17II; the Winter Postil and yet another Summer Postil (1544) are in WA 21; with WA 52 containing the House-Postil of 1544. Luther's postils were translated into English in volumes 7-14 of the older »Standard Edition« of his works, ed. J. N. Lenker (Minneapolis 1904-09). These eight volumes were reprinted by Baker Book House of Grand Rapids under the title *Sermons of Martin Luther* (1983).
15 WA 10I/1, 71,7, a phrasing which is similar to the reflection on the Nativity recommended by Ignatius Loyola, namely, that Christ began his life in poverty and after much suffering died on the cross, »and all this for me.« *Spiritual Exercises*, no. 116.

work of translation by Luther and his assistants led to numerous editions of distinct parts of the Scripture, before the completion of the whole Bible in 1534. Each book of the Bible came with Luther's preface, which sought to aid pastors and the literate laity to make religiously fruitful their encounter with the world of biblical revelation.[16]

It is well known that Luther wrote catechisms that were immensely successful.[17] Here Luther follows the classic sequence of commandments, Creed, prayer, and sacraments, in works which created the ethos of faith and piety that is cherished by Lutheran Christians to this day.

In 1523 Luther began composing new vernacular orders of service for morning and evening prayer.[18] Shortly after came revised liturgies for baptism, marriage, and burial, all of which Cavallotto has translated and commented upon in his Italian anthology. Luther was musically gifted, and he delighted in preparing vernacular hymns that express major themes of Christian piety.[19] His book of prayers was first printed in 1522 and it included both his earlier instruction on meditating on the passion of Christ and a catechetical exposition of the commandments, Creed, and Our Father.[20] Even more pertinent to daily prayer by ordinary people is the 1535 booklet *A Simple Way to Pray*, which is included in Cavallotto's anthology.

Thus, for both pastors and people, Luther produced an ample, comprehensive corpus of works for popular religious formation. Sad to say, a widespread interpretation of Luther, which lives on even today, is not notably different from the image formed by 19th century liberalism. Here Luther is seen above all as the exponent of emancipation from ecclesiastical authority and its laws and prescriptions. It is certainly true that Luther wrote profound passages on Christian freedom, but for him this is primarily the liberation given by Christ the Savior to the heart weighed down with sin and fearful before God. From 1524 onward, Luther expressed repeated concern over what he saw as abuses of the cry for »Christian liberty,« when others used it to justify causes that seemed

---

[16] The full set of Luther's prefaces are given in English in LW 35, 225-411. In Italian, the Marietti publishing house recently brought out a complete translation of Luther's biblical prefaces. *Prefazioni alla Bibbia*, ed. Marco Vannini (Casale Monferrato 1987).

[17] In English, in Tappert, ed., *The Book of Concord*, Small Catechism, pp. 337-356; Large Catechism, pp. 357-461. The following Study in this collection draws on these catechisms to illustrate Luther's teaching on the church and sanctification.

[18] See the recent exposition by J. Neil Alexander, »Luther's Reform of the Daily Office,« *Worship* 57 (1983), 348-369.

[19] Luther's liturgical chants and hymns are given in representative selection in LW 53, 149-341.

[20] On pp. 198-202, below, the following study in this collection treats Luther's catechesis on the church in this early instruction.

to Luther to have little relation to the epistle to the Galatians, the fundamental document on Christ's gift of freedom through faith.

Another element in an all-too-popular image of Luther is that with his rediscovery of the priesthood of all believers he destroyed any claim to authority by the church's hierarchy. To be sure, Luther was an implacable polemicist against the papal claims to give a normative interpretation of Scripture and to lay down laws binding Christian consciences. Luther countered the claims of social privilege by members of the clerical estate. But a complete account of his work must also include at least a reference to Luther's doctrine of the pastoral ministry and ordination. Pastors are called by Christ and are commissioned to speak in his name, when they address the Gospel and the words of absolution to believers.[21]

Cavallotto's volume illustrates one of the main goals of all of Luther's polemic, namely, to clear away the obstacles standing in the way of effective reform of pastoral care and the renewal of popular lived religiosity. In any general presentation of Luther, accuracy demands that the image of the great reformer highlight the religious and pastoral dimension of his dedicated work in a moment of widespread religious crisis in Europe.[22]

For interpreting Luther, a phrase is particularly helpful which we find in a letter of 1516, when he was first becoming known around Wittenberg. Luther explained his approach to his work of biblical interpretation to Georg Spalatin, the Latin Secretary of the Prince-Elector of Saxony, assuring the latter, *Pro re theologica et salute fratrum haec facio*.[23] The texts presented by Cavallotto show us

---

[21] This has been brought out in the study of Ramon Arnau García, *El ministro legado de Cristo, según Lutero* (Valencia 1983), a work which looks carefully at Luther's sermons on the occasion of ordinations to the pastoral ministry, with their references to the pastor speaking *an Christi statt*. I reviewed Arnau García's book in *Theological Studies* 46 (1985), 366-368.

[22] The notes in Cavallotto's anthology refer to the main studies of the pastoral problems and abuses marking the religious situation on the eve of the Reformation, e.g., by J. Lortz and B. Moeller. It is especially refreshing in Cavallotto to read a work on Luther and the German reform which incorporates references to the theses of the French historian Jean Delumeau. Still, we must take note of a counter-current in recent history writing in English, in which late-medieval lived religiosity and the church are judged more positively than is customary in Continental scholarship. See, for instance, Francis Oakley, *The Western Church in the Later Middle Ages* (Ithaca, N.Y. 1979) and John Bossy, *Christianity in the West, 1400-1700* (Oxford 1985). My own inclination is less toward viewing European Christianity in the early 16th century as more decadent and rife with abuses than in other eras, but much more toward attending to the way in which the realities of religion and church were then being subjected to the more severe evaluations of members of the educated elite. Luther belonged to the new generation of critical observers of the ecclesiastical scene who were then emerging. What is new, and what provoked the crisis, is their application to their religious world, to both popular and institutional practice in the church, of more demanding criteria. Also, the »new men« of the early 16th century showed a lower level of tolerance for the indolence of popes and bishops, whose positions of ecclesiastical authority should have been used for promoting reform of the church.

[23] »For theology and for the salvation of my brothers I am doing this.« Letter of 19 October 1516, WABr 1, 71,42

how Luther's mature work contributed to a theologically grounded pastoral practice and to helping his brothers and sisters in central moments of their life of faith, that is, when they receive the sacraments, suffer the assaults of temptation, and prepare themselves for death. An essential part of Luther's image is his work to meet these needs of his contemporaries with an instruction which was more clear, better focused, and also more exigent than what already existed.

Let us attempt now to characterize in a global way the underlying theology of Luther's pastoral instruction. Three elements seem to be fundamental.

First, in the disposition of the material, Luther's instruction is centered on the Apostles' Creed, which he always expounds in terms of the three basic articles of creation, redemption, and sanctification, with reference to the three divine persons.[24] The Creed orients the Christian toward appropriating in living faith the truth that the Father has made him and preserves him as his creature, and this with loving regard. The second article recalls that the Son of God has become our Lord Jesus Christ, who »suffered for us, died for us, rose for us,« so that we may share in the joy of redemption.[25] It is the Holy Spirit who, according to the third article, gathers us sinners into the church, where every day the same Spirit carries out a work of forgiveness of sins and sanctification, of enlightenment and inspiration, by means of the preached word, the sacraments, and Christian doctrine.[26] One sees that Luther's instruction is not particularly innovative. Actually, he transmits the basics of a classic form of lived religiosity.

A second note of this popular instruction was in fact the main reason for its popular impact. Luther overcame the problem of catechetical diffusiveness into a great number of articles and explanations. His instruction is notably focused on a center that is soteriological in character. Almost every page of Luther's popular instruction treats of Christ crucified and of his victory over sin, death, and the murderous powers of the devil. This pastoral program seeks to open the way for troubled souls to pass over to having a share in this victory of Christ the Savior.[27]

The third basic aspect of Luther's instruction is his emphasis on the mediation in this world of God's grace and gifts. We recall how late-medieval scholastic theology was fascinated by the absolute power of God and by the possibility that

---

[24] For example, from the texts in Cavallotto, Luther's own confession of faith (1528): WA 26, 499-509; LW 37, 360-372; the expositions of the faith in Luther's catechisms of 1529: WA 30I, 362-368 & 182-192; T. Tappert, ed. *The Book of Concord*, 344f, 411-420; and »A Simple Way to Pray« (1535): WA 38, 373-375; LW 43, 209-211.

[25] »A Simple Way to Pray,« LW 43, 211.

[26] In the 1528 Confession, LW 37, 365-372; WA 26, 505-509. In the catechisms, *Book of Concord*, 344f & 411-420; WA 30I, 296-298 & 187-192. In »A Simple Way to Pray,« LW 43, 211; WA 38, 374-375. In this collection, the following Study treats Luther's catechetical teaching on the Holy Spirit and sanctification.

[27] This is especially clear in the works in Cavallotto's anthology on comfort in temptation, on countering discouragement in prayer, and on preparing for death.

God could intervene directly in any part of life and at any moment. This mode of theological thought and questioning tended to reduce the importance of the secondary causes that God has instituted and incorporated into the historical, inner-worldly order of redemption and sanctification.[28] Luther shows no interest in speculating on the myriad possibilities open to the absolute power of God, but instead gives himself passionately to treating the concrete means that Christ has historically instituted for the daily mediation of his grace of salvation. The believer is taught to lay hold of the word of the Gospel in faith, including the expression of this word in the sacraments. These are events in the church and are the privileged parts of the concrete dispensation for the communication of God's grace and mercy.[29]

The question can arise among Catholics whether this retrieval of the pastoral works of Luther is part of the discovery of a »Catholic Luther« or at least of an »ecumenical Luther« in an era no longer scarred by confessional polemic. However, the use of such labels seems to be of doubtful value, in view of the fact that seven of the nine works presented by Cavallotto come from the period 1526-1540. These are thus contributions made by Luther to the upbuilding of the reformed territorial church of Electoral Saxony. From the moment of the protest of Saxony and its allies at the Diet of Speyer in 1529, these churches have been called »protestant«. These territorial churches presented their doctrine and reform program to the Diet of the German Empire in the Augsburg Confession of 1530 and asked that the bond of unity with the other estates not be broken off. This request, however, was met by the refusal of a majority of the princes and bishops of the Empire, of Emperor Charles V, and of the papal legate Cardinal Lorenzo Campeggio.[30] Luther's contributions to the revitalization of popular or lived religiosity is an essential part of early German protestantism.

---

[28] This has been set forth by Erwin Iserloh, in *Gnade und Eucharistie in der philosophischen Theologie des Wilhelm von Ockham* (Wiesbaden 1956). It is common today to speak of the late-medieval Franciscan theology of Duns Scotus, William of Ockham, and Gabriel Biel as promoting a »covenantal« view of causality and of the mediation of redemption. This is to emphasize at the same time the contingency and the reliability of the order that God has freely established. See, for instance, Alister E. McGrath, *Iustitia Dei. A History of the Christian Doctrine of Justification*, vol. 1, *From the Beginnings to 1500* (Cambridge 1986), 49-50, 65-66, 87-89, 115-118, 121-128. As suggested in Study 1 of this collection, p. 9, n. 23, above, the terminology of »covenant« can be misleading when applied to the *via moderna*'s teaching on the disposition by which the fallen human being can become prepared for God's saving grace.

[29] Contrary to what Cavallotto suggests *(Scritti pastorali minori*, 240, n. 22), one must emphasize that »the keys« (cf. Matt 16:19) are for Luther an essential component of the church, because in virtue of them the pastor may pronounce in the name of Christ the efficacious words of forgiveness of sins. In fact, a decisive step in Luther's maturing as a theologian is precisely the accentuation of the sacramental word in his publications of 1518, as shown in this collection in Study 6, above. Cavallotto himself remarked on the contrast between Luther's emphasis on the role of the sacraments in preparing for death and Johann von Staupitz's almost complete silence about the sacraments in his work on the same topic (*Scritti*, 7).

[30] The crucial decisions of 1530 are the subject of Studies 10 and 11, below, in this collection.

But today, in the wake of the Second Vatican Council, the Catholic Church acknowledges that protestant churches treasure and transmit »many elements of sanctification and of truth«.[31] Luther, along with others, made a constructive contribution to the very churches that preserve to this day the »elements« that Vatican II acknowledges. We see this contribution concretely in his pastoral works, with their notable Christian instruction on the faith and the sacraments. To this day, the churches of the Lutheran reformation remain outside the Catholic communion, but the Catholic Church professes that she is linked with Lutherans in numerous ways and that they have been brought »into a certain, though imperfect, communion with the Catholic Church«.[32] All this has grounded a fruitful and promising dialogue between the Catholic Church and the churches of the Lutheran confessional family in the past twenty-five years.[33]

But from the historical point of view, the pastoral writings of Luther the Reformer ground a conclusion about the quality of his particular contribution to the sixteenth century catechetical and pastoral renewal. Given the trinitarian structure in the background, the soteriological focus on Christ in the center, and the repeated emphasis on the mediations of God's forgiveness, grace, and encouragement – with such basic elements, Luther created a pastoral instruction that is of perennial value. Furthermore, Luther's expansive outreach to the full span of moments and situations of Christian living suggests that his is an exemplary work of theological service of pastoral care. It deserves recognition from all who concern themselves with Christian teaching and the fostering of lived Christianity.

---

[31] The Second Vatican Council, Dogmatic Constitution on the Church (*Lumen Gentium*), no. 8; Decree on Ecumenism (*Unitatis Redintegratio*), nos. 19-23.

[32] *Lumen Gentium*, 15; *Unitatis Redintegratio*, 3 (cited).

[33] I reviewed this dialogue in »Ecclesiological Issues in the Lutheran-Catholic Dialogue (1965-1985),« in R. Latourelle, ed., *Vatican II: Assessment and Perspectives*, 3 vols. (New York/Mahwah 1988-89), 2, 305-346.

9

HOLY SPIRIT – CHURCH – SANCTIFICATION: INSIGHTS FROM LUTHER'S INSTRUCTIONS ON THE FAITH

The students of Erwin Iserloh have learned from their revered mentor a helpful approach to the reading of Luther's works.[1] This approach, based on a distinction between Luther's different historical contexts, differentiates between the positions he advanced in the period 1519-25, as the Reformation was breaking out, and a series of somewhat different positions found in works of Luther's later years.[2]

Sad to say, Luther's principal reformatory writings, such as *On the Papacy in Rome* (1520), *The Babylonian Captivity of the Church* (1520), *To the Christian Nobility of the German Nation* (1520), and *The Bondage of the Will* (1525), contain a series of doctrinal positions that impede the agreement in faith aimed at in ecumenical dialogue between Lutherans and Catholics.[3] But at the same time Iserloh-students are accustomed to take note of the self-corrective process that marked the development of the Reformation. The later Luther, and then especially the Augsburg Confession of 1530, advanced a series of more balanced doctrinal formulations that in effect notably reduce the sharp oppositions arising from earlier Reformation positions on justification, ecclesiology, sacraments, and the church's ministerial office.[4] Even during Luther's lifetime, Lutheranism came

---

[1] This text is substantially the lecture I gave, at the invitation of the Faculty of Catholic Theology of the University of Münster, 15 May 1990, in honor of Prof. Erwin Iserloh, on the occasion of his 75th birthday.

[2] See E. Iserloh's exposition in H. Jedin, gen. ed., *Handbuch der Kirchengeschichte*, 4 (Freiburg 1967), 66-72, 222-233, 263-274; in English, *History of the Church*, 5 (New York 1980), 64-71, 213-225, 253-265. More concisely: E. Iserloh, *Geschichte und Theologie der Reformation* (Paderborn 1980), 37-39, 72-76, 105-115. Also in E. Iserloh, »Martin Luther. Fragen an uns – Fragen an ihn,« in P. Manns, ed., *Martin Luther »Reformator und Vater im Glauben«* (Stuttgart 1985), 60-73, esp. 67f. – Also, according to Iserloh, Luther's central Reformation insight into God's saving righteousness occurred prior to, and does not necessarily lead to, the polemics of 1519-25.

[3] E. Iserloh states this viewpoint in »Martin Luther. Fragen an uns,« 72.

[4] E. Iserloh said in 1981 that, in view of the fact that Luther moved on from much of the onesidedness of his 1519-21 positions, one should not appeal to the latter texts without regard for the larger corpus of his later works. »450 Jahre Confessio Augustana. Eine Bilanz,« *Catholica* 35 (1981), 4; also, *Kirche – Ereignis und Institution* (Münster 1985), 2, 304. – A good example of a study that distinguishes between the different phases of Reformation doctrine is Vinzenz Pfnür, *Einig in der Rechtfertigungslehre? Die Rechtfertigungslehre der Confessio Augustana (1530) und die*

to express aspects of a common doctrinal heritage shared with Catholics, and this latter body of doctrine has provided the basis for the fruitful ecumenical dialogue of recent decades.

My aim in this study is to further exemplify this situation, especially by presenting a series of constructive ecclesiological positions found in Luther's works of instruction on the Christian faith. In his various catechetical writings, Luther repeatedly set forth the essential nature and the mission of the church in the context of his exposition of the third article of the Creed, that is, in the framework of a comprehensive doctrine of the Holy Spirit and the Spirit's work of sanctification. The retrieval of this complex of ecclesiological insights seems to be especially urgent today, not only because this topic is rarely treated in Luther scholarship with the attention it deserves, but also because the role of the church is becoming increasingly important in ecumenical dialogues. Also, we need to offset the reconfessionalizing tendencies of our day, whether in the Roman Catholic or Lutheran communities, which seem inclined more toward neglecting than toward exploiting the rich ecclesiological potential of Luther's constructive works.[5] In what follows I hope to show that anyone who deals with ecclesiological topics can be positively stimulated and enriched by Luther's insights.[6]

Insights from the Early Years of the Reformation, 1520-21

We can begin by pointing out a rather simple fact, namely, that Luther's critical, anti-institutional ecclesiological writings of 1520-21, such as those directed against Augustine von Alveld, Jerome Emser and Thomas Murner, and Ambrosius Catharinus,[7] were accompanied by a continuation and further diffusion of Luther's constructive presentation of the basics of the Christian faith.[8] I refer especially to a vernacular work that Luther brought out in the first

---

Stellungnahme der katholischen Kontroverstheologen zwischen 1530 und 1535 (Wiesbaden 1970), an investigation first suggested by J. Ratzinger and then carried through as a dissertation under the direction of E. Iserloh.

[5] An example of such a tendency on the Lutheran side would be K. Schwarzwäller, »Rechtfertigung und Ekklesiologie in den Schmalkaldischen Artikeln,« *Kerygma und Dogma* 35 (1989), 84-105.

[6] We do well to recall here that Luther saw the catechism as providing both doctrine and material for prayer. The catechetical topics not only teach about the Holy Spirit, but are as well occasions for the same Spirit to be interiorly heard and for one to converse and deal with the Spirit. This has been set forth by Martin Nichol, *Meditation bei Luther* (Göttingen 1984), 150-167.

[7] *Von dem Papstum zu Rom wider den hochberühmten Romanisten zu Leipzig*, WA 6, 285-324; *On the Papacy in Rome*, LW 39, 55-104. *Auf das überchristliche ... Buch Bocks Emsers Antwort*, WA 7, 621-688 (including the section »An den Murnarr«, pp. 681-688); *Answer to the Hyperchristian ... Book by Goat Emser*, LW 39, 143-224. *Ad librum ... Ambrosii Catharini, defensoris Silvestri Prieratis acerrimi, Responsio*, WA 7, 705-778.

[8] M. Brecht has set this forth, under the title »Das reformatorische Programm,« in *Martin Luther*, 1, *Sein Weg zur Reformation 1483-1521* (Stuttgart 1981), 333-351.

half of 1520, *Eine kurze Form der zehn Gebote, ... des Glaubens und ... des Vater Unsers (A Short Form of the Ten Commandments, of the Faith, and of the Our Father).*⁹ The portions of this booklet that expound the Commandments and the Our Father were not new in 1520, for on these topics Luther simply had the contents of earlier publications reprinted. But the catechetical interpretation of the Creed (»the Faith«) was newly composed for the booklet of 1520. Thus, by May 1520 a work was circulating which we may view as Luther's first catechism. The popularity of the work is evident from its twelve reprintings in just a few years. Further, this treatment of the commandments, the Creed, and prayer was soon incorporated into Luther's book of prayers (*Betbüchlein*, 1522) and in this larger work went through some thirty editions during Luther's lifetime. Therefore, a complete picture of Luther's contribution to the outbreak of the Reformation must include his noteworthy effort to develop and spread basic instruction in Christian doctrine. Luther remained a catechist, even in a phase of his life that was more deeply marked historically by controversy and by his well-known polemical exaggerations on the church and its constitution.

The content of Luther's catechetical ecclesiology of 1520 deserves our consideration. This instruction is especially noteworthy because in it we find Luther pointedly telling pastors and believers, first, to anchor their view of the church firmly in the doctrine of the Holy Spirit, and, second, to envisage the church as a *communio* – necessary to salvation – of shared spiritual gifts. However, the importance of these points will be more easily grasped, if we briefly consider some aspects of Luther's polemic in this same period.

Luther's anti-institutional and anti-papal writings of 1520-21 depict the church as hidden and spiritual.¹⁰ The church, as Scripture and the Creed treat it, is strictly speaking not an object of sight, for it is not corporeal. Instead, it is »an assembly of hearts in one faith.« Christianity has been »separated by Christ himself from all physical and external places and locations and given a spiritual place.«¹¹ »No one can see or feel the holy Christian church.«¹² What Christ says about the church leads to the conclusion that the church is without sin and is

---

9 WA 7, 204-229.

10 E. Iserloh summarized the main elements of this polemical ecclesiology in »Martin Luther und die römische Kirche,« in E. Iserloh & G. Müller, eds., *Luther und die politische Welt* (Stuttgart 1984), 173-186, esp. 181f. H.-J. Prien sketched the development of Luther's ecclesiological thinking down to 1521 in »Grundgedanken der Ekklesiologie beim jungen Luther,« *Archiv für Reformationsgeschichte* 76 (1985), 96-111., The most recent exposition of Luther's notion of the church in 1520-21 is K. Hammann's Munich dissertation, *Ecclesia spiritualis. Luthers Kirchenverständnis in den Kontroversen mit Augustin von Alveldt und Ambrosius Catharinus* (Göttingen 1989).

11 WA 6, 293,4.36; LW 39, 65 & 66.

12 WA 7, 685,3; LW 39, 220.

therefore an invisible, spiritual reality that one can only grasp in faith.[13] Luther's statements in his book on the papacy against Alveld and in his response to Catharinus have been frequently cited and treated as fundamental to his ecclesiology. Here he holds that the church is not bodily, for its unity is unity by and in the Holy Spirit, not a unity based on a place or a person.[14]

This then is Luther's ecclesiology of the hidden church of true believers, which clearly is not an institution. It is an ecclesiology of the complete number of those who have laid hold of God's saving word in faith. It is as well an ecclesiology in which hardly any role is attributed to an office of rule and direction. One may ask, however, whether Luther set forth the nature of the church in these works with sufficient clarity to guard against an understanding of the church, not as hidden, but as invisible because it is located in human intentions.[15] Luther's concern was of course to respond to the sharply accentuated role of the papacy in the ecclesiology of his first Roman opponents, especially the view set forth by the papal court-theologian Silvester Prierias.[16] But Luther met one extreme view of the church with another extreme conception.

Luther maintains in 1520-21 that the community of those redeemed by Christ is not bound to a specific place or person. Instead, he characterizes the church as *creatura Evangelii*, and explains, in a frequently cited passage, »The whole life and substance of the church is in the word of God.«[17]

---

[13] Against Catharinus: »Necesse est ... Ecclesiam sine peccato invisibilem et spiritualem sola fide perceptibilem esse.« WA 7, 710,2.

[14] E.g., WA 7, 721,3.

[15] K. Hammann repeatedly pointed out passages in the works of 1520-21 in which Luther's concept of the church could be easily misunderstood. *Ecclesia spiritualis*, 85, 108 (Luther very close to a Donatist insistence on the holiness of the rightful pastor), 122f, 235. Another Lutheran exposition of the difficulties and unsolved problems of an ecclesiology based on Luther's polemic is T. Koch, »Das Problem des evangelischen Kirchenverständnisses nach dem Augsburger Bekenntnis,« in B. Lohse & O.H. Pesch, eds., *Das Augsburger Bekenntnis von 1530 damals und heute* (Munich & Mainz 1980), 125-143.

[16] The *Dialogus* of Prierias, a wide-ranging criticism of Luther's Ninety-Five Theses of 1517, is now available in a new edition in *Dokumente zur Causa Lutheri*, vol. 1, *Das Gutachten des Prierias und weitere Schriften gegen Luthers Ablaßthesen (1517-1518)*, ed. P. Fabish und E. Iserloh, Corpus Catholicorum 41 (Münster 1988), 52-107. Basic for the development of Luther's counterpointed ecclesiology is the emphasis Prierias places on the Pope as visible head of the church in his opening four *fundamenta* (pp. 53-56). Study 7, above in this volume, treats the first Roman responses to Luther. For understanding Prierias's onesidedness, it is important relate him to the broad reaction of Roman theologians, especially the Dominicans, after 1511, to the threat of renewed conciliarism in connection with the *conciliabulum* of Pisa. Just before dealing with Luther, this theology had been marshalling quite forcefully all the arguments for the superior authority of the pope over a general council. This aspect of the early Reformation argument has been set forth in Ulrich Horst, *Zwischen Konziliarismus und Reformation. Studien zur Ekklesiologie im Dominikanerorden* (Rome 1985).

[17] »Tota vita et substantia Ecclesiae est in verbo Dei« WA 7, 721,12. As Luther said just before about the church, »Per solum Evangelium concipiatur, formetur, alatur, generetur, educetur, pascatur, vestiatur, ornetur, roboretur, armetur, servetur« (721,10).

One can, however, take a more comprehensive view of Luther's teaching at this time, and so take into consideration his earliest catechetical work. Thereby, the one-sided and polemical conception of the church is complemented by other themes, and the whole gains balance and considerable enrichment. Most important, Luther's teaching is protected against misunderstanding. This occurs in *Eine kurze Form*, first, by the insertion of the church, this hidden and spiritual reality, into the framework of the work of the Triune God in the economy of salvation. In the third article of the Creed, the Holy Spirit, who is truly God, is further characterized as the one »by whom the Father and the Son touch, awaken, call, and engender me and all their chosen ones, and in Christ make us living, holy, and spiritual, and so bring us to the Father.«[18] The foundation of Luther's teaching on the church is therefore the Trinity, which effects our salvation by the earthly missions of Son and Holy Spirit.

Luther's doctrine on the community of salvation, as set forth in the catechism of 1520 is, to be sure, a doctrine about what is believed, but this faith relates to an earthly reality. The believer is instructed to say, »I believe that there is on earth, as far as the world extends, not more than one holy community of the Christian church.« As is usual with Luther, »church« is then elucidated by the term *communio sanctorum*, taking this in the personal sense of *sancti*, but also relating the *communio* to the expansive work of the Holy Spirit on earth. The church is »the community or assembly of holy, pious, believing persons on earth, which the same Holy Spirit assembles, preserves, and rules, daily increasing it by the sacraments and Word of God.«[19]

This carefully constructed paragraph of doctrine clearly includes the notion of the church as »creature of the word.« But the principal specification of the community of salvation is given by the efficient cause, the Holy Spirit, which constitutes the church by assembling it and then preserves, rules, and daily increases what has come to be. Luther considers the instrumental cause and mentions it, but in a subordinate manner. On the basis of this text, we could well consider laying down a rule of discourse that would oblige one to complement every mention of the slogan *creatura verbi* by a reference to the church as *creatura Spiritus sancti*. Ecclesiology would thus be deepened, while remaining rooted in Luther's instructional texts.

Luther's 1520 instruction on the church, grounded in the mission of the Holy Spirit, then developed further in three concise but substantive paragraphs. Each one of them contrasts with Luther's more polemical works of the same period by setting forth a positive aspect of ecclesiology. Also, each point refers to visible aspects of human life in community.

The church gathered by the Holy Spirit is, first, necessary for salvation. To come to the Father through Christ, a person cannot avoid the earthly

---

[18] WA 7, 218,29.
[19] WA 7, 219,1-5.

community of salvation.[20] Consequently Luther speaks of the absolute necessity that persons of a different faith and sinners come to be reconciled and united with this community. The work of the Spirit surely aims at something deeper than communality of intention between people, but this work nonetheless includes being in agreement with this community, »in one faith, word, sacrament, hope, and love.«[21]

The community of salvation is, according to Luther's instruction in 1520, a living network of spiritual exchange. Here one does not live for oneself alone, but »each one bears one another's burdens« (Gal 6:2).[22] Luther emphasizes how in the church »all prayers and good works of the whole community come to my aid and help every single believer.«[23] This is a natural characteristic of a community ultimately based on the divine Trinity and more immediately brought into being and maintained by the *communicatio Spiritus sancti* (2 Cor 13:13).

A third elaboration of Luther's ecclesiological instruction of 1520 comes with reference to the next phrase of the Creed, »the forgiveness of sins.« This catechesis teaches the Christian to say, »I believe that there is in the same community, and nowhere else, forgiveness of sins, and that outside it, however many and great one's good works might be, they are no help toward forgiveness of sins.«[24] This saving gift of God is central to the life of this community, because Christ gave over the keys to her, along with the promise that the words of binding and loosing on earth would have heavenly validity. Thus, the historic act of institution by Christ on earth regarding forgiveness of sins lays a further ecclesial foundation and is the source of a basic component of the church's life.

Fundamental Insights into Luther's Pneumatological Ecclesiology in His Main Works of Christian Instruction

Setting out from Luther's teaching in 1520, we turn now to the larger complex of catechetical texts in which Luther further developed and notably deepened his notion of the church and its mission or role. Our sources in this section are

---

[20] In a parallel passage in the Church Postil of 1522, Luther emphasizes the church in treating how and where one »finds Christ.« WA 10I/1, 140,7-9.14-16.

[21] WA 7, 219,7.

[22] WA 7, 219,5. Luther first cited Gal 6:2 with reference to the fruits of the sacrament of the altar, in his 1519 *Sermon on the Blessed Sacrament and the Brotherhoods* (WA 2, 745,24-35; LW 35, 54f). This will recur in his instruction on the sacrament in his catechetical sermon of May 1528 (WA 30I, 27,10f). U. Stock treated the 1519 passage in *Die Bedeutung der Sakramente in Luthers Sermonen von 1519* (Leiden 1982), 309-311, 358-361.

[23] WA 7, 219,13.

[24] WA 7, 219,17.

fourfold: (1) the interpretations of the Creed that Luther gave in four sets of sermons, first in March 1523, and then in May, September, and December 1528;[25] (2) Luther's own extensive confession of faith, in the last part of his final major work against Zwingli in 1528;[26] (3) Luther's two catechisms of 1529;[27] (4) selected sermons, especially those of Pentecost in 1529, 1531, and 1538.[28]

I offer now the results of a careful reading of this complex of Luther texts.[29] These findings will be principally summarized in three ecclesiological theses, for each of which a short explanation will be given.

Thesis 1: According to the Creed, the proper locus of the church is the Holy Spirit's structured work of sanctification.

It is generally known that Luther's instructions in the faith tend forcefully toward promoting the personalization of belief. His interpretation of the Creed in the Small Catechism of 1529, highlighting as it does the laying hold of how God's work relates to me and my salvation, is famous in the Christian world:

> I believe that God created me and all that exists; that he has given me and still sustains my body and soul.... I believe that Jesus Christ ... is my Lord, who has redeemed me, a lost and condemned creature.... I believe that by my own reason or strength I cannot believe in Jesus Christ, my Lord, or come to him. But the Holy Spirit has called me through the Gospel, enlightened me with his gifts, and sanctified and preserved me in true faith, just as he calls, gathers, enlightens, and sanctifies the whole Christian church on earth and preserves it in union with Jesus Christ in the one true faith.[30]

Thus we simply presuppose that a principal work of the Holy Spirit is the eliciting of this personalized saving faith.[31] When Luther preached in Smalkalden

---

[25] WA 11, 48-54; WA 30I, 2-94.

[26] WA 26, 499-509; LW 37, 360-372.

[27] Large Catechism: WA 30I, 182-192; BS 646-662; *The Book of Concord*, ed. T. Tappert et al. (Philadelphia 1959), 411-420. Small Catechism: WA 30I, 292-299; BS 510-512; *Book of Concord*, 344f.

[28] WA 29, 359-376; WA 34I, 458-468; WA 46, 423-433.

[29] Strangely, out of these texts M. Beyer uses only the confession of 1528 in »Luthers Ekklesiologie,« in H. Junghans, ed., *Leben und Werk Martin Luthers von 1526 bis 1546* (Berlin & Göttingen 1983), 93-117, 755-765. I have taken numerous positive suggestions for grasping the sense of these texts from E. Herms, *Luthers Auslegung des Dritten Artikels* (Tübingen 1987). The main differences between my interpretation and that of Herms are, first, that I make no use here of the notion of »revelation,« since it became theologically important only after Luther's time; second, I lay more emphasis on the equipping of the church with gifts or the means of grace (see my second thesis, below); and, third, in the third major section, below, I offer a more extensive account of the components of sanctification, which is the main purpose of the Holy Spirit's work in and through the church.

[30] *Book of Concord*, 345; BS 510-512.

[31] See, for instance, Luther's confession of 1528: WA 26, 505,35; LW 37, 366. His Pentecost sermons of 1529 repeatedly touched on this aspect of the Spirit's work: WA 29, 363,6, 364,16 (»Discrimen inter Christum et Spiritum sanctum: Christus redet es mündlich durch das Wort der Gnade, ipse [Spiritus] mit der Tat scribit in cor«), 365,20 (»Spiritus sanctus loquitur eitel Flammen in corda nostra«), 374,14.

in February 1537, he interpreted the third article of the Creed wholly in terms of the personal experience and feeling of how the truth of creation and redemption relates to me.[32]

But Luther's catechesis goes further, as he regularly sets forth the whole office and work of the Holy Spirit, and thus comes to expound a doctrine of the church as the assembly of those whom the Spirit intends to sanctify.[33] According to Luther, the name »Holy Spirit« means precisely to show that this Spirit has sanctification as a specific work, and so »must be called Sanctifier, the One who makes holy.«[34]

The work of sanctification has according to Luther a given content and structure, which the confession of faith sets forth.[35] First the Holy Spirit's work is closely linked to the saving works of the Father and the Son: »The Father wills it, the Son merits it, and the Holy Spirit carries it out.«[36] Luther can also formulate this so as to direct one's gaze both back to Christ and ahead to the church: »What Christ merited by his passion, that the Holy Spirit carries out by his church.«[37] In his catechetical sermon of 1523, Luther first spoke of the Spirit as participant in creation as wrought by the Father and in the making of Christians as effected by the incarnate Son, but he then went on to speak of the proper work of the Spirit, which is to bring the church into being.[38] This then is sanctification it its broadest outline.

---

[32] WA 45, 22,8-15. Further: »Das heist den Heiligen Geist haben, die Schöpfung und Erlösung also fühlen und in das Herz schreiben, denn solches tut allein der Heilige Geist« (23,2-4). Earlier Luther had distinguished different kinds of faith, making use of the traditional distinction between *credere Deo* (»eine Merkung,« by which one takes note of an objective fact) and *credere in Deum* (»cordialis Zuversicht et tota fiducia in Dei gratiam«). Sermon on the Creed, 1523; WA 11, 49,5. Also, in *Eine kurze Form* (1520): WA 7, 215,6-10.17.

[33] For example, in the catechetical sermons of May 1528: »Pater creavit et filius reconciliavit; Spiritus sanctus facit, quod sit Christiana ecclesia per totum mundum.« WA 30I, 9, 34f. In the New Testament, the Acts of the Apostles shows forth the doctrine and work of the Holy Spirit. »Summa illius libri: Spiritus sanctus sua opera et doctrina apostolorum congregat ecclesiam illamque unanimem construit et custodit in fide Christi.« Sermon on Pentecost Tuesday, 1529; WA 29, 374,19-21.

[34] »Ein Heiliger oder Heiligmacher.« Large Catechism: BS 653f; *Book of Concord*, 415.

[35] A helpful exposition of this matter is R. Jansen, *Studien zur Luthers Trinitätslehre* (Bern & Frankfurt 1976), 36-48.

[36] Catechetical Sermon of March 1523; WA 11, 54,1-5.

[37] »Quod Christus sua passione meruit, das richtet Spiritus sanctus aus per suam ecclesiam.« Catechetical Sermon of September 1528; WA 30I, 45,12.

[38] »Pater creavit coelum et terram cum spiritu sancto. Filius fit homo et facit Christianos cum spiritu sancto. Proprium opus spiritus sancti est, quod ecclesiam facit.« WA 11, 53,30-34.

But the inner structure of God's sanctifying work is our special concern, for Luther presents this structure in a way that makes clear the specific locus of the church.

Beginning in the catechetical sermons of 1528, Luther repeatedly gave instructions on how the Holy Spirit carries out his broadly based work of sanctifying. Naturally Luther assumes the priority of the outward spoken word, as he had posited with all desirable clarity against Andreas Karlstadt.[39] But in his instruction in the faith, Luther emphasizes the trinitarian order, as the Large Catechism nicely summarizes:

> Just as the Son obtains dominion by purchasing us through his birth, death, and resurrection, etc., so the Holy Spirit effects our sanctification through the following: the communion of saints or Christian church, the forgiveness of sins, the resurrection of the body, and life everlasting.[40]

In this regard Luther can go so far as to emphasize the set order shown by the Creed. This is not surprising, since the notion of a determined temporal or logical order within the economy of salvation is an important component of Luther's overall thought and teaching.[41] Luther may not have produced a system of theology, but he often set forth his teaching in a quite systematic manner. With relation to the third article of the Creed, he emphasized on Pentecost 1531, »The Holy Spirit will not break his chosen order.«[42] This concerns first the priority of the second article over the third, since *Christum cognoscere* precedes the *dona Spiritus*. But the order is also internal to the third article, with its sequence of acting person and resulting outcomes of this action. Luther finds here an excellent order, with the Holy Spirit coming first and then being followed by the church and the forgiveness of sins.[43] For the Spirit sanctifies believers now

---

[39] *Against the Heavenly Prophets* (1525), especially WA 18, 136-139 (LW 40, 146-149), where the notion of God's intended order, with the priority of the outward word, occurs several times, e.g., WA 18, 136,14.24.

[40] *Book of Concord*, 415; BS 654, 9-13. This view of the unity of the whole third article of the Creed was echoed in Luther's sermon on Pentecost Monday 1529: »Opus Spiritus sancti est facere ecclesiam Christianam, remissionem peccatorum, resuscitare carnem a mortuis et dare vitam aeternam.« WA 29, 363,14-16.

[41] This has been set forth in investigations published by Erwin Iserloh, e.g. on Christ being first sacrament and only then example. »Sacramentum et exemplum. Ein augustinisches Thema lutherischer Theologie,« in E. Iserloh & K. Repgen, eds., *Reformata Reformanda*, Festschrift Hubert Jedin (Münster 1965), 1, 247-264. Also, on Luther's set way of relating God's grace and gift in the doctrine of justification. »Gratia und Donum. Rechtfertigung und Heiligung nach Luther's Schrift 'Wider den Löwener Theologen Latomus' (1521),« in L. Abramowski & J.F. Goeters, eds., *Studien zur Geschichte und Theologie der Reformation*, Festschrift Ernst Bizer (Neukirchen 1969), 141-156.

[42] WA 34I, 465,25.

[43] »Ergo optime ordinatum in simbolo: spiritum sanctum, Ecclesiam, remissionem peccatocrum.« WA 34I, 465,28.

through the church by the forgiveness of sins until the moment of final sanctification in the resurrection.

The locus of the church is therefore the third article of the Creed. Consequently a complete account of Luther's ecclesiology must include the church's relation to the divine work of sanctification. We note briefly that on several occasions Luther emphasized the relevance of the third article by contrasting it with the Father's and the Son's already completed works of creation and redemption. Sanctification by the Holy Spirit is the work that is presently being carried out in a continuous, ongoing manner.[44] In the third main section, below, we will offer an account of the nature of sanctification as Luther describes it.

Thesis 2: According to Luther, the Holy Spirit carries out his work of sanctification, not only by assembling believers, but as well by richly equipping his community with gifts.

We can assume as well known that fact that Luther interpreted the creedal phrase *communio sanctorum* in a personal way, with reference to the total community of saints or believers. He saw the phrase as a helpful gloss, added to the Creed in the patristic era, to specify the preceding term *sancta ecclesia*. Its purpose was to guard against a misunderstanding of the church as an institution or in terms of the hierarchy. Luther's ecclesiological thinking and teaching was in fact basically shaped by this personalizing interpretation of *communio sanctorum* as *communio credentium*.

But the reference to persons does not suffice. In Luther's conception of the church, it is necessary first to include the specific actions of the Holy Spirit in the lives of these persons. As we already noted in the 1520 catechetical work, »this community or gathering of the saints is assembled by the same Holy Spirit, maintained and ruled ..., and daily increased by the sacraments and Word of God.«[45] Or in the Small Catechism: »The Holy Spirit has called me ... just as he calls, gathers, enlightens, and sanctifies the whole Christian church on earth and preserves it in union with Jesus Christ in the one true faith.«[46] Luther described the activity of the Holy Spirit in constituting the church with a set complex of verbs. The Spirit makes the church by assembling or bringing it together and by calling. Then he gives it enduring being by maintaining, ruling, and increasing it.[47]

---

[44] Catechism Sermons of May and December 1528; WA 30I, 10,32f and 94,10-13. Then in the Large Catechism as well: BS 659,44-660,3; *Book of Concord*, 419.

[45] WA 7, 219,2-5.

[46] *Book of Concord*, 345; BS 512,5-8.

[47] Assembling (*versammeln*): WA 7, 219,4; 26, 506,30 (LW 37, 367); 29, 374,19.25; 30I, 92,27; BS 512,6, 655,31, 659,47-660,5 (*Book of Concord*, 345, 416, 419). Calling (*berufen*): BK 512,6, 655,31. Maintaining (*behalten*): WA 7, 219,4; 31, 10,33; BS 512,5; WA 46, 424,33. This last text also echoes the notion of the church as *creatura verbi*: »Evangelium adhuc conservat Ecclesiam« 432,12. Ruling (*regieren*): WA 7, 219,4; 30I, 45,11. Increasing (*vermehren*): WA 7, 219,5; 46,

9. Spirit - Church - Sanctification

But once more we must move on with Luther and attend to the benefits or gifts with which the Holy Spirit equips his community of salvation. The special significance of this step is that the theme of the gifts given the church lays the basis for understanding how Luther ascribes to the church a subordinate instrumental service in the work of the Holy Spirit.

Luther spoke quite simply in the catechetical sermons of May 1528 of the equipping of the church with different gifts: »The Holy Spirit rules by the word and gives the church various gifts.«[48] Seven months later Luther says the same thing, but he also adds a significant remark against the *Schwärmer*. The Apostles' Creed clearly shows the ecclesial manner and means by which sanctification is given. The Spirit does not justify believers outside the church, as the fanatics hold, who gather in out-of-the-way corners in their conventicles. The Creed is dead set against this, for upon naming the Holy Spirit it speaks immediately of the Christian church, »in which all the Spirit's gifts are found.«[49]

Even though Luther's thinking was deeply rooted in the letters of St. Paul, these gifts are not primarily the charisms of 1 Cor 12 and its parallel texts. Instead, the gifts are the means of grace, as is indicated by the text just cited in which Luther attacked the *Schwärmer*.

A number of treatments of Luther's ecclesiology have dealt with the difficulty that arises from the fact that our great exponent of the hiddenness of the church also at times systematically listed these gifts or means of grace, treating them as public marks or »notes« of the church of Christ on earth.[50] In this study the task is easier, since we can abstract from Luther's writings in the genre of apologetics, in which he argued that the outward marks testify to the authenticity of the reformed territorial churches. His constructive presentations of the Christian faith were simpler and much more direct. The issue was not the complex of heuristic signs of a legitimate church, but instead the mediation of new life as Christ's work of salvation is carried out on earth.

In December 1528 Luther summarized the meaning of the Creed's third article with a specific accent on the church. Thus, the Holy Spirit sanctifies me now through the word and sacraments that are in the church and he will completely

---

424,33f (»Deus vero quotidie auget et conservat suam Ecclesiam, adiicit quosdam, corroborat et reficit«).

[48] WA 30I, 10,12f.

[49] »In qua sunt omnia eius dona.« WA 30I, 94,1-4. The Large Catechism notes the variety of gifts the Holy Spirit has given the community of saints. BS 657,31; *Book of Concord*, 417.

[50] In 1520-21 Luther spoke of outward signs of the church in his works against Alveld and Catharinus: WA 6, 301,3-10 (LW 39, 75); WA 7, 726,32-727,14. K. Hammann has treated these passages in *Ecclesia spiritualis*, 96-99, 156-161. The most important of Luther's later expositions of the notes of the church came in *On Councils and the Church* (1538) and in *Wider Hanswurst* (1541): WA 50, 628-633, 641-643 (LW 41, 148-154, 164-166); WA 51, 479-487 (LW 41, 194-199). F.W. Kantzenbach gave us a good treatment of this aspect of Luther's work in »Strukturen in der Ekklesiologie des älteren Luther,« *Lutherjahrbuch* 35 (1968), 48-77.

sanctify us on the last day.⁵¹ Luther brought out the role of the church more emphatically by introducing in this context the image of the church as the mother who generates her offspring and bears them to the moment of birth. New life begins from the word that is in mother church and is spoken there. This begins the process of sanctification, which culminates in the two highpoints of the forgiveness of sins and the resurrection.⁵²

The forgiveness of sins is for Luther a comprehensive doctrine that refers as well to the excellent gifts given the church. All the means of grace have here their place in the Creed, for here faith embraces all the means of forgiveness, that is, baptism, the sermon, the sacrament of the altar, absolution and all other words of consolation, and all the ministries. This part of the Creed is thus descriptive of the ecclesial space outside of which no sanctification is given.⁵³

The sequence of thought that links mother church, the word, and the means by which sins are forgiven, gained normativity by being included in Luther's Large Catechism.⁵⁴ Less well known, and more fascinating, is the image Luther used in a Pentecost sermon of 1538. He accentuated the conviction of faith that the Holy Spirit will be faithful to the end in solidarity with the church. To be sure, the biblical signs of the Spirit's presence and action have ended, but in a transferred sense the tongues of fire, the cloud, and the dove are still present. For the Spirit now works through the signs that are the ecclesial means of grace.⁵⁵

---

51 WA 30I, 94,16f.

52 »Sicut pater est Creator meus et Christus dominus meus, sic Spiritus sanctus est sanctificator meus: sanctificat enim me per sequentia opera, per remissionem peccatorum, resurrectionem carnis usw. Christiana ecclesia et mater tua, illa zeugt dich per verbum et trägt dich. Et hoc facit Spiritus sanctus, qui de Christo testimonium perhibet.« WA 30I, 91,16-21. E. Herms treated the notion of church as mother concisely but sensitively. *Luthers Auslegung des dritten Artikels*, 109-111. A later reference to church as mother came in a sermon by Luther on Isa 60 in 1545: WA 49, 672,30f.

53 »Postea habes in Christianitate 'Remissio peccatorum'. In hòc articulo conclusus est baptismus et praedicatio in lecto, Sacramentum altaris, Absolutio et omnes loci consolatorii. Omnia ministeria comprehenduntur in hoc articulo, per quae Christianitas remittit peccata, praesertim ubi Evangelium praedicatur, non praecepta seu traditiones usw. Extra illam Ecclesiam, sacramenta usw. non est sanctificatio.« WA 30I, 92,18-93,3. As is characteristic of Luther's mature instruction, no mention is made of the priesthood of all believers, but instead reference is made to the ministries of the church. S. Cavallotto pointed this out in »Il 'Credo ecclesiam' dalla Professione di fede di Lutero (1527-28) agli Articoli di Schwabach (1529),« *Asprenas* (Naples) 30 (1983) 383-416, esp. 401 and 403f.

54 BS 655,2-8, with 657,26-38 and 658,10-18; *Book of Concord*, 416, 417f.

55 »Et dicimus: Credo in Spiritum sanctum. Non abiit a Christiana Ecclesia usque ad finem mundi. Sic incepit die Pentecostes ignitis linguis, quae cessaverunt, et alia signa, doch nicht alle.... Et tamen visibiliter nobiscum est. Manet apud nos lingua ignita, Wolken, columba, quia praedicatio Evangelii, baptismus, absolutio, Trost, Unterrichtung omnium statuum.... Ipse praedicat, baptisat, quomodo filius morte sua, et ipse sanctificat. Et hoc videmus, scilicet dari Sacramentum, baptisari, audimus verbum praedicari. Hoc nemo facit nisi Spiritus sanctus.« WA 46, 424,5-14.

»The Holy Spirit is the one who outwardly and visibly baptizes, makes use of the word, and applies the keys. These are his tongues of fire.«[56] Mother church is thus splendidly equipped with gifts, all of which owe their earthly institution to Jesus Christ, but which now are efficacious for sanctification by reason of the constant action of the Holy Spirit.

Thesis 3: The Holy Spirit sanctifies believers through the community he has assembled and equipped.

I already cited part of a text in which Luther specifies the manner in which the Holy Spirit works as »through the church.« The whole text, from Luther's 1528 catechetical sermons, is as follows:

> What Christ merited by his passion, that the Holy Spirit carries out through his church. Consequently the work of the church is the forgiveness of sins. For she announces the Gospel, baptizes, and offers the forgiveness of sins.[57]

The Holy Spirit is thus the executor who carries out the work of Christ in order to complete the economy of salvation. But in this project the Spirit makes use of the cooperation of the community that he has called together.[58] In the Large Catechism, Luther's resumé of the third article says this with all desirable clarity:

> This, then, is the article that must always remain in force. Creation is past and redemption is accomplished, but the Holy Spirit carries on his work unceasingly until the last day. For this purpose, he has appointed a community on earth, through which he speaks and does all his work.[59]

One can then easily list the ministerial works that the church carries out under the influence of the Holy Spirit. Mother church is above all a preaching church, but also a baptizing church and a church that forgives sins. The Holy Spirit sanctifies us, according to the Large Catechism, in that »he first leads us into his holy community, placing us on the bosom of the church, where he preaches to us

---

[56] »Is est spiritus sanctus, qui greifflich, sichtbarlich baptisat, verbi ministerium, usum clavium. Sind sein feurig zungen.« WA 46, 425,3-5 (as copied down directly from Luther's sermon).

[57] »Quod Christus sua passione meruit, das richt Spiritus sanctus aus per suam Ecclesiam. Ergo opus Ecclesiae est remissio peccatorum. Praedicat enim Evangelium, dat Baptismum et remissionem peccatorum.« WA 30I, 45,12-14.

[58] Another avenue leading to this conclusion is Luther's use of the image of mother to designate the church and to indicate her activity – as we showed in the previous section.

[59] *Book of Concord*, 419; BS 659,44-660,3. E. Herms speaks in fact of an unmistakable shift of emphasis in Luther's catechetical texts from the creation of the church by the Holy Spirit to the use that the same Spirit makes of the church in his proper work of sanctification. *Luthers Auslegung des dritten Artikels*, 108.

and brings us to Christ.«⁶⁰ The church first opens up the knowledge of Christ: »First you knew nothing of Christ, but then the Christian church announced Christ to you.«⁶¹ The church then confers baptism. We can recall that the creedal article on the forgiveness of sins includes all the means of grace and ministries of forgiveness. What can surprise a modern reader is that Luther unhesitatingly ascribes to the church an activity with the means and ministries instituted by Christ. For they are the ways »by which Christianity forgives sins, especially where the Gospel is announced.«⁶²

Luther underscored even more the importance of the role of the church in a passage treating the eschatological completion of our sanctification, in which the opposition of rebellious flesh will be finally overcome. But even now, notwithstanding its opposition to our true good, the flesh is being sanctified by faith and by the church, in a process extending onward to the start of eternal life.⁶³ Luther does not shy away from linking faith and the church, namely, two religious realities that a later Protestantism at times considers separable, if not mutually exclusive.

Luther has no difficulty with the church in his instruction on the faith. This is especially clear in his resumé of the third article in December 1528. One asks, how then does the Holy Spirit sanctify me? The answer:

> Through faith, namely, that the church does exist; for through the church the Spirit sanctifies me, through her the Spirit speaks and bestirs those who preach, so that they announce the Gospel. Further, the Spirit works in your heart through the sacraments, so that you believe the word and come to be a member of the church.⁶⁴

In this context, just ten lines later, we come upon the passage treated above in which Luther attacks the *Schwärmer*, underscoring both the ecclesial character of justification and the full array of gifts of the Spirit that are in the church.⁶⁵

---

⁶⁰ *Book of Concord*, 415; BS 654,13-17.

⁶¹ WA 30I, 92,14.

⁶² »Omnia ministeria comprehenduntur in hoc articulo, per quae Christianitas remittit peccata, praesertim ubi Evangelium praedicatur.« WA 30I, 92,21-93,1.

⁶³ »In hac vita sumus mixti, halb hundt halb ruede, quia circumferimus nobiscum carnem imbecillem et peccatricem, quae nobis insidiatur, illa autem sanctificatur per fidem et ecclesiam Dei usque ad aeternam vitam, in qua tota nostra caro munda, sancta erit.« WA 30I, 93,23-26.

⁶⁴ »Quomodo me sanctificat? Quod credo esse Ecclesiam sanctam, per hanc sanctificat me, per hanc Spiritus loquitur et treibt praedicatores, ut praedicent Evangelium. Item dat tibi in cor per sacramenta, ut credas verbo et fias membrum Ecclesiae.« WA 30I, 93,11-14. The same thing is taught in the Large Catechism about the holy community of the Christian people: »Through it he [the Holy Spirit] gathers us, using it to teach and preach the Word. By it he creates and increases sanctification, causing it daily to grow.« *Book of Concord*, 417; BS 657,44-47.

⁶⁵ WA 30I, 94,1-4.

Therefore, one must conclude that Luther's constructive exposition of Christian doctrine ascribes a definite sphere of activity to the church. The Holy Spirit carries out the work of sanctification in such a way as to use the services of the ecclesial community he has assembled and equipped with gifts.[66]

Insights into Sanctification from Luther's Instructions

The third main part of this study can begin with Luther's catechetical work of 1520, in which he briefly described the work of the Holy Spirit as awakening human beings, calling them, and making them alive, holy, and spiritual in Christ.[67] As he repeated his expositions of the Creed, Luther moved steadily toward interpreting the whole third article as a unity under the master-concept sanctification.[68]

A first step toward understanding Luther's view of sanctification can be made with the help of his Pentecost Monday sermon of 1529. Holiness consists, on the one hand, in the non-imputation of enduring sinfulness, which though is not an unreal situation of God dealing with sinners »as if« they were sinless. For the Holy Spirit is in fact creating a new person, both in one's self-understanding and, in the course of time, in one's moral behavior. The understanding or heart is struck by the gospel of Christ, which announces a wholly benign and gracious message. The Holy Spirit actualizes this message of Christ and brings about a profound change in the understanding. The believer is thereby made strong

---

[66] If one wanted to speak of the church as exercising an »instrumental« influence on sanctification, the notion at least would not be alien to Luther. In 1523, in a defense of the singular role of faith in justification against Johann Cochlaeus, Luther readily admitted that faith does not rule out the several other causes of justification to which Cochlaeus had appealed. »Christus meruit, ut iustificemur, Spiritus sanctus exequitur meritum Christi, ut iustificemur. Verbum est instrumentum, quo exequitur Spiritus meritum Christi, similiter et sacramentum et praedicator. Sed formalis iustificatio relinquitur soli fidei.« WA 11, 302,25-28. Here, word, sacrament, and preacher are instruments of the Spirit, through which he carries out justification. Later, Luther articulates a similar »through which« with regard to the church's role in sanctification.

[67] *Eine kurze Form*, WA 7, 218,29. The approach taken here to understanding the nature of sanctification in Luther is consciously diverse from that of Regin Prenter in »Luthers Lehre von der Heiligung,« in V. Vajta, ed., *Lutherforschung heute* (Berlin 1958), 64-74. Prenter ascribes the progressive overcoming of sin so much to the dynamic of *fides Christi* that Luther's doctrine of the *donum* and of the gifts of the Holy Spirit are hardly mentioned, and the third creedal article is not given the attention it deserves. I also differ from E. Herms over sanctification, since he presents it as primarily a process of developing knowledge and certitude. *Luthers Auslegung des dritten Artikels*, 65-92.

[68] In the Large Catechism, we read that the third article could be given no better title than »On Sanctification.« BS, 653,32f; *Book of Concord*, 415. In what follows, we will not develop further a formulation of Luther's that appeared in 1523 but then was not repeated, namely, that the *communio sanctorum* is holy »quia sanctificata est per Deum, quia sanctitatem quam Deus habet, dat eis.« WA 11, 53,26f.

against death, sin, and all evil.⁶⁹ Thus there comes to pass what Luther described so simply in the Large Catechism, after referring to what Christ gained by his death and resurrection: »Therefore, to sanctify is nothing else than to bring to the Lord Christ to receive this blessing, which we could not obtain by ourselves.«⁷⁰

Thus, the sanctifying work of the Holy Spirit is to bring believers to Christ so they may receive from him the benefits of new life.⁷¹ The holiness thus conferred has according to Luther four component parts. It is, first, the forgiveness of sins by means of God's word of grace; second, the personalization of one's relation to God, by the Holy Spirit's imprinting of the love of God upon a believing heart; third, the penitential life, expelling sin and renewing daily behavior in accord with God's commandments; and, fourth, the expectation of complete sanctification in resurrection unto eternal life.

Luther's different expositions of the creedal third article speak regularly of these components of holiness. Each element naturally gives rise to questions about the church, once it is established that the assembled community exercises a subordinate activity serving the Spirit of sanctification. We have already seen how Luther's texts on the role of the church guard one from understanding holiness in an individualistic manner, for sanctification is essentially connected with incorporation into the community of salvation.⁷² Here, however, our concern is to garner insights from Luther into the nature of the holiness mediated to the believer from the Holy Spirit by that community.

We have already referred to the first component of holiness, the forgiveness of sins, in this study, for example, in connection with the conferral of the keys and in treating the larger complex of the means of grace, by which mother church is

---

⁶⁹ Beyond the non-accounting of the *reliquiae peccati*, holiness consists in this, »ut homo fiat novus, alium intellectum habeat, novos mores. Video Spiritus sanctus non verum qui cum legibus umgehe, sed sanctificat hominem, ut iuvet a morte, peccato, ab omnibus malis. Dominus annunciat per Evangelium eitel freundliche Dinge. Das treibt der Spiritus sanctus mit der Tat und treibt nach.« The forgiveness of sins and eternal life, as Christ proclaimed them, come to be impressed on the heart by the Holy Spirit: »Discrimen inter Christum et Spiritum sanctum: Christus redet es mündlich durch das Wort der Gnaden. Ipse [Spiritus] mit der Tat scribit in cor.« WA 29, 361,21-364,4.16-18.

⁷⁰ *Book of Concord*, 415f; BS 654,38-42.

⁷¹ This, of course, fits with what Luther saw as the ordered connection between the second and third articles of the Creed. See pp. 204f, above. K. Schwarzwäller brought out the christological orientation of the office of the Holy Spirit, who brings the believer to Jesus Christ, preserves him in faith in Christ, and sees him through death unto the fullness of life in the kingdom of Christ. »Delectari assertionibus. Zur Struktur von Luthers Pneumatologie,« *Lutherjahrbuch* 38 (1971), 26-58, at p. 55. In a similar vein, M. Lienhard, »La doctrine du Saint-Ésprit chez Luther,« *Verbum Caro* 19 (1965), no. 76, 11-38, at pp. 30f.

⁷² See, on this, G. Ebeling, »Luthers Ortsbestimmung der Lehre vom Heiligen Geist,« in *Word und Glaube*, 3 (Tübingen 1975), 316-348, at 323-326.

equipped for carrying out her role in the Spirit's work of sanctification.[73] These means or gifts have their place in Luther's doctrinal instruction as aspects of the creedal confession of the forgiveness of sins. The Creed gives clear testimony that in the work of the Spirit the first component of holiness is the forgiveness of sins.[74] Luther remarks on the fine order or sequence of the third article, as it moves from confessing the Holy Spirit to affirming the church and the forgiveness of sins. For forgiveness is how the Spirit sanctifies the church.[75] Like the third article as a whole, the element of forgiveness of sins is of ongoing relevance for believers, since it perdures just like the heavens above and the lordship of Christ.[76] The conferral of forgiveness is according to the Large Catechism both our daily need and an uninterrupted work carried out in us and for us by the Spirit.[77] Luther could consequently generalize about the daily life of the church as a service of forgiveness:

> Therefore everything in the Christian church is so ordered that we may daily obtain full forgiveness of sins through the word and through signs appointed to comfort and revive our consciences as long as we live.[78]

In Luther's instruction, the forgiveness of sins is righteousness itself and holiness. This conception contrasts with the scholastics' erroneous notion of an inherent *gratia gratum faciens*, which cannot stand with the principle of the *extra nos* of Christ himself and of his work of reconciliation. He alone makes the sinner pleasing (*gratum*) to God. The Holy Spirit distributes this grace by working in the sinner in order to make him attentive to the message of Christ.[79]

---

[73] See above, pp. 202, 206-209.

[74] In K. Schwarzwäller's reading, the forgiveness of sins becomes the central theme of the third article, both as principal work of the Holy Spirit and as the goal of all ecclesial activities. »Delectari assertionibus,« 39.

[75] »Ergo optime ordinatum in simbolo: Spiritum sanctum, Ecclesiam, remissionem peccatorum. Nam ecclesia per remissionem est sancta. Denn das ist die Heiligkeit, scilicet remissionem peccatorum.« Sermon on Pentecost 1531, WA 34I, 465,28-30.

[76] »Sicut natus puer vivit usque ad senectutem sub coelum, ita etiam sub hoc Christo vivendum est fide, auf das wir wissen, daß wir eine beständige Vergebung haben, quae non cessat, sed perpetuo durat haec iustitia.« WA 34I, 468,23-25.

[77] BS 659,7-10.16-20; *Book of Concord*, 418.

[78] *Book of Concord*, 418; BS 658,25-29.

[79] »Gratum faciens ist Christus et remissionem peccatorum, quod audistis Spiritum sanctum de eo praedicare, ut sciamus, quis sit et quid adferat: durch das sumus grati, non per charitatem.« WA 34I, 467,11-13. Characteristic of Luther's polemic against the place of *caritas* in scholastic doctrine is the insinuation, made just before these lines, that papal teaching holds that one can love God above all things by his own powers and thus in effect Christ is not needed in sanctification (467,5-10).

This is the way God confers grace, whereby God *propter Christum* no longer imputes sin and thus righteousness comes to be as *iustitia aliena*.[80]

Forgiveness of sins is thus an essential characteristic of Christianity or the church, since forgiveness is, as Luther confessed his faith in 1528, the content of all the words of grace. As faith lays hold of such a word, God's forgiveness transforms the person and thus we have »a kingdom of grace and true indulgence.«[81] The essential connection between the church and forgiveness is then the central point of Luther's first resumé of the third article in the Large Catechism.

> All this then is the office and work of the Holy Spirit, to begin and daily to increase holiness on earth through these two means, the Christian church and the forgiveness of sins.[82]

The second principal component of holiness, according to Luther, stands in apparent contrast with the grace of Christ outside the justified believer. For this great exponent of the *extra nos* of salvation also transmitted a dense doctrine of the heart's transformation as it comes to faith. Luther's many-sided description of the *fides qua*, which the Spirit elicits in the heart, occurred, paradoxically, as he set forth the traditional doctrine of faith, that is, the *fides quae* of the Creed.

One often meets in interpretations of Luther the view that he explained faith with a creative emphasis on the *pro me* reference of the work of Christ. But Luther also went beyond this emphasis, as he gave his account of faith a greater depth. He could, for example, teach the Augustinian distinction between *credere Deo* (taking testimony as true) and *credere in Deum* (dealing with God in trust, the giving of self, and a conviction that God will treat me in accord with the testimony).[83] But Luther's accounts of *credere in Deum* can also bear the imprint of his own characteristic teaching, as in the catechetical sermons of 1523: »What then is to believe *in* God the Father? It is a heartfelt confidence and complete

---

[80] In Luther's teaching God's *gratia* brings complete forgiveness of sins by non-imputation, because through the word and faith a believer is united with Christ the Savior, becomes the object of the *favor Dei*, and sin no longer torments the conscience. Most informative on this are Luther's 1521 work, *Against Latomus* (especially WA 8, 106-108; LW 32, 228-231) and his 1536 Disputation on Justification (especially WA 39I, 93,26-95,8 and 98,3-14; LW 34, 163f and 166f. I treat this in Study 4, above, pp. 70-74 and 77f.

[81] »Ein Königreich der Gnaden und des rechten Ablasses.« This is the content of the Gospel, baptism, and the sacrament of the altar, all of which offer the forgiveness of sins and bring about the presence of Christ, his Father, and their Spirit. WA 26, 507,7-11; LW 37, 368. Similarly in the sermons on the catechism in May 1528: »Ideo est una ecclesia Christiana, in qua est remissio peccatorum. Si etiam quis cadit, ut sciat misericordiae et gratiae regnum Christi esse, non peccati, irae, mortis aeternae.« WA 30I, 10,34-37.

[82] *Book of Concord*, 418; BS 659,16-20.

[83] *Eine kurze Form*, 1520; WA 7, 215,1-19.

trust in the grace of God.«⁸⁴ Therefore, an essential component of holiness is a *cordialitas* in relation to Christ and the Father, as the Holy Spirit elicits this personal relation.

The Holy Spirit is at work in the church through the word and the sacraments, but anthropologically the proper locus of the Spirit is the human heart, where his work hits home and brings about a transformation. It is due to the Spirit that the ecclesially mediated message of redemption becomes a living reality in the believing heart. The word is spoken on discrete occasions and at times meets opposition, but the Holy Spirit speaks so as to enflame the heart and this fire endures.[85]

The Spirit's work brings forth consolation, strength, and joy, with delight in the confession of Christ. This is holiness, with its own special vitality. Thus the Spirit makes holy, who is holiness in person.[86] According to the Large Catechism the outward work of the Spirit is the revelation of the grace of God through the church, but there is an inner work intimately linked to announcing the message: »The Holy Spirit reveals and preaches that word, and by it he illumines and kindles hearts so that they grasp and accept it, cling to it, and persevere in it.«[87]

A central dynamic of the Spirit of sanctification is, according to Luther's Pentecost Tuesday sermon of 1538, to enter into human hearts that have been addressed in the sacrament or by absolution and there to take possession. Thus: *corda credentium sunt Spiritus sancti corda*.[88] In such hearts the fire of the Spirit is transforming, so that a new person comes to be endowed by the Spirit with a characteristic power of discernment and vitality.[89]

But a full account of this instilling of *cordialitas* by the Spirit must include as well that which John Henry Newman expressed in his own personal motto, *Cor*

---

[84] »Est cordialis zuversicht et tota fiducia in Dei gratiam.« WA 11, 49,7f. A little later in the same text, Luther brings out the personal aspect of faith as a relationship to the three divine persons. »Nemo sentit, quam dulcis sit Deus, Christus, nisi Spiritus revelavit. A Patre veniunt omnia et ad omnia iterum Spiritus sanctus est, cum quo tangit cor nostrum, ut cognoscamus Christum et cum hoc Patrem, ut fit in praedicatione Evangelii, quod cum audit, cor habet fiduciam in Christum et tandem sentit sic voluisse patrem« (52,32-36).

[85] Sermon of Pentecost Monday 1529; WA 29, 365,20f.

[86] On Pentecost Tuesday 1529, Luther gave a profile of the Holy Spirit. »Ille autem Spiritus est spiritus qui nos solatur, confirmat, freimutig und freüdig macht, indem der heilig macht, der heilig ist.« Outward ceremonies are not his »office,« but instead »animus fervens doctrinae et confessionis Christi, sicut in apostolis videmus in Actibus. Hoc est sanctum illius spiritus opus.« WA 29, 374,11-16. See also the account of the gift of the Spirit in Luther's confession of 1528: WA 26, 505,13-17; LW 37, 365f.

[87] *Book of Concord*, 416; BS 655,5-8.

[88] WA 46, 426,14-17.

[89] This is one »qui omnia iudicat [cf. 1 Cor 2:15], et geht in Leben und Sterben hin und fragt nach niemand.« WA 46, 427,16.

ad cor loquitur. For Luther explained in the Large Catechism that those who by daily study impress the Creed upon their minds are thereby made able to see in the world around them the result of God's love.

> He gives us all these things so that we may sense and see in them his fatherly heart and his boundless love toward us. Thus our hearts will be warmed and kindled with gratitude to God and a desire to use all these blessings to his glory and praise.[90]

Therefore, corresponding to the *cordialitas* of the believing heart, there is God's own *cordialitas* toward us, which comes to personal realization in us through the Spirit's work of sanctification.

A third main component of sanctification goes beyond forgiveness and a personalized relationship to God in faith, for holiness also includes a new behavior and style of life by the believer. The Spirit brings about holiness, that which Luther defined concisely on Pentecost Monday 1528: *ut homo fiat novus, alium intellectum habeat, novos mores*.[91] There are, however, two distinct contexts in Luther's thinking in which one finds meaning ascribed to the transformed human behavior that results from the Spirit's influence.

First, there is the connection, repeatedly treated in Luther's catechetical work, between the Creed and the Decalogue.[92] We meet a notable emphasis on this in the catechetical sermons of September 1528, and then it comes back in the treatment of the Creed in the Large Catechism of 1529.[93]

The main point of Luther's reflection is the inability of human nature outside faith to do what God demands in the commandments. The precepts of God's law accordingly reveal our human weakness, while the Creed, because it sets forth in more ample form the Gospel itself, shows the source and the means by which one obtains power and strength to observe the commandments.[94] The Ten Commandments demand too much from the fallen offspring of Adam; »therefore, God comes to my help, saying that if I believe in him, his Son, and his Holy Spirit, he will then give that Spirit, who then by his grace will observe the commandments.«[95] In this vein, Luther can go so far as to say that the very

---

[90] *Book of Concord*, 413; BS 650,15-20. Luther's concluding point about the Creed comes back to this same point: »Here you have everything in richest measure. In these three articles God himself has revealed and opened to us the most profound depth of his fatherly heart, his sheer, unutterable love.« *Book of Concord*, 419; BS 660,28-32. In Study 3, p. 57, above, I cited an earlier text on the Father's heart, known through the heart of the Son, as revealed on the cross.

[91] WA 29, 363,24.

[92] This was brought out in masterful fashion by the late Albrecht Peters in »Die Theologie der Katechismen Luthers anhand der Zuordnung ihrer Hauptstücke,« *Lutherjahrbuch* 43 (1976), 7-35, which treats the third article on pp. 22-25.

[93] WA 30I, 43,27-44,26 and BS 646,10-22; *Book of Concord*, 411.

[94] WA 11, 48,23 and 30I, 43,28.36.

[95] Catechetical Sermons, September 1528; WA 30I, 44,20.

purpose of Christ's sacrifice is that we might come to live according to the commandments, which then the implementing work of the Holy Spirit brings about. The commandments instruct in the best possible way of life. »Then the Creed shows where one obtains the strength with which to live a holy life.«[96]

Thus, lived holiness of life, made possible by the Holy Spirit, moves a basic dynamic of the economy of salvation toward its completion. Here the Decalogue plays a significant part, for it sketches the profile of the renewed heart and the human behavior that the Holy Spirit then brings to realization in holiness.

The second context that throws light on the believer's new conduct, as effected by the Holy Spirit, is that of the progressive overcoming of endemic sin. Sanctification by the Spirit takes place each day, according to Luther, both in the conferral of complete forgiveness by means of the divine word of grace and as well in the Holy Spirit's opposition through his gifts against our flesh with its impurity and destructive drives.[97] The Spirit, who implements the work of Christ, makes his assembled community strong in faith and fruitful in those attitudes and deeds that are the fruits of the Spirit.[98]

In this context Luther can even commend the scholastic doctrine of infused *caritas*, for the Holy Spirit certainly does confer a set of gifts that includes charity. Naturally, he insists that forgiveness by grace and *propter Christum* has priority over the gift of *caritas* and that one place no trust before God in this gift, but still it would be wrong to neglect this gift and its results, that is, how the Spirit makes one zealous and devout in the love of God.[99]

Systematically, Luther developed this aspect of sanctification with the aid of the duality of *gratia* and *donum*. The gift is precisely that by which the Holy Spirit promotes the gradual healing of the sinner.[100] Two of Luther's later texts are also informative on the significance of the practical renewal of conduct in sanctification. The third main part of *On Councils and the Church* (1539) rests on a two-phase scheme in its exposition of the Holy Spirit's work in believers. The second phase, that of daily expulsion of sin and the eliciting of good works, follows the outline of the Decalogue in showing what the gifts of the Holy Spirit do bring forth as lived holiness of life.[101] In the same work, Luther made express reference to the Creed as he criticized his Antinomian disciples. They are at fault for appropriating only part of the divine economy set forth in the Creed. While

---

[96] WA 30I, 45,1.12, 46,9f.
[97] Catechetical Sermons, December 1528; WA 30I, 93,23-26.
[98] The implied reference here is to Gal 5:22. BS 657,44-658,1; *Book of Concord*, 417.
[99] Pentecost Sermon, 1531; WA 34I, 464,9-28.
[100] See the texts and study referred to in n. 80, above, to which one can add Luther's instructive preface to the Epistle of the Romans: WADB 5, 622,17-22; 7, 9,10-29; LW 35, 369f.
[101] WA 50, 624,30-33, 625,23-29, 626,15-627,15; LW 41, 143-144, 145-147.

they may preach well on the second article on redemption by Christ, they completely neglect the third article. They have no doctrine of sanctification, that is, of the new life brought forth by the Holy Spirit in virtue of his gifts and of the resulting transformation of our old Adam by the penitential life.[102]

The fourth component of sanctification is dependent on Luther's insistence on the fundamental unity of the creedal third article. Consequently, the final resurrection is the culmination of the Spirit's work of imparting holiness.

Thus the believer lives in a mid-time, in which the Spirit has begun his work and is pushing it forward, but has not completed it. Holiness looks to its own eschatological perfection, and so the believer longs for what has not yet come, namely, resurrection and eternal life.[103] At the end the Spirit will sanctify the body in resurrection and this will put an end to our prayer for forgiveness of guilt, which has its place now when holiness is only beginning. After death the Spirit will bring his work to conclusion by wholly expelling sin, *et tunc erit mea sanctificatio. Ideo etiam erit mera vita.* But to come to this holiness one must cling fast to the word and sacraments and remain a part of the community of salvation: »If you die after remaining in the church, then he will raise you up and totally sanctify you.«[104]

The eschatological outlook of faith, guided by the Creed, is precisely the expectation of resurrection »to complete and perfect holiness in a new, eternal life.« What we are now, according to the Large Catechism, is partial and imperfect, but it will then be perfect.

> In that life are only pure and holy people, full of goodness and righteousness, completely freed from sin, death, and all evil, living in new, immortal, and glorified bodies.[105]

This then is the fundamental orientation of the work of the Holy Spirit, that is, to a time when the church with its ministry of forgiveness of sin will come to an end.

Concluding Reflections

Recently K. Hammann declared that Luther's action in May 1521 of branding the pope the Antichrist was a major turning point, because it unleashed the theological energies of those who then went on to rethink on a biblical basis the

---

[102] WA 50, 599,26-35; LW 41, 113f.
[103] Catechetical Sermons, May 1528; WA 30I, 10,34.
[104] Catechetical Sermons, December 1528; WA 30I, 93,7 and 94,6 (»Si moreris et manes in ecclesia, tum te resuscitabit et penitus te sanctificabit«).
[105] *Book of Concord*, 418; BS 659,5-7,12-16.

nature and role of the church.[106] After this study of Luther's own instruction in the faith, one is prompted to rank Luther himself high on the list of those sixteenth century thinkers who contributed fresh insights in ecclesiology. Admittedly, Luther did not offer a theological account of the structure of the church, as for example we find indicated in Article 28 of the Augsburg Confession, with its exposition of episcopal authority.[107] But Luther was quite insightful on themes located on a deeper level of ecclesiological teaching. By way of conclusion, I note three points of Luther's continuing importance.

First, Luther consistently made the doctrine of the church part of the third article of the Creed, in close connection with faith's convictions about the Holy Spirit. This is of special importance for Western Christianity, because of the questionable tendency in the medieval and modern West to emphasize the church's relation to certain founding actions of Jesus Christ during his public ministry, for example, his promises to Peter or the saying to his followers recorded in Luke 10:16 (»He who hears you hears me.«). It is more promising to follow Luther's way of relating the church less to the will of its founder and more to the outpouring of the Spirit on Pentecost. We note that modern Lutheran theology may well have something to learn by returning to its own basic documents, like Luther's catechisms, and then following their lead in rightly situating the church in the economy of salvation.[108]

Second, Luther is helpful toward overcoming any temptation to a Donatist misunderstanding of the church's contribution to sanctification. For the church and her ministers do not impart their own holiness to those being sanctified. Luther quite rightly emphasizes the gifts or endowments, by means of which mother church bears and nourishes the new life of believers. The immanent holiness of the church does not count here, but instead the mediation of God's salvation through the means of grace given over to the stewardship of the church. These gifts and means, being also part of the third article, are the ongoing

---

106 *Ecclesia spiritualis*, 229.

107 See, for example, E. Iserloh, »'Von der Bischofen Gewalt': CA 28,« in E. Iserloh & B. Hallensleben, eds., *Confessio Augustana und Confutatio. Der Augsburger Reichstag 1530 und die Einheit der Kirche* (Münster 1980), 473-488. – Regarding Luther, we now have the just-published collection, M. Brecht, ed., *Martin Luther und das Bischofsamt* (Stuttgart 1990), in which new light on Luther's thinking about the episcopal task in the church is especially found in M. Wriedt's study, »Luthers Gebrauch der Bischofstitulatur in seinen Briefen,« ibid., 73-100.

108 André Birmelé's major investigation of the Lutheran-Catholic fundamental difference repeatedly expounds the Lutheran understanding of the mediation of salvation without any mention of the Holy Spirit or of the third article of the Creed. *Le salut en Jésus-Christ dans les dialogues oecuméniques* (Paris & Geneva 1986), 156, 197, 228, 238-253, 291. Instead one notes a connection between the Holy Spirit and the church in the theological conceptions of certain Catholics whom Birmelé cites, e.g., P. Smulders (p. 229), B. Sesboué (233), and J.M. Tillard (234). The Lutheran representatives whom Birmelé cites tend to work out the mediation of salvation in a manner alien to Luther, by placing it in the framework of creator/creature, that is, within the first article of the Creed.

modalities of the Holy Spirit's activity. Word and sacrament do link the church with the ministry of Jesus, but their effectiveness rests on their being part of the Holy Spirit's own phase of the economy of salvation. On this point Lutherans and Catholics are in basic agreement, since both traditions have their roots in Augustine and the anti-Donatist tradition of Western Christianity.[109]

A third enrichment of any systematic ecclesiological proposal can come from Luther's specification of the task of the church as the service of sanctification. Retrieval of the primacy of holiness should contribute notably both to revitalizing ecclesiological reflection in theology and to the renewal of the churches' pastoral practice. Also, Luther's notion of the components of sanctification, as sketched in our third section above, deserves attention too. The task of the church relates to forgiveness of sins, personalizing faith's relation to God, a penitential observance of the commandments, and an impatient expectation of the eschatological salvation of body and soul. To relate the ministry of the whole church to such a complex of blessings – this would notably enhance for all Christians both their theology of the church and their lives as people assembled in the church.

---

[109] It is doubtful whether this elementary consideration, based on a long-range view of the history of doctrine, plays its proper role in the overall conception of A. Birmilé's *Le salut*.

PART III

THE EARLY LUTHERAN CHURCH IN DIALOGUE

10

ABUSES UNDER INDICTMENT
AT THE DIET OF AUGSBURG 1530

The Augsburg Confession of 1530, a primary and constitutive affirmation of faith for the Lutheran churches of the world, has been studied in recent years with greater intensity than ever before. Nonetheless, one avenue of approach to the Confession has not been travelled by other scholars. This concerns the way in which the Confession laments a number of »abuses« in the papal church. I take up this topic in the present essay. But first, I offer a sketch of the contemporary context of study by noting some major areas of recent study of the text and context of the Confession submitted by the princes and imperial cities that had espoused the Lutheran reformation in 1530.

The Augsburg Confession in Recent Research

Writings on the Diet of Augsburg of 1530 have in recent decades clustered around two poles. First, a vigorous theological discussion of the Augsburg Confession itself began in the 1970s and crested with the 450th anniversary celebrated in 1980. In this context, a strong ecumenical motivation surfaced, in the hope that the anniversary could become a milestone on the road to restoration of ecclesial communion between the Roman Catholic Church and the Lutheran churches of the world. Could the Confession be acknowledged as expressing the common core of faith and doctrine adhered to by Lutherans and Catholics? Considerable attention was directed to the question whether the Roman Catholic Church could formally recognize the Augsburg Confession as a profession of authentic Christian faith.[1] This discussion led to a widely-held

---

[1] Numerous collaborative volumes on the Confession presented theological and ecumenical analyses. H. Meyer, H. Schütte et al., eds., *Katholische Anerkennung des Augsburgischen Bekenntnisses?* (Frankfurt 1977); translated in large part in J.A. Burgess et al., eds., *The Role of the Augsburg Confession. Catholic and Lutheran Views* (Philadelphia & New York/Ramsey, N.J. 1980). H. Fries, E. Iserloh, et al., *Confessio Augustana: Hindernis oder Hilfe?* (Regensburg 1979). F. Hoffmann & U. Kühn, eds., *Die Confessio Augustana in ökumenischem Gespräch* (Berlin/DDR 1980). B. Lohse & O.H. Pesch, eds., *Das »Augsburger Bekenntnis« von 1530 damals und heute* (Munich & Mainz 1980). E. Iserloh & B. Hallensleben, eds., *Confessio Augustana und Confutatio. Der Augsburger Reichstag 1530 und die Einheit der Kirche* (Münster 1980). P. Meinhold, ed., *Kirche und Bekenntnis* (Wiesbaden 1980). *La Confession d'Augsbourg. 450e anniversaire. Autour d'un*

conviction that the Augsburg Confession is largely susceptible of a »catholic« interpretation, both in its overall intention and in its individual articles.

Furthermore, a form of Catholic recognition of this primary Lutheran Confession did in fact occur. Catholic theologians gave numerous convincing demonstrations of the basic coherence of the Confession with the perennial faith of the church.[2] This scholarly theological basis then underlay important declarations in 1980 by the Catholic bishops of West Germany, by Cardinals Johannes Willebrands and Joseph Ratzinger, and by Pope John Paul II. The German bishops said that the Confession shows that the Catholic-Lutheran consensus is more than a partial agreement on just some truths; it is rather »an agreement on the central truths of faith,« an agreement which grounds the hope that ongoing dialogue will lead to overcoming the divisive effect of the differences that remain.[3] Pope John Paul, speaking on June 25, 1980, noted the failure 450 years before to successfully build the bridge of reconciliation that the Augsburg Confession had proposed, but went on in a positive vein:

colloque. Le Point théologique, 31 (Paris 1980). H. Meyer & H. Schütte, eds., *Confessio Augustana, Bekenntnis des einen Glaubens* (Paderborn & Frankfurt 1980); translation edited by G.W. Forell & J.F. McCue, *Confessing One Faith: a Joint Commentary on the Augsburg Confession* (Minneapolis 1981). K. Lehmann & E. Schlink, eds., *Evangelium – Sakramente – Amt. Die ökumenische Tragweite der Confessio Augustana* (Freiburg/B. & Göttingen 1982). The best short report on the question of a Catholic recognition of the Confession is P. Gauly, *Katholisches Ja zum Augsburger Bekenntnis?* (Freiburg/B. 1980). – A helpful review of the broader span of recent work on the 1530 Diet is given by H. Neuhaus, in »Der Augsburger Reichstag des Jahres 1530. Ein Forschungsbericht,« *Zeitschrift für historische Forschung* 9 (1982), 167-211.

[2] The joint commentary edited by Meyer & Schütte (in English by Forell & McCue) exemplifies such work, especially in its ten thematic chapters on the doctrines expressed in the Confession. A short formulation of the results of such study is the declaration, »All Under One Christ,« issued by the Lutheran-Roman Catholic International Joint Commission, in *Origins* 9 (1980), 685-689. Two individual Catholic contributions stand out for their treatment of the considerable Catholic-Lutheran agreement that, in spite of contrary appearances, can be ascertained: O.H. Pesch, »Rechtfertigung des Sünders und Gerechtigkeit der Welt,« in Lohse & Pesch, eds. *Das Augsburger Bekenntnis damals und heute*, 215-236, and L. Ullrich, »Ist die katholische Meßopferlehre ein Hindernis für eine katholische Anerkennung des Augsburgischen Bekenntnis?« in Hoffmann & Kühn, eds., *Die Confessio Augustana im ökumenischen Gespräch*, 191- 220. An informative retrospective view of the ecumenical theology resulting from the Augustana anniversary is given by L. Ullrich in E. Koch, L. Ullrich, U. Kühn, »Der wissenschaftliche Ertrag des Confessio-Augustana-Gedenkjahres 1980,« *Theologische Literaturzeitung* 106 (1981), 706-731.

[3] Cited from E. Iserloh, »450 Jahre Confessio Augustana. Eine Bilanz,« *Catholica* 35 (1981), 14, which also cites – on pp. 15f – the interventions of the two Cardinals. In Augsburg, on June 29, 1980, Cardinal Willebrands voiced his conviction that what Lutherans and Catholics hold in common is both more profound in nature and wider in extent than the issues of divergent belief. Cardinal Ratzinger said on the same occasion that the Augsburg Confession documents »den elementaren Grundkonsens« in which Lutherans and Catholics are one in essential matters of faith. Later in 1980, on Nov. 17, Pope John Paul addressed Lutheran leaders in Mainz and incorporated into his address what the German bishops had declared about the existence of »a full accord on fundamental and central truths.« The later papal address is given in *Origins* 10 (1980), 398f.

We are all the more grateful that today we see with even greater clearness that at that time, even if there was no success in building a bridge, the storms of that age spared important piers of that bridge. The intense and long-standing dialogue with the Lutheran Church, called for and made possible by the Second Vatican Council, has enabled us to discover how great and solid are the common foundations of our Christian faith.[4]

One observer summarized the outcome of this effort as the ascertaining of a large measure of communality in faith between Lutheran and Catholics, which however goes hand in hand with differences not yet resolved.[5] The papal affirmation, made with reference to the dialogue with adherents of the Augsburg Confession, should not blind us to the *sic et non* character of Catholic attitudes to the Confession itself. Some have pointed out the ecclesiological minimalism or deficit of the Confession.[6] A spokesman for Orthodoxy, steeped in the Fathers and in theology based in the liturgy, raised a whole series of doctrinal objections against the Confession, which should give pause to those urging Roman Catholic recognition.[7] A Catholic observer asked whether the modern reading of the Confession as a document of Christian unity takes seriously enough the potential for division latent in the same document's fierce protest, based on the Lutheran doctrine of justification, against abusive aspects of the church of its day.[8] This latter remark, especially, can be kept in mind in the study we are presenting here. In fact, one difficulty with the recent discussion of a Catholic acknowledgment

---

[4] Cited from *Origins* 10 (1980), 166; also given in the documentary collection of papal and Vatican statements, T.F. Stransky & J.B. Sherrin, eds., *Doing the Truth in Charity* (New York & Ramsey N.J. 1982), 326. The statement was given in German in *L'Osservatore Romano*, June 27, 1980, and reviewed by U. Ruh, »Ein Bekenntnis wird lebendig. Zum 450. Jubiläum der Confessio Augustana,« *Herder Korrespondenz* 34 (1980), 384. It is found in French in the Vatican Unity Secretariat's *Service d'Information*, no. 44 (1980), 100. In Italian: *La Traccia* 1 (1980), 521, and in *Civiltà Cattolica* 131 III (1980), 159.

[5] »Hohes Maß an Gemeinsamkeit – weiterhin unbewältigte Probleme.« U. Ruh, »Ein Bekenntnis wird lebendig,« 383.

[6] Erwin Iserloh singled out the lacunae of the Confession and recalled the fact that even some Lutherans see problems in its stance against ecclesial institutionalism. »450 Jahre Confessio Augustana,« 6-10. A particularly incisive statement of this issue is T. Koch's study, »Das Problem des evangelischen Kirchenverständnisses nach dem Augsburger Bekenntnis,« in Lohse & Pesch, eds., *Das Augsburger Bekenntnis damals und heute*, 125-143.

[7] E. Timiadis, »Une Texte inachevé,« in *Le Confession d'Augsbourg*, 197-226. Here we read, »La Confession d'Augsbourg flotte et hésite entre la loyauté e la rupture définitive. C'est un texte indécis, irrésolu. A certains égards ... désapprouve ce qu'ailleurs elle admet« (p. 199); »Quel critère permettra de discerner une communauté authentique de tant d'assemblées hétéroclites? La réponse de la Confession d'Augsbourg nous semble insuffisante« (p. 215); »Est-ce trop de dire que dans les articles de la Confession ... il y a une certaine ambiguité et une certaine incohérence?« (p. 221). L. Ullrich noted this intervention at length in »Der wissenschaftliche Ertrag,« *Theologische Literaturzeitung* 106 (1981), 717f.

[8] L. Ullrich, ibid., 719.

of the Confession is that its declarations on abusive practices in worship and church order, the topic of the present essay, were only rarely treated in the ecumenical studies of recent years.

A second stream of recent study is a collaborative work of historical scholarship concentrating on the dialogue, or unity-negotiations, conducted at the Diet of Augsburg.[9] Beginning on August 16, 1530, Lutheran and Catholic representatives worked energetically, and with some substantial successes, to overcome the divergence between the Augsburg Confession, presented on June 25, and the Catholic *Confutatio*, read on behalf of Emperor Charles V on August 3. Negotiations carried on by a »joint commission« treated the doctrinal differences, especially on August 16-17, and in fact dramatically narrowed the differences on sin, justification, good works, and repentance, but from this point on the discussions became more difficult and an impasse was reached by August 21 which further exchanges only confirmed. But the sticking points were not directly matters of faith, professed belief, and doctrine. Instead, the impediments were a cluster of concrete forms and structures of church life.

It is no exaggeration to say that the Lutheran-Catholic dialogue on faith and doctrine in 1530 reached a notable consensus. There was then, for a time, a Catholic acceptance and recognition of what the Lutherans professed in the Augsburg Confession. As Martin Luther remarked some years later, »I'm concerned that we will never again come so close to each other as we did at Augsburg in 1530.«[10] The dialogue in 1530 did not lead to the reconciliation of church bodies, but it was nonetheless a doctrinal exchange that had an astounding measure of success.

Approaching the Question of the Abuses

This essay and the one that follows offer a fresh look at the Lutheran-Catholic exchanges of mid-1530 over doctrine and church reform. I ask about what was in fact proposed and why the proposals came to be rejected. These two essays rest

---

[9] The recent stage of research began with Gerhard Müller's study, »Johann Eck und die Confessio Augustana,« *Quellen und Forschungen aus italienischen Archiven und Bibliotheken* 38 (1958), 205-242, and continued in works by Eugène Honée and Vinzenz Pfnür, with further contributions of G. Müller. This work reached a climactic moment with the text-edition and analysis of E. Honée in *Der Libell des Hieronymus Vehus zum Augsburger Reichstag 1530* (Münster 1988). Study 11 in this collection is my account of these negotiations, which I take as the first Lutheran-Catholic ecumenical dialogue, and the essay will include references to all of the recent studies in their specific context. They are also listed in our Bibliography. Herbert Immenkötter made the initial results easily accessible to the general reader in *Um die Einheit im Glauben: Die Unionsverhandlungen des Augsburger Reichstages im August und September 1530* (Münster 1973).

[10] Probably in 1536 or 1537, when rumors were circulating about Pope Paul III's intention to convoke a general council, Luther expressed his doubts that anything significant would come of such an event. What happened in 1530 had been more promising, and by now the latter looks like a great lost opportunity. »Ich habe Sorge, daß wir nimmermehr so nahe werden zusammen kommen, als zu Augsburg 1530.« WA *Tischreden*, 4, 495,22f.

on the conviction that a religiously meaningful »recognition« is primarily an act of acknowledgment of a church or group of churches. Such recognition rests on a global perception of the way a body of people hold together, of how they worship, and of what forms, inspires, and consoles them. These essays offer especially a fresh perception of the sixteenth-century Lutheran church body, that is, of a group of reformed territorial and urban churches that articulated a notable self-expression in the Augsburg Confession and in the dialogue that followed in August 1530. Written by a Catholic historical scholar and ecumenist, these essays aim first to help Catholic readers look afresh at the churches of the Augsburg Confession and to grasp their early religious motivation, their sense of values held in faith, their aspirations for reform, and their arguments for legitimacy as a realization of the Church of Jesus Christ.

These essays are not engaged in nostalgic reflection over a case of what-might-have-been. My main interest is not simply the project or set of proposals that missed by a hair's breadth being a success.[11] Instead, the underlying issue is the original ecclesial identity of the two churches that failed to resolve their differences at one point on their way into distinct and separate existences in 1530.

Emperor's Charles V's draft recess of September 22, 1530, proposed to end the Diet of Augsburg with a declaration that the Lutheran Confession had been refuted and that its signers had six months to consider acceptance of the articles proposed to them at the point of impasse in late August. Also, no further doctrinal innovations nor any more changes in religious practice were to be introduced in their domains.[12] When the adherents of the Reformation dissented from this recess, it became unmistakably clear that the religious unity of the German Empire and of Western Christendom was on the way to dissolution.

But why did it come to this? Why was Charles V so severely frustrated in realizing the aims he had proposed for the Diet in his conciliatory summons of January 21, 1530? The Diet was to be a forum for a respectful hearing of the views and positions of the estates and for considerations of those steps that would lead to agreement and unity in one church under Christ.[13]

In early 1530 Charles V was riding the crest of a series of diplomatic successes – assertion of firm control over Spain, victory over France, reconciliation with

---

[11] Michael Root has recently called attention to how the Augsburg Confession actually served as »a concrete proposal for a reconciliation,« which Lutherans made to Emperor Charles V and to the Catholic authorities. »The Augsburg Confession as Ecumenical Proposal: Episcopacy, Luther, and Wilhelm Maurer,« *Dialog* 28 (1989), 223-232. We will return to this theme, both in this essay and the one that follows, especially in connection with Melanchthon's direct exchanges with Cardinal Legate Campeggio.

[12] K.E. Förstemann, *Urkundenbuch zu der Geschichte des Reichstages zu Augsburg im Jahre 1530*, 2 (Halle 1835), 474f.

[13] Ibid., 1 (1833), 7f. The wording of the imperial summons is woven into the Preface of the Augsburg Confession, nos. 2-4. *The Book of Concord*, ed. T.G. Tappert et al. (Philadelphia 1959), 25.

Pope Clement VII, solidification of his power in Italy – but the goal of restoring religious unity in the German Empire eluded him.

Why did it come to this? In quest of an answer, we have probed into the attitudes and mentalities of the spokesmen for the churches, those who struggled with the religious questions and arguments of the Diet of Augsburg in 1530. For this investigation we have for the most part put to the one side their directly doctrinal and systematic theological views. Studies of their theological development and positions exist already in sufficient number. Moreover, we know from recent research that a considerable doctrinal agreement was attained in the August committee work on Articles 1-21 of the Augsburg Confession and *Confutatio*. The irreconcilable differences emerged when the negotiators took up the matters of religious practice treated by the two basic position papers in articles 22-28. The insoluble problems turned up under these headings:
- Communion under both forms (Art. 22)
- marriage of priests (Art. 23)
- the Mass (Art. 24)
- confession (Art. 25)
- distinction of foods, i.e. fasting laws (Art. 26)
- monastic vows (Art. 27)
- episcopal authority (Art. 28).

On these matters the Lutheran side claimed it had simply undertaken the reform of abuses and defective traditions then undermining right religious practice.[14] But not everything the Protestants called abuses were admitted to be such by their Catholic partners in discussion. The final article of the imperial *Confutatio* of August 3 had concluded with an assertion of a firm will and intent to correct abuses, curtail infringements of right order, and restore Christian religious practice once more to its original fervor and splendor.[15] Thus both sides professed a commitment to reform of abuses, but they differed over which practices and institutions should properly be judged abuses.

The nagging differences at Augsburg in 1530 were over concrete realities of religious practice. »Practice« is not meant here in the narrow sense of purely external activity, but includes both the preaching and instruction associated with specific forms of lived religion and the underlying beliefs that came to light when the legitimacy of forms was contested and/or defended. Differences, expressed imperfectly in the doctrinal articles of the Confession and its rebuttal, documented themselves in the concrete and visible forms of ecclesial practice.[16]

---

[14] Augsburg Confession, Introduction to Part 2. *Book of Concord*, 48f.

[15] *Confutatio*, art. 28. *Die Confutatio der Confessio Augustana vom 3. August 1530*, ed. Herbert Immenkötter (Corpus catholicorum 33; Münster 1979), 202f.

[16] H. Immenkötter, *Der Reichstag zu Augsburg und die Confutatio* (Münster 1979), 37. W. Maurer has pointed out the impossibility of sustaining a complete separation of the doctrinal and practical parts of the confession. *Historischer Kommentar zur Confessio Augustana*, 2 (Gütersloh 1978), 74.

At Augsburg the divisive issues between the two churches had a concrete focus.

This indicates that important light can be thrown on the Augsburg impasse, and on the deeper grounds of the Lutheran-Catholic religious division, by probing into the attitudes and judgments held by the participants at Augsburg on conditions of worship and religious practice in the pre-Reformation Church. How did they perceive and judge popular instruction on the eve of the Reformation? What was their assessment of Eucharistic practice and popular devotions? How did they portray conditions in late-medieval German parishes, religious and monastic communities, and ecclesiastical courts? How did those who spoke at Augsburg in 1530 evaluate the pastoral ministry then being carried out by priests and the administration of dioceses by bishops and their associated officials?

I have reviewed some of the principal expository documents connected with the Diet, both from the preparatory stages and from the transactions in Augsburg down to the beginning of negotiations on August 16, 1530, taking note of the positions taken on religious conditions on the eve of the Reformation. What came to expression here is in my judgment an important component in the self-understanding of Lutherans and Catholics at a critical juncture in their history. In this study I begin on the Protestant side and move through various Lutheran statements, such as the preparatory apologias from outside Saxony, the Saxon preparatory drafts, and Luther's *Admonition to the Clergy*, to the Augsburg Confession itself. The present essay will conclude by reviewing some key reactions to the Confession, first from Martin Luther and then from the side of the Catholic majority at the Diet of 1530.

This ordering of the materials in a roughly chronological sequence should facilitate insights both into the specific historical character of the Augsburg Confession and into some distinctive differences between Protestant claims and the responses stimulated by the statement of these claims. All through this presentation, however, my principal purpose is to retrieve from the mental worlds of the Augsburg participants their perceptions, reports, assessments, and claims about religious practice in the era just preceding the outbreak of the Reformation struggles. Thereby I hope to illuminate the Diet of Augsburg and the epochal document, the Lutheran Confession, from a fresh perspective and to gain new insights into the outlooks of those who labored in mid-1530 to save the religious unity of the West.

Preparatory Apologias from outside Saxony

This section will review a summary of claims and assertions about the pre-Reformation Church made by representatives of some of the estates and cities that took their stand with Electoral Saxony by signing the Augsburg Confession. We will review seven such preparatory reports from areas outside Saxony where the Lutheran reformation had established itself in the 1520s. Our selection will include three apologias commissioned by Margrave Georg of Brandenburg-

Ansbach: that is, individual papers by Johann Rurer of Ansbach and Kaspar Löner, then of Hof, and the corporate report of four members of the clergy in Kulmbach.[17] We also use two preparatory statements extant from the city of Heilbronn, describing the new church order recently instituted there.[18] And from Nürnberg we use a corporate report prepared by the preachers of the city (ready by May 7, 1530) and a defense of the Nürnberg reforms which Andreas Osiander submitted to the city council on June 22.[19]

The first modern editor of these documents, Wilhelm Gussmann, underscored their special value as reflections of first-generation Lutheranism. These reports tell of a cluster of common religious convictions stemming from Luther, of a large range of agreement on those institutions of late-medieval religion that are to be attacked and rejected, and of some interesting differences of emphasis.[20] These documents are similar to the Saxon preparatory apologia, commonly known as the Torgau Articles, prepared by the Wittenberg theologians in March-April, on which the second half of the Augsburg Confession was based. In the end these non-Saxon apologias made little contribution to the final polishing of the Augsburg Confession of the Lutheran group of estates. Still, the preparatory apologias from outside Saxony remain of value for their expression of the views of people on the Lutheran side in the momentous exchanges of the Augsburg Diet.[21]

---

[17] The Margrave called for contributions in preparation for the Diet in a letter to the church superintendents of his domains on January 29, 1530. Wilhelm Gussmann, *Quellen und Forschungen zur Geschichte des Augsburgischen Glaubensbekenntnisses*, 1/1 (Leipzig-Berlin 1911), 274f. Eventually forty-nine apologias for the Reformation were sent in by way of response to this request. We use the three texts given by Gussmann in his Vol. 1/2: pp. 3-47 (Rurer), pp. 96-168 (Löner), and pp. 47-96 (clergy of Kulmbach). Thirteen other Brandenburg-Ansbach reports – five in complete texts and eight in excerpts – are given in Wilhelm F. Schmidt and Karl Schornbaum, eds., *Die Fränkische Bekenntnisse. Eine Vorstufe der Augsburgischen Konfession* (Munich 1930), 474-654. G. Seebass recently called attention to the need of a systematic study of these early reformation documents. »Die reformatorische Bekenntnisse vor der Confessio Augustana,« in P. Meinhold, ed., *Kirche und Bekenntnis* (Wiesbaden 1980), 26-55, at p. 52.

[18] Gussmann, 1/1, 173-180, a preliminary description of the religious changes and how they can be defended, and 180-203, a comprehensive account of the reforms. The latter paper was brought to Augsburg with a view to submitting it to Charles V (Gussmann, 1/1, 169-171). Heilbronn formally joined the signers of the Augsburg Confession on July 14 or 15, 1530 (ibid., 163).

[19] Texts in Gussmann, 1/1, 278-294 and 297-312. The latter piece is now available in a critical edition prepared by Bernhard Schneider in Andreas Osiander, *Gesamtausgabe*, ed. Gerhard Müller, vol. 4, *Schriften und Briefe, Mai 1530 bis Ende 1532*, ed. G. Müller & G. Seebass (Gütersloh 1981), 68-102.

[20] Gussmann, 1/1, 204f., 210, 231ff.

[21] Johann Rurer of Ansbach was at Augsburg to advise Margrave Georg (ibid., 81). The Nürnberg delegation, which included A. Osiander from about June 27 into late July (ibid., 140), was a powerful counterpoise to Melanchthon's conciliatory approach to the issues of the Diet.

1) Two themes of a general character accompanied the explanation of the religious changes recently introduced in these lands of the early Lutheran reformation. First, the changes were attributed to *popular biblical instruction*. The Bürgermeister and Council of Heilbronn related that their daily lessons in the word of God brought them to realize how many horrid abuses were plaguing the Church. Fearing the Gospel warning to servants who know their master's wishes but do nothing to fulfil them (Lk 12:47), these urban leaders felt they had to take action to introduce a new church order based on sound doctrine.[22] In a similar vein, Andreas Osiander located the real beginning of reform in the opening of fresh access to understanding Holy Scripture through the linguistic work of Reuchlin and Erasmus. Thereby people came to recognize and detest the abuses that had recently arisen in the Church. Luther's sermons and German writings then attacked the abuses so sharply that church leaders lost their credibility and people welcomed the religious changes.[23] Thus the pre-Reformation Church is implicitly characterized as closed to Scripture and lacking an awareness of the low state of the Church. The Reformation sprang from the critical ferment arising from encounter with the biblical word.

A second general theme in the non-Saxon reports is the characterization of pre-Reformation religious life as *false worship* based on the observance of various human enactments. The Nürnberg preachers highlighted Christian freedom, deducing from St. Paul an admonition against human traditions, such as outward observances regarding foods, garb, and special days, which turn believers from true worship of God to the idolatrous cultivation of externals.[24] All three reports submitted to Margrave Georg used a schematic contrast between false worship before the Reformation and true worship now being introduced. »False worship« was especially found in those practices concocted by human ingenuity with the aim of attaining forgiveness of sins and eternal life. After giving such a definition, Johann Rurer of Ansbach offered Margrave Georg a short catalogue of practices verging on idolatry.

> These are the works of all human precepts, namely, keeping the rule and statutes in monasteries and convents, not wearing this or that kind of garment, not eating this or that kind of food, or not touching any money; similarly, building churches or chapels, founding regular singing of the *Salve*, or endowing benefices and Masses, such as an annual requiem on the date of death, or one with procession and holy water; praying the Rosary and Psalter; commissioning images, panels, bells, or organs for churches, setting up confraternities; making pilgrimages to this or that shrine; holding processions in the church or through the town and fields; lighting candles; fasting on

---

[22] Gussmann, 1/2, 181 and 183.
[23] Gussmann, 1/1, 297; Osiander, *Gesamtausgabe*, 4, 68f.
[24] Gussmann, 1/1, 288. A broad concern of the Reformation was to promote true worship, while suppressing what it saw as the idolatrous veneration of innerworldly localizations of sacred power. This has been treated with some amplitude by Carlos M.N. Eire, in *War Against the Idols. The Reformation of Worship from Erasmus to Calvin* (Cambridge 1986).

vigils of saints' days; getting holy water and blessed salt; eating no meat on papal fast days. These and similar works are nothing else but false and vain worship of God.²⁵

Here we see the acid of Reformation criticism attacking important outgrowths of medieval European popular piety. The immediate target is less the faith and doctrine and much more the folk religion of vast numbers of believers. Explosive shibboleths, »false worship«, »human enactments,« serve to indict the recent past and to rally those leading the movement of reform.

2) The preparatory statements assert that doctrinal confusion, error, and ignorance reigned before the coming of the Reformation. The Nürnberg preachers began their report by showing how all salvation comes from the word of God by which we were created and redeemed. Although Christ commanded the proclamation of his gospel to all creatures, recently people were forbidden to speak of the faith by which we are saved. Such was the collapse of Christianity.

> O God, who can tell of the horrid seduction that we have witnessed up to now? Thereby it finally came to the point that no one had any understanding of God's word, of Christian freedom, of the power of the law and sin, of the efficacy of faith and rightly ordered worship, of the Church, of what are sacraments, and of sin and how it is forgiven. So thoroughly had Satan and his accomplices ruined and confused all things necessary to salvation through our own concocted works, righteousness, and innumerable laws.²⁶

Andreas Osiander began his report in defense of the Nürnberg reformation with a ten-point catalogue²⁷ of doctrinal errors flourishing before the changes:

- free choice was stressed and our need of the Spirit concealed;
- observance of the law was preached as the way to merit heaven;
- works of piety, such as pilgrimages, veneration of images, use of candles, etc., were placed ahead of the commandments of God;
- duties of one's calling were not presented as ways of serving God;
- repentance was made into a work to be performed by our native abilities;
- complete, auricular confession was demanded;
- satisfactory works were required for actual sins;
- baptism was devalued into forgiveness merely of original sin and had no relevance for the rest of life;
- the »gospel« was referred to stories about Christ's miracles and example, not to the good news of Christ by which we are justified;
- teaching on the Eucharist stressed the concomitant presence of Christ's blood under the form of bread and how to make worthy preparation, not mentioning Christ's saving words addressed to us.

---

[25] Gussmann, 1/2, 35. K. Löner's long syllabus of practices of false worship made up the second of the three main parts of his report (ibid., 110-142). Similarly, the clergy of Kulmbach began with a short exposition of true worship (ibid., 48-55) and then went one-by-one through all the notions and practices of false worship which had been corrected by their reformation (ibid., 55-81).
[26] Gussmann, 1/1, 286.
[27] Gussmann, 1/1, 288-300; Osiander, *Gesamtausgabe*, 4, 72-76.

Osiander went on to depict the malaise that spread as people became aware of these abuses. Some recalled the New Testament prophecies about the deceptions to arise in the last days and this combined with the emergence of sectarian preachers to cause the threat of tumult. In such a situation the lay civic leaders of Nürnberg had to take action on behalf of reform.[28]

Thus the apologias from outside Saxony were clear and outspoken in defending measures taken to correct erroneous preaching and instruction. A new popular catechesis was needed. The basics of Christianity had to be clarified to overcome an intolerable situation of doctrinal confusion.

3) Each one of these reports gave prominence to abuses connected with the celebration of *the Mass* prior to the coming of the Reformation. The most complete listing was given by Johann Rurer of Ansbach in his report for Margrave Georg.[29] Beginning from the basic Lutheran teaching that the Lord's Supper is a testament of forgiveness and not a propitiatory sacrifice,[30] Rurer then named the following abuses:

- daily offering of Christ's body and blood for the sins of the living and the dead;[31]
- payments for the celebration of Mass;[32]
- celebrating or hearing Mass in order to gain temporal benefits;
- obligatory founded Masses that must be said even if the priest lacks desire and devotion;
- reception of Communion by the priest alone;
- Mass in a language the people do not understand and without a sermon;[33]
- saying Mass for the dead who can no longer hear, believe and communicate;[34]
- the sacrilege of withholding one form from lay people;[35]
- restricting the reception of Communion to the Eater season;
- unnecessary attention to reservation of the Eucharist in the tabernacle;

---

[28] Gussmann, 1/1, 304; Osiander, *Gesamtausgabe*, 4, 86f.

[29] Gussmann, 1/2, 14-28.

[30] The Kulmbach pastors gave a full contestation of the doctrine of Eucharistic sacrifice (ibid., 64-73).

[31] The Heilbronn apologia spoke of the offering of Mass as »ein Gruel vor Gott« (ibid., 191).

[32] Osiander called stipends simony and explained that Nürnberg now has eliminated the Masses formerly held only for money (Gussmann, 1/1, 310).

[33] The Nürnberg preachers say that now the words of Christ's testament are openly sung and read, in accord with his mandate to proclaim his message from the housetops, Mt 10:27 (ibid., 289).

[34] Similarly, in Heilbronn's apologia (Gussmann, 1/2, 193-195).

[35] K. Löner was especially incensed over the withholding of the chalice, calling it robbing the Sacrament of its better part (ibid., 121). See also the report of the Nürnberg preachers, art. 3 (Gussmann, 1/1, 189f.) and Osiander's concise protest (ibid., 310).

– the idolatrous worship connected with processions of the Blessed Sacrament on Thursdays and other days.

Such a syllabus of abuses leaves no doubt that the Reformation broke sharply with a broad range of customs and practices of late-medieval Eucharistic worship. We note, however, that Rurer's abuses manifest different degrees of nearness to basic convictions. The daily offering flows more directly from belief in the sacrificial nature of Eucharistic worship than does the system of stipends and foundations. Eucharistic reservation and processions had a concrete logic about them after the early-medieval anti-Berengarian definitions, a logic not supporting infrequent lay reception and mandatory withholding of the chalice. An adequate discussion with Rurer could not be global but would have to engage in sensitive sifting of the material in question.

4) The Lutheran reformation also brought renewal of baptism and two aspects of the new rite were defended in the apologias. Each point involved criticism of pre-Reformation practice.

Both Johann Rurer and Kaspar Löner defended the recent simplification of the baptismal rite by pointing to superstitious abuses connected with the added rites with salt, spittle, and chrism, especially the popular belief that these were necessary if baptism is to have its effect.[36] A special form of this error is that the Holy Spirit is conferred by the baptismal anointing with chrism.

The Reformation introduction of baptism in the vernacular was defended against a stubborn and senseless insistence on the use of Latin. The apologists cited 1 Cor 14 against the use of a tongue contributing nothing to the instruction and edification of the people and to their confirmation in faith.[37]

5) Another target of these reports was the complex of *blessed objects* ritually consecrated by the Church and then used superstitiously by the people.

Kaspar Löner named the misused objects, that is, salt, holy water, candles, palms, ashes, the Easter fire, and blessed bread and meat, and charged that both the ritual blessing and popular use of the objects were blasphemous in seeking from these creatures both cleansing from sin and protection from Satan.[38] The Kulmbach clergy cited both canon law and scholastic theologians to demonstrate that religious use of these objects had official sponsorship. But such use, they charged, attributes divine power to creatures and robs God of due honor. In addition, the Kulmbach reformers pointed to the well-known and widespread practices of sorcery with blessed water and salt.[39]

---

[36] Gussmann, 1/2, 10 (Rurer) and 117f (Löner). For Löner, these beliefs shift trust away from Christ and rob his true baptism of its power. The Heilbronn apologia insinuated that the inventors of these additions were trying to improve on the well-conceived original institution by Christ (ibid., 187f).

[37] Gussmann, 1/1, 290 (Nürnberg preachers); 1/2, 10f (Rurer), 118 (Löner), 187 (Heilbronn).

[38] Ibid., 137f.

[39] Ibid., 73-75.

Again one is forcefully reminded of the sharp break made by the Reformation with the everyday realities of popular religion as these were in vogue before the changes set in motion by Luther's message and teaching.

6) Each of these Lutheran apologias for the Diet of Augsburg offered justification for the Reformation abolition of the obligation of *clerical celibacy*. These sections of the Brandenburg-Ansbach reports were largely doctrinal disquisitions on the divine institution of marriage, the impossibility for most people to live out a vow of chastity, and the evidence for a married clergy in the New Testament and early Christianity.[40] The conclusion could be stated, as by Johann Rurer, in a succinct thesis: for the Church to forbid priests to marry is contrary to God's word and command, against Christian freedom, opposed to numerous ancient councils, and so stems not from the Holy Spirit but from the devil's prompting of human inventiveness.[41] Or testimony could be given to a firm, heartfelt conviction that those bound by the Church to an impossible chastity should flee this Babylonian captivity and state of certain spiritual ruin to a new life in the divinely instituted state of marriage, in which alone authentic chastity is found.[42] In any case, no one was to be held to keeping a vow extracted at the time of priestly ordination.

The preachers of Nürnberg directed a further attack against *monastic institutions* as being in fact contrary to what was, or should have been, the intention of those contributing to their foundation. First, monastic life does not promote the greater honor of God, because it knows nothing of that faith that turns away from good works and achieved holiness to rely totally on God. Second, the founders themselves did not act in a Christian manner but erroneously sought salvation through their benefactions to monasteries, which in fact led more to their damnation. Third, goods of the larger community should support only preachers of the word and the handicapped poor, while all others should work for their daily bread. Consequently, the Reformation spokesmen called for civil authority to suppress the institutions of religious and monastic life and apply their properties to new purposes.[43]

7) The preparatory reports from the newly reformed areas presented a biblical basis for *ecclesiastical office* and thence drew sharply critical conclusions about papal and episcopal claims to authority.

---

[40] Ibid., 28-30 (Rurer) and 58-64 (Kulmbach preachers). Also from the Nürnberg preachers, in Gussmann, 1/1, 291.

[41] Gussmann, 1/2, 28.

[42] Ibid., 64 (from the clergy of Kulmbach).

[43] Gussmann, 1/1, 291-293. A century before, the Nürnberg city council had urged effective implementation of reform and regular observance in the local Augustinian convent. Letters from the council, in 1419, 1434, and 1448, had called on the Bavarian Augustinian Provincial and the order's Superior General in Rome to take action. The councillors' hope is that God will be praised and the city be blessed by reason of reformed observance. See Hellmut Zschoch, *Klosterreform und monastische Spiritualität im 15. Jahrhundert* (Tübingen 1988), 10-12, 30-32.

The Kulmbach pastors contrasted the papal claim to *maiestas* with Jesus' words at the Last Supper that his apostles were sent to serve, not to rule as lords. Their commission was to preach Christ and his message of repentance and forgiveness of sins. People should heed only those ecclesiastics who follow out this divine commission.[44] According to the other reports, the power of the keys associated with the commission to preach is not a jurisdictional authority over consciences but the power to absolve from sin.[45]

Consequently, the claim made by ecclesiastical leaders to jurisdiction is rejected as a blasphemy against God. The preachers of Nürnberg call for the bishops to show whence they got power to institute ceremonies and impose them on consciences once freed by Christ. St. Paul convinced others that his authority was God-given, but since the bishops can never do this, one must retort that they are arrogating to themselves a power God did not give them and on their own they are encroaching on God's authority.[46]

8) The apologias solicited by Margrave Georg were to treat, among other points, whether and on what basis Christian civil authorities were entitled to suppress long-standing abuses in the Church and to disregard charges by bishops that such actions infringed upon their jurisdiction.[47] This request prompted at least one striking indictment of pre-Reformation *episcopal neglect and malfeasance*.

George Rurer's paper culminated in an article on the suppression of abuses.[48] Principally, the article is an account of the basis for intervention by civil authority. The protests of bishops are to be expected, since reform has brought application of painful medicine to serious wounds on the body of the Church. These bishops are blind and insensitive to the Christian zeal of reform-minded rulers. They have shown no heed for the gospel and true worship for so long that, according to Rurer, their present protest cannot be due to zeal for God's honor and concern for the salvation of their flocks. No, they are pained over the loss of empty honors and the income they used to have from consecrations, benefices, investitures, commendations, requiem Masses, and all the other taxes and fees they are no longer collecting.[49]

---

[44] Gussmann, 1/2, 82-85.

[45] Ibid., 44 (Rurer) and 107f (Löner).

[46] Gussmann, 1/1, 293f. Both in the Augsburg Confession, art. 28 and in private and official negotiations, Melanchthon sought to ground a real role for bishops in administering the Church and in transmitting doctrine. We see already, especially regarding the Nürnbergers, some of the reasons why Melanchthon's allies from the cities did not support him on this point. On the basic position of the Augsburg Confession, to which we will return, one can consult the contributions of E. Iserloh and H. Meyer, with comments from the audience (B. Lohse, G. Kretschmar, W. Kasper), in E. Iserloh & B. Hallensleben, eds., *Confessio Augustana und Confutatio*, 473-523.

[47] Gussmann, 1/1, 274.

[48] Gussmann, 1/2, 36-47.

[49] Ibid., 45.

Rurer closed his apologia for the Reformation by drawing a striking contrast. On the one hand, he drew from Scripture the profile of the zealous and responsible shepherd who promotes good preaching, carefully examines candidates for the pastorate, and visits them annually to oversee their ministry of word and sacrament. On the other hand are the indolent and heedless bishops of his times.

> They do not preach the divine word, nor do they allow it to be rightly preached. Instead they oppose, prohibit and persecute the word, and do not tolerate that the sacraments be administered and received in a manner conformable to the content and power in them from the teaching, institution and precept of Christ. They do not abolish the abuses affecting the sacraments. They exercise no discretion in ordaining priests and appointing pastors and preachers, but admit ignorant men who lack understanding of Scripture and give them benefices, invest them, and confirm them in office. Then the bishops forbid them to marry, which God left free to all, and with this prohibition force priests into whoring and concubinage. They thus cause dishonor and insults to the Lord our God, disgrace and ridicule to our Christian faith, and a colossal scandal by ruining countless men and bringing them to perdition.[50]

Given such negligence, a Christian prince is clearly obligated to undertake reform.

After our survey of these first-generation Lutheran statements on behalf of the reforms undertaken, it seems less important that they in fact contributed little to the wording of the Augsburg Confession. Independently of any connection with the text of the official declaration made June 25, 1530, these reports witness to a powerful conviction that the reforms recently initiated with local, civil sponsorship have swept aside manifold corruptions of religion in obedience to God's word. Here we see the will and force lying behind the adoption of the Augsburg Confession by Margrave Georg and the cities of Nürnberg and Heilbronn. One is all the more amazed that the August committee-work toward ecclesial unity had its partial measure of success, in view of the broad span of charges and the rhetorical vehemence of the indictment of traditional religion in the preparatory Lutheran reports. Their rhetoric was biting, and one understands how the mentality they document produced difficulties for those participants in the Diet who brought more irenic and conciliatory dispositions and who resonated more with Charles V's desire to save the religious unity of the German Empire.

Our first encounter with the Lutheran mentalities of 1530 reveals a powerful determination to correct the malfunctioning of religious institutions of the late-medieval Church. But we also perceive a strong doctrinal element, one suggesting insights into and convictions about how one comes to share in the grace of redemption. The bases of traditional worship and popular piety are under challenge. Beyond this, and perhaps even more important for understanding the opposition those claims met, is the calling in question of basic visible structures,

---

50 Ibid., 46f.

such as hierarchical authority, Masses for the dead, and celibacy, which for centuries were both constitutive and significative of the unity of Western Christendom. Working with their broad understanding of »abuses«, these apologists were seeking to legitimate a broad socio-cultural upheaval – and doing this with no little rancor.

Saxon Preparatory Statements

In the genesis of the Augsburg Confession, the decision to include the concise doctrinal articles 1-21 was made after considerable work had already been done on draft statements on worship and external church order.[51] As of May 2, 1530, when Prince-Elector John and his entourage arrived in Augsburg, the Saxon apologia for the Reformation consisted of a draft preface[52] and a list of articles defending practical reforms of church life in the Elector's domain.[53] The leitmotif of this early material prepared for presentation to Charles V was quite simply that of abuses in the Church and their reformation. Consequently, these early Saxon preparatory statements, the preliminary forms of articles 22-28 of the Augsburg Confession, offer us a sharply drawn portrait of pre-Reformation conditions. Reflective study yields six general themes.

1) Melanchthon's earliest draft preface began by referring to the widespread realization of the existence of many serious and long-standing abuses in the Church. The draft noted that particular points had been listed by the estates of the Empire in the *gravamina* of 1521 and that the Papal Legate to the Diet of Nürnberg in 1522-23 had uttered on behalf of the Pope the promise to correct as many of these abuses as possible.[54] Melanchthon's subsequent revision of this preface brought to the fore the precedents and backing for imperial activity in

---

[51] The Saxon preparation for the Diet was initiated by Prince-Elector John's letter of March 14, 1530, to his Wittenberg theologians. CR 2, 25-28. Also WABr 5, 263-266. We will discuss below why it later became urgent to begin the confession with doctrinal articles.

[52] BS 35-39, a revision and expansion of the draft preface printed on the lower portion of BS 36-39 and given in CR 2, 63f.

[53] The Torgau Articles, given in CR 4, 985-999, and Förstemann, *Urkundenbuch*, 1, 68-84. Probably, additional drafts were also on hand by May 2 on faith and works (CR 4, 1005-1008; BS 75-78; Förstemann, 1, 84-87) and on the power of the keys (CR 4, 1002-1005; Förstemann, 87-91). English translations of these materials are given in H.E. Jacobs, *The Book of Concord*, 2 (Philadelphia 1883), 75-90. The fundamental study of this material is Theodor Brieger. »Die Torgauer Artikel,« in *Kirchengeschichtliche Studien Hermann Reuter ... gewidmet* (Leipzig 1890), 268-320. The results of scholarly study of the Torgau Articles is reflected in the section covering 1530 in the *Register* prepared by H. Scheible in *Melanchthons Briefwechsel*, 1 (Stuttgart 1977).

[54] CR 2, 63. The *gravamina* of 1521 are found in *Deutsche Reichstagsakten*, jüngere Reihe, 2 (Gotha 1896), 670-704; a partial English translation is in Gerald Strauss, *Manifestations of Discontent in Germany on the Eve of the Reformation* (Bloomington, Ind. 1971), 52-63. The papal message is found in *Deutsche Reichstagsakten*, 3 (1901), 390-399, and in English in John Olin, *The Catholic Reformation: Savonarola to Ignatius Loyola* (New York 1970), 118-127.

10. Abuses under Indictment, 1530

fostering and preserving true religion,[55] and then suggested something of the long history of abuses by mentioning some of the leading proponents of church reform.[56] The revision repeated the reference to contemporary common knowledge, the 1521 *gravamina*, and Pope Adrian's promise of reforming action. Therefore, the Emperor should pay no heed to anyone who might rashly deny the existence of abuses and the need of reform.[57]

Melanchthon's earliest draft preface gave this account of the fundamental problem:

> Compared with the other abuses, the worst was that in almost all schools, monasteries, and churches little was preached and taught about the principal parts of the Christian faith. Instead, they expounded for the people a great deal of harmful doctrine on a way of worship that burdened consciences terribly. Human enactments, the orders, veneration of saints, pilgrimages, indulgences, and other unneeded and inept things received more frequent and more insistent treatment – to the ruin of souls – than the content of the gospel with its power to comfort consciences.[58]

The revision of this passage omitted this catalogue but made reference to the articles to follow on preaching and life in Saxony, in which the Emperor could readily see, as in a mirror, the abuses that had been corrected. Indulgence preaching did receive special mention, both because it represented a cluster of abuses (preaching instant salvation, deception of the people, exercise of power by monks appointed quaestors) and because it had occasioned Luther's original protest.[59] The ensuing controversy over indulgences brought Luther to speak of other, more central doctrines which had been languishing on the periphery of the preaching of the day, that is, how one attains grace, forgiveness of sins, and the consolation through Christ of an otherwise disturbed conscience.[60]

A parallel analysis of the main problem of the pre-Reformation church appeared in Melanchthon's short treatise on faith and works written some time in the preparation for the Diet and later reworked as article 20 of the Confession. Genuine good works had been all but forgotten:

> It is public knowledge what kind of good works were taught formerly by the monks: the Rosary, gulden Masses, and the like, were the only things preached. Little was taught about true good works such as the office of civil authority, obedience and serious respect for such authority, each one's calling, as well as suffering and heartfelt prayer and trust in God in time of need. Their books prove this, full as they are of

---

[55] BS 35,3-33.
[56] BS 36,8-29, naming Augustine, Gregory, Cyprian and Pope Innocent III.
[57] BS 36,30-35.
[58] CR 2, 63.
[59] BS 37,5-38,1.
[60] BS 38,1-12.

foolish and harmful questions and devoid of useful teaching. Consequently the whole world had long been crying out for another teaching.[61]

This stress on external devotional acts left the people famished for the central truths of Christianity, a hunger which the new preaching is now filling.

Thus, as the Saxon reformation prepared to present itself before Charles V, it began from the existence of broad misunderstandings about Christian essentials. A connecting line was drawn to link the changes in Lutheran Saxony with the outcry over corruption voiced in the »hundred *gravamina*« collated nine years before as the culmination of eighty years of German unrest. Lutheranism sought recognition as a movement that was beginning to set right this many-sided reality of error, false worship and abuse of power.[62] Given this point of departure, its apologists came inevitably to give a »bill of particulars« indicting the pre-Reformation Church. In an evaluative vein, one must point out that the Saxon appeal to the earlier protest documents does not in itself guarantee a congruence between the Lutheran reforms and the earlier complaints of the estates expressed in the *gravamina*. Careful study of the latter is first called for, before one can judge just how traditional was the Lutheran movement. Of course, the legitimacy of the movement does not stand or fall on the score of its congruence with recent German clamoring for reform.

We turn now to note the main points formulated in the Torgau Articles, composed for the Prince-Elector in March-April, 1530, by Luther, Melanchthon, Justus Jonas, and Johann Bugenhagen (»the Wittenberg theologians«), which Melanchthon's draft prefaces were originally meant to introduce.

2) Among the corrupt practices the Reformation had set aside, the Wittenberg theologians list four which were of such dire consequence that those observing them could not avoid sin. These abusive practices had been introduced by human doctrines and human legal enactments. Realizing the true nature of these ordinances, the Saxon Elector could not sanction their further observance, since »one is to obey God rather than men« (Acts 4:19).[63]

Two of these ordinances entailing sin were innovations introduced into the Church contrary to an express divine precept. (i) The law of priestly celibacy goes against St. Paul's formulation of a divine command, »It is better to marry than to burn« (1 Cor 7:9), and departs from both the practice and conciliar legislation of the early Church. In Germany the law had been imposed by violent means, and the results have not been good.[64] (ii) The practice of lay reception of

---

[61] CR 4, 1006f; also BS 75,25-76,34.

[62] As mentioned above on p. 228, the response to the Augsburg Confession issued from the Catholic side on August 3, 1530, did not deny the fact of abuses but espoused instead their reform, along with the correction of excesses, the renewal of a leadership sunk to low ebb, and the revitalization of religion now cooled.

[63] CR 4, 987.

[64] Ibid., 990f.

Communion under only one form goes contrary to Jesus' express command, »Drink this, all of you« (Mt 26:27), and to the practice observed a long time before it mysteriously disappeared.[65]

(iii) The widespread and documentable teaching that the Mass is a good work gaining both grace and temporal benefits for its beneficiaries gave rise to a shameful commerce in stipends, to proud boasting by sacrificing priests (of how they make others blessed), to frequent offering of Mass without devotion but solely out of avarice, and to pernicious neglect of trusting faith in Christ's testamentary legacy of grace and forgiveness of sin.[66] This indictment of pre-Reformation Eucharistic belief and practice served as the Saxon justification for holding only community Masses and for sponsoring frequent instruction and admonition on the correct use of the Sacrament, that is, as the place of exercising faith in Christ's consoling gift of himself.[67] Once more, the argument is stated that community celebration and the primacy of faith were normative in the early Church, at least to the time of Jerome and Augustine, and that no one knows how the contrary practices with stipends and private Masses came to be accepted.[68] Still, the innovations have, it is claimed, spawned a multitude of sins.

(iv) Prince-Elector John has also refused to sanction the continuance of religious orders in his territories because of three sinful aspects of their given structure: people are taught to undertake life in the cloister in order thereby to satisfy for sins and merit grace; the vow of celibacy is contrary to human nature and to an express divine command; and members of these orders must engage in perverse worship through Masses for the dead, invocation of the saints, and the like. Consequently, Saxon authorities cannot in conscience take actions to restore religious houses or to penalize those who recently departed from such houses in non-canonical ways.[69]

Such are the issues on which the Wittenberg theologians claimed that the Reformation was freeing Christians from sinful structures of the pre-Reformation Church. The Saxon apologists know that some will contest their position with the counter-claim that these changes made without papal approval constitute a far

---

[65] Ibid., 991.
[66] Ibid., 991f.
[67] We put aside for the present a short tract on illegitimacy of the private Mass which K.E. Förstemann published as part of these early articles in his *Urkundenbuch*. 1, 91-93 (in English in Jacobs, *Book of Concord*, 2, 90-92). The tract belongs to a later stage of the discussion, when the Lutherans were preparing to negotiate specific points. We follow Brieger, »Die Torgauer Artikel,« 283-285, and WABr 5, 303-305, in taking it as written by Luther, probably in late July, for the guidance of his colleagues in Augsburg.
[68] CR 4, 992f.
[69] Ibid., 996f.

worse sin, namely, schism.⁷⁰ This occasioned discussion of basic issues about the nature of church unity, which we will relate below. But one anticipatory response should be mentioned here. The Wittenbergers answered that it would be far more appropriate to accuse those of schism who have and are acting contrary to »the whole order of Christendom« and to prescriptions of councils by forbidding marriage to priests, going against God's word by instituting new forms of worship, and departing from sound ancient practice by the sale of Masses.⁷¹ If charges of schism are made, the defenders of the old order should realize their own vulnerability! The abusive practices they have sponsored constitute a serious rupture in continuity with Christian beginnings. Here one senses how Reformation theological method was deeply affected by the disputation and even more by the pamphleteering done by its early exponents and enemies.

3) A second class of practices treated in the Torgau draft includes matters of human law which do not intrinsically involve sin but which were being so badly misused in the late-medieval Church that the Saxon authorities can no longer sanction their observance. Principally this argument concerned the observance of fasting and abstinence on days set by church law, but it also touched the liturgical calendar of holy days, certain prescribed hymns, pilgrimages, and other devotional practices.⁷²

The abuse lay not in these practices themselves, which originally had served the good purpose of co-ordinating community practices and disposing people to receive God's word. The problem concerned instead a cluster of understandings that vitiated these practices by taking them for good works meriting grace and forgiveness and by construing them as necessary to being a Christian. When these practices are understood as meritorious, they constitute a blasphemous offense against the central message of freely-given salvation by Christ to be received by us in faith.

> So these people who have taught that we gain grace through works of our own choosing, such as prescribed fasting or feasts or the like, have greatly dishonored Christ by attributing to their own chosen works the glory belonging to Christ. They have also thereby caused the people not to recognize Christ and his grace.⁷³

The false evaluation of these church practices comes under Christ's stricture against human enactments, especially Mt 15:9 (*frustra me colunt mandatis hominum*) and those who insist on them fall under Paul's censure of those

---

⁷⁰ Ibid., 987.
⁷¹ Ibid., 988.
⁷² Ibid., 988, 990.
⁷³ Ibid., 989.

condemning Christians in matters of food and drink and festivals (Col 2:16).[74]

A similar abuse lay in the veneration of saints. To devoutly petition something from them or to ask something of God in virtue of their merits also derogates from the honor due to Christ and offends against his claim to be the sole mediator (1 Tim 2:5; Mt 11:28 [»Come to me, all you who are burdened«]). Saints do have roles to play in the lives of Christians, precisely as models of faith and of the life of good works in one's calling. But there is no basis for the intercessory role given them in pre-Reformation piety.[75] We are again made aware that the Lutheran claim to have corrected abuses entails a broad construction of what is abusive that at times clashes with convictions undergirding the religion of the people of late-medieval Europe.

4) A special issue for the Saxon apologia was the practice of confession and absolution from sin, which has not been abolished by the reform but only changed in two aspects. In fact, Lutheranism could claim to have rediscovered this rite. In the new order, integral self-accusation by the penitent is no longer required, since this pre-Reformation practice was not grounded in Scripture, was in fact impossible, and served only to torment consciences with scrupulous anxiety.[76] Second, the Saxon Church no longer sets a specific time of the year for confession and so avoids the earlier abuse of driving people to acts signifying repentance when they have no intention of turning from sin. Still, in the renewed church order, confession is required before one receives Holy Communion, but no one is strictly compelled to communicate. The frequent instructions given on confession aim to highlight the power of the word of absolution, in which one hears Christ's own heavenly verdict »not guilty«. Thus troubled and assailed consciences are taught the consolation found in believing acceptance of the word of absolution.[77]

By establishing for confession a regime of freedom, the Saxon reformers claimed to have re-established the proper setting for this event of consoling grace though Christ's compassionate and liberating word of forgiveness of sin.[78]

5) The Torgau Articles introduce their treatment of *episcopal authority* with the plea that the Prince-Elector did not himself oust the Saxon bishops, but that their authority had collapsed under the weight of abuses which the people would

---

74 Ibid.
75 Ibid., 998.
76 Ibid., 993.
77 Ibid., 993f. Here, of course, is a notable result of Luther's teaching on *fides sacramenti* and on the power of absolution, as that emerged in his works of 1518. Study 6 in this collection treats this topic in depth.
78 According to Melanchthon's draft prefaces, this doctrine, »wie man die Gewissen durch Glauben an Christum trösten solle,« was historically the momentous message Luther came to disseminate in the wake of the controversy over indulgences. CR 2, 64, and BS 38,10f.

tolerate no longer. First, the Elector had to take over matters belonging to church courts, because they had been discredited by the way they leveled improper excommunications.[79] Second, whereas church leaders were earlier guilty of total dereliction of their duty of supervising doctrine and rebuking false teachers, now they perversely want to exercise jurisdiction by suppressing true doctrine! The Prince-Elector surely cannot consent to such a misuse of power.[80] Third, the Elector can have no obligation in conscience to aid the bishops in disciplining priests who have married. As patron, he is instead obliged to protect ministers of his church against prelates attempting to use their authority improperly. His primary duty is to see to the appointment and maintenance of capable priests in the office of pastor.[81] Fourth, the ecclesiastical judiciary was discredited by bad decisions in a whole host of marriage cases.[82]

Regarding ordination, the Saxon argument was that no one could rightly be obliged to seek ordination at the hands of the bishops now in office, because they require their ordinands to swear two sinful oaths, namely, promises not to teach Lutheran doctrine and not to marry. Other questions on the nature of ordination and ministry could be raised, but they are put aside in the interests of public peace and concentration on the central points of Christian teaching.[83]

Thus the apologia prepared for the Elector's use in the Diet included a forceful indictment of the pre-reformation episcopate for neglect of duty and misuse of authority. Where the bishops were derelict, there the authority of the Prince has initiated action to promote the genuine Christian doctrine stemming from Luther; where their courts discredited themselves, there secular courts have extended their reach; where bishops now try to act contrary to God's will, there the Elector impedes their projects. But the Saxons did not call in question the rightfulness of the episcopal office as a basic structure of the Church.

6) We noted above that the Torgau Articles included a defense against charges that the ecclesiastical changes initiated in Saxony were tantamount to schism. This prompted, early in the draft apologia, a reflection on the unity of the

---

[79] CR 4, 994. In a draft presentation of the power of the keys from about this time, Melanchthon insisted on the spiritual powers of churchmen, that is, their authority to preach the gospel and to discipline public sinners. Excommunication should be leveled against those who refuse to accept correction of their open vices and those found at the time of annual visitation not to have received Communion for a year or longer. CR 4, 1002-1004; in English in Jacobs, *Book of Concord*, 2, 88-90.

[80] CR 4, 994.

[81] Ibid., 994f.

[82] Ibid., 995. In the tract on the power of the keys, Melanchthon called for clear delineation of religious and secular authority. Marriage matters, especially the impediments, were best committed to the civil power. Ibid., 1004f.

[83] Ibid, 995f.

Church. The treatment brought in its train two implied criticisms of the late-medieval Church.

The Wittenbergers make the point that uniform observance of human enactments is not the ultimate constituent of ecclesial unity. Diversity in external practices must have a place. A fortiori, those who dissent from false teachings and ordinances are not cut off from the body of the Church. Scripture testifies both to the primacy of the interior bond with Christ and to the regime of freedom that ought to envelop all human legal prescriptions.[84]

Implicitly the apologia of the Wittenberg theologians is charging (1) that the pre-Reformation Church was imposing serious obligations going beyond norms set by revelation and (2) that this was based on the false conception of ecclesial unity as constituted by externally uniform practice.

Such considerations raise the key issue of the criteria of a community's membership in the Catholic communion. It will be instructive to follow closely the give-and-take of negotiations at Augsburg to see whether these notions found any resonance on the imperial or Catholic side and whether the Protestant side proved capable of applying these principles creatively to cases of proposed diversity within ecclesial unity.

The Torgau Articles show the strategy that the Prince-Elector of Saxony was preparing to follow at the Diet. As of May 1, as he neared Augsburg, his plan was to emphasize practical matters of worship and church order. He was claiming continuity between his reform and earlier German outcries for renewal of Church and society. Selected abusive practices and structures came under indictment as contrary to Scripture. The Elector was ready to plead the gains of the Reformation in terms of easily understood items like peace of conscience by sacramental absolution and the upgrading of lay vocations. The bishops were charged with malpractice, but the charge did not contest the right and propriety of the episcopate to have a carefully defined role in the Church.[85] The document will acknowledge that important changes have been introduced, but if principles of legitimate pluralism were granted, they need not be divisive. The strategy aimed to direct attention away from the heresy indictment against Luther that underlay *Exsurge Domine* and the Edict of Worms. The discussion at the Diet should instead see Saxony as a reformed territorial church and consider its claim

---

[84] Ibid., 987f.

[85] M. Root insists on the Saxon willingness, documented in the Torgau Articles and after, to acknowledge a spiritual jurisdiction for bishops. »The Augsburg Confession as Ecumenical Proposal,« *Dialog* 28 (1989), 223f. This is grounded in the evidence, but one notes that regarding supervision of doctrine, the Saxons approach the dialogue already holding strong convictions about just how the bishops must judge and decide numerous issues of true and false teaching connected with the practical reforms. The Reformation party knows what accords with the Gospel and what goes contrary to it. An episcopal »magisterium«, to use a later term, is not given any notable scope in the Lutheran ecclesiological proposal. One could ask, retrospectively, whether this dimension of episcopal ministry was not already preempted by the Saxon theologians.

for tolerance in the unity of the Empire. Recognition is sought for its newly achieved life as a Christian society.

Luther's Admonition to the Clergy

As an outlaw of the Empire, Martin Luther could not appear personally at the Diet, but his presence was nonetheless felt through both publications and correspondence. At Castle Coburg, in late April, he composed his *Admonition to All the Clergy Assembled at Augsburg*,[86] and copies of this work went on sale in Augsburg about June 7.[87] The bookseller quickly sold his five hundred copies, and by June 11 the imperial authorities forced the Augsburg city council to prohibit both local reprints and any further sale in Augsburg of copies printed elsewhere.[88] Of course, the five hundred copies continued to be read and passed around during the Diet.

On June 12, Justus Jonas, a member of the Saxon group, wrote Luther from Augsburg that many were reading his prophetic *Admonition*, albeit with divergent reactions.[89] The next day Jonas wrote Luther again praising the »powerful apologia,« while noting that the vehemence of Luther's words was likely to elicit yet more bitter hatred from some. Jonas felt it was an inspired work, rebuking the haughtiness of the higher clergy, forcefully asserting »the article on necessity,« and reducing the opponents to silence.[90] The Strassbourg reformers Bucer and Capito were put off by Luther's *Admonition*, not only because in passing it accused them of sedition, but especially because of Luther's glorification of himself and his doctrine.[91]

1) In tone, Luther's exhortation oscillates between two poles. There are some moderate appeals for the bishops to take advantage of an opportunity given them

---

[86] WA 30II, 268-356. In English translation by Lewis W. Spitz: LW 34, 9-61. In a letter to Melanchthon on April 29, Luther reported that the preparation of his »oratio ad clerum« was going well, except that he was struggling to hold back aggressive notions which were threatening to make the tract too polemical (WABr 5, 298,15-18). On May 12 Luther reported that he had finished his »invectivam contra ecclesiasticos« and sent it off to Wittenberg for printing (ibid., 316,6f).

[87] Reported by Justus Jonas on June 13 (ibid., 361,1ff).

[88] Reported in letters from members of the delegations representing Strassbourg and Nürnberg (ibid., 363, n. 4). Still, the work went through nine printings in 1530 (WA 30II, 238-240).

[89] WABr 5, 358,131ff.

[90] Ibid., 361,14-25. Twelve days later, writing to Luther a few hours before the presentation of the Augsburg Confession to Charles V, Jonas spoke again of the *Admonition* as a »liber ... propheticus et sanctissimus« (ibid. 392,41f).

[91] Cited, ibid., 363, n. 5. Capito termed Luther's work »in episcopis librum odiosissimum.« The accusation of sedition probably lay in Luther's mentioning urban confiscations of church properties (WA 30II, 312,12; LW 34, 35).

for repentant turning to God and for compassion on their badly-used people and priests. Luther would elicit their sympathy for a population lacking sound Christian instruction, exploited by indulgence preachers, and made frantic to pile up works of satisfaction. Special pity is deserved by parish pastors forced to forgo marriage and caught in miserable unchastity.[92]

But far more often Luther levels blunt accusations of malfeasance and guilt at the bishops, whom he judges responsible for a lamentable corruption of Christian belief and practice.

> All of you clergy bear the guilt for this unspeakable thievery and robbery of money, for such an inconceivable multitude of misled hearts and consciences, for such a most horrible outrageous lie and blasphemy of the suffering of Christ, of the gospel, of grace and of God himself, perpetrated through indulgences. This is true not only of you who accepted money from it, but also of you who kept silent about it and willingly looked on at such raging of the devil.[93]

> For such shameless violation is not to be tolerated that whatever you choose must be known as an innovation and what you do not so choose must not be called an innovation. You are suppressing the truth against your own consciences.[94]

> It is exactly as though baptism had been a temporary human work, just as the Anabaptists teach, and not an everlasting covenant of God. Tell me here, what good is left among you?... For you have taught nothing right, but have taught everything contrary to baptism, the sacrament, and penance. That is clear.[95]

> Who, then, is the church? Are you? Then show the seals and credentials or prove it another way with deeds and fruits. Why are not also we the church, since we are baptized as well as you, teach, preach, have the sacraments, believe, pray, love, hope, and suffer more than you? Or are you the church because you introduce nothing but novelties and thereby change, blaspheme, persecute, and murder God's Word and, in addition, occupy the foundations and monasteries like church robbers? Yes, you are the devil's church.[96]

> We both know that you are living without God's Word, but that we have God's Word. It is therefore our deepest desire and humble request that you will give honor to God, acknowledge yourselves for what you are, repent, and mend your ways. If not, do away with me. If I live, I shall be your plague. If I die, I shall be your death. For God has set me on you. I must be, as Hosea says, a bear and a lion in the way of

---

[92] WA 30II, 273,12ff, 282-284, 290,3-15, 324,7; LW 34, 11, 16f, 20f, 41f. At the very end Luther begs the bishops to change: »Men's hearts are already too much embittered....This makes it necessary to sooth, mollify, and quiet them with humble confession and solemn reformation and not to jolt and irritate them further« (LW 34, 60, translating WA 30II, 354,7-10).
[93] LW 34, 17, translating WA 30II, 284,17-285,6.
[94] LW 34, 29, translating WA 30II, 303,14ff.
[95] LW 34, 32, translating WA 30II, 308,6-11.
[96] LW 34, 39, translating WA 30II, 321,6-12.

Assur. You shall have no rest in the presence of my name until you reform yourselves or go to ruin.[97]

The prevalent tone is the bitterness of angry denunciation.[98] Luther acted out the role of prophet called to confront leaders hardened in their evil. When he spoke late in the *Admonition* of a negotiated settlement which would allow the restoration of episcopal jurisdiction in exchange for free preaching of the gospel, he immediately noted that the bishops' power had fallen into discredit by reason both of the abuses they sponsored and the measures they took against him and God's word.[99] In fact, Luther left little or no ground for respectful discussion of accommodations.

In content, Luther's message to Augsburg interwove two related complexes or clusters of topics: religious practices and preaching before the Reformation, and the performance in office of the bishops of the Church.

2) In composing his *Admonition*, Luther first made a simple catalogue of devotional practices in vogue in late-medieval parishes, which he set in contrast with topics central to Christian life and practice.[100] These lists then became, with some small revisions, the final section of the published *Admonition*.[101] Luther claimed that this jungle of pious practices was taken as enshrining articles of faith and so had to be carried out by pastors and people. The genuine articles on faith, conversion, and Christian living were not preached. Essentials were marginalized and forgotten, while peripheral religious practices came to dominate church life.[102]

As Luther developed his pamphlet after the Elector and his entourage had left Coburg in late April, he went through a familiar series of late-medieval devotional and doctrinal dislocations of authentic Christianity. Indulgences

---

[97] LW 34, 49, translating WA 30II, 339,12-340,2.

[98] Upon hearing that Johann Eck had published a lengthy anti-Lutheran heresy catalogue that was circulating in Augsburg, Luther wrote to Melanchthon on May 19: »Eccium acriter odi cum sua Sathana, homicidam et mendacem...« (WABr 5, 322,12f). Luther sees himself ranged against men who serve as allies and instruments of the devil.

[99] WA 30II, 340-342; LW 34, 49-51. – R. Decot's just-published study of Luther's *Admonition* brings out its coherence, notwithstanding all the invective, with the Saxon proposal of a settlement with the bishops of the Empire based on negotiated concessions to be given to the Lutherans in exchange for the restoration of their jurisdiction in reformed territories. See »Luther's Kompromißvorschlag an die Bischöfe auf dem Augsburger Reichstag 1530,« in M. Brecht, ed., *Martin Luther und das Bischofsamt* (Stuttgart 1990), 109-119.

[100] WA 30II, 249-255. These lists were given by Förstemann in his *Urkundenbuch*, 1, 98-108, as part of the Torgau Articles, but have been universally accepted since Brieger's analysis in 1890 (»Die Torgauer Artikel,« 282f) as Luther's jottings in preparation for the *Admonition*.

[101] WA 30II, 345-351; LW 34, 52-58.

[102] WA 30II, 346f, 353; LW 34, 53, 59.

defrauded the people, while obscuring Christ's redemption, undercutting faith, and making outlandish claims for the Pope's power.[103] Confession featured tortuous attempts at the complete recounting of sins, while nothing was said about how absolution comforts consciences.[104]

Situating repentance in human satisfactory efforts drove people into the frantic multiplication of devotional works, most of which involved innovations (saints' intercession, forms of prayer, pilgrimage sites, confraternities, relics) unknown in earlier times.[105] Sermon books brought no corrective but made things worse, especially by placing the Virgin Mary in Christ's place as a refuge in need and source of comfort.[106] The Mass was vitiated by commercial traffic in stipends for the sacrifice and all but total suppression of Communion and the remembrance of Christ.[107] Withholding the chalice from the laity innovated directly against the precept of Christ,[108] while priestly celibacy was contrary to human nature, the rightful esteem due to women, and the overall cause of public decency.[109]

Central in this picture of things out of joint was the pitiably low state of Christian instruction:

> Everything was so confused and upside-down with sheer discordant doctrines and strange new opinions that no one could know any longer what is certain or uncertain, what it means to be a Christian or not a Christian. The old doctrine of faith in Christ, of love, of prayer, of the cross, of comfort in affliction lay trodden under. Indeed, there was no doctor in the whole world who would have known the whole Catechism, that is the Lord's Prayer, the Ten Commandments and the Creed, to say nothing of understanding and teaching it, as it is now taught and learned, praise God, even by young children. For proof of this I refer to all the books of both theologians and jurists. If you can learn from them correctly one part of the Catechism, I will let myself be put on the wheel and be shredded.[110]

These bishops have done no teaching of basic Christianity, and so the center of Christian consciousness was captured by childish peripherals.[111] Such was

---

103 WA 30II, 281-286; LW 34, 16-18.
104 WA 30II, 287f; LW 34, 19.
105 WA 30II, 288-292, 295-298; LW 34, 19-22, 24-26.
106 WA 30II, 298f; LW 34, 26f.
107 WA 30II, 293f, 305f; LW 34, 22f, 30.
108 WA 30II, 320f; LW 34, 38f.
109 WA 30II, 323-329; LW 34, 40-43. In his May 19 letter to Melanchthon, Luther expressed the intention of telling all about clerical unchastity if he were to write on vows again (WABr 5, 322,18ff).
110 LW 34, 28, translating WA 30II, 301,5-15.
111 WA 30II, 331,12ff, 346,15ff, 353,4-17; LW 34, 45, 53, 59. Luther's indictment of devotional religion differs from the Zwinglian and Calvinist affirmation of the utter transcendence of God and their refocusing of faith on the supreme source of all things – to the exclusion of intermediaries not »spiritual« and/or linguistic. On this, we have the recent exposition of Carlos Eire, *War Against the Idols*, 83-85, 197-220, 228-233. Luther's concern is much more the devotional displacement in this world of the main themes of normative catechesis, that is, instruction on the commandments, creed, prayer, and dominical sacraments (with an emphatic statement of the presence of the body and blood of Christ in the Lord's Supper).

Luther's indictment of pre-Reformation religion.

3) Woven into Luther's narrative of doctrinal and devotional confusion are a series of direct accusations of abuses perpetrated by the bishops in the performance of their office. In using the spiritual penalty of excommunication, they have infringed on the rightful area of secular authorities, at times arbitrarily condemning the innocent, especially by frequent misuse of the Church's ban to enforce collection of tithes and fees owed to ecclesiastics.[112] Corruption abounds because endowments are applied to perverse purposes never intended by the donors and founders.[113] The bishops, who exercise no supervision over pilgrimage sites, neglect Christian teaching themselves and commission auxiliary bishops who in ordaining pay no heed to the capabilities especially for preaching of those on whom they lay hands.[114] Luther gave a brief sketch of the true bishops, but then began his »negotiations« with the observation that his addressees do not perform the episcopal office and are unfit for preaching and ministering to consciences.[115]

Such was the written apologia for the Reformation movement that Luther sent to Augsburg in 1530. His *Admonition* was in fact a bitter, at times compulsive, denunciation of late-medieval popular religion as exploitative and perverse, for which the blame falls on a guilty leadership. And the message is delivered with sovereign assurance of rectitude and possession of the truth.[116]

One can see in Luther's *Admonition* the outline of a Saxon strategy: acceptance of a restoration of episcopal jurisdiction in exchange for freedom in preaching the gospel. The strategy itself was burdened by the ill-defined nature of »freedom for the gospel.« But the tone of Luther's work also suggests that he had little hope for the success of the formula. These bishops, the princely pastors of Germany, are in effect written off under a hailstorm of accusations of corruption. One wonders how many could read this work and then still take seriously the Saxon Elector, Luther's patron and protector, in his appeal for tolerance and coexistence in the Empire.

---

[112] WA 30II, 309-312; LW 34, 32-34.

[113] WA 30II, 313-319; LW 34, 35-38.

[114] WA 30II, 297,1, 332f.; LW 34, 25, 45.

[115] WA 30II, 335,5-15, 340,3ff; LW 34, 47, 49.

[116] M. Root cites the texts of early 1530 that provide the evidence that the *Admonition* rests on Luther's »apocalyptic conviction that his struggle with Rome was an event of the Last Days.« »The Augsburg Confession as Ecumenical Proposal,« *Dialog* 28 (1989), 227f. An insightful statement on Luther's apocalyptic rhetoric and the beginning of the Reformation is K.-V. Selge's »Das Autoritätengefüge der westlichen Christenheit im Lutherkonflikt 1517 bis 1521,« *Historische Zeitschrift* 223 (1976), 591-617. To a degree, this influence of apocalyptic, along with the dire polemic issuing from such influence, stands in contrast with Luther's calm and balanced instruction on the church and its sanctifying mission, which we find especially in his sermons and catechetical works of 1528-29. See Study 9, above, in this collection.

Historians regularly point to Luther's impact in late-August 1530 in stiffening the resistance of the Protestant side against concessions demanded of them in the last phases of the negotiations over differences.[117] Our review of Luther's *Admonition to the Clergy* serves to remind us of his earlier impact on the Diet. With five hundred copies of his tract circulating, Luther was certainly a force in Augsburg, instilling confidence on the Protestant side, especially in their rejection of late-medieval popular religion, and moving bishops and others on the Catholic side to the pained outrage of those whipped by denunciations.[118] We will return to Luther and to his further messages to those assembled in Augsburg after we review the Augsburg Confession itself with an eye to its assertions about pre-Reformation religious practice.

The Augsburg Confession[119]

We turn now to the document of June 25, 1530, in which the Lutheran estates, seven princes of the Empire and two imperial cites, presented to Charles V an account of their belief and reformed ecclesial practice. Patent in the statement, they claimed, was »that we have introduced nothing, either in doctrine or in ceremonies, that is contrary to Holy Scripture or the universal Christian church.«[120] The Confession begins with twenty-one succinct articles of faith which serve to demonstrate that the doctrine professed and preaching approved in these territories is conformed to biblical and traditional norms. Therefore, the Lutherans should not be treated as heretics and not be expelled from the catholic communion.[121] The second part of the Confession, articles 22-28, describes and justifies the changes in life and worship undertaken through reform of certain

---

[117] For example, H. Immenkötter, *Um die Einheit im Glauben*, 54, 56, especially with reference to Luther's letters of August 26 to the Prince-Elector and to Melanchthon. WABr 5, 572-579. The first of these letters is translated in LW 49, 403-412. These are treated in context in Study 11, pp. 311f, below.

[118] Sixteen years later Melanchthon noted in his oration at Luther's funeral that good people have asserted, »asperiorem fuisse Lutherum quam debuerit.« Melanchthon did not deny that a sinful aggressivity at times marked Luther's words and actions (CR 11, 729f). The tone and content of Luther's writings from Coburg in 1530 exemplify quite well what Melanchthon referred to. I am grateful to Prof. James M. Weiss of Boston College for this reference.

[119] In the following notes we use the conventional abbreviation CA in referring to the confession, adding an Arabic number to indicate the article, and a second Arabic number when the reference is to a specific sentence of an article. The German and Latin texts are in BS 44-137, and the English translation is in the *Book of Concord*, ed. T.G. Tappert et al. (Philadelphia, 1959), 24-96. The Confession was read on June 25 in German, the official language of the Diet, in spite of the fact that Charles V and his main advisors did not know German.

[120] CA, Conclusion, 5.

[121] CA, Conclusion of Part I.

abusive practices that had crept in over the years.¹²²

Clearly, the Augsburg Confession differs in content, tone, and purpose from the Saxon preparatory apologia reviewed above. What occurred between May 2, the date the Prince-Elector and his retinue arrived in Augsburg, and June 25? Why did the Lutheran group come to insist so forcefully on their fundamental orthodoxy? Why is the Confession so mild and irenic?¹²³

For Melanchthon and his associates, the stay in Augsburg began quite traumatically with the discovery that Johann Eck of Ingolstadt had prepared for Charles V a comprehensive catalogue of Lutheran heresies and seditious teachings. This work, *The 404 Articles*, had also been published and was circulating in Augsburg, where the participants in the forthcoming Diet were assembling.¹²⁴

Eck's type of work was not uncommon in the early days of Reformation controversy, and the imperial summons to the Diet provoked the preparation of at least fourteen other such dossiers aimed at grounding the accusation and conviction of the Protestant teachers for heresy and sedition.¹²⁵ Especially galling to the Saxons was the fact that Eck's articles did not present Lutheran teachings as distinctive from the doctrines of Zwingli, the Anabaptists, and the radical spiritualists, but instead depicted Luther as the fountainhead of these latter movements. Eck tarred with the same brush »Luther himself, obviously an intimate of the devil, Luther's adherents, and those who moved from the foolishness of his errors to worse absurdities.«¹²⁶ The Lutherans found themselves lumped together with those against whom they had been battling for five years.

---

¹²² See p. 228, above, where the topics of CA, Part II, are listed.

¹²³ Out of the considerable secondary literature on Melanchthon's redactional work of May-June, 1530, we list the following major contributions: H. Bornkamm, *Der authentische Text der Confessio Augustana* (= *Sitzungsberichte der Heidelberger Akademie der Wissenschaften*, Phil.-Hist. Klasse, 1956, no. 2); W. Maurer, »Studien über Melanchthons Anteil an der Entstehung der Confessio Augustana,« *Archiv für Reformationsgeschichte* 51 (1960), 158-207; Vinzenz Pfnür, *Einig in der Rechtfertigungslehre* (Wiesbaden 1970), 1-221; W. Maurer, *Historischer Kommentar zur Confessio Augustana*, 2 vols. (Gütersloh 1976-78), in English as *Historical Commentary on the Augsburg Confession*, tr. H. George Anderson (Philadelphia 1986).

¹²⁴ Melanchthon mentioned Eck's »great heap of propositions« in his first report to Luther from Augsburg (WABr 5, 305,20). The critical text of Eck's notorious work is W. Gussmann, *Quellen und Forschungen zur Geschichte des Augsburger Glaubenskenntnisses*, 2 (Kassel 1930). The genesis of Eck's articles began with the request of the Dukes of Bavaria, by letter of February 19, 1530, that the theological faculty of Ingolstadt supply a summary of Luther's heresies and scandalous utterances for possible use at the forthcoming Diet. The text of this letter is given by Gussmann, 2, 196f.

¹²⁵ See the catalogue given by H. Immenkötter, *Die Confutatio* (Corpus catholicorum 33), 15. Eck's was the only one of these works printed. Some of the manuscripts contain excerpts from Eck's articles.

¹²⁶ *404 Articles*, Conclusion; Gussmann, 2, 151.

Further, Eck portrayed the Lutheran movement as responsible for a wide range of errors, many already condemned, which were destructive of substantial elements of Christian belief and life.[127] And this was circulating just after Luther had issued his large and small catechisms to instruct believers in the substance of their belief and duties. Eck had also depicted Lutheran teaching as responsible for a breakdown of civil order in Germany,[128] paying no heed to the fact that Luther had written against the marauding bands of the peasants in 1525 and that the reforming visitations of Saxon parishes in the late 1520's were sanctioned under the authority of the Prince.

Eck's intervention struck a tone of belligerence on the eve of the Diet. There were those who favored harsh measures of repression, even the use of armed force, against the estates and cities fallen into heresy, and Eck's articles could well be used to convince Charles V to pursue such a policy.[129] The Protestant hopes for a *modus vivendi* were in jeopardy, and it became imperative to mount a convincing defense against Eck's allegations.

Soon after May 2, Philip Melanchthon set to work transforming the Saxon preparatory tracts into a firm statement of orthodox faith.[130] For this he had

---

[127] Among the seventy-two section headings Eck provided to indicate the objects of Lutheran destructiveness, we find these: In Christum (arts. 66-82), In Spiritum Sanctum (arts. 83f.), In crucem Domini (arts. 88-90), In evangelia (arts. 107-110), In Nicaenum concilium (arts. 145f.), In Vetus testamentum (arts. 152-158), Contra opera (arts. 198-202), In eucharistiam (arts. 235-243), In claves (arts. 261-263), Vota (arts. 299-313). B. Dittrich treats the *404 Articles* as the natural way to approach the Augsburg Confession, singling out Eck's portrayal of the Lutheran movement as destructive of civil, patristic, and conciliar authority, citing art. 374 (an alleged Luther-word), »Cuilibet christiano permissum est iudicare super omni doctrina, quia non tenemur credere conciliis et papae.« *Das Traditionsverständnis in der Confessio Augustana und in der Confutatio* (Leipzig 1983), 6-12, citing p. 11, n. 50.

[128] Further headings included these: Contra obedientiam et principes (arts. 332-341), Seditio (arts. 342-348, 375-379), In nobiles (arts. 350f.), Contra jura (arts. 380-383).

[129] The memoranda of the Papal Legate, Cardinal Lorenzo Campeggio, to the Emperor in the first half of May 1530 sketch out a series of punitive legal measures to apply toward the extirpation of heresy in Germany: renewal of the Edict of Worms, interdiction of the University of Wittenberg, privation of princely privileges, destruction of heretical books, inquisitorial prosecution of heretical teachers – as in Spain, expulsion of heretical advisors from princes' courts and urban councils (*Nuntiaturberichte aus Deutschland*, 1. Abtl., 1533-59, 2. Ergänzungsband, ed. Gerhard Müller [Tübingen, 1969], 457-471, esp. 464-467). However, Campeggio also urged Charles to prepare himself, in case legal severity is not effective, to apply yet stronger measures, that is, »metter la mano al ferro et al foco et radicius extirpare queste male et velenose« (ibid., 464). The leading enemies of the Lutheran cause, Duke Georg of Albertine Saxony, the Bavarian Dukes, and Price-Elector Joachim of Brandenburg, went to confer with Charles V in Innsbruck in May. Melahchthon characterized their discussion: »Ibi habentur de nostris cervicibus comitia. Orabis igitur Deum ut dissipet consilis gentium quae bella volunt« (Letter to Luther, May 11, 1530; WABr 5, 314,8ff). Shortly after, the welcome news came that the Emperor was not swayed by them but was still bent on preserving neutrality as he entered the Diet (WABr 5, 335,9, 339,10).

[130] See Melanchthon's laconic description of his work on May 11, when he sent an early draft for Luther's inspection: »Mittitur tibi apologia nostra, quamquam verius confessio est... Ea dixi, quae arbitrabar maxime vel prodesse vel decere. Hoc concilio omnes ferre articulos fidei complexus sum, quia Eckius edidit *diabolikotatas diabolas* contra nos. Adversus has volui

recourse to the seventeen Schwabach Articles, which had been prepared in mid-1529 to articulate the Lutheran position at the Marburg Colloquy with the Zwinglians. Melanchthon's work of revision and expansion produced both notable changes in the Schwabach Articles and the composition of new articles. Melanchthon clarified points in the original articles by additions, and formulated specific answers to charges of destructive heterodoxy.[131] Revising the first article, on the Trinity, Melanchthon underscored the traditional character of Lutheran faith by stating its explicit adherence to the Nicene decree on the three divine Persons.[132] Further, he added a series of anathemas against ancient and modern heresies in which however Zwingli was not noted by name.[133] However, the correspondence of Luther and Melanchthon in these crucial months is emphatic on the line of demarcation separating Lutherans and Zwinglians, a line clearly believed to run between orthodoxy and blatant heresy.[134]

The overall tone of Melanchthon's Confession is notably irenic. Luther read it in an early stage and remarked that stylistically it was gentle and delicate in a way

---

remedium opponere« (WABr 5, 314,2-6). The composition of a succinct exposition of normative faith and doctrine was not a new kind of activity for adherents of Luther's reform in 1530. G. Seebass set forth the series of such documents which preceded the Diet of 1530 (Melanchthon's *Loci* of 1521, visitation-documents in 1527, Luther's personal confession of faith in his last work against Zwingli in 1528 [WA 26, 499-509; LW 37, 360-372], Luther's catechisms of 1529, etc.). »Die reformatorische Bekenntnisse vor der Confessio Augustana,« in P. Meinhold, ed., *Kirche und Bekenntnis* (Wiesbaden 1980), 26-55.

[131] Looking at the final form of CA, the following purposes are served by articles composed new in Augsburg. Art. 14, on a minister being »rite vocatus,« clarifies Art. 5 on the ministry through which justifying faith is given. Arts. 18-19, on human freedom, give precision to Art. 2 on original sin and respond to Eck's allegations of determinism and of a Lutheran attribution of the causality of sin to God (*404 Articles*, arts. 48, 86, 331). The first part of Art. 21, on the positive role of the saints as examples of faith, responds to Eck's allegations that Lutheran teaching utterly expelled the saints from Christian devotion. Gussmann gives a full list of the anti-Eckian passages of CA (*Quellen und Forschungen*, 2, 49f).

[132] Contrast CA 1 (BS, 51) with Art. 1 from Schwabach (BS, 52), where Nicea is not mentioned. B. Dittrich places this profession of the Nicene faith at the head of his chapter on the Confession's formal reception of older doctrinal and theological traditions. *Das Traditionsverständnis*, 36-55.

[133] Ancient heresies are condemned in CA 1, 2, 7, and 12, while Anabaptist teachings are explicitly rejected in CA 5, 9, 12, 14, and 17. CA 10 confesses the presence and giving of the body and blood of Christ in the Lord's Supper and disapproves those who teach otherwise, such as Zwingli. The softer handling of Zwingli, shown in the omission of a condemnation of him by name, was part of the price paid for gaining the signature of Landgrave Philip of Hesse to the Confession. Philip still harbored hopes of forging an anti-Hapsburg alliance between the Lutheran estates and the Swiss cities.

[134] Luther and Melanchthon were personally convinced that Zwingli was teaching heresies on original sin, infant baptism, the *usus* of the sacraments, and on the mediation of grace by the external word, in addition to his denial of the Real Presence. Furthermore, Zwingli had acted hypocritically at Marburg in October 1529, and in mid-1530 had become a tool of the devil. So WABr 5, 336,34f, 330,32-64, 340,36-41.63f, 475,8ff.

he could never have written.¹³⁵ Melanchthon himself was aware that he was stating the Lutheran position with restraint and showing extreme tact in his choice of words. He expected to be criticized for being too gentle against adversaries such as those the Lutherans were facing.¹³⁶ The important thing, however, was to convince Charles V and to gain his agreement to a policy of toleration in the Empire.

The restraint of the Augsburg Confession involves more than a prudent avoidance of polemical and injurious language. Luther later noted that there was no article against purgatory and no unmasking of the papal Antichrist.¹³⁷ We know that the deliberations accompanying Melanchthon's compositional work in Augsburg did treat at length the basis and role of papal authority in the Church. But it was decided not to incorporate a statement of the Lutheran position on the papacy in the Confession in order not to upset Charles V and run the risk of his simply refusing to negotiate with the Lutheran party at the Diet.¹³⁸

The political and diplomatic aims of the Confession are especially clear in the Preface and Conclusion, both composed in Augsburg by the Saxon Chancellor, Gregor Brück. Instead of beginning with Melanchthon's early prefatory references to long-standing discontent over abuses in the Church,¹³⁹ the Confession presents itself as the estates' response to the Emperor's call for their »judgments, opinions, and beliefs with reference to the said errors, dissensions, and abuses« in faith and religious practice. It is hoped that the other estates will also make written presentations and that amicable discussion may reconcile those

---

135 »Ich hab M. Philipsen Apologia uberlesen, die gefellet mir fast wol, und weis nichts dran zu bessern noch endern. Wurde sich auch nicht schicken, denn ich so sanfft und leise nicht tretten kann. Christus unser herr helffe, das sie viel und grosse frucht schaffe, wie wir hoffen und bitten« (Letter of May 15 to the Prince-Elector, WABr 5, 319,5-9). In the second clause, *fast* is equivalent to the modern German word *sehr*. Basically, Luther liked the CA very much.

136 »Ego apologiam paravi scriptam summa verecuncia, neque his de rebus dici mitius posse arbitror« (Letter of May 21 from Melanchthon to J. Camerarius; CR 3, 57). »Non dubitabam, quin Apologia nostra videretur futura lenior, quam mereatur improbitas adversariorum. Ego tamen complexus sum ea, quae sunt in causa praecipua« (Letter of June 19, also to Camerarius; CR 2, 119).

137 Letter of July 21 to J. Jonas; see n. 181, below.

138 B. Dittrich works out the complex political and apologetical motivation underlying the appeal to older traditions in the Confession. *Das Traditionsverständnis*, 55-84. The Augsburg discussion about whether or not to speak to the issue of the papacy was related by a key participant, Chancellor Brück, in 1537 (WABr 12, 116). Consequently, CA 28, on ecclesiastical authority (»De potestate ecclesiastica«; German title,»Von der Bischofen Gewalt«), makes no reference to the Pope, although it is forthright on episcopal authority *iure divino* to preach the gospel, forgive sins, censure doctrine, and ban sinners (CA 28, 21).

139 Scattered references to existing discontent over abuses do occur in CA: Conclusion to Part I, no. 5; 23,1-2; 24,10; 27,60.

who differ. If unity is not achieved at the Diet, the estates look ahead to participating in a general council.[140] The Confession makes a first step toward a broader agreement, by demonstrating that Lutheran beliefs are not erroneous and that the troublesome dissensions are caused – unjustifiably – by the fact that manifest abuses have been corrected in the signers' territories.

The question arises whether the new purposes influencing the redaction of the Augsburg Confession brought about any notable softening of the positions taken earlier, in the Torgau Articles, on abuses and the reform of worship and church life. We can answer immediately that Melanchthon's revisions in the second part of the Confession brought no substantial changes in the indictment leveled against pre-Reformation religiosity. In fact, the abuses were set in even sharper relief by the claim that they in fact constituted the heart of the matter in the present dispute. The Confession's transition from the doctrine of faith, Articles 1-21, to the practice of religion is made in this manner.

> Since this teaching is grounded clearly on the Holy Scripture and is not contrary or opposed to that of the universal Christian church, or even of the Roman church (in so far as the latter's teaching is reflected in the writings of the Fathers), we think that our opponents cannot disagree with us in the articles set forth above....The dispute and dissension are concerned chiefly with various traditions and abuses.[141]

> From the above it is manifest that nothing is taught in our churches concerning articles of faith that is contrary to the Holy Scriptures or what is common to the Christian church. However, inasmuch as some abuses have been corrected (some of the abuses having crept in over the years and others of them having been introduced with violence), we are obliged by our circumstances to give an account of them and to indicate our reasons for permitting changes in these cases.[142]

My own reflections on the second part of the Augsburg Confession lead me to identify five distinct patterns of analysis and argumentation about recent religious practice. »Abuses« are judged and assessed in the Confession in five ways, or according to five types of diagnosis. After reviewing these I will return to a consideration of Melanchthon's audacious assertion, *Tota dissentio est de paucis quibusdam abusibus*. But first let us review the Confession's five perspectives on the pre-reformation practice of religion.

1) Three cases stand out where the Lutherans criticize religious practices because the actions were vitiated by erroneous theological interpretations. The Church's prescribed fasts and cycle of feasts were being presented wrongly and

---

[140] CA, Preface, nos. 6-11, 15-21. An important motive for the Lutheran estates' persistent demand that their confession be read, and not just handed over, was the defense of their honor before the Diet against the accusations then circulating that they were tolerating false doctrine in their lands (Letter of the Nürnberg envoys, June 25; CR 2, 128). Again we are reminded of the impact of Eck's *404 Articles*.
[141] CA, Conclusion to Part I (*Book of Concord*, 47f, translating the German text).
[142] CA, Introduction to Part II (*Book of Concord*, 48, from the German).

consequently were being observed for the wrong reasons, namely, as works of a meritorious and/or satisfactory character and as necessary to being a Christian in good standing.[143] Second, this erroneous notion of merit and satisfaction was also attached to the taking and observance of monastic vows and was leading to a false evaluation of life under vows as »the state of Christian perfection.«[144] Third, erroneous doctrine also vitiated the Mass, especially its private celebration without community, by taking it as a sacrifice for actual sins with multiple beneficiaries.[145]

Therefore, key parts of the self-presentation of the Lutheran estates and cities in 1530 attacked the doctrinal superstructure erected by theology and preaching to justify and motivate certain religious practices. The latter have been rendered harmful by false constructions placed upon them. These understandings must now be dismantled and replaced with teachings having solid biblical backing, that is, that Christ alone merits and satisfies, that faith is an entry into a realm of freedom and equality, and that the Lord's Supper is Christ's testament of forgiveness for those actually participating by hearing and partaking of his gifts. But to make room, the contrary teachings must be rejected and practices interpreted in their light must be either suppressed or radically reinterpreted in accord with true doctrine. Such was a first form of the Lutheran protest against abuses.

2) Some of the most striking passages of the Augsburg Confession describe pre-Reformation cases of displacement or marginalization of themes or topics which should be central in Christian instruction. Priorities were askew in catechesis. The late-medieval stress on devotional practices – in all their kaleidoscopic variety – went hand in hand with a *mirum silentium* about faith in Christ, which is the authentic way to peace and consolation.[146] The multiplication of

---

[143] CA 15,2-4; 26,1-3.19-21.29; 28,34-39. Most of the recent ecumenical studies of the Confession include treatment of the no-longer-divisive issue of meritorious good works done in the power of God's justifying grace. But the church's authority to lay down obligatory practices has not received extensive attention in recent study. Pp. 258f, 266-268, and 274 of this essay will enlarge this theme, while the next Study in this collection will show how central this issue of law-making authority was in the dialogue – and its breakdown – following the public readings of the Augsburg Confession and the imperial Confutation.

[144] CA 14,4; 27,11-13.36.46-60. In the intense study of the Confession around 1980, B. Lohse contributed an account of the background of the Reformers' rejection of monastic life under vows and offered a revised, positive Lutheran evaluation of this form of Christian life. »Mönchtum, 1, Zum Verständnis von CA 27,« in Meyer & Schütte, eds., *Confessio Augustana*, 281-292 (in English in Forell & McCue, eds., *Confessing One Faith*, 286-296).

[145] CA 24,21-23.29-30. We recall the 1980 study of L. Ullrich, who works out a contemporary confrontation between the Confession's critique of the sacrifice of the mass and a developed Catholic doctrine of the eucharist. In large part, what the Reformation rejects is not identical with church teaching on the mass. »Ist die katholische Meßopferlehre ein Hindernis für eine katholische Anerkennung des Augsburgischen Bekenntnis?« in F. Hoffmann & U. Kühn, eds., *Die Confessio Augustana im ökumenischen Gespräch* (Berlin/DDR 1980), 191-220.

[146] CA 20,3-8.19-20.

private Masses also obscured faith and true service of God.[147] In confession, no one could experience comfort and peace through God's Word of absolution, so great was the emphasis on complete enumeration of sins and on satisfactions.[148] Instruction on meritorious observances extinguished a rightful stress on the merit of Christ and on the duties of the worldly callings.[149] Praise of monastic life detracted from the central components of a personal relation to God and service of him in family and society according to his commandments.[150]

Therefore, another phase of the Lutheran protest charged that pre-Reformation practice pushed numerous chief topics of authentic Christianity to the periphery of lived religion through a profusion of devotions and a stress on stipulated external observances. The Reformation, therefore, represents in its own self-understanding a decisive return to the Christian center, God's redemptive grace in Christ, through the clearing away of distracting trifles and obfuscating practices.

3) The hierarchical officers of the medieval church are charged in the Confession with making excessive claims to authority. This charge plays a major role in Article 28, albeit in a framework of notable clarity on the respective competencies God has given to those who rule the secular and spiritual realms.[151] The Confession looks back on earlier infringements on the secular realm by ecclesiastics, but its principal argument attacks the episcopal claim of power to institute ordinances in the Church which are meritorious of grace and satisfactory for sin and/or which bind under penalty of sin.[152] Over against this the Confession affirms the doctrine of justification through the merit of Christ alone and »the teaching of Christian liberty.«[153] There are to be rules of community order in the Church and obedience to bishops and pastors, but the *opinio necessitatis*, namely that these norms bind in conscience, must be destroyed.[154] Also, laws prescribing actions which themselves offend against

---

[147] CA 24,23.
[148] CA 25,4-5.
[149] CA 26,4-11.
[150] CA 27,48-59.
[151] CA 28,4-22. E. Iserloh has demonstrated convincingly that CA 28 affirms episcopal jurisdiction as a supervisory authority over local pastors. Some Lutheran interpretations have been reductionist here, in a manner not justified by Melanchthon's text: »Von der Bishofen Gewalt: zu CA 28« (see above, n. 46).
[152] CA 28,2.38-50.
[153] CA 28,36.51.
[154] CA 28,53-60.64.

divine precepts, such as Communion *sub una forma* and celibacy, dramatically exemplify this hierarchical overreach.[155]

This third aspect of the Lutheran protest struck at an alleged arrogance of power in the pre-Reformation hierarchy. The episcopal office is not contested in principle, but a sharp censure is leveled against the extension of episcopal authority far beyond the scope it is claimed to have by biblical warrant. Hierarchs have been acting on the basis of a fundamental error about the limits of Christian obligation. The remedy is to redefine the office in order to make it consonant with the renewed doctrine of Christian freedom now flourishing in Lutheran territories.

4) The Confession notes with little or no rancor a series of instances of negligent performance in office by the leadership of the pre-Reformation church. It admonishes the bishops for their failure to correct fiscal abuses concerning the Mass.[156] In the religious orders, superiors have not observed numerous norms and even some canons: for instance, those diminishing the obligating force of vows taken at a young age.[157] Article 28 makes passing reference to the oppression bishops exercise through reserving the absolution of certain sins to themselves and issuing violent excommunications.[158]

In this fourth phase of its protest, the Lutheran Confession offered a relatively brief account of episcopal malfeasance in office, which is quite mild when compared with the charges of corruption voiced in the apologias from outside Saxony and with the denunciatory invective of Luther's *Admonition to the Clergy*. The Confession, however, is not just being tactful and politic before an assembly that included numerous prince-bishops. Its restraint on episcopal performance seems more due to the conviction that the real problem lies elsewhere. Whether bishops be conscientious or careless means little in comparison with their erroneous conceptions and convictions about lawmaking, Christian obligation, and how grace is given and satisfaction made for sin.

5) The Confession could not be clearer in its contestation of particular institutions of the pre-Reformation Church. It is direct and succinct in rejecting five structures of Christian practice stemming from decisions contrary to identifiable norms. (i) Invoking the aid of the saints is contrary to the unique and exclusive mediatory role of Christ.[159] (ii) Communion under one form goes

---

[155] CA 28, 69f. This theme will recur below in our treatment of the fifth model of the abuses.
[156] CA 24,14-20, Latin text.
[157] CA 27,3-6.27-33.
[158] CA 28,2.
[159] CA 21. The question of the saints was discussed in depth by P. Manns, in Iserloh & Hallensleben, eds., *Confessio Augustana und Confutatio*, 596-640 (with comments from the floor, pp. 641-651), and was taken up by G. Kretschmar and R. Laurentin in Meyer & Schütte, eds., *Confessio Augustana*, 256-280 (in English in Forell & McCue, eds., *Confessing One Faith*, 262-285). These studies show this point of Lutheran doctrine to be embedded in the context of late-medieval piety and also profoundly intertwined with fundamental convictions about justification and faith. The prospects for ecumenical rapprochement were explored by the United States Lutheran-Catholic dialogue commission in the 1980s, but at the present time (December 1990),

directly against Christ's mandate that all drink from the cup.[160] (iii) Making celibacy obligatory on all in major orders was a bad decision, as is indicated by widespread clerical incontinence, by the deathbed torments of priests, and by the violence with which the law was introduced. The cumulative evidence is that priests are by God's will free to marry.[161] Consequently, the monastic vow of chastity is also rejected.[162] (iv) A private Mass, offered only to fulfil the obligation connected with the stipend, is a contemporary form of the unworthy eating and drinking censured by St. Paul in 1 Cor 11:27.[163] (v) The requirement of integral confession must be dropped in the face of the demonstrable impossibility of its observance.[164]

The Lutheran protest, in this fifth phase, rejected concrete institutionalized practices sanctioned by custom and law in the Church. Specific decisions, reached in a past distant enough to be obscure to people of 1530, had been rolled back in the reformed life of the Lutheran territories. New patterned actions of conduct in worship and clerical life-style had been introduced amid an elation of release for those experiencing the new, but causing consternation to others over the shattering of sacred traditions. In 1530, before the Reformation argument was reduced to opposed doctrinal systems, these practical matters constituted the true radicality of the new movement. Here issues were public and concrete, touching people intimately, even physically, in their relationship with God. Here, in the second part of the Augsburg Confession, the Reformation argued that it was fully justified, fully responsible, in changing these parts of people's lives and worship.

After this review of the Lutheran syllabus of abuses, we can return to the central claim advanced by the Confession, namely, that while its doctrine is in substance traditional, the critical points at issue are certain abusive practices now being reformed. The reforms, the Lutherans assert, should be acknowledged as authentically Christian and, starting from that acknowledgement, arrangements should be made for harmonious coexistence in a unified empire and church.

What, then, are we to say about Melanchthon's audacious claim, *Tota dissentio est de paucis quibusdam abusibus*? A first observation, based simply on the full text

---

the results of this exchange have not been published. – However, even in 1530, the dialogue of late August narrowed considerably the area of dispute between the two sides, as will be related in Study 11, below, pp. 293f.

[160] CA 22,1f.10; 28,70. This seemingly innocuous issue loomed very large in the exchanges of late August in the mixed committees striving to narrow the distance separating the two sides and build a bridge of reconciliation. See below, pp. 296f, 299-301, 304, 306 and 311.
[161] CA 23,1-13.18-25.
[162] CA 27,18.36-40.
[163] CA 24,12f.
[164] CA 25,7-12.

of the Confession, is that the concept *abusus* is not a univocal term. In fact, it denotes a variety of issues which in their formal structure are quite distinct. Notably different kinds of diagnosis contributed to the Lutheran syllabus of abuses. Therefore, the conciliatory intentions expressed in the transitional passages linking the two parts of the Augsburg Confession were burdened by a broad ambiguity in the central concept *abusus*.

Secondly, when the meaning of *abusus* is reduced to more manageable proportions of a strict sense, as did occur in Melanchthon's private negotiations with Cardinal Campeggio, we are left mainly with the fifth category of specific institutionalized practices.[165] As we indicated above, these practice are far from being of minor importance, as Melanchthon's adjectives *paucis quibusdam* would indicate. In fact, on the Lutheran side, in the non-Saxon apologias and in Luther's *Admonition to the Clergy*, these practices were seen as documenting a horrid fall of the Church into corruption and sin. Melanchthon's claim was, therefore, neither adequate to the importance of things strictly termed abuses nor congruent with the mentalities of his colleagues on the Lutheran side.

Some might want to write off Melanchthon's conciliatory claim as an unworthy product of an anxious fear of incurring Charles V's displeasure.[166] As he wrote, was he frantically searching for arguments, even specious ones, that would lure Charles away from advisors urging severity against the Lutherans? Certainly there is evidence that Melanchthon suffered a painful siege of depression and anxiety toward the end of his redactional work on the Confession.[167] But his claim about the true location of the division was not just a

---

[165] On June 26 and July 5 Cardinal Campeggio reported to Rome that the Lutheran side had approached him and proposed terms for a restoration of harmony to the Church. Essential would be the concession to the Lutheran territories of Communion under both forms, clerical marriage, a revision of the Canon of the Mass, and the calling of a general council. *Nuntiaturberichte*, I. Abtl., 1. Ergänzungsband, 70, 76. In reporting to Luther on June 26, Melanchthon named the key issues as both forms, marriage, and private Mass with the last being the least promising for eventual concessions (WABr 5, 397,16; = CR 2, 140). Three letters from Melanchthon's negotiations with Campeggio are given in CR 2, 169-174, in which we note the claim, »Dogma nullum habemus diversum ab Ecclesia Romana« (Letter of July 4; on the dating, see *Nuntiaturberichte*, 76, n.10; CR 2, 170). Melanchthon's revised list of conditions for peace, in his letter of July 7 to Campeggio, were both forms in Communion, toleration of marriage by priests and monks, and the calling of a conference of learned and good men to establish a new *ratio* concerning the Mass (CR 2, 173).

[166] Wilhelm Gussmann's representatively Lutheran reaction was that Melanchthon's claim shows him both naive and cowardly in his quest of peace (*Quellen und Forschungen*, 2, 52, 54). H. Bornkamm stated baldly that under pressure Melanchthon inserted a falsehood in the confession in the »Tota dissentio...« sentence (*Religion in Geschichte und Gegenwart*, 3rd ed., 1, 735). J. von Walter's anniversary account of the Augsburg Diet included the charge that in his dealings with Campeggio, especially in his letter of July 4 (see the previous note). Melanchthon denied the gospel. »Der Reichstag zu Augsburg 1530,« *Lutherjahrbuch* 12 (1930), 68.

[167] Melanchthon wrote on June 13 to Luther; »Ego paene consumor miserrimis curis,« and on June 26, »Versamur hic in miserrimis curis et plane perpetuis lacrymis« (CR 4, 1009, and 2, 140; = WABr 5, 365,16, 369,2). Jonas wrote in the same vein on June 18 and 25, also to Luther (WABr 5, 368,69, 392,44).

flimsy barricade thrown up in defense. With the benefit of historical hindsight, we know that the negotiations of August 16-17 greatly reduced the apparent gap between the opposing sides. Face-to-face exchanges, especially between Melanchthon and Eck, brought clarification and unexpected agreement on points of doctrine.[168] Regarding the »abuses,« there were problems, but the possibility of accommodation was by no means excluded in principle. If anything, the August negotiations proved Philip Melanchthon almost wholly correct in his claim that the abuses were the heart of the controversy, but not right in his statements that these were matters susceptible of easy solution.

The Augsburg Confession must be judged a considerable success. It did come very close to vindicating the claim it put forth in 1530. In part, the success was achieved because of its calculated omissions in content and its purposeful moderation in language and tone. A key factor is the Confession's forthright profession of central Christian truths, a profession given an extra degree of sharpness by use of anathemas. The heart of Luther's teaching is presented in concrete terms as a new piety, reformed worship, and the regime of freedom enveloping practices outside the core of New Testament prescriptions. The Confession was a diplomatic document, serving a specific political strategy. In this context, its omissions can be judged more leniently, since total disclosure is simply not expected by those engaged in discourse in the political and diplomatic spheres.

But, as we know, unity amid a pluralistic church was not achieved in 1530. But before ascribing the failure to Melanchthon and his Confession, we should look carefully at the exchanges and decisions taken after the reading of the Augsburg Confession on June 25, 1530. We can make a start by reviewing some key reactions to the Confession expressed in the six weeks after it was read and submitted.

Luther's Reactions to the Confession

From his temporary residence at Coburg, Luther followed the events of the Diet as closely as he could through correspondence. He took up his role as advisor to his prince with a memo of early May on Lutheran conduct in case Charles V required the Protestant participants in the Diet to observe abstinence days, to halt evangelical preaching, and to attend Mass.[169] Melanchthon repeatedly asked Luther's advice, pointedly remarking in one letter that those with him in Augsburg were not much help on the momentous topics being treated.[170] In June, when there was a break in the correspondence, Melanchthon

---

[168] This initial success is recounted in Study 11 of the this collection, pp. 291-294, below.
[169] WABr 5, 313f.
[170] Letter of July 27 (ibid., 508,11).

eventually pleaded with Luther to exercise direction of his friends who depended on his authoritative guidance and needed his consoling words amid the threats and hostility surrounding them at the Diet.[171] Luther did write touching letters of encouragement from Coburg, and their ensemble would provide a good basis for a study of his ideal of adamantine trust in God's providential care.[172]

The Augsburg Confession itself was a first major item in this correspondence between Augsburg and Coburg. On May 11 a first draft was sent for Luther's review and both the Elector and Melanchthon asked for his suggested emendations.[173] Eleven days later, while he was recasting the article on episcopal authority, Melanchthon expressed again his desire that Luther go over the articles on doctrine.[174] The day after the Confession was presented to Charles V, Melanchthon dutifully sent Luther a copy of the text read, and at the same time opened discussions on the second major theme of this correspondence, namely, the possibility of concessions if Charles V sets conditions for peace and unity. Luther was asked to set down some guidelines for his followers to use in the give-and-take of negotiations. The first topics were quite practical: Communion under both forms, clerical marriage, and the suppression of private Masses. Just how firm should the Lutherans be in demanding these?[175] In July Melanchthon requested position papers from Luther on »traditions«, that is, ecclesiastical laws, as well as on vows.[176]

How, then, did Luther evaluate the Augsburg Confession? In answering, one has to take care with the nuances, but the central point is Luther's early fundamental approval of the document, an assessment that escalated, after he studied the June 25 text, to enthusiasm and delight. On May 15, after reviewing a draft, he said he liked it and had no emendations to offer.[177] On July 3, after a careful reading, Luther repeated his approval (*placet vehementer*) and chided

---

171 Ibid. 397,11. Luther responded sharply on June 29, rejecting the notion that he was an authoritative leader and alleging that Melanchthon's worries stemmed from a lack of faith (ibid. 406,43-47.65ff).

172 Some examples: letters of May 20 and June 30 to the Prince-Elector (WABr 5, 324-327, 421f); letters of June 19 and late July to Jerome Weller (ibid., 373-375, 518-520); letter of June 30 to Spalatin (ibid., 413-415); letter of June 30 to Brenz, with advice for Melanchthon (ibid., 417-419); letter of August 5 to Chancellor Brück (ibid., 530-532).

173 Ibid., 311, 314. Melanchthon's submissiveness is concise but complete: »Tu pro tuo spiritu de toto scripto statues« (314,7).

174 Ibid., 336,29f. Melanchthon indicates that he can exercise more freedom in treating matters of practice.

175 Letter of June 26 (ibid., 397).

176 Letters of July 14 and 20 (ibid., 476,15, 490,11).

177 Ibid., 319,5-9, cited in n. 135, above.

Melanchthon for expecting to be treated differently than Christ, the stone rejected.[178] The implication is that the Confession is the witness of a genuine disciple and is bound to be rejected by corrupt leaders. In the following days Luther expressed exultation in being alive in a time when Christ had been confessed and proclaimed so wonderfully before the world in the estates' enunciation of their doctrine and church life.[179]

In two ways, however, Luther restricted his approval of the Augsburg Confession. First, he uttered explicit reservations on at least two occasions. On June 29, just after receiving the text, he said he was disinclined to discuss further concessions to the papal party, since in his judgment more than enough was already conceded in the Confession itself.[180] Then, on July 21, upon hearing that Charles V was asking whether the Lutherans had any further articles to submit, Luther asserted that Satan, working in midst of the opponents, had seen that the Confession lacked total candor by reason of its omission of forthright rejections of purgatory, the cult of the saints, and especially of the papal Antichrist.[181] This is more than an offhand remark, since Luther published strongly polemical statements on each of these three points in the weeks after he saw the text of the Confession.[182] Still, these directly critical statements by Luther are not revocations of his positive assessment, but rather indications of the limitations of the Confession in view of its quite complex set of aims. Luther's basic judgment was that it gave authentic witness to Jesus Christ and to his significance in the lives of his followers.

A second line of Luther's criticism of the Augsburg Confession is more subtle. Four times in mid-July Luther told his friends in Augsburg that he had no expectation that the exchanges at the Diet would lead to doctrinal agreement. Events, he claims, are showing him right in his predictions that the best the

---

[178] Ibid., 435,4.

[179] Letter of July 6 to C. Cordatus (ibid., 442,12); letter of July 9 to the Prince-Elector (ibid., 453,9); letter of July 9 to Jonas (»Christus publica et gloriosa confessione declamatus est...«, ibid., 458,12); letter of July 15 to the four colleagues in Augsburg (ibid., 480,13).

[180] »Accepi Apologiam vestram, et miror quid velis, ubi petis, quid et quantum cedendum Pontificibus....Pro mea parte plus satis cessum est in ista Apologia...« (ibid., 405,17). Luther notes that politically it might be necessary for the Elector to submit in some matters in order to avoid a greater evil (405,18) but doctrinally it is time to stand fast (405,24).

[181] »Nunc video, quid voluerint istae postulationes, an plus articulorum haberetis offerendum. Scilicet Satan adhuc vivit, et bene sensit Apologiam vestram leise treten et dissimulasse articulos de purgatorio, de sanctorum cultu, et maxime de antichristo Papa« (ibid., 495).

[182] On purgatory, in *Widerruf vom Fegfeuer*, written June 30-July 15, which arrived in printed form in Augsburg on August 13 (WA 30II, 360-390). On the saints, in the final section of *Sendbrief vom Dolmetschen*, finished before September 12 (ibid. 643-646; English: LW 35, 198-202). On the papal Antichrist, in passages of *Von den Schlüsseln*, written by August 25, circulating in printed form in October (WA 30II, 470,39, 480,21, 484,4, 496,17, 506,8).

Lutheran side can hope for is a political settlement allowing them to teach as they have been doing, while the papal side continues in its errors and evil.[183] These statements on doctrinal agreement being a chimera are, we suggest, Luther's dissenting judgment on Melanchthon's claims in the Confession that the heart of the controversy is disciplinary or practical but not doctrinal. Luther does not agree, for who can reconcile Belial with Christ? Luther was perceptive on this point, it would seem – at least as we look back from our later historical vantage point. But he was speaking on the subject before the official response had been given from the other side and before the important doctrinal negotiations of August 16-17, 1530. The latter negotiations in fact almost proved Luther wrong.

Another phase of Luther's reaction to the Augsburg Confession is found in the positions he took in letters and published works in the six weeks after the presentation of the Confession on June 25. Some of these works provide more material for our review of indictments of pre-Reformation life and worship. On June 29 Luther set the tone for this period, when he told Melanchthon that the question of further concessions was driving him into intense study and reflection, which however was only increasing his certainty and deepening his conviction of the rightness of their doctrine and position.[184] His missives to the brethren in Augsburg breathed this spirit of uncompromising tenacity.

Luther treated five points of doctrine and practice in this period. (1) Purgatory has no biblical basis but represents an intolerable dogmatizing of an unbinding patristic opinion. The church of foundations, monasteries, altars, and chapels – all in service of requiems offered for souls – is in fact ruled by lies and greed. Worse, this church does not teach about dying in the embrace of Christ's mercy and it has abused the precious prayers of faith found in the Psalms by having these recited for the souls in purgatory.[185] (2) No quarter is to be given in battling the private Mass, even if some claim to celebrate it purely as an expression of gratitude to God. It is blatantly contrary to Christ's institution to have Mass without a community to hear about and commemorate his death. This abuse of the sacrament and of the priesthood is structural and the best of intentions

---

[183] On July 9, to Jonas, Luther says that the drama is nearing its end: »Non sane ut de dogmatibus unquam fiat concordia (quis enim Belial cum Christo speret conciliari?)... sed quod optem paeneque sperem, dissentione dogmatica suspensa, politicam concordiam fieri posse« (WABr 5, 458,5ff; also 470,2ff, 480,23ff, 496,15). The same point is made by Luther in an open letter to Archbishop Albrecht of Mainz, circulating in Augsburg in late July (WA 30II, 399,3, 400,8).

[184] »Ego dies ac noctes in ista causa versor, cogitans, volvens, disputans et totam Scripturam lustrans, et augescit mihi assidue ipsa *plerophoria* [1 Thes 1:5] in ista doctrina nostra, et confirmor magis et magis, dass ich mir (ob Gott will) nu nichts mehr werd nehmen lassen, es gehe druber, wie es wolle« (WABr 5, 405,22).

[185] *Widerruf vom Fegfeuer*, WA 30II, 360-390, esp. 369,14-25, 372,19-26, 377,1-13, 386,3-17, 388,2-23.

cannot make it acceptable.[186] (3) Christ's ordinance of Communion under both forms is also fully binding, whatever may be the discipline in one's locale. If the chalice is forbidden to lay people, then they must either emigrate or restrict themselves to spiritual communion. No obedience to a magistrate has any value in this case, in view of the contrary mandate of Christ.[187] (4) When Melanchthon asked whether life under monastic rule might be admitted as a non-meritorious act of thankful worship, Luther responded that we humans have no authority to declare some acts to be worship of God. God alone determines how He is to be worshiped. Also, the choice of monastic life is an option for singularity which can easily lead people to despise God's own ordinances, such as the family, which are much holier.[188]

5) In mid-July Melanchthon was having difficulty formulating the Lutheran position on the nature and extent of law-making authority in the Church. There was apparently no consensus on the implications of article 28 among the signers of the Confession and this made Melanchthon feel ill-prepared for the expected negotiations over a restoration of episcopal jurisdiction in Lutheran territories. The nub of the problem was the reconciliation of the principle of evangelical freedom with the maintenance of obedience in the Church. Is there some principle (*causa*) that grounds obedience?[189] In response, Luther first reaffirmed the God-given distinction between the realms of ecclesiastical and political governance. Further, an ecclesiastical authority as such can make no binding

---

[186] Letter to Spalatin, July 27 (WABr 5, 502,2-21). Similarly, in Luther's July 27 letter to Melanchthon (ibid. 498,5) and in his memo on Communion for Queen Maria of Hungary (ibid., 528,17-21). Luther's memo against the private Mass, included in older editions of the Torgau Articles, is probably from this time (ibid. 504f; in English, in *The Book of Concord*, ed. H. Jacobs, 2, 90-92). See Brieger, »Die Torgauer Artikeln,« 283-285.

[187] Memo by Luther, about August 4, 1530 (WABr 5, 527-529), in response to questions (ibid., 511) posed on behalf of the Emperor's sister, Queen Maria of Hungary. The Queen's evangelical leanings were well known, since she always had a Latin Bible with her, even on the hunt, and would open it to read during sermons if the preacher made insufficient use of Scripture (ibid.). In response to the suggestion by Campeggio that the Lutheran territories might be granted a dispensation by the Pope for the lay chalice, Luther cited a vulgar remark of Nicholas Amsdorf. When the Lord has commanded, Luther asserts, one need have no care for the dispensation of some impudent servant. Letter of July 15 (ibid., 480,34).

[188] Melanchthon's question, which he himself thought was to be answered negatively, is in his letter of July 28 (ibid., 510,6), in which Melanchthon is following up a question placed initially in his letter of July 20 (ibid., 490,11). Luther's answers of August 3 and 4: ibid., 523,3-524,16 and 526,37-56.

[189] Melanchthon to Luther, July 14: »Mitto tibi quaestionem de traditionibus, de qua velim te copiose respondere. Nulla me res magis exercet in omnibus nostris disputationibus quam illa« (ibid., 476,15). After giving a spectrum of five positions on how prescribed practices could be binding (476,31-477,64), Melanchthon anticipated Luther's appeal to Christian liberty and continued: »Si est obedientia necessaria, libertas nulla est; pugnant inter se libertas et obedientia. Hic nodus explicandus est; nam illa libertas videtur dissolvere prorsus obedientiam, quod non convenit« (ibid., 477,69).

ordinances without the consent of the Church. Actually, Luther charges, the bishops have not been seeking to be representative spokesmen for the corporate will of the Church in its self-governance, but have lusted after arbitrary domination of the Church. They were guilty of oppressing the Church by a political style of governance and until they repent of this horrid sin and tyranny they are to resisted at every turn.[190]

On July 27 Melanchthon answered Luther, asking him to review more carefully the possibility that ecclesiastical law might be justified, if its imposition were purified of base motives and the prescribed practices were observed simply as acts of worship and praise of God.[191] Luther responded on August 4, reaffirming his position against the binding power of church law with yet more cogent reasoning. If one goes through the scheme of the four causes, one finds no ecclesial principle that serves to justify an authority to make binding laws. The true scope of the Church – sin, forgiveness, holding to the word in the Spirit, righteousness before God, eternal life – is simply alien to laws regulating external practice.[192] Correlatively, the scriptural word is both necessary and sufficient in binding us to obligatory practices of self-discipline and thankful worship. What is left for a putative church authority to impose is either the specific manner of our practice – which God wills to be free – or matter outside God's word, such as purgatory, pilgrimages, brotherhoods, and prayers to the saints – which are wicked. Thus nothing is left to be instituted as binding tradition, no matter what the motive might be for its imposition or observance.[193] In the next section it will be important to note carefully the position taken in response not to these precise arguments but to the Lutherans' general position on church authority.

These five positions, which Luther articulated for his brethren between the reading of the Augsburg Confession and the beginning of negotiations in mid-August, reveal for us the deeper basis for Luther's conviction that there would be no agreement between the Lutherans and Catholics at the Diet. We note especially how his positions focus on specific religious practices that were firmly institutionalized in the late-medieval Church. The erroneous doctrines and base

---

[190] Letter of July 21 to Melanchthon (ibid., 492-495). Shortly before writing this letter, Luther composed his forty *Propositiones adversus totam synagogam Sathanae et universas portas inferorum*, which were quickly printed in Nürnberg and arrived in Augsburg on July 22 in the form of a one-page placard in Latin. In these, great emphasis falls on the argument that Scripture has provided sufficiently for the Church in matters of faith and has set severe limits for church authority in matters of worship and church life. Malicious nonobservance of these limits transformed the pre-Reformation Church into an oppressive tyranny. WA 30II, 420-424, esp. theses 9-20 (421,1ff).

[191] WABr 5, 508,9-19.
[192] Ibid., 529f.
[193] Letter of August 4 (ibid., 525-527).

attitudes were incarnate in patterned actions of worship, life-style, and procedure affecting Christian practice on a daily basis. Again we see the radicality of the Lutheran protest.[194] One gauge of the seriousness of Luther's contestation of church structures was the respectful request made by the Prince-Elector on July 27 that Luther refrain for a while from publishing things liable to upset those with whom the Protestants are dealing in the Diet.[195] We turn now to see what in fact that »other side« had to say in its official response to the Lutheran protest.

Initial Catholic Reactions[196]

The available evidence indicates that two factors loomed large in the deliberations of the Diet immediately after the reading and submission of the Augsburg Confession on June 25. The Papal Legate, Campeggio, showed little initial interest in what the Lutherans had professed publicly, because he was treading the more promising path of private exchanges with Philip Melanchthon.[197] In the first days of July these contacts produced formulae of relatively simple conditions for a reconciliation of at least Electoral Saxony with the Roman Church.[198] As of July 6 the Legate was optimistic that dissensions

---

[194] It would, however, be hasty to conclude that Luther's demands in effect barred all possibility of agreement and reconciliation. In 1531, Tommaso de Vio, Cardinal Cajetan, responded to a request of Pope Clement VII by submitting a list of the concessions that could be made to the Lutherans in the framework of their restoration to unity. Clerical marriage and Communion under both forms could be allowed. For the mass, the Roman canon may not simply be dropped, but use of another canon may be admitted. Finally, for the whole Church it may be declared that purely ecclesiastical laws do not bind the conscience seriously. The text of Cajetan's memo was published by W. Friedesburg. »Aktenstücke über das Verhältnis der Römischen Kurie zur Reformation 1524 and 1531,« *Quellen und Forschungen aus italienischen Archiven und Bibliotheken* 3 (1900), 16-18. I translated it under the title, »Guidelines for Concessions to the Lutherans.« *Cajetan Responds* (Washington, D.C. 1978), 201-203.

[195] Ibid., 498,18. The immediate occasion for this attempt to muzzle Luther were the *Propositiones* (see n. 190, above), which arrived in Augsburg on July 22.

[196] We use the term »Catholic« here and in the following pages as a simple designation of the side opposed to the Lutherans. The more accurate terms used in German literature, *Ständemehrheit* (majority-block of estates) and *altgläubige* (adherents of the »old« faith), do not translate smoothly into English. We realize that in the events we are describing the precise point at issue was the claim of the signers of the Augsburg Confession to have done nothing which would justify their exclusion from the Catholic communion of the Church.

[197] Campeggio reported to Rome on June 26 and July 5 on these exchanges (*Nuntiaturberichte*, 1, I. Ergänzungsband, 70, 76). After discussion in consistory, the papal secretary Salviati wrote to the Legate on July 13 that no concessions were to be made to the Lutherans (ibid., 80f). But Campeggio had already been moved, apparently by pressure from the Catholic majority in Augsburg, to break off his negotiations with Melanchthon (ibid., 84). Later the issue of a negotiated, diplomatic settlement came up once more.

[198] Melanchthon's letters to Campeggio are in CR 2, 169-174. See n. 165, above. H. Immenkötter gathered the evidence that shows that Melanchthon's approach to the Legate was made with the knowledge of the Saxon Prince-Elector and the other signers of the Augsburg Confession (*Die Confutatio*, 29).

could be settled and unity re-established, but in just a few days circumstances caused these negotiations to break down. Still, in the first days after June 25 the Legate paid little heed to the Augsburg Confession itself.

Others deliberated over procedure. The majority of the imperial estates had already decided not to submit a confession of faith corresponding to the Lutheran document. Their faith, they claimed, could not be questioned, since they held loyally to the teaching and traditions of the Church. On June 27, they recommended two steps. First, theological experts should examine the Lutheran Confession and where necessary provide a refutation on the basis of the gospel and church teachings. Second, the Emperor should take resolute action toward reforming the abuses pointed out by the Lutherans and should put reform on a wider basis by drawing up a catalogue of the complaints of secular and ecclesiastical lords over conditions in Church and Empire.[199]

After an exchange of memoranda between the Catholic estates, Campeggio, and the Emperor, it was decided to have the articles of the Lutheran Confession examined carefully by learned and prudent men working under the Cardinal Legate. This group should sift through what had been submitted, separating truth from error. Teachings diverging from the faith should be refuted, but with judicious arguments and evangelical admonitions apt to lead the adherents of the Confession to a change of heart. Also, the responsible ecclesiastics, that is, the Pope and his Legate, should take up the cause of reform and deal with the abuses. At best this should be done quickly, so that it would not appear to be done at the Lutherans' insistence but because of the Pope's sense of his duty to provide for the good estate of Christendom. If, however, the Lutherans prove obstinate – for instance, by refusing to submit to what the theologians and the Emperor determine about their articles or by refusing to acknowledge the authority of an eventual general council – then the Catholic side must be ready to apply rigor and even prepare for war.[200]

The group of theologians commissioned to examine the Augsburg Confession were men who had come to Augsburg as advisors to various princes and prince-bishops. Among their number were men already well known for writings opposing Luther and the other reformers. They included the following: Johann Eck, *peritus* for the Bavarian Dukes and an experienced controversialist; Johann Fabri of Constance, presently advisor to the Emperor's brother, Ferdinand of Austria, and later to be bishop of Vienna; Johann Cochlaeus, chaplain to Duke

---

[199] Memorandum of the Catholic estates, edited by T. Brieger, *Zeitschrift für Kirchengeschichte* 12 (1891), 126f. In mid-July a *gravamina* committee began work at the Diet, leading to a new list of complaints against the Roman Curia and to a draft imperial constitution on internal reform. See W. Gussmann, *Quellen und Forschungen*, 1, 14-21; S. Ehses, »Kardinal Lorenzo Campeggio auf dem Reichstag von Augsburg 1530,« *Römische Quartalschrift* 18 (1904), 372-382; G. Pfeilschifter, *Acta reformationis catholicae*, 1 (Regensburg 1959), 453f., 489-548.

[200] »Proposita R.D. Legato ex resolutione concilii Caes. Maiestatis,« ca. June 30, 1530 (*Concilium Tridentinum*, 4, ed. S. Ehses [Freiburg 1904], XXXVIf).

Georg of Albertine Saxony and prolific opponent of the German Protestants; Bartholomew von Usingen, an Augustinian who had been Luther's teacher in Erfurt in 1501-1505; the Dominicans Johann Mensing of Frankfurt/Oder and Johann Dietenberger of Koblenz; and Arnold von Wesel of Cologne, who submitted a key draft for the official *Confutatio* of August 3.[201] Campeggio had conceived of the task given this group as first, a careful demonstration that the Protestants were espousing errors already condemned, especially by the Council of Constance, and second, a comparison of the official Lutheran Confession with earlier Lutheran teachings in order to bring to light any other errors for which the five princes and cities should be held responsible. This refutation should then be enunciated as the Emperor's definitive judgment on the religious dissensions in his realm.[202]

The first draft of a Catholic response to the Augsburg Confession, the *Responsio theologorum* (early July), apparently covered only the first four articles of the Confession. The approach corresponded generally to Campeggio's proposed method. The Lutheran princes and cities were commended for specific points found orthodox but were to be admonished by the Emperor for tolerating the dissemination by their preachers and theologians of other, false teachings, many of which had not been listed in the Augsburg Confession.[203]

Two particular points in this earliest draft reveal the mentality of its band of authors. (1) The Lutheran profession of the Nicene Trinitarian faith became an occasion for accusing them of unjustifiably diverging from practices obligatory by reason of a common consensus of the Catholic Church. The Sacrifice of the Mass, the Lenten fast, prayers to saints, and liturgies for the dead have all been attacked by Lutheran preachers as unbiblical. But we accept the Trinity of divine persons not from Scripture but from the Church, »and therefore we should profess and practice the other things the Catholic Church teaches, receives, commends, and institutes, even if they are not found explicitly in Scripture.«[204] The Emperor should point to Christ's promises to his Church, which make it the pillar and ground of truth (1 Tim 3:15), and so he should urge the princes to stop giving credence to fallible individual teachers who in their pride dare to oppose the teachings and practices of this same Church.[205] Here ecclesiological

---

[201] A full roster of the *confutatores* is given by H. Immenkötter, *Die Confutatio*, 17-23.

[202] Ibid., 26. Only excerpts of Campeggio's recommendation are given by Ehses, *Concilium Tridentinum*, 4, XXXVf.

[203] CR 27, 85, 89, 91, 95.

[204] Ibid., 86.

[205] Ibid., 87. The obligation to follow the Church is grounded in Jn 14:26, 16:13, Mt 16:18, and 1 Tim 3:15. On Art. 2 of the Augsburg Confession, the *Responsio* lists five erroneous but divergent teachings on original sin and baptism (from Luther, Melanchthon, Zwingli, Eberhard Vuidensee, and the *Catabaptistae*), and then observes characteristically: »Et quis tandem erit errorum modus aut finis, si unicuique iuxta somnia sua novam opinionem effingere, et in populum evulgare liceat? Satius est igitur et multo salubrius, unam certam Ecclesiae sententiam sequi et amplecti, quam per tot opinionum ambages misere in errorum pelago fluctuare« (ibid., 90). This concern, however, was not found solely among the *confutatores*. Melanchthon foresaw a

10. Abuses under Indictment, 1530

considerations come to the fore in response to the Lutheran Confession. Notable also is the concern to defend matters of everyday worship and practice.

2) Article 4, on justification being wholly God's gift, occasioned, among other points, the charge that the Lutherans were calumniating Catholics, especially monks, by accusing them of a Pelagian disregard of divine grace. The Catholic spokesmen claim to know quite well the New Testament teachings on God's gifts from above, and their side professes that good works – otherwise of no worth – are only meritorious because they are begun, accompanied, and completed by God's grace given by merit of Christ's passion.[206] The Catholics were clearly not without answers in response to Lutheran charges of an erroneous doctrine of merit. There was a basis for further exchanges and possibly a reduction of differences.

It is not clear just when the cumbersome *Responsio theologorum* was set aside, but it must have been in very early July because by July 12 a complete draft response to the Lutheran Confession, the *Catholica responsio*, was submitted to the Emperor by the *periti*, who were now working under the chairmanship of Johann Fabri. But the deliberations of the following week unleashed from the majority group of estates a small storm of criticism of this second attempt to answer the Augsburg Confession. The document was far too long; it included many points not germane to the precise purpose of refuting the Lutherans' stated views; its polemical tone was insulting and more destructive of than conducive to peace.[207]

The *Catholica responsio* of June 12 represented the high-water mark of the influence at the Diet of Eck's *404 Articles* and similar heresy catalogues. Throughout this draft response the Lutheran princes were briefly commended for professing the traditional faith of the Church but were then called upon to admonish Luther and his colleagues for a host of divergent doctrines. Abundant citations of the erroneous teachings of the Reformers showed the wide gap thought to separate those on the Lutheran side from the traditional faith.[208] The

---

similar outcome if an episcopate were not restored in Lutheran lands (Letters of September 4, 6, and mid-October, 1530; CR 2, 341, 347, 433). If there were a violent outcome, the Lutherans would be driven into an alliance with the Zwinglians, and Melanchthon foresaw this leading to a detestable »maxima confusio dogmatum et religionum« (ibid., 382).

206 CR 27, 96. The *Responsio* cites these texts on the role of grace: 1 Cor 4:7, 15:10; Jn 3:27, 6:44; Jas 1:17; 2 Cor 3:5; and the traditional prayer beginning »Actiones nostras, quaesumus, Domine, aspirando praeveni et adiuvando prosequere...«

207 H. Immenkötter gives pertinent excerpts from this criticism out of his work in archival material (*Die Confutatio*, 38f).

208 The edition of the *Catholica responsio* by Johannes Ficker, *Die Konfutation des Augsburgischen Bekenntnisses* (Leipzig 1891), 1-140, gives full documentation of these citations taken over by the *confutatores* from Eck's *404 Articles*. Unfortunately, only pages 1-51, printed by Ficker for his *Habilitation*, were available to the present author.

Catholica responsio rested on the assumption that the Augsburg Confession represented quite inadequately what comprised Lutheran doctrine and preaching. In addition, the Lutherans were charged with being responsible for sectarian teachings and tumults troubling Germany for the past ten years.[209] However the approach of the *responsio* was unacceptable to the majority of the imperial estates, who demanded that the theologians adhere closely to the actual text submitted to the Diet and that they avoid injurious and insulting statements.[210] Consequently, on about July 20 the group of men working under Fabri made a fresh start on their work of examination and refutation. The product of their work, the *Confutatio*, was read in the name of Charles V on August 3, 1530, as his official response to the Lutheran Confession.[211]

The *Confutatio* took shape under great pressure of time and amid shifting conceptions of just what kind of document it was to be. On July 22 the decision was finally made to issue the response in the name of the Emperor himself. On August 1 the wording was revised to reduce the document from the legal status of a final, binding decision to that of an official report on the Emperor's religious position which, however, left open the possibility of negotiations. The document differs from the Augsburg Confession in not being a confession of faith or an apology for reform. It is strictly a response and reaction to what the Lutherans had presented.

Although the *Confutatio* was drawn up largely by men who had for a decade been turning out polemical retorts to the Reformation, it is marked by restraint and objectivity. It acknowledges much in the Lutheran Confession as sound and it makes a conscious effort to ground its alternative positions in Scripture and early patristic and conciliar texts. The *Confutatio* passed over opportunities for further confrontation and so evinced a sincere desire for peace. While being firmly critical on numerous doctrinal and disciplinary points, it did not preclude further discussion, clarification, and even rapprochement.[212]

We turn now to review the specific responses of the imperial *Confutatio* to the Lutheran indictment of abuses in the life and worship of the pre-Reformation

---

[209] Preface (Ficker, *Die Konfutation*, 2f).

[210] Their recommendation of July 19 is given by Brieger, *Zeitschrift für Kirchengeschichte* 12 (1891), 152-155.

[211] A fine edition of this work, with the official German text and the Latin base-text has been edited by Herbert Immenkötter as Vol. 33 of *Corpus catholicorum* (Münster, 1979). In subsequent footnotes we refer to this edition as CC 33, with added Arabic numbers indicating page and line numbers of the Latin text.

[212] Our information on the *Confutatio* comes largely from the preface of H. Immenkötter's edition, while our evaluative remarks depend on his *Um die Einheit im Glauben* (Münster 1973), 11-21, and his »Die Confutatio – ein Dokument der Einheit,« in E. Iserloh & B. Hallensleben, eds., *Confessio Augustana und Confutatio. Die Augsburger Reichstag 1530 und die Einheit der Kirche* (Münster 1980), 205-213.

Church. We follow the five-point analysis used above in presenting material from the Augsburg Confession.

1) The *Confutatio* does not accept the erroneous character of the interpretations that the Lutherans claimed were vitiating certain religious practices. The doctrine of merit is upheld for those good works done with the assistance of divine grace given through the power of Christ's passion.[213] The *Confutatio* extols fasting in accordance with church ordinances for its contribution to self-discipline, and holds that satisfactory works are integral to repentance.[214] Vows have good biblical and historical backing, and with the aid of grace their observance brings merit of eternal life.[215] Monastic life does not detract from Christ's honor, since this religious observance is dedicated to Christ and to his gospel and so merits eternal life. Private Masses, the *Confutatio* asserts, do redound to the glory of God and the benefit of both the living and the dead. Consequently the Lutheran suppression of these Masses deserves a sharp reprehension.[216]

In this first phase of its response the *Confutatio* offered direct rejection of the Lutheran indictment as doctrinally unsound. The controverted practices can be set in a good light, if one only attend to their biblical justification and to certain details of the doctrinal superstructure. Correct interpretations can be supplied, and so the practices are to be continued. The Lutheran charges of erroneous interpretation have met serious rebuttal. But this was not the end. An exchange was to follow which would open up new issues: for instance, whether each side has adequately understood the other position, whether fuller definition of terms might reveal important common convictions, whether certain practices – or their suppression – might be tolerated from a distance while not being actually espoused, and whether one side or the other, or even both, might develop their positions to be inclusive of each other.

2) The *Confutatio* declined to be drawn into a discussion of the alleged displacement or marginalization of central points of Christian instruction. It did not meet head on the Lutheran claim of promoting a revitalization of Christianity from its center. In 1530 this issue fell outside the scope of the task given to the Catholic *periti* and so the charges and claims made by the Lutherans were quietly allowed to stand.

3) The *Confutatio* made some forthright responses to the Lutheran charge of hierarchical overreach. In tone, Article 28 of the Augsburg Confession was found excessively harsh. More importantly, grounds were given for the existence in the

---

[213] Arts. 4, 6, 20 (CC 33, 85,11, 86,11, 93,14-17, 123,11f).
[214] Arts. 12, 26 (CC 33, 181,7, 107,10ff).
[215] Art. 27 (CC 33,186-197, esp. 191,7-13 and 195,5-13).
[216] Art. 24 (CC 33, 163,1-14).

Church of a power of governance and disciplinary correction.[217] Where the Lutherans appealed to Christian freedom, the rebuttal saw license.[218] The ordinances enacted by church authority promote desirable ends, such as the worship of God and personal discipline and do not detract from the righteousness of faith and from divine commandments.[219]

This line of defense might appear to accentuate and even harden differences between the two sides. But one should recall that the *Confutatio* was not responding to Luther and his missives from Coburg but instead to the Confession of June 25 with its clear doctrine of ecclesiastical authority by divine right. A shared conviction lay beneath the difference over the extent of this authority's lawmaking power. Also, the *Confutatio* concluded its own Article 28 with a ringing call for reform, specifically mentioning the correction of excesses, or encroachments, by those having authority in Church and state.[220] It is not too much to state that there was, at Augsburg in the high summer of 1530, important common ground on which to base further discussion of the rightful exercise of authority in the Church.

4) The *Confutatio* did not directly touch issues of episcopal performance in pastoral office, but it was not unmindful of the need of reform in the Church. Regarding the Mass, it asserted that all sensible people greatly desired its reform.[221] The Lutheran princes and cities were told to support ordered reform of the monasteries in their domains and to see to the correction of monks rather than connive in the destruction of their way of life.[222] And in the final paragraph of the last article the *Confutatio* gave a ringing endorsement of reform. Excesses of both ecclesiastical and secular leaders are to be corrected and their negligence set right. Religion has declined and infringements of right order cry out for correction. The Emperor, at least, will not flag in his pursuit of a renewed Christianity.[223]

In the *Confutatio*, therefore, we hear some scattered expressions of aspirations

---

[217] Art. 28 (CC 33, 197,11, 199,8-15). Also in art. 26 (179,3ff).
[218] Art. 28 (CC 33, 201,5ff).
[219] Art. 26 (CC 33, 177,12-16, 179,20-181,9).
[220] Art. 28 (CC 33, 203,11f). This passage came from the Emperor's advisors, Granvella and Valdes, who reviewed the text in the final days before it was prepared for reading.
[221] Art. 24 (CC 33, 161,16f).
[222] Art. 27 (CC 33, 197,3-6).
[223] Art. 28 (CC 33, 203,7-17). This endorsement of reform indicates well the idealistic hopes of Emperor Charles V. On August 12, 1530, he spoke to the Venetian envoy to the Diet of his aspiration of having a great council during his reign to correct the grave disorders plaguing Christendom (cited by J. von Walter, »Der Reichstag zu Augsburg 1530,« *Lutherjahrbuch* 12 [1930], 5).

for reform. The will to change was not totally absent, and the Diet's *gravamina* commission was beginning work on the details of a comprehensive reform plan. Further probes would be necessary to ground a judgment on the congruence of these reform ideas with what the Lutherans had presented in their indictments of abuses. Also, just how strong were the reform intentions of the German bishops? It is not clear that the imperial reform movement could easily absorb the church renewal taking hold in the Lutheran territories. Still, it is clear enough that the Lutherans were not the only ones present in Augsburg in 1530 for whom reform of the Church was an important issue.

5) The *Confutatio* opposed the Lutheran contestation of particular institutions, at times with direct denials that they were abuses. (i) In questioning the legitimacy of prayer to the saints, the Lutherans have fallen into an error condemned on numerous occasions by the Church.[224] (ii) It is wrong to call Communion under one form an abuse, in view of the backing it has from Scripture, history, and practical pastoral considerations.[225] (iii) Nor should celibacy be called an abuse, because it too is well grounded both in the tradition and in considerations on the nature of priestly ministry.[226] (iv) The abrogation of private Masses receives severe censure as destructive of important values.[227] (v) Integral confession, the *Confutatio* claims, is necessary to salvation and is the key moment in the Church's system of discipline.[228] Generally, the Catholic rebuttal does not accept the Lutheran argument for legitimate diversity on these matters. In fact, the second part of the Lutheran Confession is said in passing to be about »pretended abuses«.[229]

One senses in these sections of the *Confutatio* dealing with specific institutions a special vigor born of outrage over the Lutheran charges and changes. Firm convictions had come under fire and the response was a series of direct reprehensions. The everyday visibility of the contested practices and ways of life added to the urgency of defense and counterargument. The authors of the *Confutatio* would in no way allow the term »abuses« to be applied to religious activities woven deeply into their own worship, ministry, and everyday living. The web of the authors' own lives was under attack, and the forthrightness of their response is understandable. Here the Reformation indictment and the

---

[224] Art. 21 (CC 33, 125,4-11).
[225] Art. 22 (CC 33, 133-139). The real abuse for the *Confutatio* is instead the disobedience of giving both forms to lay people (133,7).
[226] Art. 23 (CC 33, 143-159, esp. 143,13ff and 151,5-9).
[227] Art. 24 (CC 33, 163,1-7).
[228] Art. 25 (CC 33, 175,19ff). Carl Peter contrasted the Augsburg Confession and the *Confutatio* on this point in his diachronical study of the Reformation debate on integral confession of moral sins. »From *Sermo* to *Anathema*: a Dispute about Confession of Mortal Sins,« in N.H. Minnich et al., eds., *Studies in Church History in Honor of John Tracy Ellis* (Wilmington, Del. 1985), 576-580.
[229] Art. 26 (CC 33, 185,1f.10-13 and 192,1f).

Catholic response clashed with considerable intensity, leaving a situation sure to daunt even the most skillful of mediators.

Conclusion

Throughout my presentation, I have interspersed reflective considerations on the mentalities revealed in our texts. Clearly, many of the participants in the Diet of Augsburg did not harbor attitudes conducive to a reconciliation of the differences between the estates. We have seen abundant evidence that this clash of attitudes was most sharp when dealing with practical matters of worship and church organization. On these points the crucial arguments, ever present just beneath the surface, concerned, first, the law-making competence of ecclesiastical authority, and, second, the criteria of legitimacy of concrete forms of religious practice. On these points, the participants at Augsburg in 1530 were divided to a point beyond easy reconciliation. But on the surface, the arguments we have seen show a remarkable symmetry.

On the Lutheran side one finds a forceful movement of polemical attack, across a wide front, against allegedly corrupt and abusive aspects of pre-Reformation religious life. The reformers argued from their conception of pristine biblical forms to the discrediting of existing popular practices and ecclesial traditions. In the preparatory apologias and in Luther's *Admonition*, polemic became at times compulsive. Accusations were hurled with abandon, based on certitude about God's will for the life of Christian believers. Luther's consummate self-assurance stands out amid the attitudes we have researched. He denounced with full earnestness, rising on occasion to apocalyptic cries, as he charged the hierarchy with greed, blasphemy, arbitrary rule, and downright hypocrisy. Little wonder that peace did not prevail in mid-1530.

But the enduring Lutheran monument from the Diet is the moderate and measured statement of the Augsburg Confession. I find it a worthy and even attractive articulation of the reformatory impulse. The Confession does not encompass the whole of the Lutheran movement and it remains burdened by the ambiguity of its key term »abuses«. Still, Melanchthon made his indictment in a firm, judicious manner. Its case for reform deserves recognition.

On the Catholic side we met the belligerent approach of Johann Eck and his associates in heresy-hunting. They too were compulsive, self-assured, and given to broad denunciations. But sounder minds prevailed in July 1530 and accordingly the *Confutatio* was also shaped into a document of moderate and measured argumentation. Much like its Lutheran counterpart, neither was it comprehensive. It was burdened, I would judge, by its failure to address questions about norms controlling popular religion. On abuses and their reform the *Confutatio* had good random remarks, but reform was not a major theme. Its writers were not reformers and so they lacked important common ground with Melanchthon and his colleagues.

Still, the *Confutatio* was a significant Catholic response to the first phase of the

Lutheran reformation. Compared with the majority of early Catholic controversial works, it was controlled and judicious in both tone and content. It urged values of considerable religious importance: continuity, consensus, authority. The *Confutatio* spoke well for those who remained committed to tradition and to historically developed forms of life and worship. Its advocacy of such structures – against some Lutheran charges of inherent sinfulness – also deserves recognition. The prosecution should consider carefully this response given to its indictment.

11

THE LUTHERAN *FORMA ECCLESIAE* IN THE COLLOQUY AT AUGSBURG, AUGUST 1530

In an ecumenical age such as our own, we read the history of the Reformation with different leading questions from those asked by our forebears. The promising dialogues between our churches today stir a natural interest in the colloquies of the sixteenth century. These colloquies are less well known than the great disputations of the Reformation era, for example, the Leipzig Disputation of 1519 and the Zürich Disputation of 1523. But there were colloquies or dialogues as well, at which appointed spokesmen worked, briefly but unsuccessfully, to prevent the emerging religious divisions from hardening into fixed ecclesial and political oppositions.[1] Beginnings exercise a special fascination and consequently a small, but notable, body of literature has developed around the first such Reformation-era bilateral colloquy. This took place between Lutheran and Catholic representatives at the German imperial Diet of Augsburg in 1530, after the submission of the Lutheran Augsburg Confession on June 25 and the reading of the imperial *Confutatio* on 3 August.[2]

My earlier study of Lutheran-Catholic relations in the decisive months of 1530 attended to the immediate preparations for the Diet and to the exchange of argument into early August. That study investigated the conflicting assessments made by the participants regarding concrete forms of religious practice, such as mass stipends, private masses, communion under one form, ritual blessings of objects for devotional use, clerical celibacy, integral confession of sins, fasting

---

[1] The papers of the Wolfenbüttel Symposium of March 1979 reflect recent scholarship on these sixteenth-century bilateral colloquies. See the edition, edited by Gerhard Müller, *Die Religionsgespräche der Reformationszeit* (Gütersloh 1980). Also, more recently, M. Hollerbach, *Das Religionsgespräch als Mittel der konfessionellen und politischen Auseinandersetzung* (Bern-Frankfurt 1982).

[2] The basic narrative is Herbert Immenkötter, *Um die Einheit im Glauben: Die Unionsverhandlungen des Augsburger Reichstages im August und September 1530* (Münster 1973). Immenkötter advances the prior research of G. Müller, E. Honée, and V. Pfnür, whose contributions will be noted in the pages that follow. After Immenkötter's book, the most significant new contribution is E. Honée's analytic and documentary work, *Der Libell des Hieronymus Vehus zum Augsburger Reichstag 1530* (Münster 1988). Honée has drawn together his main insights in »Hieronymus Vehus. Seine Vermittlerrolle während der Augsburger Einigungsverhandlungen,« in R. Decot, ed., *Vermittlungsversuche auf dem Augsburger Reichstage* (Stuttgart 1989), 29-49.

laws, and the institution of religious and monastic life under vows. The Lutherans offered a searing indictment of this complex of practices and structures, making evident just how imperative was their call for reform, a reform which the bishops had not undertaken. The Catholic *Confutatio* offered defenses of selected practices and institutions, maintaining they were not abuses but instead were fully warranted and had hierarchical approval.[3] The present essay considers the colloquy of August 1530, giving special attention to the give-and-take of discussion on these controverted practices and structures of church life.

Philip Melanchthon gave a useful point of focus to my earlier study, when he wrote in the Confession of June 25 that, since the Lutheran faith is orthodox and in continuity with past ages, the real argument lies elsewhere: »The dispute and dissension are concerned chiefly with various traditions and abuses.«[4] For the middle phases of the Diet, especially for the colloquies of August 7 to 31, another phrase penned by Melanchthon can serve well to name the central issue. On or about August 12, Melanchthon proposed that the Lutheran leader, Elector Johann of Saxony, request the naming of a relatively small joint commission to work toward greater agreement between the Lutheran and Catholic positions on doctrine and rites. The Saxon and Lutheran goal in such an exchange would be to show that the real differences were – or could be brought – within the bounds of what the other side could tolerate, at least until the convocation of a General Council. Dogma will not be critical, since Melanchthon is sure that the Lutherans can make patent their essential orthodoxy. In the service of doctrinal continuity and good order, the Lutheran side would accept the restoration of episcopal jurisdiction. From the other side the specific concessions to request are the chalice for the laity, marriage for the clergy and religious, and »our mass« (that is, only the reformed, communitarian celebration, with private masses being suppressed). In fact, if the other side granted only the chalice and clerical marriage, that could suffice, for »thus our *forma ecclesiae* would remain.«[5] The colloquies of August 1530 were in fact a lively exchange over the continuation, in certain territories and cities of Germany, of the *forma ecclesiae* recently constituted by reforms inspired by Luther, for which responsible established authorities were asking tolerant recognition from the Emperor Charles V, the

---

[3] »Abuses under Indictment at the Diet of Augsburg 1530,« Study 10, above, in this collection, originally published in *Theological Studies* 41 (1980), 252-302.

[4] Augsburg Confession, Conclusion to Part 1, cited from T.G. Tappert et al., eds., *The Book of Concord* (Philadelphia, 1959), 48, translating the German. In Melanchthon's Latin: »Tota dissensio est de paucis quibusdam abusibus« (BS 83). The German text was read before the Diet on 25 June 1530, in the name of five princes of the Empire and the free cities of Nürnberg and Reutlingen, but both German and Latin texts were submitted to the Emperor Charles V.

[5] Cited from the essential source collection, K.E. Förstemann, ed., *Urkundenbuch zu der Geschichte des Reichstages zu Augsburg im Jahre 1530*, 2 vols. (Halle 1833; reprinted Osnabrück 1966), 2, 239. For the dating near 12 August, I follow H. Scheible, *Melanchthons Briefwechsel*, 1 (Stuttgart-Bad Cannstadt 1977), 423.

papal legate Lorenzo Cardinal Campeggio, and the majority block of princes and prince-bishops attending the Diet.

Before we study the conflicting assessments made in August 1530 concerning the Lutheran *forma ecclesiae*, let us attempt a brief evocation of the mood or climate of the colloquy of 1530. Then our account of the actual dialogue will follow its three phases, at the end of which our reflection will probe the contributing causes of the final impasse at Augsburg in 1530.

The Climate of Dialogue

Two small details suggest something of the partial openness of Catholic authorities to some concessions to certain German Protestants. In May and October 1529, Miguel Mai, the imperial ambassador to the court of Pope Clement VII, reported how Clement had expressed a readiness to grant certain Lutheran demands and to condone some at least of their practical and liturgical innovations, if he could thereby avoid having to convoke a General Council.[6] The Emperor Charles V did not share the Pope's abhorrence of a Council, but he had other motives for magnanimity. In late July 1530 he was once discussing religious policy with his brother, Archduke Ferdinand, and the Papal Legate Campeggio. Ferdinand gave vent to his forthright disapproval of Lutheran doctrine, to which Charles reportedly responded with a reproof and a reminder that kings should be outstanding for mercy and sympathy in dealing with their subjects. And Campeggio took Charles's side in admonishing Ferdinand.[7]

Clearly, the notoriously irresolute Clement VII was not firmly set on a policy of accommodation with even a small group of German Protestants. But there was a context in which such accommodation was the lesser of two evils for the second Medici Pope. And in July 1530 Charles V was not determined on some form of peaceful coexistence with the imperial estates then sponsoring Lutheran reforms. But a susceptibility was present, if the toleration of Lutheran doctrine and worship could be integrated into Charles's larger dynastic and imperial aims. Some form of negotiated settlement with the Lutheran party was not out of the question when the colloquies began in August 1530.

Looking to Charles V, one can point to three political and personal factors that favored dialogue and negotiation with the Lutherans in 1530. First, Charles was not ready to make the outlay of funds required for the use of military force to suppress heresy and compel obedience to his edicts in Germany. Other goals,

---

[6] Cited in P. de Gayangos y Arce, ed., *Calendar of Letters, Despatches, and State Papers Relating to the Negotiations between England and Spain*, 4/1 (London 1879), 23f and 283. Karl Brandi cited Mai's original Spanish on the first such utterance by Clement: *Kaiser Karl V.*, 2 vols. (Munich 1937-39), 2, 198.

[7] Related in a letter of the Wittenberg theologian Justus Jonas to Luther, 27 July 1530. WABr 12, 120; also WABr 5, 427,19-24. Jonas reported how his observations convinced him of Charles's humane and generous manner, contrasting with Ferdinand's harshness. WABr 5, 427,16-19.

especially the defence of Austria and Hungary against the Turk, ranked ahead of securing religious unity in Germany.⁸ Second, Charles was open to persuasion by the Lutheran protestation of orthodoxy. He was impressed by their confession of central Christian truths, while at the same time apparently not informed in detail about the doctrinal issues that had engaged Catholic theologians in controversy with Luther in the 1520s, such as the divine right of the papacy, eucharistic sacrifice, and the coexistence with divine grace of free choice and merit.⁹ Charles's concentration on the foundational truths may well have been due to the third factor, his Latin Secretary, Alfonso de Valdés.

Valdés was a devoted Erasmian and the protégé of Charles V's recently deceased Chancellor, Mercurino Gattinara. Valdés wanted to see his master sponsor peace within Christendom and a spiritually based reform of Church and society.¹⁰ Shortly after the Emperor's solemn entry into Augsburg on June 15, Melanchthon and Valdés began discussions of the issues facing the Diet. For Melanchthon this was not an unwelcome distraction from the final revisions of the Augsburg Confession. Instead, this personal contact with the Emperor's entourage allowed Melanchthon to pursue a line of action and argument already thought out among the Saxon policy-makers, including Luther.

Valdés received from Melanchthon assurances that an easy resolution of the Lutheran problem was within reach. The formula for peace would have the Catholic authorities accepting Lutheran requests for the chalice, clerical marriage, and only community masses, while the Lutherans would re-establish episcopal jurisdiction.¹¹ Valdés related this proposal to Charles even before the Lutheran confession was read out on June 25. The prospect pleased the Emperor, and when Campeggio was informed, he too evinced interest and willingness to explore

---

⁸ W. Reinhard, »Die kirchenpolitische Vorstellungen Kaiser Karls V.: Ihre Grundlagen und ihr Wandel,« in E. Iserloh and B. Hallensleben, eds., *Confessio Augustana und Confutatio* (Münster 1980), 86-94. The Diet of 1530 became a watershed for church history, but one does well to ponder the fact that Augsburg was chosen as the site in order to facilitate Charles's negotiation of loans from the Fugger Bank to fund war against the Turk and to defray the cost of votes for his brother Ferdinand as King of the Romans and thus to secure the Hapsburg dynasty. H. Neuhaus, in his report on recent research, listed seven issues concerning the structure and procedures of imperial government that the Diet of 1530 was expected to settle, in addition to the religious question. »Der Augsburger Reichstag des Jahres 1530. Ein Forschungsbericht,« *Zeitschrift für historische Forschung* 9 (1982), 192-209.

⁹ Sometime early in the Diet, Charles told his sister, Queen Maria of Hungary, that his earlier information about the diabolical errors of the Lutherans had been proven false, since they hold to all the twelve articles of the Apostles' Creed. He is thus ready to hear what the theologians say about the controverted externals. Cited in P. Rassow, *Die Kaiser-Idee Karls V.* (Berlin 1932), 38f.

¹⁰ On Valdés, a fundamental interpretation is M. Bataillon's chapter, »El erasmismo al servicio de la politica imperial...,« in *Erasmo y España*, 2nd ed. (Mexico City, 1966), 364-431.

¹¹ Earlier, on June 3, Melanchthon had written in the same vein to the Prince Elector of Mainz, Archbishop Albrecht. *Melanchthons Werke in Auswahl* (Gütersloh, 1951 –), 7/2, 163-167.

Melanchthon's proposal.¹² The legate assured his Lutheran visitor that he had delegated authority to grant some parts of Germany communion under both forms and a relaxation of celibacy for the diocesan clergy. Rome had provided, clearly to forestall if need be clamors for a general council.

But the initial movement toward such a settlement came to a halt by decision of Campeggio in early July, because of the obstruction of princes such as the dukes of Bavaria and Duke Georg of Albertine Saxony.[13] However, a seed had been planted which could sprout again, and Valdés remained a force for moderation in the circle around Charles V. The Latin Secretary had the advantage of advocating an inexpensive and magnanimous solution to the problems posed by Luther and his protectors.

As papal legate, Campeggio influenced policy-making all through the Diet of 1530, but he showed some flexibility. In early May he had offered Charles V a lengthy memorandum on the Emperor's duty to apply a range of sanctions, and even military force, against the German heretics, but in late June, when he informed the Pope of Melanchthon's proposal of reconciliation by mutual concessions, Campeggio brought forth warrants for granting at least the chalice and a married clergy.[14] Campeggio, however, worked closely with a group of theologians, headed by Johann Fabri and Johann Eck, who were fresh from the front lines of doctrinal warfare with Luther. Here were men determined to catalogue publicly the Lutheran heresies and subversive notions. Fabri served Archduke Ferdinand, and Eck the Bavarian dukes; along with Duke Georg, this group constituted a force quite unfavorable to a dialogue of understanding with the Lutherans over doctrine and church reforms. The Catholic Estates, however, were not a solid phalanx against the Lutherans. Some, like the bishops of Augsburg and Mainz, were more tolerant. On the other hand, the Estates were not ready to support Charles V in any measures likely to reinforce his power in the Empire. Even the opposition between him and the Lutherans could have its political usefulness.[15]

---

12 Melanchthon wrote to Luther on 19 June that Valdés had informed Charles and Campeggio about the proposal. CR 2, 119. A fuller report went out in the dispatch of 21 June from the Nürnberg delegates to the Diet (ibid., 122f). On 12 July Valdés wrote to the Cardinal of Ravenna about his exchanges with Melanchthon, in a text published by G. Bagnatori, »Cartas inéditas de Alfonso de Valdés sobre la Dieta de Augsburgo,« *Bulletin hispanique* 57 (1955), 362-364.

13 Melanchthon on his conference with the legate (8 July): »Summa fuit orationis illius, se nihil posse discernere, nisi de voluntate Principum Germaniae: tametsi quarundam rerum relaxandarum potestatem habeat, qua invitis Principibus uti non sit utile« (CR 2, 174f). A letter earlier in the same day had named the chalice and celibacy as matters for possible concessions by Campeggio (ibid., 174). E. Honée treated this in »Die römische Kurie und der 22. Artikel der Confessio Augustana,« *Nederlands archief voor kerkgeschiedenis* 50 (1969-70), 148-159.

14 *Nuntiaturberichte aus Deutschland*, 1533-1559, *Ergänzungsbände* 1530-1531, ed. G. Müller, 2 vols. (Tübingen 1963-69), 2, 457-471 (8 and 12 May), 1, 70-73 (26 June).

15 A. Kohler, »Die innerdeutsche und die ausserdeutsche Opposition gegen das politische System Karls V.,« in Heinrich Lutz, ed., *Das römisch-deutsche Reich im politischen System Karls V.* (Munich 1982), 112-116.

On the Lutheran side, the Saxon Elector had come to the Diet well prepared to make a case for his reformation. Since mid-1529 he had been insisting on adherence to the Schwabach Articles, enshrining Luther's affirmation of the Real Presence, as a condition for any Protestant alliance including Electoral Saxony. After the *protestatio* of Speyer in 1529, Saxony, along with Nürnberg, Hesse, and Brandenburg, sent a delegation to Charles to make clear the intent of their protest, and to differentiate it from unchristian and rebellious behavior. In early 1530 Elector Johann gained his allies' adherence to the Schwabach Articles and commissioned a new delegation to inform Charles that this group anathematized Zwingli, while requesting respect for their efforts to reform intolerable abuses. The Schwabach Articles were even submitted to Charles in Innsbruck in March 1530 in the hopes of thereby demonstrating Lutheran orthodoxy and opposition to the outrageous teaching of the Swiss.[16] Furthermore, there is ample evidence that the recurring Saxon formula for concessions leading to unity had been worked out before Augsburg in lengthy consultations which included the Elector, Chancellor Gregor Brück, and Luther.[17]

There was tension, however, in the Lutheran camp. Landgrave Philip of Hesse remained attracted to Zwingli and thereby sowed doubts in the Saxon group about his constancy as their partner in the developing alliance.[18] The free city of Nürnberg would clearly not agree to a reintroduction of episcopal jurisdiction, and Melanchthon's diplomacy eventually came under sharp attack from this quarter.[19] In late June the Electoral Saxon theologian Justus Jonas had confronted

---

[16] W. Steglich, »Die Stellung der evangelischen Reichsstände und Reichsstädte zu Karl V. zwischen Protestation und Konfession 1529/30,« *Archiv für Reformationsgeschichte* 62 (1971), 161-192.

[17] Melanchthon wrote on August 31 that nothing had been conceded to the Emperor beyond what Luther had agreed to, »re bene ac diligenter deliberata ante conventum« (CR 2, 334). Brück wrote in 1537 about lengthy discussions on the papacy and episcopal jurisdiction which accompanied the composition of the *Confessio* (cited in WABr 12, 116). A recent exposition of the Saxon plan and effort for a negotiated settlement is H. Scheible, »Melanchthon und Luther während des Augsburger Reichstags 1530,« in P. Manns, ed., *Martin Luther »Reformator und Vater im Glauben«* (Stuttgart 1985), 40-45. Martin Brecht's new account of Luther's life from 1521 to 1532 appears to neglect these texts and so views Melanchthon's attempts at mediation as Philip's personal program and – from Luther's point of view – judges them harshly. *Martin Luther, 2, Ordnung und Abgrenzung der Reformation* (Stuttgart, 1986), 374-390.

[18] Philip did sign the Augsburg Confession, but he also expressed orally his reservations about its profession of the eucharistic Real Presence (WABr 5, 427,29f). Melanchthon's early letters from Augsburg expressed recurrent worries over Philip's steadfastness. CR 2, 39 (4 May), 60f (22 May), 92-96 (appealing to Philip, 11 June), 101-103 (another appeal, in mid-June), and 126 (25 June).

[19] On Aug. 29 Melanchthon told Luther »Valde reprehendimur a nostris, quod iurisdictionem reddimus Episcopis« (CR 2, 328). On Sept. 1 he identified the Nürnbergers as those accusing him of seeking the reintroduction of papal tyranny (ibid., 336). Gerhard Müller related the bitter protest of Lazarus Spengler of Nürnberg against Melanchthon's ecclesiastical diplomacy at Augsburg in »Die Anhänger der Confessio Augustana und die Ausschussverhandlungen,« in Iserloh and Hallensleben, eds., *Confessio Augustana und Confutatio*, 233-236.

11. The Lutheran *forma ecclesiae*, 1530

Melanchthon with arguments against accepting the authority of bishops in Lutheran territories and on June 28 Jonas joined with theologians of three other signatories of the Lutheran Confession to propose the preparation of a short list of non-negotiable positions in order to set down clear limits for Melanchthon's conciliatory efforts.[20]

A further factor was Martin Luther himself, isolated at Castle Coburg. By 1530 the German Reformation was no longer the immediate product of Luther's explosive tracts of 1520-21, but instead a complex movement being implemented and institutionalized under considerable influence of territorial rulers. Doctrine and religious urgency had to coexist with, and at times suffer the constraints of, the political dynamics of governing and relating to other public authorities. In 1530 Luther could chafe under such restraints, and some of his tracts from Coburg were in tone, if not in content, out of harmony with the Saxon diplomatic appeal for recognition and toleration of the new form of church life.[21]

Thus, on both sides a *complexio oppositorum* generated tensions during the August bilateral dialogues of 1530. The span of viewpoints on the Lutheran side concerned ways of interpreting and further elucidating the irenic Confession of June 25, with its concentration on fundamentals of doctrine and reform and its selected omissions.[22]

The Catholic tensions were played out in July as Fabri and his theological team composed two draft responses to the Lutheran Confession which Charles

---

[20] M. Liebmann, *Urbanus Rhegius und die Anfänge der Reformation* (Münster 1980), 273f. Liebmann sketches well the span of different views in the Lutheran camp regarding possible concessions through negotiations (ibid., 265-302).

[21] Mark U. Edwards has written sensitively about Luther's relation to what his reform was becoming in this period, e.g. in »The Older Luther, 1526-1546,« in G. Dünnhaupt, ed., *The Martin Luther Quincentennial* (Detroit 1985), 48-62, and *Luther's Last Battles: Politics and Polemics 1531-46* (Ithaca, N.Y. 1983), 20-67. On Luther's writings at the Coburg, see Study 10, above in this collection, pp. 246-251, 262-268. That account ended with the Elector Johann's request on July 21 that Luther desist for a while from polemical publications.

[22] Luther was basically very pleased with the Confession's proclamation of Christ, as he wrote to the Elector on 9 July (WABr 5, 453,10-454,26). But on that same day, in Augsburg, Melanchthon and the other Saxon theologians formulated an apologia for their Confession's omission of such topics as predestination, freedom and necessity, the priesthood of all believers, the *ius divinum* of papal primacy, indulgences, and the number of the sacraments. These points, which Melanchthon calls »die gehässigen und unnöthigen Artikel,« are matters of academic disputation, while the Confession is an account of what is being preached publicly in the territories of the signers (CR 2, 182f). Later, Luther noted that the Confession avoided forthright rejections of purgatory, the saints, and' the papal Antichrist (WABr 5, 496,1-3). In recent studies, R. Bäumer has highlighted the Augsburg Confession's concealment of points on which the Lutherans differed sharply with Catholic convictions, especially on the mass as the sacrificial offering that benefits the living and the dead. »Vermittlungsbemühungen auf dem Augsburger Reichstag,« *Theologie und Glaube* 70 (1980), 308, n.34, 312, n.64, 330, n.184. See also Bäumer's »Bekenntnis des einen Glaubens? Zur Diskussion um das Augsburger Bekenntnis,« *Theologie und Glaube* 71 (1981), 364-367.

V's advisors rejected as being too polemical.[23] By the beginning of August, a third text, restrained and for the most part well argued, was ready and found acceptable. This became the imperial *Confutatio*, an article-by-article assessment of the Augsburg Confession that was read before the Diet on August 3.[24]

The *Confutatio* concluded by admonishing the Lutheran princes and cities to distance themselves from the errors pointed out in the body of the declaration and to return to obedient profession of the faith of the Catholic and Roman Church.[25] Charles V had his appeal repeated in afternoon meetings with the Lutheran leaders on August 4 and 5. In response, the signers of the Confession of June 25 asserted they were not convinced by what they had heard on August 3 and that they needed a copy of the *Confutatio* for examination. From the imperial side, a copy was in effect refused, since it was offered on condition that it should not be printed or subjected to any counterarguments.[26]

Melanchthon had not been present at the reading of the *Confutatio*, but the reports he received on its allegedly poor content and style only served to strengthen him and his associates in assurance about their cause.[27] Other information, upon reflective consideration, made Melanchthon realize that the Emperor's response had in fact conceded the correctness of the main doctrines professed by the Lutherans. Where the refutation accused them of error, it was calumniating them.[28] At this time, Melanchthon sought to reopen his dialogue

---

[23] Alfonso de Valdés was one critic of the draft responses of mid-July as »mas invectiva que respuestas ny admonition christiana« (Letter of July 21 to Accolti), and he had a hand in softening the final version of the *Confutatio* so that it conformed to the attitude of Charles V (Letter of Aug. 1; Bagnatori, »Cartas inéditas,« pp. 364, 366).

[24] *Die Confutatio der Confessio Augustana*, ed. H. Immenkötter (Corpus Catholicorum, 33; Münster, 1979), in which pp. 34-48 describe the genesis of the imperial response. A decade later Luther recalled how forthcoming the *Confutatio* had been, in that it had admitted that the Augsburg Confession had a good biblical basis. *Wider Hans Worst*, 1541; WA 51, 473,22-28; LW 41, 190. The *Confutatio* has been studied from a helpful point of view in B. Dittrich, *Das Traditionsverständnis in der Confessio Augustana und in der Confutatio* (Leipzig 1983), esp. pp. 107-213.

[25] *Confutatio*, ed. Immenkötter, 204-207.

[26] Förstemann, *Urkundenbuch*, 2, 179-181. H. Immenkötter traced the equivalent refusal of a copy of the *Confutatio* to the interventions by Campeggio, who wanted the refutation to have something of the character of an imperial edict requiring obedience, not counterargument (*Um die Einheit im Glauben*, 14f, 22f).

[27] Letter of 6 Aug. to Veit Dietrich, who was with Luther at Coburg (CR 2, 253). Martin Bucer criticized the refutation's use of Old Testament texts as arguments for communion under one form and for the sacrifice of the mass and found the case for the saints' intercession quite weak. Letter of Aug. 14 from Augsburg to Ambrosius Blaurer in Constance; *Briefwechsel der Brüder Ambrosius und Thomas Blaurer*, ed. T. Schiess, 1 (Freiburg 1908), 214f.

[28] Memoranda to the Prince Elector, from around Aug. 4 and 12, in which, for example, Melanchthon wrote, »unsere Artikel, in effectu, die fürnehmen approbirt sind. Ob schon etlich zusätz daran gehängt sind, so sind doch die unsern nicht verworffen« (CR 2, 258). See also Förstemann, *Urkundenbuch*, 2, 240, where Melanchthon predicts that the Emperor will not contest Lutheran doctrine in the proposed colloquy, where it should be easy to refute the several calumnies by the *Confutatio*.

with Campeggio over a negotiated set of mutual concessions to restore unity. Campeggio's reply was negative in tone and most of its substance, but did leave a door slightly ajar by referring to the remote possibility that Rome could tolerate married priests.[29]

What though was to be done to overcome the impasse created by the Lutheran refusal to accept the *Confutatio* as a judgment on their doctrine and rites?[30] The direct appeals by the Emperor to the Lutheran leaders were not succeeding, and so the Estates aligned with the Emperor proposed that they take up dealings with the Lutherans. On August 6 this was accepted and seventeen members of the Diet, Electors, princes, and bishops, were named to undertake a work of mediation between the Lutherans and the Emperor who was now identified with the *Confutatio*.[31]

The First Phase of Dialogue

The exchanges of August 7-14 were not, strictly speaking, a colloquy on doctrine and rites, but they did bring to the surface certain issues of fundamental importance. The committee of seventeen repeatedly admonished their opposite numbers, the seven Lutheran princes, to submit to the refutation of their Confession and to return to a relationship of peace and concord with the Emperor. The Lutherans pleaded their inability, on grounds of conscience and Scripture, to do this. Each side called on the other to recommend some other means likely to move the discussion forward toward resolution, and finally, on August 13, the Lutherans proposed the formation of smaller commissions, which would represent the two sides and include some theologians. Thus was born the

---

[29] Melanchthon wrote on Aug. 4 to the legate's secretary Luca Bonfio (CR 2, 248f). Campeggio described his response in his dispatch to Rome on 11 Aug.: *Nuntiaturberichte*, ed. Müller, 1, 108-110.

[30] Luther had described for the Elector Johann the limits within which Charles V could be acknowledged as a proper judge concerning religious issues: »so fern und ausgenomen das sein K[eyserliche] M[aiestät] nicht widder die schrifft odder Gotts wort richte« (Letter of 9 July; WABr 12, 118,47f). A verse of Ps 118, »Nolite confidere in principibus«, should instil reserve vis-à-vis imperial claims (ibid., 119,56-59). When consulted again in August, Luther drew up a five-point memorandum that even noted the prohibition in Justinian's Code against judging one's own case, which seems to apply, now that the *Confutatio* had been presented in Charles's name (ibid., 122f). Charles was under no illusions, and had informed the Pope on July 14 that the dissidents would not accept him as rightful judge in the case before the Diet. *Corpus Documental de Carlos V*, ed. M. F. Alvarez, 5 vols. (Salamanca 1973-81), 1, 228.

[31] V. von Tetleben, *Protokoll des Augsburger Reichtages 1530*, ed. H. Grundmann (Göttingen 1958), 102f. Tetleben was counsellor of the Archbishop of Mainz. E. Honée relates the composition of this commission, »der große Ausschuß,« and the goals set for it, in *Der Libel des Hieronymus Vehus zum Augsburger Reichstag 1530* (Münster 1988), 55f.

project of a colloquy on the controverted doctrines and practices with the aim of establishing greater agreement.[32]

In the first phase of the August negotiations, the Catholics urged the non-theological consideration of the likelihood of war, bloodshed, and destruction, if the Lutherans did not recant their errors. Charles V, they intimated, would not be derelict in his duty as guardian of the Church in the West. The seventeen promised as well that if agreement on doctrine were attained, then reform of abuses could come up for deliberation and common decision.[33] Responding to the Lutheran appeal to conscience, Joachim, Margrave of Brandenburg, spoke for the seventeen in warning that this only leads to schism and the multiplication of sects, much to the detriment of the Church. The pointed question was posed whether the Lutheran theologians and preachers deserved to have more influence in the formation of the consciences of their rulers than the teachings and ordinances of the holy and universal Church. The dissenting leaders should take care not to be led astray.[34] Thus, this side evinced notable concern for authority, unity, and broad consensus.

But the Lutherans retorted that their position, formulated in the written Confession they had submitted, rested on solid biblical arguments, while the *Confutatio* had not been given them for reflective study of its validity. For them to change at this point would be to shift from firm ground to sandy uncertainty. And some future deliberation on abuses held little attraction, since they had already realized the needed reforms in notable areas.[35] If the present dissension is lamentable, the blame falls on those who omitted holding synods for the supervision of preaching and on the bishops who neglected their duty of regulating worship and devotional practice.[36]

After such counter-statements, the Reformation party broached the idea of a colloquy on specific doctrinal, ecclesiastical, and ritual issues. The idea had come from Melanchthon in his memorandum of around August 12 on a forum in

---

[32] Tetleben, *Protokoll*, 103f, 108-117; Förstemann, *Urkundenbuch*, 2, 183-191, 201-217. Meetings of the seventeen with the Lutheran princes and their advisers, e.g. Chancellor Brück of Saxony, were held on August 7, 9, 11, and 13, with the days between given to each side's preparation of proposals and responses.

[33] Opening statement of the seventeen. Tetleben, *Protokoll*, 103.

[34] Intervention by Joachim, in the name of the seventeen, on August 11. Förstemann, *Urkundenbuch*, 2, 188-191.

[35] Ibid, 183-187, esp. 184.

[36] Ibid. 213f. H. Lutz observed that the German bishops of this time, as a body, were so enmeshed in feudal power structures and financial arrangements as to be unsusceptible to real reform – in contrast with the Spanish bishops of the same age, with whom Charles V had just had seven years' contact. »Kaiser, Reich und Christenheit: Zur weltgeschichtlichen Würdigung des Augsburger Reichstages 1530,« in Iserloh and Hallensleben, eds., *Confessio Augustana und Confutatio*, 11-13, 21-24.

which Lutheran orthodoxy would be demonstrated and at least interim tolerance gained for the reformed configuration of the church's life. Campeggio might be persuaded to use his dispensing power, if only a dialogue of explanation and mutual understanding could dissipate the accusations of heresy. On August 14 this proposal was included in the report of the seventeen to the full assembly of Catholic Estates, which then approved naming a smaller body which would include some jurists and theologians and would deal with a similar body named by the Lutheran princes.

The Second Phase of Dialogue

On the evening of August 14, Charles V consulted Cardinal Campeggio about the proposed new form of discussion and with his agreement gave approval for the formation of two commissions of seven members who would represent and speak for each of the major religious parties of the Diet. The competency of the commissions was strictly consultative and the results of their work to narrow down differences and formulate agreements would have to be approved both by the respective groups of the Estates and by Charles V himself, who would act only in concert with the papal legate. Meetings of the groups of seven were held on six consecutive days, August 16-21, followed by separate reporting sessions on August 22. For the colloquy, each side mandated two princes, two high-ranking officials with legal expertise, and three theologians for dialogue on specific controverted issues of doctrine and religious practice.[37]

The first two days of the colloquy, devoted to the twenty-one doctrinal articles of the Augsburg Confession went amazingly well. The Council of Nürnberg heard from its envoys to the Diet that on August 16 the tone was friendly and peaceable, with the Catholic side behaving well. Eck and Melanchthon had begun on occasion to collide in heated argument, but the princes forced them to keep

---

[37] Tetleben, *Protokoll*, 117-119; F.W. Schirrmacher, ed., *Briefe und Acten zu der Geschichte des Religionsgespräches zu Marburg 1529 und des Reichstages zu Augsburg 1530* (Gotha 1876), 211-213, 216-223, 229-240. The Catholics chose Duke Heinrich of Braunschweig and Bishop Christoph von Stadion of Augsburg, the Cologne chancellor, Bernhard Hagen, and the Chancellor of Baden, Hieronymus Vehus (spokesman), and the theologians Johann Eck, Johann Cochlaeus, and Conrad Wimpina. When Charles V commissioned Duke Heinrich to chase down the departed Philipp of Hesse, Duke Georg of Albertine Saxony took Heinrich's place. The Lutherans were Prince Johann Friedrich of Saxony and Margrave Georg of Brandenburg-Ansbach, the Saxon Chancellor Gregor Brück (spokesman) and Chancellor Sebastian Heller of Ansbach, and the theologians Philip Melanchthon, Johann Brenz, and Erhard Schnepf of Hesse. Fatefully, no member represented Nürnberg and the other cities, by now six in number, on the Lutheran side. The Catholic spokesman, H. Vehus, has been treated biographically in H. Immekötter, *Hieronymus Vehus Jurist and Humanist der Reformationszeit* (Münster 1982). Vehus's precious work of recording the proceedings is treated in the extensive introduction to E. Honée, *Der Libell des Hieronymus Vehus zum Augsburger Reichstag 1530* (Münster 1988), a study nicely condensed by the author in »Hieronymus Vehus. Seine Vermittlerrolle während der Augsburger Einigungsverhandlungen,« in R. Decot, ed., *Vermittlungsversuche auf dem Augsburger Reichstage 1530* (Stuttgart 1989), 29-49.

on track toward interpreting Lutheran faith and doctrine in a mutually acceptable manner.[38] Campeggio wrote to Rome on the 20th that, contrary to his own misgivings before the colloquy, good results had emerged so far, with the Lutherans turning back to the truth and the number of serious differences being considerably reduced.[39]

With historical hindsight, one can point to some causes of the initial successes of the colloquy at Augsburg. Shortly before the formation of the two commissions of seven, a memorandum by the Saxon theologians, Melanchthon, Spalatin, Jonas, and Agricola, had insistently reminded Elector Johann of his Christian and princely duty to seek peace by all possible means. On the one hand, the religious divisions have already occasioned mob violence and could lead to yet more disorder. On the other hand, a settlement would benefit immensely the spread of the true doctrine of justification and of Christ's Gospel. With peace, the needed discipline can be imposed on the common people. So, for their own later peace of conscience, the Lutherans must leave no means unexplored which can lead to peace. With steadfastness concerning the primary doctrines on faith and works, Christian freedom, and the meaning of the Lord's Supper, all as set forth in the Confession, they should reduce their practical demands to the minimum allowable by Scripture and the good of souls. They should be ready to accept a degree of public conformity in ritual matters and a restoration of episcopal supervision over priests, over marriage cases, and over the discipline of excommunication against public sinners. The Emperor could well be asked to determine the disposition of former monastic houses and properties.[40]

While the Lutherans pondered the imperatives connected with public peace and Christian instruction, Johann Eck re-examined their profession of faith and apologia for reformed rites and structures. A memorandum written between August 8 and 13 reveals his readiness to think beyond the *Confutatio* of August 3. On sin, justification, and merit, Eck indicates some ways of interpreting the Lutheran position in an acceptable manner: for instance, by specifying that justifying faith is faith active in love. On sacramental penance, he admits that part of the dispute is little more than a terminological difference. CA 25 had dissented from the obligation to make a complete enumeration of one's sins in confession, but this, of course, has to be understood as applying to the sins one is conscious

---

[38] CR 2, 288.

[39] *Nuntiaturberichte*, ed. Müller, 1, 115.

[40] CR 2, 281-285; Schirrmacher, *Briefe und Acten*, 287-291; Förstemann, *Urkundenbuch*, 2, 244-248. For the date of approximately August 14 for this document, see Immenkötter, *Um die Einheit im Glauben*, 29, n.4. Immenkötter remarks incisively that the final recommendation on property betrays the political *naïveté* of the theologians composing this memorandum. Anton Schindling gives an informative account of the application of former church and monastic properties to new purposes in cities where the Reformation scored successes. »Die Reformation in den Reichsstädten und die Kirchengüter: Strassburg, Nürnberg und Frankfurt im Vergleich,« in J. Sydow, ed., *Bürgerschaft und Kirche* (Sigmaringen 1980), 67-80.

of having committed. Lutheran ecclesiology needs more explicitation on the Church as a *corpus mixtum*, and its doctrine of the saints, denying their invocation, stands in serious need of correction. Eck is ready to argue for the sacrifice of the mass and religious vows, but he makes clear that communion under both forms, married priests, and the mitigation of certain church laws could be accepted under conditions one could work out.[41] Thus, a Catholic leader, concentrating on Melanchthon's irenic Confession of 1530, was well prepared for the give-and-take of dialogue in the service of broader agreement both on the primary articles and on the *forma ecclesiae*.

As the dialogue began on 16 August, Chancellors Vehus and Brück expressed their respective understandings of the limited mandate given the two commissions and agreed to deal peaceably with the issues. The Lutheran side proposed following the method of an article-by-article comparison of their Confession with the imperial *Confutatio*, but they then agreed to a simpler procedure, one less likely to ignite disputes, of reviewing just their Augsburg Confession. Articles 1-12 were discussed in the later part of the first meeting, and on August 17 the commission worked through to Article 21 and thus completed its review of Lutheran faith and doctrine.[42]

In the scattered documentation of the Augsburg Diet of 1530, reports abound on the outcome of the first two days of doctrinal dialogue.[43] Hieronymus Vehus presented the results to Charles V according to a four-part scheme: on eight articles, immediate and full agreement; seven articles required discussion and

---

[41] Eck examined the Augsburg Confession article by article in »Iudicium doctoris Eccii de Augustana confessione,« for the Archbishop of Mainz and Duke Georg, ed. Schirrmacher, *Briefe und Acten*, 203-208. G. Müller dates this between August 8 and 15 in »Johann Eck und die Confessio Augustana. Zwei unbekannte Aktenstücke vom Augsburger Reichstag 1530,« *Quellen und Forschungen aus italienischen Archiven und Bibliotheken* 38 (1958), 216-218. A second study of the CA by Eck, »Oblata confessione Augustensi Protestantium Eckius pacis amans hanc offert concordiam,« was edited G. Müller (ibid., 225-239), who maintained it was prepared for Campeggio at the same time. But later scholarship has concluded that Eck wrote this during the Diet of Worms in December 1540. See G. Pfeilschifter, *Acta Reformationis Catholicae*, 3 (Regensburg 1968), 304.

[42] Förstemann, *Urkundenbuch*, 2, 220-229; Tetleben, *Protokoll*, 124f; Vehus, »Acta der sieben,« ed. E. Honée, in *Der Libell des Hieronymus Vehus*, 208-221. Also, »Acta septem deputatorum,« in the partial edition of S. Ehses, *Römische Quartalschrift* 19 (1905), Section Geschichte, 132-135. The latter report, sent to Rome by Campeggio, says the Lutherans were told, »debeant ipsi proponere, in quibus articulis a nobis dissentirent, item in quibus punctis conscientiae eorum gravarentur, et quae media hic haberi possent, quibus nihilominus catholicae ecclesiae unitas conservaretur« (p. 132). There appears here a sensitivity to Lutheran appeals to the dictates of conscience. Soon the evaluation of *media* for preserving ecclesial unity will prove decisive for the outcome of the colloquy.

[43] Especially valuable is Vehus's report, »Acta der sieben,« ed. Honée, *Der Libell*, 213-221. In addition to the other texts mentioned in the previous note, reports are also in Förstemann, *Urkundenbuch*, 2, 230-233 (by Brück); in CR 2, 299f (Melanchthon to Luther, 22 Aug.); in H. Vehus's report for Charles V, »Sumarischer usszug,« ed. E. Honée, *Der Libell*, 299-301; and in a »Summa tractatus,« in Schirrmacher, *Briefe und Acten*, 218-222.

further Lutheran elucidation in order to bring about agreement; on three articles, discussion was postponed for later treatment in the context of the reform of abuses; finally, on three articles, considerable agreement was reached, but unresolved differences remain.[44]

The most startling result of this dialogue is undoubtedly the nearly complete consensus on the doctrine of justification, which emerged from the exchanges and elucidation of Articles 4, 5, 6 and 20 of the Augsburg Confession. Eck, with Wimpina seconding, had insisted that justifying faith is faith active in love, and that the graced actions of the justified person are meritorious before God. Melanchthon was open to further specification on faith, but maintained that *meritum* had a checkered history because of scholastic theses on the congruous merit of justification and theories of meriting forgiveness by acts of penitential satisfaction. Eck retorted with a small barrage of arguments against *sola fide*, in the face of which Melanchthon stated his case for faith alone, urging for example that it properly directs one's attention away from self to God's grace. Eck maintained that charity *is* God's grace. Brenz explained that 'sola' only meant to exclude merit of forgiveness, not the sacraments and not the good works done by the righteous out of loving gratitude. Eck then proposed an inclusive formula: »Justification or forgiveness of sins is had formally by sanctifying grace and faith, but instrumentally by the word and the sacraments.« This clarification, with faith not standing alone, the Lutheran side acknowledged as a possible articulation of their faith. But the question of merit was not resolved.[45]

Further agreements emerged on ministry, on the church's inclusion of sinners as members, and on the eucharistic presence of Christ. But Article 12, on the component parts of sacramental penance, gave rise to a first unresolved issue. The Lutheran two-part account would combine contrition, emphasizing fear and felt sorrow, with faith – that is, assurance of forgiveness through absolution. The Catholics urged the traditional three-part analysis: contrition, absolution, and satisfaction. After discussion, the Lutherans found they could live with a three-

---

[44] Vehus, »Sumarischer usszug,« ed. Honée, *Der Libell*, 299-301.

[45] For the give-and-take of dialogue, Förstemann, *Urkundenbuch*, 2, 223-227. The consensus formula is from the »Summa tractatus«: »Iustificatio seu remissio peccatorum fiat per gratiam gratum facientem et fidem formaliter, per verbum et sacramenta instrumentaliter« (Schirrmacher, *Briefe und Acten*, 219; also, Vehus, »Acta der sieben,« ed. Honée, *Der Libell*, 214f). Melanchthon wrote to Luther on 22 Aug. that Eck had not condemned *sola fide*, but had argued that it confused and upset lay people. They had agreed to say we are justified by grace and faith, »sed ille stultus non intelligit vocabulum gratiae« (CR 2, 300). V. Pfnür has made the fundamental study of this discussion, with all its antecedents in the development of Lutheran theology and its sequel in which the agreement did not hold. *Einig in der Rechtfertigungslehre?* (Wiesbaden, 1970). H. Scheible recently contributed to a deeper understanding of the Augsburg dialogue on justification in his essay, »Melanchthons Auseinandersetzung mit dem Reformkatholizismus,« in R. Decot, ed., *Vermittlungsversuche auf dem Augsburger Reichstag 1530* (Stuttgart 1989), 79-82, adding a newly discovered short text by Melanchthon, written ca. July 1, 1530, that gives his main reasons for insisting that *fides* is the causal moment in justification and for not admitting *caritas* or *dilectio* as modes of justification itself. *Vermittlungsversuche*, 88f.

part account if it were open to their way of interpreting the component parts. But on satisfactory acts of penance there was continuing discord over whether they were essential or not for forgiveness.[46]

Article 20, on good works, posed no difficulty where it asserted both the necessity of good works in the life of the righteous person and that works proceeding from faith and grace do please God and lead to a recompense from him. But the Lutherans would not revoke their protest against ascribing merit to such works and placing any trust in them.[47]

Finally, there were the saints, whose example Article 21 of the Augsburg Confession had commended. But prayer invoking the saints for help was declared to have no biblical warrant and to derogate from Christ's pre-eminent role as heavenly advocate. Discussion brought out that the Lutherans would even admit that the saints are active intercessors for us in heaven and that this should be celebrated on their feast days. However, for direct prayer to the saints, the Lutherans maintained reserve, at least in not accepting the practice for themselves because of Scripture's silence and the many abuses in popular devotions.[48]

How are we to assess the initial achievement of the committee of fourteen at Augsburg in 1530? It is tempting to construct, on the three remaining differences, the edifice of a fundamental *dissensus* over the human person's role in his or her own salvation and in the salvation of others. Do not the differences over merit and satisfactory works reveal profound differences that the »peace offensive« of mid-1530 momentarily obscured? To be sure, the two sides were really different in the religious attitudes each wanted to inculcate, as the Catholics insisted on grace giving a new dignity to the actions of the righteous person, while the Lutherans stressed looking away from self in exclusive dependence on God and

---

[46] »Summa tractatus,« in Schirrmacher, *Briefe und Acten*, p. 220; Vehus, »Acta der sieben,« ed. Honée, *Der Libell*, 216-218; more concisely, Vehus, »Sumarischer usszug,« ibid., 300. W. Köhler edited a note, possibly by Melanchthon, which interprets the three parts of penance in an evangelical manner, e.g. »in confessione magis respiciendum est ad fidem absolutionis quam ad ipsum opus confessionis.« »Brentiana und andere Reformatoria,« Part IX, *Archiv für Reformationsgeschichte* 21 (1924), 99.

[47] »Summa tractatus,« ed. Schirrmacher, *Briefe und Acten*, 221; Vehus, »Acta der sieben,« ed. Honée, *Der Libell*, 219; Vehus, »Sumarischer usszug,« ibid., 300, where a comment is added to the effect that the difference here is merely verbal: »Est mere contencio verbalis, ist ein worttkampff.« Melanchthon's report to Luther, written on August 22, relates that Eck in fact ascribed very little to merit: »quamquam est exiguum quod merito tribuit, nos tamen ne illud quidem recipimus« (CR 2, 300).

[48] »Summa tractatus,« ed. Schirrmacher, *Briefe und Acten*, 222; Vehus, »Acta der sieben,« ed. Honée, *Der Libell*, 220f; Vehus »Sumarischer usszug,« ibid., 300f; W. Köhler also found brief notes by Melanchthon on what could and could not be ascribed to the saints (»Brentiana und andere Reformatoria,« 101f). Luther related in 1531 that in the discussion Johann Brenz denied, against Eck, that prayers to the saints had a basis in Scripture. *Warnung an seine lieben Deutschen*, WA 30III, 312,19 – a reference given by M. Brecht, »Johann Brenz auf dem Augsburger Reichstag 1530,« in R. Decot, ed., *Vermittlungsversuche auf dem Augsburger Reichstag 1530* (Stuttgart 1989), 20.

his word of absolution. Still, some of those close to the proceedings did not think that the parties were deceived about their agreement on the various inclusive formulae. A report apparently prepared for Charles V expressed hope for eventual agreement on the relation between forgiveness and satisfaction for past sins.[49] John Eck stated later in August that the differences ascertained early in the colloquy were more verbal than real.[50]

On the Lutheran side, the discussion showed their movement away from blanket condemnation of invoking the saints, a view that would have prevented them from living in ecclesial concord with others who pray to the saints. In effect, the colloquy on Article 21 ended with a Lutheran *non possumus nos*, which posed the question whether a rite could be tolerated in the Catholic Church which omitted liturgical prayers to saints. We are reminded that participants in religious colloquy do not aim at remaking the mentality of the partner in their own image, but rather at discovering heretofore obscured points of contact and deeper grounds for compatibility and *communio*.[51]

Three doctrinal articles had been passed over, since they seemed to belong more logically among the practical reforms for which Augsburg Confession, Articles 22-28, had offered a potent apologia. Article 11, on confession of sin, was to be included under Article 25, with its treatment of the discipline of confession, esteem for absolution, and ministry of the keys, as these were taught and practiced in Lutheran parishes. Article 14, on reserving ministry exclusively to those »regularly called,« would be treated with Article 23 on the marriage of priests. And Article 15, on the binding power of ecclesiastical ordinances, such as those on feast days, fasting, and vows, was to come up in the context of Articles 26, 27, and 28, on law-making, religious vows, and episcopal authority.[52] Difficult issues concerning the *forma ecclesiae* and the norms of its institutional life were to dominate discussion in the last four days of the colloquy of the fourteen. Would this further discussion bring more moments of *rapprochement* and a more limited and workable formulation of the differences?

The two sides agreed initially to treat the Lutheran reforms as a global whole, presumably because a common issue underlay all of them, namely, the rightful

---

[49] »... tamen speratur ad concordiam« (Förstemann, *Urkundenbuch*, 2, 234, n.12). Eck had said earlier that the difference over satisfaction is »lis verbalis non realis differentia« (»Iudicium,« for the Archbishop of Mainz and Duke Georg, in Schirrmacher, *Briefe und Acten*, 205).

[50] Förstemann, *Urkundenbuch*, 2, 292. Earlier Eck felt that agreement could be reached on merit if the Lutherans would introduce another *solum*, by saying merit arises »solum ex Deo, ex misericordia Dei, ex gratia assistente, preveniente et cooperante« (»Iudicium,« ed. Schirrmacher, *Briefe und Acten*, 203).

[51] The two previous paragraphs extend the considerations offered by V. Pfnür, *Einig in der Rechtfertigungslehre?* pp. 267-270, where one finds cited further utterances of those (even Johann Cochlaeus) who believed the colloquy did ascertain a wide-ranging agreement on justification.

[52] »Summa tractatus,« ed. Schirrmacher, *Briefe und Acten*, 220f.

and advantageous use of law-making authority in the Church. The particular reforms of alleged abuses concerned the introduction of communion under both forms (Augsburg Confession, Article 22), marriage of priests (Art. 23), a reformed, communitarian, and evangelical celebration of the Lord's Supper (Art. 24), the discipline of confession with emphatic instruction on absolution (Art. 25), non-meritorious observance of »human traditions« such as the fasting laws (Art. 26), restoration of a regime of freedom under divine law for monks and religious (Art. 27), and the proper scope of episcopal governance of the churches (Art. 28). In his memorandum of around August 12, Melanchthon proposed that the Lutherans should seek toleration of the changes they had introduced concerning these matters, since none of the changes goes contrary to the divinely ordered structure of the Church and its life. What is *de iure divino* remains fully intact in Lutheran territories, since the new practices only affect a number of abuses introduced by papal law.[53]

So on August 18 the Lutheran seven submitted a written proposal that they should be allowed communion under both forms, marriage for their clergy, and the reformed celebration of mass, at least until a general council could make further regulations. To maintain unity and good order, the Lutheran leaders would work out agreements with the bishops on the other articles, namely, on fasting, ceremonies, and the details of the exercise of episcopal authority. This would ensure clerical obedience, episcopal jurisdiction, and a good degree of conformity in doctrine and practice.[54] Thus the Lutheran group placed on the table the earlier Saxon design of a negotiated settlement, with the implication that their *forma ecclesiae* could well include real authority for bishops, if only recognition be given to the reforms they felt were mandated by Scripture and the requirements of godly worship in the Church.

The initial Catholic response, given orally, charged the Lutherans with failing to speak directly to the key issue of episcopal authority and offering no assurances on the restoration of church properties recently confiscated. After the Lutherans conferred among themselves, Chancellor Gregor Brück reaffirmed the primacy of the first articles, because the bishops' past connivance in abuses concerning clerical morals and the mass, along with opposition to the Gospel, had brought about the collapse of their authority. A fruitful discussion of

---

[53] Förstemann, *Urkundenbuch*, 2, 239. My earlier study found the term »abuse/*Missbrauch*,« as the *Confessio* uses it, burdened with ambiguity, half-concealing five distinct modes of critical analysis. The »abuses« include actions the recent tradition interprets wrongly, the marginalization of central catechetical themes, hierarchical overreach in governance, episcopal malpractice, and institutional practices that must be contested. See Study 10, above in this collection, pp. 256-260.

[54] Förstemann, *Urkundenbuch*, 2, 249; Tetleben, *Protokoll*, 125f; »Acta septem deputatorum,« ed. Ehses, *Römische Quartalschrift*, 19 (1905), Section Geschichte, p. 135; . The Nürnberg envoys had been apprised of the content of the proposal of Aug. 18 and had agreed to it as a starting point in the colloquy on reforms, but they made no binding commitment to it as a design for settlement (CR 2, 290f).

bishops and their power to make laws must build on a commitment to reform the clergy and worship. The Catholics conferred, and Vehus voiced their conviction that the latter points were decisive; agreement on them could lead to easy solutions concerning clergy and worship. To overcome the impasse between demands for reforms and insistence on hierarchy, the groups agreed to exchange full written expositions of their respective proposals in documents which came to be called *media concordiae*.[55]

With one Lutheran proposal already made, the Catholic side was able by the next morning, August 19, to produce and submit a document. A new Lutheran statement was finished on the morning of August 20 and submitted that afternoon.[56] These two proposals remained fundamental for the rest of the August colloquy, even with the several elucidations and adaptations given after August 19-20.

The Catholic *media* did include the substance of the concessions that Cardinal Campeggio was empowered to make, namely, the chalice for the laity and a married diocesan clergy. But these were to be granted by Pope and Emperor as dispensations hedged in with extensive restrictions. Furthermore, the Catholic proposal began by firmly stating that episcopal authority must be maintained and respected. No place was left for independent reforming activity by civil rulers. After referring to a council for the definitive regulation of the communion rite and marriage for priests, the proposal concluded, in words surely not approved wholeheartedly by Campeggio, with a ringing call for early convocation of a general council, to be held in Germany for the reform of the Church in head and members.

Among the stipulations hemming in the concession of the chalice, the Catholic side called on the Lutherans to have it taught that reception under both forms is not a divine command obligating every communicant. The people should learn that the whole Christ is received even under one form and those wishing to receive communion in the traditional way should not be hindered by their clergy or others.[57] The tradition should be maintained of celebrating both community

---

[55] For the exchange on August 18 of charges and defenses: Tetleben, *Protokoll*, 125f; Förstemann, *Urkundenbuch*, 2, 236-238; »Acta septem deputatorum,« 136f; Vehus, »Acta der sieben,« ed. Honée, *Der Libell*, 222-226.

[56] Förstemann, *Urkundenbuch*, 2, 250-255 (Catholic) and 256-263 (Lutheran); Vehus, »Acta der sieben,« ed. Honée, *Der Libell*, 226-233 (Catholic), 234-241 (Lutheran). Tetleben gives Latin summaries, *Protokoll*, 126f (Catholic) and 128-130 (Lutheran). Eck and Vehus composed the Catholic *media* in the early hours of Aug. 19. The redactors of the Lutheran document are not known, but Melanchthon was surely involved. See Honée, »Die theologische Diskussion,« 70-72. E. Honée contrasts the order and structure of the two documents. *Der Libell des Hieronymus Vehus*, 72f.

[57] These points had been included in a memorial by Johann Fabri of Vienna of ten stipulations that should govern any concession of the chalice. Edited by Gerhard Müller in »Um die Einheit der Kirche. Zu den Verhandlungen über den Laienkelch während des Augsburger Reichstages 1530,« in E. Iserloh and K. Repgen, eds., *Reformata Reformanda*, Festschrift Hubert Jedin, 2 vols. (Münster 1965), 1, 425-427. Johann Cochlaeus had been very reserved toward granting the chalice, since it would signify a schismatic difference between nations professing the same faith.

and private masses, with the usual prayers of the offertory and canon. Given the decade of controversy over sacrifice, the people should hear instructions on the true meaning of offering the victim to God. Although priests who recently married will not be subject to penalties, no permission is given for further clerical marriages and the authorities should try to install celibate priests as pastors. Civil authorities are not to interfere with the regular round of observances in monastic and religious houses and they should show no tolerance for renegade religious who do not regularize their status with church authority. Religious houses now standing empty, along with their properties and income, should come under ecclesiastical administration at least until the council.

Thus the Catholic *media concordiae* of August 19 called for considerable restoration of traditional order and form in the churches in the Lutheran territories. Concessions were offered for some adaptations, but a thoroughly unconciliatory attitude can be sensed in the initial negotiating posture.

The Lutheran counterproposal was more specific on the discipline of fasting, holy days, and confession. It formulated several responses to the Catholic *media*, both warding off insinuations of negligence and already accepting some of the many conditions laid down. The document is on the whole forthcoming in the face of Catholic demands, but also fails in places to meet the stated issue directly. The Lutheran concern for public order and discipline is evident in points going beyond the Catholic statement. The Lutheran proposal of August 20 also concludes with a call for a general council of reform to be held in Germany.

The Lutheran *media* agreed not to brand wrong those receiving communion under one form or to subject communicants to a coercion alien to the Gospel. However, the fundamental rightfulness of receiving both forms will be taught in a moderate, uncontentious way, since this agrees with Christ's institution. Confession of sins is to precede reception of communion, as Article 25 of the Augsburg Confession had stated, and of course reverential handling of the sacrament will continue. But the Lutherans left room for Catholic misgivings by failing to state the concomitant presence of the whole Christ under just one form, and by making no mention of private masses. The *media* spoke vaguely of »the usual ceremonies according to Christ's institution,« in response to the Catholic insistence on the prayers of the offertory and canon with instruction on offering sacrifice.[58]

Reported by R. Bäumer in »Vermittlungsbemühungen auf dem Augsburger Reichstag,« *Theologie und Glaube* 70 (1980), 315f.
[58] Förstemann, *Urkundenbuch*, 2, 256f; Vehus, »Acta der sieben,« ed. Honée, *Der Libell*, 234f. In a copy of this document preserved in Schwäbisch Hall, Johann Brenz noted concerning confession of sins, »Absolucion ist die Zusagung des' Evangeliums.« Related by M. Brecht, »Johann Brenz auf dem Augsburger Reichstag 1530,« in R. Decot, ed., *Vermittlungsversuche auf dem Augsburger Reichstag*, 20. In a remark given in Tetleben, *Protokoll*, 128, the Lutheran proposal is censured for being »perplexum, amfibologicum et dubium,« and thus deceptive. But the Lutheran circumspect choice of words had serious motives. On Aug. 20 and 21, Melanchthon drew up memoranda critical of the Catholics for not speaking openly on the mass. If they meant »hoc opus dici sacrificium tale, quod ex opere operato mereatur aliis gratiam,« then sharp controversy must ensue. But agreement can be had if the offering is first the giving over of

The Lutheran proposal of August 20 repeated the conclusion of Article 22 of the Confession that one should judge clerical marriage as Christian and correct, all the more because of the widespread corruption of priests not given the high grace of chastity. In Lutheran territories, when the present corps of married priests starts to die out, there will be need of able and learned replacements and how will sufficient numbers be found among the celibates, especially if the bishops do their duty in suppressing concubinage? The ordered life of marriage would impose discipline upon an otherwise corrupt clergy and the coming council should consider admitting this. Monastic and religious houses still functioning will not be disturbed, but the council should consider giving greater freedom to their inmates regarding departure or remaining. The houses from which monks and religious have all departed are better left under the administration of their secular patrons, so that income from them may go to support their ex-members, pastoral ministers, and schools. The eventual council should receive a full accounting of this interim administration, but its deliberation should ponder what disposition of these matters redounds most to God's glory.[59]

The Lutheran *media concordiae* speaks clearly to the question of episcopal governance of the Church, and to the ordering of fasts and feasts. No approval, of course, is given to past episcopal failure to supervise preaching and sacramental administration, to the bishops' careless selection of ordinands, and to their neglect of firm discipline with the clergy. But pastors and preachers, in the future, should be presented for approval by the local ordinary, render him obedience, and be subject to his penalties when guilty of certain transgressions. Bishops should be unhindered in laying down excommunications in cases falling within the rightful scope of their jurisdiction, but they also should not encroach on areas properly under the governance of the secular estates. Sale of meat will be prohibited every Friday and Saturday and on eight other days of abstinence annually. The Lenten fast should be mitigated out of consideration for the poor and manual workers. However, such observances are required as a Christian pattern of good order, not as a service of God imposing a serious burden on conscience. Thirty-four holy days are listed for retention, and assurance is given that confession of sin pertains to Lutheran popular religiosity, albeit with stress on the consolation imparted by absolution.[60]

Christ's consolation to the believer which then leads to thanksgiving by the whole Church. Thus the prayers of the canon, which say »nos offerimus corpus,« need discriminating review. The text is given by W. Köhler in »Brentiana und andere Reformatoria,« Part XII, *Archiv für Reformationsgeschichte* 24 (1927), 295-297. The dating is given by H. Scheible, *Melanchthons Briefwechsel*, 1, 427.

[59] Förstemann, *Urkundenbuch*, 2, 257-259; Vehus, »Acta der sieben,« ed. Honée, *Der Libell*, 235-237.

[60] Förstemann, *Urkundenbuch*, 2, 259-263; Vehus, »Acta der sieben,« ed. Honée, *Der Libell*, 238-241.

An exchange of comments followed in the latter part of the session of August 20 and all through that of the next day. The two groups of seven reduced their differences, but some intractable problems remained. Furthermore, the language became acrimonious on occasion as charges were levelled and demands made which touched the lived religiosity of the colloquy's participant members.

After receiving the Lutheran *media* of August 20, the Catholic seven conferred apart for an hour. Then Chancellor Vehus gave voice to their dissatisfaction with the Lutheran proposal on the rite of communion and the mass.[61] It had not specified whether their required confession of sin before communion was confession as traditionally practiced, with enumeration of all of one's sins. Further, the Lutherans made no commitment to affirming the rightfulness of receiving communion under one form, a teaching which after all the Council of Basel had required of the Hussites when it granted them the chalice. Vehus warmed to his subject, presenting arguments serially much as had been done in books by Eck and Cochlaeus during the 1520s. Brück would later claim that the disputatious manner went against the guidelines for the colloquy. Vehus claimed that the Lutheran position on communion under both forms was tantamount to reserving rectitude for only their own small group while condemning all other nations and all their ancestors. Adopting an argument more common to the Lutherans, he claimed that their position is sure to disturb and burden the consciences of many good people who have long followed the rite set down by the Church. The Lutheran leaders should encourage their theologians to imitate St Augustine, who was not ashamed to publish his *Retractationes*.

On the mass, Vehus was more succinct. The Lutheran *media* had made no commitment to the offertory and canon of the mass or to interpreting the meaning of sacrifice in popular instruction. Furthermore, they gave no assurances that private masses would not be outlawed. After questioning the Lutherans as to whether they were ready to replace their present married priests with celibates, as the Catholic proposal had laid down, Vehus concluded. He had made clear that the Lutheran proposal as it then stood could not be further transmitted to the larger body of the Estates, who would surely find injurious the Lutheran rejection, or even condemnation, of religious rites they practiced as traditional.[62]

Brück fended off Vehus's criticism by referring to the commission's agreement to work out *media concordiae*, not to engage in contentious argument. The Lutherans had set down, after conscientious review, that to which they could commit themselves, and their document should be taken seriously. Disputation is not a proper response. If wrangling argument is to be reintroduced, the Lutherans will not be found weak or unprepared, especially regarding their

---

61 E. Honée studied Vehus's critique in detail in »Die theologische Diskussion,« 75-79.
62 Förstemann, *Urkundenbuch*, 2, 265f; Vehus, »Acta der sieben,« ed. E. Honée, *Der Libell*, 242-246; »Acta septem deputatorum,« ed. Ehses, *Römische Quartalschrift* 19 (1905) Section Geschichte, 139-141.

communion rite. Brück reminded the Catholics that they were facing a group which had worked out a solid position on the Lord's Supper – a reference to the recent long argument with Zwingli. He gave assurances that any Protestant irreverence toward Christ's body was something the Lutheran leaders lamented deeply. After a brief account of Lutheran confession as telling the priest the major matters burdening one's conscience so that he could give counsel and absolution, Brück proposed that the session should end, to give his side time to consider what more might be said about the mass and clerical marriage.[63] Vehus agreed to close the meeting, but gave a parting admonition that the Lutherans should reconsider the approach to Holy Communion by which they in effect condemn all who have communicated under one form and who continue to observe this rite.

The last meeting of the two commissions of seven, on August 21, began with Vehus offering a brief resumé of the shortcomings the Catholic side found in the Lutheran proposal on communion. The essential lacunae were narrowed down to three: the concomitant presence of the whole Christ under only one form, the basic rectitude of reception under one form, and the assurance that pastors in Lutheran domains would readily accede to the wishes of persons desiring to receive communion under one form.[64]

In the discussion, the Lutherans first reaffirmed their own seriousness about the proposal submitted on August 20, and indicated that if the Catholic seven would not transmit that document to the Estates then what remained was to appeal for a decision by a General Council. However, an oral elucidation was given to the effect that Lutheran doctrine does not divide Christ in a Nestorian manner, but teaches the presence of the whole Christ, body and blood, humanity and divinity, even under one form.[65]

A lengthy exchange on the rite of communion followed. The Lutheran side submitted a prepared sheet explaining that they did not mean to condemn people past and present who received communion under one form »in certain cases of necessity.« The institutional provision by Christ does oblige both priests and laity to partake of both bread and cup. But when this precept of Christ cannot be observed, then those receiving under one form are not guilty of any wrongdoing.[66]

---

[63] Förstemann, *Urkundenbuch*, 2, 267. Vehus, »Acta der sieben,« ed. Honée, *Der Libell*, 246f; »Acta septem deputatorum,« 141f.

[64] Förstemann, *Urkundenbuch*, 263, for the reference to the brief resumé; but for the contents we have Vehus, »Acta der sieben,« ed. Honée, *Der Libell*, 249.

[65] Förstemann, *Urkundenbuch*, 2, 268f. Melanchthon had jotted down a brief account of Nestorius's view of Christ's two persons, and recommended that the Lutheran side speak of the whole Christ in the sacrament so as to leave no room for suspicion that they divided Christ (ibid., 271f). Actually, Zwingli was the sixteenth-century theologian most given to emphasis on the different components of the one Christ.

[66] Johann Brenz had prepared a short memorandum on the rite with both forms, stating that it is a »ceremoniale preceptum dispensabile in quibusdam casibus necessitatis,« and the Lutheran elucidation took this over (Vehus, »Acta der sieben,« ed. Honée, *Der Libell*, 250). But if the

A long argument ensued over the meaning of a »case of necessity« excusing one from blame for receiving under one form. In the give-and-take of explanation, questioning, and further elucidation, the Catholic side somehow came to think the Lutherans were moving away from their insistence on the obligatory character of reception under both forms. If this be the case, the Lutherans should not simply refrain from condemning users of one form, but also have it taught openly that this traditional rite is correct. The Catholic seven went apart to confer and brought back a written paragraph stating what the means of agreement seemed to be in the present, more advanced, stage of dialogue.[67]

The new proposal would have the Lutherans, in the interim until the next council, teaching that neither rite is prescribed by divine command. The Catholics would undertake to instruct people on the rightfulness of the Lutheran rite, once permission for the chalice is given them. Thus, all imputations of blame would be ruled out. Also, the Lutherans are to teach, as agreed, that the whole Christ is present under each form, and their pastors are to refuse no one seeking communion under one form.

The Lutheran seven needed no time for reflection or consultation, but could respond straightway with a sharp rejection of this latest Catholic proposal. The Lutherans can confess the whole Christ under even one form, but this is all.[68] The text showed that the Catholic seven had heedlessly stumbled into challenging the fundamental Lutheran belief that a divine command, clearly stated in Scripture (*Bibite ex hoc omnes*), governed the administration and reception of Holy Communion. On such a clear imperative there could be no fudging by speaking of a neutral matter left to the Church to regulate, whatever leniency might be appropriate in judging ordinary people.

Further discussion on August 21 took up the canon of the mass, but the tone deteriorated and the sides let their annoyance with each other be felt. At one point the Lutherans listed three objections to the canon: it is wrongly made a mortal sin to omit it from mass, the canon makes the mass a sacrifice, and it includes the invocation of saints. Some progress could be made on the last point since the saints of the canon are commemorated, not invoked for aid. But the Lutherans remained firm in the face of a brief attempt to explain the »mysterial« or representative nature of eucharistic sacrifice.[69] There was no time for further discussion of conditions for a relaxation of celibacy, but discussion was on a

---

necessity arises by reason of an abusive law of the unreformed Church, then a serious accusation remains, even if those coerced into the abusive practice are excused from guilt.

[67] The paragraph, in effect a new Catholic *media*, is given in Förstemann, *Urkundenbuch*, 274, and in Vehus, »Acta der sieben,« ed. Honée, *Der Libell*, 251f.

[68] The report on this decisive moment in the colloquy: »Aber derselb begrif Ist Irn gnaden und zugewannten abgewendt, unnd um glimpfs willen.« Förstemann, *Urkundenbuch*, 270. A dishonorable retreat from duty before God had been proposed.

[69] Schirrmacher, *Briefe und Acten*, 235.

better level in the final moments as each side asked the other to report on the dialogue to their principals and to present the *media* and their amendments in a good light, so as to promote peace and unity.⁷⁰

On August 22 separate meetings were held in which each group of seven reported to the larger groups of Estates and counsellors on the six days of dialogue. Sometime during the day, the Elector Johann had four wagons packed and he sent part of his entourage back to Saxony. This became known to the Catholic Estates, who quickly sent the Elector a message begging him to remain at the Diet and to allow dialogue to continue in the hope of reconciling the opposed demands that faced each other as the fourteen had concluded.⁷¹ A petition also went from the Catholic Estates to the Emperor requesting his approval for the naming of a smaller commission to continue working toward an acceptable design for unity.⁷²

In addition to the reports to those in Augsburg who had commissioned the fourteen, other reports were composed on August 22 or shortly thereafter, which cast light on the situation as the second phase of dialogue ended. The allies of Electoral Saxony had reacted critically over not being consulted on the specific concessions offered by the Lutheran seven in the *media* of August 20. The delegates of Nürnberg and Hesse wrote immediately to their respective superiors for instructions on lines to be followed in any further negotiations.⁷³ Melanchthon wrote on August 23 to inform leaders in Reutlingen, so that they could articulate a position on the apparently central question of episcopal jurisdiction.⁷⁴

---

⁷⁰ Förstemann, *Urkundenbuch*, 2, 270f.
⁷¹ The Nürnberg envoys reported the departures in their dispatch of August 23 (CR 2, 302). On the 26th they told of the Catholic Estates' request that Johann should continue the dialogue (ibid., 312). Tetleben also recorded the fact of the appeal to the Saxon Elector (*Protokoll*, 130f).
⁷² Ibid., 131.
⁷³ The Nürnberg delegates had protested at the reporting session of August 22. If the colloquy continues, such proposals are to be agreed upon before being submitted to the other side. The Nürnberg council was asked to review the *media* of the 20th after the fact (CR 2, 301). The Hessian report and request for instruction are implied by Philip of Hesse's responses of Aug. 29 (ibid., 323-327). On the ensuing protests by the Nürnberg Council and Philip, see Immenkötter, *Um die Einheit im Glauben*, 51-54. Nürnberg's response was that the Protestant *media* makes unacceptable concessions on restoring religious and monastic houses, on obligatory confession before Holy Communion, on fasting and abstinence laws, on the saints, and especially on restoring jurisdictional authority to the bishops. The Nürnberg memorial is edited by H.-U. Hofmann in Andreas Osiander, *Gesamtausgabe*, eds. G. Müller & G. Seebaß, v. 4 (Gütersloh 1981), 145-153.
⁷⁴ Letter to Matthew Alber (CR 2, 302f). W. Gussmann relates the sharply negative reaction of Alber and his colleagues in Reutlingen to the main concessions under discussion. See *Quellen und Forschungen zur Geschichte des augsburgischen Glaubensbekenntnisses*, 2 vols. in 3 (Leipzig-Berlin 1911-31), 1/1, 158-162. For the text of Alber's draft response, ibid., 1/2, 315-319.

Melanchthon also related the outcome of the colloquy of the fourteen with accustomed lucidity to Luther in a letter of August 22.[75] On both forms, the other side made a concession contingent on the Lutherans saying there was no precept that binds people to one rite of communion. While excuses can be made for those to whom only one form is offered, Melanchthon had refused to deny the Lord's imposition of a binding precept: *Ego non potui hoc recipere.* One may not be obliged to receive communion, but are not those who do receive then bound to the rite instituted by Christ? Would Luther please state his considered view of this particular question? The colloquy, Melanchthon reports, did not have a real exchange over the mass, vows, and celibacy. The other side simply laid down conditions on these points which the Lutherans rejected. Still the Lutheran seven, out of a sense of the urgency of preventing war, did offer to obey the bishops, accept their jurisdiction, and introduce the »ordinary ceremonies.«

Also on August 22, Elector Johann formally asked Luther's opinion on positions to be taken in further negotiations.[76] Copies of the two *media* of August 19 and 20 were sent to the Reformer, along with three questions on specific demands. (1) Can the Lutheran side admit that communion under one form is not a matter of precept? The other side insists on this, arguing that it is needed for maintaining order among their own people, that is, by a Lutheran admission of the licitness of the rite practiced in Catholic lands. (2) Can the Lutheran authorities withdraw their prohibition of private masses? This would not be an order reinstituting such masses, but only the admission that princely authority does not extend to such a matter of liturgical practice. (3) Can the traditional canon of the mass also be permitted, along with appropriate explanatory comments? In effect, the wider recognition of the reformed *forma ecclesiae* came to depend on three quite specific issues of eucharistic practice and doctrine.

The Third Phase of Dialogue

From August 23 to 30, two smaller commissions of three members from each side served as the forum for Lutheran-Catholic negotiations.[77] The six met on August 24, 26, 28, and 30, devoting part of the meeting on the 28th to drafting a brief report on the latest conditions proposed by the Catholic side, but not

---

75 CR 2, 299-300.
76 WABr 12, 124f.
77 The basic sources for this phase are in Förstemann's *Urkundenbuch*, 2, 290-313, and Vehus's report, »Acta unnd handlung der dryer von gemeinen stenden verordneten,« ed. Honée, *Der Libell*, 254-280. A narrative account is given in Immenkötter, *Um die Einheit im Glauben*, 56-66, and Honée offers an analysis in *Der Libell*, 74-80. The Lutheran members of their committee of three were Chancellors Brück and Heller, and Philip Melanchthon. The Catholics were Chancellors Vehus and Hagen, and Johann Eck.

accepted by the Lutherans. On August 30 letters from Martin Luther arrived, answering questions posed to him by Melanchthon and Elector Johann, and thereby the Reformer forcefully confirmed and consolidated Protestant resistance against the latest Catholic proposal. On August 31 the Catholic Estates came to realize the intractability of the situation that had emerged, and they made this known to Charles V, which thereby signalled the end of the effort toward reconciliation begun on August 6.

The failure of the commission of six was due first to the lack of any fresh proposals from the Catholic side by which to attract the Lutherans toward more accommodations. Also, the three Lutheran spokesmen were severely restricted from offering any further concessions, especially at the behest of Lüneburg, Hesse, and Nürnberg. This resistance against further adaptations of reformed practices then took on new strength from Luther's forceful intervention. From the Protestant perspective, all that then remained was to negotiate an arrangement for peaceful coexistence, at least until the council, of groups of territories which are divided over doctrine, ritual, and church order.

A lengthy discourse by Chancellor Vehus occupied most of the first session of the six on August 24.[78] Whereas Johann Eck had urged treatment of the three unresolved doctrinal points, that is, satisfaction, merit, and invocation of the saints, Vehus insisted on attacking the larger complex of problems that had emerged in the earlier colloquy regarding the reform of abuses.

However, Vehus's actual demands on the 24th coincided both in content and in spirit with the Catholic *media concordiae* of August 19. Familiar adaptations were called for to hedge in acceptance of the Lutheran rite of communion. One result of further reflection may be found in Vehus's reference to the *dissensus* over communion as involving matters of faith, and not simply liturgical practice. He appealed to the Saxon visitation articles of 1528, with their provision of consideration for weaker consciences, as an authority for continuing to honor the request of those desiring communion under only one form.[79] Vehus specified that commitments to reverent use of the sacrament were needed because in certain cities people were receiving communion at evening celebrations of the Lord's Supper without concern for the eucharistic fast from food and drink. On the mass itself, Vehus repeated the demand put forward on August 19 for use of the traditional canon, along with instructions on sacrifice. However, the question of applying the benefits or fruits of the mass to specific persons and purposes could be remanded for doctrinal and practical settlement at the next council. This

---

[78] Förstermann, *Urkundenbuch*, 2, 292-298; Vehus, »Acta unnd handlung,« ed. Honée, *Der Libell*, 257f, 260-263.

[79] The text is »Unterricht der Visitatoren an die Pfarhern ym Kurfurstentum zu Sachssen,« found in WA 24, 195-240. The instruction treats the accommodations to be made on both forms at pp. 214-216. This is presented as a temporary work of patient love for people not yet convinced of the Lord's precept. However, if they become vociferous in their opposition to the truth, they are to be excluded from communion.

latter concession would have been made at the suggestion of a theologian with an acute sense of what was and what was not taught as already binding doctrine by the Church.[80]

Vehus repeated the already known conditions for temporary tolerance of married priests in Lutheran territories, adding some rebuttals of arguments advanced by the Lutherans against justifications of obligatory celibacy. For instance, according to Vehus the »high gift« of chastity can be sought in earnest prayer, and priests can dispose themselves for continence by greater self-discipline and care to avoid occasions of sin, such as dances. The Lutheran pastors who broke their vow of celibacy are, strictly speaking, not validly married, and they are canonically suspended from their office and benefice. However, such men may remain in their posts temporarily, until the coming council makes its determination.

Existing monasteries and religious houses in Lutheran territories are to be left intact and not be subjected to pressures such as those exerted by the Nürnberg reformers upon the convents of Saint Clare and Saint Catherine.[81] Renegade religious, desirous of returning to life under their rule, should be allowed, out of respect for their consciences, to rejoin a community without application of the canonical penalties. In a variation on earlier demands, Vehus proposed on August 24 that the Emperor should be asked to stipulate how local authorities are to handle vacated religious houses and their properties.

Vehus also called for wider powers of local bishops regarding pastoral appointments. Where the Lutheran *media* had spoken of an obligatory »presentation« by patrons of nominees to the bishop, it should be added that the bishop may by right examine the candidate and then decide upon his admission to the post in question.[82] Also the Lutheran list of abstinence days in the proposal of August 20 is to be somewhat expanded, while striking the unacceptable teaching that these laws about »ceremonies« do not bind the consciences of church members.[83] Indicative of Catholic doctrinal concerns were

---

[80] Eck wrote to Melanchthon on Aug. 27 that he was personally certain about the doctrine of the Mass's benefits, but he had nonetheless argued before the Estates that it could be left undecided until the council (CR 2, 316f).

[81] See Gottfried Seebass, »The Reformation in Nürnberg,« in L.P. Buck and J.W. Zophy, eds., *The Social History of the Reformation*, Festschrift Harold J. Grimm (Columbus, Ohio 1972), 35. Before the Reformation the Nürnberg authorities had already imposed considerable restrictions on religious houses in the city. G. Strauss, *Nuremberg in the Sixteenth Century*, 2nd ed., (Bloomington, Ind. & London 1976), 157f. At St. Clare's however, the Reformation measures toward suppressing religious life met the tenacious resistance of the Abbess Caritas Pirkheimer. Gerta Krabbel gives extensive passages from Caritas's diary in her account of this struggle. *Caritas Pirkheimer: Ein Lebensbild aus der Zeit der Reformation*, 5th ed. (Münster 1982), 86-208.

[82] The Nürnberg delegates related this part of Vehus's proposal (letter of 26 August; CR 2, 313).

[83] B. Dittrich calls attention to this significant Lutheran-Catholic difference as documented in the Confession and *Confutatio*. The latter does not say that obeying church laws gains grace and salvation, but that such laws constitute a pedagogy needed by people desiring to walk in the way of godliness. *Das Traditionsverständnis in der Confessio Augustana und in der Confutatio* (Leipzig

the final demands that Corpus Christi be added to the list of holy days and that the season of Advent be specified as the time for instruction and preaching on Christ's coming in judgment.[84]

Understandably, Brück's opening remarks on August 26 were critical of the Catholics. They had already heard in the last part of the previous phase of dialogue why the Protestant side could not accept their demands. Why then did they even ask for a new round of discussion when they had nothing new to propose?[85]

This sharp rejoinder gave notice of a new spirit of resistance in the Lutheran camp. Melanchthon had already come under fire on August 22 for the concessions offered in the *media* of August 20. On the 23rd, the Nürnberg delegates wrote home about their misgivings over what they perceived as Saxony's and Brandenburg's overeagerness to reach some kind of agreement with the Catholic, imperial party.[86] One report of Lutheran provenance states that for the colloquy between the two groups of three Melanchthon was strictly enjoined to make no more concessions, since his offers regarding episcopal jurisdiction had already exceeded what Lüneburg, Hesse, and Nürnberg would approve.[87]

These demurs did not, however, prevent Melanchthon from thinking out a decidedly forthcoming response to what Vehus said on August 24. For an inner-Lutheran conference on the 25th he sketched ways in which the Lutheran side could still stand on fundamental principles, such as Christ's ordinance of both forms and the inalienable freedom of clerics to marry, but still enter into further discussion on these points. For all practical purposes, the Lutherans had already said that in view of certain circumstances they excused from wrongdoing both those offering and those receiving communion under only one form. On the mass, one may question whether princes are not encroaching upon priests' consciences by prohibiting private celebration of mass. Also, the Catholic readiness to suspend discussion of the applied benefits of the mass was an opening for discussing the revision of the offertory and canon where these texts spoke of

1983), 27-30, 180-185. The traditional warrant for such law-making authority was Jesus' promise of the keys and the power to bind and loose (Matt 16:19, 18:19). Luther delivered a forceful rebuttal of such an argument, between 20 July and 25 Aug. 1530, in »Von den Schlüsseln,« WA 30/2, 435-464 (in English: LW 40, 325-377). M. Brecht sees here the basic reason why Luther did not speak in favor of admitting episcopal jurisdiction. *Martin Luther, 2, Ordnung und Abgrenzung der Reformation* (Stuttgart 1986), 386.

[84] Vehus, »Acta unnd handlung der dryer,« ed. Honée, *Der Libell*, 262f.

[85] Brück published the text of his intervention in *Geschichte der Handlungen zu Augsburg*, ed. K.E.Förstemann, in *Archiv für Geschichte der kirchlichen Reformation* (Halle, 1831), 109-118. We use the excerpt given in *Dr. Martin Luthers Sämtliche Schriften*, ed. J.G. Walch, 23 vols. (2nd edn., St. Louis 1880-1910), 16, 1438-55.

[86] CR 2, 301f.

[87] Schirrmacher, *Briefe und Acten*, 242f.

such benefits. If the Lutheran theologians are permitted to compose the requested »glosses« on sacrificial terms in the canon, then there is room for negotiations.[88]

However, the Lutheran conference of August 25 was a decisive defeat for Melanchthon and the conciliatory wing of the Lutheran party. The Chancellor of Duke Ernst of Lüneburg attacked Melanchthon's proposal on several points. Erhard Schnepf of Hesse added his objections as well. The Nürnberg delegates took the position, along with Lüneburg, Hesse, and the other cities, that discussion should cease on accommodations such as Melanchthon envisaged. There is no sense in seeking Catholic approval for the reforms already undertaken, and no reason for letting the other side dictate adaptations. The one issue remaining is to work out some formal arrangement for living side by side as territories not at one in belief, worship, and church order.[89] Thus, the Lutheran three could not come to the meeting of August 26 with any constructive response to Vehus's proposals.

Because Vehus had repeated such well-known demands on August 24, Gregor Brück could respond with clearly grounded refusals on August 26.[90] Those who implement reform will not admit into their Churches a divisive and confusing diversity in the communion rite. Private masses contrary to Christ's institution are rightly prohibited, since they constitute acts of public blasphemy. The Catholic demand for such masses would in effect shift attention toward priests' meritorious work of sacrifice and away from Christ's redemptive passion – a sinful act for those who know the true meaning of the mass. The offer to treat application of mass-fruits at the council reveals an uncertainty which undercuts private masses, since these are celebrated only so that they can be applied to the needs of some stipend-giver. The canon cannot be made obligatory, because it adds many unnecessary prayers over and above the substance of the mass, which is found in Christ's words of institution.

Brück questioned whether those who broke vows by marrying are more guilty than the popes and bishops who imposed such a vow contrary to Christ's word that not all receive the grace of chastity (Matt 19:11) and Paul's assertion that it is better to marry than to burn (1 Cor 7:9). Remanding to the Emperor the determination of how vacated religious houses are to be administered can be discussed, once the Lutherans are told what he might have in mind. Vehus's suggested elaborations on episcopal jurisdiction and ceremonies need not be answered, since the Lutheran position remains what was submitted on August 20 in their *media*.

---

[88] Melanchthon's sketch was edited by K. Schornbaum, »Zur Geschichte des Reichstages von Augsburg im Jahre 1530,« *Zeitschrift für Kirchengeschichte* 26 (1905), 144-146.
[89] Letter of the Nürnberg representatives, 26 Aug. (CR 2, 313f).
[90] See n. 85, above.

The crucial passage in Brück's presentation of 26 August came at the end, in the recommendation that a report on the unresolved problems should be given to the Estates, so that they in turn could address the Emperor on the urgent need to bring about an early convocation of a general council. If then the Estates also wanted to discuss an interim arrangement for peaceful coexistence of the two parties, the Lutheran group would gladly take up this complex of questions.

In the discussion following Brück's statement, John Eck spoke some key words.[91] The Catholic three has no mandate for negotiating practical ways of maintaining the peace. Now certainly the Emperor, along with the Electors and other Estates, wants a council, but these authorities also hold that the Christian world can proceed to a council only when heresy and disobedience have ceased in Germany. The innovations recently introduced must be suppressed and earlier doctrines and traditional practices must first be reinstituted.[92]

We are informed through the Nürnberg delegates about the inner-Lutheran consultation on August 27, at which the three delegated spokesmen made their report. After discussion, it was confirmed that the Lutherans would present no more *media* and would protest against the demand of a wholesale restoration of pre-Reformation conditions. Brück was to draft a written statement for submission the next day. Also, it was suggested that another paper should be prepared to answer the imperial *Confutatio*, to the extent that the Lutherans grasped its content during the reading of August 3.[93]

The next day, August 28, Brück handed over his statement.[94] It ascertains that the Catholics are demanding a number of specific changes which the Reformation party, after careful examination, finds unacceptable. Beyond this, the other side has broached a massive new demand for a return to pre-reformation ways as a

---

[91] Förstemann, *Urkundenbuch*, 2, 301.

[92] Campeggio had stressed this provision earlier in his discussions with Charles V, as the Legate reported in dispatches of 14 and 29 July to Rome. *Nuntiaturberichte*, ed. Müller, 1, 83, 90. Charles V had spoken of such a rollback in his letter to Clement VII of 14 July, indicating that it was a condition for the granting of a council in the face of Lutheran demands. *Corpus Documental de Carlos V*, ed. M. Fernández Alvarez, 5 vols. (Salamanca 1973-81), 1, 228f. These conditions suggest that an aura of unreality surrounds many of the references made in 1530 to the coming council.

[93] CR 2, 320f. The last recommendation amounts to the commissioning of Melanchthon's *Apologia Confessionis Augustanae*, a first draft of which was ready in the second half of September 1530. Publication followed, after revision and expansion, in Spring 1531. M. Brecht has recently shown that Melanchthon had begun drafting counter-statements to the *Confutatio* before late August, and that these early texts provide what amounts to a commentary on the dialogue between August 16 and 30. The first forms of the *Apologia* are thus a neglected source for historical work on the Augsburg negotiations on doctrine and the *forma ecclesiae*. »Die ursprüngliche Gestalt der Apologie der Confessio Augustana und ihre Entstehung,« in R. Decot, ed., *Vermittlungsversuche auf dem Augsburger Reichstag 1530* (Stuttgart 1989), 50-67.

[94] Förstemann, *Urkundenbuch*, 2, 306-310; Vehus, »Acta unnd handlung der dryer,« ed. Honée, *Der Libell*, 269-275.

condition for the long-awaited council. But this further imposition also has to be rejected. The Lutheran authorities have shown more than adequate justification for the doctrine they promote and the reforms they were constrained to undertake, given papal and episcopal neglect in supervising the life of the Church. Past imperial diets have issued calls for a council, precisely to heal divisions over doctrine and church practices. A year ago, at the end of the Diet of Speyer, the Lutheran estates made a formal appeal related to these questions and directed it to both the Emperor and the next council. While such an appeal is pending, Brück maintains, it goes against tradition and law to demand suppression of that which the council is to review. The Catholics show no respect for this duly formulated appeal and are trying to impose a solution before the council makes its decisions. If this had been required in the past, hardly any councils would have been held. So the Catholics should make no more calls for wholesale suppression of reforms, but instead turn to the requirement of the hour, the interim arrangement of terms of peace. In this interim, the Lutheran princes and cities will hold to their confession without additional glosses, in a manner for which they hope to give a good accounting to His Imperial Majesty and to Almighty God.

The Catholic three responded by once again insisting that they had no mandate from their principals authorizing them to negotiate terms of peace for the time until the council meets. The only point they can discuss in this regard is the specification of what the Lutherans must suppress and reinstate in order to prepare for the council.[95] But since the Lutheran three have just submitted a written formulation of their position, which includes arguments against this interim rollback to the pre-Reformation state of affairs, the Catholics would be willing to report on this to the majority of the Estates. However, the group of six also agreed that the declaration the Lutherans had brought to this meeting would not serve by itself for such a report, because it did not specify the particular conditions or demands over which the dialogue on reforms had run aground. And so the Catholic three offered to formulate a statement of these unresolved issues, so that the six could agree to this text before the meeting of the 28th ended.[96]

Thus, the final report on the theological colloquy intends to state the particular measures Vehus had called for on August 24 and the Lutherans then refused on August 26.[97] In the text, warrants and arguments are left out, so that

---

[95] Tetleben, *Protokoll*, 135f; Vehus, »Acta unnd handlung der dryer,« ed. Honée, *Der Libell*, 275f.

[96] H. Immenkötter has reconstructed the sequence of the deliberations on Aug. 28. *Um die Einheit im Glauben*, 64f.

[97] German texts are given in Förstemann, *Urkundenbuch*, 2, 274-276 (under the wrong date); in Vehus, »Acta unnd handlung der dryer,« ed. Honée, *Der Libell*, 278f; and in Schirrmacher, *Briefe und Acten*, 244-6. E. Honée edited a Latin text sent to Rome in »Die Vergleichsverhandlungen zwischen Katholiken und Protestanten im August 1530,« *Quellen und Forschungen aus italienischen Archiven und Bibliotheken* 42-43 (1963), 432f.

the sticking points themselves stand in clear light. However, haste took a toll, and the resulting document is so incomplete that one observer even called it »yet another *media*.«[98]

Over and above the Lutheran confession of the concomitant presence of the whole Christ under each form of the Eucharist, the Catholics call for the affirmation that those receiving under just one form are guilty of no wrongdoing. Also Lutheran authorities must not hinder those so desiring from receiving under one form, at least until the coming council. Communion under both forms will also be administered only during mass, unless a serious case of necessity dictates otherwise.[99]

The traditional ceremonies, vestments, chants, and readings are to be observed during both private and community masses. The traditional prayers of both the offertory and the canon are to be used, conformably with a *pius atque Christianus sensus*. Disputed questions in this area, such as the basis for applying masses to a given intention and their *ex opere operato* efficacy, can be remanded to the coming council.

Priests already married may be tolerated in Lutheran territories, if the Emperor sees fit to accept this. He should, however, give special consideration to the fact that a reimposition of obligatory celibacy would deprive the Lutherans of the pastors they need.[100]

Finally, religious and monastic communities still functioning in the Lutheran territories must be left intact, with no hindering of ex-members from returning, should they so desire. Regarding houses which have been vacated, including their properties and the persons forced to leave them – on these points the Emperor should decide what provisions are to be made.[101]

On August 29 the Catholic three made a full report to the majority block of Estates on the three sessions of dialogue on August 24, 26, and 28.[102] The report,

---

[98] Tetleben, *Protokoll*, 136.

[99] From earlier discussion it is clear that the final provision intends to rule out reservation of the Eucharist under the form of wine and the carrying of it under both forms to the sick.

[100] The four texts (see above, n. 97) do not agree in their formulation of this condition.

[101] The omission of any treatment of episcopal jurisdiction, the binding power of fasting laws, and the calendar of fasts and feasts make this a quite incomplete listing of the unresolved problems as of August 28. One can surmise that the text was meant to be taken as an elucidation of selected points in the Catholic *media* of Aug. 19, while leaving unmodified the other conditions of the earlier *media*. The main fact not taken into consideration in the document of August 28 is that the Lutheran position on bishops had broken down, and that their *media* of 20 August was no longer representative. This appears most dramatically in a memorandum by the Hessian theologian Erhard Schnepf from around this time which gives the biblical warrants which seem to him to demolish Melanchthon's case for reintroducing episcopal authority in Lutheran lands. Förstemann, *Urkundenbuch*, 2, 311-313.

[102] The report is Vehus's »Acta unnd handlung der dryer,« ed. Honée, *Der Libell*, 254-280. The Nürnberg delegates heard that several Catholic Estates found offensive the Lutheran position paper of August 28, incorporated into Vehus's report, predicting that it would be sure to anger Charles V as well (CR 2, 319).

however, did not snuff out all hopes of agreement, in spite of its recital of rejections and appeals to a future council. It was agreed that Duke Heinrich of Braunschweig would make a personal princely appeal to Elector Johann at the supper they were planning to have together that evening. Concretely, Heinrich would propose the naming of new commissions of seven members each to take up the unresolved issues concerning liturgy and clerical and religious life. Would not the presence of some princes and bishops, in a fourth phase of dialogue, contribute to more fruitful negotiations?[103]

So another important day of decision for the Lutheran party was August 30. A consultation reviewed the suggestion that further discussion might well overcome the impasse reached by the committees of three. On this day, also, the courier arrived from the Coburg, bringing from Martin Luther the awaited answers to questions sent to him on August 22. Later in the day, the group of six delegates held their final meeting.[104]

Luther argued from basic principle in his response to the Elector.[105] The Reformation position on the cluster of practices now at issue rests on clear biblical norms. One is to teach nothing and institute no practice in a binding manner without the certainty given by God's word.[106] Once God's word has been spoken and heard, then a Christian has no authorization for accepting an alternative arising by human enactment. One after the other, Luther brands as human inventions what the Catholic side had demanded. Communion under one form is such an invention (*ein lauter Menschenfund*), which as well goes against an utterly clear word of Christ.[107] Private masses are human inventions which must be banned from divine worship. A prince who is a believing Christian must give way to Scripture's prohibition of private celebrations. The sale of masses under the rubric of sacrifice and *opus operatum* makes them human enactments as well,

---

[103] Schirrmacher, *Briefe und Acten*, 248; Tetleben, *Protokoll*, 136. For the Estates, the alternative was to refer the whole matter for settlement by the Emperor, entailing what for many of them would be an undesired increment in his power.

[104] At approximately the same time, the memorial of the Nürnberg city council arrived in Augsburg, which forcefully rejected the accomodations to Catholic demands that had been offered by the Lutheran seven-man committee in their *media* of August 20. See n. 73, above.

[105] WABr 5, 572-574.

[106] In a short note on the same day to Justus Jonas in Augsburg, Luther concluded, »Sed viriliter agite neque cedite adversariis quidquam, nisi quod evidenti Scriptura probaverint« (ibid., 580,16-18).

[107] In his letter of the same day to Melanchthon, Luther counters the Catholic insinuation that the small reformed party condemns the whole world for practicing communion under only one form. The Protestant charge is rather that Catholic authorities have reduced the Church to captivity, much like the Jews in Babylon, where God's people were impeded from practicing their religion in its integrity. The call for help in maintaining a tranquil Catholic people is to be countered by attacking theologians like Eck for their complicity in violating the sacrament and thus condemning God's word (WABr 5, 577,25-578,34).

and this the prayers of the canon clearly confirm. In no way may such a rite be allowed, which one cannot grasp as the biblically mandated memorial of Christ's passion.

In another letter arriving on August 30, Luther expressed his satisfaction and gratitude over Melanchthon's refusals of the conditions laid down by the Catholics in the meetings of the commissions of seven. At the same time Luther was uneasy over what might follow from the restoration of episcopal jurisdiction, for instance, if cases arose in which Lutherans disobeyed their bishops.[108] The papacy is the real problem for Luther, and its continued existence means for him that the Reformation doctrine of justification and the church has in fact not been acknowledged and agreed to. In a summary judgment on the Diet, Luther concludes that it was quite enough that his side had given its public account of faith and then uttered a plea for peace. There is no sense extending oneself in an impossible attempt to convert the enemies of the truth.[109]

The committees of three met for what was apparently a brief session on August 30.[110] The Lutherans related that their principals had carefully examined the proposal for yet another round of dialogue. But they see no purpose in further negotiation. They have already deliberated with great care over the unresolved issues, and at present conscience will permit no further concessions. Their written declaration of August 28 stated the case against an interim restoration of pre-reformation doctrine, worship, and church order and thus an argument from allegedly prescriptive rights of possessors has no validity. When, however, discussion begins on provisions for peaceful coexistence, the Lutherans will gladly participate.

The Catholic three agreed to inform the Estates about this decision to break off the theological colloquy. This was done on the morning of August 31, and the report was consolidated by a narrative of the specific Lutheran refusals.[111] An

---

[108] In his letter to the Elector Johann, Luther had undercut an important component of the Lutheran offer to conform to the calendar of fasts and feasts obligatory in the Western Church. In his view, the ordering of such matters should be determined by secular authorities. God has placed such outward matters under the rule of reason, not his divine law, and in the realm of reason established government has the decisive word. WABr 5, 574,83-91.

[109] »Summa, mihi in totum displicet tractatus de doctrinae concordia, ut quae plane sit impossibilis, nisi papa velit papatum suum aboleri. Satis est, nos redimus rationem fidei et petere pacem; convertere eos ad veritatem quare speramus?« WABr 5, 578,42-53.

[110] Schirrmacher, *Briefe und Acten*, 248; Honée, »Vergleichsverhandlungen,« 433f. Melanchthon mentioned in a letter the next day that at the session on the 30th Eck had wryly lamented that Charles V had not instituted inquisitorial measures against the Lutherans immediately upon his arrival in Germany. Then he would have heard their monstrous heresies and responded by wiping them out. But now he is forming his view of them from Brück's feigned orthodoxy and Melanchthon's sweet reasonableness, and has become a very mild emperor. Melanchthon adds that he and Eck get along in a friendly way (CR 2, 335).

[111] Schirrmacher, *Briefe und Acten*, 248.

account which Johann Eck gave to Cardinal Campeggio about this time on the remaining difficulties may well have been used in this final report to the Estates.¹¹² In his memorandum Eck gives an approving account of the Lutherans' readiness to accept bishops, introduce abstinence days and holy days, and promote confession of sin. But the sides disagreed on what disposition to make of monastic properties. This issue the Catholics could well remand to the Emperor for a decision. The Lutherans had not agreed to the limiting conditions under which existing marriages of their clergy are to be tolerated, but for Eck this also can be referred to the Emperor for further deliberation and regulation. But on the Eucharist, Eck lists five problems for which he could apparently offer no solution. The Lutherans refuse to teach the liceity of one form; they will not allow variations in the communion rite within the same community; they reject private masses; they oppose the canon of the mass; and they are intractable when the Catholics show how sacrifice should be explained. And the last-named problem remains, even though questions about the benefits of the mass and their application can be remanded to a council for decision.¹¹³

The Catholic Estates then agreed that no more could be done through dialogue with the Lutheran party. That afternoon, they met with Emperor Charles V to report on what had transpired since August 7. Their colloquies had come to a dead end, and so it was left to Charles to take action in the service of unity in the Church and peace in Germany.¹¹⁴

Conclusions

The end of August marked the completion of a significant phase of the Imperial Diet of 1530 in Augsburg. Further efforts in early September had no success in negotiating an accommodation between the Lutheran and Catholic parties.¹¹⁵ On September 22 Charles V presented to the Diet a draft recess

---

112 The text was edited by G. Müller, »Johann Eck und Die Confessio Augustana,« *Quellen und Forschungen aus italienischen Archiven und Bibliotheken*, 38 (1958), 240-242. H. Immenkötter proposed that Eck's report was composed on August 30 (*Um die Einheit im Glauben*, 94, n.8).

113 On these eucharistic issues Eck saw and stated the Lutheran-Catholic conflicts quite clearly. Thus, there is reason to moderate the negative judgments of H. Immenkötter and R. Bäumer on Eck's excessive penchant for reducing serious differences to issues of variant terminology. So Immenkötter, *Um die Einheit im Glauben*, 58f, 70, n.13; and Bäumer, »Vermittlungsbemühungen,« *Theologie und Glaube* 70 (1980), 320f.

114 Tetleben, *Protokoll*, 137f.

115 This effort centered on an eight-point plan, formulated at the behest of Archduke Ferdinand by Georg Truchsess von Waldburg and Hieronymus Vehus and revised by Cardinal Campeggio. A basic account is H. Immenkötter, *Um die Einheit im Glauben*, 71-80. Recent studies include G. Müller, »Duldung des deutschen Luthertums? Erwägungen Kardinal Lorenzo Campeggios vom September 1530,« *Archiv für Reformationsgeschichte* 68 (1977), 158-172; and E. Honée, »'Pax politica' oder Wiedervereinigung im Glauben?«, in R. Bäumer, ed., *Reformatio ecclesiae*, Festschrift Erwin Iserloh (Paderborn 1980), 440-466.

declaring the Lutheran Confession refuted and demanding that its signers state within six months whether they accept the adaptations proposed to them in late August. And in their domains they are to introduce no further innovations in doctrine and worship.[116] The Lutherans' dissent from this recess sealed the failure of the 1530 attempts at religious reconciliation. Even the extensive doctrinal agreements on Articles 1-21 of the Augsburg Confession did not receive the codification needed for them to serve later as a basis for further relations between the Catholic and Lutheran groups.

Reflection on the details of this first colloquy of the Reformation era indicates four major reasons why it failed in its quest for doctrinal consensus and a mutually acceptable pattern of diversity in the *forma ecclesiae* regarding worship, clergy, and church order.

1) A notable difference made itself felt all through the August colloquy regarding the norms regulating religious practice. The Lutheran documents repeatedly appeal to the dictates of a conscience that was formed by Scripture. The Catholics, for their part, insist that regulations set down by church authorities do bind in conscience. Melanchthon, around August 12, stated his assumption that the dialogue on reform of the abuses did not concern provisions of divine law. Nonetheless his side argued that it was bound in conscience by what God had determined on the communion rite, marriage for priests, and the mass. The Catholic response at one point (August 11) called in question the authority the Lutheran princes ascribed to their theologians as interpreters of Scripture and God's will. In forming consciences, more weight should be ascribed, according to the Catholic argument, to what the Church has determined. And, in the face of this contention, Martin Luther countered with the powerful shibboleth, »human enactments,« in reference to unacceptable ecclesiastical encroachments upon the area where God has determined how he is to be worshipped. The two parties differed notably over what serves as the immediate source of norms regulating liturgy, the clergy, and church order.[117]

2) Among the particular issues of unresolved controversy, the Lutheran insistence on the chalice is emblematic of the previous difference over norms. Communion under both forms could be granted in the reformed territories – this the Catholic side stated quite clearly. But the sticking point was the

---

[116] Förstemann, *Urkundenbuch*, 2, 474f.

[117] One observer of the clash over norms was Johannes Dietenberger, O.P., who set to work in late August composing treatises on the issues that had surfaced during the Diet. He especially argues against Reformation claims for *sola Scriptura* and *sacra Scriptura sui ipsius interpres*, with arguments for an ongoing teaching work of the Holy Spirit, to carry the church beyond the bare letter of Scripture. Consequently, doctrine and practice are shaped in post-apostolic times by unwritten apostolic traditions, the Fathers, general councils, and universal customary practices, by all of which the full meaning of revelation comes to expression. Dietenberger's treatises were collected in *Phimostomus scripturariorum* (1532), now edited by E. Iserloh and P. Fabisch, as Corpus Catholicorum 38 (Münster 1985). See also U. Horst, »Das Verhältnis von Schrift und Tradition nach Johannes Dietenberger,« *Theologie und Philosophie* 46 (1971), 223-247.

qualification of communion under both forms. Was it a precept binding all ministers of, and participants in, the sacrament (so the Lutherans)? Or was this left open by Christ, for the church to regulate according to changing conditions (so the Catholics)? The Catholic gaffe on August 21 occasioned an especially sharp clash over this matter, as the Lutherans straightway refused to link the offering of the chalice to communicants with instruction that receiving under only the form of bread was also admissible. This Lutheran refusal then became a first fixed element in the emerging *dissensus*. This point of Lutheran contestation of a Catholic demand makes especially clear how the Lutheran leaders felt themselves bound by imperatives derived directly from Scripture (e.g. *Bibite ex hoc omnes*). One senses little comprehension on the Catholic side for such a personal encounter with God's revealing word and for the sense of solemn obligation arising from such a communication.

3) The provisions recommended by the Catholics for the celebration of mass, and the ensuing refusals by the Lutherans, reveal an opposition which was in all likelihood much deeper than most of the dialogue participants realized. There was a *dissimilitudo ingens* over the meaning of the Mass.[118] Melanchthon's memoranda of August 20-21 stated a view of the controversy which would be widely shared on the Lutheran side.[119] Eucharistic sacrifice is taken as an egregious case of a meritorious work before God, one running counter to the primacy of Christ's consoling gift which believers can only receive in gratitude. The Catholics would reject such an understanding of the mass as woefully inadequate because theologically ill-informed. This would eventually have manifested itself in the instructions or glosses on sacrificial terms in the canon, had Catholic theologians got to the point of formulating them. Such instructions would emphatically attribute the sacrifice primarily to Jesus Christ, the eternal priest, who makes present his once-for-all offering, so that his people may incorporate themselves into his action.[120] But the Lutheran doctrine of the Lord's Supper rested on a perception of the people of the Church as those needing, and recurrently receiving, Christ's testamentary gift of forgiveness through the words, gestures, and gifts of communion. Thus, the eucharistic *dissensus* was also ecclesiological.

4) Finally, our attention is drawn to the way the Lutheran case for the renewed *forma ecclesiae* recurrently appealed to elements of incipient confessionalization

---

[118] Urbanus Rhegius said this in 1539, speaking of how far apart even in 1530 the two sides were on the number of masses and the *intentio* of eucharistic celebration (cited by M. Liebmann, *Urbanus Rhegius und die Anfänge der Reformation*, 279, n. 434).

[119] See above, n. 58, in this Study.

[120] So K. Schatzgeyer in various works on the mass in the 1520s. See *Schriften zur Verteidigung der Messe*, ed. E. Iserloh and P. Fabisch (Corpus Catholicorum, 37; Münster 1984), 59f., 82, 229, 462-465, 495, 582, 613. Also Tommaso de Vio Cardinal Cajetan, *De sacrificio missae* (1531), trans. J. Wicks, *Cajetan Responds* (Washington, DC 1978), 189-200.

and modernization.[121] The Saxon theologians had urged accommodation, so as to maintain the proper climate for catechizing the people in true doctrine and for imposing Christian discipline on an otherwise unruly populace.[122] The Lutheran *media* of August 20 showed evident concern for enforcing public order in reformed territories. The case for married priests stressed how lawful marriage would impose control on a lower clergy otherwise given to concubinage and random sexual excursions. Episcopal jurisdiction recommended itself to Melanchthon because he could foresee the eventual application by bishops of the sanction of excommunication on lay people and priests who proved obstinate in their unruliness. Furthermore, the Lutherans intended to legislate a unified rite of communion under both forms in their territories, as Brück stated on August 28. As we noted early in this essay, by 1530 the Lutheran reformation was not simply the product of Luther's early broadsides.

The measures just indicated exemplify facets of a major historical process which began unfolding in Europe in the sixteenth century. The Lutheran leadership, both rulers and theological advisers, were, as early as 1530, promoting indoctrination in more conscious orthodoxy and the imposition of more disciplined behavior upon their people. The Catholics did not perceive or acknowledge this process, which they would hardly have opposed in principle. Instead, the Catholics fixed on details in which the Lutheran program departed from more recent tradition. The details were indicative of significant differences over Scripture, the Eucharist, and the church. But they also obscured the Catholic perception of a Lutheran intention and of a process unfolding in Lutheran lands which some Catholics of 1530 could have appreciated.

But, we must also note, many German Catholics at the Diet of Augsburg in 1530 could give only lip service to the indictment of abuses and the clamor for reform of Church and society. A new Catholic generation had to emerge, and evangelical idealism had to be injected from Spain and Italy, before »reform« ceased being a century-old cliché and began to motivate personal living and ecclesial service. Sad to say, the eventual Tridentine reform, also a confessionalizing and modernizing process, took place behind the barricades thrown up against later generations living according to the Lutheran *forma ecclesiae*.

---

[121] The classic article on confessionalization is E. W. Zeeden, »Grundlagen und Wege der Konfessionsbildung in Deutschland im Zeitalter der Glaubenskämpfe,« *Historische Zeitschrift* 185 (1958), 149-199; reprinted in E.W. Zeeden, ed., *Gegenreformation* (Darmstadt 1973), 85-134. On modernization, W. Reinhard, »Gegenreformation als Modernisierung? Prolegomena zu einer Theorie des konfessionellen Zeitalters,« *Archiv für Reformationsgeschichte* 68 (1977), 226-252.

[122] See above, p. 290; also, 295 and 298.

ACKNOWLEDGMENTS
OF PLACES OF FIRST PUBLICATION

1. »Approaching Luther's Reform«
   Written for this volume.

2. »Justification and Faith in Luther's Theology«
   Theological Studies 44 (1983), 3-29.

3. »The Heart Clinging to the Word«
   Spiritualities of the Heart, ed. Annice Callahan rscj (Mahwah, N.J. & New York: Paulist Press, 1990), 79-96. Copyright, Society of the Sacred Heart, U.S. Province. Used by Permission.

4. »Living and Praying as *simul iustus et peccator*:
   A Chapter in Luther's Spiritual Teaching«
   Gregorianum 70 (1989), 521-548.

5. »Martin Luther's Treatise on Indulgences, 1517«
   Theological Studies 28 (1967), 481-518.

6. »*Fides sacramenti – fides specialis*: Luther's Development in 1518«
   Gregorianum 65 (1984), 53-87.

7. »Roman Reactions to Luther: the First Year (1518)«
   Catholic Historical Review 69 (1983), 521-562.

8. »Luther and Lived Religiosity«
   Gregorianum 70 (1989), 121-126, in Italian.

9. »Holy Spirit – Church – Sanctification: Insights from Luther's Instructions on the Faith«
   Vierteljahresschrift für ökumenische Theologie Catholica 45 (1991), No. 2; original in German. Used by permission of Aschendorff Verlag, Münster.

10. »Abuses Under Indictment at the Diet of Augsburg 1530«
    Theological Studies 41 (1980); 253-302.

11. »The Lutheran *forma ecclesiae* in the Colloquy at Augsburg, August 1530«
    Christian Authority. Essays in Honour of Henry Chadwick, ed. G. Evans (Oxford: Clarendon Press, 1988), 160-203. Used by Permission of Oxford University Press.

APPENDIX

Books Reviewed on Luther and the Reformation
by Jared Wicks (A Selection, 1966-1991)

Aland, Kurt, *Martin Luther's 95 Theses* (St. Louis 1967), in *Theological Studies* 29 (1968), 331-333.

Alberigo, Giuseppe, *La Riforma protestante. Origini e cause*, 2nd ed. (Brescia 1988), in *Civiltà Cattolica* 140 (1989), I 404.

Arnau-García, Ramón, *El Ministro legado de Cristo, según Lutero* (Valencia 1983), in *Theological Studies* 46 (1985), 366-368.

Atkinson, James, *Martin Luther – Prophet to the Church Catholic* (Exeter & Grand Rapids 1983), in *Catholic Historical Review* 71 (1985), 74-75, and in *Heythrop Journal* 26 (1985), 443-444.

Beer, Theobald, *Der fröhliche Wechsel und Streit. Grundzüge der Theologie Martin Luthers* (Einsiedeln 1980), in *Theologische Revue* 78 (1982), 1-12, and in *Gregorianum* 63 (1982), 162-164.

Beyna, Werner, *Das moderne katholische Lutherbild* (Essen 1969), in *Theological Studies* 31 (1970), 224.

Bluhm, Heinz, *Martin Luther: Creative Translator* (St. Louis 1965), in *Theological Studies* 27 (1966), 730-731.

Bornkamm, Heinrich, *Luther in Mid-Career 1521-1530* (Philadelphia 1983), in *Catholic Historical Review* 71 (1985), 69-71.

Bossard, Stefan N., *Zwingli-Erasmus-Cajetan: Die Eucharistie als Zeichen der Einheit* (Wiesbaden 1978), in *Theological Studies* 41 (1980), 238-239.

Boyer, Charles, *Luther: sa doctrine* (Rome 1970), in *Theological Studies* 32 (1971), 689-691.

Boyle, Marjorie O., *Rhetoric and Reform: Erasmus' Civil Dispute with Luther* (Cambridge, Mass. 1983), in *Theological Studies* 45 (1984), 742-744.

Brenz, Johannes, *Explicatio Epistolae Pauli ad Romanos*, v. 1, ed. Stefan Strom (Tübingen 1986), in *Gregorianum* 69 (1988), 556-557.

Burger, Christoph, *Aedificatio, Fructus, Utilitas. Johannes Gerson als Professor der Theologie und Kanzler der Universität Paris* (Tübingen 1986), in *Gregorianum* 69 (1988), 796-798.

Cavallotto, Stefano, *Lutero: scritti pastorali minori* (Naples 1987), in *Gregorianum* 70 (1989), 120-126.

The Church, Mysticism, Sanctification and the Natural in Luther's Thought, ed. Ivar Asheim (Philadelphia 1967), in *Theological Studies* 29 (1968), 544-545.

Die Confutatio der Confessio Augustana vom 3. August 1530, ed. H. Immenkötter, Corpus Catholicorum, 33 (Münster 1979), in *Catholic Historical Review* 67 (1981), 120-122.

Dietenburger, Johannes, *Phimostomos Scripturariorum*, ed. Erwin Iserloh & Peter Fabisch, Corpus Catholicorum, 38 (Münster 1985), in *Gregorianum* 67 (1986), 577-579.

Dittrich, Bernhard, *Das Traditionsverständnis in der Confessio Augustana und in der Confutatio* (Leipzig 1983), in *Theological Stuies* 45 (1984), 772.

Dokumente zur Causa Lutheri (1517-1521). 1. Teil: Das Gutachten des Prierias und weitere Schriften gegen Luthers Ablaßthesen (1517-1518), ed. P. Fabisch & E. Iserloh, Corpus Catholicorum, 41 (Münster 1988), in *Catholic Historical Review* 75 (1989), 697-699.

Ebeling, Gerhard, *Luther: an Introduction to his Thought* (Philadelphia 1970), in *Journal of the American Academy of Religion* 39 (1971), 364-368, and in *Journal of Ecumenical Studies* 8 (1971), 420-422.

Ebeling, Gerhard, *Umgang mit Luther* (Tübingen 1983), in *Heythrop Journal* 26 (1985), 442-443.

Eck, Johann, *Enchiridion locorum communium adversus Lutherum et alios hostes ecclesiae (1525-1543)*, ed. Pierre Fraenkel, Corpus Catholicorum, 34 (Münster 1979), in *Archivum Historiae Pontificiae* 19 (1981), 386-390.

Eck, Johann, *De sacrificio missae libri tres (1526)*, ed. Erwin Iserloh et al. Corpus Catholicorum, 36 (Münster 1982), in *Bibliotheque d'humanisme et Renaissance* 46 (1984), 226-228.

Edwards, Mark U. & George Tavard, *Luther – a Reformer for the Churches* (Philadelphia & New York 1983), in *Catholic Historical Review* 71 (1985), 66-67.

Forsberg, Juhani, *Das Abrahamsbild in der Theologie Luthers: Pater fidei sanctissimus* (Stuttgart 1984), in *Theologische Revue* 83 (1987), 43-44.

Führer, Werner, *Das Wort Gottes in Luthers Theologie* (Göttingen 1984), in *Theologische Revue* 85 (1989), 207-209.

Garcia Villoslada, Ricardo, *Raices historicas del luteranismo* (Madrid 1969), in *Catholic Historical Review* 57 (1971), 639-640.

Geist und Geschichte der Reformation, Festschrift Hanns Rückert, ed. Heinz Liebing et al. (Berlin 1966), in *Theological Studies* 29 (1968), 545-548.

Gritsch, Eric, *Martin – God's Court Jester* (Philadelphia 1983), in *Catholic Historical Review* 71 (1985), 67-68.

Hacker, Paul, *Das Ich im Glauben bei Martin Luther* (Graz 1966), in *Theological Studies* 28 (1967), 374-376.

Hamm, Berndt, *Frömmigkeitstheologie am Anfang des 16. Jahrhunderts. Studien zu Johannes von Paltz und seinem Umkries* (Tübingen 1982), in *Gregorianum* 65 (1984), 200-204.

Harran, Marilyn J., Luther on Conversion, the Early Years (Ithaca, N.Y. 1983), in Theological Studies 45 (1984), 180-182.

Hasler, August, Luther in der katholischen Dogmatik (Munich 1968), in Theological Studies 30 (1969), 140-142.

Heinz, Johannes, Justification and Merit. Luther versus Catholicism (Berrien Springs, Mich. 1984), in Theologische Revue 85 (1989), 211-213.

Hendrix, Scott, Ecclesia in via: Ecclesiological Developments in Medieval Psalms Exegesis and the »Dictata super psalterium« (1513-15) of Martin Luther (Leiden 1974), in Theological Studies 36 (1975), 184-186.

Hendrix, Scott, Luther and the Papacy (Philadelphia 1981), in Archivum Historiae Pontificiae 20 (1982), 427-430.

Immenkötter, Hubert, Der Reichstag zu Augsburg und die Confutatio (Münster 1979), in Catholic Historical Review 67 (1981), 120-122.

Janz, Denis R., Luther and Late Medieval Thomism (Waterloo, Ont. 1983), in Catholic Historical Review 72 (1986), 100-102.

Joest, Wilfried, Ontologie der Person bei Luther (Göttingen 1967), in Theological Studies 30 (1969), 289-311.

Johannes Eck (1486-1543) im Streit der Jahrhunderte, ed. Erwin Iserloh (Münster 1988), in Theologische Revue (forthcoming)

Kadlec, Jaroslav, Studien und Texte zum Leben und Wirken des Prager Magisters Andreas von Brod (Münster 1982), in Gregorianum 63 (1982), 750-752.

Kaliner, Walter, Katechese und Vermittlungstheologie im Reformationszeitalter. Johann VIII., Bischof von Meissen, und seine »Christliche Lehre« (Leipzig 1981), in Gregorianum 64 (1983), 363-365.

Katholische Theologen der Reformationszeit, ed. Erwin Iserloh, v.1 (Münster 1984), in Catholic Historical Review 72 (1986), 107-108.

Katholische Theologen der Reformationszeit, ed. Erwin Iserloh v.2 (Münster 1985), in Catholic Historical Review 73 (1987), 461-462.

Klausnitzer, Wolfgang, Das Papstamt im Disput zwischen Lutheranern und Katholiken (Innsbruck 1987), in Heythrop Journal 31 (1990), 347-348.

Kunzler, Michael, Die Eucharistielehre des Hadamer Pfarrers Gerhard Lorich (Münster 1981), in Gregorianum 63 (1982), 591-592.

Léonard, Emile G., A History of Protestantism, 1, The Reformation (Indianapolis 1968), in Theological Studies 29 (1968), 774-776.

Liebmann, Maximillian, Urbanus Rhegius und die Anfänge der Reformation (Münster 1980), in Archivum Historiae Pontificiae 18 (1980), 434-438.

Lienhard, Marc, Luther témoin de Jésus-Christ: les étapes et les thèmes de la christologie du réformateur (Paris 1973), in Theological Studies 35 (1974), 758-759.

Lutero in Italia, ed. Lorenzo Perrone (Casale Monferrato 1983), in Theological Studies 46 (1985), 176-177.

Luther: Theologian for Catholics and Protestants, ed. George Yule (Edinburgh 1985), in Heythrop Journal 24 (1988), 526-527.

Luther's Ecumenical Significance, ed. Peter Manns & Harding Meyer (Philadelphia & New York 1984), in *Catholic Historical Review* 71 (1985), 72-74.

McSorley, Harry, *Luthers Lehre vom unfreien Willen* (Munich 1967), in *Theological Studies* 29 (1968), 542-544.

McGrath, Alister, *The Intellectual Origins of the Protestant Reformation* (Oxford 1987), in *Theological Studies* 49 (1988), 745-747.

Martin Luther »Reformator und Vater im Glauben«, ed. Peter Manns (Stuttgart 1985), in *Theologische Revue* 83 (1987), 40-43.

Marranzini, Alfredo, *Dibattito Lutero-Seripando su »Giustizia e libertà del Cristiano«* (Brescia 1981), in *Theological Studies* 43 (1982), 723-725.

Marx, Gerhard, *Glaube, Werke und Sakramente im Dienst der Rechtfertigung in den Schriften von Berthold Pürstinger, Bischof von Chiemsee* (Leipzig 1982), in *Gregorianum* 64 (1983), 361-363.

Nicol, Martin, *Meditation bei Luther* (Göttingen 1984), in *Theologische Revue* 85 (1989), 213-214.

Oberman, Heiko, *Werden und Wertung der Reformation* (Tübingen 1977), in *Journal of Religion* 59 (1979), 118-120.

Ökumenische Erschließung Martin Luthers, ed. Peter Manns & Harding Meyer (Paderborn 1983) & *Luther's Ecumenical Significance* (Philadelphia & New York 1984), in *Heythrop Journal* 27 (1987), 86-88.

Olivier, Daniel, *La foi de Luther* (Paris 1978), in *Theological Studies* 41 (1980), 214-216.

von Paltz, Johannes, *Werke*, v.1, *Coelifodina*, ed. C. Burger & F. Stasch, and v.2, *Supplementum Coelifodinae*, ed. B. Hamm (Berlin 1983), in *Gregorianum* 65 (1984), 200-204; v. 3, *Opuscula*, ibid. 71 (1990), 592-595.

Pani, Giancarlo, *Martin Lutero: Lezioni sulla lettera ai Romani* (Rome 1983), in *Theologische Revue* 83 (1987), 209-211.

Pelikan, Jaroslav, *Spirit versus Structure: Luther and the Institutions of the Church* (New York 1968), in *Church History* 39 (1970), 249-250.

Pfnür, Vinzenz, *Einig in der Rechtfertigungslehre?* (Wiesbaden 1970), in *Theological Studies* 32 (1971), 689-691.

Power, David N., *The Sacrifice We Offer. The Tridentine Dogma and Its Reinterpretation* (New York 1987), in *Catholic Historical Review* 74 (1988), 504-506.

Preus, J. Samuel, *From Shadow to Promise: Old Testament Interpretation from Augustine to the Young Luther* (Cambridge, Mass. 1968), in *Theological Studies* 30 (1969), 715-717.

Reformation Europe, A Guide to Research, ed. Steven Ozment (St. Louis 1982), in *Archivum Historicum Societatis Iesu* 52 (1983), 309-310.

Schatzgeyer, Kaspar, *Schriften zur Verteidigung der Messe*, ed. Erwin Iserloh & Peter Fabisch, Corpus Catholicorum, 37 (Münster 1984), in *Gregorianum* 66 (1985), 351-353, and in *Archivum Historiae Pontificiae* 23 (1985), 398-399.

Schmitt, Paul, *La Réforme catholique. Le Combat de Maldonat* (Paris 1985), in *Catholic Historical Review* 73 (1987), 607-609.

Schwarz, Reinhard, *Vorgeschichte der reformatorischen Bußtheologie* (Berlin 1968), in *Theological Studies* 30 (1969), 714-715.

von Staupitz, Johann, *Sämtliche Schriften*, 1/1, *Tübingen Predigten*, ed. Richard Wetzel (Berlin 1987), in *Theologische Revue* (forthcoming).

Steinbach, Wendelin, *Opera exegetica*, v.2, *Commentarii in Epistolam ad Hebraeos pars prima*, ed. Helmut Feld (Wiesbaden 1984), in *Gregorianum* 66 (1985), 576-577.

Steinbach, Wendelin, *Opera exegetica*, v.3, *Commentarii in Epistolam ad Hebraeos pars altera*, ed. Helmut Feld (Stuttgart 1987), in *Gregorianum* 70 (1989), 153-155.

Steinmetz, David, *Luther and Staupitz. An Essay in the Intellectual Origins of the Protestant Reformation* (Durham, N.C. 1980), in *Catholic Historical Review* 68 (1982), 341-342.

Steinmetz, David C., *Luther in Context* (Bloomington, Ind. 1986), in *Theologische Revue* 85 (1989), 210-211.

Stock, Ursula, *Die Bedeutung der Sakramente in Luthers Sermonen von 1519* (Leiden 1982), in *Theological Studies* 44 (1983), 717-719.

Thesaurus Lutheri: Auf der Suche nach neuen Paradigmen der Luther-Forschung, ed. Tuomo Mannermaa et al. (Helsinki 1987), in *Heythrop Journal* (forthcoming).

Todd, John, *Luther, A Life* (New York 1982), in *Catholic Historical Review* 69 (1983), 602-603.

Vercruysse, Jos, *Fidelis populus* (Wiesbaden 1968), in *Theological Studies* 30 (1969), 713-714.

Zschoch, Hellmut, *Klosterreform und monastische Spiritualität im 15. Jahrhundert. Conrad von Zenn (d. 1460) und sein »Liber de vita monastica«* (Tübingen 1988), in *Gregorianum* 70 (1989), 363-364.

Zum Gedenken an Joseph Lortz (1887-1975). Beiträge zur Reformationsgeschichte und Ökumene, ed. Rolf Decot und Rainer Vinke (Stuttgart 1989), in *Gregorianum* 72 (1991), 381-383.

Zumkeller, Adolar, *Erbsünde, Gnade und Verdienst nach der Lehre der Erfurter Augustinertheologen des Spätmittelalters* (Würzburg 1984), in *Gregorianum* 66 (1985), 573-576.

Zur Mühlen, Karl-Heinz, *Reformatorische Vernunftkritik und neuzeitliches Denken. Dargestellt am Werk M. Luthers und F. Gogartens* (Tübingen 1980), in *Gregorianum* 62 (1981), 196-197.

BIBLIOGRAPHY OF STUDIES CITED

Alexander, J. Neil. »Luther's Reform of the Daily Office,« *Worship* 57 (1983), 348-369.
Alfaro, Juan. »Certitude de l'esperance et 'certitude de la grace,'« *Nouvelle Revue théologique* 94 (1972), 3-42.
Althaus, Paul. *Die Theologie Martin Luthers* (Gütersloh 1962).
– *Die Ethik Martin Luthers* (Gütersloh 1966).
– *The Theology of Martin Luther* (Philadelphia 1970).
– *The Ethics of Martin Luther* (Philadelphia 1972).
Anderson, H. George, et al., eds. *Justification by Faith*, Lutherans and Catholics in Dialogue, 7 (Minneapolis 1985).
Arnau García, Ramon. *El ministro legado de Cristo, según Lutero*, Series Valentina, 14 (Valencia 1983).
Asendorf, Ulrich. »Die Einbettung der Theosis in die Theologie Martin Luthers,« in S. Peura & A. Raunio, eds., *Luther und Theosis. Vergöttlichung als Thema der abendländischen Theologie* (Helsinki & Erlangen 1990), 81-102.

Bäumer, Remigius. »Die Diskussion um Luthers Thesenanschlag,« in A. Franzen et al., *Um Reform und Reformation*, Katholisches Leben und Kirchenreform im Zeitalter der Glaubensspaltung, 27/28 (Münster 1968), 53-95.
– *Martin Luther und der Papst*, Katholisches Leben und Kirchenreform im Zeitalter der Glaubensspaltung, 30 (Münster 1970, 5th ed. 1987).
– »Vermittlungsbemühungen auf dem Augsburger Reichstag,« *Theologie und Glaube* 70 (1980), 304-330.
– »Bekenntnis des einen Glaubens? Zur Diskussion um das Augsburger Bekenntnis,« *Theologie und Glaube* 71 (1981), 364-367.
Bataillon, Marcel. *Erasmo y España*, 2nd ed. (Mexico City, 1966).
Bayer, Oswald. *Promissio. Geschichte der reformatorischen Wende in Luthers Theologie*, Forschungen zur Kirchen– und Dogmengeschichte, 24 (Göttingen 1971, reprint Darmstadt 1990).
– »Natur und Institution. Eine Besinnung auf Luthers Dreiständelehre,« *Zeitschrift für Theologie und Kirche* 81 (1984), 352-382.
Baylor, Michael. *Action and Person. Conscience in Late Scholasticism and the Young Luther*, Studies in Medieval and Reformation Thought, 20 (Leiden, 1977).

Becker, Hans-Jürgen. Die Appellation vom Papst an ein allgemeines Konzil, Forschungen zur kirchlichen Rechtsgeschichte und zum Kirchenrecht, 17 (Cologne & Vienna 1988).

Beer, Theobald. Der fröhliche Wechsel und Streit. Grundzüge der Theologie Martin Luthers (Einsiedeln 1980).

Beintker, Horst. Die Überwindung der Anfechtung bei Luther, Theologische Arbeiten, 1 (Berlin 1954).

Beyer, Michael. »Luthers Ekklesiologie,« in H. Junghans, ed., Leben und Werk Martin Luthers von 1526 bis 1546 (Berlin & Göttingen 1983), 93-117, 755-765.

Birmelé, André. Le salut en Jésus-Christ dans les dialogues oecuméniques, Cogitatio fidei, 141 (Paris & Geneva 1986).

Bizer, Ernst. Fides ex auditu, 3rd edition (Neukirchen 1966).

Boehmer, Heinrich. Luthers Romfahrt (Leipzig 1914).

Bornkamm, Heinrich. Der authentische Text der Confessio Augustana (= Sitzungsberichte der Heidelberger Akademie der Wissenschaften, Phil.-Hist. Klasse, 1956, no. 2).

– »Augsburger Bekenntnis,« in Religion in Geschichte und Gegenwart, 3rd ed., 1, 733-736.

– »Thesen und Thesenanchlag Luthers,« in Geist und Geschichte der Reformation. Festschrift Hanns Rückert, Arbeiten zur Kirchengeschichte, 38, ed. Heinz Liebing et al. (Berlin 1966), 179-218.

Borth, Wilhelm. Die Luthersache (causa Lutheri). Die Anfänge der Reformation als Frage von Politik und Recht, Historische Studien, 414 (Lübeck & Hamburg 1970).

Bossy, John. Christianity in the West, 1400-1700 (Oxford 1985).

Brandi, Karl. Kaiser Karl V., 2 vols. (Munich 1937-39).

Brecht, Martin. »Der rechtfertigende Glaube an das Evangelium von Jesus Christus als Mitte von Luthers Theologie,« Zeitschrift für Kirchengeschichte 89 (1978), 45-77.

– Martin Luther, 3 vols. (Stuttgart 1981-87).

– Martin Luther. His Road to Reformation, 1483-1521 (Philadelphia 1985).

– »Johann Brenz auf dem Augsburger Reichstag 1530,« in R. Decot, ed., Vermittlungsversuche auf dem Augsburger Reichstag 1530. Melanchthon – Brenz – Vehus, Veröffentlichungen des Insituts für europäische Geschichte, Beiheft 26 (Stuttgart 1989), 9-28.

– »Die ursprüngliche Gestalt der Apologie der Confessio Augustana und ihre Entstehung,« in R. Decot, ed., Vermittlungsversuche auf dem Augsburger Reichstag (Stuttgart 1989), 50-67.

– ed., Martin Luther und das Bischofsamt (Stuttgart 1990).

Brieger, Theodor. »Die Torgauer Artikel,« in Kirchengeschichtliche Studien Hermann Reuter gewidmet (Leipzig 1890), 268-320.

Brown, Dorothy Catherine. Pastor and Laity in the Theology of Jean Gerson (Cambridge 1987).

Burger, Christoph. Aedificatio, Fructus, Utilitas. Johannes Gerson als Professor der Theologie und Kanzler der Universität Paris, Beiträge zur historischen Theologie, 70 (Tübingen 1986).

Burgess, Joseph A. et al. eds. The Role of the Augsburg Confession. Catholic and Lutheran Views (Philadelphia & New York/Ramsey, N.J. 1980).

Camelot, T. »Sacramentum fidei,« in Augustinus Magister (Paris 1954), 2, 891-896.

Cavallotto, S. »Il 'Credo ecclesiam' dalla Professione di fede di Lutero (1527-28) agli Articoli di Schwabach (1529),« Asprenas (Naples) 30 (1983), 383-416.

Chantraine, Georges. Erasmus et Luther: Libre et serf arbitre, Le Sycomore, ser. Horizon, 5 (Paris-Namur 1981).

La Confession d'Augsbourg. 450e anniversaire. Autour d'un colloque, Le Point théologique, 31 (Paris 1980).

Congar, Yves M.-J. »Regards et réflexions sur la christologie de Luther,« in Chrétiens en dialogue, Unam Sanctam, 50 (Paris 1964), 453-489.

— »Considerations and Reflections on the Christology of Luther,« in Dialogue between Christians (Westminster, Md. 1966), 372-406.

— »Intentionalité de la foi et sacrament,« in H.J. Auf der Maur et al., Fides Sacramenti-Sacramentum Fidei. Festschrift Pieter Smulders (Assen 1981), 177-191.

Creutzberg, Heinrich A. Karl von Miltitz (Freiburg/B. 1907).

Decot, Rolf. Vermittlungsversuche auf dem Augsburger Reichstag 1530. Melanchthon – Brenz – Vehus. Veröffentlichung des Instituts für Europäische Geschichte, Beiheft 26 (Stuttgart 1989).

— »Luthers Kompromißvorschlag an die Bischöfe auf dem Augsburger Reichstag 1530,« in M. Brecht, ed., Martin Luther und das Bischofsamt (Stuttgart 1990), 109-119.

Decot, Rolf, and Rainer Vinke, eds. Zum Gedenken an Joseph Lortz (1887-1975). Beiträge zur Reformationsgeschichte und Ökumene. Veröffentlichungen des Instituts für Europäische Geschichte, Beiheft 30 (Stuttgart 1989).

Dettloff, Werner. Die Lehre von der acceptatio divina bei Johannes Duns Scotus, Franziskanische Forschungen, 10 (Werl 1954).

— Die Entwicklung der Akzeptations- und Verdienstlehre von Duns Scotus bis Luther, Beiträge zur Geschichte der Philosophie und Theologie des Mittelalters, 40/2 (Münster 1963).

Dietterle, Johannes, »Die Summae confessorum (sive de casibus conscientiae) von ihren Anfängen bis zum Silvester Prierias,« in ten parts, Zeitschrift für Kirchengeschichte, Volumes 24 (1903) through 28 (1907).

Dittrich, Bernhard. Das Traditionsverständnis in der Confessio Augustana und in der Confutatio, Erfurter theologische Schriften, 51 (Leipzig 1983).

Ebeling, Gerhard. *Luther. Einführung in sein Denken* (Tübingen 1964).
- *Luther, Introduction to his Thought* (Philadelphia 1970).
- »Der Mensch als Sünder: die Erbsünde in Luthers Menschenbild,« in *Lutherstudien* (Tübingen 1971-), 3, 74-107.
- »Luthers Ortsbestimmung der Lehre vom Heiligen Geist,« in *Word und Glaube*, 3 (Tübingen 1975), 316-348.

Edwards, Mark U. *Luther and the False Brethren* (Stanford, Cal. 1975).
- *Luther's Last Battles: Politics and Polemics 1531-46* (Ithaca, N.Y. 1983).
- »The Older Luther, 1526-1546,« in G. Dünnhaupt. ed., *The Martin Luther Quincentennial* (Detroit 1985), 48-62.

Eire, Carlos M. N. *War Against the Idols. The Reformation of Worship from Erasmus to Calvin* (Cambridge 1986).

Ernst, Wilhelm. *Gott und Mensch am Vorabend der Reformation: eine Untersuchung zur Moralphilosophie und -theologie bei Gabriel Biel*, Erfurter theologische Studien, 28 (Leipzig 1972).

Evennett, H. Outram. *The Spirit of the Counter-Reformation*, ed. J. Bossy (Cambridge 1968 & Notre Dame 1970).

Farge, James K. *Orthodoxy and Reform in Early Reformation France. The Faculty of Theology of Paris, 1500-1543*, Studies in Medieval and Reformation Thought, 32 (Leiden 1985).

Flatten, Heinrich. *Der Häresieverdacht im Codex iuris canonici*, Kanonistische Studien und Texte, 21 (Amsterdam 1963).

Flörken. Norbert. »Ein Beitrag zur Datierung von Luthers 'Sermo de indulgentiis pridie Dedicationis,'« *Zeitschrift für Kirchengeschichte* 82 (1971), 344-350.

Forell, George W., and James F. McCue, eds. *Confessing One Faith: a Joint Commentary on the Augsburg Confession* (Minneapolis 1981).

Fraenkel, Pierre. »Luther et le langage de la théologie,« *Revue de théologie et de philosophie* 119 (1987), 17-32.

Fransen, Piet. »Réflexions sur l'anathème au Concile de Trente,« *Ephemerides theologicae Lovanienses* 29 (1953), 657-672.

Fries, Heinrich, Erwin Iserloh, et al. *Confessio Augustana: Hindernis oder Hilfe?* (Regensburg 1979).

Gauly, Peter. *Katholisches Ja zum Augsburger Bekenntnis?* (Freiburg/B. 1980).

Gebhardt, Bruno. *Die Gravamina der Deutschen Nation gegen den römischen Hof* (2nd ed., Breslau 1895).

Gerrish, Brian. »'To the Unknown God': Luther and Calvin on the Hiddenness of God,« *Journal of Religion* 53 (1973), 263-292.

Gogan, Brian. *The Common Corps of Christendom. Ecclesiological Themes in the Writings of Sir Thomas More*, Studies in the History of Christian Thought, 26 (Leiden 1982).

Grendler, Paul F. »Schools, Seminaries, and Catechetical Instruction,« in John W. O'Malley, ed., *Catholicism in Early Modern Europe. A Guide to Research* (St. Louis 1988), 315-330.

Hacker, Paul. *Das Ich im Glauben* (Graz 1966).
- *The Ego in Faith. Martin Luther and the Origin of Anthropocentric Religion* (Chicago 1970).
Hamm, Berndt. »Frömmigkeit als Gegenstand theologiegeschichtlicher Forschung,« *Zeitschrift für Theologie und Kirche* 74 (1977), 464-497.
- *Frömmigkeitsthologie am Anfang des 16. Jahrhunderts*, Beiträge zur historischen Theologie, 65 (Tübingen 1982).
Hammann, Konrad. *Ecclesia spiritualis. Luthers Kirchenverständnis in den Kontroversen mit Augustin von Alveldt und Ambrosius Catharinus*, Forschungen zur Kirchen- und Dogmengeschichte, 44 (Göttingen 1989).
Happee, J. *Mediteren met Luther. De weg van meditatie en gebed* (Deventer 1983).
Hasler, August. *Luther in der katholischen Dogmatik*, Beiträge zur ökumenischen Theologie, 2 (Munich 1968).
Hendrix, Scott. *Luther and the Papacy. Stages in a Reformation Conflict* (Philadelphia 1981).
Hennig, Gerhard. *Cajetan und Luther*, Arbeiten zur Theologie, II, 7 (Stuttgart 1966).
Hermann, Rudoph, *Luthers These »Gerecht und Sünder zugleich«* (Gütersloh 1930, reprint 1960).
- »Das Verhältnis von Rechtfertigung und Gebet nach Luthers Auslegung von Röm 3,« in *Gesammelte Studien* (Göttingen 1960), 11-43.
Herms, Eilert. *Luthers Auslegung des Dritten Artikels* (Tübingen 1987).
Herrmann, Fritz. »Miscellen zur Reformationsgeschichte. Aus Mainzer Archiven,« *Zeitschrift für Kirchengeschichte* 23 (1902), 263-268.
- »Luthers Tractatus de indulgentiis,« *Zeitschrift für Kirchengeschichte* 28 (1907), 370-373.
Hof, Otto. »Luthers Unterscheidung zwischen dem Glauben und der Reflexion auf den Glauben,« *Kerygma und Dogma* 18 (1972), 249-324.
Hoffmann, Fritz, and Ulrich Kühn, eds. *Die Confessio Augstana in ökumenischen Gespräch* (Berlin/DDR 1980).
Hollerbach, Marion. *Das Religionsgespräch als Mittel der konfessionellen und politischen Auseinandersetzung*, Europäische Hochschulschriften, III, 165 (Bern-Frankfurt 1982).
Honée, Eugène. »Die Vergleichsverhandlungen zwischen Katholiken und Protestanten im August 1530,« *Quellen und Forschungen aus itelienischen Archiven und Bibliotheken* 42-43 (1963), 412-434.
- »Die römische Kurie und der 22. Artikel der Confessio Augustana. Kardinal Lorenzo Campeggios Verhalten zur protestantischen Forderung des Laienkelches während des Augsburger Reichstages 1530,« *Nederlands archief voor kerkgeschiedenis* 50 (1969-70), 140-196.

- »Die theologische Diskussion über den Laienkelch auf dem Augsburger Reichstag 1530. Versuch einer historischen Rekonstruktion,« *Nederlands archief voor kerkgeschiedenis* 53 (1972-73), 1-96.
- »'Pax politica' oder Wiedervereinigung im Glauben?« in R. Bäumer, ed.. *Reformatio ecclesiae*, Festschrift Erwin Iserloh (Paderborn 1980), 440-466.
- *Der Libell des Hieronymus Vehus zum Augsburger Reichstag 1530*, Reformationsgeschichtliche Studien und Texte, 125 (Münster 1988).
- »Hieronymus Vehus. Seine Vermittlerrolle während der Augsburger Einigungsverhandlungen,« in R. Decot, ed., *Vermittlungsversuche auf dem Augsburger Reichstage. Melanchthon – Brenz – Vehus*. Veröffentlichungen des Insituts für Europäische Geschichte, Beiheft 26 (Stuttgart 1989), 29-49.

Honselmann, Klemens. *Urfassung und Drucke der Ablassthesen Martin Luthers und ihre Veröffentlichung* (Paderborn 1966).
- »Wimpina's Druck der Ablaßthesen Martin Luthers 1528,« *Zeitschrift für Kirchengeschichte* 97 (1986), 189-204.

Horst, Ulrich. »Das Verhältnis von Schrift und Tradition nach Johannes Dietenberger,« *Theologie und Philosophie* 46 (1971), 223-247.
- *Zwischen Konziliarismus und Reformation. Studien zur Ekklesiologie im Dominikanerorden*, Institutum Historicum FF. Praedicatorum, Dissertationes Historicae, 22 (Rome 1985).

Immenkötter, Herbert. *Um die Einheit im Glauben: Die Unionsverhandlungen des Augsburger Reichstages im August und September 1530*, Katholisches Leben und Kirchenreform im Zeitalter der Glaubensspaltung, 33 (Münster 1973).
- *Der Reichstag zu Augsburg und die Confutatio*, Katholisches Leben und Kirchenreform im Zeitalter der Glaubensspaltung, 39 (Münster 1979).
- »Die Confutatio – ein Dokument der Einheit,« in E. Iserloh & B. Hallensleben, eds., *Confessio Augustana und Confutatio. Die Augsburger Reichstag 1530 und die Einheit der Kirche* (Münster 1980), 205-213.
- *Hieronymus Vehus, Jurist and Humanist der Reformationszeit*, Katholisches Leben und Kirchenreform im Zeitalter der Glaubensspaltung, 42 (Münster 1982).

Iserloh, Erwin. *Gnade und Eucharistie in der philosophischen Theologie des Wilhelm von Ockham*, Veröffentlichungen des Instituts für Europäische Geschichte, 8 (Wiesbaden 1956).
- *Luthers Thesenanschlag: Tatsache oder Legende?* Institut für Europäische Geschichte, Vorträge, 31 (Wiesbaden 1962).
- *Luther zwischen Reform und Reformation. Der Thesenanschlag fand nicht statt*, Katholisches Leben und Kämpfen im Zeitalter der Glaubensspaltung, 23/24 (Münster 1966).
- Josef Gladzik, and Hubert Jedin. *Handbuch der Kirchengeschichte*, ed. H. Jedin, vol. 4, *Reformation, Katholische Reform und Gegenreformation* (Freiburg 1967).
- *The Theses Were Not Posted. Luther Between Reform and Reformation* (Boston & London 1968).

- »Sacramentum et exemplum: ein augustinisches Thema lutherischer Theologie,« in E. Iserloh & P. Manns, eds., *Reformata Reformanda*, Festschrift Hubert Jedin (Münster 1965), 1, 247-264.
- »Gratia und Donum, Rechtfertigung und Heiligung nach Luthers Schrift 'Wider den Löwener Theologen Latomus' (1521),« in L. Abramowski & J.F.G. Goeters, eds., *Studien zur Geschichte und Theologie der Reformation*, Festschrift Ernst Bizer (Neukirchen 1969), 141-156; reprinted in Iserloh, *Luther und die Reformation* (Aschaffenburg 1974), 88-105.
- *Luther und die Reformation. Beiträge zu einem ökumenischen Lutherverständnis* (Aschaffenburg 1974).
- Josef Gladzik, and Hubert Jedin. *History of the Church*, ed. H. Jedin and John Dolan, vol. 5, *Reformation and Counter Reformation* (New York 1980).
- *Geschichte und Theologie der Reformation* (Paderborn 1980).
- and Barbara Hallensleben, eds. *Confessio Augustana und Confutatio. Der Augsburger Reichstag 1530 und die Einheit der Kirche*, Reformationsgeschichtliche Studien und Texte, 118 (Münster 1980).
- »'Von der Bischofen Gewalt': CA 28,« in *Confessio Augustana und Confutatio*, 473-488.
- »450 Jahre Confessio Augustana. Eine Bilanz,« *Catholica* 35 (1981), 1-16.
- »Der fröhliche Wechsel und Streit,« *Catholica* 36 (1982), 101-114.
- »Luther und die Kirchenspaltung,« in H. Geisser et al., *Weder Ketzer noch Heiliger. Luthers Bedeutung für den ökumenischen Dialog* (Regensburg 1982), 73-92, and *Katechetische Blätter* 108 (1983), 27-41.
- »Martin Luther und die römische Kirche,« in E. Iserloh and G. Müller, eds., *Luther und die politische Welt*, Historische Forschungen, 9 (Stuttgart 1984), 173-186.
- »Martin Luther. Fragen an uns – Fragen an ihn,« in P. Manns, ed., *Martin Luther »Reformator und Vater im Glauben«* (Stuttgart 1985), 60-73.

Jansen, Reiner. *Studien zu Luthers Trinitätslehre*, Basler und Berner Studien zur historischen und systematischen Theologie, 26 (Bern & Frankfurt 1976).
Jedin, Hubert. *Geschichte des Konzils von Trient*, 4 vols. in 5 (Freiburg/B. 1958-75).
- *A History of the Council of Trent*, Vols. 1-2 (London and New York 1957-61).

Joest, Wilfred. *Gesetz und Freiheit* (Göttingen 1951, 4th ed. 1968)
- *Ontologie der Person bei Luther* (Göttingen 1967).

Kalkoff, Paul. *Forschungen zu Luthers römischen Prozess*, Bibliothek des königlichen preußischen historischen Instituts in Rom, 2 (Rome 1905).
- »Luther vor dem Generalkapitel zu Heidelberg,« *Zeitschrift für Kirchengeschichte* 27 (1906), 320-323.
- »Die von Kajetan verfasste Ablassdekretale und seine Verhandlungen mit dem Kurfürsten von Sachsen in Weimar,« *Archiv für Reformationsgeschichte* 9 (1911), 142-171.

— »Zu Luthers römischen Prozess,« Zeitschrift für Kirchengeschichte 33 (1912), 40-46.

Kantzenbach, F.W. »Strukturen in der Ekklesiologie des älteren Luther,« Lutherjahrbuch 35 (1968), 48-77.

Kleinaidam, Erich. »Ursprung und Gegenstand der Theologie bei Bernard von Clairvaux und Martin Luther,« in Wilhelm Ernst et al., eds., Dienst der Vermittlung, Erfurter theologische Studien, 37 (Leipzig 1977), 221-247.

Koch, E., L. Ullrich, and U. Kühn. »Der wissenschaftliche Ertrag des Confessio-Augustana-Gedenkjahres 1980,« Theologische Literaturzeitung 106 (1981), 706-731.

Koch, Traugott. »Das Problem des evangelischen Kirchenverständnisses nach dem Augsburger Bekentnis,« in B. Lohse & O.H. Pesch, eds., Das Augsburger Bekenntnis von 1530 damals und heute (Munich & Mainz 1980), 125-143.

Kohler, Alfred. »Die innerdeutsche und die ausserdeutsche Opposition gegen das politische System Karls V.,« in Heinrich Lutz, ed., Das römisch-deutsche Reich im politischen System Karls V., Schriften des historischen Kollegs, 1 (Munich 1982), 107-127.

Kolde, Theodor. »Luther und sein Ordensgeneral in Rom in den Jahren 1518 und 1520,« Zeitschrift für Kirchengeschichte 2 (1878), 472-480.

— Die deutsche Augustiner-Congregation und Johann von Staupitz (Gotha 1879).

Krabbel, Gerta. Caritas Pirkheimer: Ein Lebensbild aus der Zeit der Reformation, Katholisches Leben und Kämpfen im Zeitalter der Glaubensspaltung, 7, 5th ed. (Münster, 1982).

Kretschmar, Georg, and R. Laurentin. »Der Artikel vom Dienst der Heiligen in der Confessio Augustana,« in H. Meyer & H. Schütte, eds., Confessio Augustana. Bekenntnis des einen Glaubens (Paderborn & Frankfurt 1980), 256-280.

Kroeger, Matthias. Rechtfertigung und Gesetz. Studien zur Entwicklung der Rechtfertigungslehre beim jungen Luther, Forschungen zur Kirchen- und Dogmengeschichte, 20 (Göttingen 1968).

Krüger, Gustav. »Luthers Tractatus de indulgentiis,« Theologische Studien und Kritiken 90 (1917), 507-520.

Ladaria, Luis. Antropología teológica (Rome & Madrid 1983).

— Antropologia teologica (Casale Monferraro & Rome 1986).

Lang, Albert. »Die Gliederung und Reichweite des Glaubens nach Thomas von Aquin und den Thomisten,« Divus Thomas (Freiburg/ Switzerland) 20 (1942), 207-236, 334-346, and 21 (1943), 79-97.

Lehmann, Karl, and E. Schlink, eds. Evangelium – Sakramente – Amt. Die ökumenische Tragweite der Confessio Augustana, Dialog der Kirchen, 2 (Freiburg/B. & Göttingen 1982).

— and Wolfhart Pannenberg, eds. Lehrverurteilungen-kirchentrennend? vol. 1, Rechtfertigung, Sakramente und Amt im Zeitalter der Reformation und heute, Dialog der Kirchen, 4 (Freiburg & Göttingen, 1986).

Liebmann, Maximillian. *Urbanus Rhegius und die Anfänge der Reformation*, Reformationsgeschichtliche Studien und Texten, 117 (Münster 1980).

Lienhard, Marc. »La doctrine du Saint-Ésprit chez Luther,« *Verbum Caro* 19 (1965), no. 76, 11-38.

— *Luther. Témoin de Jésus-Christ*, Cogitatio fidei, 73 (Paris 1973).

Liske, Xavier. »Zur Geschichte des Augsburger Reichtages 1518,« *Forschungen zur deutschen Geschichte* 18 (1878), 638-648.

von Loewenich, Walther. *Luther's Theology of the Cross* (original, Munich 1929; translation from the 5th edition of 1967, Minneapolis 1976).

Lohse, Bernhard, and Otto Hermann Pesch, eds. *Das »Augsburger Bekenntnis« von 1530 damals und heute* (Munich & Mainz 1980).

— »Mönchtum, 1, Zum Verständnis von CA 27,« in H. Meyer & H. Schütte, eds., *Confessio Augustana. Bekenntnis des einen Glaubens* (Paderborn & Frankfurt 1980), 281-292.

— »Cajetan und Luther — Zur Begegnung von Thomismus und Reformation,« *Kerygma und Dogma* 32 (1986), 150-169.

— »Die bleibende Bedeutung von Joseph Lortz' Darstellung 'Die Reformation in Deutschland',« in Rolf Decot and Rainer Vinke, eds., *Zum Gedenken an Joseph Lortz (1887-1975)* (Stuttgart 1989), 337-351.

Lortz, Joseph. *Die Reformation in Deutschland*, 2 vols. (Freiburg 1939-40).

— »Zur Problematik der kirchlichen Mißstände im Spät-Mittelalter,« *Trierer Theologische Zeitschrift* 58 (1949), 1-26, 212-227, 257-279, 347-357; reprinted in *Erneuerung und Einheit. Aufsätze zur Theologie- und Kirchengeschichte*, ed. P. Manns (Stuttgart 1987), 295-370.

— »Luthers Römerbriefvorlesungen: Grundanliegen,« *Trierer theologische Zeitschrift* 71 (1962), 129-153, 216-247; reprinted in *Erneuerung und Einheit*, 540-596.

— »Martin Luther, Grundzüge seiner geistigen Struktur,« in E. Iserloh et al., eds., *Reformata Reformanda*, Festschrift Hubert Jedin (Münster 1965), 1, 214-246; reprinted in *Erneuerung und Einheit*, 597-629.

— »Zum Kirchendenken des jungen Luther,« in L. Scheffczyk et al., eds., *Wahrheit und Verkündigung*, Festschrift Michael Schmaus (Munich 1967), 947-986; reprinted in *Erneuerung und Einheit*, 678-717.

— »Reformatorisch und Katholisch beim jungen Luther (1518/19),« in G.M. Beyschlag & E. Wölfel, eds., *Humanitas–Christianitas*, Festschrift Walther von Loewenich (Witten 1968), 47-62; reprinted in *Erneuerung und Einheit*, 630-645.

— »Sakramentales Denken beim jungen Luther,« *Lutherjahrbuch* 36 (1969) 9-40; reprinted in *Erneuerung und Einheit*, 646-677.

— »The Basic Elements of Luther's Intellectual Style,« in J. Wicks, ed., *Catholic Scholars Dialogue with Luther* (Chicago 1970), 3-33.

— *Erneuerung und Einheit. Aufsätze zur Theologie- und Kirchengeschichte*, ed. P. Manns, Veröffentlichungen des Instituts für Europäische Geschichte, 126 (Stuttgart 1987).

Lutz, Heinrich. »Kaiser, Reich und Christenheit: Zur weltgeschichtliche Würdigung des Augsburger Reichstages 1530,« in E. Iserloh and B. Hallensleben, eds., *Confessio Augustana und Confutatio* (Münster 1980), 7-35.

McCue, James F. »*Simul iustus et peccator* in Augustine, Aquinas, and Luther: Toward Putting the Debate in Context,« *Journal of the American Academy of Religion* 48 (1981), 81-96.

McGrath, Alister E. *Iustitia Dei. A History of the Christian Doctrine of Justification*, vol. 1, *From the Beginnings to 1500* (Cambridge 1986).

– *The Intellectual Origins of the European Reformation* (Oxford 1987).

McSorley, Harry. »Was Gabriel Biel a Semipelagian?« in L. Scheffczyk et al. eds., *Wahrheit und Verkündigung*, Festschrift Michael Schmaus (Munich 1967), 2, 1109-20.

– *Luther: Right or Wrong? An Ecumenical-Theological Study of Luther's Major Work, The Bondage of the Will* (New York and Minneapolis 1969).

– »Luther and Trent on the Faith Needed for the Sacrament of Penance,« in E. Schillebeeckx, ed., *Sacramental Reconciliation* (*Concilium*, no. 61; New York 1971), 89-98.

Mannermaa, Tuomo, ed. *Thesaurus Lutheri. Auf der Suche nach neuen Paradigmen der Luther-Forschung*, Veröffentlichungen der finnischen theologischen Literaturgesellschaft, 153 (Helsinki 1987).

– »In ipsa fide Christus adest,« in *Der im Glauben gegenwärtige Christus. Rechtfertigung und Vergottung*, Arbeiten zur Geschichte und Theologie des Luthertums, N.F. 8 (Hannover 1989), 11-93.

– »Der im Glauben gegenwärtige Christus und die Heiligkeit des Christen,« in *Der im Glauben gegenwärtige Christus* (Hannover 1989), 56-93.

– »Theosis als Thema der finnischen Lutherforschung,« in S. Peura and A. Raunio, eds., *Luther und Theosis. Vergöttlichung als Thema der abendländischen Theologie* (Helsinki & Erlangen 1990), 11-26.

Manns, Peter. »Fides Absoluta – Fides Incarnata. Zur Rechtfertigungslehre Luthers im Großen Galaterkommentar,« in E. Iserloh & K. Repgen, eds., *Reformata Reformanda*, Festschrift Hubert Jedin (Münster 1965), 1, 265-312; reprinted in P. Manns, *Vater im Glauben. Studien zur Theologie Martin Luthers*, ed. R. Decot (Stuttgart 1988), 1-48.

– »Absolute and Incarnate Faith. Luther on Justification in the Galatians' Commentary of 1531-1535,« in J. Wicks, ed., *Catholic Scholars Dialogue with Luther* (Chicago 1970), 121-156.

– »Die Heiligenverehrung nach CA 21,« in E. Iserloh & B. Hallensleben, eds., *Confessio Augustana und Confutatio* (Münster 1980), 596-640.

– »Was macht Luther zum 'Vater im Glauben' für die eine Christenheit?« in P. Manns, ed., *Martin Luther Reformator und Vater im Glauben*. Veröffentlichungen des Instituts für Europäische Geschichte, Beiheft 18 (Stuttgart 1985), 1-24.

– »Zum Gespräch zwischen M. Luther und der katholischen Theologie,« in T. Mannermaa, ed., *Thesaurus Lutheri. Auf der Suche nach neuen Paradigmen der Luther-Forschung* (Helsinki 1987), 63-154.

Marcocchi, Massimo. »Spirituality in the Sixteenth and Seventeenth Centuries,« in John W. O'Malley, ed., *Catholicism in Early Modern Europe. A Guide to Research* (St. Louis 1988), 163-192.

Maurer, Wilhelm. »Studien über Melanchthons Anteil an der Entstehung der Confessio Augustana,« *Archiv für Reformationsgeschichte* 51 (1960), 158-207.

– *Historischer Kommentar zur Confessio Augustana*, 2 vols. (Gütersloh 1976-78).

– *Historical Commentary on the Augsburg Confession*, tr. H. George Anderson (Philadelphia 1986).

Meinhold, Peter, ed. *Kirche und Bekenntnis* (Wiesbaden 1980).

Meyer, Harding, Heinz Schütte, et al., eds., *Katholische Anerkennung des Augsburgischen Bekenntnisses?* (Frankfurt 1977).

– and Heinz Schütte, eds., *Confessio Augstana, Bekenntnis des einen Glaubens* (Paderborn & Frankfurt 1980).

– »Das Bischofsamt nach CA 28,« in Erwin Iserloh and Barbara Hallensleben, eds., *Confessio Augustana und Confutatio. Der Augsburger Reichstag 1530 und die Einheit der Kirche* (Münster 1980), 489-498.

Moeller, Bernd. »Frömmigkeit in Deutschland um 1500,« *Archiv für Reformationgeschichte* 56 (1965), 5-31.

– »Piety in Germany around 1500,« in S. Ozment, ed., *The Reformation in Medieval Perspective* (Chicago 1971), 50-75; also in G. Strauss, ed., *Pre-Reformation Germany* (London & New York 1972), 13-42.

– »Korreferat zu Wolfgang Reinhard: Luther und die Städte,« in E. Iserloh & G. Müller, eds., *Luther und die politische Welt* (Stuttgart 1984), 113-121.

– »Was wurde in der Frühzeit der Reformation in den deutschen Städten gepredigt?« *Archiv für Reformationsgeschichte* 75 (1984), 176-193.

– »Die letzten Ablaßkampagnen. Der Widerspruch Luthers gegen den Ablaß in seinem geschichtlichen Zusammenhang,« in H. Boockmann et al., eds., *Lebenslehren und Weltentwürfe im Übergang vom Mittelalter zur Neuzeit* (Göttingen 1989), 539-567.

Mostert, Walter. »Scriptura sacra sui ipsius interpres. Bemerkungen zum Verständnis der Heiligen Schrift bei Luther,« *Lutherjahrbuch* 46 (1979), 60-96.

Müller, Gerhard. »Johann Eck und die Confessio Augustana,« *Quellen und Forschungen aus italienischen Archiven und Bibliotheken* 38 (1958), 205-242.

– »Ekklesiologie und Kirchenkritik beim jungen Luther,« *Neue Zeitschrift für systematische Theologie* 7 (1965), 100-128, reprinted in *Causa Reformationis*, ed. G. Maron & G. Seebass (Gütersloh 1989), 472-500.

– »Um die Einheit der Kirche. Zu den Verhandlungen über den Laienkelch während des Augsburger Reichstages 1530,« in E. Iserloh and K. Repgen, eds., *Reformata Reformanda*, Festschrift Hubert Jedin, 2 vols. (Münster 1965), 1, 393-427.

– »Duldung des deutschen Luthertums? Erwägungen Kardinal Lorenzo Campeggios vom September 1530,« *Archiv für Reformationsgeschichte* 68 (1977), 158-172.
– ed. *Die Religionsgespräche der Reformationszeit*, Schriften des Vereins für Reformationsgeschichte, 191 (Gütersloh 1980).
– »Die Anhänger der Confessio Augustana und die Ausschussverhandlungen,« in E. Iserloh and B. Hallensleben, eds., *Confessio Augustana und Confutatio* (Münster 1980), 243-257.
Müller, Karl. »Luther's römischer Prozess,« *Zeitschrift für Kirchengeschichte* 24 (1903), 46-61.

Naz, Raoul. »Maître du sacré-palais,« *Dictionnaire de droit canonique* 6 (1957), 711-712.
Neill, Thomas P. *The Makers of the Modern Mind* (Milwaukee 1949).
Neuhaus, Helmut. »Der Augsburger Reichstag des Jahres 1530. Ein Forschungsbericht,« *Zeitschrift für historische Forschung* 9 (1982), 167-211.
Nicol, Martin. *Meditation bei Luther*, Forschungen zur Kirchen- und Dogmengeschichte, 34 (Göttingen 1984).
Nilsson, K.O. *Simul. Das Miteinander von Göttlichem und Menschlichem in Luthers Theologie*, Forschungen zur Kirchen- und Dogmengeschichte, 17 (Göttingen 1966).

Oakley, Francis. *The Western Church in the Later Middle Ages* (Ithaca, N.Y. 1979).
Oberman, Heiko A. *The Harvest of Medieval Theology* (Cambridge, Mass. 1963).
Olivier, Daniel. *La foi de Luther*, Le Point théologique, 27 (Paris 1978).
– *Luther's Faith: the Cause of the Gospel in the Church* (St. Louis 1982).
O'Malley, John W. »Erasmus and Luther: Continuity and Discontinuity as Key to Their Conflict,« *Sixteenth Century Journal* 5 (1974), 47-65.
– »The Feast of Thomas Aquinas in Renaissance Rome,« *Rivista di Storia della Chiesa in Italia* 35 (1981), 1-27.
– ed. *Catholicism in Early Modern History. A Guide to Research* (St. Louis 1988).

Pannenberg, Wolfhart. »Über Lortz hinaus?« in R. Decot and R. Vinke, eds., *Zum Gedenken an Joseph Lortz (1887-1975)* (Stuttgart 1989), 93-105.
Paulus, Nikolas. *Johann Tetzel der Ablassprediger* (Mainz 1899).
– *Geschichte des Ablasses im Mittelalter*, 3 vols. (Paderborn 1922-23).
Perrone, Lorenzo, ed. *Lutero in Italia*, Dabar: Saggi di storia religiosa, 1 (Casale Monferrato 1983).
Pesch, Otto Hermann. *Die Theologie der Rechtfertigung bei Martin Luther und Thomas von Aquin*, Walberberger Studien, Theologische Reihe, 4 (Mainz 1967, reprint 1984).
– »Existential and Sapiential Theology: The Theological Confrontation between Luther and Thomas Aquinas,« in J. Wicks, ed., *Catholic Scholars Dialogue with Luther* (Chicago 1970), 61-81.

- »Gottes Gnadenhandeln als Rechtfertigung des Menschen,« in *Mysterium Salutis*, ed. Johannes Feiner & Magnus Löhrer, vol. IV/2 (Einsiedeln 1973), 831-920.
- »Rechtfertigung des Sünders und Gerechtigkeit der Welt,« in B. Lohse & O.H. Pesch, eds., *Das Augsburger Bekenntnis damals und heute* (Munich & Mainz 1980), 215-236.
- *Hinführung zu Luther* (Mainz 1982).

Peter, Carl J. »From *Sermo* to *Anathema*: a Dispute about the Confession of Mortal Sins,« in Nelson H. Minnich, et al., eds., *Studies in Church History in Honor of John Tracy Ellis* (Wilmington, Del. 1985), 566-588.
- »The Church's Treasures (*thesauri ecclesiae*) Then and Now,« *Theological Studies* 47 (1986), 251-272.

Peters, Albrecht. »Die Theologie der Katechismen Luthers anhand der Zuordnung ihrer Hauptstücke,« *Lutherjahrbuch* 43 (1976), 7-35.
- »Die Spiritualität der lutherischen Reformation,« in W. Lohff and L. Mohaupt, eds., *Volkskirche – Kirche der Zukunft?* (Hamburg 1977), 132-148.

Peura, Simo, and A. Raunio, eds. *Luther und Theosis. Vergöttlichung als Thema der abendländischen Theologie*, Schriften der Luther-Agricola-Gesellschaft, A, 25 (Helsinki & Erlangen 1990).
- »Die Teilhabe an Christus bei Luther,« in S. Peura and A. Raunio, eds. *Luther und Theosis. Vergöttlichung als Thema der abendländischen Theologie* (Helsinki & Erlangen 1990), 121-161.

Pfnür, Vinzenz. *Einig in der Rechtfertigungslehre? Die Rechtfertigungslehre der Confessio Augustana (1530) und die Stellugnahme der katholischen Kontroverstheologen zwischen 1530 und 1535*, Veröffentlichungen des Instituts für Europäische Geschichte, 60 (Wiesbaden 1970).

Pfürtner, Stephanus. *Luther und Thomas im Gespräch* (Heidelberg 1961).
- *Luther and Aquinas on Salvation* (New York 1964).

Pollet, Jacques. *Huldrych Zwingli et la Réforme en Suisse* (Paris 1963).

Poschmann, Bernhard. *Der Ablaß im Licht der Bußgeschichte*, Theophaneia, 4 (Bonn 1948).

Prenter, Regin. »Luthers Lehre von der Heiligung,« in V. Vajta, ed., *Lutherforschung heute. Referate und Berichte des 1. Internationalen Lutherforschungskongresses* (Berlin 1958), 64-74.

Prien, H.-J. »Grundgedanken der Ekklesiologie beim jungen Luther,« *Archiv für Reformationsgeschichte* 76 (1985), 96-111.

Rahner, Karl. »Remarks on the Theology of Indulgences,« *Theological Investigations*, 2 (Baltimore 1963), 173-201.
- »Gerecht und Sünder zugleich,« in *Schriften zur Theologie*, 6 (Einsiedeln 1965), 262-276.
- »Justified and Sinner at the Same Time,« in *Theological Investgations*, 6 (Baltimore & London 1969), 218-230.

Rapp, François. Réform et Réformation à Strasbourg. Église et Societé dans le diocese de Strasbourg (1450-1525), Collection de l'Institut des Hautes Etudes alsaciennes, 23 (Paris 1974).

Rassow, Peter. Die Kaiser-Idee Karls V., Historische Studien, 217 (Berlin 1932).

Reinhard, Wolfgang. »Gegenreformation als Modernisierung? Prolegomena zu einer Theorie des konfessionellen Zeitalters,« Archiv für Reformationsgeschichte 68 (1977), 226-252.

– »Die kirchenpolitischen Vorstellungen Kaiser Karls V.: Ihre Grundlagen und ihr Wandel,« in E. Iserloh and B. Hallensleben, eds., Confessio Augustana und Confutatio (Münster 1980), 86-94.

Root, Michael. »The Augsburg Confession as Ecumenical Proposal: Episcopacy, Luther, and Wilhelm Maurer,« Dialog 28 (1989), 223-232.

Ruh, Ulrich. »Ein Bekenntnis wird lebendig. Zum 450. Jubiläum der Confessio Augstana,« Herder Korrespondenz 34 (1980), 382-387.

Rupp, Gordon. The Righteousness of God (London 1953).

Scheible, Heinz. »Melanchthon und Luther während des Augsburger Reichstags 1530,« in P. Manns, ed., Martin Luther »Reformator und Vater im Glauben« (Stuttgart 1985), 40-45.

– »Melanchthons Auseinandersetzung mit dem Reformkatholizismus,« in R. Decot, ed., Vermittlungsversuche auf dem Augsburger Reichstag 1530, Veröffentlichungen des Instituts für Europäische Geschichte, Beiheft 26 (Stuttgart 1989), 68-90.

Schindling, Anton. »Die Reformation in den Reichsstädten und die Kirchengüter: Strassburg, Nürnberg und Frankfurt im Vergleich,« in J. Sydow, ed., Bürgerschaft und Kirche, Stadt in der Geschichte, 7 (Sigmaringen, 1980), 67-80.

Schmaus, Michael. Der Glaube der Kirche, 2 vols. (Munich 1969-70).

– Dogma, vol. 6, Justification and the Last Things (Kansas City & London 1977).

Schwab, Wolfgang. Entwicklung und Gestalt der Sakramententheologie bei Martin Luther, Europäische Hochschulschriften, XXIII, 79 (Frankfurt/M. & Bern 1977).

Schwager, R. »Der fröliche Wechsel und Streit,« Zeitschrift für katholische Theologie 115 (1983), 27-66.

Schwarzwäller, Klaus. »Delectari assertionibus. Zur Struktur von Luthers Pneumatologie,« Lutherjahrbuch 38 (1971), 26-58.

– »Rechtfertigung und Ekklesiologie in den Schmalkaldischen Artikeln,« Kerygma und Dogma 35 (1989), 84-105.

Seebass, Gottfried. »The Reformation in Nürnberg,« in L. P. Buck and J. W. Zophy, eds., The Social History of the Reformation, Festschrift Harold J. Grimm (Columbus, Ohio 1972), 17-40.

– »Die reformatorische Bekenntnisse vor der Confessio Augustana,« in P. Meinhold, ed., Kirche und Bekenntnis (Wiesbaden 1980), 26-55.

Selge, Kurt-Victor. Review of Gerhard Hennig, *Cajetan und Luther* (Stuttgart 1966), in *Archiv für Reformationsgeschichte* 60 (1969), 271-274.
- *Normen der Christenheit im Streit um Ablaß und Kirchenautorität 1518-1521*. 1. Teil, *Das Jahr 1518*. Habilitationsschrift, Heidelberg 1968.
- »Das Autoritätengefüge der westlichen Christenheit im Lutherkonflikt 1517 bis 1521,« *Historische Zeitschrift* 223 (1976), 591-617.
- »La chiesa in Lutero,« in *Martin Lutero*, ed. M. Marcocchi (Milan 1984).
Setton, Kenneth M. »Pope Leo and the Turkish Peril,« *Proceedings of the American Philosophical Association* 113 (1969), 367-424; reprinted as essay no. IX in K.M. Setton, *Europe and the Levant in the Middle Ages and the Renaissance* (London 1974).
Smith, Thurman L. »Luther and the Iserloh Thesis from a Numismatic Perspective,« *Sixteenth Century Journal* 20 (1989), 183-201.
Stakemeier, Adolf. *Das Konzil von Trient über die Heilsgewissheit* (Heidelberg 1947).
Steglich, Wolfgang. »Die Stellung des evangelischen Reichsstände und Reichsstädte zu Karl V. zwischen Protestation und Konfession 1529/30,« *Archiv für Reformationsgeschichte* 62 (1971), 161-192.
Steinmetz, David C. *Misericordia Dei. The Theology of Johannes von Staupitz in its Late Medieval Setting*, Studies in Medieval and Reformation Thought, 4 (Leiden 1968).
- *Luther and Staupitz. An Essay in the Intellectual Origin of the Protestant Reformation*, Duke Monographs on Medieval and Renaissance Studies, 4 (Durham, N.C. 1980).
Stock, Ursula. *Die Bedeutung der Sakramente in Luthers Sermonen von 1519*, Studies in the History of Christian Thought, 27 (Leiden 1982).
Strauss, Gerald. *Nuremberg in the Sixteenth Century*, 2nd edition (Bloomington, Ind. & London 1976).
Strayer, J.R. »The Fourth and the Fourteenth Centuries,« *American Historical Review* 77 (1972), 1-14.
Strohl, Henri. *Luther jusqu'en 1520*, 2nd ed. (Paris 1962).

Tentler, Thomas N. *Sin and Confession on the Eve of the Reformation* (Princeton 1977).
Timiadis, E. »Une Texte inachevé,« in *Le Confession d'Augsbourg, 450e anniversaire. Autour d'un colloque*, Le Point théologique, 31 (Paris 1980), 197-226.

Ullrich, Lothar. »Ist die katholische Meßopferlehre ein Hindernis für eine katholische Anerkennung des Augsburgischen Bekenntnis?« in F. Hoffmann & U. Kühn, eds., *Die Confessio Augustana im ökumenischen Gespräch* (Berlin/DDR 1980), 191-220.

Vercruysse, Jos E. »Gesetz und Liebe. Die Struktur der Heidelberg Disputation Luthers (1518),« *Lutherjahrbuch* 48 (1981), 7-43.
- »Word and Sacrament in Luther's Theology,« in *Luther et la Réforme allemande dans une perspective oecuménique*, Les Études théologiques de Chambésy, 3 (Chambésy-Geneva 1983), 197-211.
- »Jacobus Latomus und Martin Luther: Einführendes zu einer Kontroverse,« *Gregorianum* 64 (1983), 515-538, reprinted in *Katholische Theologen der Reformationszeit*, ed. E. Iserloh, 2 (Münster 1985), 7-26.
von Voltelini, Hans. »Die Bestrebungen Maximilians I. um die Kaiserkrone 1518,« *Mitteilungen des Instituts für österreichische Geschichtsforschung* 11 (1890), 41-85, 574-626.
Volz, Hans. *Martin Luthers Thesenanschlag und dessen Vorgeschichte* (Weimar 1959).

Wagner, Georg. »Der letzte Türkenkreutzzugsplan Kaiser Maximilians I. aus dem Jahre 1517,« *Mitteilungen des Instituts für österreichische Geschichtsforschung* 77 (1969), 314-353.
von Walter, J. »Der Reichstag zu Augsburg 1530,« *Lutherjahrbuch* 12 (1930), 1-90.
Wiesflecker, Hermann. *Kaiser Maximilian I. Das Reich, Österreich und Europa*, 4, *Gründung des habsburgischen Weltreiches. Lebensabend und Tod* (Munich 1981).
Wicks, Jared. *Man Yearning for Grace. Martin Luther's Early Spiritual Teaching* (Washington, DC 1968 and Wiesbaden 1969).
- »Luther through Catholic Eyes,« *Chicago Studies* 8 (1969), 275-285.
- »Luther (Martin),« *Dictionnaire de Spiritualité*, vol. 9 (1976), cols. 1206-1243.
- *Cajetan Responds. A Reader in Reformation Controversy* (Washington 1978).
- *Cajetan und die Anfänge der Reformation*, Katholisches Leben und Kirchenreform im Zeitalter der Glaubensspaltung, 43 (Münster 1983).
- *Luther and His Spiritual Legacy*, Theology and Life, 7 (Wilmington, Del. 1983).
- »Temi di ecclesiologia nel dialogo luterano-cattolico (1965-1985),« in R. Latourelle, ed., *Vaticano II Bilancio e prospettive*, 2 vols. (Assisi 1987), 2, 883-919; in English in R. Latourelle, ed., *Vatican II: Assessment and Perspectives*, 3 vols. (New York/Mahwaw, N.J. 1988-89), 2, 305-346.
- »Reformation Studies,« *New Catholic Encyclopedia*, vol. 18, Supplement 1978-88 (Palatine, Ill. 1989), 415-424.
- »Simul iustus et peccator,« *Dictionnaire de Spiritualité*, vol. 14 (1989), cols. 921-931.
Witek, John W. »From India to Japan: European Missionary Expansion, 1500-1650,« in John W. O'Malley, ed., *Catholicism in Early Modern Europe. A Guide to Research* (St. Louis 1988), 193-210.
Wriedt, Markus. »Luthers Gebrauch der Bischofstitulatur in seinen Briefen,« in Martin Brecht, ed., *Martin Luther und das Bischofsamt* (Stuttgart 1990), 73-100.

Zeeden, Ernst Walter. »Grundlagen und Wege der Konfessionsbildung in Deutschland im Zeitalter der Glaubenskämpfe,« *Historische Zeitschrift* 185 (1958), 149-199; reprinted in E.W. Zeeden, ed., *Gegenreformation*, Wege der Forschung, 311 (Darmstadt 1973), 85-134.

Zschoch, Hellmut, *Klosterreform und monastische Spiritualität im 15. Jahrhundert. Conrad von Zenn (d. 1460) und sein »Liber de vita monastica«*, Beiträge zur historischen Theologie, 75 (Tübingen 1988).

Zur Mühlen, K.-H. »Zur Rezeption der Augustinischen Sakramentsformel 'Accedit verbum ad elementum, et fit sacramentum' in der Theologie Luthers,« *Zeitschrift für Theologie und Kirche* 70 (1973), 50-76.

– *Reformatorische Vernunftkritik und neuzeitliches Denken*, Beiträge zur historischen Theologie, 59 (Tübingen 1980).

INDEX

Abelard, Peter 41
Absolution 2, 23-24, 26, 34, 45, 50n, 53, 78, 98, 122-129, 130, 131, 133, 134, 141, 142, 144, 145, 171, 172, 182, 208, 236, 243, 249, 258, 292, 294, 295, 296n, 298
Abstinence. *See* Fasting laws
Abuses, in church practice 17, 41-42, 97-98, 223, 225, 228, 231-237, 238-245, 247-250, 252, 256-261, 273-276, 296-280
Acceptatio divina 8, 102
Adrian VI, Pope 238, 239
Agricola, Johann 290
Aland, Kurt 87n
Albrecht of Brandenburg, Archbishop 19, 46, 87-92, 93n, 94, 96, 99n, 101n, 102n, 149, 150, 153, 158n, 179n, 186, 265n, 282n, 283
Alexander, J. Neil 192n
Alexander of Hales 8
Alfaro, Juan 117, 118n
Althaus, Paul 39n, 118n
Alveld, Augustine von 198, 200
Ambrose, St. 65
Amsdorf, Nicholas 266n
Anabaptists 252
Anthropology, biblical 63-69
Antichrist 184, 218, 255, 264
Antinomians 28, 68, 73, 78, 217
Apocalyptic 186, 276
Apologia of the Augsburg Confession 308n
Arnau García, Ramon 193n
Arnoldi, Bartholomew, of Usingen 7, 270
Asendorf, Ulrich 37n
Attrition 145
Augsburg Diet (1530) 3, 12, 195, 223-316 *passim*

Augsburg Confession 38, 195, 197, 219, 223-226, 227, 229, 237, 251-263, 290
  Catholic recognition of 223-225, 227
Augustine, St. 9, 29, 65, 83, 104, 126n, 137, 158, 212, 239n, 299
Authority, ecclesiastical 152, 219, 228, 235, 238, 243, 245, 258-259, 295, 296, 298, 305
  See also Jurisdiction, ecclesiastical
  Law, ecclesiastical

Bäumer, Remigius 87n, 159n, 178n, 285n, 297n, 313n
Balthasar, Hans Urs von 6
Baptism 34, 55, 69, 74-76, 78, 98, 141, 190, 208, 209, 234, 247
Bayer, Oswald 2n, 4, 16n, 23n, 50n, 74n, 119n, 125n, 129n, 136n, 137n, 174n
Baylor, Michael G. 22n, 47n
Becker, Hans-Jürgen 178n, 183n
Beer, Theobald 6
Beintker, Horst 140n
Belloc, Hilaire 5n
Bernard of Clairvaux, St. 29, 41, 101n, 128n, 137, 138n, 145
Bernardi, Bartholomew 121n
Beyer, Michael 203n
Bible, instruction on 231
Bible, Luther's translation 191-192
Biel, Gabriel 7-9, 20n, 102n, 104n, 106n, 114, 127n, 195n
Binding and loosing (Mt. 16:19) 24, 26, 123, 124, 126, 127, 136, 138, 142, 144, 168, 169n, 171, 173, 202
  See also Absolution
Birmelé, André 219n, 220n

Bishops, German 41, 236-237, 243-244, 246-248, 250, 288, 298
Bizer, Ernest 50n, 135n
Boehmer, Heinrich 91n
Bonaventure, St. 168
Bondage of the will 27, 30-33
Bonfio, Luca 287n
Bornkamm, Heinrich 91n, 251n, 262n
Borth, Wilhelm 150n, 153n, 154n, 160n, 163n
Bossy, John 193n
Brecht, Martin 23n, 50n, 91n, 108n, 118n, 126n, 174n, 189n, 198n, 219n, 284n, 293n, 297n, 306, 308n
Brenz, Johann 289n, 292, 297, 300n
Brieger, Theodor 238n, 241n, 266n
Brown, Dorothy Catherine 190n
Brück, Gregor 255, 284, 288n, 289n, 291, 295, 299, 300, 303n, 306, 307, 308
Bucer, Martin 246, 286n
Bugenhagen, Johann 240
Burger, Christoph 190n

Cajetan, Cardinal Tommaso de Vio 2n, 11, 50n, 116n, 130-135, 137, 138, 139, 142, 146-147, 152, 155, 156n, 158, 159, 160, 161, 162, 163, 164-181, 182, 183, 185, 187, 268n, 315n
  Augsburg Treatises (1518) 131-134, 160, 166-175, 187
Camelot, T. 126n
Campeggio, Lorenzo, Cardinal 158n, 195, 253n, 261n, 262n, 268, 269, 270, 281, 283, 286n, 289, 290, 291n, 308n, 313
Canon Law, doctrinal authority 158, 185
Capito, Wolfgang 246
Caraffa, Olivero, Cardinal 158n
Catechetical works, Luther's 11, 38n, 57, 190, 192, 198, 199, 203-211, 254n
Catharinus, Ambrosius 198, 200n
Catholic interpretations of Luther 4-6, 82-83, 96, 116
»Catholic Luther« 195
Catholica responsio (July 1530) 271-272, 285-286
Cavallotto, Stefano 189-196, 208n

Celibacy, clerical 228, 235, 238, 240, 241, 242, 244, 249, 259, 260, 263, 268n, 275, 279, 282-283, 287, 291, 295, 296, 297, 298, 299, 300, 305, 306, 307, 309, 313, 316
Certainty of salvation 29, 32, 101, 117-118, 121, 140
Certitude of grace 49, 117-118, 121, 132, 133, 139, 170, 172, 173
Chalice, for laity. *See* Communion under one form
Chantraine, Georges 30n
Charles V, Emperor 161, 163n, 195, 227, 240, 253, 255, 261, 262, 264, 272, 274n, 280, 281, 282, 283, 284, 287, 288n, 289, 290, 308n, 309, 310n, 313
Christian life 2, 69-70, 106, 108
  See also Spirituality, penitential
Christology, Luther's 23, 25-26, 33-34, 56-57, 110, 174
Church, Christian 78, 194, 197-220, 232
  Donatist misunderstanding 219-220
  hidden, 199-200, 207
  marks of 207
  as mother 208
  unity of 242, 245
Civil authority 236, 239
Clement VI, Pope 168, 176, 181, 182
Clement VII, Pope (formerly Giulio de' Medici) 281, 308n
Clerical privileges 193
Coat of arms, Luther's 43
Cochlaeus, Johann 211n, 269, 289n, 296n, 299
Communio sanctorum 206
Communion under one form 228, 233, 241, 259, 260, 263, 266, 268n, 275, 279, 280, 282-283, 291, 295, 296, 297, 299, 300, 303, 304, 306, 309, 311, 313, 314-315, 316
Conciliarism 41
Concupiscence. *See* Sin, remaining
Confession of sin 10, 16-17, 47-49, 53, 64, 66, 80, 81, 103, 119, 120, 123, 129, 190, 228, 232, 243, 249, 258, 260, 275, 279, 290, 294, 296, 298, 299, 313
Confessionalization 315-316

Index

Confutatio, imperial (Aug. 3, 1530) 226, 228, 269, 272-276, 277, 280, 286, 288, 290, 291
Congar, Yves 34n, 126n
Conrad of Zenn 62n
Contarini, Gasparo 141
Conscience 22, 26, 71, 72, 236, 239, 249, 258, 287-288, 305, 314
Consolation 72, 76, 142, 239, 249, 258, 298
Contrition 53, 61, 93, 103, 104, 105, 106, 109, 120, 123, 124, 126, 128, 132, 133, 142, 145, 171, 172, 173, 292
Controversialists, Catholic 39, 115, 269-272
Conversion 1, 2, 16-23, 45, 46-49, 55, 67, 72-74, 83, 88, 104, 105, 107, 109, 112, 119-122, 232
Council, general, of the church 159, 183, 256, 281, 296, 300, 308, 309
Creatura evangelii, church as 200, 201
Creed, the 73, 80, 194, 198, 199, 201, 203-211, 213, 216, 218, 249
Creutzberg, Heinrich A. 183n
Crusade proposal (1518) 161-162, 165, 186
Cum postquam, papal bull (1518) 182, 184-185, 186, 187
Cyprian, St. 239n

Death, preparation for 141, 191, 194, 265
Decalogue 38n, 101n, 216-217, 249
Decot, Rolf 248n
Delfini, Giovanni A. 176n
Delumeau, Jean 193n
Dettloff, Werner 102n
Dialogue, Lutheran-Catholic, 20th century 40, 59-60, 118, 196, 197-198, 220, 223-226, 259n
  in 1530, 226, 262, 279, 280-281, 287-316
Dietenberger, Johann 270, 314n
Dietterle, J. 110n
Discipline, imposed on the people 290, 295, 303, 307, 316
  on priests 298
Dispositions for receiving sacraments 172, 182
Disputation on indulgences (1517), Luther's proposed approach 88, 92, 94, 157, 159, 178
Dittrich, Bernhard 254n, 255n, 286n, 305n

Dominicans 151, 153, 159, 184

Early teachings, Luther's 16-23, 45-49, 62, 118-122
Ebeling, Gerhard 21n, 63n, 118n, 212n
Ecclesiology 3, 197-202, 291
  See also Church, Christian
Eck, Johann 50n, 67, 111n, 170n, 184n, 185n, 252, 253, 254n, 269, 276, 283, 289n, 290, 292, 293n, 294, 296n, 299, 303n, 304, 308, 311n, 313
404 Articles (1530) 252-254, 271
Edwards, Mark U. 53n, 285n
Eire, Carlos M. N. 231n, 249n
Emser, Jerome 198
Erasmus, Desiderius 28, 30, 31, 141, 158n
Ernst, Wilhelm 20n
Estates 39, 74, 76, 232, 258
Eucharist. *See* Lord's Supper
Evennett, H. Outram 40n
Exchange with Christ 23, 26-27, 36-37, 76
Excommunication 154-155, 162, 179, 244, 250, 259, 290, 316
Experience 27-29, 41, 81

Fabri, Johann 269, 271, 283, 285, 296n
Facienti quod in se est Deus non denegat gratiam 8, 10, 20, 144
Faith 2, 17, 26-27, 33, 44, 49-53, 117-118
  active in love 290, 291
  infused and acquired 132, 172
  reflexive 143-144
  See also Fides sacramenti
Farge, James K. 149n
Farnese, Alessandro, Cardinal (later, Pope Paul III) 161
Fasting laws 228, 231, 242, 256, 270, 273, 279, 294, 295, 305, 313
Fathers of the church, doctrinal authority 158, 185
Ferdinand, Archduke of the Holy Roman Empire 281, 283, 313n
Fides sacramenti 2, 23-25, 26, 49-53, 117-147, 170-176, 178, 179, 182, 187, 243n

See also *Non sacramentum sed fides sacramenti iustificat*
Fides specialis 137, 138, 139, 140-141, 142, 146, 147, 177
See also *Pro me*
1518, Luther's thought in 2, 23-26, 45, 122-147, 174
Flatten, Heinrich 155n
Flörken, Norbert 49n, 120n
Florence, Council of 133, 134, 172
Forgiveness of sin 23-25, 34-35, 49-53, 64, 69, 71-73, 75, 78, 83, 100, 105, 122-129, 202, 206, 208, 209-210, 212-214, 232, 239, 292
Fraenkel, Pierre 70n
Francis I, King 183
Fransen, Piet 156n
Frederick the Wise, Prince-Elector 3n, 9, 11n, 130, 138, 153-154, 158n, 160, 161, 163, 164, 165, 167, 177n, 178n, 182, 183, 184, 185, 186, 191
Freedom, Christian 11, 28, 37-38, 76-77, 192-193, 232, 235, 257, 258, 262, 266, 274, 290, 306
Fugger Bank 150

Gattinara, Mercurino 282
Gauly, Peter 224n
Gebhardt, Bruno 161n
Georg, Duke of Albertine Saxony 253n, 270, 283, 289n
Georg, Margrave of Brandenburg-Ansbach 229, 230n, 231, 233, 236, 237, 289n
Gerrish, Brian 32n
Gerson, Jean 121, 146n, 190
Ghinucci, Girolamo, Bishop 130, 155, 156, 158, 160, 179
God, eternal will 32
hidden 21
sovereign 40
See also Trinity, of divine persons
Gogan, Brian 157n
Gospel, proclamation of 34, 72, 78, 211, 232, 242, 290
See also Word, God's

Grace, healing 18, 19, 20, 62, 70, 72, 100, 103, 105, 106, 108, 109, 112, 114, 116, 121, 149, 169
infused 75, 100, 213, 217
preparation for (scholastic doctrine) 8, 20
See also *Gratia et donum*
Granvella, Nicolas de 274n
Gratia et donum 35-36, 63, 70-74, 83, 217
Gravamina of German nation 161, 186, 240, 275
Gregory the Great, St. 67, 239
Grendler, Paul F. 40n
Gussmann, Wilhelm 230, 261n

Hacker, Paul 6, 143
Hagen, Bernhard 289n, 303n
Hamm, Bernd 121, 190n
Hammann, Konrad 199n, 200n, 207n, 218
Happee, J. 80n
Hasler, August 82n, 118n
Heart, believing 43-57
  Christ's 56-57
  God's 56-57, 216
  submissive 53-57
Hecker, Gerhard 164
Heidelberg Disputation 95, 154
Heilbronn 230, 231, 237
Heinrich of Braunschweig, Duke 289n, 311
Heller, Sebastian 289n, 303n
Hendrix, Scott 19n, 151n, 159n, 167n, 180n
Hennig, Gerhard 181n
Heresy, Luther suspect of 155-157, 160
  Luther accused of 157, 163, 175n
  Zwingli's 254
Hermann, Rudolph 62n, 64n, 70n, 73n
Herms, Eilert 203n, 209n
Hermann, Fritz 89n, 90n, 91n
Hof, Otto 118n, 143n
Hollerbach, Marian 279n
Holy days 242, 256, 294, 298, 313
Holy Spirit 3, 31, 35, 37, 43, 53, 56, 57, 69, 71, 72, 73, 75, 77, 78, 80, 81, 82, 107n, 127, 137, 138, 144, 147, 194, 197-198, 201, 203-211, 212, 213, 215, 235

Index

Honée, Eugène 226n, 279n, 283n, 287n, 289n, 299n, 313n
Honselmann, Klemens 87n
Horst, Ulrich 200n, 314n
Human enactments 231, 234, 235, 236, 240, 242, 266, 274, 295, 311-312, 314
Hutten, Ulrich von 155n

Ignatius Loyola, St. 141, 191n
Images, religious 231, 232
Immenkötter, Herbert 226n, 228n, 251n, 270n, 271n, 272n, 279n, 286n, 290n, 302n, 309n, 313n
Imputation 27, 36, 66, 72, 77, 98, 117, 119, 211, 214
Indulgences 10, 11, 17, 19, 23, 45-47, 87-88, 93, 96, 97-114, 119-121, 122, 123, 126, 130, 131, 149, 162, 167-170, 175, 178-179, 180, 181-182, 239, 247, 248
Innocent III, Pope 239n
Intercession by the Church 100, 102, 104, 105, 106, 108-109, 111-114, 116
Iserloh, Erwin 1n, 4, 6n, 25n, 35n, 45n, 71n, 82, 87, 88n, 91n, 92n, 96n, 111n, 143n, 183n, 195n, 197, 199n, 205n, 219n, 224n, 225n, 236n, 258n
Ius divinum 295
Iustitia divina 151
Iustus ex fide vivit (Rom. 1:17) 24, 49-50

Jansen, Reiner 204n
Jedin, Hubert 118n
Jesus Christ 26, 28, 33, 36, 38, 39, 40, 41, 43, 44, 50, 54, 55, 57, 63n, 69, 71, 72, 73, 76, 80, 124, 140, 205, 209, 212, 218
 Christus actuosissimus 25-26, 120
 merits of, 97, 110
 in the Psalms, 107n
 See also Christology, Luther's
Joachim, Prince-Elector of Brandenburg 253n, 288
Joest, Wilfried 25n, 63n, 71n, 73n, 77n, 118n, 143n, 144
Johann, Prince-Elector of Saxony 238n, 244, 245, 248n, 252, 263, 284, 285n, 286n, 287n, 290, 302, 303, 304, 311, 312n
Johann Friedrich, Prince of Saxony 289n
John Paul II, Pope 224
Jonas, Justus 240, 246, 281n, 290
Judgment, God's word as 17, 26, 47, 119-120, 123
Jurisdiction, ecclesiastical 236, 280, 282, 290, 295, 307, 316
 See also Authority, ecclesiastical
Justification 15-42, 50, 59-60, 99, 108, 112, 129, 290

Kalkoff, Paul 154n, 162n, 163n, 165n, 181n
Kantzenbach, F. W. 207n
Karlstadt, Andreas 30, 54, 128, 139, 153, 178n, 205
Kasper, Walter 236n
Keys, power of 100, 101, 102, 105, 109, 110, 127, 128, 131, 169, 176, 212, 236, 294
 See also Binding and loosing
Kleinaidam, Erich 145n
Kleinknecht, H. 68n
Kluckhorn, August 161n
Koch, Traugott 200n
Köhler, Walther 90n
Kohler, Alfred 283n
Kolde, Theodor 153n, 164n
Kretschmar, Georg 236n, 259n
Kroeger, Matthias 2n, 16n, 24n, 121n, 123n, 169n
Krüger, Gustav 90n, 91n, 95n, 97

Ladaria, Luis 82
Lang, Albert 156n
Lang, Johann 151, 153n, 158n
Lasco, Oswald de 98n
Late-medieval piety 41, 229, 230, 232, 235, 237, 243, 248
Late-medieval theology 3, 7-9, 41
Latomus, Jacob 68-70
Laurentin, René 259n
Law, ecclesiastical 236, 240, 242-243, 258-259, 263, 266-268, 274, 276, 294, 295, 305

Law, God's 18, 22, 64, 68, 72, 106, 216-217, 232
Leipzig Disputation (1519) 279
Leo X, Pope 68, 92n, 101n, 130, 151, 152, 157n, 159, 161, 162, 165n, 176, 177, 179, 180, 181-182, 185n, 186, 187
Liberum arbitrium 8-9, 20, 29, 30, 40, 232, 282
  See also Bondage of the Will
Liebmann, Maximillian 285n
Lienhard, Marc 25n, 212n
Link, Wenceslaus 138, 175-176
Liske, Xavier 162n
Loewenich, Walter von 175n
Lohse, Bernhard 115n, 131n, 133n, 134n, 166n, 175n, 179n, 186n, 236n, 257n
Lombard, Peter 124, 133, 172
Löner, Kaspar 230, 232n, 233n, 234
Löscher, Valentin E. 88
Lord's Supper 24, 34, 51, 52, 54-55, 82, 125, 141, 144, 208, 228, 232, 233-234, 290, 292, 295, 300, 304
  See also Mass
Lortz, Joseph 1n, 5-6, 21n, 42n, 103n, 115, 118n, 141, 142, 145n, 193n

Luther's works:
  Acta Augustana (1518) 135-139, 141, 177, 178n, 180-181
  Admonition to the Clergy Assembled at Augsburg (1530) 38n, 229, 246-251
  Against Latomus (1522) 15, 35-36, 68, 69, 70, 71, 72n, 73n, 79, 214n
  Against the Antinomians (1539) 81
  Against the Heavenly Prophets (1525) 30
  Answer to the Hyperchristian Book of Goat Emser (1522) 198n
  Antinomian Disputations (1537-38) 28, 33, 36n, 61n, 68, 72n, 80
  Appeal to a Better Informed Pope (1518) 155, 178-179, 187
  Appeal to a General Council (1518) 155, 183-184
  Assertio omnium articulorum (1521) 65, 68
  Auf des Bocks zu Leipzig Antwort (1521) 176n
  Baptism, Order of (1523) 190
  Baptism, Sermon on the Sacrament (1519) 52, 67n, 74-76, 141
  Babylonian Captivity of the Church (1520) 51n, 127n, 197
  Blessed Sacrament and the Brotherhoods, Sermon (1519) 52, 141
  Bondage of the Will (1525) 15, 30-32, 39, 197
  Catechetical Sermons (1523, 1528) 203-210, 214n, 216, 217-218
  Church Postil (1522) 44
  Comfort When Facing Grave Temptations (1521) 191
  Confession of Faith (1528) 190, 194n, 203, 254n
  Confession of Sins, Short Order (1529) 190
  Councils and the Church (1539) 72, 74n, 79, 207n, 217
  Decem praecepta predicata populo (1518) 101n
  Dictata super Psalterium (1513-15) 21-22, 47f, 101n, 107n
  Disputatio de veste nuptiali (1537) 78n
  Disputation (Sept. 25, 1516) 121
  Disputation against Scholastic Theology (1517) 49n, 106n
  Disputation on Justification (1536) 35n, 37n, 49n, 72n, 77, 80, 214n
  Disputation on Man (1536) 37
  Eine kurze Form der Gebote, des Glaubens, und des Vater Unsers (1520) 199, 201-202, 204n, 211, 214
  Enarratio Psalmi LI. See Psalm 51, Exposition
  Freedom of a Christian (1520) 15, 28, 76-77
  Galatians, Commentary (1519) 74n, 140
  Galatians, Lectures (1531, 1535) 27, 36, 38n, 53
  Genesis, Lectures (1535-45) 45n, 53, 55n
  Hebrews, Lectures (1517-18) 24, 25n, 50, 51, 104n, 125, 127n, 143, 144n, 174
  Heidelberg Disputation (1518) 15, 21n, 22, 25, 95, 128n, 154, 175

Luther's Works (continued):
Instructio pro confessione peccatorum (1518) 144
The Keys (1530) 55n, 264n
Large Catechism (1529) 57-58, 78, 190, 192n, 194n, 203-210, 211-216, 218
Leipzig Disputation (1519) 185
Lombard, Peter, Marginal Notes to, 124n
Marlburg Colloquy (1529) 55
Marriage, Order of (1529) 190
Meditation on the Passion of Christ (1519) 52, 57, 80
Nativity of Christ, Sermon (1533) 43-44
Ninety-five Theses (1517) 45-46, 62, 87, 91, 92, 93n, 94, 95, 96, 98n, 105n, 112n, 114, 120n, 122, 134n, 149, 156-157, 159, 181
Operationes in Psalmos (1519-21) 32n, 56n, 139
Our Father, Exposition (1519) 52, 191
Papacy in Rome (1520) 197, 198, 199-200, 207n
Penance, Sermon on the Sacrament (1519) 52, 141, 174
Penitential Psalms, Commentary (1517) 11, 46, 48, 67, 119
Pentecost Sermons 57n 203, 205, 208-209, 213, 215-217
Postils (1522-1544) 44, 191
Prayer Book (1522) 192, 199
Preface to German Works, vol. 1 (1539) 80
Preface to Latin Works, vol. 1 (1545) 45n, 108n
Preparation for Death, Sermon on (1519) 52, 141, 191
Pro veritate inquirenda et timoratis conscientiis consolandis (Disputation, 1518) 23-24, 125-129, 135, 141, 142n, 143, 145, 174n
Propositiones adversus totam Synagogam Satanae (1530) 267n, 268n
Psalm 51, Exposition (1532, 1538) 16, 27-28, 34, 35n, 45n, 53, 56, 60-61, 63-64, 68-69, 71, 72, 73n, 79
Psalm 126, Expository lecture (1533) 81

Resolutiones of the Leipzig Disputation (1519) 32n, 61n, 67, 69
Resolutiones of the Ninety-five Theses (1518) 24, 25n, 92n, 113n, 122-123, 131-132, 143, 151, 152, 154, 157, 160, 165-171, 181, 187
Responsio ad librum A. Catharini (1522) 198n, 199-200, 207n
Responsio to Prierias (1518) 2n, 114n, 158, 159, 187
Rhapsodia de loco justificationis (1530) 38n
Romans, Lectures on (1515-16) 16-23, 48-49, 61, 64-66, 79, 98n, 101n, 103n, 107, 108n, 109
Romans, Prefaces to (1522, 1529) 35n, 71, 72n, 73n, 79n, 217n
Sendbrief vom Dolmetschen (1530) 264n
Sermo de digna praeparatione (1518) 144n
Sermo de duplici iustitia (1519) 128n
Sermo de poenitentia (1518) 124-125, 129, 131-132, 143n, 145, 165, 166, 171, 174
Sermon (Feb. 24, 1517) 26, 120
Sermon (Feb. 2, 1518) 123-124
Sermon (Oct. 30, 1519) 140n
Sermon at first Mass of a new priest (1518) 51, 123-124
Sermon on Excommunication (1518) 154-155, 166n
Sermon on Justification (Jan. 1, 1517) 107
Sermon on Zaccheus (May 30, 1517) 49, 120
Sermon von dem Ablass und Gnade (1518) 151
Simple Way to Pray (1535) 80, 191, 192, 194n
Smalkald Articles (1537) 33
Small Catechism (1529) 38n, 189, 192, 194n, 203
That These Words of Christ, »This is my Body,« Still Stand Firm (1527) 54, 55
Treatise on Indulgences (1517) 2, 19, 47, 62, 87-116, 120-121, 122, 149, 169
Warnung an seine lieben Deutschen (1531) 293n

Luther's Works (continued):
 Wider Hans Worst (1541) 207n, 286n
 Widerruf vom Fegfeuer (1530) 264n, 266
 Winkelmesse und Pfaffenweihe, Von der (1533) 78
 Worthy Reception of the Sacrament (1521) 51
Lutz, Heinrich 288n

McCue, James F. 63n
McGrath, Alister 9n, 65n, 195n
McSorley, Harry 20n, 30n, 118n, 175n
Mai, Miguel 281
Mainz, University faculty 89-90, 150
Mannermaa, Tuomo 37n, 63n
Manns, Peter 38n, 82, 83n, 105n, 260n
Marburg Colloquy (1529) 55, 254
Marcocchi, Massimo 40n
Maria, Queen of Hungary 266n, 282n
Marriage of priests
 See Celibacy, clerical
Mary, Blessed Virgin 44, 249
Mass, canon of 268n, 301, 303, 304, 306, 313
 fruits applied 304, 305n, 306, 309, 313
 private 241, 257, 258, 260, 263, 265, 273, 275, 279, 280, 282, 297, 299, 303, 306, 307, 309, 311, 313
 reform of (in the *Confutatio*) 274
 requiem 231, 233, 238, 270
 as sacrifice 233, 241, 249, 251, 270, 282, 291, 297, 299, 301, 304, 311, 313, 315
Maurer, Wilhelm 228n, 252n
Maximilian I, Emperor 130, 155, 161, 162, 163n, 166n, 181n, 184, 185, 186
Medici, Guilio de' (later, Pope Clement VII) 163n, 166n
Meditation 9, 11, 44, 56
Melanchthon, Philip 91, 238-240, 243n, 244n, 249n, 251n, 252-262, 263-267, 269, 271n, 277, 282-287, 289-293, 295, 296n, 297n, 300n, 302, 303, 304, 306, 307, 308n, 310n, 311n, 312, 314, 315
 See also Augsburg Confession
Mensing, Johann 270

Merit 8, 144, 292, 293, 304
Meyer, Harding 236
Miltitz, Karl von 152, 181, 183, 184
Ministry, church 39, 193, 197, 236, 292, 294
Modernization 316
Moeller, Bernd 42n, 52n, 94n, 96n, 99n, 116n, 193n
Monastic life 231, 235, 258, 266, 274, 295, 297, 298, 305, 307, 310
 See also Vows, monastic
Mostert, Walter 65n
Müller, Gerhard 19n, 226n, 279n, 284n, 291n, 313n
Müller, Karl 156n, 163n
Murner, Thomas 198

Naz, Raoul 150n
Neill, Thomas P. 5n
Nemini (canon) 150
Nestorius 300
Neuhaus, Helmut 224n, 282n
Newman, John Henry 215
Nicholas V, Pope 158n
Nicol, Martin 56n, 80n, 81n, 198n
Nilsson, K. O. 63n
Non sacramentum sed fides sacramenti iustificat 23, 126, 137, 145, 171
Norms of doctrine 2n, 4, 158, 185, 186
 of religious practice 276, 314
Nürnberg 230, 231, 232, 233, 235, 237, 284, 301, 306, 307, 308

Oakley, Francis 42n, 193n
Oberman, Heiko A. 20n, 102n, 127n
Objects, blessed 234, 279-280
Ockham, William 7, 106n, 195n
Ockhamist theology 7-9, 41, 174
Oecolampadius, Johann 54
Olivier, Daniel 34n
O'Malley, John W. 21n, 40n, 158n
Ordinary procedure, canonical, against Luther, 155-162, 176, 181, 184
Osiander, Andreas 230, 232, 233n

Paltz, Johann von 9-11, 122, 127n, 145-146, 190
Pannenberg, Wolfhart 116
Papal authority 151, 152, 157, 177, 193, 249, 312
   by divine right 282
   to grant indulgences 100, 150
Passion of Christ 9, 56
Pastoral writings, Luther's 2, 11, 52, 141, 173-174, 189-196
Paul III, Pope (formerly Alessandro Farnese) 226n
Paulus, Nikolas 94, 109n, 170
Peasants' Revolt (1525) 3, 30, 253
Peccatum regnans/regnatum 35, 37, 60n, 72-73, 79, 83
Pelagianism 20, 271
Penance, lifelong 1, 2, 19, 36, 37-38, 40-41, 45, 46-49, 61, 70, 73-74, 83, 93, 99, 103, 104, 106-108, 110, 149, 212
Penance, sacrament 10, 23-24, 46, 49, 51, 103, 105, 122-129, 142, 290
Penances, imposed 99-100, 102, 105, 110, 114-115, 142, 151, 167, 232, 273
Peraudi, Raymond, Cardinal 94, 99n, 109n, 116n
Perusco, Mario de 155
Pesch, Otto H. 29n, 82, 118n, 178n, 224n
Peter, Carl J. 116n, 124n, 171n, 275n
Peters, Albrecht 83n, 216n
Peura, Simo 37n
Pfeilschifter, Georg 291n
Pfnür, Vinzenz 197n, 226n, 279n, 292n, 294n
Pfürtner, Stephanus 118n
Philip of Hesse, Landgrave 254n, 284, 302n
Pilgrimages 231, 232, 239, 249, 250, 267
Pirkheimer, Caritas 305n
Pius II, Pope 183
Pius IX, Pope 5n
Pollet, Jacques 141
Poschmann, Bernhard 109
Practice in the church 4, 128, 228
Prayer 2, 61, 63, 69, 74, 78-81, 191, 192, 239

Prenter, Regin 73n, 211n
Prien, H.-J. 199n
Prierias, Silvester 3n, 96, 114n, 134, 150, 152, 156-160, 163, 165n, 175, 179, 185, 186, 187, 200n
Priesthood 122, 124, 127-128
Pro me 25, 26-27, 118, 138, 146, 203, 214
Processions 231, 233
Profession of faith, Luther's (1528) 190, 203, 214, 254n
Promise, Christ's 2, 24, 52, 125, 127, 129, 136, 144, 271
   See also Binding and loosing
Property, church and monastic 290, 295, 298, 310, 313
Purgatory 93, 100, 101, 101, 102, 103, 104, 105, 106, 111-114, 255, 264, 265, 267

Rab, Herman 155
Rahner, Karl 82, 109n
Rapp, François 42n
Ratzinger, Joseph 6, 117, 224
Reception of Luther 3-4, 11, 28, 39-42, 81-83, 115-116, 219-220, 285
Reconciliation with God 123, 126, 142
Reformation breakthrough, Luther's 2n, 44, 49-50, 108n, 197n
Reinhard, Wolfgang 282n, 316n
Repentance. *See* Conversion
Responsio theologorum (July 1530) 270-271, 285-286
Resurrection, final 206, 212, 218
Rhegius, Urbanus 315n
Righteousness 15, 16-17, 22-23, 25-26, 33, 35-39, 47, 49, 60, 63, 66, 69, 97
Roman Catholic doctrine and practice 156-157, 159
Root, Michael 227n, 245n, 250n
Ruh, Ulrich 225n
Rupp, Gordon 107n
Rurer, Johann 230, 231, 233, 234, 235, 236, 237

Sacraments 23, 26, 34, 39, 49, 50-52, 55, 78, 80, 119, 122, 127, 128-129, 131, 132, 135, 170, 194, 195, 196, 197, 207, 210, 220, 232, 247, 292
 See also Absolution, Baptism, Lord's Supper
Saints, invocation of 241, 243, 249, 259, 267, 270, 275, 291, 293, 301, 304
 merits of 97
 veneration of 239, 243, 264
Sanctification 198, 203, 204-218, 220
Satisfaction for sin 95, 97, 98, 99, 100, 110-111, 151, 232, 247, 258, 273, 292-293, 304
Schatzgeyer, Kaspar 315n
Scheible, Heinz 280n, 284n, 292n
Scheurl, Christoph 92n, 94, 96
Schindling, Anton 290n
Schmaus, Michael 82
Schnepf, Erhard 289n, 307, 310n
Scholastic theology 7-9, 20, 41, 65, 69, 117, 121-122, 125, 128, 140, 194, 213, 217, 292
 Luther's polemic against 16, 19-21
Schultze, Hieronymus, Bishop 90n, 92n, 113n, 152
Schwab, Wolfgang 23n, 50n, 118n, 121n, 125n, 127n, 129n, 137n, 138n, 172n, 174n
Schwabach Articles (1529) 254, 284
Schwärmer 207, 210
Schwager, R. 77n
Schwarzwäller, Klaus 212n, 213n
Scotist theology 121, 128, 176
Scotus, John Duns 176n, 195n
Scripture, authority of 157, 158, 185, 287-288, 290, 295, 311, 314, 315
 message of 27-28, 63-70
 self-interpreting 64, 314n
Seebass, Gottfried 230n, 305n
Selge, Kurt-Victor 2n, 4, 134n, 159n, 165n, 170n, 176n, 184, 185n, 250n
Sensus ecclesiae 133, 167-168, 169-170, 173, 176
Simul iustus et peccator 2, 18, 59-83
Sin, remaining 17-19, 29, 35, 37, 47, 59-60, 61-62, 64-70, 74, 93, 97, 98, 99-103, 104, 105, 106, 108, 110, 111, 113, 119, 121, 211
 See also *Peccatum regnans/regnatum*, Struggle against sin
Sixtus IV, Pope 99n, 102n
Smith, Thurman L. 91n
Sorbonne 149n, 183
Soteriology 33-34, 41, 80, 194, 196
Spalatin, Georg 113n, 120n, 153n, 178n, 193, 290
Spengler, Lazarus 43n, 284n
Spirituality, penitential 2, 9, 41, 49, 63, 66n, 115, 116, 118-122
Stadion, Christoph von, Bishop 283, 289n
Stakemeier, Adolf 118n
Staupitz, Johann von 113n, 122, 152, 153, 177, 180n, 190, 195n
Steglich, Wolfgang 284n
Steinmetz, David C. 18n, 190n
Stock, Ursula 52n, 141n, 202n
Strauss, Gerald 303n
Strayer, James R. 42n
Strohl, Henri 89n
Struggle against sin, lifelong 35, 61-62, 68, 70, 72, 74-81, 93, 98, 100, 103, 104, 106-108, 111, 115, 119, 217
Subjectivism 2, 5, 6, 147
Suffrages for the departed, indulgences as 95, 100, 106, 108-109, 111-113, 181-182
Summary procedure, canonical, against Luther 162-164, 176

Temptation 81, 194
Tentler, Thomas N. 127n, 145
Testament, Christ's 50, 125, 157
Tetzel, Johann 45, 87, 88, 89, 93n, 96, 101n, 111n, 120n, 149, 151, 152, 153, 164n
Theology, proper 27, 28, 41, 63
»Theology-for-piety« 9-11, 121-122, 147, 190
Theology of the cross 43, 80, 98, 117, 119, 120, 154
Thérèse of Lisieux, St. 83
Thesaurus ecclesiae 95, 109, 110, 131, 134, 168, 175, 177, 182
Theses on indulgences, non-posting on Oct. 31 (1517) 87n, 91n

Thomas Aquinas, St. 28, 132n, 133n, 158, 168n, 170, 176, 180
Thomist theology 41, 121, 158, 180
Thought patterns, Luther's 21-23
Timiadis, E. 225
Tongues of fire, pentecostal 208-209
Torgau Articles 238, 240, 244
Trent, Council of 39-40, 60n, 117-118, 146, 316
Trinity, of divine persons 194, 196, 201, 202, 204, 205, 215, 216, 254, 270
Truchsess von Waldburg, Georg 313n
Trutvetter, Jodocus 7, 92n

Ullrich, Lothar 224n, 225, 257n
Unigenitus, papal bull (1343) 168, 169, 170, 175, 177, 179, 181

Valdés, Alfonso de 274n, 282-283, 286n
Vatican Council, Second 196
Vehus, Hieronymus 289n, 291, 296, 299, 303n, 304, 306, 307, 310n, 313n
Vercruysse, Jos. E. 68n, 146n, 154n, 175n
Vocation, worldly 39
  See also Estates
Vogelsang, E. 17n, 95n
Volta, Gabriele della 151, 152, 164, 177
Voltelini, Hans von 161n
Volz, Hans 87, 89n, 91n, 97n
Vows, monastic 228, 257, 263, 273, 291, 294
  See also Monastic life
Vuidensee, Eberhard 271n

Wagner, Georg 161n
Walter, Johann von 261n
Weiss, James M. 251n
Wesel, Arnold von 270
Wicks, Jared 1, 2n, 4n, 16n, 17n, 19n, 46n, 59n, 97n, 107n, 108n, 109n, 115n, 118n, 119n, 120n, 130n, 138, 141n, 166n, 196n, 280n, 295n
Wiesflecker, Hermann 161n
Willebrands, Johannes, Cardinal 224
Wimpina, Konrad 87n, 96, 111n, 151, 289n
Witek, John W. 40n
Wittenberg University 153, 160
Word, God's 78, 80, 205, 215, 232, 237, 247
  See also Absolution
  Gospel, proclamation of
Works, good 37-39, 40, 77, 107n, 239, 242, 257, 271, 273, 292, 293
Wriedt, Markus 219n

Yearning for grace 18, 19, 21, 29, 47, 48, 62, 64, 70, 73, 79, 80, 106, 107n, 109, 114, 119, 120-121

Zeeden, Ernst Walter 316n
Zschoch, Hellmut 62n, 235n
Zürich Disputation (1523) 279
Zur Mühlen, Karl-Heinz 37n, 126n
Zwingli, Ulrich 54, 141, 252, 254, 271n, 284, 300

www.ingramcontent.com/pod-product-compliance
Lightning Source LLC
Chambersburg PA
CBHW052141300426
44115CB00011B/1474